ADVANCED DATA STRUCTURES

[Concepts and Applications]

Anuradha A. Puntambekar
M.E. (Computer)
Formerly Assistant Professor in
P.E.S. Modern College of Engineering,
Pune

ADVANCED DATA STRUCTURES

First Edition : December 2020

© Copyright with Author
All publishing rights (printed and ebook version) reserved with Technical Publications. No part of this book should be reproduced in any form, Electronic, Mechanical, Photocopy or any information storage and retrieval system without prior permission in writing, from Technical Publications, Pune.

Published by :

Amit Residency, Office No.1, 412, Shaniwar Peth, Pune - 411030, M.S. INDIA
Ph.: +91-020-24495496/97, Email : sales@technicalpublications.org
Website : www.technicalpublications.org

ISBN 978-93-332-2383-6

PREFACE

The importance of **Advanced Data Structures** is well known in various engineering fields. Overwhelming response to my books on various subjects inspired me to write this book. The book is structured to cover the key aspects of the subject **Advanced Data Structures**.

The book uses plain, lucid language to explain fundamentals of this subject. The book provides logical method of explaining various complicated concepts and stepwise methods to explain the important topics. Each chapter is well supported with necessary illustrations, practical examples and solved problems. All the chapters in the book are arranged in a proper sequence that permits each topic to build upon earlier studies. All care has been taken to make students comfortable in understanding the basic concepts of the subject.

Representative questions have been added at the end of each section to help the students in picking important points from that section.

The book not only covers the entire scope of the subject but explains the philosophy of the subject. This makes the understanding of this subject more clear and makes it more interesting. The book will be very useful not only to the students but also to the subject teachers. The students have to omit nothing and possibly have to cover nothing more.

I wish to express my profound thanks to all those who helped in making this book a reality. Much needed moral support and encouragement is provided on numerous occasions by my whole family. I wish to thank the **Publisher** and the entire team of **Technical Publications** who have taken immense pain to get this book in time with quality printing.

Any suggestion for the improvement of the book will be acknowledged and well appreciated.

Author

A. A. Puntambekar

Dedicated to God.

SYLLABUS

UNIT - I Trees

Tree - basic terminology, General tree and its representation, Representation using sequential and linked organization, Binary tree-properties, Converting tree to binary tree, **Binary tree traversals -** inorder, preorder, Post order, Level wise-depth first and breadth first, Operations on binary tree. Binary Search Tree (BST), BST operations, Threaded binary tree- concepts, Threading, Insertion and deletion of nodes in in-order threaded binary tree, In order traversal of in-order threaded binary tree. **Case Study -** Use of binary tree in expression tree-evaluation and Huffman's coding .

Unit - II Graphs

Basic Concepts, Storage representation, Adjacency matrix, Adjacency list, Adjacency multi list, Inverse adjacency list. Traversals-depth first and breadth first, Introduction to greedy strategy, Minimum spanning tree, Greedy algorithms for computing minimum spanning tree - Prims and Kruskal Algorithms, Dikjtra's single source shortest path, Topological ordering. **Case study -** Data structure used in webgraph and google map.

Unit - III Hashing

Hash Table - Concepts-hash table, Hash function, Bucket, Collision, Probe, Synonym, Overflow, Open hashing, Closed hashing, Perfect hash function, Load density, Full table, Load factor, Rehashing, Issues in hashing, Hash functions - Properties of good hash function, Division, Multiplication, Extraction, Mid-square, Folding and universal, Collision resolution strategies - Open addressing and chaining, Hash table overflow - Open addressing and chaining, Extendible hashing.

Dictionary - Dictionary as ADT, Ordered dictionaries.

Skip List - representation, Searching andoperations - Insertion, Removal.

Unit - IV Search Trees

Symbol table - Representation of symbol tables - Static tree table and dynamic tree table, Introduction to dynamic programming, Weight balanced tree, Optimal Binary Search Tree (OBST), OBST as an example of dynamic programming, Height balanced tree - AVL tree.

Unit - V Indexing and Multiway Trees

Indexing and multiway trees - Indexing, Indexing techniques, Types of search tree - Multiway search tree, B-Tree, B+Tree, Trie tree, Splay tree, Red-black tree, K-dimensional tree, AA tree. **Set-**set ADT, Realization of set and operations. **Heap-**basic concepts, Realization of heap and operations, Heap as a priority queue, Heap sort.

Unit - VI File Organization

Sequential file organization - Concept and primitive operations, **Direct access file -** Concepts and primitive operations, **Indexed sequential file organization -** Concept, Types of indices, Structure of index sequential file, **Linked organization -** Multi list files, Coral rings, Inverted files and cellular partitions. **External sort -** Consequential processing and merging two lists, Multiday merging - A k way merge algorithm.

TABLE OF CONTENTS

Solved University Question Papers **(S - 1) to (S - 44)**

1 Trees

Syllabus

***Tree** - basic terminology, General tree and its representation, Representation using sequential and linked organization, Binary tree-properties, Converting tree to binary tree, **Binary tree traversals** - inorder, preorder, Post order, Level wise-depth first and breadth first, Operations on binary tree. Binary Search Tree (BST), BST operations, Threaded binary tree- concepts, Threading, Insertion and deletion of nodes in in-order threaded binary tree, In order traversal of in-order threaded binary tree. **Case Study** - Use of binary tree in expression tree-evaluation and Huffman's coding .*

Contents

1.1 Basic Terminology

SPPU : May-10, Dec.-10, Marks 5

Definition of a Tree :

A tree is a finite set of one or more nodes such that -

i) Root node : It is a specially designated node.

ii) There are remaining n nodes which can be partitioned into disjoint sets T_1, T_2, T_3,... T_n where T_1, T_2, T_3,... T_n are called subtrees of the root.

The concept of tree can be represented by following figure -

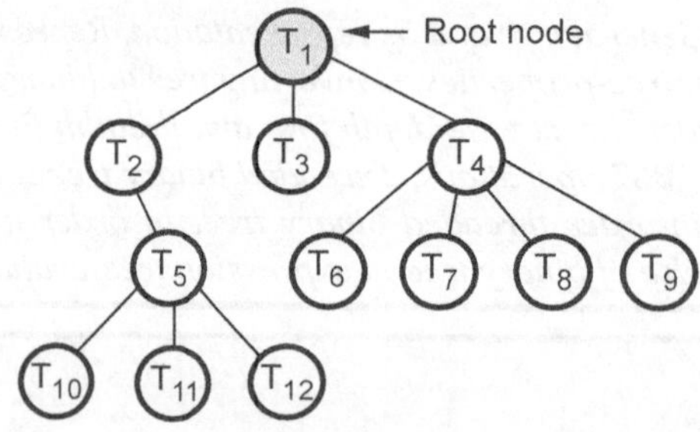

Fig. 1.1.1 Tree

Let us get introduced with some of the definitions or terms which are normally used.

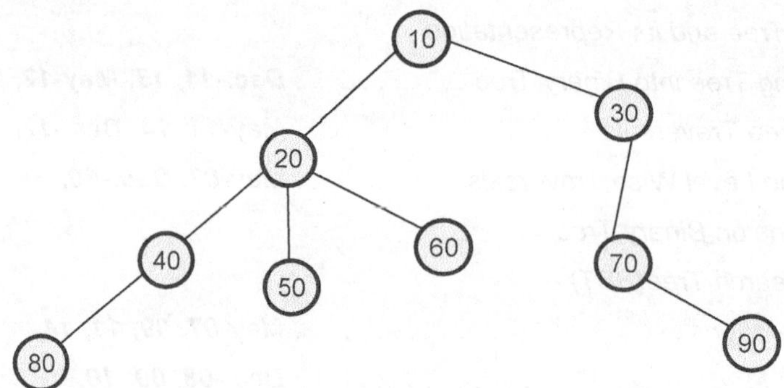

Fig. 1.1.2 Binary tree

From Fig. 1.1.2,

1. Root

Root is a unique node in the tree to which further subtrees are attached. For above given tree, node 10 is a root node.

2. Parent node

The node having further sub-branches is called parent node. In Fig. 1.1.3, 20 is parent node of 40, 50 and 60.

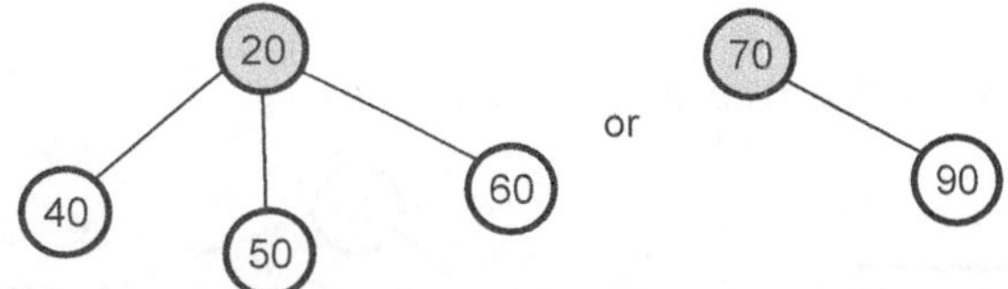

Fig. 1.1.3 Binary tree representing parent node

3. Child nodes

The child nodes in above given tree are marked as shown below.

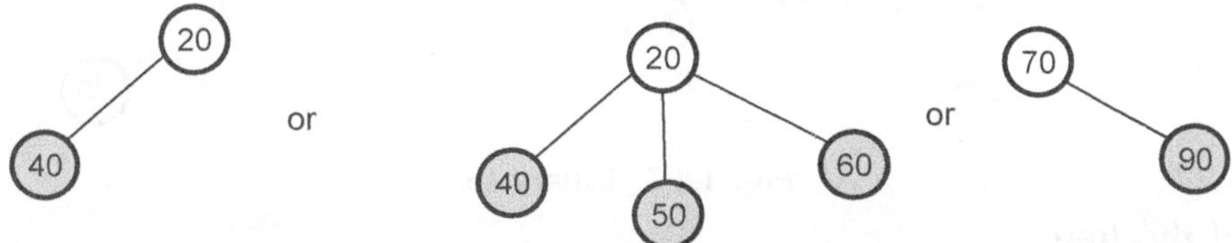

Fig. 1.1.4 Binary tree representing child node

4. Leaves

These are the terminal nodes of the tree.

For example

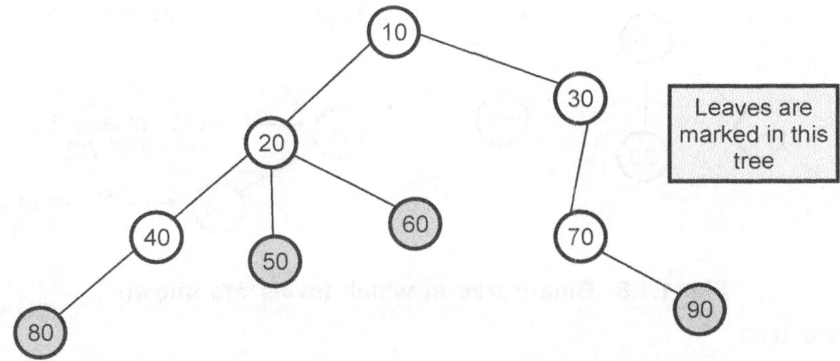

Fig. 1.1.5 Binary tree with left nodes

5. Degree of the node

The total number of sub-trees attached to that node is called the degree of a node.
For example

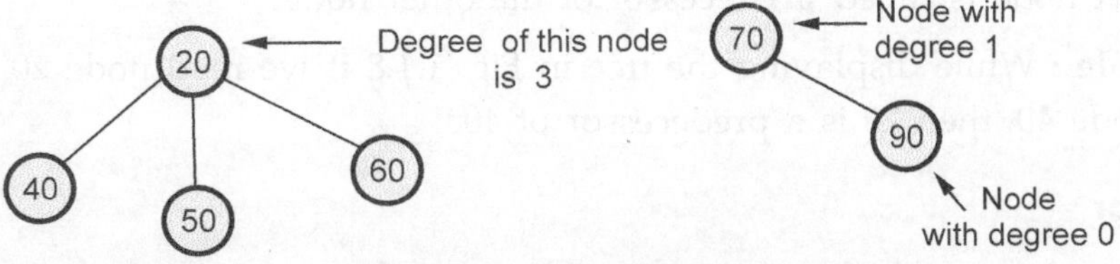

Fig. 1.1.6 Binary tree

6. Degree of tree

The maximum degree in the tree is degree of tree.

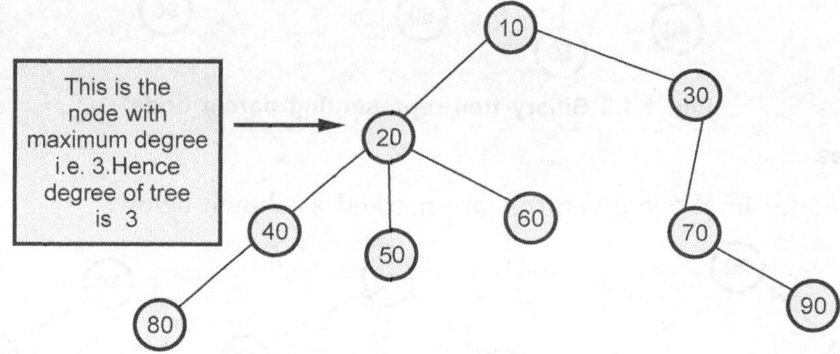

Fig. 1.1.7 Binary tree

7. Level of the tree

The root node is always considered at level zero.

The adjacent nodes to root are supposed to be at level 1 and so on.

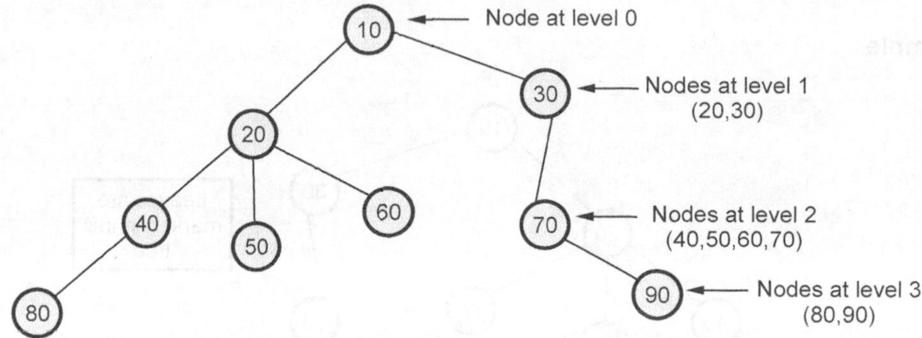

Fig. 1.1.8 Binary tree in which levels are shown

8. Height of the tree

The maximum level is the height of the tree. In Fig. 1.1.8 the height of tree is 3. Sometimes height of the tree is also called **depth** of tree.

9. Predecessor

While displaying the tree, if some particular node occurs previous to some other node then that node is called **predecessor** of the other node.

For example : While displaying the tree in Fig. 1.1.8 if we read node 20 first and then if we read node 40, then 20 is a predecessor of 40.

10. Successor

Successor is a node which occurs next to some node.

For example : While displaying tree in Fig. 1.1.8 if we read node 60 after reading node 20 then 60 is called successor of 20.

11. Internal and external nodes

Leaf node means a node having no child node. As leaf nodes are not having further links, we call leaf nodes **external nodes** and non leaf nodes are called **internal nodes**.

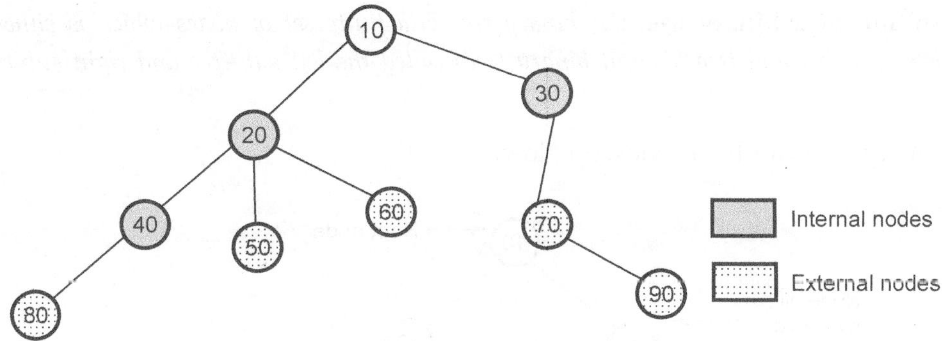

Fig. 1.1.9 Representing internal and external nodes

12. Sibling

The nodes with common parent are called siblings or brothers.

For example

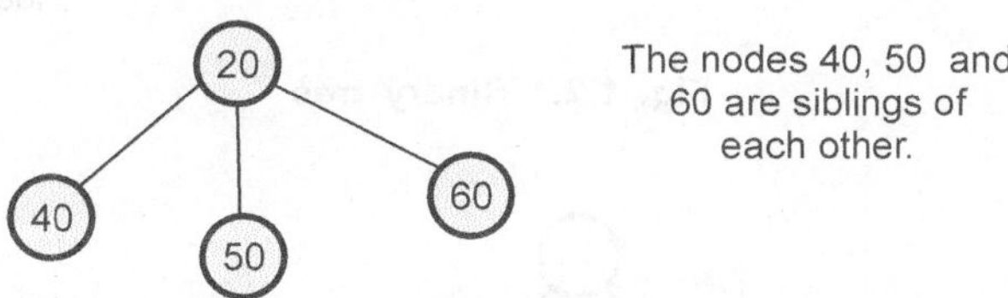

Fig. 1.1.10

In this chapter we will deal with special type of trees called binary trees. Let us understand it.

University Questions

1. *Write the concept of - Skewed binary tree.* **SPPU : May-10, Marks 2**
2. *What is binary tree ? How is it different than a basic tree ? Explain with figures.* **SPPU : Dec.-10, Marks 5**

1.2 Properties of Binary Tree

SPPU : May-06, Marks 4

In the trees, we can have any number of child nodes to a parent node. But if we impose some restriction on number of child nodes i.e. if we allow at the most two children nodes then that type of tree is called binary tree. Let us formally define binary trees,

Definition of a binary tree : *A binary tree is a finite set of nodes which is either empty or consists of a root and two disjoint binary trees called the left sub-tree and right sub-tree.*

The binary tree can be as shown below.

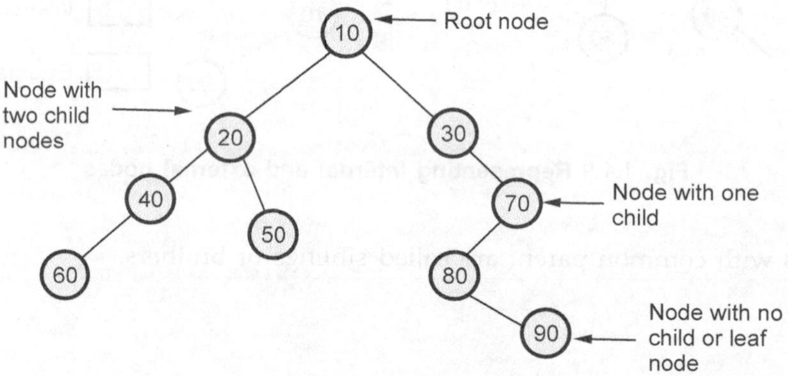

Fig. 1.2.1 Binary tree

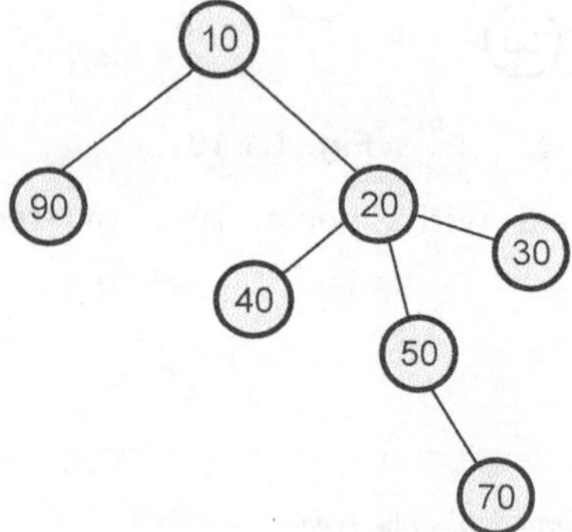

Fig. 1.2.2 Not a binary tree

Left and Right Skewed Trees

The tree in which each node is attached as a left child of parent node then it is **left skewed tree**. The tree in which each node is attached as a right child of parent node then it is called **right skewed tree**.

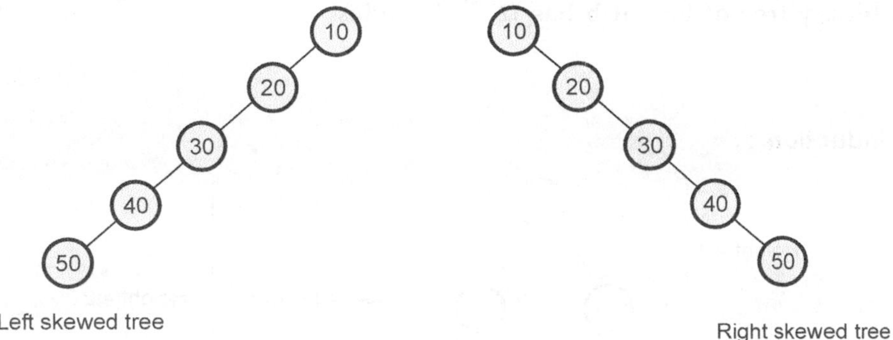

Fig. 1.2.3 Skewed trees

Properties of Binary Trees

Various properties of binary trees are -

i) For a binary tree maximum number of nodes at level L are 2^L.

Proof :

Basis of Induction : As we know, root node is a unique node present at 0th level. That means, if L = 0, Maximum number of nodes are $2^L = 2^0 = 1$.

The binary tree is a tree in which each node has maximum two nodes. Hence if level m = 1 then maximum nodes are, $2^L = 2^1 = 2$.

L = 0 then maximum nodes are 1.

When L = 1, then maximum nodes are two i.e. n_l and n_r.

Inductive step :

$$
\begin{aligned}
\text{As,}\quad \text{Maximum\_nodes}(0) &= 1. \\
\text{Maximum\_nodes}(1) &= 2 * \text{maximum\_nodes}(0) \\
\therefore\quad \text{Maximum\_nodes}(k) &= 2 * \text{maximum\_nodes}(k-1) \\
&= 2 * \quad (2 * (2 * \ (2 * \ (\ldots 2 * \text{maximum-nodes}(0))))) \\
&= 2^k.
\end{aligned}
$$

This proves that maximum number of nodes at level L are 2^L.

ii) A full binary tree of height h has (2^{h+1}–1) nodes.

Proof :

Basis of induction :

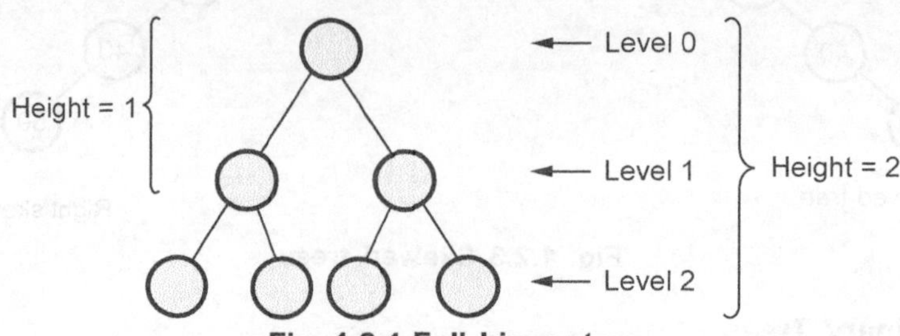

Fig. 1.2.4 Full binary tree

For the binary tree, total number of nodes at level m are 2^m. In above figure, total nodes at level 0 are 1, at level 1 are 2 and at level 1 are 4. Thus total number of nodes in the given binary tree are,

$$\text{total\_nodes} = 2^0+2^1+2^2+2^3+...2^m$$

$$= \sum_{i=0}^{m}$$

If height h = 0, then

total_nodes = $2^{h+1}-1 = 2^{0+1}-1 = 1$ node i.e. root.

If height h = 1, then

total_nodes = $2^{h+1}-1 = 2^{1+1}-1 = 3$ nodes when h = 1.

Induction hypothesis :

Assume total_nodes $\leq 2^{h+1}-1$ for a full binary tree when h = k.

Inductive step :

Now a tree T has two subtrees T_L and T_R. These subtrees are also the full binary trees with the heights $h(T_L)$ and $h(T_R)$.

Hence

$$T = T_L \cdot T_R$$

$$T = \text{total\_nodes}\ (T_L) + \text{total\_nodes}\ (T_R) + 1$$

Here 1 is added for root nodes, and T denotes total number of nodes.

$\therefore \quad T = (2^{h(T_L)+1}-1)+(2^{h(T_R)+1}-1)+1 \quad \because$ induction hypothesis

$$= (2^{h(T_L)+1} + 2^{h(T_R)+1}) - 1$$

$$= (2(2^{\max(h(T_L)+1,\, h(T_R)+1)})) - 1$$

$$= 2 \cdot 2^{h(T)} - 1 \qquad \because \max(h(T_L) + 1, h(T_R)+1 = h(T)$$

$$T = 2^{h(T)+1} - 1$$

Thus total number of allowed nodes in a full binary tree of height h are $\mathbf{2^{h(T)+1} - 1}$ is proved.

iii) Total number of external nodes in a binary tree are internal nodes + 1. i.e. e = i + 1.

Proof : We assume

e = External nodes

i = Internal nodes.

$\therefore$ We have to prove e = i + 1.

Basis of induction :

If there is only one node i.e. root node

(n)

$$i = 0$$
$$\therefore e = 0 + 1$$
$$e = 1$$

i.e. Only one external node is present.

Thus, e = i+1 is true.

Whenever we add the nodes to a binary tree we add two external nodes and then previous external node becomes an internal node.

For example

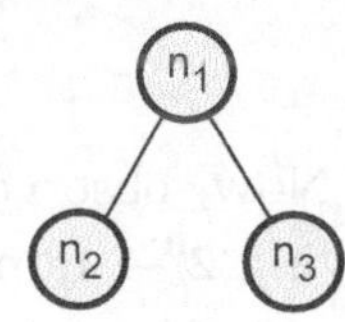

Again, i = 1, e = 2

Hence, e = i + 1
i.e. 2 = 2 is true.

Inductive step :

As soon as we add two external nodes previous external node becomes an internal node.

i.e $\quad e_{new} = e_{prev} + 1$

$\quad = (i_{prev} + 1) + 1$

$e_{new} = i_{new} + 1 \qquad \therefore i_{new} = i_{prev} + 1$.

Thus $\quad$ e = i + 1 is true.

University Questions

1. *Prove that maximum possible nodes in a binary tree of height is 2h–1 .*

   SPPU : May-06, Marks 4

2. *Prove that for binary tree maximum number of nodes at level L are 2L .*

   SPPU : May-06, Marks 4

1.3 Representation of Binary Tree **SPPU : May-10, Dec.-11, 12, 13, Marks 8**

There are two ways of representing the binary tree.

1. Sequential representation. 2. Linked representation.

Let us see these representations one by one.

1. Sequential representation of binary trees or array representation :

Each node is sequentially arranged from **top to bottom** and from **left to right.** Let us understand this matter by numbering each node. The numbering will start from root node and then remaining nodes will give ever increasing numbers in level wise direction. The nodes on the same level will be numbered from left to right.

The numbering will be as shown in following figure.

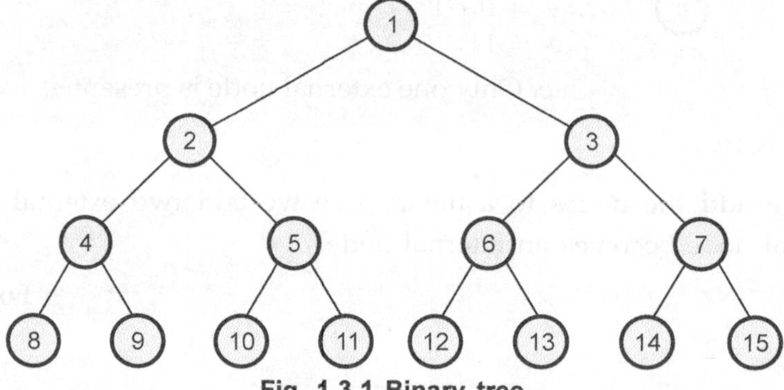

Fig. 1.3.1 Binary tree

Now, observe Fig. 1.3.1 carefully. You will get a point that a binary tree of depth **n** having $\mathbf{2^n – 1}$ number of nodes. The tree is having the depth 4 and total number of nodes are 15. Thus remember that in a binary tree of **depth n** there will be maximum $\mathbf{2^n – 1}$ nodes. And so if we know the maximum depth of the tree then we can represent binary tree using arrays data structure. Because we can then predict the maximum size of an array that can accommodate the tree.

Thus array size can be >=n. The root will be at index 0. Its left child will be at index 1, its right child will be at index 2 and so on. Another way of placing the elements in the array is by applying the formula as shown below.

When n=0 the root node will placed at 0th location

Parent(n) = floor(n–1)/2

Left(n) = (2n+1)

Right(n) = (2n+2).

Where n>0

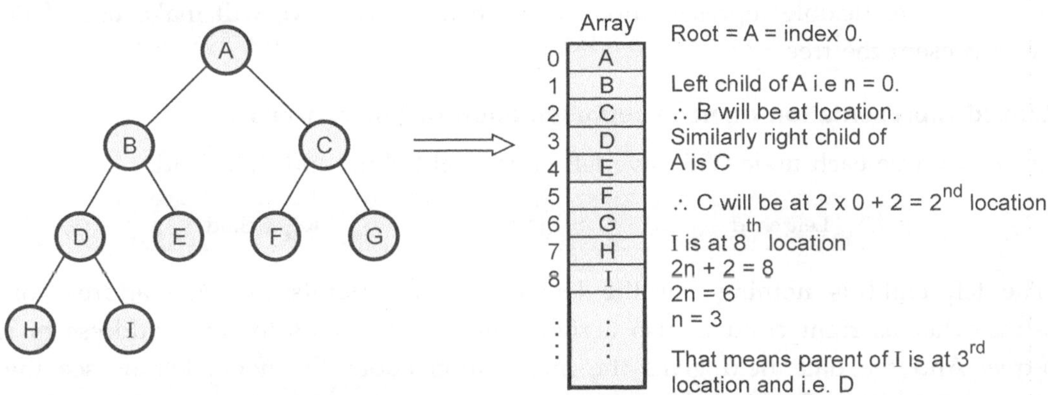

Fig. 1.3.2 Sequential representation of binary tree

Advantages of sequential representation

The only advantage with this type of representation is that the direct access to any node can be possible and finding the parent, left or right children of any particular node is fast because of the random access.

Disadvantages of sequential representation

1. The major disadvantage with this type of representation is wastage of memory.

For example : In the skewed tree half of the array is unutilized. You can easily understand this point simply by seeing Fig. 1.3.3

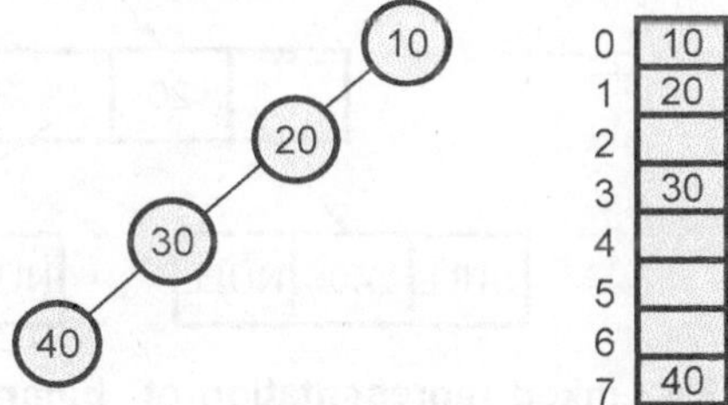

Fig. 1.3.3

2. In this type of representation the maximum depth of the tree has to be fixed because we have already decided the array size. If we choose the array size quite larger than the depth of the tree, then it will be wastage of the memory. And if we

choose array size lesser than the depth of the tree then we will be unable to represent some part of the tree.

3. The insertions and deletion of any node in the tree will be costlier as other nodes have to be adjusted at appropriate positions so that the meaning of binary tree can be preserved.

As these drawbacks are there with this sequential type of representation, we will search for more flexible representation. So instead of array we will make use of linked list to represent the tree.

2. Linked representation or node representation of binary trees :

In binary tree each node will have left child, right child and data field.

The left child is nothing but the left link which points to some address of left sub-tree whereas right child is also a right link which points to some address of right sub-tree. And the data field gives the information about the node. Let us see the 'C' structure of the node in a binary tree.

```
typedef struct node
{
 int data;
 struct node *left;
 struct node *right;
}bin;
```

The tree with linked representation is as shown below.

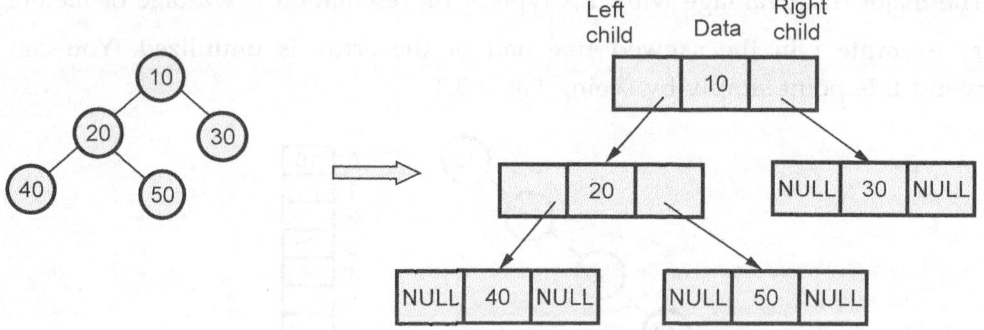

Fig. 1.3.4 Linked representation of binary tree

Advantages of linked representation

1. This representation is superior to our array representation as there is no wastage of memory. And so there is no need to have prior knowledge of depth of the tree. Using dynamic memory concept one can create as many memory (nodes) as

required. By chance if some nodes are unutilized one can delete the nodes by making the address free.

2. Insertions and deletions which are the most common operations can be done without moving the other nodes.

Disadvantages of linked representation

1. This representation does not provide direct access to a node and special algorithms are required.
2. This representation needs additional space in each node for storing the left and right sub-trees.

Example 1.3.1 *Represent the following binary tree using array.* **SPPU : Dec.-13, Marks 3**

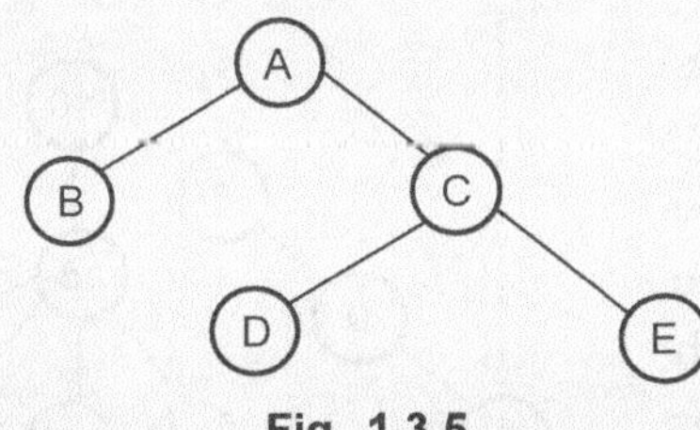

Fig. 1.3.5

Solution : The root node will be at 0th location. We will use following formula to find the location of parent node, left child node and right child node.

Parent (n) = floor (n–1)/2

Left (n) = (2n+1)

Right (n) = (2n+2)

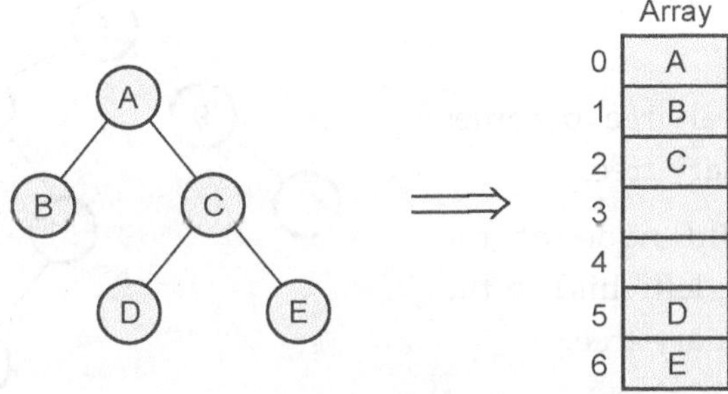

Fig. 1.3.5 (a)

University Questions

1. *Explain the concept of representation of a binary tree using an array.* **SPPU : May-10, Marks 4**
2. *Explain binary tree representation with example.* **SPPU : Dec.-11, Marks 4**

3. *Explain the following :*

   i) What is array representation of given binary tree ?

   ii) What is linked representation of given binary tree ? What are important observations of linked representation ?

   SPPU : Dec.-12, Marks 8

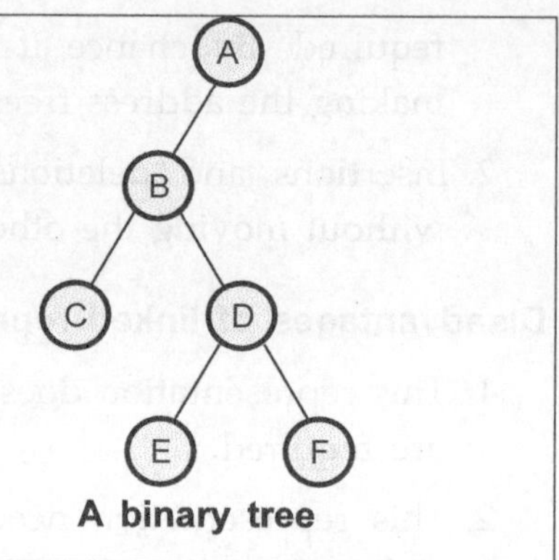

A binary tree

1.4 General Tree and its Representation

General trees are those trees in which there could be any number of nodes that can be attached as a child nodes. The number of subtrees for each node may be varying. For example - in Fig. 1.4.1 is a **General tree.**

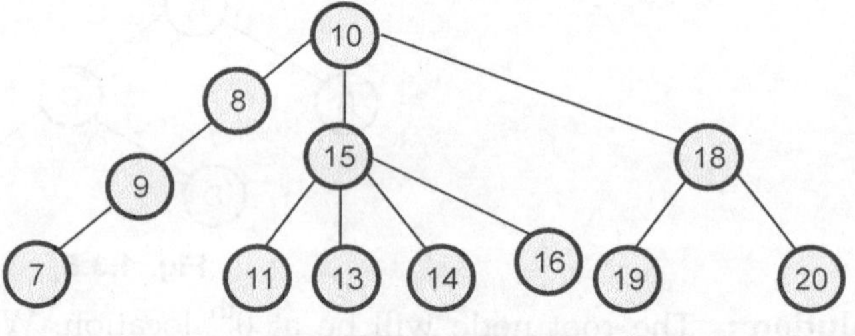

Fig. 1.4.1 General tree

1.5 Converting Tree into Binary Tree

We can convert the given general tree into equivalent binary tree as follows -

i) The root of general tree becomes the root of the binary tree.

ii) Find the first child node of the node attach it as a left child to the current node in binary tree.

iii) The right sibling can be attached as a right child of that node.

Let us convert the given general tree in Fig. 1.5.1 into equivalent binary tree.

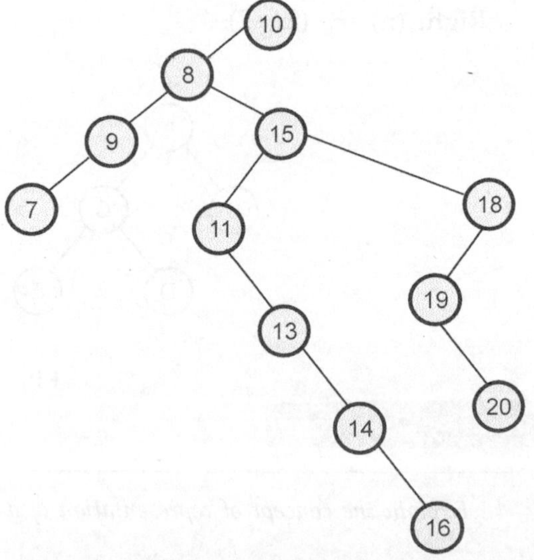

Fig. 1.5.1 Binary tree

Example 1.5.1 *Convert following generalized tree into a inary tree.*  **SPPU : Dec.-13, Marks 3**

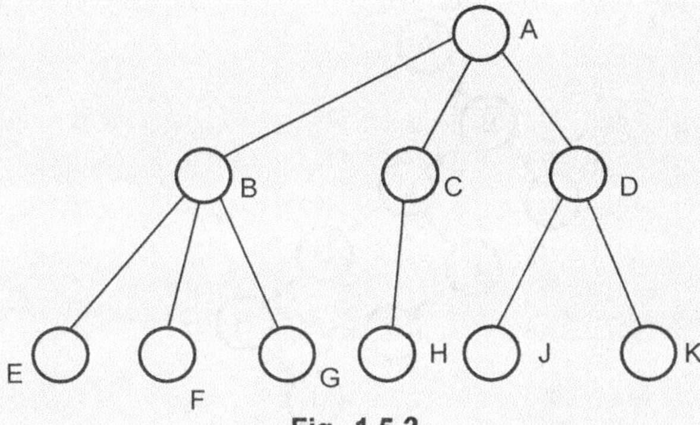

Fig. 1.5.2

Solution :

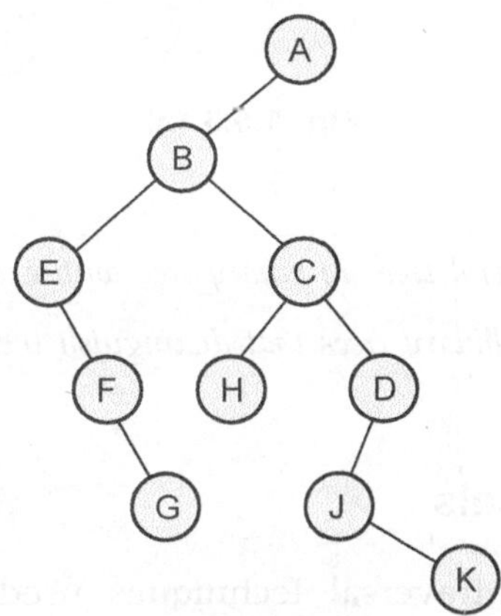

Fig. 1.5.2 (a)

Example 1.5.2 *Convert the following tree into Binary tree.*  **SPPU : May-14, Marks 6**

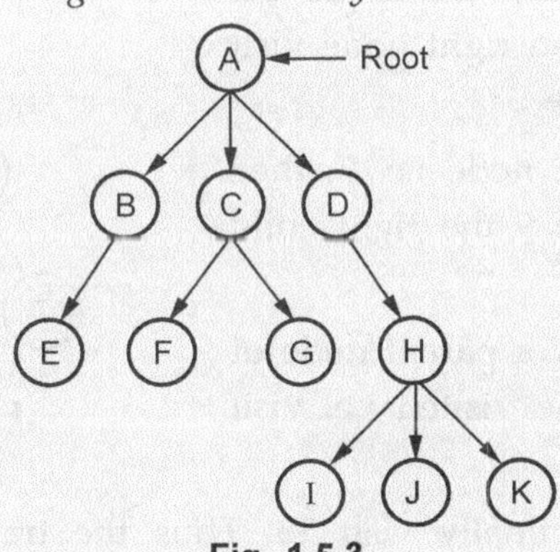

Fig. 1.5.3

Solution : The rules are

i) The root of general tree becomes root of the binary tree.

ii) The first left child becomes left child of the tree.

iii) The right sibling is attached as right child.

The binary tree will be -

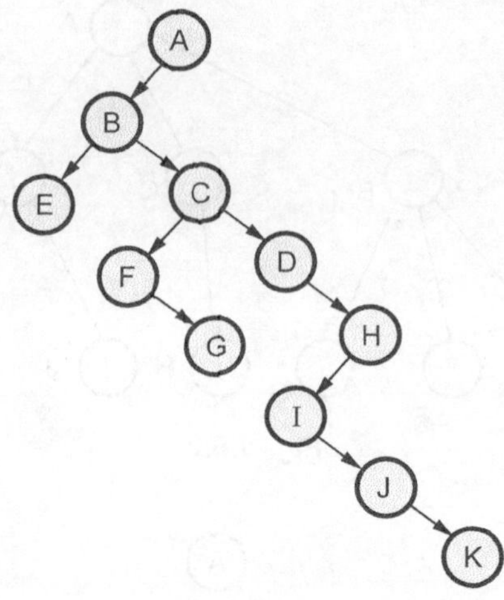

Fig. 1.5.3 (a)

University Questions

1. *Explain how to convert general trees to binary tree with example.* **SPPU : Dec.-11, Marks 5**
2. *What are the properties for binary trees that distinguish them from general trees ?* **SPPU : May-12, Marks 6**

1.6 Binary Tree Traversals

SPPU : May-11, 14, Dec.-12, Marks 9

Concept : There are three traversal techniques used for binary tree. These are - Inorder, Preorder and Postorder traversals. Let us discuss these traversals in detail

1. Inorder traversal : In this technique the leftnode, parent and then right node visit is followed. For example

I) Here visit the leftmost node i.e. 7, then its parent node 8 then 9 the right child will be visited.

II) The root node (actually a parent node of left sub-branch) will be visited i.e. visit 10.

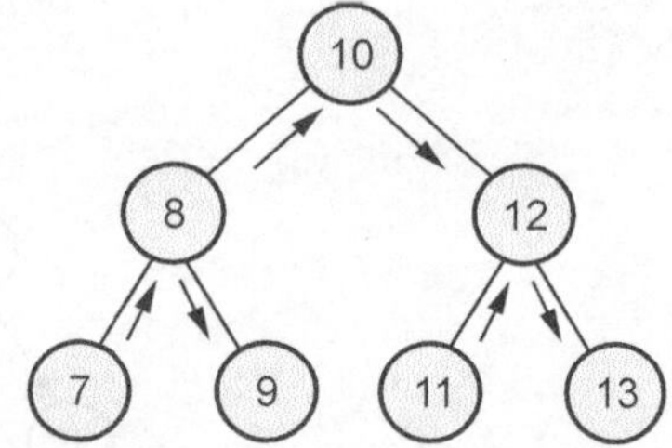

Fig. 1.6.1 Binary tree

III) Visit 11 then 12 and finally visit 13. Thus the traversal of right subbranch is performed.

Hence, Inorder sequence is **7, 8, 9, 10, 11, 12, 13**

2. Preorder traversal : In this method visit parent node the left and then right node.

I) Visit 10

II) Visit 8, then 7 finally 9

III)Visit 12 then 11 and finally 13.

Hence preorder traversal is **10, 8, 7, 9, 12, 11, 13.**

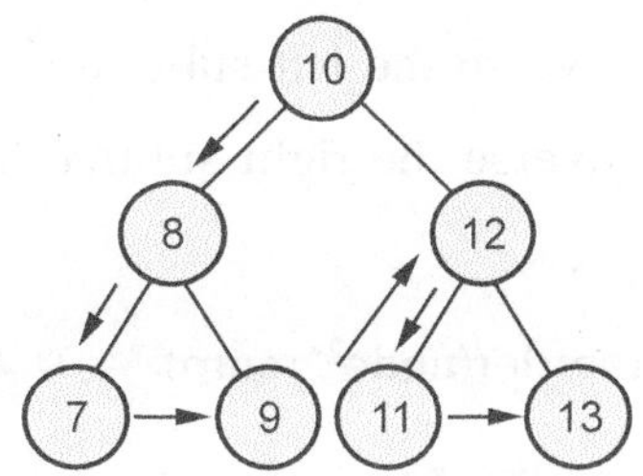

Fig. 1.6.2 Binary tree

3. Postorder traversal : In this technique visit left node then right node and finally parent node.

I) Visit 7, then 9 and then 8.

II) Visit 11, then 13 and then 12.

III)Visit node 10.

The Postorder sequence is : **7, 9, 8, 11, 13, 12, 10.**

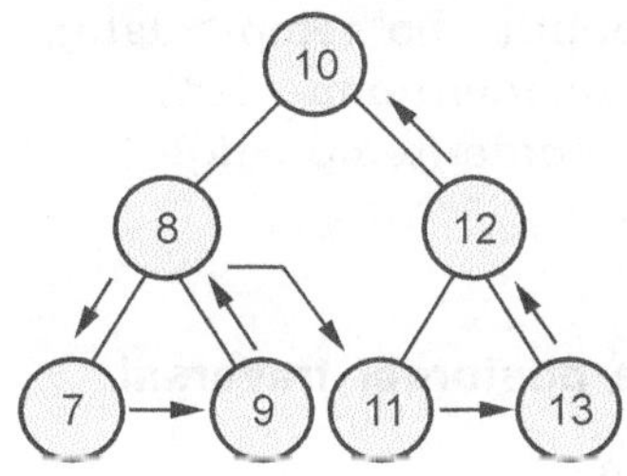

Fig. 1.6.3

Algorithms and C Functions

1. Recursive inorder traversal

Algorithm :

1. If tree is not empty then

    a. traverse the left subtree in inorder

    b. visit the root node

    c. traverse the right subtree in inorder

C Function

```
void inorder(node *temp)
{
 if(temp!=NULL)
 {
      inorder(temp->left);
      printf(" %d",temp->data);
      inorder(temp->right);
 }
}
```

2. Recursive preorder traversal

Algorithm :

1. If tree is not empty then

    a. visit the root node

b. traverse the left subtree in preorder

c. traverse the right subtree in preorder

C Function

```
void preorder(node *temp)
{
 if(temp!=NULL)
 {
        printf(" %d",temp->data);
        preorder(temp->left);
        preorder(temp->right);
 }
}
```

3. Recursive postorder traversal

Algorithm :

1. If tree is not empty then

a. traverse the left subtree in postorder

b. traverse the right subtree in postorder

c. visit the root node

C function

```
void postorder(node *temp)
{
 if(temp!=NULL)
 {
        postorder(temp->left);
        postorder(temp->right);
        printf(" %d",temp->data);
 }
}
```

Example 1.6.1 *Consider the following tree given in the problem. Show a Postorder, Preorder and In order Traversal of tree.* **SPPU : May-14, Marks 3**

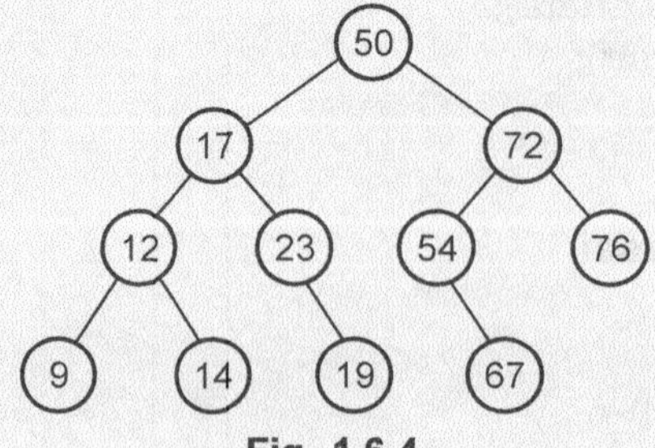

Fig. 1.6.4

Solution : Preorder Sequence : 50, 17, 12, 9, 14, 23, 19, 72, 54, 67, 76.

Inorder Sequence : 9, 12, 14, 17, 23, 19, 50, 54, 67, 72, 76.

Postorder Sequence : 9, 14, 12, 19, 23, 17, 67, 54, 76, 72, 50.

1.6.1 Non Recursive Traversals

We will consider following tree as an example.

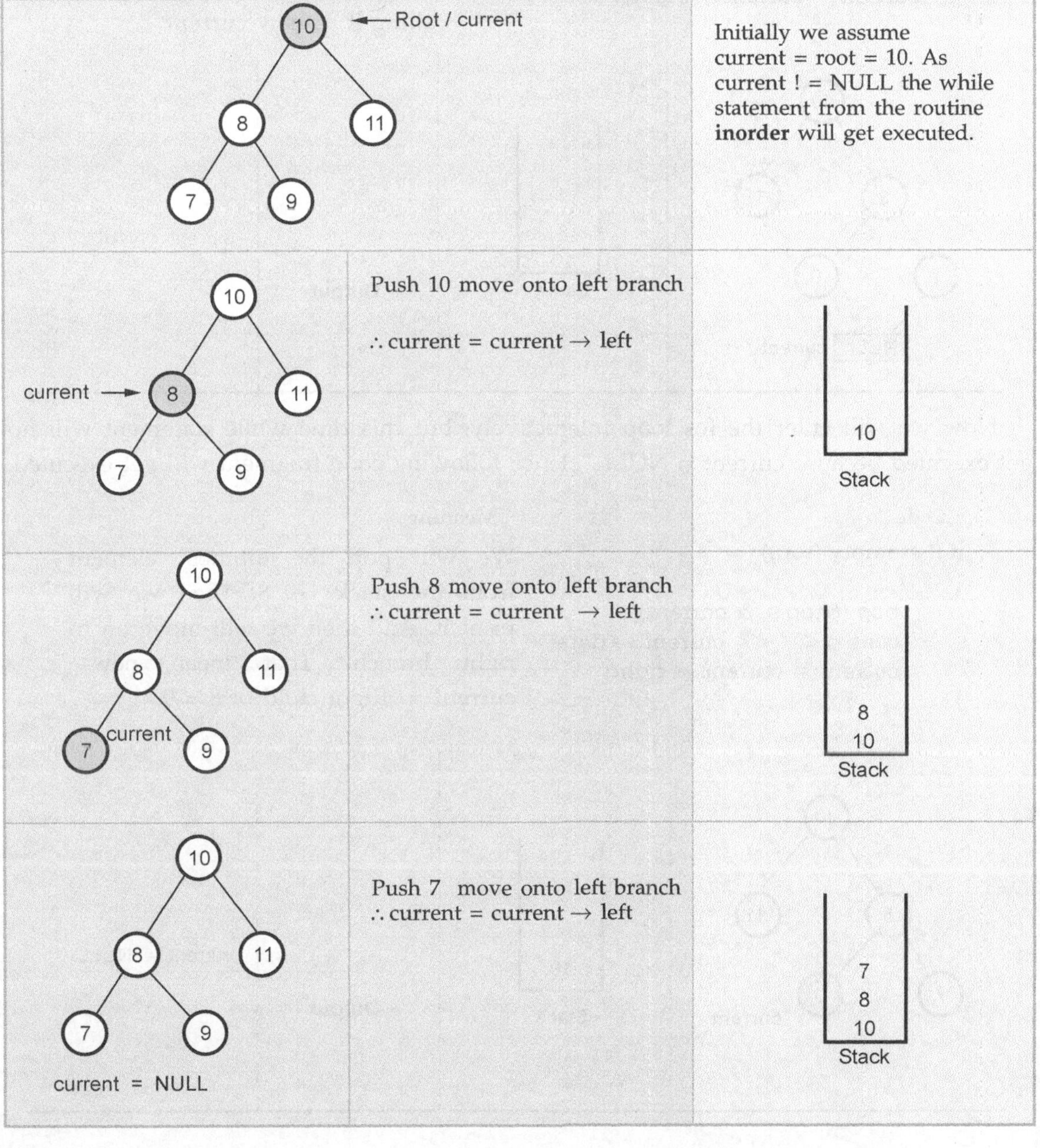

Now as **current** becomes **NULL**, we will come out of the while statements and following code fragment will get executed.

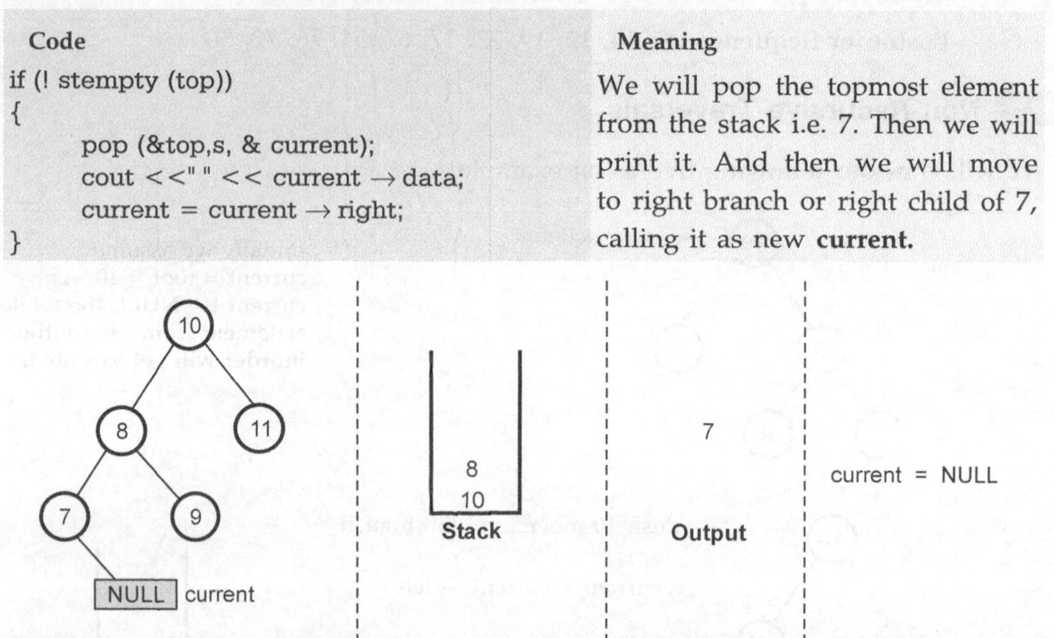

Code	Meaning

`if (! stempty (top))`
`{`
`    pop (&top,s, & current);`
`    cout <<" " << current → data;`
`    current = current → right;`
`}`
	We will pop the topmost element from the stack i.e. 7. Then we will print it. And then we will move to right branch or right child of 7, calling it as new **current.**

Now we will enter the for loop interactively, but this time while statement will not get executed because current = NULL. Hence following code fragment will get executed.

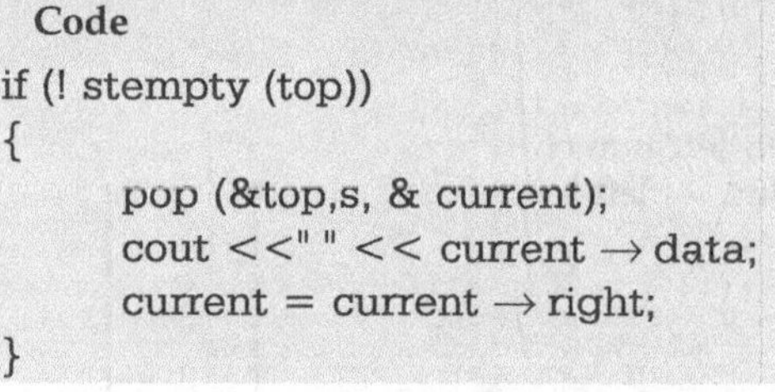

Code	Meaning

`if (! stempty (top))`
`{`
`    pop (&top,s, & current);`
`    cout <<" " << current → data;`
`    current = current → right;`
`}`
	We will pop the topmost element from the stack i.e. 8. Then we will print it. And then we will move on to right branch. That mean new **current** = Right child of 8 = 9.

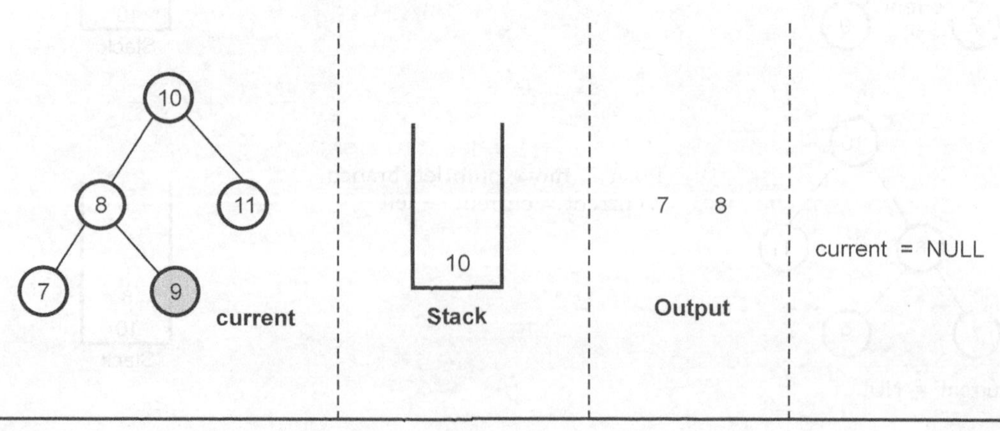

Now we will enter the for loop iteratively and while loop will be executed because current = 9. Hence 9 will be pushed onto the stack. And now current = current → left. As there is no left child for the node current; current = NULL. Hence following code fragment will be executed.

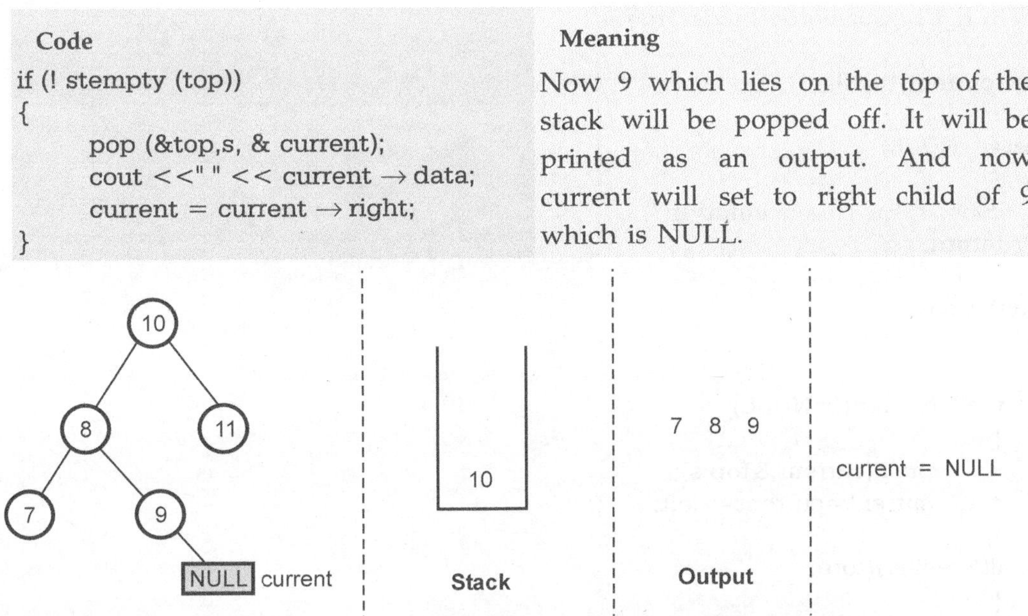

Code	Meaning

`if (! stempty (top))`
`{`
`pop (&top,s, & current);`
`cout <<" " << current → data;`
`current = current → right;`
`}`
	Now 9 which lies on the top of the stack will be popped off. It will be printed as an output. And now current will set to right child of 9 which is NULL.

Now we will enter the for loop interactively but this time while statement will not be executed. The if statement will be executed. According to this code fragment, 10 will be popped off, it will be printed as an output and we will move on to the right branch of 10. Hence now, current = 11 As an output we will get **7 8 9 10 .**

Again we will enter the for loop interactively. The while statement will be executed because current = 12. We will push 11 onto the stack. And move onto the left branch of 11. But there is no left child to 11. Hence value of **current** becomes **NULL**. Then if statement will get executed. According to it, 11 will be popped off, it will be printed as an output and we will move onto right branch of 11.

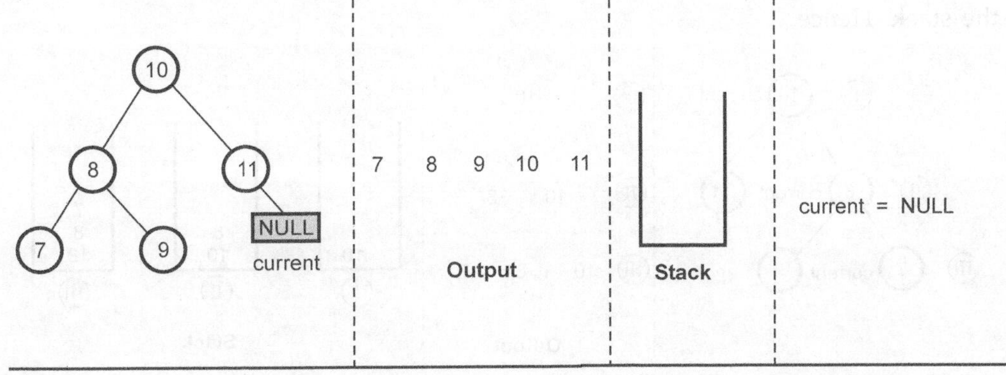

Again we will enter the for loop iteratively. But current = NULL ; hence **while** statements will not be executed, stack is empty; hence if statements will not be executed. Hence **else** will be executed, by which control returns to main function. Thus we will get **7 8 9 10 11** as an output of nonrecursive inorder traversal.

```
void TREE_CLASS::inorder(node *root)
{
 node *current,*s[10];
 int top=-1;
 if(root==NULL)
 {
        cout<<"\n Tree is empty\n";
        return;
 }
 current=root;
 for(;;)
 {
        while(current!=NULL)
        {
               push(current,&top,s);
               current=current->left;
        }
        if(!stempty(top))
        {
               pop(&top,s,&current);
               cout<<" "<<current->data;
               current=current->right;
        }
        else
               return;
 }
```

Non-recursive Preorder Traversal

The logic for preorder traversal is similar to the inorder traversal. But the only difference is that we will print the value of each visited current node before pushing it onto the stack. Hence

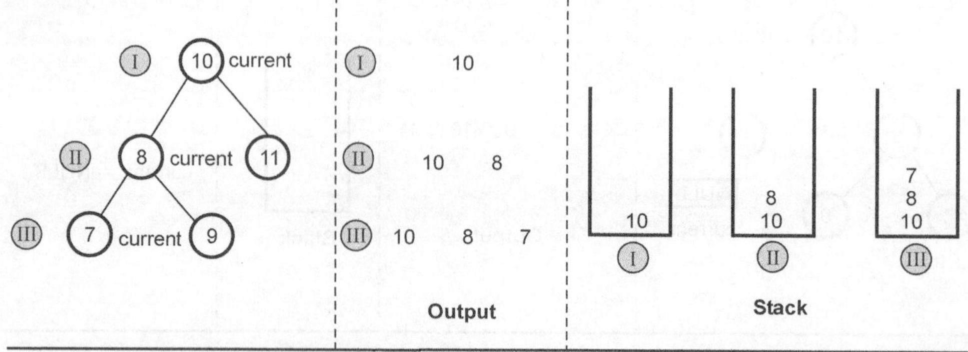

Visiting each node, calling it as current, printing it as an output, pushing current node onto the stack and moving on to the left child. These are the sequence of operation which we must follow at every stage. Above is the scenario for stage I, II and III.

Now if we move on to left branch of 7 we will get current = NULL. We will pop 7 check if it has any right. As 7 has no right child. We will pop the next element i.e. 8. As 8 has a right child i.e. 9, we will print 9 as an output and push it on to the stack. The stack will now be

Then 9 will be popped off, but 9 has no right child so we will pop 10. The 10 has right child i.e. 11. Hence print 11 as an output and push it onto the stack.

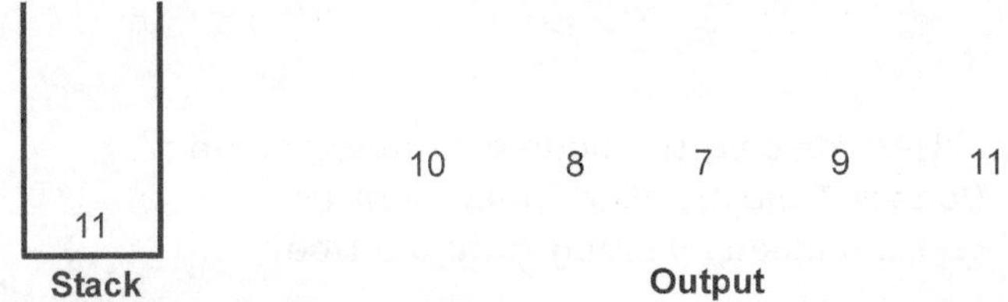

Finally 11 will be popped off. The node 11 has no left or right child so nothing will be pushed. As a result we get **10 8 7 9 11** as an output for nonrecursive preorder traversal.

```
void TREE_CLASS::preorder(node *root)
{
 node *current,*s[10];
 int top=-1;
 if(root==NULL)
 {
       cout<<"\n The Tree is empty\n";
       return;
 }
 current=root;
 for(;;)
 {
       while(current!=NULL)
       {
        cout<<" "<<current->data;
        push(current,&top,s);
        current=current->left;
       }
       if(!stempty(top))
```

```
        {
         pop(&top,s,&current);
         current=current->right;
        }
        else
         return;
 }

}
```

Nonrecursive Postorder Traversal

In the nonrecursive postorder traversal we have to add extra field in the stack structure. This field keeps a check on whether the node is visited once or not. If we visit that node for the first time then we set that check to 1, if we again visits that node then we reset that check. This extra logic we have to put because we traverse to the left node first, then right node and then the parent node.

```
void TREE_CLASS::postorder(node *root)
{
struct stack
 {
       node *element;//Here placing the node containing value
       int check;       //check 1 means visiting left subtree
                        //check 0 means visiting right subtree
}st[10];
int top=-1;
node *current;
if(root==NULL)
{
       cout<<"\n The Tree is empty\n";
       return;
}
current=root;
for(;;)
{
        while(current!=NULL)
        {
               top++;
               st[top].element=current;
               st[top].check=1;//visiting the left subbranch
               current=current->left;
        }
        while(st[top].check==0)
        {
               current=st[top].element;
               top--;
               cout<<"  "<<current->data;
```

```
            if(stempty(top))
             return;
        }
        current=st[top].element;//pushing the element onto the stack
        current=current->right;
        st[top].check=0;//visiting right subtree
    }
}
```

University Questions

1. *Write pseudocode for printing the elements of a binary search tree in ascending order non-recursively.* **SPPU : May-11, Marks 6**
2. *Write non-recursive algorithm for traversal of binary tree.* **SPPU : Dec.-12, Marks 9**

1.7 Depth and Level Wise Traversals **SPPU : May-07, Dec.-10, Marks 8**

The tree can be traversed along with its depth as well as along with its breadth. Let us discuss about it.

1.7.1 Depth First Search(DFS)

Concept : In this traversal technique the tree is traversed according to its depth and the visited vertex in this depthwise traversal are printed. For example

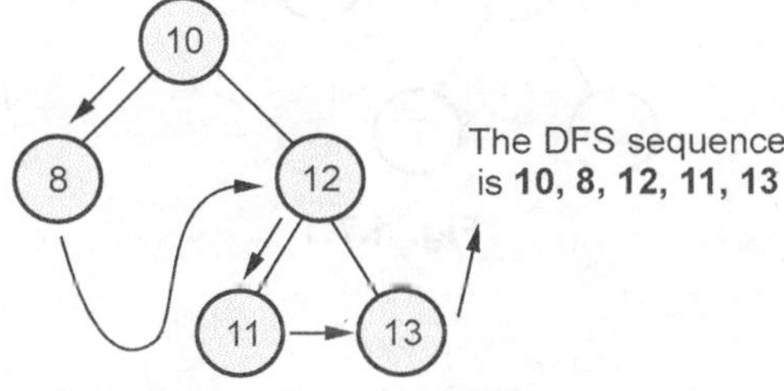

For displaying the tree in depth first search manner, we have to start from the root node. From that node moving along the edge, and we have to move towards the leaf node and display the data. The depth first traversal is same as **preorder traversal.**

To perform this traversal we need an additional data structure called **stack.**

Algorithm :

Step 1 : Visit the root node . Push it onto the stack.

Step 2 : Pop the node and display it as output.

Step 3 : If its right child is not NULL, push it onto the stack.

Step 4 : If its left child is not NULL push it onto the stack.

Step 5 : Repeat step 2 to Step 4 until stack is not empty.

Pseudo Code :

```
Algorithm DFS(root)
{
	temp=root;
	if(temp!=NULL)
	{
		display "temp->data";
		DFS(temp->left);
		DFS(temp->right);
	}
}
```

Example 1.7.1 *Consider following tree and obtain its DFS sequence.*

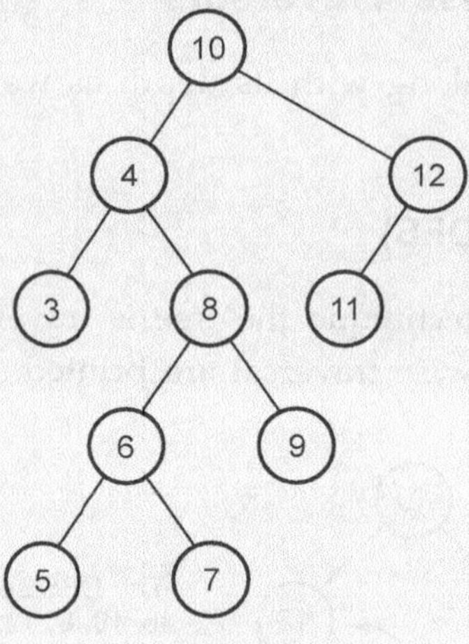

Fig. 1.7.1

Solution :

Action	Stack	Output
Step 1 : We will visit 10 and push it onto the stack. Pop the node display it as output.	10	
		10

Step	Description	Stack	Output
Step 2 :	We will visit right child of popped node push it. Then we will visit left child of 10, push it onto the stack.	4 12	
	Pop the node, display it as output.	12	10, 4
Step 3 :	We will visit right child of node 4, push it onto the stack. Now we will visit left child of node 4, push it onto the stack.	3 8 12	
	Pop the node and display it as output.	8 12	10, 4, 3, 8
Step 4 :	As 3 has no left or right child, nothing will be pushed. Pop the top node from the stack and display it as output.	12	10, 4, 3, 8
Step 5 :	We will visit right child of 8, push it onto the stack. Then we will visit left child of 6, push it onto the stack.	6 9 12	
	Pop the top node from the stack and display it as output.	9 12	10, 4, 3, 8, 6
Step 6 :	Visit right child of 6 i.e. 7, push it onto the stack. Visit left child of 6 i.e. 5, push it onto the stack.	5 7 9 12	
	Pop the top node from the stack and display it as output.	7 9 12	10, 4, 3, 8, 6, 5

		Stack	Output
Step 7 :	As 5 has no left or right child nothing will be pushed onto the stack. Pop the top element of stack and display it as output.	9 12	**10, 4, 3, 8, 6, 5, 7**
Step 8 :	As 7 has no left or right child nothing will be pushed onto the stack. Pop 9. Display it.	12	**10, 4, 3, 8, 6, 5, 7, 9**
Step 9 :	Again 9 is a leaf node nothing will be pushed. Pop 12, Print it.		**10, 4 , 3, 8, 6, 5, 7, 9, 12**
Step 10 :	There is no right child of 12. But 12 has left child. So Push 11 onto the stack. Pop 11 and display it.		**10, 4, 3, 8, 6, 5, 7, 9, 12, 11**

Now all the nodes are visited. The stack is empty. Hence we get DFS sequence as. **10, 4, 3, 8, 6, 5, 7, 9, 12, 11.**

C++ Program

```
/*******************************************************************
Program to create a binary tree and display it using Depth First Traversal.
Both the recursive and non recursive versions of DFS are considered in
this program
*******************************************************************/
#include<iostream.h>
#include<conio.h>
#define size 50

/* Declare a node for binary tree */
class tree
{
        private:
        typedef struct node
        {
                int data;
                struct node *left;
                struct node *right;
```

```
            }btree;
            public:
            btree  *stack[size];
            int top;
            btree *root,*New;
            tree();
            ~tree();
            void create();
            void insert(node*,node*);
            void push(btree *Node);
            void Dfs(btree *);
            void Dfs_Rec(btree *);
            btree* pop();
            void remove(btree *);
};

/*
------------------------------------------------------------------------
The constructor defined
------------------------------------------------------------------------
*/
tree::tree()
{
      root=NULL;
      top=-1;
}
/*
------------------------------------------------------------------------
The create function
------------------------------------------------------------------------
*/
void tree::create()
{
      New=new btree;
      New->left=NULL;
      New->right=NULL;
      cout<<"\n Enter The Element ";
      cin>>New->data;
      if(root==NULL)    /* Tree is not Created */
       root=New;
      else
       insert(root,New);
}

/*
```

```
----------------------------------------------------------------------------
The insert Function
----------------------------------------------------------------------------
*/
void tree::insert(node *root,node *New)
{
char ch;
 cout<<"\n Where to insert left/right of "<<root->data<<" ";
 ch=getche();
 if ((ch=='r')||(ch=='R'))
 {
      if(root->right==NULL)
       {
            root->right=New;  //attaching new node as a right child
       }
      else
       insert(root->right,New);  //moving on the right branch
}
 else
 {
      if (root->left==NULL)
      {
            root->left=New;   //attaching new node as a left child
      }
      else
            insert(root->left,New); //moving on the left branch
 }
}
/*
----------------------------------------------------------------------------
      The recursive Dfs function
----------------------------------------------------------------------------
*/
void tree::Dfs_Rec(btree *root)
{
      btree *temp;
      temp = root;
      if (temp!= NULL )
      {
            cout<<" "<<temp->data;
            Dfs_Rec(temp->left);
            Dfs_Rec(temp->right);

      }
}
/*
```

```
------------------------------------------------------------------------
        The non recursive Dfs function
------------------------------------------------------------------------
*/
void tree::Dfs(btree *root)
{
        btree *temp;
        top = -1; /* Initialize Stack */
        temp = root;
        if ( temp == NULL )
        {
                cout<<"The Tree is Empty\n";
                getch();
                return ;
        }
        push(temp);
        while ( top != -1)
        {
                                temp = pop();
                                cout<<" "<<temp -> data;
                                /* push Right Child if any */
                                if ( temp -> right)
                                push(temp -> right);
                                /* Move on to left child, if any and push it */
                                if ( temp -> left )
                                {
                                        temp = temp -> left;
                                        push(temp);
                                }
        }
}
/*
------------------------------------------------------------------------
        The push function
------------------------------------------------------------------------
*/
void tree::push(btree *Node)
{
                if ( top+1 >= size )
                cout<<" Stack is Full\n";
                top++;
                stack[top] = Node;
}
/*
------------------------------------------------------------------------
The pop function
------------------------------------------------------------------------
```

```
*/
btree* tree::pop()
{
        btree *Node;
        if ( top == -1 )
        cout<<"Stack is Empty\n";
        Node = stack[top];
        top--;
        return(Node);
}
/*
-----------------------------------------------------------------------
The destructor defined
-----------------------------------------------------------------------
*/
tree::~tree()
{
 remove(root);
}
/*
-----------------------------------------------------------------------
The remove function for de allocating the memory
-----------------------------------------------------------------------
*/
void tree::remove(btree *root)
{
 if(root!=NULL)
 {
  remove(root->left);
  remove(root->right);
 }
 delete root;
}

/*
-----------------------------------------------------------------------
The main function
-----------------------------------------------------------------------
*/
void main()
{
    tree tr;
    char ans='y';
    cout<<"\n Program for Depth First Traversal\n";
        do
        {
        clrscr();
```

```
        tr.create();

        cout<<"\n Do u Want To enter More Elements?(y/n)\n";
        ans=getch();
        }while(ans=='y');
        cout<<"\n\n The Non Recursive Depth First Traversal is ...\n";
        tr.Dfs(tr.root);
        cout<<"\n\n The Recursive Depth First Traversal is ...\n";
        tr.Dfs_Rec(tr.root);
        getch();
}
```

Output

```
Program for Depth First Traversal

Enter The Element 10

Do u Want To enter More Elements?(y/n)

Enter The Element 8

Where to insert left/right of 10 l
Do u Want To enter More Elements?(y/n)
Enter The Element 9

Where to insert left/right of 10 l
Where to insert left/right of 8 r
Do u Want To enter More Elements?(y/n)

Enter The Element 7

Where to insert left/right of 10 l
Where to insert left/right of 8 l
Do u Want To enter More Elements?(y/n)

Enter The Element 5

Where to insert left/right of 10 l
Where to insert left/right of 8 l
Where to insert left/right of 7 l
Do u Want To enter More Elements?(y/n)

Enter The Element 6

Where to insert left/right of 10 l
Where to insert left/right of 8 l
Where to insert left/right of 7 l
```

```
Where to insert left/right of 5 r
Do u Want To enter More Elements?(y/n)

Enter The Element 12

Where to insert left/right of 10 r
Do u Want To enter More Elements?(y/n)

Enter The Element 11

Where to insert left/right of 10 r
Where to insert left/right of 12 l
Do u Want To enter More Elements?(y/n)

Enter The Element 13

Where to insert left/right of 10 r
Where to insert left/right of 12 r
Do u Want To enter More Elements?(y/n)


The Non Recursive Depth First Traversal is ...
10 8 7 5 6 9 12 11 13

The Recursive Depth First Traversal is ...
10 8 7 5 6 9 12 11 13
```

Analysis : The time and space complexity of DFS is O(n).

1.7.2 Breadth First Search(BFS)

Concept : This is a searching technique in which all the nodes of the same level are displayed.

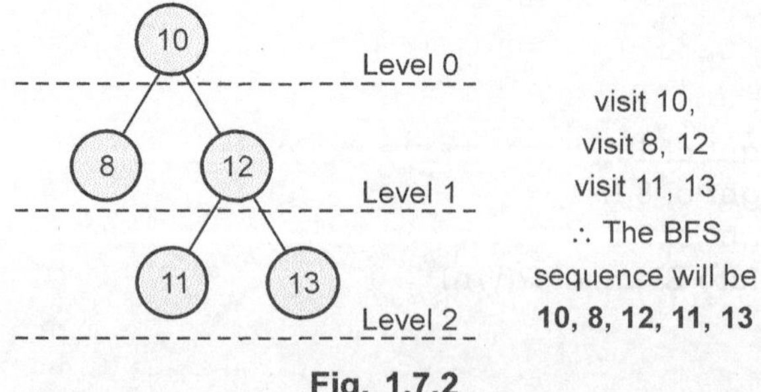

Fig. 1.7.2

In this traversal method, we start from the root node and go on printing the data in level wise manner.

An additional data structure called **queue** is required to perform this traversal.

Algorithm :

Step 1 : Visit the root node . Insert it in Queue from the rear end.

Step 2 : Delete the node from front end of the queue and display it as output.

Step 3 : If its left child is not null insert the left child in the queue.

Step 4 : If Its right child is not null, insert the right child in the queue.

Step 5 : Repeat step 2 to Step 4 until queue is not empty and all nodes are visited.

Pseudo Code :

```
Algorithm BFS()
{
        btree *temp, *dummy;
        dummy = new btree;
        if ( dummy == NULL)
           cout<<"Insufficient Memory\n";
        dummy->left = root;
        dummy->right = NULL;
        dummy->data = ' ';
        temp = dummy ->left;
        enque(temp);
        enque(dummy);
        temp = deque();
        while ( front != rear)
        {
                if ( temp != dummy)
                {
                        cout<<" "<<temp->data;
                        if ( temp ->left != NULL)
                                        enque(temp -> left);
                        if ( temp ->right != NULL)
                                enque(temp -> right);
                }
                else
                {
                        enque(temp);
                        cout<<"\n";
                }
                temp = deque();
        }
}
```

Example 1.7.2 *Consider following tree and find its BFS sequence.*

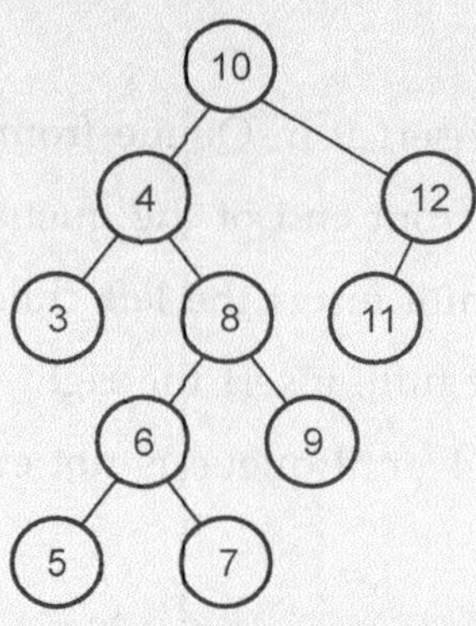

Fig. 1.7.3

Solution :

Step 1 : We will visit root node insert it in queue.

Delete the node from queue, display it as output.

∴ **BFS sequence :** 10

Step 2 : Find left and right nodes of 10, insert them in queue.

4	12

Queue

Delete the node 4 from, display as output.

∴ **BFS Sequence :** 10, 4

Step 3 : Find left and right child of 4, insert them in queue.

12	3	8

Delete 12, display as output.

∴ **BFS sequence :** 10, 4, 12

Step 4 : Find left and right child of 12, insert them in queue.

3	8	11

Delete 3, display it.

∴ **BFS sequence :** 10, 4, 12, 3

Step 5 : Find left and right child of 3.

But 3 has no left or right child.

Now delete 8, display it.

∴ **BFS sequence :** 10, 4, 12, 3, 8

Step 6 : Find left and right child of 8, Insert them in queue.

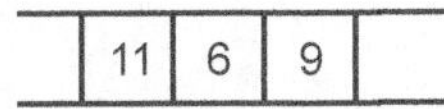

Delete 11, display it.

∴ **BFS sequence :** 10, 4, 12, 3, 8, 11

Step 7 : There is no left or right child of 11. So nothing will be inserted in queue.

Now delete 6, display it.

∴ **BFS sequence :** 10, 4, 12, 3, 8, 11, 6

Step 8 : Find left and right child of 6. Insert them in queue.

9	5	7

Delete 9, display it.

∴ **BFS sequence :** 10, 4, 12, 3, 8, 11, 6, 9

Step 9 : There is no left or right child of 9. Delete 5, display it.

∴ **BFS sequence :** 10, 4, 12, 3, 8, 11, 6, 9, 5

Step 10 : There is no left or right child of 5.

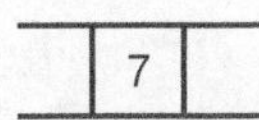

Delete 7, display it.

∴ **BFS sequence :** 10, 4, 12, 3, 8, 11, 6, 9, 5, 7

C++ Program

```
/*********************************************************************
Program to create a binary tree and print the data level wise or in a
breadth first search order.
*********************************************************************/
#include<iostream.h>
#include<conio.h>
#define size 50

/* Declare a node for binary tree */
class tree
{
        private:
         typedef struct node
         {
                int  data;
                struct node *left;
                struct node *right;
         }btree;
         btree *root,*New;
  public:
  tree();
  void create(),display();
  void insert(node *,node *);
  void enque(btree *Node);
  btree *deque ();
  btree *que[size];
  void remove(btree *);
  ~tree();
  int front,rear;
};

/*
-----------------------------------------------
The constructor defined
-----------------------------------------------
*/
tree::tree()
{
 root=NULL;
 front=rear=-1;
}
/*
-----------------------------------------------
The create function
-----------------------------------------------
*/
```

```
void tree::create()
{
 New=new btree;
 New->left=NULL;
 New->right=NULL;
 cout<<"\n Enter The Element ";
 cin>>New->data;
 if(root==NULL)     /* Tree is not Created */
       root=New;
 else
       insert(root,New);
}
/*
------------------------------------------------------------------------------------------------
The insert Function
------------------------------------------------------------------------------------------------
*/
void tree::insert(node *root,node *New)
{
char ch;
cout<<"\n Where to insert left/right of "<<root->data<<" ";
ch=getche();
if ((ch=='r')||(ch=='R'))
 {
                 if(root->right==NULL)
                 {
                  root->right=New;  //attaching new node as a right child
                 }
                 else
                 insert(root->right,New);  //moving on the right branch
 }
 else
 {
  if (root->left==NULL)
  {
       root->left=New;   //attaching new node as a left child
  }
  else
       insert(root->left,New); //moving on the left branch
 }
}

/*
------------------------------------------------------------------------------------
       The display function
------------------------------------------------------------------------------------
*/
```

```
void tree::display()
{
      btree *temp, *dummy;
      dummy = new btree;
      if ( dummy == NULL)
        cout<<"Insufficient Memory\n";
      dummy->left = root;
      dummy->right = NULL;
      dummy->data = ' ';
      temp = dummy ->left;
      enque(temp);
      enque(dummy);
      temp = deque();

      while ( front != rear)
      {
            if ( temp != dummy)
            {
                  cout<<"  "<<temp->data;
                  if ( temp ->left != NULL)
                              enque(temp -> left);
                  if ( temp ->right != NULL)
                        enque(temp -> right);
            }
            else
            {
                  enque(temp);
                  cout<<"\n";
            }
            temp = deque();
      }
}

/*
-------------------------------------------------------------------------------------
The enque function
-------------------------------------------------------------------------------------
*/
void tree::enque(btree *Node)
{
      if ( rear == size-1)
         cout<<"Queue is full\n";
      rear = rear + 1;
      que[rear] = Node;
}

/*
```

```
-----------------------------------------------------------------------------------------
The deque function
-----------------------------------------------------------------------------------------
*/
btree *tree::deque ()
{
        btree *Node;

        if ( front == rear )
            cout<<"Queue is empty\n";
        front++;
        Node = que[front];
        return(Node);
}
/*
-----------------------------------------------------------------------------------------
The destructor defined
-----------------------------------------------------------------------------------------
*/
tree::~tree()
{
 remove(root);
}
/*
-----------------------------------------------------------------------------------------
The remove function for de allocating the memory
-----------------------------------------------------------------------------------------
*/
void tree::remove(btree *root)
{
 if(root!=NULL)
 {
  remove(root->left);
  remove(root->right);
 }
 delete root;
}

/*
-----------------------------------------------------------------------------------------
        The main function
-----------------------------------------------------------------------------------------
*/
void main ()
{
   tree tr;
   char ans='y';
```

```
        do
         {
          clrscr();
          tr.create();
          cout<<"\n Do u Want To enter More Elements?(y/n)\n";
          ans=getch();
          }while(ans=='y');
         cout<<"\n\n The Breadth First Traversal is ...\n";
         tr.display();
         getch();
}
```

Output

```
Enter The Element 10

Do u Want To enter More Elements?(y/n)

Enter The Element 8

Where to insert left/right of 10 l
Do u Want To enter More Elements?(y/n)

Enter The Element 9

Where to insert left/right of 10 l
Where to insert left/right of 8 r
Do u Want To enter More Elements?(y/n)

Enter The Element 12

Where to insert left/right of 10 r
Do u Want To enter More Elements?(y/n)

Enter The Element 7

Where to insert left/right of 10 l
Where to insert left/right of 8 l
Do u Want To enter More Elements?(y/n)

Enter The Element 11

Where to insert left/right of 10 r
Where to insert left/right of 12 l
Do u Want To enter More Elements?(y/n)
```

```
Enter The Element 13

Where to insert left/right of 10 r
Where to insert left/right of 12 r
Do u Want To enter More Elements?(y/n)

The Breadth First Traversal is ...
 10
 8  12
 7  9  11  13
```

Analysis : The time and space complexity of BFS is O(n).

Difference between DFS and BFS

DFS	BFS
The nodes are visited in depthwise manner.	The nodes are visited in breadth wise manner
The additional data structure stack is required for this type of traversal.	The additional data structure queue is required for this type of traversal.

University Questions

1. *Write a pseudo C code that uses queue to print out the nodes of tree level by level i.e. all level 0 nodes, followed by all level 1 nodes, followed by all level 2 nodes and so on.*

   SPPU : May-07, Marks 8

2. *Write a C/C++ function to print given binary tree in BFS (without using recursion).*

   SPPU : Dec.-10, Marks 8

1.8 Operations on Binary Tree

Various operations that can be performed on binary tree are

1. Insertion of a node in a tree
2. Deletion of any node from the tree
3. Traversal of a tree.

Before performing these operations it is necessary to create the simple binary tree. Let us discuss the procedure for creation of a binary tree -

1. Declare the node structure for binary tree. It is as follows -

```
typedef struct bin
{
      int data;
      struct bin *left;
      struct bin *right;
}node;/*Binary tree structure*/
```

2. Write the Create Function for creation of binary tree. It is as follows -

```
void TREE_CLASS::create()
{
    char ans = 'y';
    do
    {
        New = new node;
        cout << "\n Enter The Element : ";
        cin >> New->data;
        New->left = NULL;
        New->right = NULL;
        if (root == NULL)
            root = New;
        else
            insert(root, New);
        cout << "\n Do You want To Enter More elements ? (y / n) : ";
        ans = getche();
    } while (ans == 'y' || ans == 'Y');
    clrscr();
}
void TREE_CLASS::insert(node *root, node *New)
{
    char ch;
    cout << "\n Where to insert left / right of " << root->data << ": ";
    ch = getche();
    if ((ch == 'r') || (ch == 'R'))
    {
        if (root->right == NULL)
        {
            root->right = New;
        }
        else
            insert(root->right, New);
    }
    else
    {
        if (root->left == NULL)
        {
            root->left = New;
        }
        else
            insert(root->left, New);
    }
}
```

The above can be expressed diagrammatically as follows :

Step 1 : Initially create a root node. For instance - if we want to create a root node with value 10 then.

Step 2 : Insert 8 as left child.

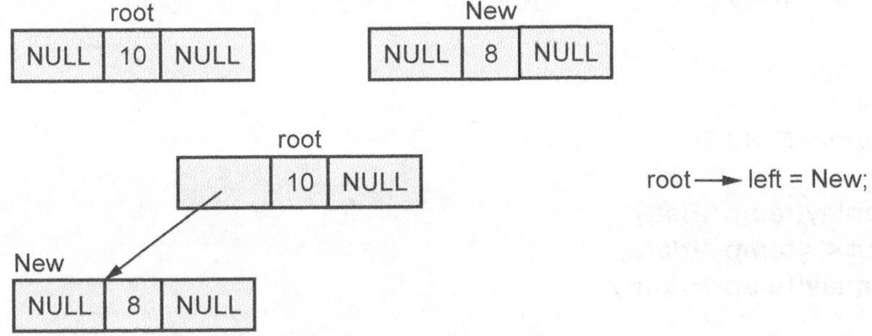

Step 3 : Insert 12 as a right child.

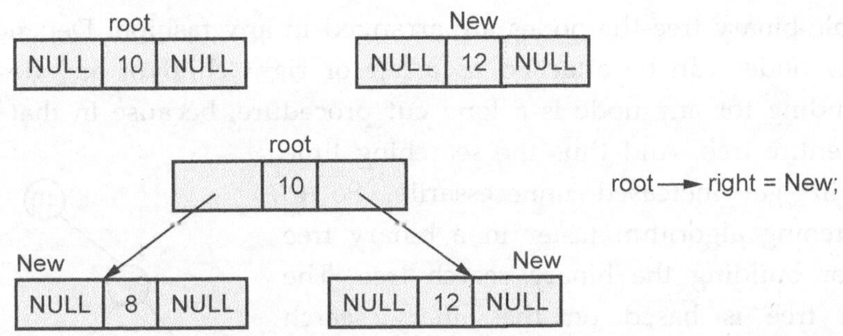

Step 4 : Insert 7 as a left child of 8.

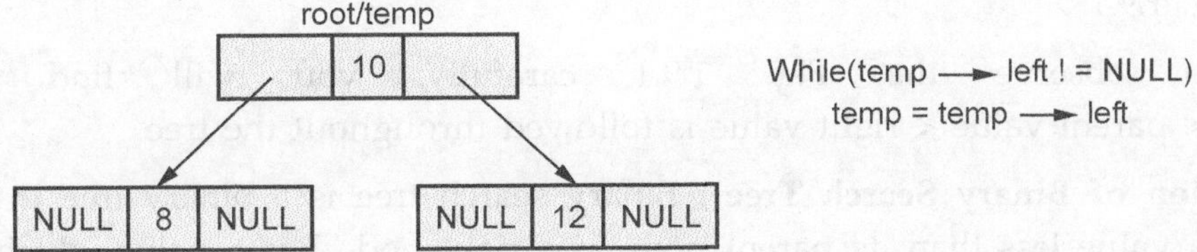

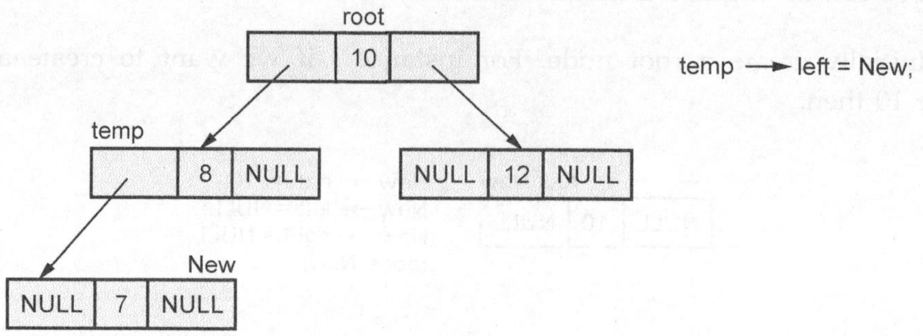

3. Write the display function using either inorder, preorder or postorder traversal -

```
void display(btree *root)
{
	btree *temp;
	temp=root;
	while(temp!=NULL)
	{
		display(temp->left)
		cout<<temp->data;
		display(temp->right);
	}
}
```

1.9 Binary Search Tree(BST)

In the simple binary tree the nodes are arranged in any fashion. Depending on user's desire the new nodes can be attached as a left or right child of any desired node. In such a case finding for any node is a long cut procedure, because in that case we have to search the entire tree. And thus the searching time complexity will get increased unnecessarily. So to make the searching algorithm faster in a binary tree we will go for building the binary search tree. The binary search tree is based on the binary search algorithm. While creating the binary search tree the data is systematically arranged. That means values at left subtree < root node value < Right subtree values. See the Fig. 1.9.1.

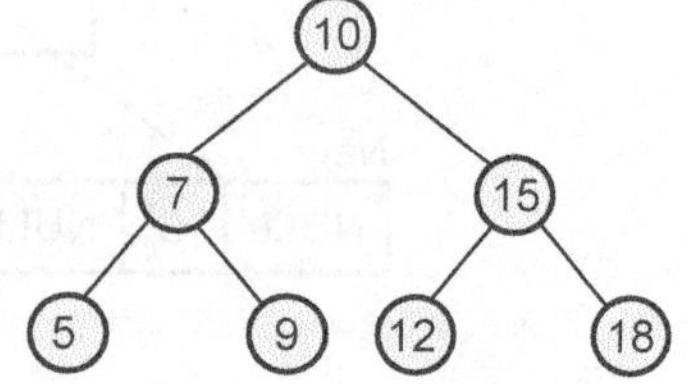

Fig. 1.9.1 Binary search tree

If you observe the Fig. 1.9.1 carefully, you will find that the left value < parent value < right value is followed throughout the tree.

Definition of Binary Search Tree : Binary search tree is a binary tree in which left node has a value less than its parent node and right node has a value which is greater than its parent node.

1.10 BST Operations

SPPU : May-07, 09, 11, 14, Dec.-08, 09, 10, Marks 12

Various operations that can be performed on binary search tree are -

1. Insertion of a node in a binary tree.
2. Deletion of some element from the binary search tree.
3. Searching of an element in the binary tree.
4. Display of binary tree.

Let us discuss each operation one by one -

1. Insertion of a node in a binary tree

Algorithm :

1. Read the value for the node which is to be created, and store it in a node called **New**.
2. Initially if (root!=**NULL**) then root=**New**.
3. Again read the next value of node created in **New**.
4. If (New->value < root->value) then attach **New** node as a left child of root otherwise attach **New** node as a right child of root.
5. Repeat step 3 and 4 for constructing required binary search tree completely.

```
void bintree::insert(node  *root,node *New)
{
        if(New->data<root->data)
         {
                if(root->left==NULL)
                 root->left=New;
                else
                 insert(root->left,New);
         }
        if(New->data>root->data)
         {
          if(root->right==NULL)
                        root->right=New;
          else
                        insert(root->right,New);
         }
}
```

Attaching left node to the current node.

If the root node has already some left child, then move on to left subtree

While inserting any node in binary search tree, first of all we have to look for its appropriate position in the binary search tree. We start comparing this new node with each node of the tree. If the value of the node which is to be inserted is greater than the value of current node we move on to the right sub-branch otherwise we move on to the left sub-branch. As soon as the appropriate position is found we attach this new node as left or right child appropriately.

In the Fig. 1.10.1 if we want to insert 23. Then we will start comparing 23 with value of root node i.e. 10. As 23 is greater than 10, we will move on right sub-tree. Now we will compare 23 with 20 and move right, compare 23 with 22 and move right. Now compare 23 with 24 but it is less than 24. We will move on left branch of 24. But as there is NULL node as left child of 24, we can attach 23 as left child of 24.

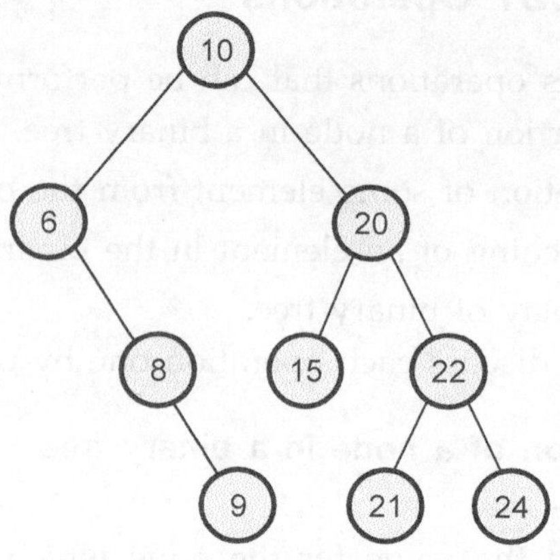

Fig. 1.10.1 Before insertion

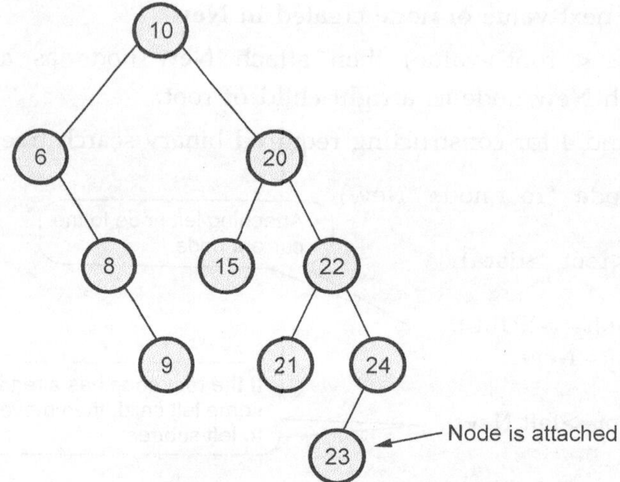

Fig. 1.10.2 After insertion

Example 1.10.1 *What is binary search tree ? Draw binary search tree for the following data : 10, 08, 15, 12, 13, 07, 09, 17, 20, 18, 04, 05.* **SPPU : Dec.-10, Marks 10, May-14, Marks 3**

Solution : Binary search tree - The binary search tree is a kind of binary tree in which the values at left subtree are less than the value of root node. Similarly values of root node is less than values of right subtree.

Let, 10, 08, 15, 12, 13, 07, 09, 17, 20, 18, 04, 05 are the given elements. The binary search tree can be constructed as shown in Fig. 1.10.3 (Refer Fig. 1.10.3 on next page).

That is final binary search tree.

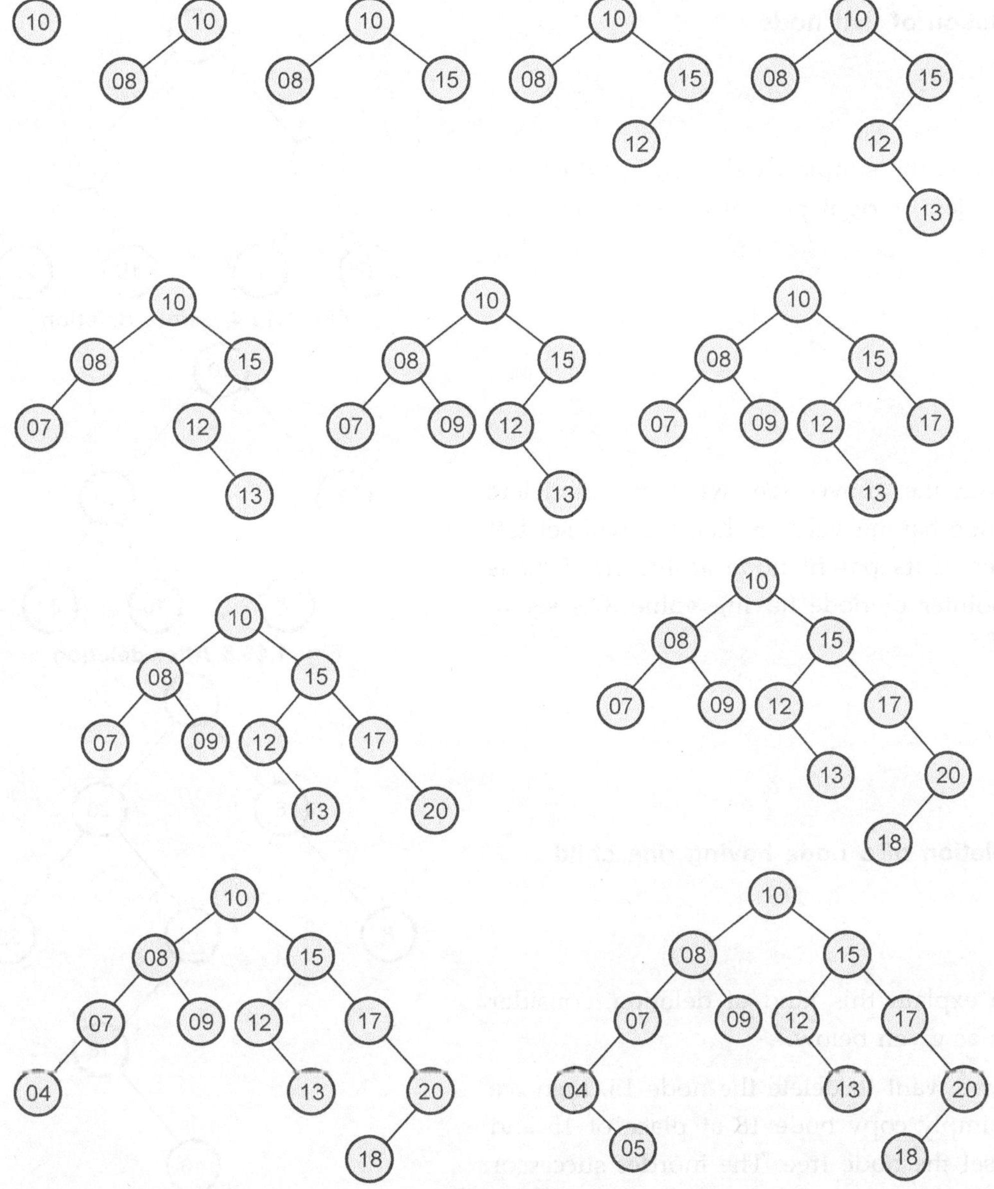

Fig. 1.10.3

2. Deletion of an element from the binary tree

For deletion of any node from binary search tree there are three cases which are possible.

i. Deletion of leaf node.

ii. Deletion of a node having one child.

iii. Deletion of a node having two children.

Let us discuss the above cases one by one.

i. Deletion of leaf node

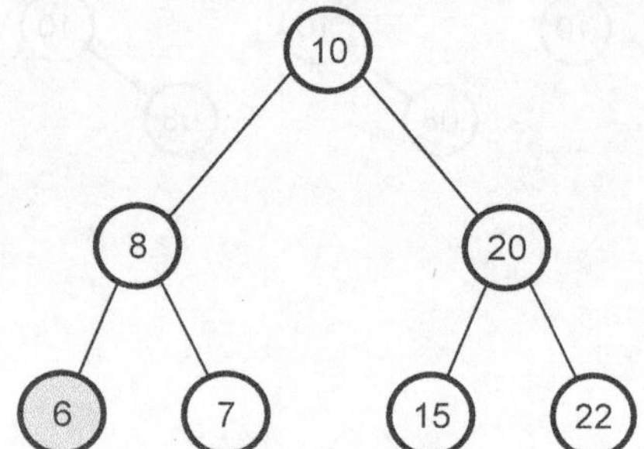

Fig. 1.10.4 Before deletion

This is the simplest deletion, in which we set the left or right pointer of parent node as NULL.

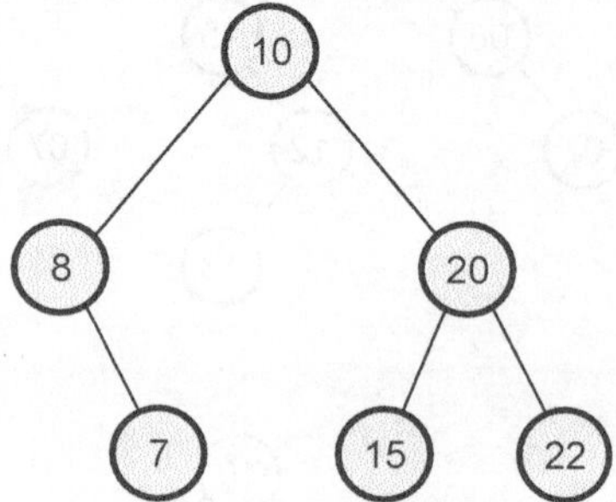

Fig. 1.10.5 After deletion

From the above tree, we want to delete the node having value 6 then we will set left pointer of its parent node as NULL. That is left pointer of node having value 8 is set to NULL.

ii. Deletion of a node having one child

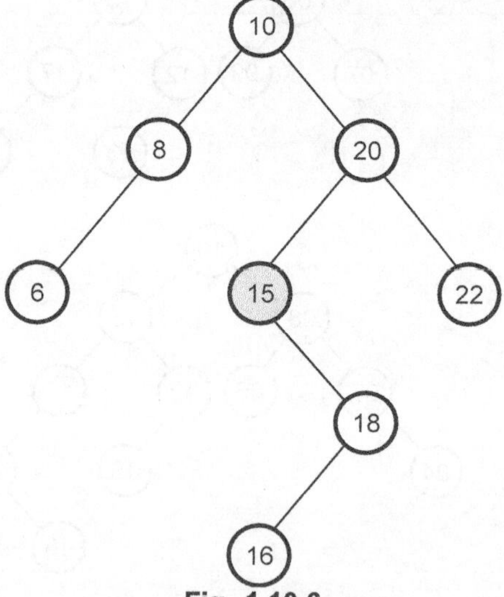

Fig. 1.10.6

To explain this kind of deletion, consider a tree as given below.

If we want to delete the node 15, then we will simply copy node 18 at place of 15 and then set the node free. The inorder successor is always copied at the position of a node being deleted.

iii. The node having two children

Again, let us take some example for discussing this kind of deletion.

Let us consider that we want to delete node having value 7. We will then find out the inorder successor of node 7. The inorder succesor will be simply copied at location of node 7. Thats it !

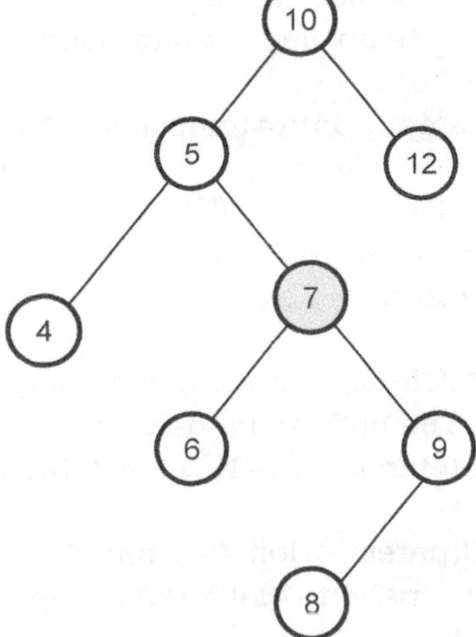

Fig. 1.10.7 Before deletion

That means copy 8 at the position where value of node is 7. Set left pointer of 9 as NULL. This completes the deletion procedure.

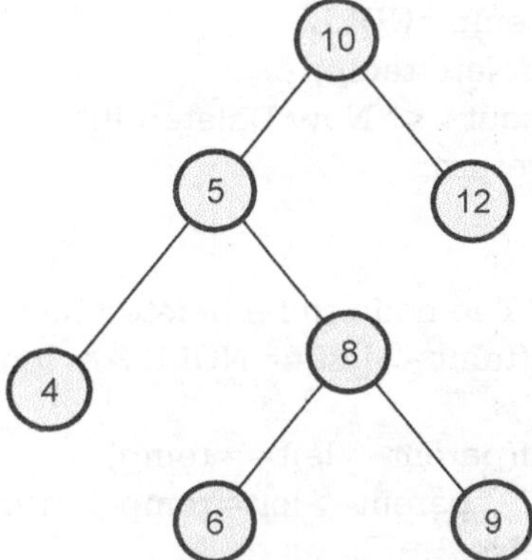

Fig. 1.10.8 After deletion

```
void bintree::del(node *root,int key)
{
 node *temp_succ;
  if(root==NULL)
   cout<<"Tree is not Created!";
  else
  {
   temp=root;
   search(&temp,key,&parent);
  //temp node is to be deleted
  /*deleting a node with two children*/
  if(temp->left!=NULL && temp->right!=NULL)
  {
   parent=temp;
temp_succ=temp->right;
   while(temp_succ->left!=NULL)
   {
```

temp is node which is to be deleted. **Parent** is a node which keeps track of parent node. **temp** and **temp_succ** is for keeping track of successor of **temp** node.

```
    parent=temp_succ;
    temp_succ=temp_succ->left;<-----------Moving to leftmost sub-tree
 }
 temp->data=temp_succ->data;
       //copying the immediate successor
 temp->right=NULL;
 cout<<" Now Deleted it!";
 return;
}
/*deleting a node having only one child*/
/*The node to be deleted has left child*/
if(temp->left!=NULL && temp->right==NULL)
{
 if(parent->left==temp)<------------- Finding the parent of temp
    parent->left=temp->left;
 else
    parent->right=temp->left;
 temp=NULL;
 delete temp;
 cout<<" Now Deleted it!";
 return;
}

/*The node to be deleted has right child*/
if(temp->left==NULL && temp->right!=NULL)
{
 if(parent->left==temp)
    parent->left=temp->right;
 else
    parent->right=temp->right;
 temp=NULL;
 delete temp;
    cout<<" Now Deleted it!";
 return;
}
/*deleting a node which is having no child*/
if(temp->left==NULL && temp->right==NULL)
{
    if(parent->left==temp)
     parent->left=NULL;
    else
     parent->right=NULL;
 cout<<" Now Deleted it!";
 return;
}
}
}
```

Copying the successor node's data to **temp** node. Thus contents of **temp** node gets deleted.

3. Searching a node from binary search tree

In searching, the node which we want to search is called a key node. The key node will be compared with each node starting from root node if value of key node is greater than current node then we search for it on right sub-branch otherwise on left sub-branch. If we reach to leaf node and still we do not get the value of key node then we declare "node is not present in the tree".

In the above tree, if we want to search for value 9. Then we will compare 9 with root node 10. As 9 is less than 10 we will search on left sub-branch. Now compare 9 with 5, but 9 is greater than 5. So we will move on right sub-branch. Now compare 9 with 8 but as 9 is greater than 8 we will move on right sub-branch. As the node we will get holds the value 9. Thus the desired node can be searched. Let us see the 'C' implementation of it.

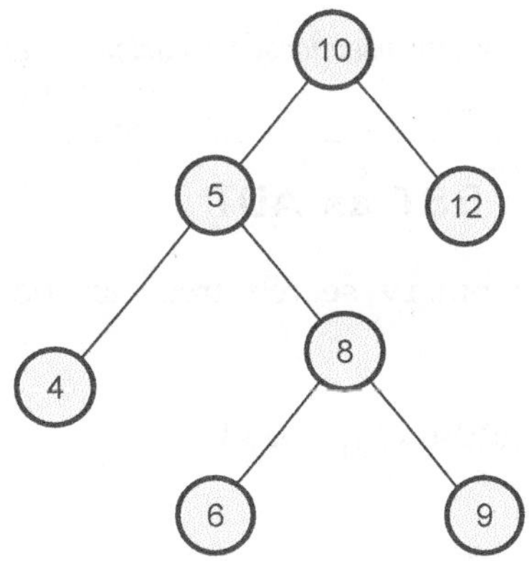

Fig. 1.10.9 After deletion

The routine is as given below.

```
void bintree::search(node **temp,int key,node **parent)
{
 if(*temp==NULL)
  cout<<endl<<"Tree is Not Created"<<endl;
 else
 {
  while(*temp!=NULL)
  {
     if((*temp)->data==key)
     {
      cout<<"\nThe"<<(*temp)->data<<"Element is Present";
      break;
     }
   *parent=*temp;//stores the parent value<------
  if((*temp)->data>key) <------------------------------
     *temp=(*temp)->left;    <----------------------
  else
     *temp=(*temp)->right;
  }
 }
 return;
}
```

- Marking the parent node
- If current node is greater than key
- Search for the left subtree

We can display a tree in inorder fashion.

University Questions

1. *Write a pseudo 'C' code for the following operations -*
   i) Insertion of a node in a binary search tree.
   ii) Deletion of a node from binary search tree. **SPPU : Dec.-08, Marks 8**
2. *Write pseudocode to delete a node in given binary search tree. Explain with example for each case.* **SPPU : May-07,09, Marks 6, Dec.-09, Marks 4, May-11, Marks 12**

1.11 BST as ADT

SPPU : May-06, 09, 10, Dec.-06, Marks 8

The binary search tree can be represented as an abstract data type. It is as given below

AbstractDataType BST

{

Instances : Binary search tree is a binary tree in which value of left child is less than its parent node and value of right child is greater than its parent node.

Operations :

1. **Create** - Using this operation a binary search tree can be created.
2. **Display** - This operation is used for displaying all the nodes of BST.
3. **Insert** - For insertion of any node in the BST, this operation is useful.
4. **Delete** - Using this operation, any node from BST can be deleted
5. **Search** - This function is used for searching any node from BST.

}

The complete implementation of BST as an ADT as follows -

```
/*****************************************************************
Program For Implementation Of Binary Search Tree and perform insertion
deletion,searching,display of tree.
*****************************************************************/
#include<iostream.h>
#include<conio.h>
class bintree
 {
      typedef struct bst
      {
       int data;
       struct bst *left,*right;
      }node;
      node  *root,*New,*temp,*parent;
  public:
```

```
 bintree()
 {
     root=NULL;
 }
 void create();
 void display();
 void delet();
 void find();
 void insert(node *,node *);
 void inorder(node *);
 void search(node **,int,node **);
 void del(node *,int);
};
void bintree::create()
{
      New=new node;
      New->left=NULL;
      New->right=NULL;
      cout<<"\n Enter The Element ";
      cin>>New->data;
      if(root==NULL)
            root=New;
      else
            insert(root,New);
}
void bintree::insert(node  *root,node *New)
{
      if(New->data<root->data)
       {
            if(root->left==NULL)
             root->left=New;
            else
             insert(root->left,New);
       }
      if(New->data>root->data)
       {
        if(root->right==NULL)
                  root->right=New;
        else
                  insert(root->right,New);
       }
}


 void bintree::display()
 {
 if(root==NULL)
```

```
        cout<<"Tree Is Not Created";
 else
        {
       cout<<"\n The Tree is : ";
       inorder(root);
        }
}

void bintree::inorder(node  *temp)
{
 if(temp!=NULL)
 {
       inorder(temp->left);
       cout<<"  "<<temp->data;
       inorder(temp->right);
 }
}
void bintree::find()
{
  int key;
  cout<<"\n Enter The Element Which You Want To Search";
  cin>>key;
  temp=root;
  search(&temp,key,&parent);
  if(temp==NULL)
   cout<<"\n Element is not present";
  else
  cout<<"\nParent of node "<<temp->data<<"is "<<parent->data;
}
void bintree::search(node **temp,int key,node **parent)
{
  if(*temp==NULL)
   cout<<endl<<"Tree is Not Created"<<endl;
  else
  {
   while(*temp!=NULL)
   {
       if((*temp)->data==key)
       {
         cout<<"\nThe"<<(*temp)->data<<"Element is Present";
         break;
       }
   *parent=*temp;//stores the parent value
   if((*temp)->data>key)
       *temp=(*temp)->left;
   else
       *temp=(*temp)->right;
```

```
  }
 }
 return;
}

void bintree::delet()
{
 int key;
 cout<<"\n Enter The Element U wish to Delete";
 cin>>key;
 if(key==root->data)
 {
  bintree();//assigning a value NULL to root
 }
 else
 del(root,key);
}
/*
--------------------------------------------------------------------
This function is for deleting a node from binary search tree There exist three possible
cases for deletion of a node
--------------------------------------------------------------------
*/
void bintree::del(node *root,int key)
{
 node *temp_succ;
  if(root==NULL)
   cout<<"Tree is not Created!";
  else
  {
   temp=root;
   search(&temp,key,&parent);
  //temp node is to be deleted
  /*deleting a node with two children*/
  if(temp->left!=NULL && temp->right!=NULL)
  {
   parent=temp;
   temp_succ=temp->right;
   while(temp_succ->left!=NULL)
   {
       parent=temp_succ;
       temp_succ=temp_succ->left;
   }
   temp->data=temp_succ->data;
          //copying the immediate successor
   temp->right=NULL;
   cout<<" Now Deleted it!";
```

```
 return;
 }
 /*deleting a node having only one child*/
 /*The node to be deleted has left child*/
 if(temp->left!=NULL && temp->right==NULL)
 {
  if(parent->left==temp)
       parent->left=temp->left;
  else
       parent->right=temp->left;
  temp=NULL;
  delete temp;
  cout<<" Now Deleted it!";
  return;
 }

 /*The node to be deleted has right child*/
 if(temp->left==NULL && temp->right!=NULL)
 {
  if(parent->left==temp)
       parent->left=temp->right;
  else
       parent->right=temp->right;
  temp=NULL;
  delete temp;
       cout<<" Now Deleted it!";
  return;
 }
 /*deleting a node which is having no child*/
 if(temp->left==NULL && temp->right==NULL)
 {
       if(parent->left==temp)
        parent->left=NULL;
       else
        parent->right=NULL;
  cout<<" Now Deleted it!";
  return;
 }
 }
 }
void main()
{
        int choice;
        char ans='N';
        bintree tr;
        cout<<"\n\t Program For Binary Search Tree ";
        do
```

```
      {
       cout<<"\n1.Create\n2.Search\n3.Delete\n4.Display";
       cout<<"\n\n Enter your choice :";
       cin>>choice;
       switch(choice)
       {
        case 1:do
               {
                tr.create();
                cout<<"Do u Want To enter More elements?(y/n)"<<endl;
                ans=getche();
               }while(ans=='y');
               break;
        case 2:tr.find();
               break;
        case 3:tr.delet();
               break;
        case 4:tr.display();
               break;
       }
   }while(choice!=5);
}
```

Output

```
      Program For Binary Search Tree
1.Create
2.Search
3.Delete
4.Display

 Enter your choice :1

 Enter The Element 10
Do u Want To enter More elements?(y/n)
y
 Enter The Element 8
Do u Want To enter More elements?(y/n)
y
 Enter The Element 7
Do u Want To enter More elements?(y/n)
y
 Enter The Element 9
Do u Want To enter More elements?(y/n)
y
 Enter The Element 12
Do u Want To enter More elements?(y/n)
y
```

```
 Enter The Element 11
Do u Want To enter More elements?(y/n)
y
 Enter The Element 13
Do u Want To enter More elements?(y/n)
n
1.Create
2.Search
3.Delete
4.Display

 Enter your choice :4

 The Tree is :   7  8  9  10  11  12  13
1.Create
2.Search
3.Delete
4.Display

 Enter your choice :2

 Enter The Element Which You Want To Search 13

The13Element is Present
Parent of node 13 is 12
1.Create
2.Search
3.Delete
4.Display

 Enter your choice :3

 Enter The Element U wish to Delete 12

The 12 Element is Present Now Deleted it!
1.Create
2.Search
3.Delete
4.Display


 Enter your choice :4

 The Tree is :   7  8  9  10  11  13
1.Create
2.Search
3.Delete
```

```
4.Display

 Enter your choice :3

Enter The Element U wish to Delete 11

The 11 Element is Present Now Deleted it!
1.Create
2.Search
3.Delete
4.Display

 Enter your choice :4

 The Tree is :  7  8  9  10  13
1.Create
2.Search
3.Delete
4.Display

 Enter your choice :3

 Enter The Element U wish to Delete 7

The7Element is Present Now Deleted it!
1.Create
2.Search
3.Delete
4.Display

 Enter your choice :4

 The Tree is :  8  9  10  13
1.Create
2.Search
3.Delete
4.Display

 Enter your choice :5
```

Programing Examples

Example 1.11.1 *Write efficient functions that takes only a pointer to the root of binary tree T, and compute :*

1) The number of nodes in T   2) The number of leaves in T.

What is running time of your algorithm ? **SPPU : May-06, Marks 8**

Solution : 1) The number of nodes in T

There are two function written -

count_nodes function has a logic for visiting each node of the tree and counting them.

display function displays the actual count value

```
/*
------------------------------------------------------------------------------
Function which counts the total number of nodes in the tree
------------------------------------------------------------------------------
*/
void tree::count_nodes(btree *temp,int *count)
{
 if(root==NULL)
      cout<"TREE IS NOT CREATED";
 if(temp!=NULL)
 {
  count_nodes(temp->left,count);
  *count++;
  count_nodes(temp->right,count);
 }
}
/*
------------------------------------------------------------------------------
The calling function - It calls the function for counting total number of nodes
------------------------------------------------------------------------------
*/

void tree::display()
{
 int *count=0;
 count_nodes(root,count);
 cout<<"Total nodes= "<<*count;
}
```

2) The number of leaves in T

There are two function written –

count_leaves function has a logic for visiting each leaf node of the tree and counting them.

display function displays the actual count value for the leaves

```
/*
------------------------------------------------------------------------------
The count_leaves Function
------------------------------------------------------------------------------
*/
```

```
void tree::count_leaves(btree *temp,int *count)
{
 if(root==NULL)
      cout<<"TREE IS NOT CREATED";
 if(temp!=NULL)
 {
 if((temp->left==NULL)&&(temp->right==NULL))
      *count=*count+1;
 else
 {
  count_leaves(temp->left,count);
  count_leaves(temp->right,count);
 }
 }
}
/*
-------------------------------------------------------------------------
 The display function
-------------------------------------------------------------------------
*/

void tree::display()
{
 int *count;
 *count=0;
 count_leaves(root,count);
 cout<<"Total nodes= "<<*count;
}
```

Example 1.11.2 *Write a pseudo C routine to find the depth of the binary tree.*

SPPU : Dec.-06, Marks 4

Solution :

```
int tree::Height(btree *temp)
{
 int d1,d2;
 if(temp==NULL)
  return 0;
 if(temp->left==NULL && temp->right==NULL)
  return 0;
 d1=Height(temp->left);//computing height of leftsubtree
 d2=Height(temp->right);//computing height of rightsubtree
  if(d1>d2)
   return d1+1;
  else
   return d2+1;
//maximum depth=height of the tree
}
```

```
/*
-----------------------------------------------------------------------------
    The display function
-----------------------------------------------------------------------------
*/

void tree::display()
{
 cout<<"The height of the tree is "<<Height(root);
}
/*
```

Example 1.11.3 *Write recursive function to find mirror image of a given binary tree. Show the contents of stack stepwise.* **SPPU : May-09, Marks 4**

Solution : Recursive function to find mirror image

```
void tree : : mirror (btree*root)
{
btree * temp:
if (root ! = NULL)
{
    mirror(root  → left);
    mirror(root → right);
    temp = root → left;
    root → left = root → right;
    root → right = temp ;
}
}
```

Stack contents - Assume the binary search tree as -

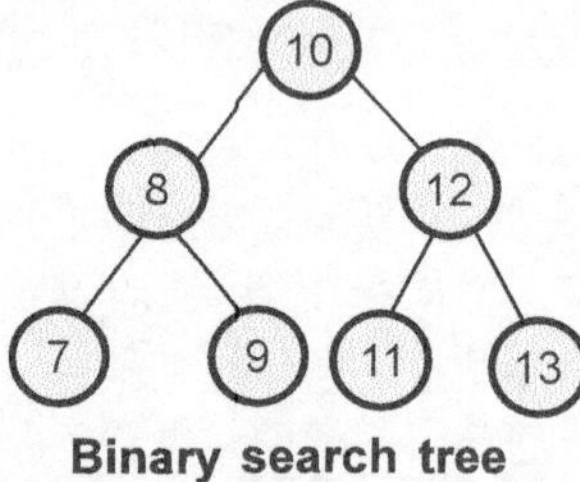

Binary search tree

Step 1 :

10

Stack

Step 2 :

8
10

Stack

Step 3 :

7
8
10

Stack

Step 4 :

The stack will be popped, node 7 has no left and right child.

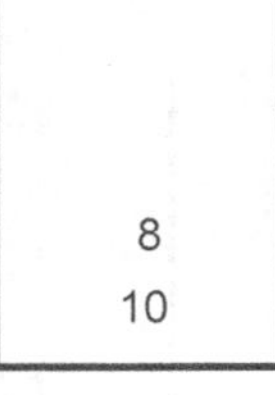

Step 5 : The stack will be popped. Then the left and right child of the node 8 will be swapped.

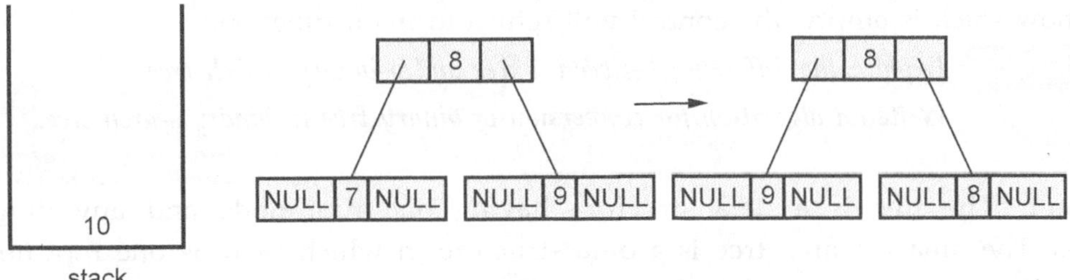

Step 6 :

Step 7 : The stack will be popped, node 11 has no left and right child

Step 8 :

The stack will be popped. Then left and right child of the node 12 will be swapped.

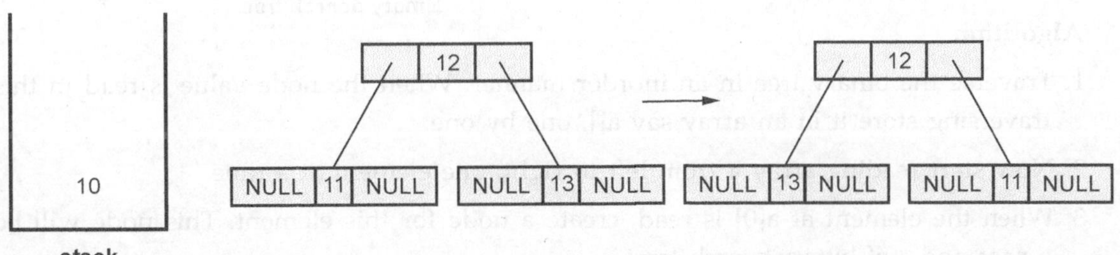

Step 9 : The stack will be popped. Then the left and right child of node 10 will be popped.

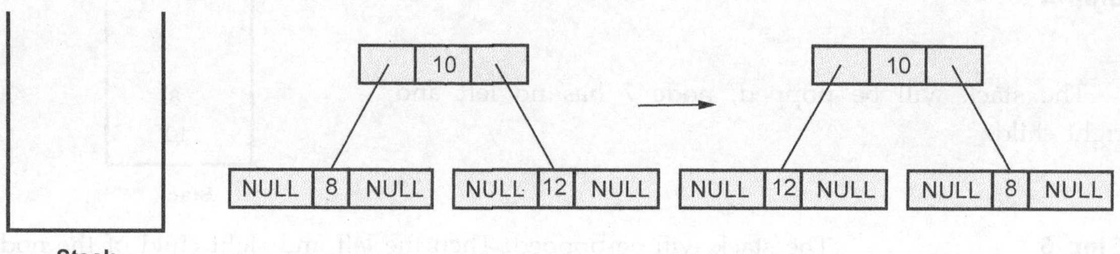

As now stack is empty, the control will return to main function.

Example 1.11.4 *Explain the difference between a tree and a binary search tree. Write an algorithm for conversion of binary tree to binary search tree.*

SPPU : May-10, Marks 8

Solution : The tree is a data structure having one root node and any number of subtrees. The binary search tree is a data structure in which there is one root node and every node has at the most two subtrees. The arrangement of nodes is based on their values. That is left node is less than parent node and right node is greater than parent node.

For example

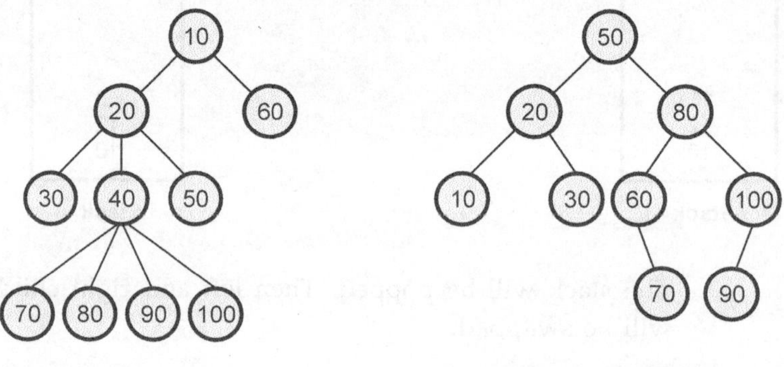

Algorithm

1. Traverse the binary tree in an inorder manner. When the node value is read in this traversing store it in an array say a[], one by one.
2. Now start reading array **a** from left to right, one element at a time.
3. When the element at a[0] is read, create a node for this element. This node will be a root node, of binary search tree.
4. Read element from array **a**. Compare each element with the nodes present in the binary search tree. If the new node has a value less than its parent node then attach it as left child otherwise attach it as right child. Repeat this step for all the elements of array **a**.
5. Display the binary search tree created in step 3 and 4.

1.12 Threaded Binary Tree

1.12.1 Concept

In previous sections we have seen that during binary tree creation, for the leaf nodes there is no sub-tree further. So we are just setting the the left and right fields of leaf nodes NULL. Since NULL value is put in the left and right field of the node it is just a wastage of the memory. So to avoid NULL values in the node we just set the threads which are actually the links to the predecessor and successor nodes. There are three types of threading possible.

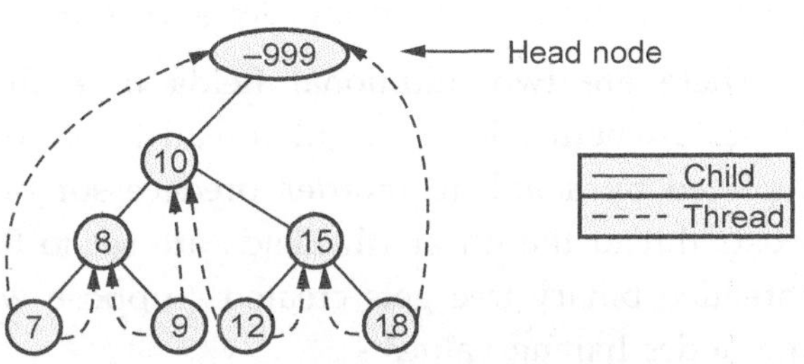

Fig. 1.12.1 Threaded binary tree

Inorder, preorder and postorder threading. We will discuss the inoder threading technique. The typical threaded binary tree looks like this

The typical 'C' structure of the node is

```
typedef struct thread
{
 int data;
int lth,rth;
struct thread *left;
struct thread *right;
}Th;
```

The basic idea in inorder threading is that the left thread should point to the predecessor and the right thread points to the successor. Here we are assuming the head node as the starting node and the root node of the tree is attached to left of head node.

Inorder predecessor - In inorder traversing of a threaded binary tree if the node. A is pointed by left thread/pointer of node B, then node A becomes inorder predecessor of node B.

In Fig. 1.12.1, the inorder predecessor of node 9 is 8.

Inorder successor - In inorder traversing of a threaded binary tree if node C is pointed by right thread/pointer of node B, then node C becomes inorder successor of node B.

In Fig. 1.12.1, the inorder successor of node 9 is 10.

1.12.2 Insertion and Deletion

1. Insertion Operation

In thread binary tree, the NULL pointers are avoided. Instead of left NULL pointer the link points to inorder predecessor of that node. Similarly instead of right NULL pointer the link points to inorder successor of that node.

There are two additional fields in each node named as lth and rth these fields indicate whether left or right thread is present. Thread present means the NULL link is replaced by a link to inorder predecessor or inorder successor. To represent that there exists thread the lth or rth Fields are set to 0. Let us take one example to explain how a threaded binary tree gets created. Suppose we want to create a threaded binary tree for the nodes haivng values -

10, 8, 6, 12, 9, 11, 14

Initially we will create a dummy node which will act as a header of the tree.

*l*th	Left	Data	Right	rth	
0	NULL	–999	NULL	0	Dummy node

Now let us take first value i.e. 10. The node with value 10 will be the root node we will attach this root node as left child of dummy node.

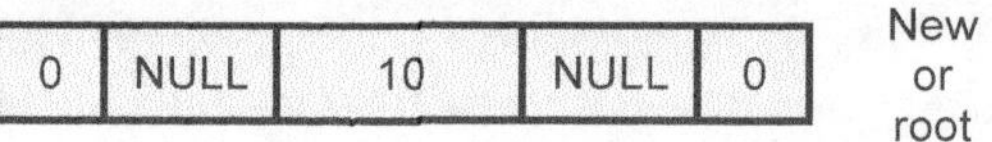

The NULL links of root's left and right child will be pointed to dummy.

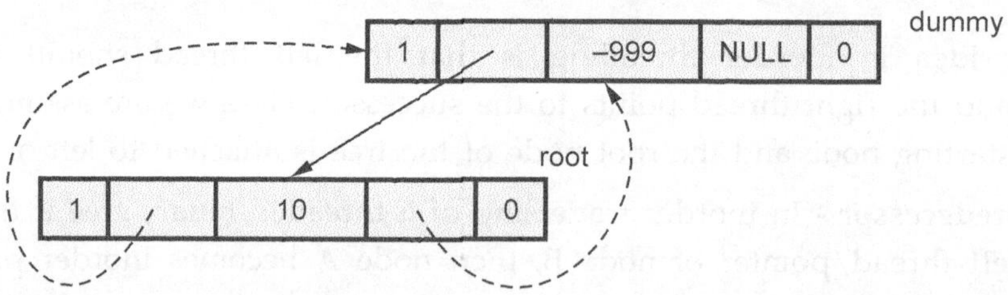

Now next comes 8. The 8 will be compared with 10, as the value is less than 10, we will attach 8 as left child of 10 and we will set root's lth field to 1, indicating that the node 10 is having left child. See then how the links are arranged.

New → left = root → left

New → right = root;

root → left = New;

root → *l*th = 1;

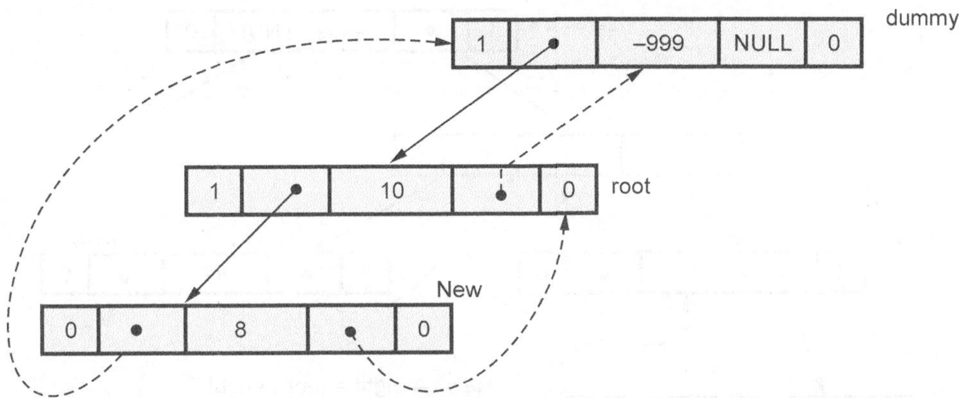

Note that the left link of node 8 points to its inorder predecessor and right link of node 8 points to its inorder successor.

Next comes 6. The value 6 will be first compared with root i.e. with 10. As 6 is less than 10, we will move on left sub-branch. The 6 will then be compared with 8, so we have to move on left sub-branched of 8. But lth of node 8 is 0, indicating that there is no left child to 8, so we will attach 6 as left child to 8.

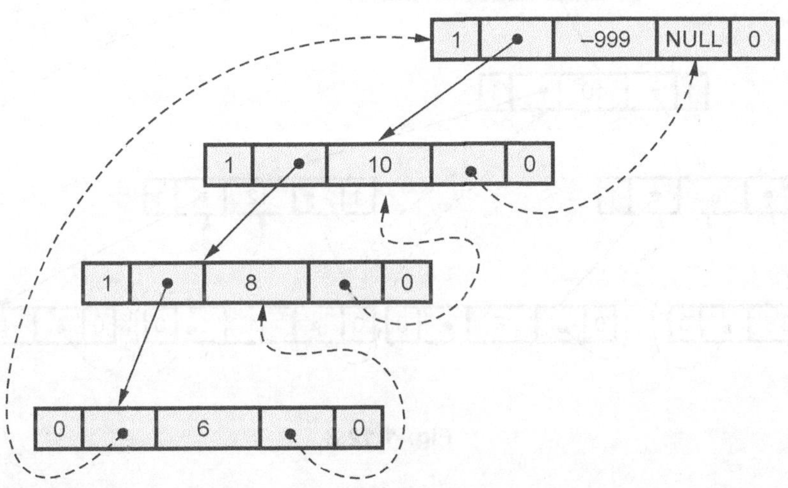

Then comes 12. We will compare 12 with 10. As 12 is greater than 10, we will attach the node 12 as right child of 10.

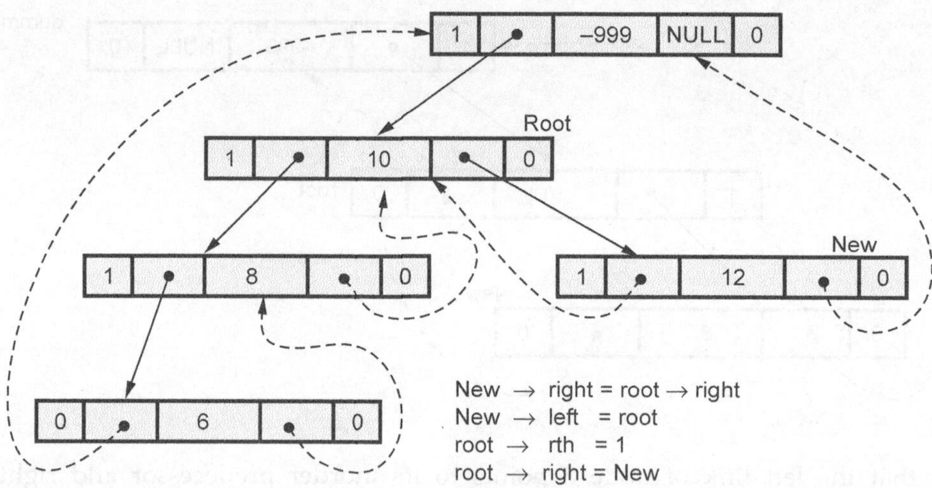

Note that the left field of node 12 points to its inorder predecessor and right field of node 12 points to its inorder sussessor. Thus by attaching 9, 11, 14 as appropriate children, the threaded binary tree will look like this -

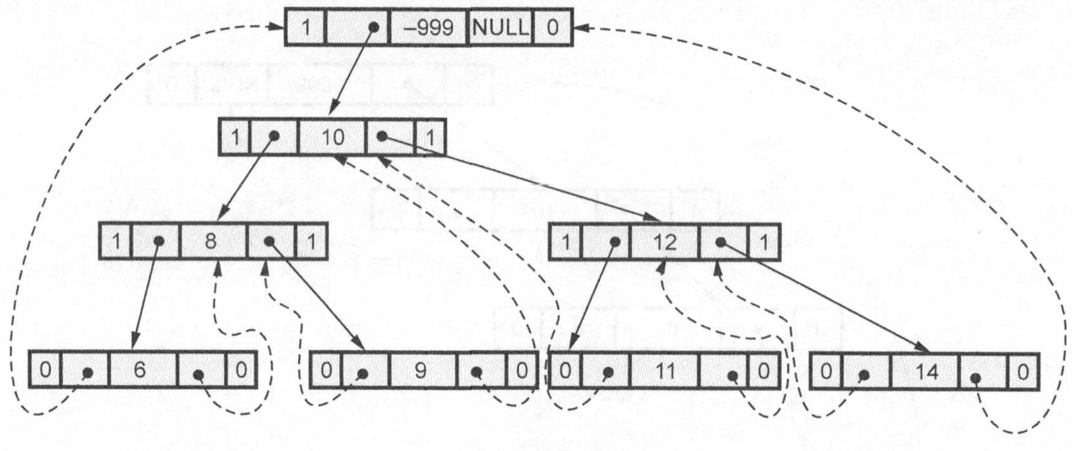

Fig. 1.12.2

Such a threaded tree is called inorder treaded binary tree.

2. Deletion Operation

The deletion operation is similar to the deletion operation in BST. The only additional thing is to adjust the left thread (*l*th) and right thread (rth) fields. For example -

Consider the given threaded binary tree as -

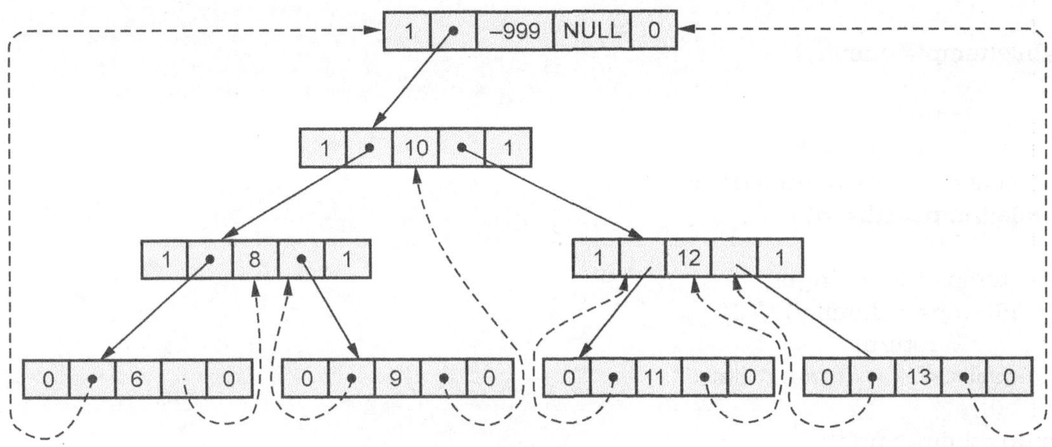

Fig. 1.12.3

If we **delete node 12** then the inorder successor 13 will occupy 12th location.

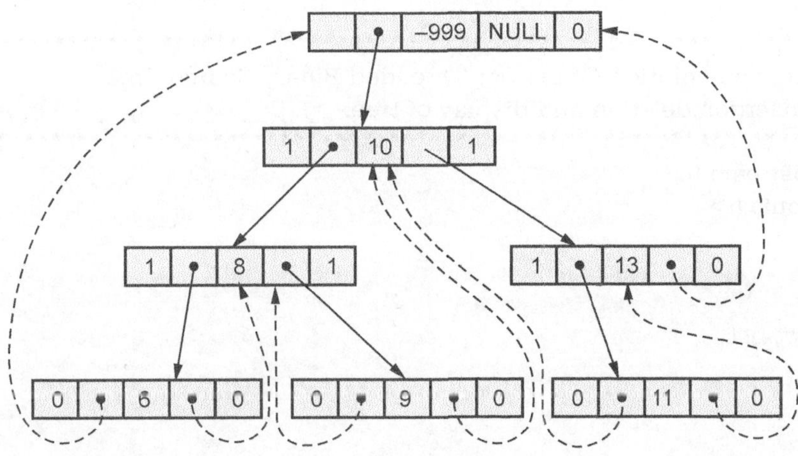

Fig. 1.12.4

1.12.3 Inorder Traversal

The inorder traversal is a technique in which left node is visited first, then its parent and finally the right node is visited. In the threaded tree, the thread field is used for traversing. For instance, if the left thread(lth) or right thread(rth) value is 1 then that means corresponding left or right child is present for that node. But if either of the value is 0 then, we have to move to successor node using corresponding thread pointer. Following C function illustrates this idea

```
void inorder(node *temp,node *dummy)
{
  while(temp!=dummy)
  {
      while(temp->lth==1)
       temp=temp->left;
      cout<<" "<<temp->data;
  while(temp->rth==0)
  {
       temp=temp->right;
      if(temp==dummy)
             return;
      cout<<" "<<temp->data;
  }
  temp=temp->right;
 }
}
```

The C++ program in which insertion and deletion operations are illustrated is as given below. Not that in this program, the tree is represented using inorder traversal.

C++ Program

```
/*************************************************************************
Program For Implementation Of Inorder Threaded Binary Search Tree
and perform insertion,deletion and display of tree.
*************************************************************************/
# include <iostream.h>
# include <conio.h>
class thread
{
 private:
 typedef struct bst
 {

  int data;
  int lth,rth;
  struct bst *left,*right;
 }node;
 node *dummy;
 node *New,*root,*temp,*parent;
public:
thread();
void create(); //All The implementation Details are hidden!
void display();
void find();
void delet();
};
/*
```

```
---------------------------------------------------------------------
The constructor defined
---------------------------------------------------------------------
*/
thread::thread()
{
 root=NULL;
}
/*
---------------------------------------------------------------------
The create function
---------------------------------------------------------------------
*/
void thread::create()
{
  void insert(node *,node *);
  New=new node;
  New->left=NULL;
  New->right=NULL;
  New->lth=0;
  New->rth=0;
  cout<<"\n Enter The Element ";
  cin>>New->data;
  if(root==NULL)
  {                          // Tree is not Created
   root=New;
   dummy=new node;
   dummy->data=-999;
   dummy->left=root;
   root->left=dummy;
   root->right=dummy;
  }
  else
  insert(root,New);
}

/*
---------------------------------------------------------------------
The display function
---------------------------------------------------------------------
*/
void thread::display()
{
  void inorder(node *,node *dummy);
  if(root==NULL)
       cout<<"Tree Is Not Created";
  else
```

```
        {
          cout<<"\n The Tree is : ";
          inorder(root,dummy);
        }
}
/*
----------------------------------------------------------------------
The find function which calls the routine for searching an element
----------------------------------------------------------------------
*/
void thread::find()
{
 node *search(node *,node *,int,node **);
 int key;
 cout<<"\n Enter The Element Which You Want To Search";
 cin>>key;
 temp=search(root,dummy,key,&parent);
 if(temp==NULL)
  cout<<"\nElement is Not Present";
 else
  cout<<" It's Parent Node is "<<parent->data;
}


/*
----------------------------------------------------------------------
The delet function which calls the routine for deletion of an element
----------------------------------------------------------------------
*/
void thread::delet()
{
 void del(node *,node *,int);
 int key;
 cout<<"\n Enter The Element U wish to Delete";
 cin>>key;
 del(root,dummy,key);
}
/*
----------------------------------------------------------------------
This function is for creating a binary search tree
----------------------------------------------------------------------
*/
void insert(node *root,node *New)
{
 if(New->data<root->data)
  {
      if(root->lth==0)
```

```
        {
                New->left=root->left;
                New->right=root;
                root->left=New;
                root->lth=1;
        }
        else
                insert(root->left,New);
 }
 if(New->data>root->data)
 {
        if(root->rth==0)
        {
                New->right=root->right;
                New->left=root;
                root->rth=1;
                root->right=New;
        }
        else
         insert(root->right,New);
 }
}
/*
--------------------------------------------------------------------
The search function
--------------------------------------------------------------------
*/
node *search(node *root,node *dummy,int key,node **parent)
{
 node *temp;
 int flag=0;
 temp=root;
 while((temp!=dummy))
 {
  if(temp->data==key)
  {
       cout<<"\n The "<<temp->data<<" Element is Present";
       flag=1;
       return temp;
  }
  *parent=temp;
  if(temp->data>key)
       temp=temp->left;
  else
       temp=temp->right;
 }
return NULL;
```

```
}

/*
--------------------------------------------------------------------
This function is for deleting a node from binary search tree
There exists three possible cases for deletion of a node
--------------------------------------------------------------------
*/

void del(node *root,node *dummy,int key)
{
 node *temp,*parent,*temp_succ;
 node *search(node *,node *,int,node **);
 int flag=0;
 temp=search(root,dummy,key,&parent);
 if(root==temp)
 {
  cout<<"\n Its Root Node Which Can Not Be Deleted!!";
  return;
 }
 //deleting a node with two children
 if(temp->lth==1 && temp->rth==1)
 {
  parent=temp;
  temp_succ=temp->right;//Finding Inorder successor
  while(temp_succ->lth==1)
  {
      flag=1;
      parent=temp_succ;
      temp_succ=temp_succ>left;
  }
  if(flag==0)
  {
      temp->data=temp_succ->data;
      parent->right=temp_succ->right;
      parent->rth=0;
  }
 else//inorder successor is on left subbranch.
            // and it has to be traversed
  {
      temp->data=temp_succ->data;
      parent->rth=0;
      parent->lth=0;
      parent->left=temp_succ->left;
  }
  cout<<" Now Deleted it!";
  return;
```

```
}
//deleting a node having only one child
 //The node to be deleted has left child
 if(temp->lth==1 && temp->rth==0)
 {
  if(parent->left==temp)
  {
      (temp->left)->right=parent;
       parent->left=temp->left;
  }
  else
  {
      (temp->left)->right=temp->right;
      parent->right=temp->left;
  }
  temp=NULL;
  delete temp;
  cout<<" Now Deleted it!";
  return;
 }

 //The node to be deleted has right child
 if(temp->lth==0 && temp->rth!=0)
 {
  if(parent->left==temp)
  {
      parent->left=temp->right;
      (temp->right)->left=temp->left;
      (temp->right)->right=parent;
  }
  else
  {
      parent->right=temp->right;
      (temp->right)->left=parent;

  }
  temp=NULL;
  delete temp;
  cout<<" Now Deleted it!";
  return;
 }
 //deleting a node which is having no child
 if(temp->lth==0 && temp->rth==0)
 {
      if(parent->left==temp)
      {
       parent->left=temp->left;
```

```
        parent->lth=0;
       }
       else
       {
         parent->right=temp->right;
         parent->rth=0;
       }
  cout<<" Now Deleted it!";
  return;
 }
}
/*
------------------------------------------------------------------------
The inorder function
------------------------------------------------------------------------
*/
void inorder(node *temp,node *dummy)
{
  while(temp!=dummy)
  {
       while(temp->lth==1)
        temp=temp->left;
  cout<<"  "<<temp->data;
  while(temp->rth==0)
  {
  temp=temp->right;
       if(temp==dummy)
        return;
       cout<<"  "<<temp->data;
  }
  temp=temp->right;
 }
 }
/*
------------------------------------------------------------------------
The main function
------------------------------------------------------------------------
*/
void main()
{
  int choice;
  char ans='N';
  thread th;
  clrscr();
  do
  {
       clrscr();
```

```
cout<<"\n\t Program For Threaded Binary Tree";
cout<<"\n1.Create \n2.Display \n3.Search \n4.Delete";
cin>>choice;
switch(choice)
{
 case 1:do
        {
         th.create();
          cout<<"\n Do u Want To enter More  Elements?(y/n)";
          ans=getch();
        }while(ans=='y');
        break;
 case 2:th.display();
        break;
 caso 3:th.find();
        break;
 case 4:th.delet();
     break;
}
cout<<"\n\nWant To See Main Menu?(y/n)";
ans=getche();
}while(ans=='y');
}
```

Output

```
      Program For Threaded Binary Tree
1.Create
2.Display
3.Search
4.Delete1

 Enter The Element 4

 Do u Want To enter More  Elements?(y/n)
 Enter The Element 2

 Do u Want To enter More  Elements?(y/n)
 Enter The Element 3

 Do u Want To enter More  Elements?(y/n)
 Enter The Element 1

 Do u Want To enter More  Elements?(y/n)
 Enter The Element 6

 Do u Want To enter More  Elements?(y/n)
 Enter The Element 5
```

```
 Do u Want To enter More  Elements?(y/n)
 Enter The Element 7

 Do u Want To enter More  Elements?(y/n)
Want To See Main Menu?(y/n)
        Program For Threaded Binary Tree
1.Create
2.Display
3.Search
4.Delete2

 The Tree is :   1  2  3  4  5  6  7

Want To See Main Menu?(y/n)

        Program For Threaded Binary Tree
1.Create
2.Display
3.Search
4.Delete3

 Enter The Element Which You Want To Search1

 The 1 Element is Present It's Parent Node is 2

Want To See Main Menu?(y/n)


        Program For Threaded Binary Tree
1.Create
2.Display
3.Search
4.Delete4

 Enter The Element U wish to Delete2

 The 2 Element is Present Now Deleted it!

Want To See Main Menu?(y/n)

        Program For Threaded Binary Tree
1.Create
2.Display
3.Search
4.Delete2
```

```
The Tree is :  1 3 4 5 6 7

Want To See Main Menu?(y/n)
```

1.12.4 Advantages and Disadvantages

Advantages of threaded binary tree :

1. In threaded binary tree there is no NULL pointer present. Hence memory wastage in occupying NULL links is avoided.
2. The threads are pointing to successor and predecessor nodes. This makes us to obtain predecessor and successor node of any node quickly.
3. There is no need of stack while traversing the tree, because using thread links we can reach to previously visited nodes.

Disadvantages of threaded binary tree :

1. Implementing threads for every possible node is complicated.

1.13 Case Study

The tree is non linear, hierarchical data structure. There are various applications of trees such as game trees, expression trees , Huffman's coding and so on. In this section we will discuss two important applications of trees as - expression tree and Huffman's Coding.

1.13.1 Expression Tree

An expression tree is a binary tree in which the operands are attached as leaf nodes and operators become the internal nodes.

For example

From expression tree :

Inorder traversal : A+B*C(Left-Data-Right)

Preorder traversal : +A*BC(Data-Left-Right)

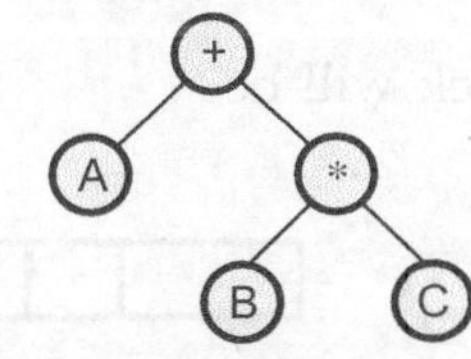

Postorder traversal : ABC*+ (Left-Right-Data)

If we traverse the above tree in inorder, preorder or postorder then we get infix, prefix or postfix expressions respectively.

Key Point *Inorder traversal of expression tree fives infix expression. The preorder traversal of expression tree gives prefix expression and post order traversal of expression tree gives postfix expression.*

Creation of an expression tree

Consider a postfix expression, stored in array **exp**

Now we will read each symbol from left to right one character at a time. If we read an operand then we will make a node of it and push it onto the stack. If we read operator then pop two nodes from stack, the first popped node will be attached as right

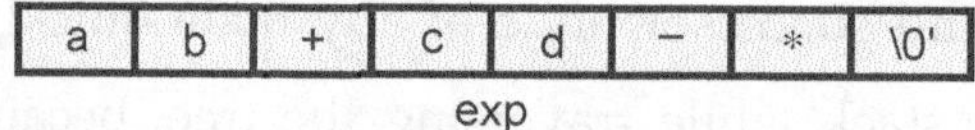

child to operator node and second popped node will be attached as a left child to operator node. For the above given expression let us build a tree.

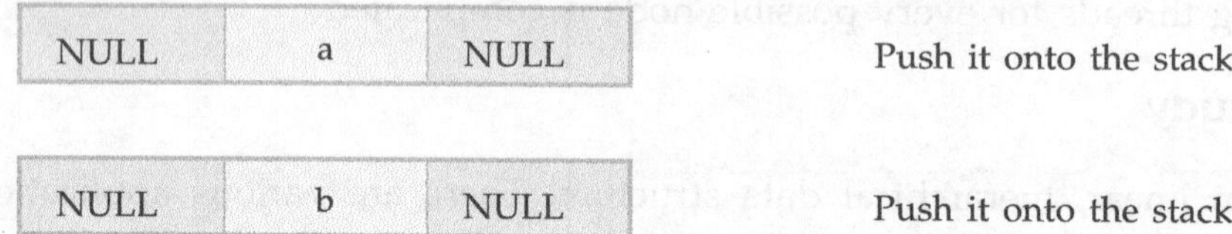

Then stack will be -

Now as we read '+' pop two operands and attach them as follows -

Now push the node '+' onto the stack.

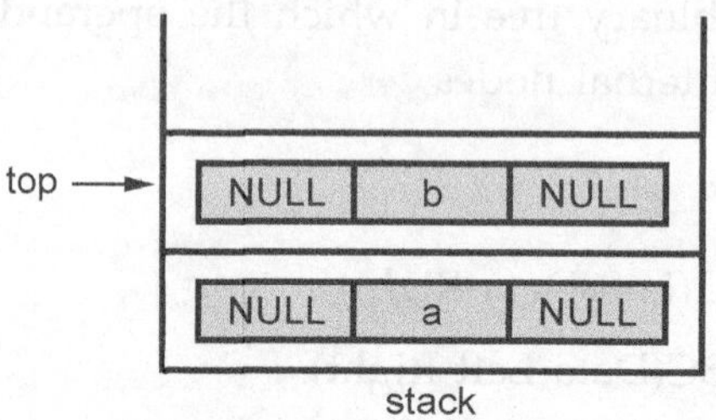

Next we read c and d. Hence stack will be -

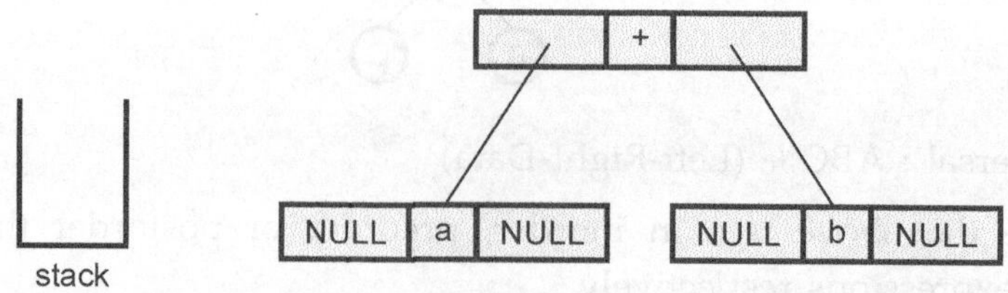

Now we read '–'. So pop two nodes

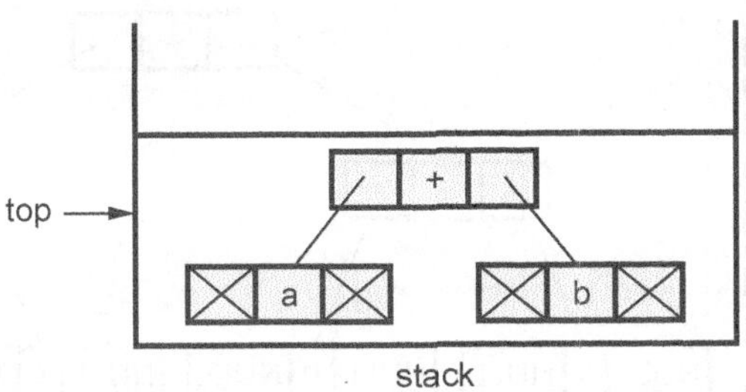

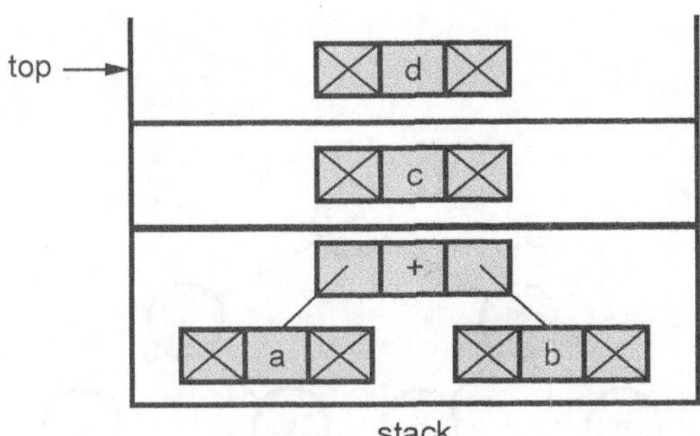

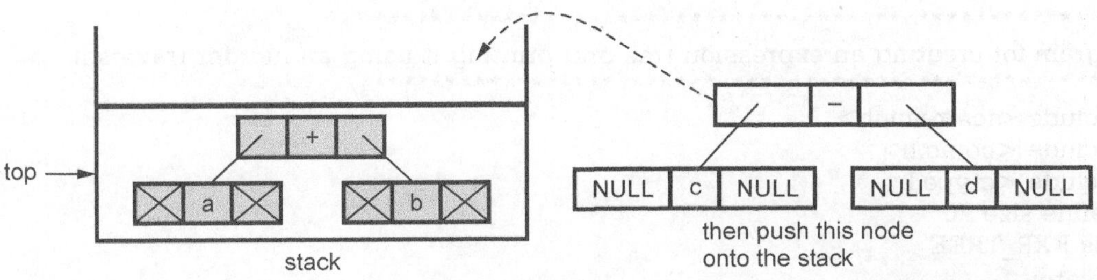

Next we read '∗'. Hence pop two nodes from the stack and attach them to ∗ node.

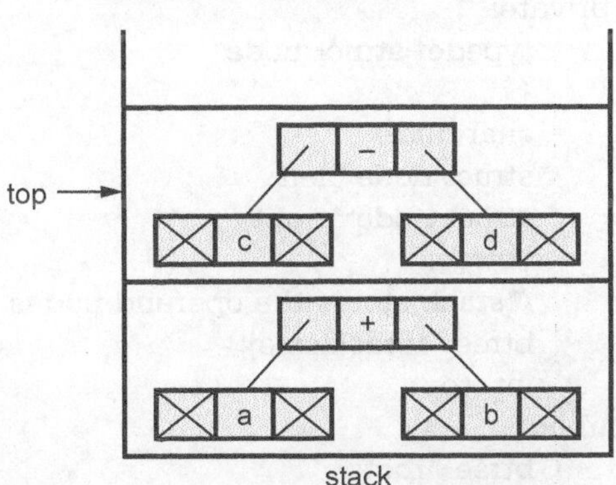

As now we read '\0', pop the content of stack. The node which we will get is the root node of an expression tree.

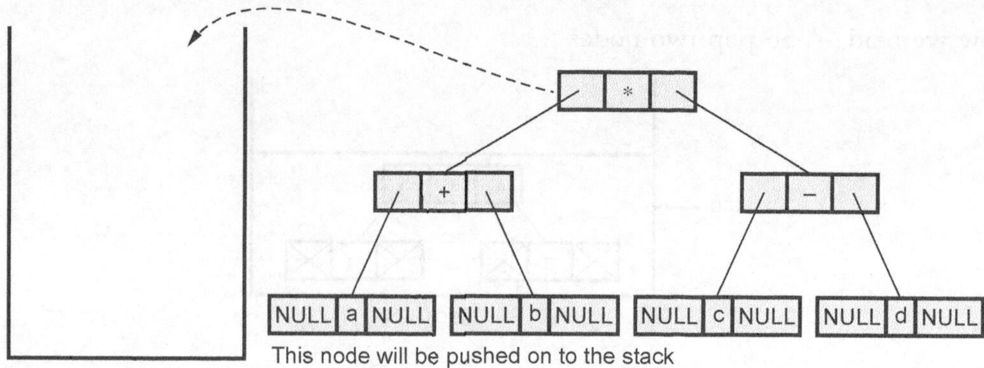

Let us implement it

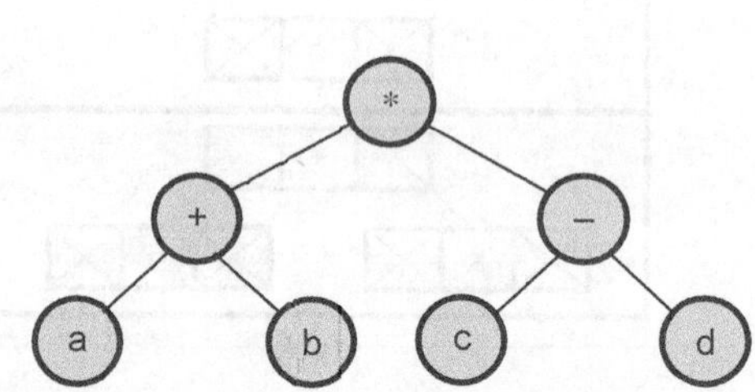

C++ Program

```
*******************************************************
Program for creating an expression tree and printing it using an inorder traversal
*******************************************************/
#include <iostream.h>
#include <conio.h>
#include <ctype.h>
#define size 20
class EXP_TREE
{private:
    typedef struct node
    {
    char data;
    struct node *left;
    struct node *right;
    }btree;
    /*stack stores the operand nodes of the tree*/
    btree  *stack[size];
    int  top;
public:
    btree *root;
    EXP_TREE();
    void create(char exp[]);
    void push(btree *);
```

```
        void display(btree *root);
        btree* pop();
};
EXP_TREE::EXP_TREE()
{
 root=NULL;
 top=-1;//initializing stack
}
void EXP_TREE::create(char exp[])
{
 int pos;
 char ch;
 pos = 0;
 ch = exp[pos];
 while ( ch !='\0')
 {
        /* Create a new node */
  root = new btree;
  root -> left = root -> right = NULL ;
  root -> data = ch;
  if (isalpha( ch) ) /* is it a operand */
        push ( root); /* push operand */
  else if ( ch=='+' ||ch=='-'||ch=='*'||ch=='/'){
 {
  /* it is operator, so pop two nodes from stack
          set first node as right child and
          set second as left child and push the
        operator node on to the stack
  */
        root->right = pop();
        root->left = pop();
        push(root);
  }
  else
        cout<<"Invalid character in expression\n";
  pos ++;
   ch = exp[pos]; /* Read next character */
 }
 root= pop();
}
void EXP_TREE::push(btree *Node)
{
        if ( top+1 >= size )
        cout<<"Error: Stack is Full\n";
        top++;
        stack[top] = Node;
}
```

```
btree* EXP_TREE::pop()
{
      btree *Node;
      if ( top == -1 )
        cout<<"Error: Stack is Empty\n";
      Node = stack[top];
      top--;
      return(Node);
}
void EXP_TREE::display(btree *root)
{
      btree *temp;
      temp = root;
      if (temp != NULL )
      {
              display(temp->left);
              cout<<" "<<temp->data;
              display(temp->right);
}
}

void main()
{

 char  exp[80]; /* exp stores postfix expression */
 EXP_TREE obj;
 clrscr();
 cout<<"Enter the postfix expression\n";
 cin>>exp;
 obj.create(exp);
 cout<<"\n The Tree is created...\n";
 cout<<"\n The inorder traversal of it is \n ";
 obj.display(obj.root);
 getch();
}
```

Output

```
Enter the postfix expression
ab+cd-*
 The Tree is created...

 The inorder traversal of it is
  a + b * c - d
```

1.13.2 Huffman's Coding

The Huffman's algorithm was developed by David. Huffman when he was a Ph.D. student at MIT. This algorithm is basically a coding technique for encoding data. Such an encoded data is **used in data compression techniques.**

- In Huffman's coding method, the data is inputted as a sequence of characters. Then a table of frequency of occurence of each character in the data is built.
- From the table of frequencies **Huffman's tree** is constructed.
- The Huffman's tree is further used for encoding each character, so that binary encoding is obtained for given data.
- In Huffman's tree is further is a specific method of representing each symbol. This method produces a code in such a manner that no code word is **Prefix** of some other code word. Such codes are called **Prefix codes** or **Prefix Free** codes. Thus this method is useful for obtaining optimal data compression.

Let us understand the technique of Huffman's coding with the help of some example.

Example 1.13.1 *Create a Huffman's tree for the given data set and find the corresponding Huffman's codes :*

Data	Weight
A	10
B	3
C	4
D	15
E	2
F	4
G	2
H	3

Solution : We will arrange the data in ascending order of weight

Step 1 : We will combine first two least values form the table. Creating a parent node.

E	2
G	2
B	3
H	3
C	4
F	4
A	10
D	15

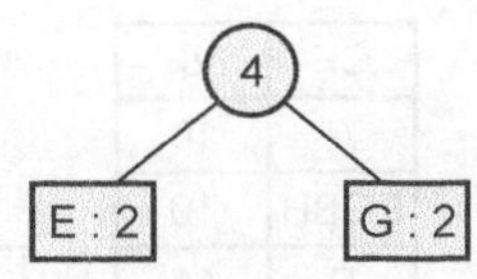

Step 2 : Remove first two entries, from the table in step 1 and add the entry of parent node created in step 1 in the table by maintaining sorted order.

B	3
H	3
C	4
F	4
EG	4
A	10
D	15

Combine first two least values to form a parent node.

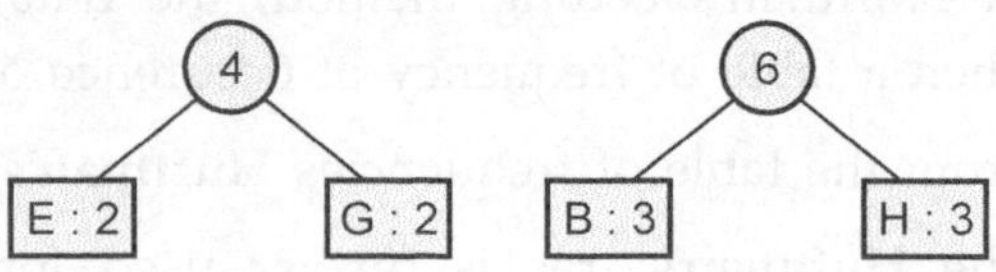

Step 3 : Remove first entries from the table and add entry of parent node at appropriate position in the table.

C	4
F	4
EG	4
BH	6
A	10
D	15

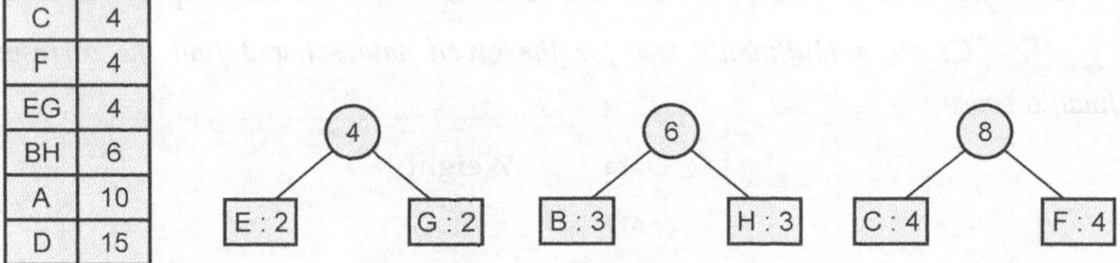

Step 4 :

EG	4
BH	6
CF	8
A	10
D	15

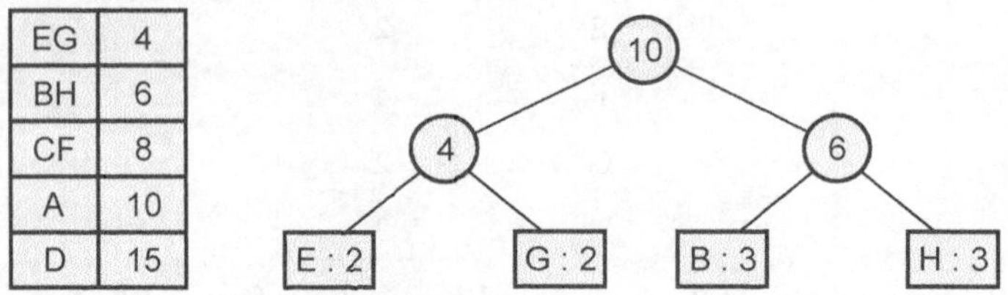

Step 5 :

CF	8
A	10
EGBH	10
D	15

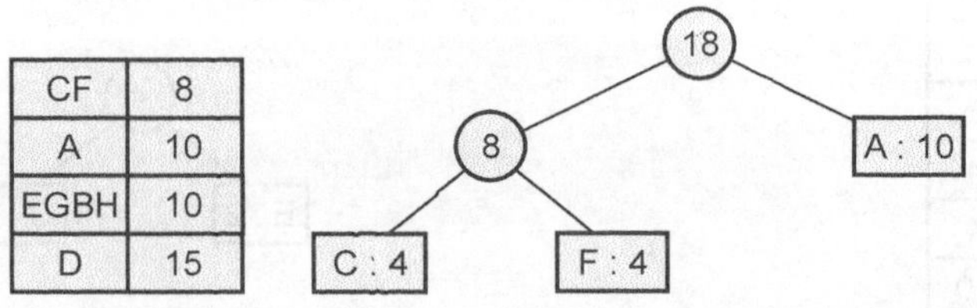

Step 6 :

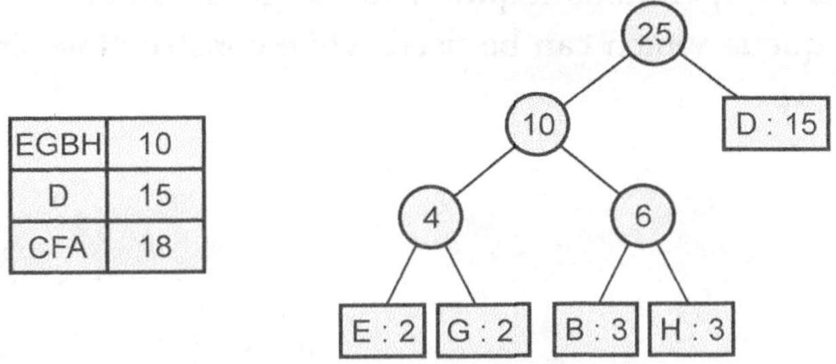

Step 7 : Huffman tree is thus obtained.

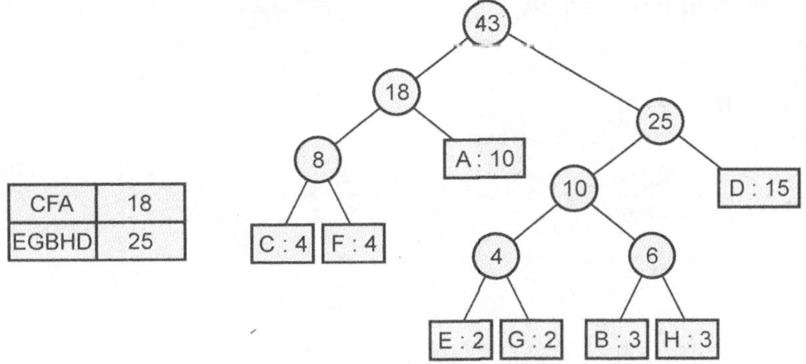

Step 8 : The left branch is coded with 0 and right branch with 1.

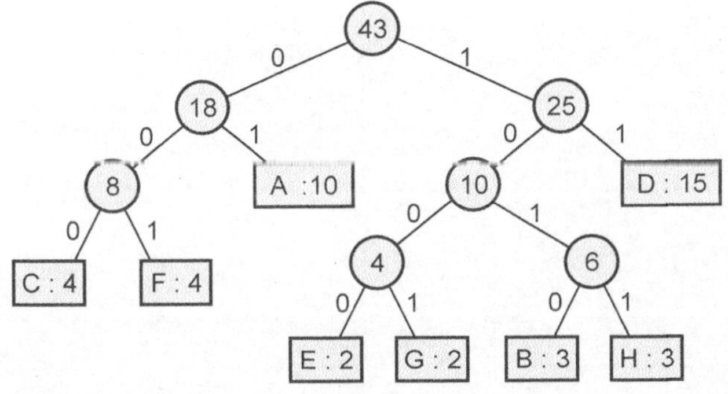

Data	Weight	Code
A	10	01
B	3	1010
C	4	000
D	15	11
E	2	1000
F	4	001
G	2	1001
H	3	1011

1.13.2.1 Algorithm

The method which is used to construct optimal prefix code is called **Huffman coding.** This algorithm builds a tree in bottom up manner. We can denote this tree by T.

Let, $|c|$ be number of leaves

$|c| - 1$ are number of operations required to merge the nodes.

Q be the priority queue which can be used while constructing binary heap.

```
Algorithm Huffman (c )
{
n = |c|
Q = c
for i ← 1  to n – 1
do
{
temp ← get _ node ()
left [temp] Get_min (Q)
right [temp] = Get_Min (Q)
a = left [temp]
b = right [temp]
F [temp] ← f [a] +f [b]
insert (Q, temp)
}
return Get_min (Q)
```

❑❑❑

2 Graphs

Syllabus

Basic Concepts, Storage representation, Adjacency matrix, Adjacency list, Adjacency multi list, Inverse adjacency list. Traversals-depth first and breadth first, Introduction to greedy strategy, Minimum spanning tree, Greedy algorithms for computing minimum spanning tree - Prims and Kruskal Algorithms, Dikjtra's single source shortest path, Topological ordering. ***Case study -*** *Data structure used in webgraph and Google map.*

Contents

2.1 Basic Concept

A graph is a collection of two sets V and E where V is a finite non-empty set of vertices and E is a finite non-empty set of edges.

- **Vertices** are nothing but the nodes in the graph.
- Two adjacent vertices are joined by **edges**.
- Any graph is denoted as G = {V, E}.
- **For example :**

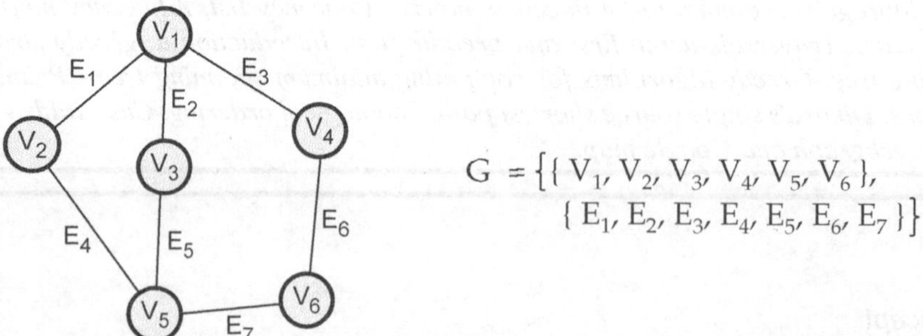

Fig. 2.1.1 Graph G

2.1.1 Comparison between Graph and Tree

Sr. No.	Graph	Tree
1.	Graph is a non-linear data structure.	Tree is a non-linear data structure.
2.	It is a collection of vertices/nodes and edges.	It is a collection of nodes and edges.
3.	Each node can have any number of edges.	General trees consist of the nodes having any number of child nodes. But in case of binary trees every node can have at the most two child nodes.
4.	There is no unique node called root in graph.	There is a unique node called **root** in trees.
5.	A cycle can be formed.	There will not be any cycle.
6.	Applications : For finding shortest path in networking graph is used.	Applications : For game trees, decision trees, the tree is used.

2.1.2 Types of Graph

Basically graphs are of two types -

1. Directed graphs 2. Undirected graphs.

In the directed graph the **directions** are shown on the edges. As shown in the Fig. 2.1.2, the edges between the vertices are ordered. In this type of graph, the edge E_1 is in between the vertices V_1 and V_2. The V_1 is called head and the V_2 is called the tail. Similarly for V_1 head the tail is V_3 and so on.

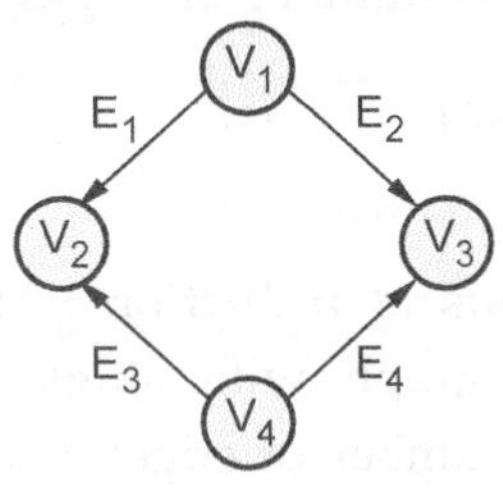

Fig. 2.1.2 Directed graph

We can say E_1 is the set of (V_1, V_2) and not of (V_2, V_1).

Similarly, in an undirected graph, the **edges are not ordered.** Please see the Fig. 2.1.3 for clear understanding of undirected graph. In this type of graph the edge E_1 is set of (V_1, V_2) or (V_2, V_1).

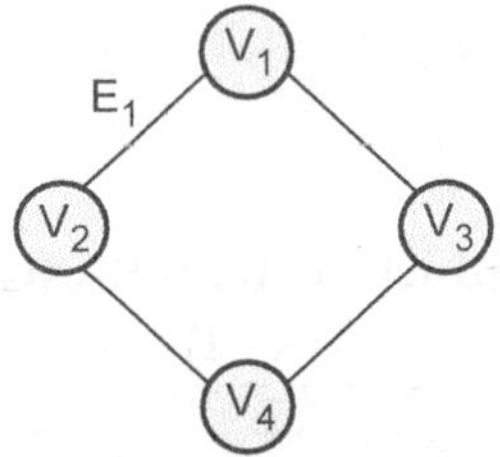

Fig. 2.1.3 Undirected graph

Similarly the object shown in the Fig. 2.1.4 is a multi-graph.

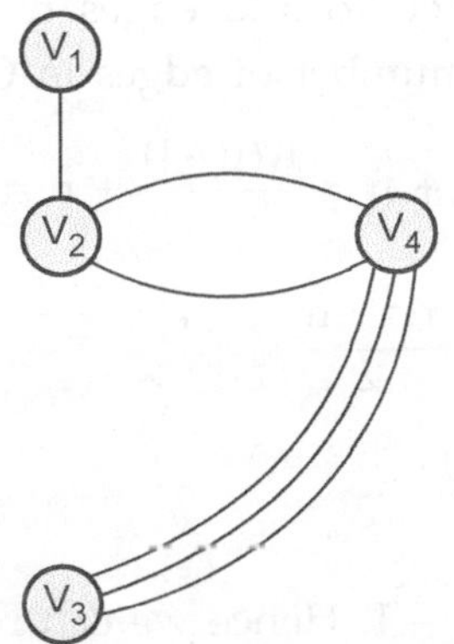

Fig. 2.1.4 A multi-graph

2.1.3 Properties of Graph

1) Complete graph : If an undirected graph of n vertices consists of $\frac{n(n-1)}{2}$ number of edges then that graph is called a complete graph.

For example : The graph shown in Fig 2.1.5 is a complete graph.

Here n = 4

$$\therefore e = \frac{n(n-1)}{2} = \frac{4(3)}{2} = 6$$

Theorem : A complete graph with n vertices has $\frac{n(n-1)}{2}$ number of edges.

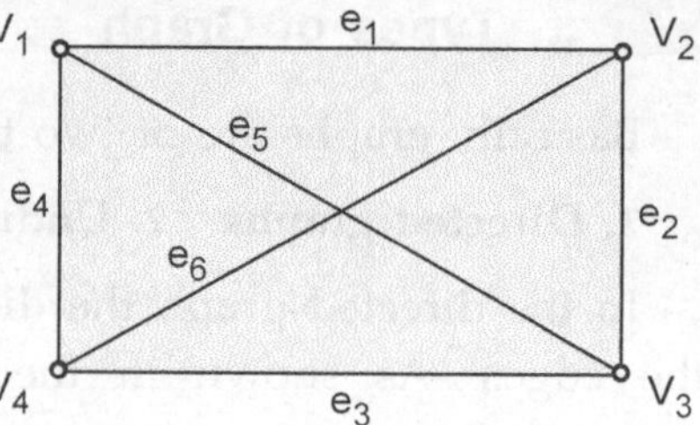

Fig. 2.1.5 Complete graph

Proof : This can be proved by principle of mathematical induction.

Basis of induction : This theorem is true for n = 1 i.e. a graph with single node because when n = 1, total number of edges = 1(1 – 1)/2 = 0.

For instance :

Fig. 2.1.6 Complete graph when n = 1

Induction hypothesis : We assume that for k vertices it is true that total number of edges $= \frac{k(k-1)}{2}$.

Inductive step : We have to show that the theorem is also true for (n + 1) vertices.

Let, G(n) be the graph with n vertices. If we add one more vertex to G(n) then to make this graph complete, we need to add edges to this newly added vertex from all the previous n vertices then total number of edges in G(n+1) will be

$$\text{Edges} = \text{Edges in G(n)} + n = \frac{n(n-1)}{2} + n = \frac{n(n-1)+2n}{2}$$

$$= \frac{n^2 - n + 2n}{2} = \frac{n^2+n}{2}$$

$$\text{Total edges in G(n + 1)} = \frac{n(n+1)}{2} \qquad \text{...(2.1.1)}$$

If we put n + 1 = k then n = k – 1. Hence we can rewrite equation (2.1.1) as

$$= \frac{(k-1)k}{2} \quad \text{i.e.} \quad \frac{k(k-1)}{2}$$

This is true by induction hypothesis. Hence total number of edges in G(n+1) graph is

$$= \frac{n(n-1)}{2} + n = \frac{n(n+1)}{2} \text{ is true.}$$

Thus it is proved by principle of mathematical induction that total number of edges in complete graph is $\frac{n(n-1)}{2}$.

2) Subgraph : A subgraph G' of graph G is a graph such that the set of vertices and set of edges of G' are proper subset of the set of edges of G.

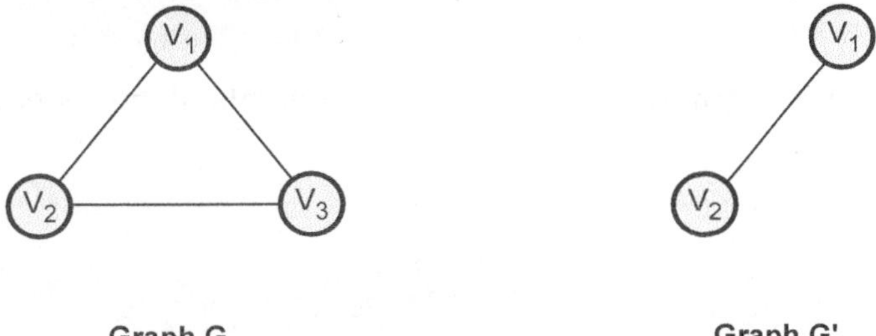

Fig. 2.1.7 Subgraph

3) Connected graph : An undirected graph is said to be connected if for every pair of distinct vertices V_i and V_j in V(G) there is an edge V_i to V_j in G.

Note that there is path from any two vertices.

For example :

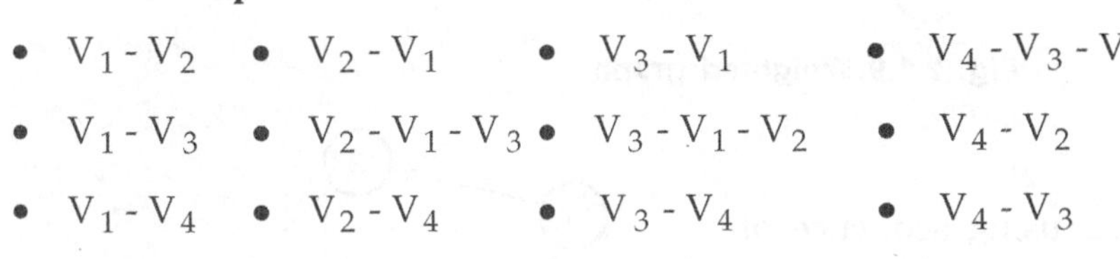

- $V_1 - V_2$
- $V_2 - V_1$
- $V_3 - V_1$
- $V_4 - V_3 - V_1$
- $V_1 - V_3$
- $V_2 - V_1 - V_3$
- $V_3 - V_1 - V_2$
- $V_4 - V_2$
- $V_1 - V_4$
- $V_2 - V_4$
- $V_3 - V_4$
- $V_4 - V_3$

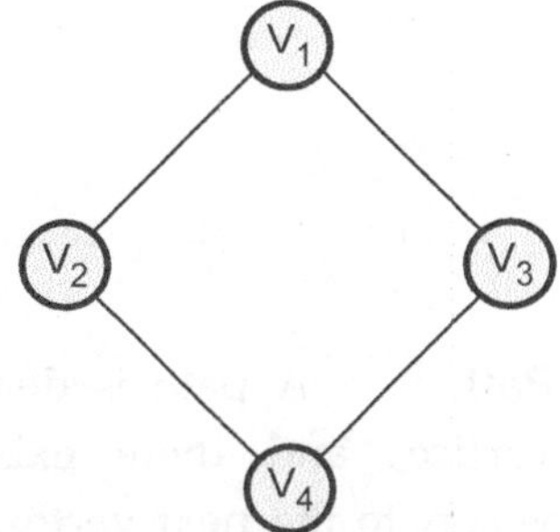

Fig. 2.1.8 Connected graph

Example 2.1.1 *Prove that the number of odd degree vertices in a connected graph should be even.*

Solution : To prove this, consider connected graphs with odd degree vertices.

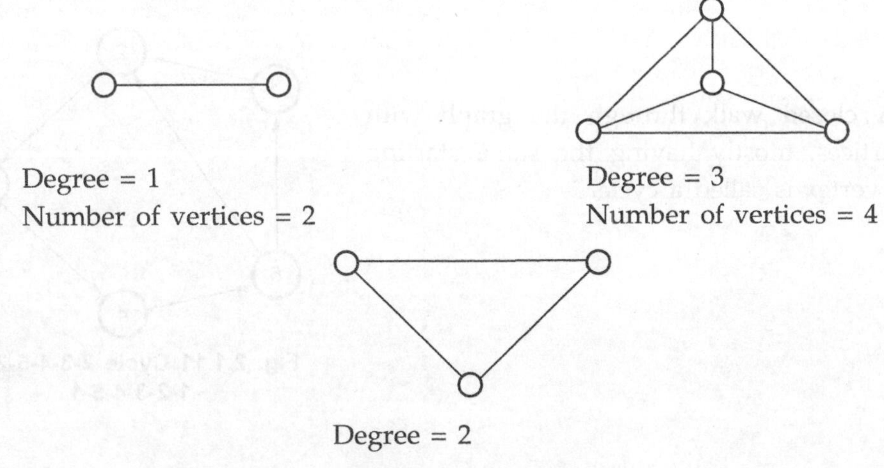

These figures show clearly that in a connected graph there are even number of vertices with odd degree.

Weighted graph

A weighted graph is a graph which consists of weights along its edges.

For example :

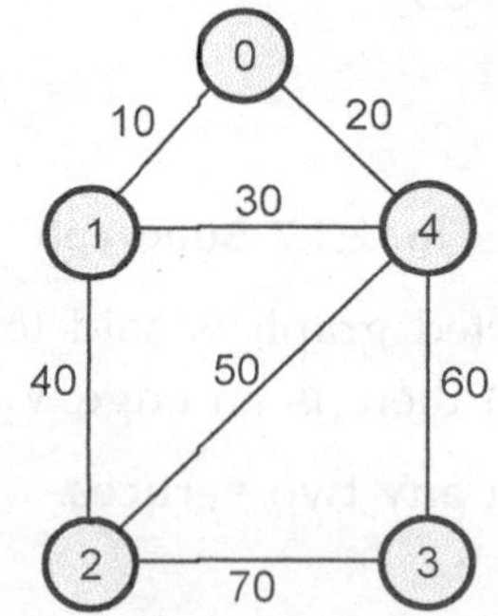

Fig. 2.1.9 Weighted graph

Path : A path is denoted using sequence of vertices and there exists an edge from one vertex to the next vertex.

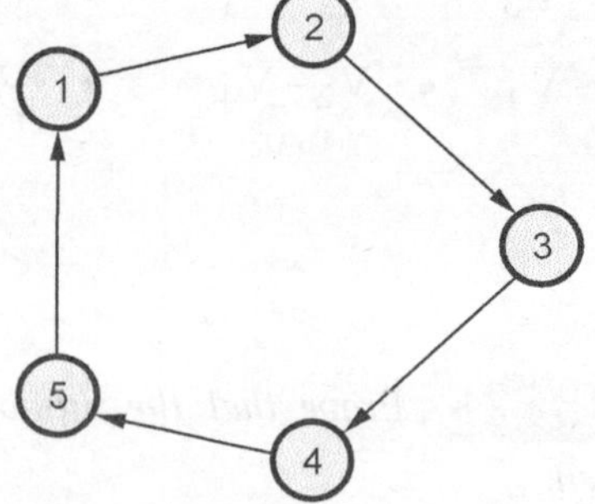

Fig. 2.1.10 Path of G is 1-2-3-4-5

Cycle : A closed walk through the graph with repeated vertices, mostly having the same starting and ending vertex is called a cycle.

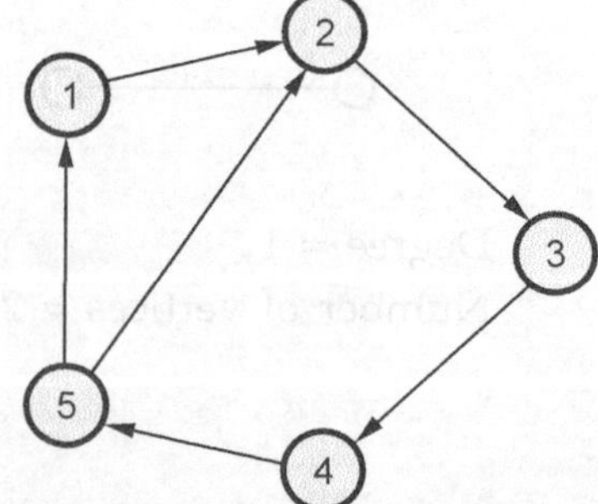

Fig. 2.1.11 Cycle 2-3-4-5-2 or 1-2-3-4-5-1

Component : The maximal connected subgraph of a graph is called component of a graph.

For example : Following are 3 components of a graph.

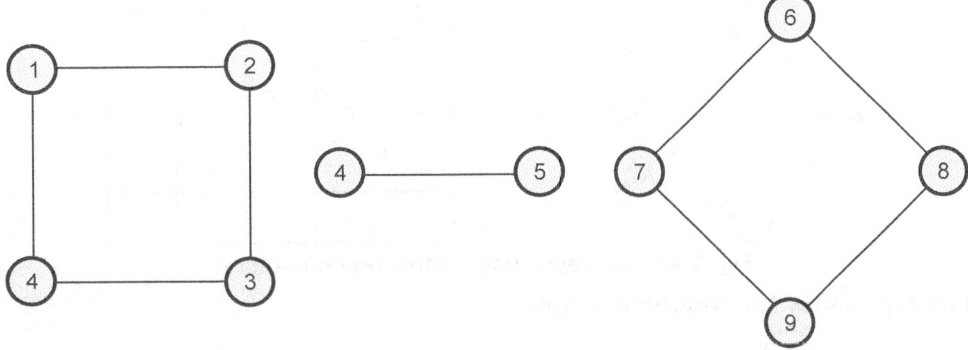

Fig. 2.1.12

In-degree and out-degree

The degree of vertex is the number of edges associated with the vertex.

In-degree of a vertex is the number of edges that incident to that vertex. Out-degree of the vertex is total number of edges that are going away from the vertex.

Vertices	In-degree	Out-degree
V_1	1	1
V_2	2	1
V_3	1	1
V_4	1	2

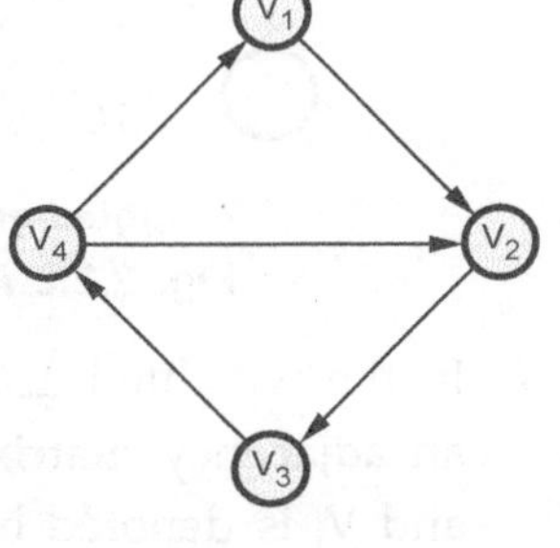

Self loop : Self loop is an edge that connects the same vertex, to itself.

Fig. 2.1.13 Self loop

2.2 Storage Representation

SPPU : May-05, 10, 11, Dec.-05, 07, 13, Marks 6

The graph can be represented using various representations. These representations are based on the data structures arrays and linked list. Let us discuss these representations in detail.

2.2.1 Adjacency Matrix

In this representation, matrix or 2 dimensional array is used to represent the graph.

Consider a graph G of n vertices and the matrix M. If there is an edge present between vertices V_i and V_j then M[i][j] = 1 else M[i][j] = 0. Note that for an undirected graph if M[i][j] = 1 then for M[j][i] is also 1. Here are some graphs shown by adjacency matrix.

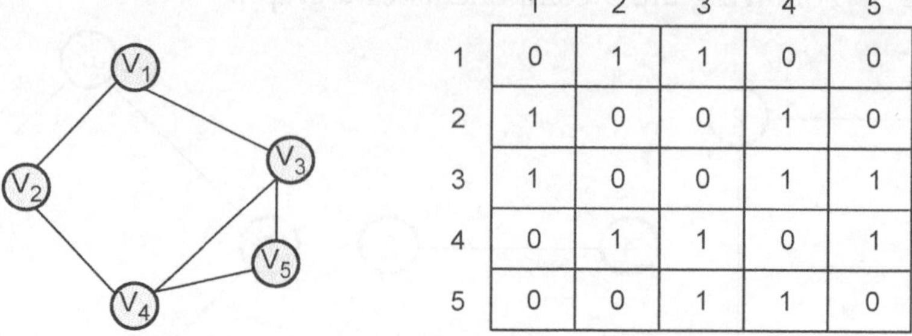

	1	2	3	4	5
1	0	1	1	0	0
2	1	0	0	1	0
3	1	0	0	1	1
4	0	1	1	0	1
5	0	0	1	1	0

Fig. 2.2.1 An adjacency matrix representation

Adjacency matrix for weighted graph

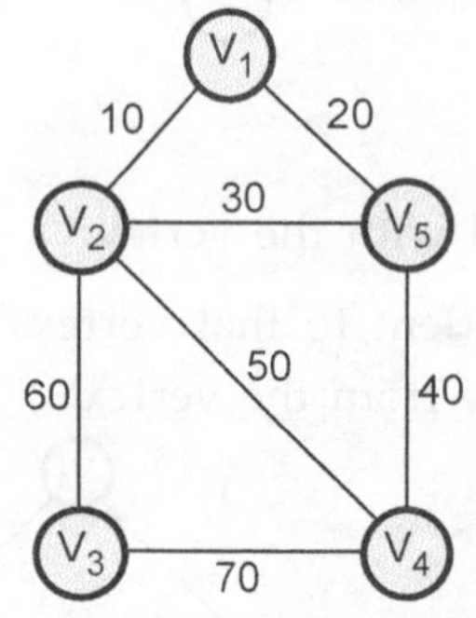

Weighted graph

	1	2	3	4	5
1	0	10	0	0	20
2	10	0	60	50	30
3	0	60	0	70	0
4	0	50	70	0	40
5	20	30	0	40	0

Adjacency matrix

Fig. 2.2.2 Adjacency matrix representation for weighted graph

- In the weighted graph, weights or distances are given along every edge. Hence in an adjacency matrix representation any edge which is present between vertices V_i and V_j is denoted by its weight. Hence M[i][j] = Weight of edge.
- If there is no edge between V_i and V_j then, M[i][j] = 0.

2.2.2 Adjacency List

In this representation, a **linked list** is used to represent a graph.

There are two methods of representing graph using adjacency list.

Method 1 : As we know the graph is a set of vertices and edges, we will maintain the two structures, for vertices and edges respectively.

For example : Now in Fig. 2.2.3, graph has the nodes as a, b, c, d, e. So we will maintain the linked list of these head nodes as well as the adjacent nodes.

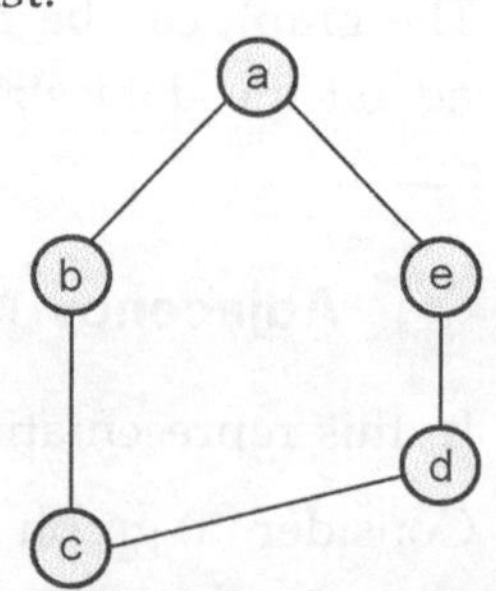

Fig. 2.2.3 Graph G

```
typedef struct head
 {
   char data;
   struct head *down;
  struct head *next;
} ;
typedef struct node
{
 int ver;
struct node *link;
};
```

Explanation : This is purely the adjacency list graph. The down pointer helps us to go to each node in the graph where as the next node is for going to adjacent node of each of the head node.

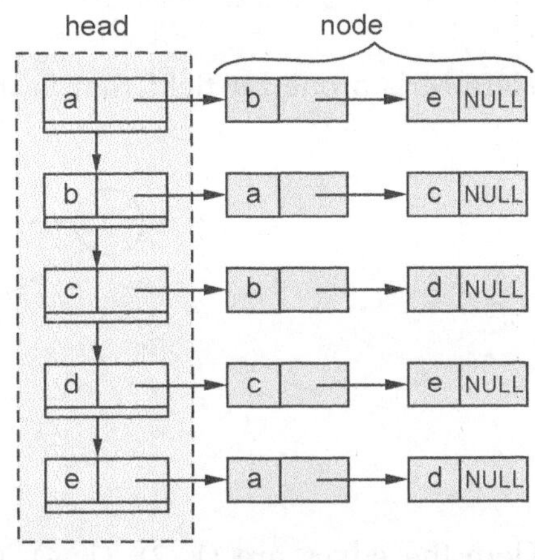

Fig. 2.2.4 Adjacency list (Method 1)

Method 2 : In this method of representing the adjacency list, we take mixed data structure. That means instead of taking the head list as a linked list we will take an array of head nodes. So only one 'C' structure will be there representing the adjacent nodes. See the Fig. 2.2.5 representing the adjacency list for the above graph. First let us see the 'C' structure.

```
typedef struct node1
{
      char vertex;
      struct node1*nex ;
}node ;
node * head [10] ;
```

Explanation : This is the graph which can be represented with the array and linked list data structures. Array is used to store the head nodes. The node structure will be the same through out.

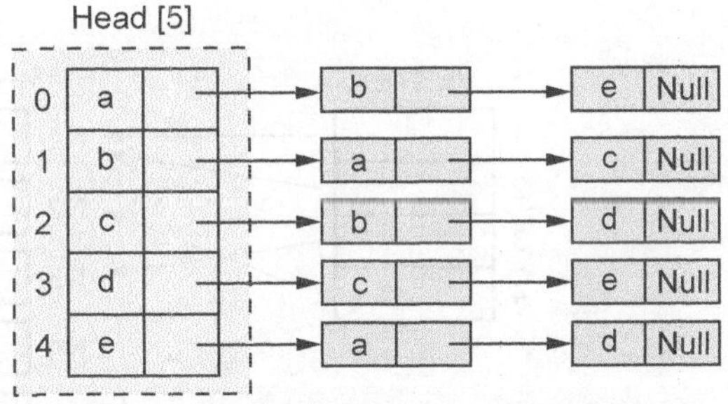

Fig. 2.2.5 Adjacency list (Method 2)

Situation in which linked representation is beneficial

The situation in which the number of nodes in the graph is not fixed and we need to create the graph dynamically, then linked representation is preferred than graph representation.

2.2.3 Adjacency Multilist

In this representation of an undirected graph each edge is represented by two entries.

In a graph, each edge is represented by two vertices but these two vertices are present in two different edges. Hence adjacency multilists can be used for each of the two nodes incident to.

The node structure is as follows -

Here M is a one bit field that is used to represent whether the edge is visited or not.

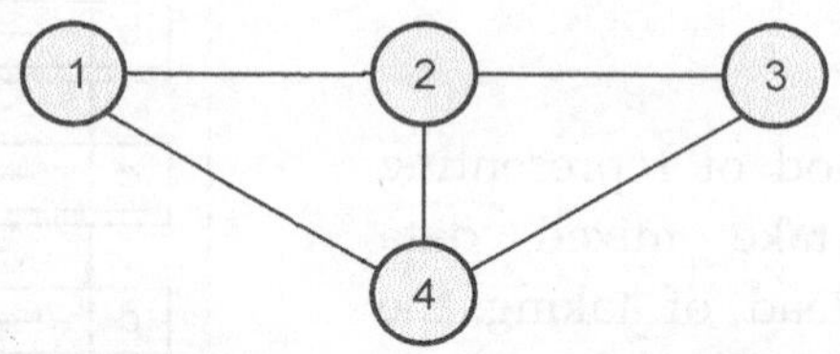

Fig. 2.2.6 Graph

Here the edges are (1, 2), (1, 4), (2, 3), (2, 4) and (3, 4). These edges are represented as nodes. The vertices are 1, 2, 3, 4.

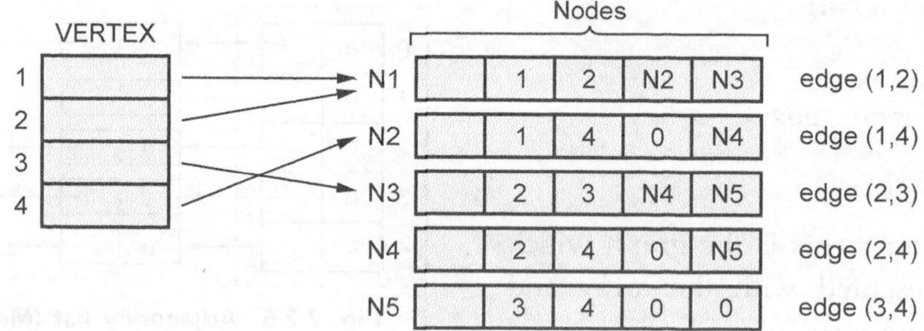

Fig. 2.2.7

In node N1 the edge (1, 2) is specified. Third field N2 is for edge (1, 4), this link is the adjacent edge of edge (1, 2) considering vertex V1 i.e., 1 Forth field-N3 is for edge (2, 3), this link is the adjacent edge of edge (1, 2) considering vertex V2 i.e. 2.

In this way remaining nodes N2, N3, N4 and N5 are created.

Now Vertex 1 is connected to (1, 2) and (1, 4) i.e. N1, N2.

Similarly Vertex 2 is connected to (1, 2), (2, 3) and (2, 4) i.e. N2, N3 and N4

$$\left.\begin{array}{l}\text{Vertex 1 : N1} \rightarrow \text{N2} \\ \text{Vertex 2 : N2} \rightarrow \text{N3} \rightarrow \text{N4} \\ \text{Vertex 3 : N3} \rightarrow \text{N5} \\ \text{Vertex 4 : N2} \rightarrow \text{N4} \rightarrow \text{N5}\end{array}\right\} \text{Adjacency Multilists}$$

2.2.4 Inverse Adjacency List

Inverse adjacency list is an adjacency list representation in which only incoming edge to a vertex is represent. For example -

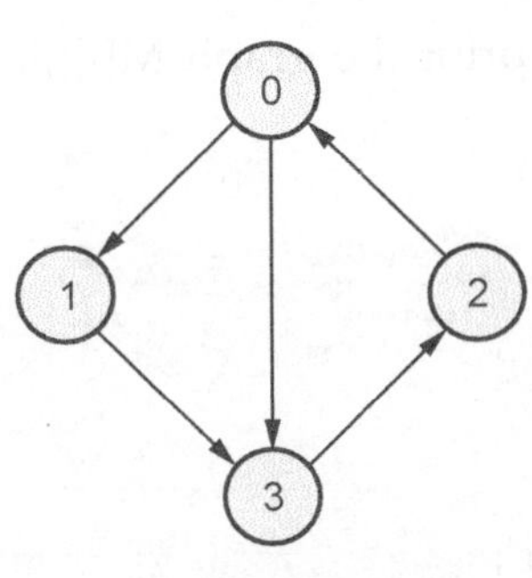

Fig. 2.2.8 Graph G

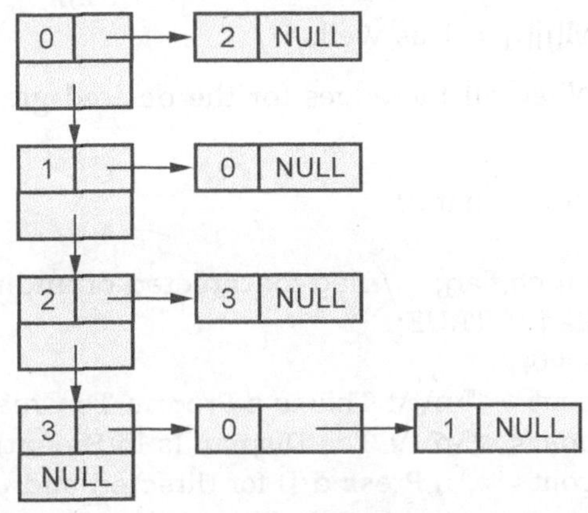

Fig. 2.2.9 Inverse adjacency list of G

University Questions

1. *Explain the following terms*

   i. Adjacency matrix of graph ii. Adjacency list of graph .

   SPPU : May-05, Dec.-05, Dec.07, Marks 4

2. *Define the following : i) A complete graph ii) A weighted graph .* **SPPU : May-10, Marks 4**
3. *Write a short note on different representation of a graph .* **SPPU : May-11, Marks 6**
4. *Explain the situation in which linked representation of a graph is more beneficial than array representation.* **SPPU : Dec.-13, Marks 2**

2.3 Graph Operations

Various operations that can be performed on the graph are

1. **Create :** The graph can be created using **adjacency matrix** or **adjacency list**.
2. **Display :** The graph can be displayed using Breadth First Search **(BFS)** or Depth First Search **(DFS)** method.

2.4 Storage Structure

SPPU : Dec.-10, 12, May-14, Marks 8

- **Graph creation using adjacency matrix**

Creation of graph using adjacency matrix is quite simple task. The adjacency matrix is nothing but a two dimensional array. The algorithm for creation of graph using adjacency matix will be as follows :

1) Declare an array of M[size] [size] which will store the graph.

2) Enter how many nodes you want in a graph.

3) Enter the edges of the graph by two vertices each, say V_i, V_j indicates some edge.

4) If the graph is directed set M[i][j] = 1. If graph is undirected set M[i][j] = 1 and M[j][i] = 1 as well.

5) When all the edges for the desired graph is entered print the graph M[i][j].

```
void Gbfs::create()
{
    int ch,flag;    //flag for directed or undirected graph
    flag = TRUE;
    n=0;
    cout<<"\n\t\t This is a Progrm To Create a Graph";
    cout<<"\n\t\t The Display Is In Breadth First Manner";
    cout<<"\n Press d/D for directed and u/U for undirected graph\n";
    ch = toupper(getche());
    if ( ch == 'D')
      flag = FALSE;

    do
    {
        cout<<"\nEnter the Edge of a graph ";
        cout<<"(And for termination type-99)\n";
        cin>>v1>>v2;
        if ( v1 == -99)
          break;
        if ( v1 >= size || v2 >= size)
                error("Invalid Vertex Value\n" );
        else
          g[v1][v2] = TRUE;
          if (flag)
                g[v2][v1] = TRUE;
    n++;//for keeping track of total number of nodes
    }while(1);
}
```

Graph creation using adjacency list

1. Declare node structure for creating adjacency list.
2. Initialize an array of nodes. This array will act as head nodes. Say '*head [10]'. The index of head [ ] will be the starting vertex.
3. The create function will create the adjacency list for given graph G as follows -

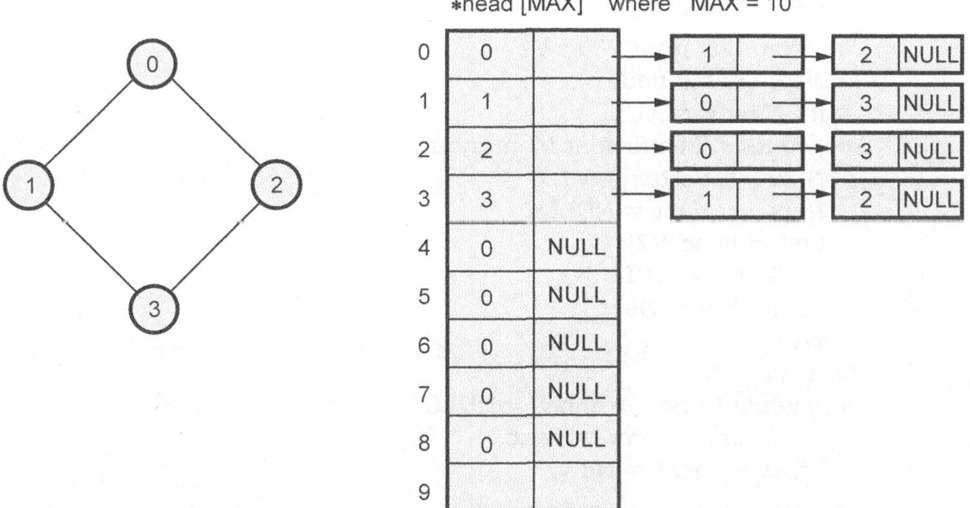

Fig. 2.4.1 Graph and its adjacency list representation

The pseudo code for create function is as follows :

```
void Lgraph::create()
{
        int V1, V2;
        char ans='y';
        node *New,*first;
        cout<<"\n\nEnter the vertices no. beginning with 0";
        do
        {
          cout<<"\nEnter the Edge of a graph \n";
             cin>>V1>>V2;
             if ( V1 >= MAX || V2 >= MAX)
                    cout<<"Invalid Vertex Value\n" ;
             else
               {
                    // creating link from V1 to V2
                    New = new node;
                    if ( New == NULL )
                      cout<<"Insufficient Memory\n";
                    New -> vertex = V2;
                    New -> next = NULL;
```

```
            first = head[V1];
            if ( first == NULL )
             head[V1] = New;
            else
             {
                 while ( first  -> next != NULL )
                   first = first -> next;
                 first  -> next = New;
             }
        // creating link from V2 to V1
            New = new node;
            if ( New == NULL )
             cout<<"Insufficient Memory\n";
            New  -> vertex = V1;
            New  -> next = NULL;
            first = head[V2];
            if ( first == NULL )
             head[V2] = New;
            else
             {
              while ( first  -> next != NULL )
                  first = first-> next;
             first -> next = New;
             }
        }
    cout<<"\nWant to add more edges?(y/n)";
    ans=getche();
   }while(ans=='y');
}
```

Example 2.4.1 *What is graph ? Draw how the following graph can be represented using linked organization :* **SPPU : Dec.-10, Marks 8**

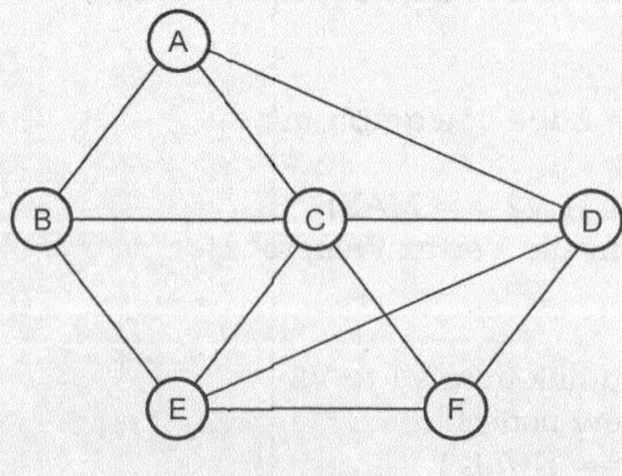

Fig. 2.4.2

Solution : Graph : The graph is a collection of nodes and vertices. The linked representation of given graph is -

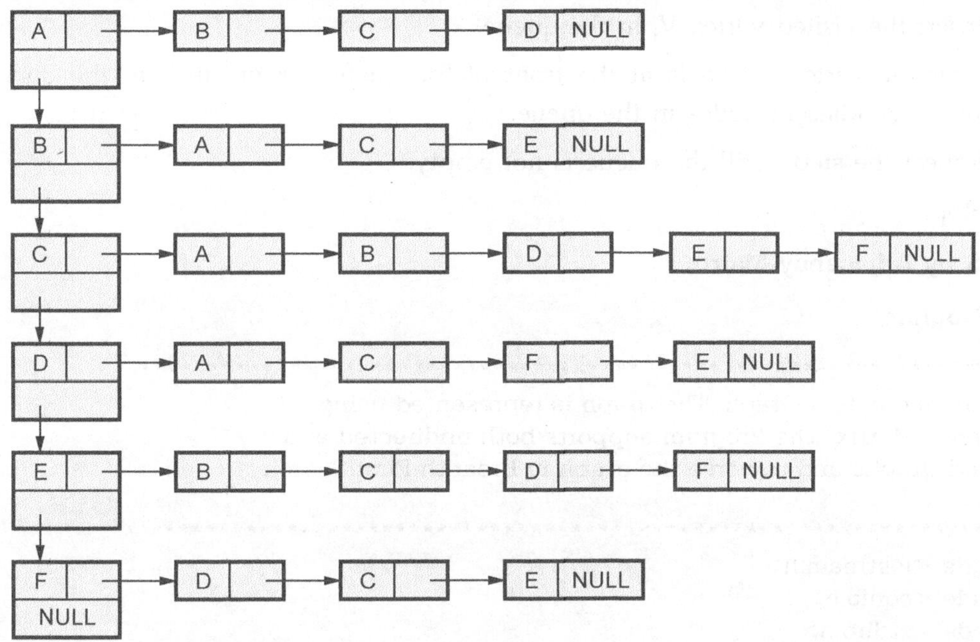

Fig. 2.4.3

University Questions

1. *What are graph storage structures ?* **SPPU : Dec.-12, Marks 4**
2. *Explain with suitable example the various storage structures for the graph.* **SPPU : May-14, Marks 6**

2.5 Traversals

2.5.1 BFS Traversal of Graph

- In BFS we start from some vertex and find all the adjacent vertices of it. This process will be repeated for all the vertices so that the vertices lying on same breadth get printed.
- For avoiding repetition of vertices, we maintain array of **visited** nodes.
- A **queue** data structure is used to store adjacent vertices.

Algorithm :

1. Create a graph. Depending on the type of graph i.e. directed or undirected set the value of the flag as either 0 or 1 respectively.

2. Read the vertex from which you want to traverse the graph say V_i.
3. Initialize the visited array to 1 at the index of V_i.
4. Insert the visited vertex V_i in the queue.
5. Visit the vertex which is at the front of the queue. Delete it from the queue and place its adjacent nodes in the queue.
6. Repeat the step 5, till the queue is not empty.
7. Stop.

1. BFS by Adjacency Matrix :

C++ Program

```
/*************************************************************************
Program to create a Graph. The graph is represented using
Adjacency Matrix. The Program supports both undirected and
Directed Graphs and traverse the graph in Breadth First Search
Order.
*************************************************************************/
#include <iostream.h>
#include <conio.h>
#include <stdlib.h>
#include<ctype.h>

#define    size  20
#define    TRUE  1
#define    FALSE  0
class Gbfs
{
 private:
 int g[size][size],v1,v2;
 int visit[size],Q[size];
 int front,rear;
 public:
 int n;
 Gbfs();
 void error(char *);
 void create(),bfs(int);
 void display();
 ~Gbfs();
};
/*
-----------------------------------------------------------------
The costructor defined
-----------------------------------------------------------------
*/
```

```
Gbfs::Gbfs()
{
 for ( v1 = 0; v1 < size; v1++)
       for ( v2 = 0; v2 < size; v2++)
              g[v1][v2] = FALSE;
 for ( v1 = 0; v1 < size; v1++)
        visit[v1] = FALSE;
}
/*
-----------------------------------------------------------------------
The destructor defined
-----------------------------------------------------------------------
*/
Gbfs::~Gbfs()
{
 for ( v1 = 0; v1 < size; v1++)
 {
       for ( v2 = 0; v2 < size; v2++)
       g[v1][v2]=FALSE;
 }
 for ( v1 = 0; v1 < size; v1++)
 visit[v1] = FALSE;
}
/*
-----------------------------------------------------------------------
The display defined
-----------------------------------------------------------------------
*/
void Gbfs::display()
{
 for ( v1 = 0; v1 < n; v1++)
 {
       for ( v2 = 0; v2 < n; v2++)
              cout<<" "<<g[v1][v2];
       cout<<endl;
 }
}
/*
-----------------------------------------------------------------------
       The error function
-----------------------------------------------------------------------
*/
void Gbfs::error( char *Msg )
{
       cout<<"\n"<<Msg;
       cout<<"Press any key to abort\n";
       getch();
```

```
	exit(1);
}

/*
------------------------------------------------------------------------
	The create function
------------------------------------------------------------------------
*/
void  Gbfs::create()
{
	int ch,flag;    //flag for directed or undirected graph
	flag = TRUE;
	n=0;
	cout<<"\n\t\t This is a Progrm To Create a Graph";
	cout<<"\n\t\t The Display Is In Breadth First Manner";
	cout<<"\n Press d/D for directed and u/U for undirected graph\n";
	ch = toupper(getche());
	if ( ch == 'D')
	  flag = FALSE;

	do
	{
		cout<<"\nEnter the Edge of a graph ";
		cout<<"(And for termination type -99)\n";
		cin>>v1>>v2;
		if ( v1 == -99)
		  break;
		if ( v1 >= size || v2 >= size)
			error("Invalid Vertex Value\n" );
		else
		  g[v1][v2] = TRUE;
		  if ( flag )
			g[v2][v1] = TRUE;
	n++;//for keeping track of total number of nodes
	}while(1);
}

/*
------------------------------------------------------------------------
	The bfs function
------------------------------------------------------------------------
*/
void Gbfs::bfs(int v1)
{
	int v2;

	visit[v1] = TRUE;
```

```
        front = rear = -1;
        Q[++rear] = v1;
        while ( front != rear )
        {
                v1 = Q[++front];
                cout<<"\n"<<v1;
                for ( v2 = 0; v2 < n; v2++)
                {
                        if ( g[v1][v2] == TRUE && visit[v2] == FALSE )
                        {
                                Q[++rear] = v2;
                                visit[v2] = TRUE;
                        }
                }
        }
}
/*
-----------------------------------------------------------------------
The main Function
-----------------------------------------------------------------------
*/
void main()
{
        int v1;
        Gbfs gr;
        clrscr();
        gr.create();
        cout<<"The Adjacency Matrix for the graph is "<<endl;
        gr.display();
        cout<<"Enter the Vertex from which you want to traverse ";
        cin>>v1;
        if ( v1 >= size )
         gr.error("Invalid Vertex\n");
        cout<<"The Breadth First Search of the Graph is \n";
        gr.bfs(v1);
        getch();
}
```

Output

```
          This is a Progrm To Create a Graph
          The Display Is In Breadth First Manner
 Press d/D for directed and u/U for undirected graph
u
Enter the Edge of a graph (And for termination type -99)

0 1
```

```
Enter the Edge of a graph (And for termination type -99)
0 2

Enter the Edge of a graph (And for termination type -99)
1 3

Enter the Edge of a graph (And for termination type -99)
2 3

Enter the Edge of a graph (And for termination type -99)
-99 -99
The Adjacency Matrix for the graph is
 0 1 1 0
 1 0 0 1
 1 0 0 1
 0 1 1 0
Enter the Vertex from which you want to traverse 0
The Breadth First Search of the Graph is
0
1
2
3
```

Explanation of logic of BFS

In BFS the queue is maintained for storing the adjacent nodes and an array 'visited' is maintained for keeping the track of visited nodes. i.e. once a particular node is visited it should not be revisited again. Let us see how our program works :

Fig. 2.5.1

Step 1 : Start with vertex 1.

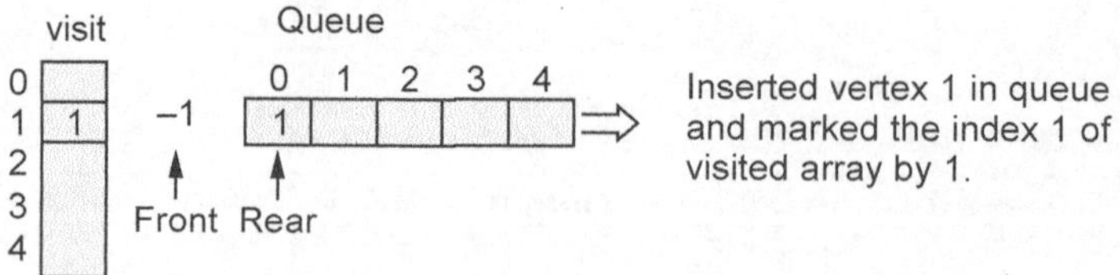

Step 2 :

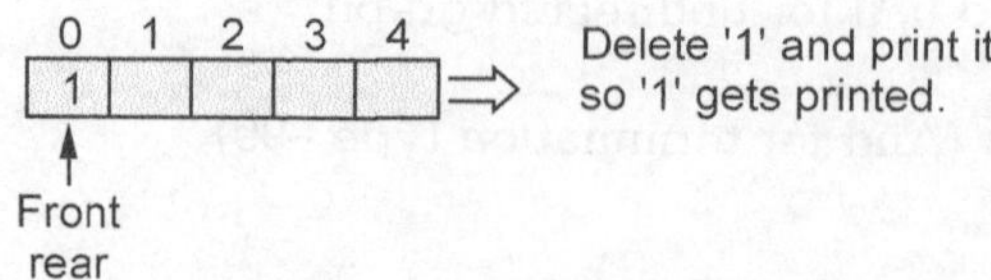

Step 3 : Find adjacent vertices of vertex 1 and mark them as visited, insert those in Queue.

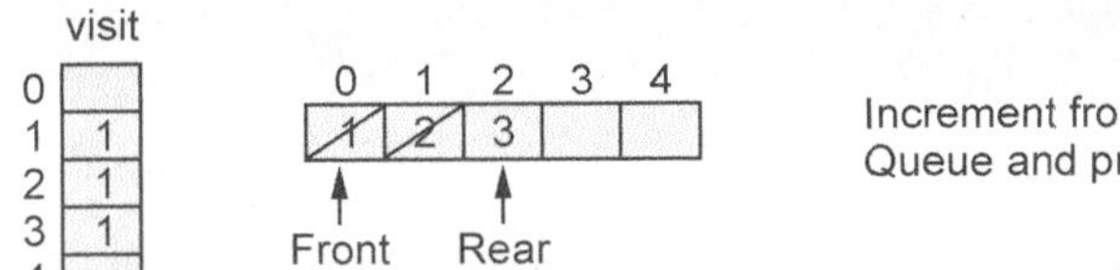

Increment front by 1 delete '2' from Queue and print it so '2' gets printed.

Step 4 : Find adjacent to '2' and insert those nodes in Queue as well as mark them as visited.

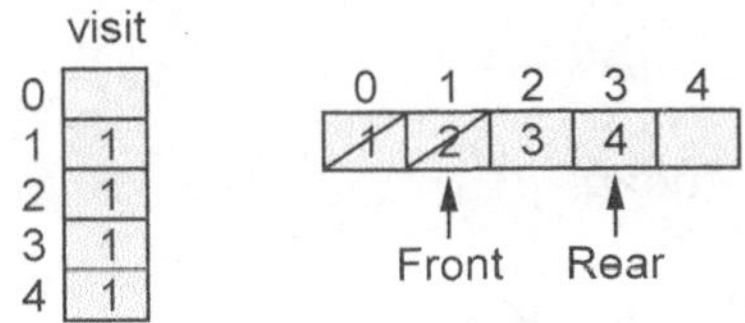

Step 5 : Increment front and delete the node print it.

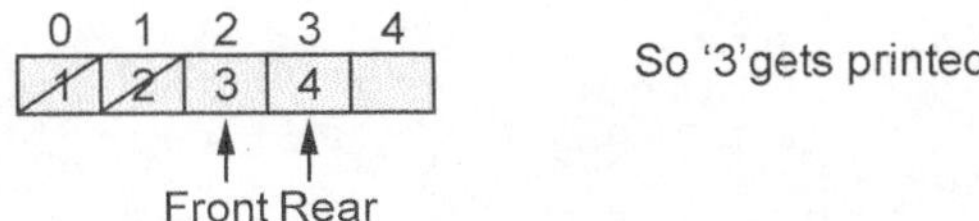

So '3'gets printed

Step 6 : Find adjacent to '3' i.e. 4 check whether it is marked as visited. If it is marked as visited do not insert in the queue.

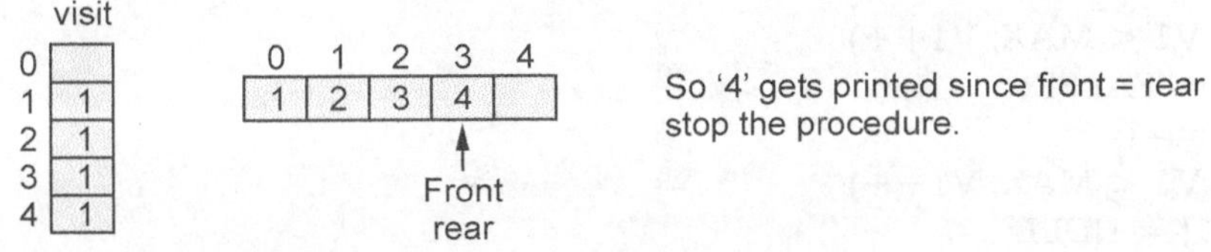

So '4' gets printed since front = rear stop the procedure.

Increment front, delete the node from Queue and print it.

So output will be - BFS for above graph as

1 2 3 4

2. BFS by Adjacency List

C++ Program

```
/*******************************************************************
      Program to create a Graph. The graph is represented using
      Adjacency List and traversing the graph in Breadth First Search
      Order.
*******************************************************************/

#include<iostream.h>
```

```
#include <conio.h>
#include <stdlib.h>

#define    MAX    10
#define    TRUE    1
#define    FALSE   0

class Lgraph
{
 private:
     typedef struct node1
            {
                int vertex;
                struct node1 *next;
            }node;
            node *head[MAX];
            int visited[MAX];
            int Queue[MAX],front,rear;
 public:
     Lgraph();
     void create(),bfs(int);
};

Lgraph::Lgraph()//constructor defined
{
 int V1;
 for ( V1 = 0; V1 < MAX; V1++)
  visited[V1] = FALSE;
 front = rear = -1;
 for ( V1 = 0; V1 < MAX; V1++)
     head[V1] = NULL;
}
/*
-----------------------------------------------------------------------
The create function
-----------------------------------------------------------------------
*/
void Lgraph::create()
{
     int V1, V2;
     char ans='y';
     node *New,*first;
     cout<<"\n\nEnter the vertices no. beginning with 0";
     do
     {
       cout<<"\nEnter the Edge of a graph \n";
       cin>>V1>>V2;
```

```
    if ( V1 >= MAX || V2 >= MAX)
            cout<<"Invalid Vertex Value\n" ;
        else
          {
            // creating link from V1 to V2
            New = new node;
            if ( New == NULL )
              cout<<"Insufficient Memory\n";
            New -> vertex = V2;
            New -> next = NULL;
            first = head[V1];
            if ( first == NULL )
              head[V1] = New;
            else
             {
            while ( first -> next != NULL )
            first = first-> next;
            first -> next = New;
            }
          // creating link from V2 to V1
            New = new node;
            if ( New == NULL )
              cout<<"Insufficient Memory\n";
            New -> vertex = V1;
            New -> next = NULL;
            first = head[V2];
            if ( first == NULL )
              head[V2] = New;
            else
             {
              while ( first -> next != NULL )
                    first = first -> next;
              first -> next = New;
            }
          }
     cout<<"\nWant to add more edges?(y/n)";
     ans=getche();
    }while(ans=='y');
}
/*
----------------------------------------------------------------------
The bfs Function
----------------------------------------------------------------------
*/
void Lgraph::bfs(int V1)
{
    int i;
```

```
        node *first;
        Queue[++rear] = V1;
        while ( front != rear)
        {
                i = Queue[++front];
                if ( visited[i] == FALSE )
                {
                cout<<endl<<i;
                visited[i] = TRUE;
                }
                first = head[i];
                while ( first != NULL )
                {
                if ( visited[first->vertex] == FALSE )
                Queue[++rear] = first->vertex;
                first = first -> next;
                }
        }

}
/*
--------------------------------------------------------------------------
        The main function
--------------------------------------------------------------------------
*/
void main ( )
{
  // Local declarations
        int V1;
        char ans;
        Lgraph gr;
        clrscr();
        Lgraph();
        gr.create();
        clrscr();
        cout<<"Enter the Vertex from which you want to traverse :";
        cin>>V1;
        if ( V1 >= MAX  )
                cout<<"\nInvalid Vertex\n";
        else
        {
        cout<<"The Breadth First Search of the Graph is \n";
        gr.bfs(V1);
        getch();
        }
}
```

Output

```
Enter the vertices no. beginning with 0
Enter the Edge of a graph
0 1

Want to add more edges?(y/n)y
Enter the Edge of a graph
0 2

Want to add more edges?(y/n)y
Enter the Edge of a graph
0 3

Want to add more edges?(y/n)y
Enter the Edge of a graph
0 4

Want to add more edges?(y/n)y
Enter the Edge of a graph
1 5

Want to add more edges?(y/n)y
Enter the Edge of a graph
2 5

Want to add more edges?(y/n)y
Enter the Edge of a graph
3 5

Want to add more edges?(y/n)y
Enter the Edge of a graph
4 5

Want to add more edges?(y/n)n
Enter the Vertex from which you want to traverse :0
The Breadth First Search of the Graph is
0
1
2
3
4
5
```

Analysis of BFS

- If the graph is created using **adjacency matrix** in BFS routine then while statement executes for n times. Inside this while statement there is a for loop which executes for all the vertices. Hence time complexity of BFS is **O(V^2)**.

- If the graph is created using **adjacency list** then each vertex V is enqueued and dequeued at most once. Scanning for all the adjacent vertices takes $O(|E|)$ time. Hence the time complexity of BFS is $\mathbf{O(|V|+|E|)}$.

2.5.2 DFS Traversal of Graph

- In depth first search traversal we start from one vertex and traverse the path as deeply as we can go. When there is no vertex further, we traverse back and search for unvisited vertex.
- An array is maintained for storing the visited vertex.

For example

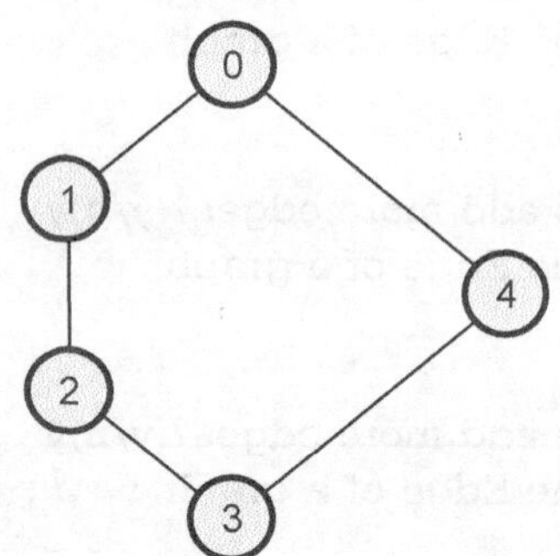

- The DFS will be (if we start from vertex 0) 0 - 1 - 2 - 3 - 4
- The DFS will be (if we start from vertex 3) 3 - 4 - 0 - 1 - 2

1) DFS by Adjacency Matrix (Recursive Program)

C++ Program

```
/*************************************************************************
    Program to create a Graph. The graph is represented using
    Adjacency Matrix. The Program supports both undirected and
    Directed Graphs and traverse the graph in Depth First Search
    Order.

*************************************************************************/

// List of include files

#include <iostream.h>
#include <conio.h>
#include<ctype.h>
#include <stdlib.h>

// List of defined constants

#define        MAX 20
#define        TRUE       1
```

```
#define           FALSE       0

// Global declarations

// Declare an adjacency matrix for storing the graph
class Gdfs
{

 private:
 int g[MAX][MAX],v[MAX];
 int v1, v2;
 public:
 int n;
 Gdfs();
 void error(char *);
 void create(),display();
 void Dfs(int);
 ~Gdfs();
};
/*
----------------------------------------------------------------------
The constructor defined
----------------------------------------------------------------------
*/
Gdfs::Gdfs()
{
 for ( v1 = 0; v1 < MAX; v1++)
       v[v1] = FALSE;
 for ( v1 = 0; v1 < MAX; v1++)
  for ( v2 = 0; v2 < MAX; v2++)
        g[v1][v2] = FALSE;
}
/*


----------------------------------------------------------------------
The destructor defined
----------------------------------------------------------------------
*/
Gdfs::~Gdfs()
{
*/
 for ( v1 = 0; v1 < MAX; v1++)
 {
      for ( v2 = 0; v2 < MAX; v2++)
      g[v1][v2]=FALSE;
 }
```

```
 for ( v1 = 0; v1 < MAX; v1++)
  v[v1] = FALSE;
}
/*
------------------------------------------------------------------------
The display function
------------------------------------------------------------------------
*/
void Gdfs::display()
{
 for ( v1 = 0; v1 < n; v1++)
  {
	for ( v2 = 0; v2 < n; v2++)
		cout<<" "<<g[v1][v2];
	cout<<endl;
  }
}


/*
------------------------------------------------------------------------
	The error function
------------------------------------------------------------------------
*/
void Gdfs::error( char *Msg )
{
	cout<<Msg;
	cout<<"Press any key to abort\n";
	getch();
	exit(1);
}

/*
------------------------------------------------------------------------
	The Create function
------------------------------------------------------------------------
*/
void  Gdfs::create()
{
	int Ch, v1, v2, Undirected;
	Undirected = TRUE;
	n=0;
	cout<<"\n This Program Is For Creation OF Graph";
	cout<<"\n And The Display Is By Depth First Search";
	cout<<"\n\tPress d/D for directed nad u/U for undirected garph\n";
	Ch = toupper(getche());
	if ( Ch == 'D')
```

```
        Undirected = FALSE;
      do
      {
            cout<<"\nEnter the Edge of a graph by two vertices \n";
            cout<<"(and type -99 terminate)\n";
            cin>>v1>>v2;
            if ( v1 == -99)
              break;
            if ( v1 >= MAX || v2 >= MAX)
                  error("Invalid Vertex Value\n" );
            else
              g[v1][v2] = TRUE;
              if ( Undirected )
                    g[v2][v1] = TRUE;
      n++;
      }
      while(1);
}
/*
------------------------------------------------------------------
      The Dfs function
------------------------------------------------------------------
*/
void Gdfs::Dfs(int v1)
{
      int v2;

      cout<<endl<<v1;
      v[v1] = TRUE;
      for ( v2 = 0; v2 < n; v2++)
            if ( g[v1][v2] == TRUE &&  v[v2] == FALSE )
                  Dfs(v2);
}
/*
------------------------------------------------------------------
      The main function
------------------------------------------------------------------
*/
void main ( )
{
      Gdfs gr;
      clrscr();
      int v1;
      gr.create();
      cout<<"The Adjacency Matrix for the graph is "<<endl;
      gr.display();
      cout<<"Enter the Vertex from which you want to traverse : ";
```

```
	cin>>v1;
	if ( v1 >= MAX )
		gr.error("Invalid Vertex\n");
	cout<<"The Depth First Search of the Graph is "<<endl;
	gr.Dfs(v1);
	getch();
}
```

Output

```
 This Program Is For Creation OF Graph
 And The Display Is By Depth First Search
	Press d/D for directed nad u/U for undirected garph
u
Enter the Edge of a graph by two vertices
(and type –99 terminate)
0 1

Enter the Edge of a graph by two vertices
(and type –99 terminate)
0 2

Enter the Edge of a graph by two vertices
(and type –99 terminate)
1 3

Enter the Edge of a graph by two vertices
(and type –99 terminate)
2 3

Enter the Edge of a graph by two vertices
(and type –99 terminate)
–99 –99
The Adjacency Matrix for the graph is
 0 1 1 0
 1 0 0 1
 1 0 0 1
 0 1 1 0
Enter the Vertex from which you want to traverse : 1
The Depth First Search of the Graph is

1
0
2
3
```

Explanation of Logic For Depth First Traversal

In DFS the basic data structure for storing the adjacent nodes is stack. In our program we have used a recursive call to DFS function. When a recursive call is invoked actually push operation gets performed. When we exit from the loop pop operation will be performed. Let us see how our program works.

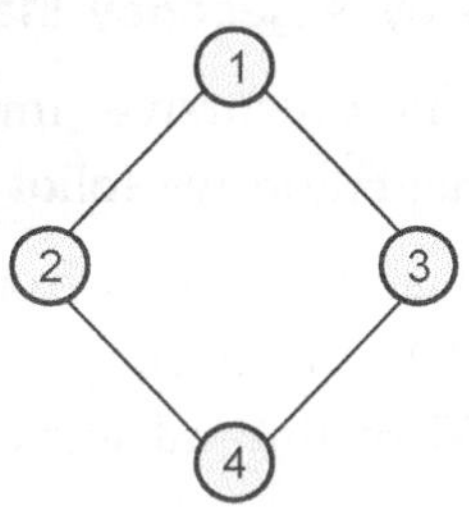

Fig. 2.5.2

Step 1 : Start with vertex 1, print it so '1' gets printed. Mark 1 as visited.

	Visited
0	0
1	1
2	0
3	0
4	0

Step 2 : Find adjacent vertex to 1, say i.e. 2 if it is not visited, call DFS(2) i.e. 2 will get inserted in the stack, mark is as visited.

	Visited
0	0
1	1
2	1
3	0
4	0

Stack: 2 ← Top

After exiting the loop 2 will be popped print '2'

Step 3 : Find adjacent to '2' i.e. vertex 4 if it is not visited call DFS(4) i.e., 4 will get pushed on to the stack mark it as visited.

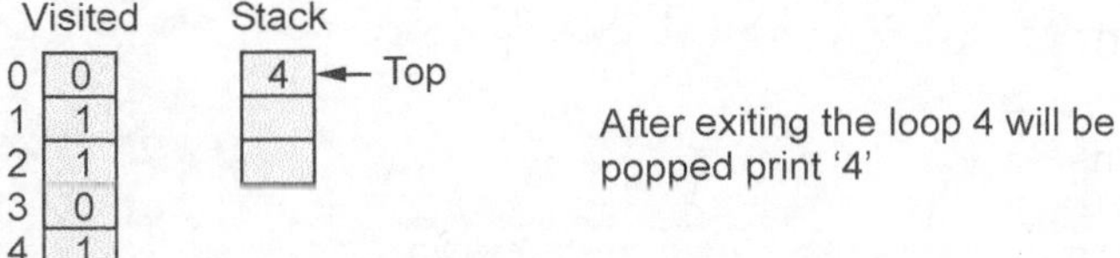

Step 4 : Find adjacent to '4' i.e. vertex 3 if it is not visited call DFS(3) i.e. 3 will be pushed onto the stack mark it visited.

	Visited
0	
1	1
2	1
3	1
4	1

Stack: 3 ← Top

After exiting the loop 3 will be popped print '3'

Since all the nodes are covered stop the procedure.

So output of DFS is

1 2 4 3

2) DFS by Adjacency Matrix (Non-recursive Program)

For non-recursive implementation of DFS, we use stack data structure. In this implementation we follow following steps

i) Push the vertex from which the searching should be started.

ii) POP the stack, print popped vertex if it is not visited. Then mark it as visited.

iii) Then find adjacent vertices to the current vertex and push them onto the stack.

iv) Repeat step (ii) and (iii) if stack is not empty.

```
/*******************************************************************
    Program to create a Graph. The graph is represented using
    Adjacency Matrix. The Program supports both undirected and
    Directed Graphs and traverse the graph in
    non-recursive Depth First Search Order.

*******************************************************************/
// List of include files

#include <iostream.h>
#include <conio.h>
#include<ctype.h>
#include <stdlib.h>

// List of defined constants

#define     MAX 20
#define     TRUE 1
#define     FALSE 0

// Global declarations

int st[10];
int top;
// Declare an adjacency matrix for storing the graph
class Gdfs
{

 private:
 int g[MAX][MAX],v[MAX];
 int v1,v2;
 public:
 int n;
 Gdfs();
 void error(char *);
 void create(),display();
```

```
 void Dfs(int);
 friend void push(int item);
 friend int pop();
 ~Gdfs();
};
/*
-----------------------------------------------------------------------
The constructor defined
-----------------------------------------------------------------------
*/
Gdfs::Gdfs()
{
 for ( v1 = 0; v1 < MAX; v1++)
       v[v1] = FALSE;
 for ( v1 = 0; v1 < MAX; v1++)
  for ( v2 = 0; v2 < MAX; v2++)
        g[v1][v2] = FALSE;
 for(v1=0;v1<MAX;v1++)
 st[v1]=0;
 top=-1;
}
/*
-----------------------------------------------------------------------
The destructor defined
-----------------------------------------------------------------------
*/
Gdfs::~Gdfs()
{
 for ( v1 = 0; v1 < MAX; v1++)
 {
       for ( v2 = 0; v2 < MAX; v2++)
       g[v1][v2]=FALSE;
 }
 for ( v1 = 0; v1 < MAX; v1++)
  v[v1] = FALSE;
}
/*
-----------------------------------------------------------------------
The display function
-----------------------------------------------------------------------
*/
void Gdfs::display()
{
 for ( v1 = 0; v1 < n; v1++)
  {
       for ( v2 = 0; v2 < n; v2++)
              cout<<" "<<g[v1][v2];
```

```
        cout<<endl;
    }
}


/*
-----------------------------------------------------------------
        The error function
-----------------------------------------------------------------
*/

void Gdfs::error( char *Msg )
{
        cout<<Msg;
        cout<<"Press any key to abort\n";
        getch();
        exit(1);
}

/*
-----------------------------------------------------------------
        The Create function
-----------------------------------------------------------------
*/
void  Gdfs::create()
{
        int Ch, v1, v2, Undirected;
        Undirected = TRUE;
        n=0;
        cout<<"\n This Program Is For Creation OF Graph";
        cout<<"\n And The Display Is By Depth First Search";
        cout<<"\n\tPress d/D for directed nad u/U for undirected garph\n";
        Ch = toupper(getche());
        if ( Ch == 'D')
          Undirected = FALSE;
        do
        {
                cout<<"\nEnter the Edge of a graph by two vertices \n";
                cout<<"(and type -99 terminate)\n";
                cin>>v1>>v2;
                if ( v1 == -99)
                  break;
                if ( v1 >= MAX || v2 >= MAX)
                        error("Invalid Vertex Value\n" );
                else
                  g[v1][v2] = TRUE;
                  if ( Undirected )
```

```
                    g[v2][v1] = TRUE;
        n++;
        }
        while(1);
}

/*
--------------------------------------------------------------------------
        The Dfs function
--------------------------------------------------------------------------
*/
void Gdfs::Dfs(int v1)
{
        int v2;
        push(v1);
        while(top!=-1)
        {
        v1=pop();
        if(v[v1]==FALSE)
        {
         cout<<endl<<v1;
         v[v1] = TRUE;
        }
        for ( v2 = 0; v2 < n; v2++)
                if ( g[v1][v2] == TRUE && v[v2] == FALSE )
                        push(v2);
        }
}
void push(int item)
{
 st[++top]=item;
}
int pop()
{
 int item;
 item=st[top];
 top--;
 return item;
}
/*
--------------------------------------------------------------------------
        The main function
--------------------------------------------------------------------------
*/
void main ( )
{
        Gdfs gr;
```

```
	clrscr();
	int v1;
	gr.create();
	cout<<"The Adjacency Matrix for the graph is "<<endl;
	gr.display();
	cout<<"Enter the Vertex from which you want to traverse : ";
	cin>>v1;
	if ( v1 >= MAX )
		gr.error("Invalid Vertex\n");
	cout<<"The Depth First Search of the Graph is "<<endl;
	gr.Dfs(v1);
	getch();
}
```

Output

```
 This Program Is For Creation OF Graph
 And The Display Is By Depth First Search
	Press d/D for directed nad u/U for undirected garph
u
Enter the Edge of a graph by two vertices
(and type -99 terminate)
0 1

Enter the Edge of a graph by two vertices
(and type -99 terminate)
0 2

Enter the Edge of a graph by two vertices
(and type -99 terminate)
1 3

Enter the Edge of a graph by two vertices
(and type -99 terminate)
2 3

Enter the Edge of a graph by two vertices
(and type -99 terminate)
-99 -99
The Adjacency Matrix for the graph is
0110
1001
1001
0110
Enter the Vertex from which you want to traverse : 2
The Depth First Search of the Graph is
2
```

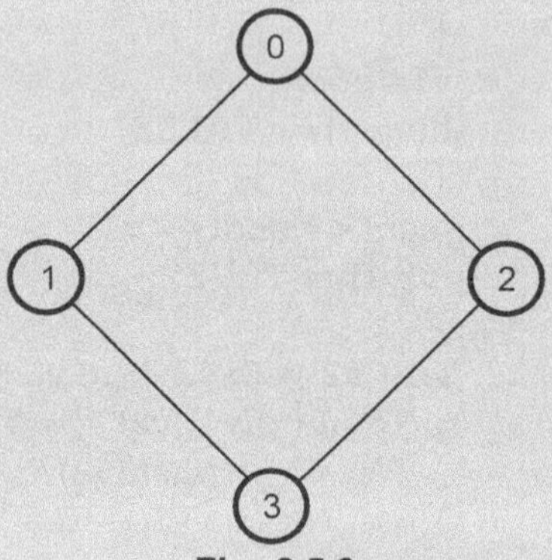

Fig. 2.5.3

```
3
1
0
```

3) DFS by Adjacency List (Recursive Program)

C++ Program

```
/**************************************************************************
      Program to create a Graph. The graph is represented using
      Adjacency List. The Program supports both undirected and
      Directed Graphs and traverse the graph in Depth First Search
      Order.
**************************************************************************/

// List of include files

#include <iostream.h>
#include <conio.h>
#include <stdlib.h>


#define     MAX 10
#define     TRUE   1
#define     FALSE  0
// Declaring an adjacency list for storing the graph
class Lgraph
{
  private:
        typedef struct node1
            {
             int vertex;
             struct node1 *next;
            }node;
        node  *head[MAX];  //Array Of head nodes
        int  visited[MAX];
       //visited array for checking whether the array is visited or not
  public:
      Lgraph();
      void create(),Dfs(int);
};
/*
-----------------------------------------------------------------
The constructor defined
-----------------------------------------------------------------
*/
Lgraph::Lgraph()
{
```

```
int V1;
for ( V1 = 0; V1 < MAX; V1++)
 visited[V1] = FALSE;
for ( V1 = 0; V1 < MAX; V1++)
 head[V1] = NULL;
}
/*
----------------------------------------------------------------------
The create function
----------------------------------------------------------------------
*/
void Lgraph::create()
{
      int V1, V2;
      char ans='y';
      node *New,*first;
      cout<<"\n\nEnter the vertices no. beginning with 0";
      do
      {
        cout<<"\nEnter the Edge of a graph \n";
            cin>>V1>>V2;
            if ( V1 >= MAX || V2 >= MAX)
                  cout<<"Invalid Vertex Value\n" ;
            else
             {
                  // creating link from V1 to V2
                  New = new node;
                  if ( New == NULL )
                    cout<<"Insufficient Memory\n";
                  New -> vertex = V2;
                  New -> next = NULL;
                  first = head[V1];
                  if ( first == NULL )
                    head[V1] = New;
                  else
                   {
                        while ( first -> next != NULL )
                          first = first-> next;
                        first -> next = New;
                   }
               // creating link from V2 to V1
                  New = new node;
                  if ( New == NULL )
                    cout<<"Insufficient Memory\n";
                  New -> vertex = V1;
                  New -> next = NULL;
                  first = head[V2];
```

```
                  if ( first == NULL )
                   head[V2] = New;
                  else
                   {
                     while ( first -> next != NULL )
                          first = first-> next;
                   first -> next = New;
                   }
              }
        cout<<"\nWant to add more edges?(y/n)";
        ans=getche();
      }while(ans=='y');
}
/*
------------------------------------------------------------------------
The Dfs function
------------------------------------------------------------------------
*/
void Lgraph::Dfs(int V1)
{
      int V2;
      node *first;
      cout<<endl<<V1;
      visited[V1] = TRUE;
      first = head[V1];
      while ( first != NULL )
            if ( visited[first->vertex] == FALSE )
                  Dfs(first->vertex);
            else
                  first = first -> next;
}

/*


------------------------------------------------------------------------
      The main function
------------------------------------------------------------------------
*/
void main ( )
{
      // Local declarations
      int V1, V2;
      clrscr();
      Lgraph gr;
      gr.create();
      clrscr();
```

```
        getch();
        cout<<endl<<"Enter the Vertex from which you want to traverse :";
        cin>>V1;
        if ( V1 >= MAX )
              cout<<"Invalid Vertex\n";
        else
        {
          cout<<"The Depth First Search of the Graph is \n";
          gr.Dfs(V1);
          getch();
        }
}
```

Output

```
Enter the vertices no. beginning with 0
Enter the Edge of a graph
0 1

Want to add more edges?(y/n)y
Enter the Edge of a graph
0 2

Want to add more edges?(y/n)y
Enter the Edge of a graph
0 3

Want to add more edges?(y/n)y
Enter the Edge of a graph
0 4

Want to add more edges?(y/n)y
Enter the Edge of a graph
1 5

Want to add more edges?(y/n)y
Enter the Edge of a graph
2 5

Want to add more edges?(y/n)y
Enter the Edge of a graph
3 5

Want to add more edges?(y/n)y
Enter the Edge of a graph
4 5

Want to add more edges?(y/n)n
```

```
Enter the Vertex from which you want to traverse :0
The Depth First Search of the Graph is

0e
1
5
2
3
4
```

4) DFS by Adjacency List (Non-recursive Program)

```
/*************************************************************************************
        Program to create a Graph. The graph is represented using
        Adjacency List. The Program supports both undirected and
        Directed Graphs and traverse the graph in non recursive
        Depth First Search Order.
*************************************************************************************/

// List of include files

#include <iostream.h>
#include <conio.h>
#include <stdlib.h>


#define      MAX  10
#define      TRUE    1
#define      FALSE  0
// Global declarations

int st[10];
int top;

// Declaring an adjacency list for storing the graph
class Lgraph
{
  private:
        typedef struct node1
             {
              int vertex;
              struct node1 *next;
             }node;
        node  *head[MAX];  //Array Of head nodes
        int  visited[MAX];
       //visited array for checking whether the array is visited or not
  public:
      Lgraph();
```

```
        void create(),Dfs(int);
        friend void push(int item);
        friend int pop();
};
/*
------------------------------------------------------------------
The constructor defined
------------------------------------------------------------------
*/
Lgraph::Lgraph()
{
 int V1;
 for ( V1 = 0; V1 < MAX; V1++)
  visited[V1] = FALSE;
 for ( V1 = 0; V1 < MAX; V1++)
  head[V1] = NULL;
 for ( V1 = 0; V1 < MAX; V1++)
  st[V1] = 0;
 top=-1;
}
/*
------------------------------------------------------------------
The create function
------------------------------------------------------------------
*/
void Lgraph::create()
{
       int V1, V2;
       char ans='y';
       node *New,*first;
       do
       {
         cout<<"\nEnter the Edge of a graph \n";
              cin>>V1>>V2;
              if ( V1 >= MAX || V2 >= MAX)
                     cout<<"Invalid Vertex Value\n" ;
              else
                {
                     // creating link from V1 to V2
                     New = new node;
                     if ( New == NULL )
                       cout<<"Insufficient Memory\n";
                     New -> vertex = V2;
                     New -> next = NULL;
                     first = head[V1];
                     if ( first == NULL )
                       head[V1] = New;
```

```
                else
                 {
                      while ( first -> next != NULL )
                        first = first -> next;
                      first -> next = New;
                 }
            // creating link from V2 to V1
                New = new node;
                if ( New == NULL )
                  cout<<"Insufficient Memory\n";
                New -> vertex = V1;
                New -> next = NULL;
                first = head[V2];
                if ( first == NULL )
                  head[V2] = New;
                else
                 {
                  while ( first -> next != NULL )
                       first = first -> next;
                  first -> next = New;
                 }
            }
      cout<<"\nWant to add more edges?(y/n)";
      ans=getche();
     }while(ans=='y');
}
/*
-----------------------------------------------------------------
The Dfs function
-----------------------------------------------------------------
*/
void Lgraph::Dfs(int V1)
{
      node *first;

      push(V1);
      while(top!=-1)
      {
      V1=pop();
      if(visited[V1]==FALSE)
      {
      cout<<endl<<V1;
      visited[V1] = TRUE;
      }
      first = head[V1];
      while ( first != NULL )
      {
```

```
            if ( visited[first->vertex] == FALSE )
              push(first ->vertex);
            first = first -> next;
          }
    }
}
void push(int item)
{
 st[++top]=item;
}
int pop()
{
 int item;
 item=st[top];
 top--;
 return item;
}

/*
---------------------------------------------------------------------
        The main function
---------------------------------------------------------------------
*/
void main ( )
{
        // Local declarations
        int V1, V2;
        clrscr();
        Lgraph gr;
        gr.create();
        clrscr();
        getch();
        cout<<endl<<"Enter the Vertex from which you want to traverse :";
        cin>>V1;
        if ( V1 >= MAX )
                cout<<"Invalid Vertex\n";
        else
        {
          cout<<"The Depth First Search of the Graph is \n";
          gr.Dfs(V1);
          getch();
        }
}
```

Output

```
Enter the Edge of a graph
1 2
```

```
Want to add more edges?(y/n)y
Enter the Edge of a graph
1 3

Want to add more edges?(y/n)y
Enter the Edge of a graph
1 4

Want to add more edges?(y/n)y
Enter the Edge of a graph
2 5

Want to add more edges?(y/n)y
Enter the Edge of a graph
3 5

Want to add more edges?(y/n)y
Enter the Edge of a graph
4 5

Want to add more edges?(y/n)n

Enter the Vertex from which you want to traverse :3
The Depth First Search of the Graph is

3
5
4
1
2
```

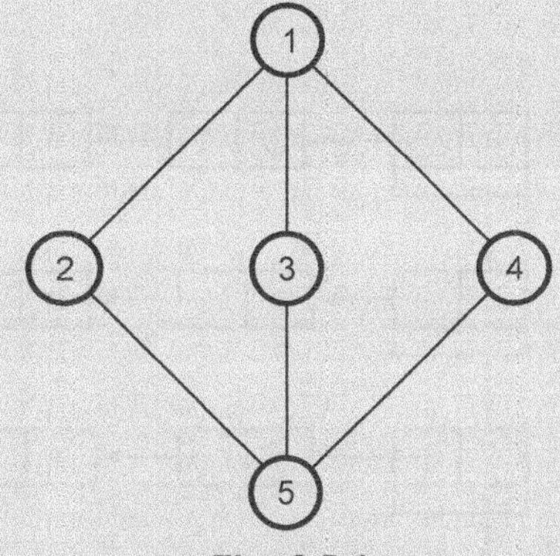

Fig. 2.5.4

Example 2.5.1 *For the graph given below, find DFS stepwise.*

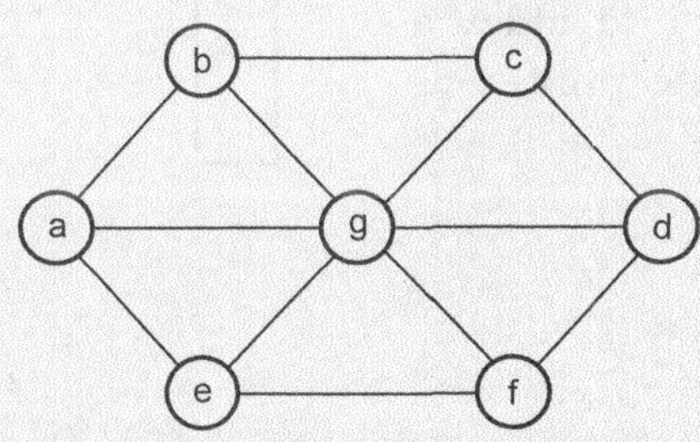

Fig. 2.5.5

Solution : We will create adjacency list for given graph.

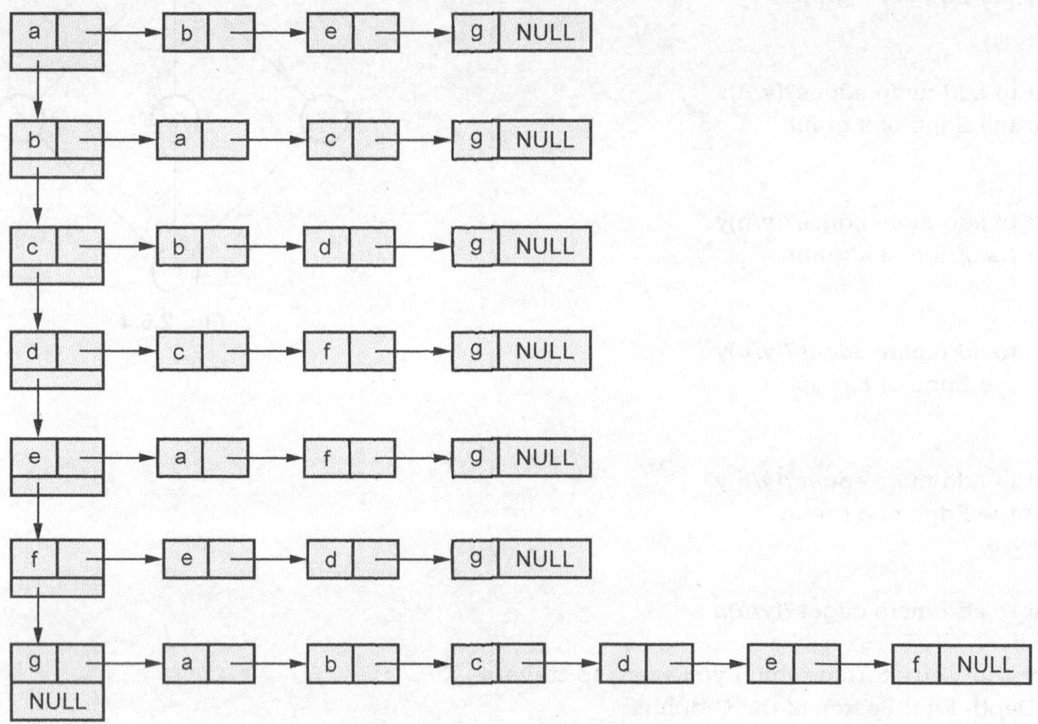

Depth first search (DFS)

Action	Stack	Visited array	Output
Step 1 : Start with vertex a, mark it visited by writing 1 to index a of visited array. The print **a** as an output.		a 1 b c d e f g	a

Step 2 : Find adjacent of b, and mark it visited. Push it onto the stack. Later b will be popped and printed.	b	a 1 b 1 c d e f g	a, b
Step 3 : Find adjacent b. The a is already visited, hence ignore. Next node will be c. Insert c onto the stack mark it as visited. Push it. Later c will be popped and printed.	c	a 1 b 1 c 1 d e f g	a, b, c
Step 4 : Find adjacent of c. Push d, mark it visited. Later d will be popped and printed.	d	a 1 b 1 c 1 d 1 e f g	a, b, c, d
Step 5 : Find adjacent of d. Push f, mark it as visited. Later f will be popped and printed.	f	a 1 b 1 c 1 d 1 e f 1 g	a, b, c, d, f

Step	Stack	Visited	Output
Step 6 : Find adjacent of f. Push e, mark it as visited. Later e will be popped and printed.	e	a 1, b 1, c 1, d 1, e 1, f 1, g	a, b, c, d, f, e
Step 7 : Find adjacent of e. Push g, mark it as visited. Later g will be popped and printed.	g	a 1, b 1, c 1, d 1, e 1, f 1, g 1	a, b, c, d, f, e, g
As all nodes are visited and stack is empty we will stop traversing.			

The DFS sequence is **a, b, c, d, f, e, g**.

Example 2.5.2 *For the graph given below, find BFS.*

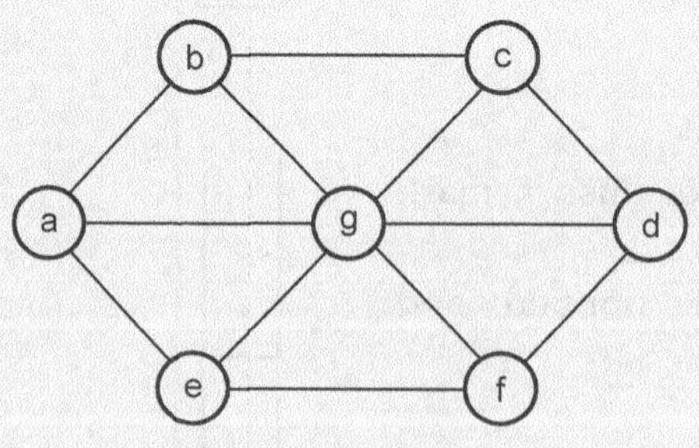

Fig. 2.5.6

Solution : We will create adjacency list for given graph.

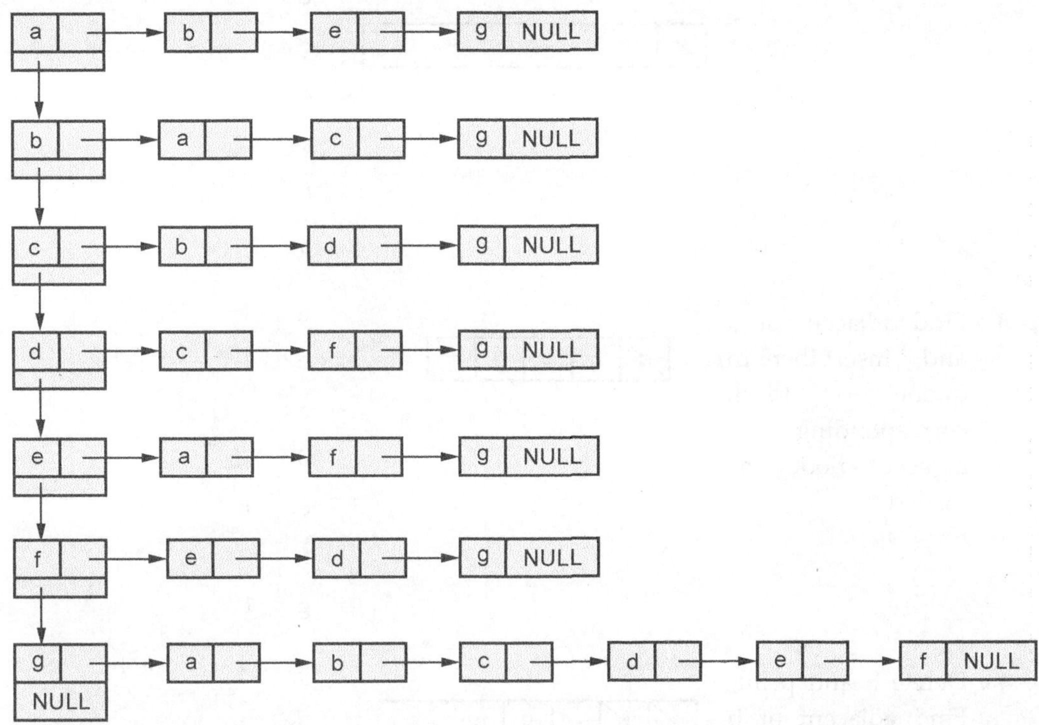

Breadth first search (BFS)

Action	Queue	Visited array	Output
Step 1 : Insert a in queue. Mark visited (a) = 1	a	a 1 b c d e f g	

Step	Queue	Visited	Output
Step 2 : Delete a and print	~~a~~	a 1 b c d e f g	a
Step 3 : Find adjacent of a and insert them in queue. Mark corresponding adjacent nodes as visited.	~~a~~ | b | e | g	a 1 b 1 c d e 1 f g 1	a
Step 4 : Delete b and print. Find adjacent of b and if those nodes are not visited then insert them in the queue. Mark corresponding nodes as visited.	~~a~~ | ~~b~~ | e | g | c	a 1 b 1 c 1 d e 1 f g 1	a, b
Step 5 : Delete e and print. Find adjacent of e and if those nodes are not visited then insert them in queue. Mark corresponding nodes as visited.	~~a~~ | ~~b~~ | ~~e~~ | g | c | f	a 1 b 1 c 1 d e 1 f 1 g 1	a, b, e

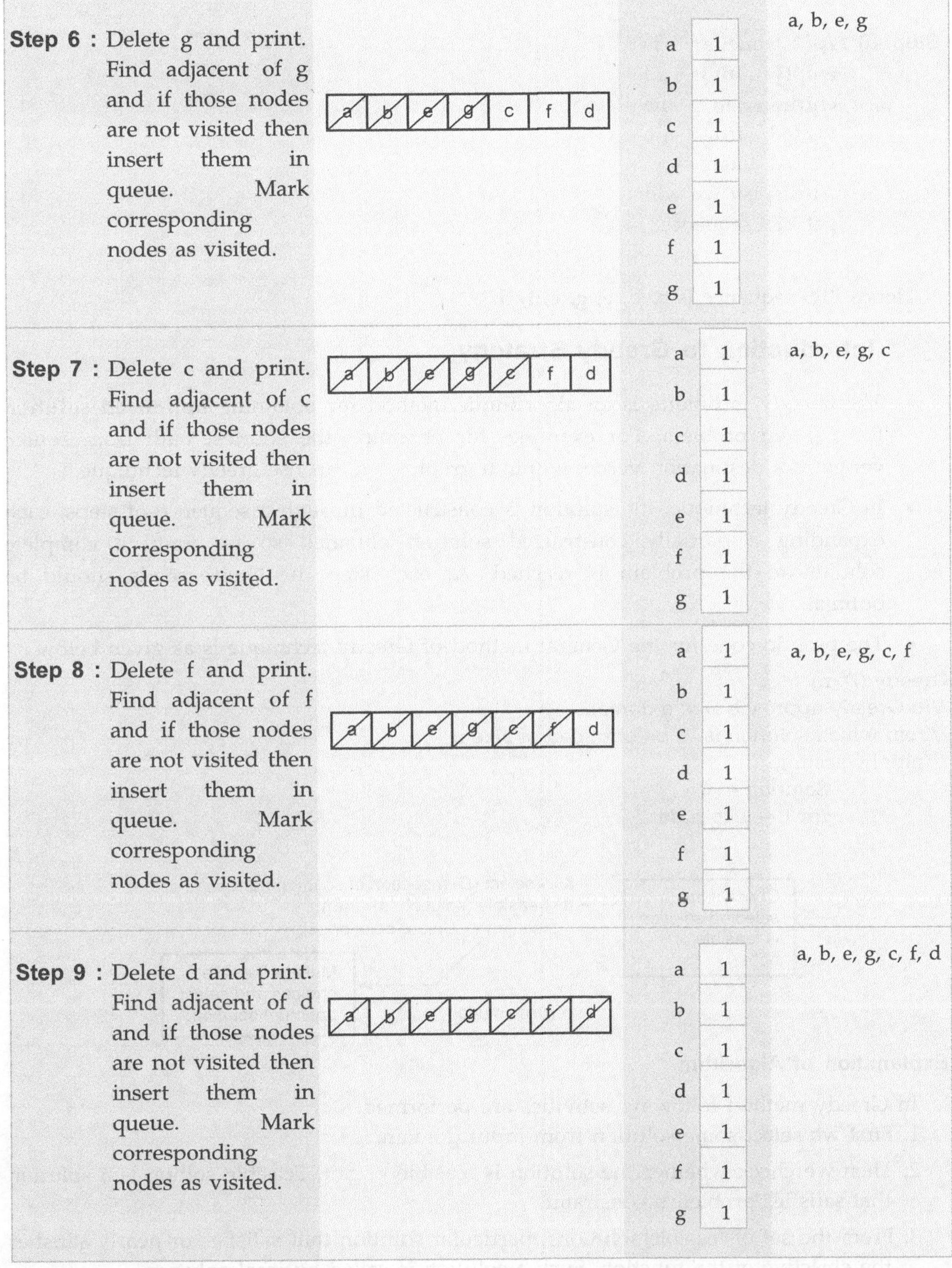

Step	Queue	Visited	Output
Step 6 : Delete g and print. Find adjacent of g and if those nodes are not visited then insert them in queue. Mark corresponding nodes as visited.	a̸ b̸ e̸ g̸ c f d	a 1, b 1, c 1, d 1, e 1, f 1, g 1	a, b, e, g
Step 7 : Delete c and print. Find adjacent of c and if those nodes are not visited then insert them in queue. Mark corresponding nodes as visited.	a̸ b̸ e̸ g̸ c̸ f d	a 1, b 1, c 1, d 1, e 1, f 1, g 1	a, b, e, g, c
Step 8 : Delete f and print. Find adjacent of f and if those nodes are not visited then insert them in queue. Mark corresponding nodes as visited.	a̸ b̸ e̸ g̸ c̸ f̸ d	a 1, b 1, c 1, d 1, e 1, f 1, g 1	a, b, e, g, c, f
Step 9 : Delete d and print. Find adjacent of d and if those nodes are not visited then insert them in queue. Mark corresponding nodes as visited.	a̸ b̸ e̸ g̸ c̸ f̸ d̸	a 1, b 1, c 1, d 1, e 1, f 1, g 1	a, b, e, g, c, f, d

Step 10 : As queue is empty and all entries in the visited array are visited them stop. At display we will get BFS sequence.

Hence BFS sequence is **a, b, e, g, c, f, d.**

2.6 Introduction to Greedy Strategy

- The Greedy technique is an algorithmic method for obtaining **optimized solution** for a given problem. For example- for obtaining the shortest path from source vertex to a destination vertex within a graph - we can use greedy technique.
- In Greedy technique, the solution is constructed through a sequence of steps, each expanding a partially constructed solution obtained so far, until a complete solution to the problem is reached. At each step the choice made should be optimal.
- The pseudo code for the General method of Greedy technique is as given below -

```
Greedy (D, n)
//In Greedy approach D is a domain
//from which solution is to be obtained of size n
//Initially assume
        Solution ← 0
        for i ← 1 to n do
        {
                s ← select (D) // section of solution from D
                if (Feasible (solution, s)) then
                  solution ← Union (solution, s);
        }
        return solution
```

Check if the selected solution is feasible or not.

Make a feasible choices and select optimum solution.

Explanation of Algorithm

In Greedy method following activities are performed.

1. First we select some solution from input domain.
2. Then we check whether the solution is feasible or not. Feasible soltion is a solution that satisfies problem's constraint.
3. From the set of feasible solutions, particular solution that satisfies or nearly satisfies the objective of the function. Such a solution is called **optimal solution.**

4. As Greedy method works in stages. At each stage only one input is considered at each time. Based on this input it is decided whether particular input gives the optimal solution or not.

Example 2.6.1 *Explain the terms, feasible solution, optimal solution and objective function*

Solution : Feasible solution - For solving a particular problem there exists n inputs and we need to obtain a subset that satisfies some constraints. Then any subset that satisfies these constraints is called **feasible solution.**

Optimal solution - From a set of feasible solutions, particular solution that satisfies or nearly satisfies the objectives of the function such a solution is called optimal solution.

Objective function - A feasible solution that either minimizes or maximizes a given objective function is called objective function.

2.6.1 Applications of Greedy Method

In this section we will discuss various problems that can be solved using Greedy approach -

1) Knapsack problem

2) Minimum spanning trees

3) Single source shortest path algorithm.

4) Huffman's Tree construction

The Greedy technique is applied to find out minimum spanning tree in a graph. Let us understand what is minimum spanning tree and how to compute it for the given graph.

2.7 Minimum Spanning Tree

SPPU : May-06, 07, 13, 14, Dec.-08, 13, Marks 16

A Spanning tree S is a subset of a tree T in which all the vertices of tree T are present but it may not contain all the edges.

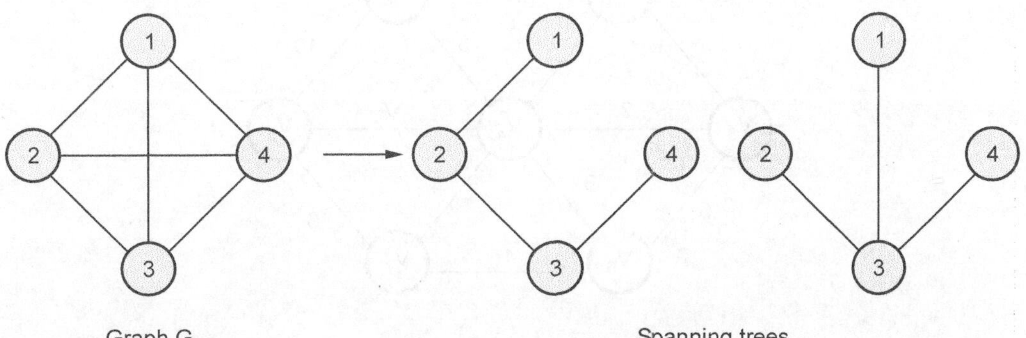

Graph G

Spanning trees

The minimum spanning tree of a weighted connected graph G is called **minimum** spanning tree if its **weight is minimum.**

We are going to discuss the two popular algorithms of minimum spanning tree, namely Prim's algorithm and Kruskal's algorithm.

1. Prim's Algorithm : In Prim's algorithm the pair with the **minimum weight** is to be chosen. Then **adjacent** to these vertices which ever is the edge having minimum weight is selected. This process will be continued till all the vertices are not be covered. The necessary condition in this case is that the **circuit should not be formed.**

ADT Operations for Prim's Algorithm

AbstractDataType Prim

{

Instances : Prim's algorithm is applied on a weighted graph G for creating a minimum spanning tree, and path length of a spanning tree can be obtained.

Operations :

1. Select an edge with minimum weight.
2. Add the vertices in the set V.
3. Then select any edge with minimum weight such that the edge is adjacent to any vertex from set V.
4. Repeat step 1, 2 and 3 until all the vertices are selected. But circuit should be formed while selecting these vertices.

}

Example 2.7.1 *For the graph given below, construct a minimum spanning tree using Prim's algorithm. Show the table created during each pass of the algorithm.*

SPPU : May-06, Marks 12 ; May-07, CSE, Marks 8 ; Dec.-08, Marks 16

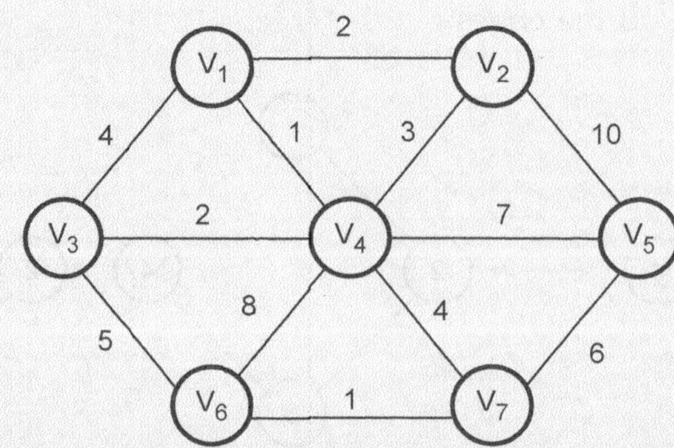

Solution : In Prim's algorithm the minimum path length is selected. Only the circuit should not be formed.

Step 1 :

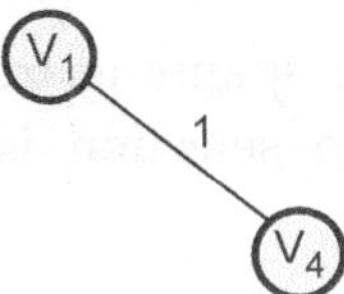

Path length = 1

Step 2 :

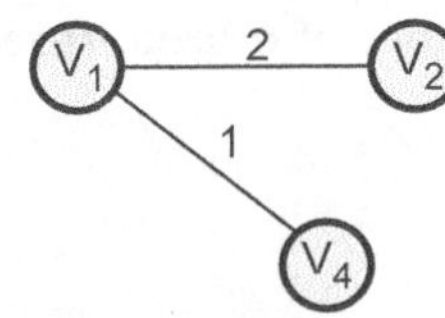

Path length = 3

Step 3 :

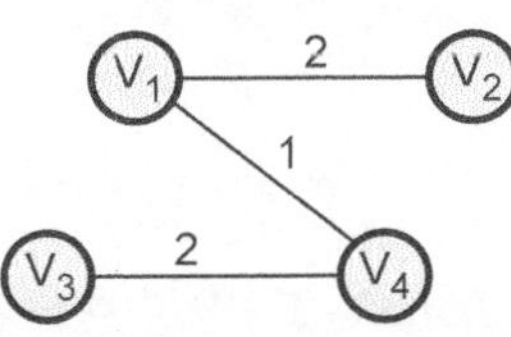

Path length = 5

Step 4 :

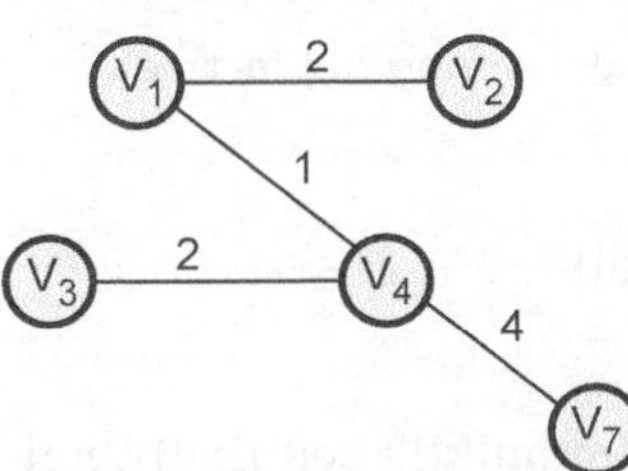

Path length = 9

Step 5 :

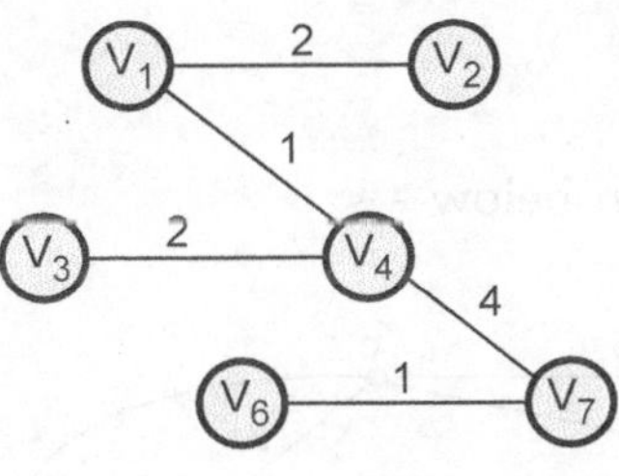

Path length = 10

Step 6 :

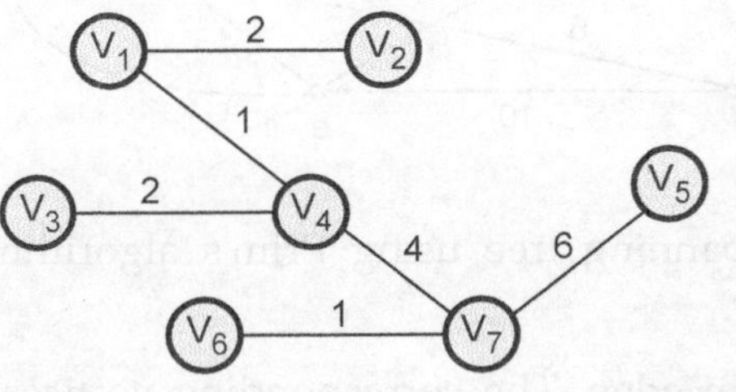

Path length = 16

Thus the minimum spanning tree with path length 16 is obtained.

Example 2.7.2 *Explain Prim's algorithm with an example.*

Solution : Prim's algorithm is to obtain the minimum spanning tree. In this algorithm the minimum edge is selected each time. The edge selection is done for adjacent vertices only.

```
Prim(G,Cost, n, tree)
{
/* G is a graph of n nodes. cost is an array of cost of edges. tree is an array of
minimum spanning tree */
min=cost[p,q] //represents minimum cost edge
tree[1][1]=p;
tree[1][2]=q;
for(i=1; i<n; i++)
{
    if(cost[i][q] < cost[i][p])
        optimum[i]=p;
    else
    optimum[i]=q // storing minimum cost
    optimum[p]=optimum[q]=0;
    for(i=2; i<n-1; i++)
{//store vertex j at optimum distance and neighbouring of j in 'tree'
        tree[i][1] = j;
        tree[i][2] = optimum[j];
        min = min+cost[j][optimum[j]];
    optimum[j]=0;
    for(k=1 to n)
    if((optimum[k]!=0)AND (cost[k,optimum[k]]>cost[k,j]))then
        optimum[k]=j;
    }
        return min;
    }
```

For example : Consider the graph as given below -

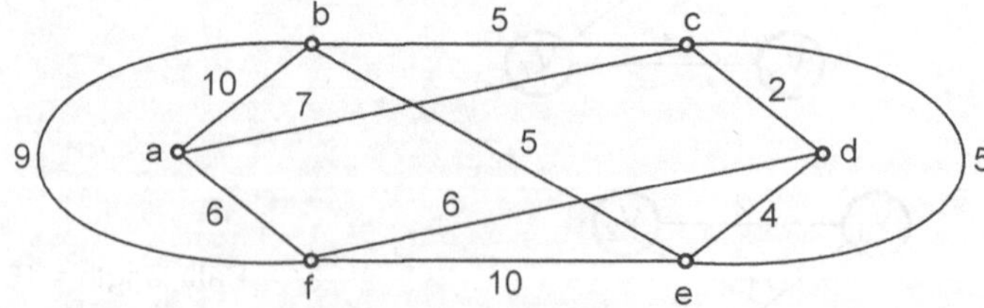

We will find the minimum spanning tree using Prim's algorithm using following rules -

1. Select the edge with minimum edge. The corresponding vertices will form the set of vertices.

2. Each time select an edge with minimum weight and the edge to be selected from the graph should be such that at least one of the vertex of the selected edge is adjacent to already selected vertices.
3. In selection of edges the circuit should not be formed.

From above graph,

First select edge c-d with minimum weight 2

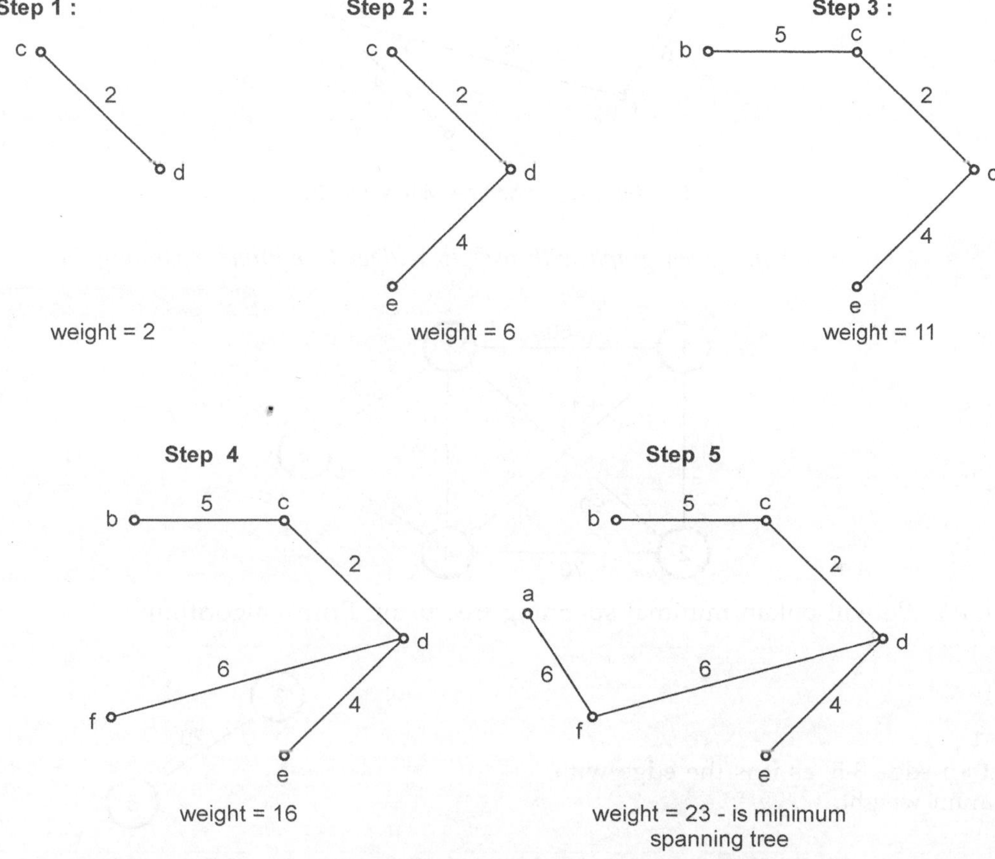

The edge selection can be summarized as below -

Edge	Set
<c-d>	{c, d}
<d-e>	{c, d, e}
<b-c>	{b, c, d, e}

<d-f>	{b, c, d, e, f}
<a-f>	{a, b, c, d, e, f}

Thus the minimum spanning tree will be -

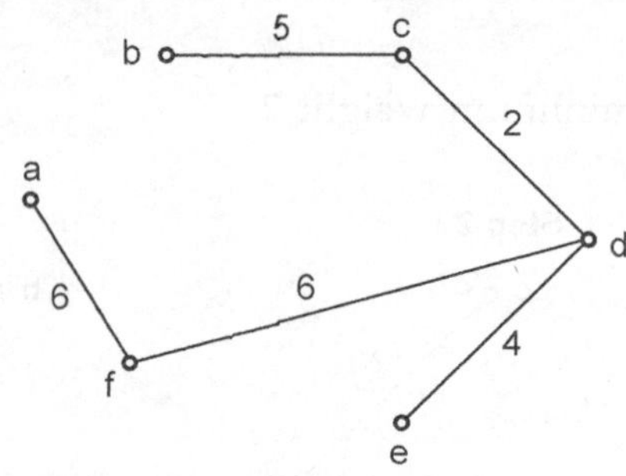

Minimum spanning tree with weight 23

Example 2.7.3 *Convert the given graph with weighted edges to minimal spanning tree.*

SPPU : May-14, Marks 3

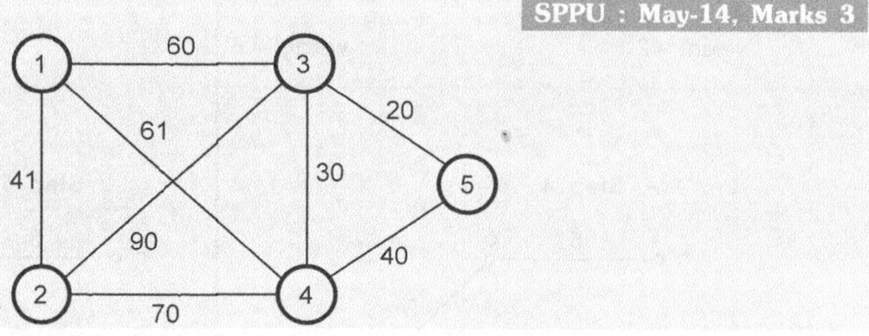

Solution : We will obtain minimal spanning tree using Prim's algorithm.

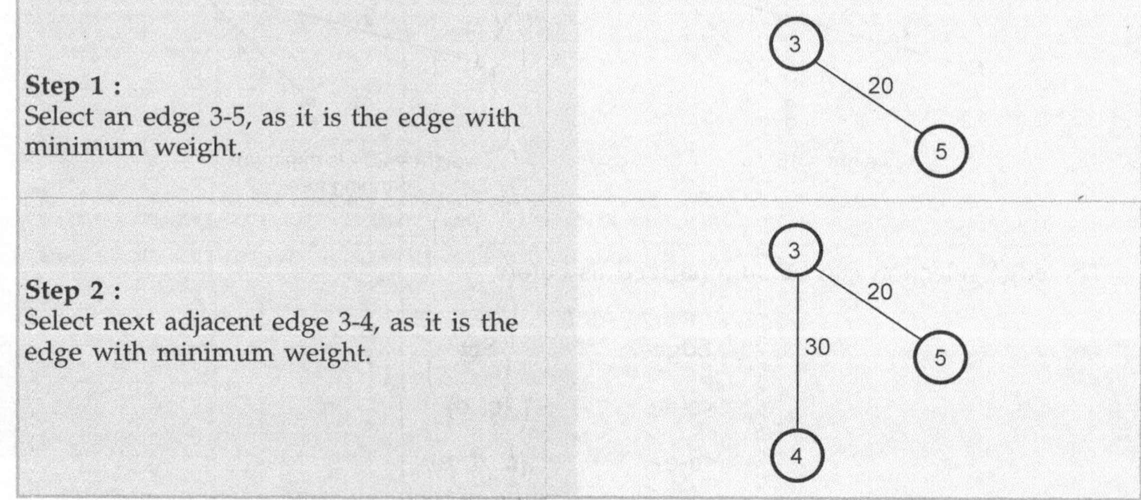

Step 1 : Select an edge 3-5, as it is the edge with minimum weight.	3 —20— 5
Step 2 : Select next adjacent edge 3-4, as it is the edge with minimum weight.	3 —20— 5, 3 —30— 4

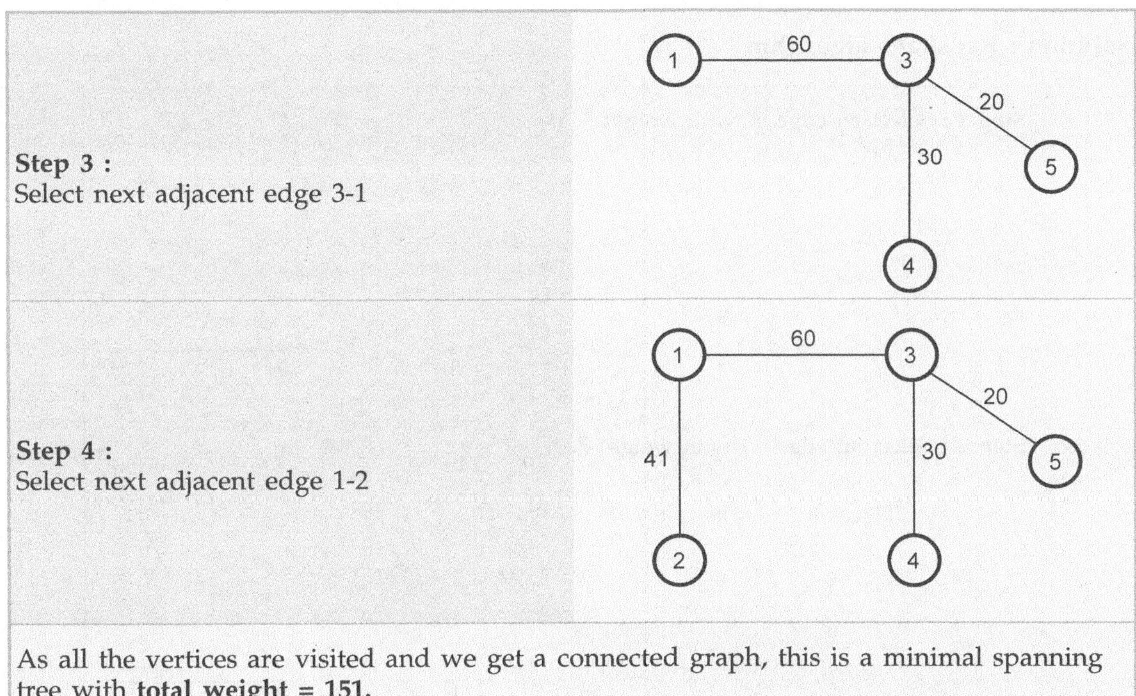

As all the vertices are visited and we get a connected graph, this is a minimal spanning tree with **total weight = 151.**

Kruskal's Algorithm : In Kruskal's algorithm the **minimum** weight is obtained. In this algorithm also the **circuit should not be formed**. Each time the edge of minimum weight has to be selected, from the graph.It is **not necessary** in this algorithm to have edges of minimum weights to be **adjacent**. Let us solve one example by Kruskal's algorithm.

Example 2.7.4 *Consider the following graph (Fig. 2.7.1)*

i) Obtain minimum spanning tree by Kruskal's algorithm.

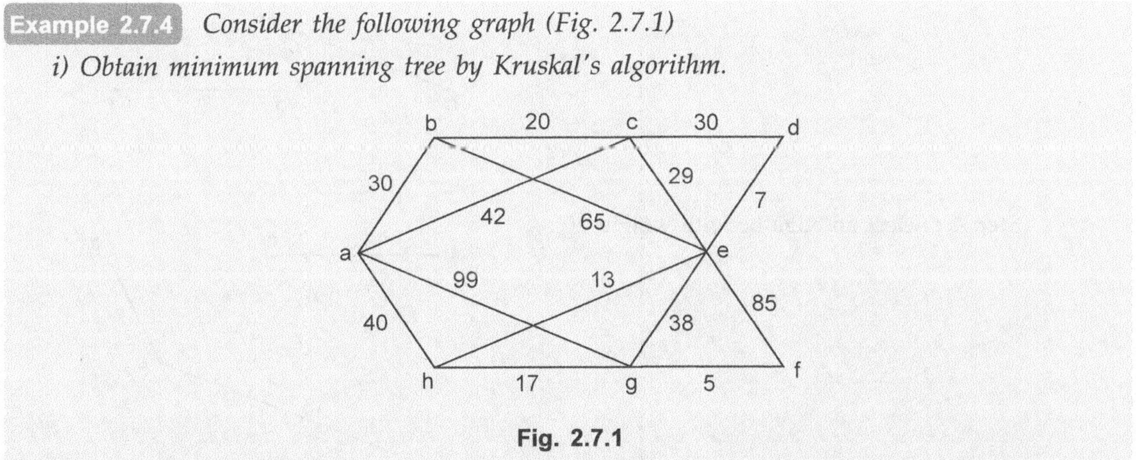

Fig. 2.7.1

Solution : Kruskal's algorithm

Step 1 : Select an edge gf with weight 5.	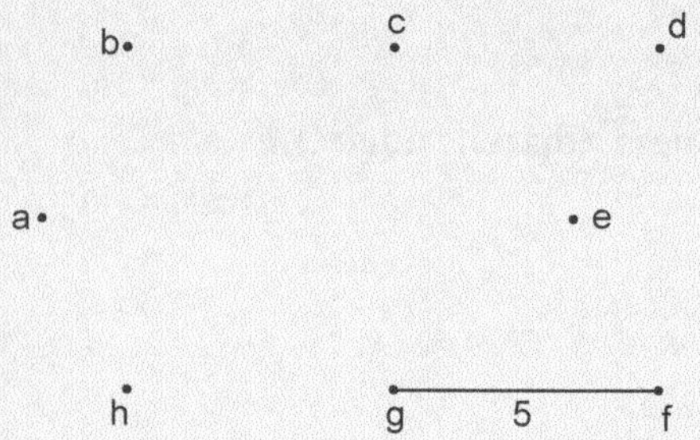
Step 2 : Select an edge ed with weight 7.	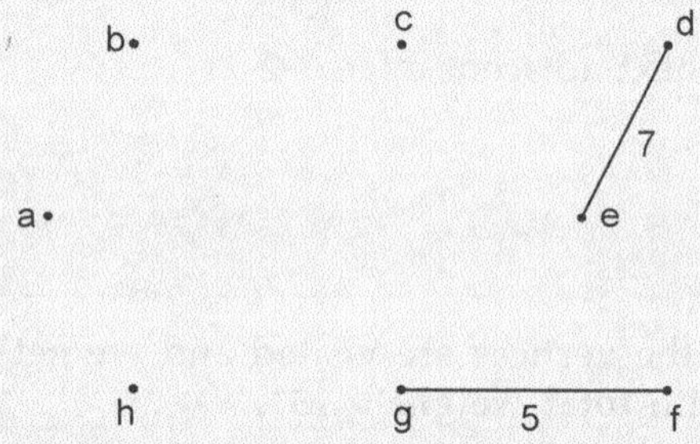
Step 3 : Select an edge eh with weight 13.	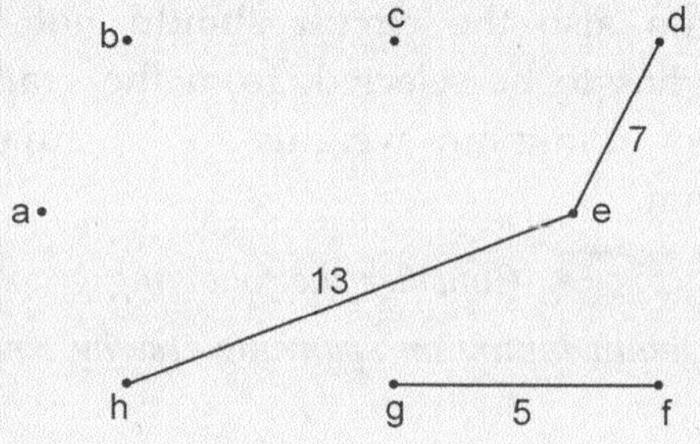
Step 4 : Select an edge bc with weight 20.	

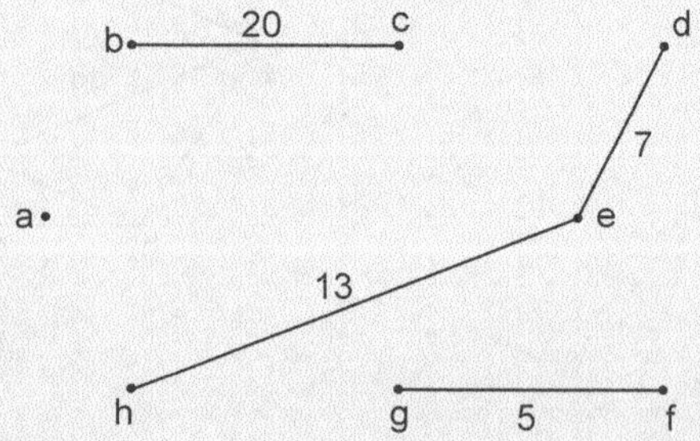

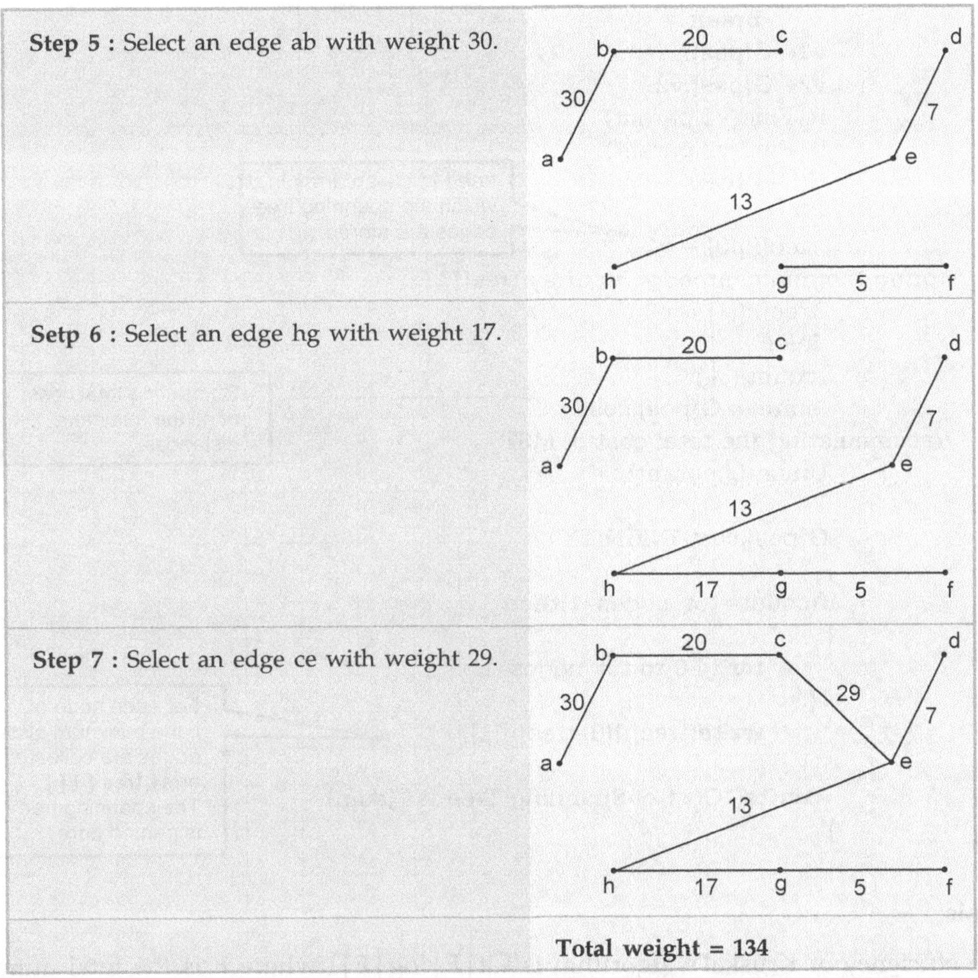

Step 5 : Select an edge ab with weight 30.

Setp 6 : Select an edge hg with weight 17.

Step 7 : Select an edge ce with weight 29.

Total weight = 134

Algorithm

```
Algorithm spanning_tree()
//Problem Description : This algorithm finds the minimum
//spanning tree using Kruskal's algorithm
//Input : The adjacency matrix graph G containing cost
//Output : prints the spanning tree with the total cost of
//spanning tree
 count←0
 k←0
 sum←0
        for i←0 to tot_nodes do
                parent[i]←i
while(count!=tot_nodes–1)do
 {
        pos←Minimum(tot_edges);//finding the minimum cost edge
                if(pos=–1)then//Perhaps no node in the graph
```

```
                break
            v1←G[pos].v1
            v2←G[pos].v2
            i←Find(v1,parent)
            j←Find(v2,parent)
            if(i!=j)then
            {
             tree[k][0] ←v1
//storing the minimum edge in array tree[]
             tree[k][1] ←v2
             k++
             count++;
             sum+←G[pos].cost
  //accumulating the total cost of MST
            Union(i,j,parent);
            }
            G[pos].cost INFINITY
            }
           if(count=tot_nodes−1)then
           {
                for i←0 to tot_nodes−1
             {
                write(tree[i][0],tree[i][1])
             }
             write("Cost of Spanning Tree is ",sum)
           }
```

tree [ ] [ ] is an array in which the spanning tree edges are stored.

Computing total cost of all the minimum distances.

For each node of i, the minimum distance edges are collected in array **tree [ ] [ ]**. The spanning tree is printed here.

Analysis

The efficiency of Kruskal's algorithm is **□(|E|log|E|)** where E is the total number of edges in the graph.

2.7.1 Difference between Prim's and Kruskal's Algorithm

Prim's algorithm	Kruskal's algorithm
This algorithm is for obtaining minimum spanning tree by selecting the adjacent vertices of already selected vertices.	This algorithm is for obtaining minimum spanning tree but it is not necessary to choose adjacent vertices of already selected vertices.

University Question

1. *What is the difference between Prim's and Kruskal's algorithms for minimum spanning trees ?* **SPPU : May-13, Marks 4, Dec.-13, Marks 3**

2.8 Dijkstra's Shortest Path

- Dijkstra's Algorithm is a popular algorithm for finding shortest path.
- This algorithm is called **single source shortest path** algorithm because in this algorithm, for a given vertex called **source** the shortest path to all other vertices is obtained.
- This algorithm applicable to graphs with non-negative weights only.

Example 2.8.1 *Obtain the shortest path for the given graph.*

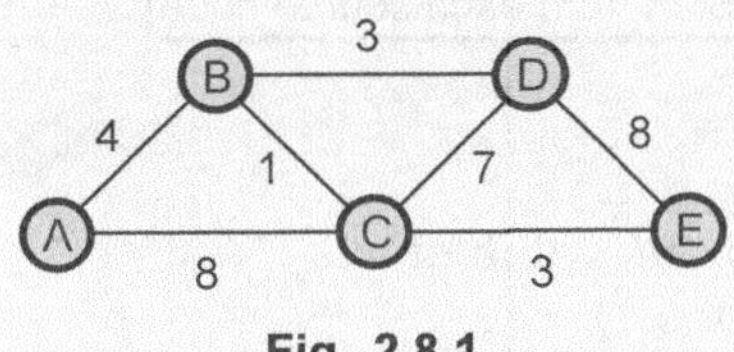

Fig. 2.8.1

Solution : Now we will consider each vertex as a source and will find the shortest distance from this vertex to every other remaining vertex. Let us start with vertex A.

Source vertex	Distance with other vertices		Path shown in graph
A	**A-B,**	**path = 4**	
	A-C,	path = 8	
	A-D,	path = ∞	
	A-E	path = ∞	
B	**B-C,**	**path = 4 + 1**	
	B-D,	path = 4 + 3	
	B-E	path = ∞	
C	C-D,	path = 5 + 7 = 12	
	C-E,	**path = 5 + 3 = 8**	
D	D-E,	path = 7 + 8 = 15	

Thus the shortest distance from A to E is obtained.

that is A - B - C - E with path length = 4 + 1 + 3 = 8. Similarly other shortest paths can be obtained by choosing appropriate source and destination.

Algorithm

```
Algorithm Dijkstra(int cost[1...n,1...n],int source,int dist[])

for i ← 0 to tot_nodes
{
        dist[i] ← cost[source,i]//initially put the
        s[i] ← 0 //distance from source vertex to i
        //i is varied for each vertex
        path[i] ← source//all the sources are put in path
}
    s[source] ← 1    ◄── Start from each source node
 for(i ← 1 to tot_nodes)
 {
        min_dist ← infinity;
        v1 ← -1//reset previous value of v1
        for(j ← 0 to tot_nodes-1)
        {
            if(s[j]=0)then
            {
                if(dist[j]<min_dist)then
                {
                 min_dist ← dist[j]
                 v1 ← j
                }
            }
        }
        s[v1] ← 1
        for(v2 ← 0 to tot_nodes-1)
        {
         if(s[v2]=0)then
         {
            if(dist[v1]+cost[v1][v2]<dist[v2])then
            {
                dist[v2] ← dist[v1]+cost[v1][v2]
                path[v2] ← v1
            }
         }
        }
    }
}
```

Finding minimum distance from selected source node.That is : source-j represents min. dist. edge

v_1 is next selected destination vertex with shortest distance. All such vertices are accumulated in array **path[ ]**

C Function

```
void Dijkstra(int tot_nodes,int cost[10][10],int source,int dist[])
{
 int i,j,v1,v2,min_dist;
 int s[10];
 for(i=0;i<tot_nodes;i++)
 {
```

```
            dist[i]=cost[source][i];//initially put the
            s[i]=0; //distance from source vertex to i
            //i is varied for each vertex
            path[i]=source;//all the sources are put in path
}
s[source]=1;
for(i=1;i<tot_nodes;i++)
{
            min_dist=infinity;
            v1=-1;//reset previous value of v1
            for(j=0;j<tot_nodes;j++)
            {
             if(s[j]==0)
             {
                   if(dist[j]<min_dist)
                   {
                    min_dist=dist[j];//finding minimum disatnce
                    v1=j;
                   }
             }
            }
            s[v1]=1;
            for(v2=0;v2<tot_nodes;v2++)
            {
             if(s[v2]==0)
             {
                   if(dist[v1]+cost[v1][v2]<dist[v2])
                   {
                          dist[v2]=dist[v1]+cost[v1][v2];
                          path[v2]=v1;
                   }
             }
            }
      }
}
```

2.9 Topological Ordering

SPPU : May-14, Marks 3

This is a direct implementation of decrease and conquer method. Following are the steps to be followed in this algorithm -

1. From a given graph find a vertex with no incoming edges. Delete it along with all the edges outgoing from it. If there are more than one such vertices then break the tie randomly.

2. Note the vertices that are deleted.

3. All these recorded vertices give topologically sorted list.

Let us understand this algorithm with some examples -

Example 2.9.1 *Sort the digraph for topological sort using source removal algorithm.*

SPPU : May-14, Marks 3

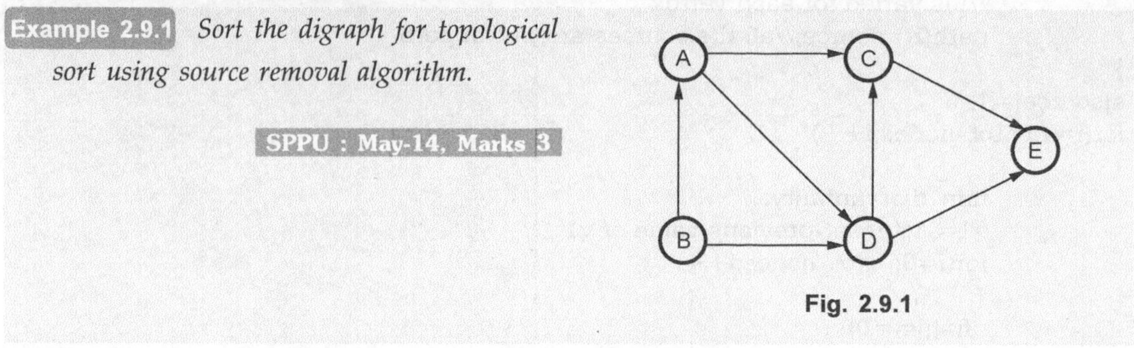

Fig. 2.9.1

Solution : We will follow following steps to obtain topologically sorted list.

Choose vertex B, because it has no incoming edge, delete it along with its adjacent edges.

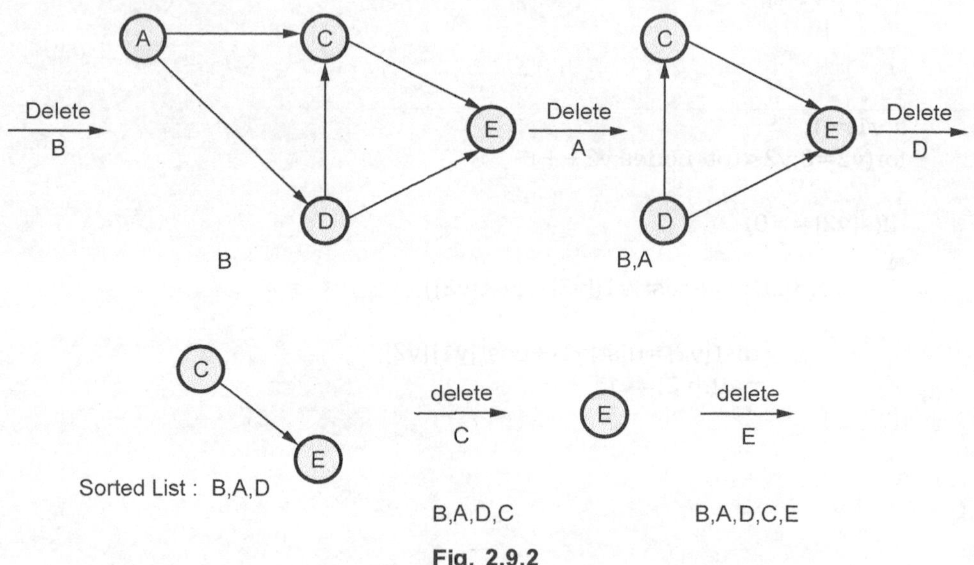

Fig. 2.9.2

Hence the list after topological sorting will be B, A, D, C, E.

C++ Program

```
#include<iostream>
#define SIZE 10
using namespace std;
class Topo
{
public:
    int G[SIZE][SIZE], i, j, k;
    int front, rear;
```

```
int n, edges;
int b[SIZE], Q[SIZE], indegree[SIZE];
Topo(int MAX)
{
	front = -1; rear = -1;
	for (i = 0; i<MAX; i++) //initialising the graph
	{
		for (j = 0; j<MAX; j++)
		{
			G[i][j] = 0;
		}
	}
	for (i = 0; i<MAX; i++)
	{
		indegree[i] = -99;
	}
}//end of Constructor
int create()
{
	n = 5;
	edges = 7;
	G[0][2] = 1;
	G[0][3] = 1;

	G[1][0] = 1;
	G[1][3] = 1;

	G[2][4] = 1;

	G[3][2] = 1;
	G[3][4] = 1;
	return n;
}
void Display(int n)
{
	int V1, V2;
	for (V1 = 0; V1<n; V1++)
	{
		for (V2 = 0; V2<n; V2++)
			cout<<" " <<G[V1][V2];
		cout<<"\n";
	}
}
void Insert_Q(int vertex, int n)
{
	if (rear == n)
		cout<<"Queue Overflow\n";
```

```
        else
        {
                if (front == -1) /*Empty Queue condition*/
                        front = 0;
                rear = rear + 1;
                Q[rear] = vertex;/* Inserting node into the Q*/
        }
}
int Delete_Q()
{
        int item;
        if (front == -1 || front > rear)
        {
                cout<<"Queue Underflow\n";
                return -1;
        }
        else
        {
                item = Q[front];
                front = front + 1;
                return item;
        }
}
int Compute_Indeg(int node, int n)
{
        int v1, indeg_count = 0;
        for (v1 = 0; v1<n; v1++)
                if (G[v1][node] == 1)//checking for incoming edge
                        indeg_count++;
        return indeg_count++;
}
void Topo_ordering(int n)
{
        j = 0;
        for (i = 0; i<n; i++)
        {
                indegree[i] = Compute_Indeg(i, n);
                if (indegree[i] == 0)
                        Insert_Q(i, n);
        }
        while (front <= rear)
        {
                k = Delete_Q();
                b[j++] = k;
                for (i = 0; i<n; i++)
                {
                        if (G[k][i] == 1)
```

```
                        {
                                G[k][i] = 0;
                                indegree[i] = indegree[i] - 1;
                                if (indegree[i] == 0)
                                        Insert_Q(i, n);
                        }
                }
        }
        cout<<"\nThe result of after topological sorting is ...";
        for (i = 0; i<n; i++)
                cout<<" "<<b[i];
        cout<<"\n";

    }
};//end of class
void main()
{
    Topo obj(10);
    obj.n = obj.create();
    cout<<"The adjacency matrix is : \n";
    obj.Display(obj.n);
    obj.Topo_ordering(obj.n);
}
```

Output

```
The adjacency matrix is :
0 0 1 1 0
1 0 0 1 0
0 0 0 0 1
0 0 1 0 1
0 0 0 0 0

The result of after topological sorting is ... 1 0 3 2 4
Press any key to continue . . .
```


2.10 Case Study

2.10.1 Webgraph and Google Map

WebGraph

Concept : The webgraph is a directed graph, whose vertices are nothing but the web pages and the directed edges between any two vertices V1 and V2 exists if there is a hyperlink present on web page V1 referring to page V2.

Example :

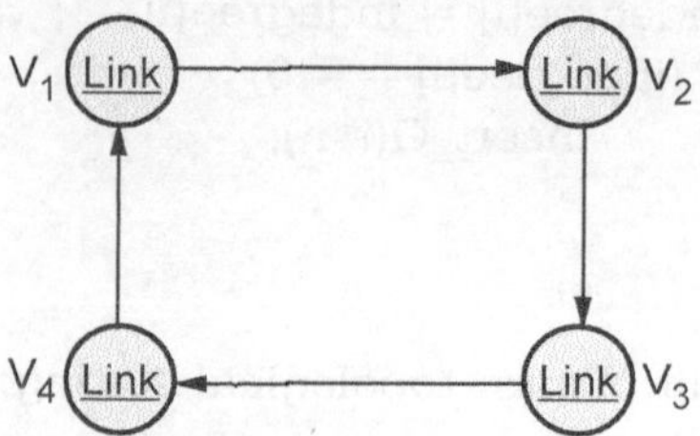

Fig. 2.10.1 Web graph

Here each node or vertex (V1, V2, V3 and V4) corresponds to webpage. These webpages contain hyperlinks. As we know, that on clicking the hyperlinks user is navigated to some other webpage. In the same manner, in above webgraph, on clicking the hyperlink on page V1, the page V2 will be displayed, on clicking hyperlink on page V2, the webpage V3 will be displayed and so on.

Applications :

1. Webgraph is used to calculate PageRank. The PageRank is an algorithm used for measuring the importance of website pages.
2. For determining the web pages of similar topics, the webgraph is used.
3. The webgraph is used to identify hubs and authorities of web pages.

Google Map

Concept :

- Google map is a service developed by Google.
- It offers services for satellite imagery, street maps, 360° views of streets and real-time traffic conditions.

Services Offered by Google Map

- Google map assists in route planning in which it offers directions for drivers, bikers, walkers and users of public transportation who want to take a trip from one specific location to another.
- Basically Google map provides **Application Programming Interface(API)** which makes it possible for website administrators to embed Google maps into their proprietary sites.
- Google maps for **Mobile** offers a location service for motorists that utilizes the Global Positioning System (GPS) location of the mobile device along with data from wireless and cellular networks.

- Using Google street view users can view and navigate through horizontal and vertical panoramic street level images of various cities around the world.
- As the user drags the map, the grid squares are downloaded from the server and inserted into the page.
- Locations are drawn dynamically by positioning a red pin on top of the map images.
- There are supplemental services that offer images of the moon, mars, and the heavens for hobby astronomers.

Technologies Used

- The Google map makes use of JavaScripts.
- The version of Google Street View for classic Google maps requires Adobe Flash.
- Google indoor maps uses JPG, .PNG, .PDF, .BMP or .GIF, for floor plan.

Notes

3 Hashing

Syllabus

Hash Table *- Concepts-hash table, Hash function, Bucket, Collision, Probe, Synonym, Overflow, Open hashing, Closed hashing, Perfect hash function, Load density, Full table, Load factor, Rehashing, Issues in hashing, Hash functions - Properties of good hash function, Division, Multiplication, Extraction, Mid-square, Folding and universal, Collision resolution strategies - Open addressing and chaining, Hash table overflow - Open addressing and chaining, Extendible hashing.*

Dictionary *- Dictionary as ADT, Ordered dictionaries.*

Skip List *- representation, Searching andoperations - Insertion, Removal.*

Contents

3.1 Concept

Hashing is an effective way to reduce the number of comparisons. Actually hashing deals with the idea of proving the direct address of the record where the record is likely to store. To understand the idea clearly let us take an example -

Suppose the manufacturing company has an inventory file that consists of less than 1000 parts. Each part is having unique 7 digit number. The number is called 'key' and the particular keyed record consists of that part name. If there are less than 1000 parts then a 1000 element array can be used to store the complete file. Such an array will be indexed from 0 to 999. Since the key number is 7 digit it is converted to 3 digits by taking only last three digits of a key. This is shown in the Fig. 3.1.1.

Observe in Fig. 3.1.1 that the first key 496700 and it is stored at 0th position. The second key is 8421002. The last three digits indicate the position 2nd in the array. Let us search the element 4957397. Naturally it will be obtained at position 397. This method of searching is called hashing. The function that converts the key (7 digit) into array position is called hash function.

Here hash function is

h(key) = key % 1000

Where key % 1000 will be the hash function and the key obtained by hash function is called hash key.

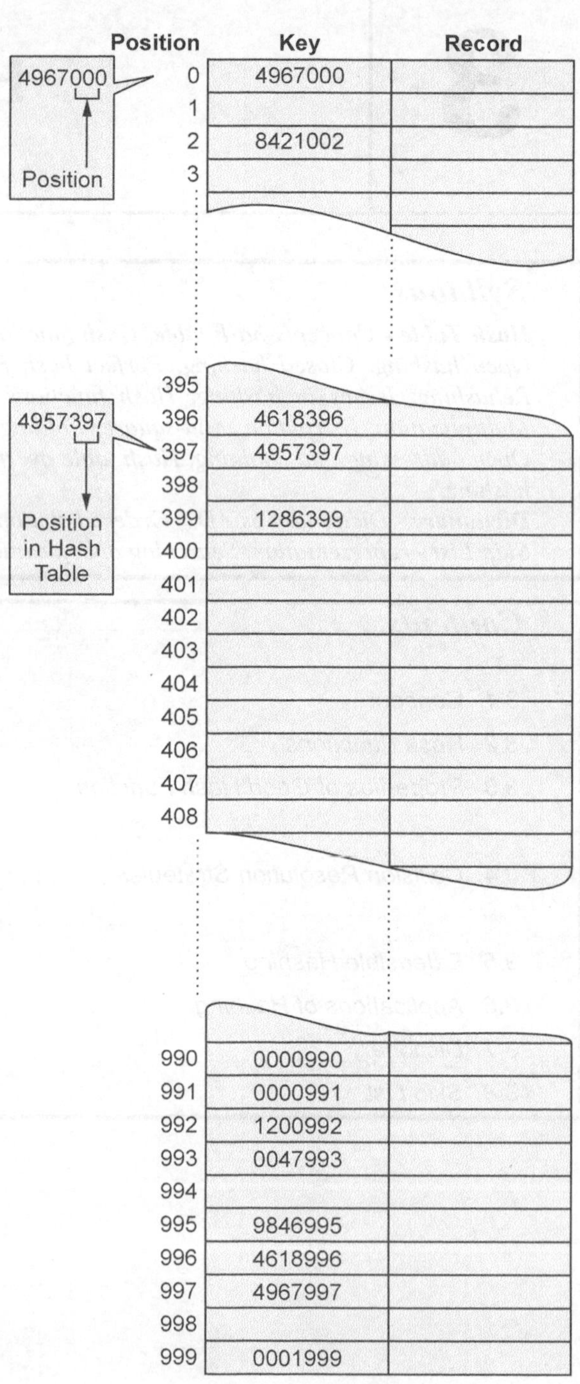

Fig. 3.1.1 Hashing

3.1.1 Basic Concepts in Hashing

1) **Hash Table :** Hash table is a data structure used for storing and retrieving data quickly. Every entry in the hash table is made using Hash function.

2) **Hash Function :**

- Hash function is a function used to place data in hash table.
- Similarly hash function is used to retrieve data from hash table.
- Thus the use of hash function is to implement hash table.

For example : Consider hash function as **key mod 5**. The hash table of size 5.

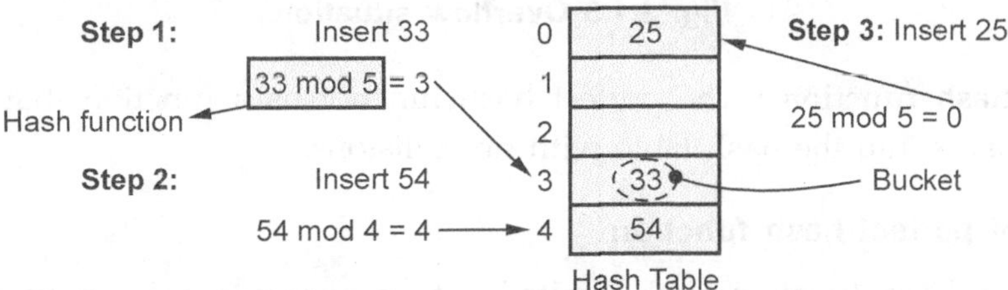

3) **Bucket :** The hash function H(key) is used to map several dictionary entries in the hash table. Each position of the hash table is called bucket.

4) **Collision :** Collision is situation in which hash function returns the same address for more than one record.

For example

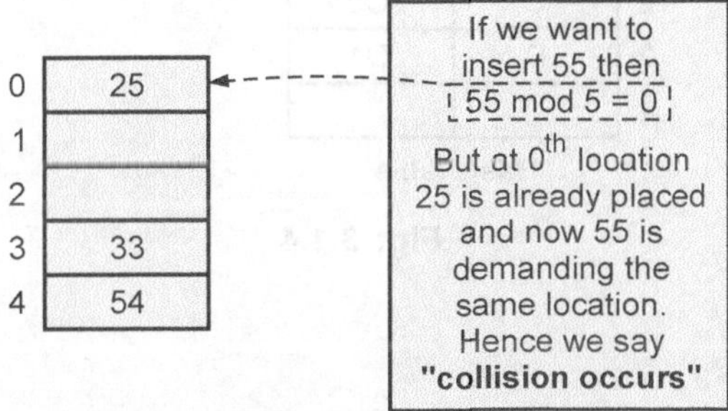

Fig. 3.1.2

5) **Probe :** Each calculation of an address and test for success is known as a probe.

6) **Synonym :** The set of keys that has to the same location are called synonyms. For example - In above given hash table computation 25 and 55 are synonyms.

7) **Overflow :** When hash table becomes full and new record needs to be inserted then it is called overflow.

For example -

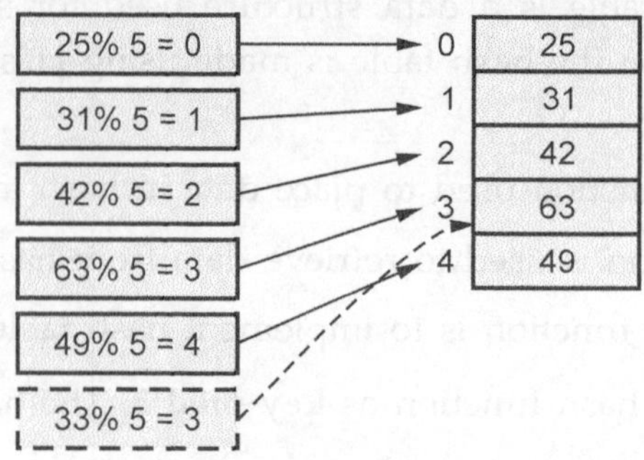

Fig. 3.1.3 Overflow situation

8) Perfect hash function : The perfect hash function is a function that maps distinct key elements into the hash table with no collisions.

Advantages of perfect hash function

1) A perfect hash function with limited set of elements can be used for efficient lookup operation.

2) There is no need to apply collision resolution technique.

9) Load factor and load density : Consider the hash table as given below -

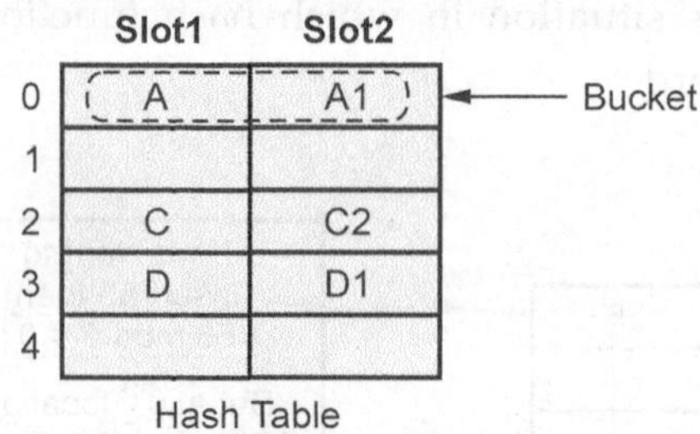

Fig. 3.1.4

Let,

- n be the total number of elements in the table.
- T is the total number of possible elements.

Element density : The element density of hash table is the ratio $\frac{n}{T}$.

Load density of load factor : The load density or load factor of hash table is

$$\alpha = \frac{n}{(sb)}$$

3.2 Hash Functions

There are various types of hash functions or hash methods which are used to place the elements in hash table.

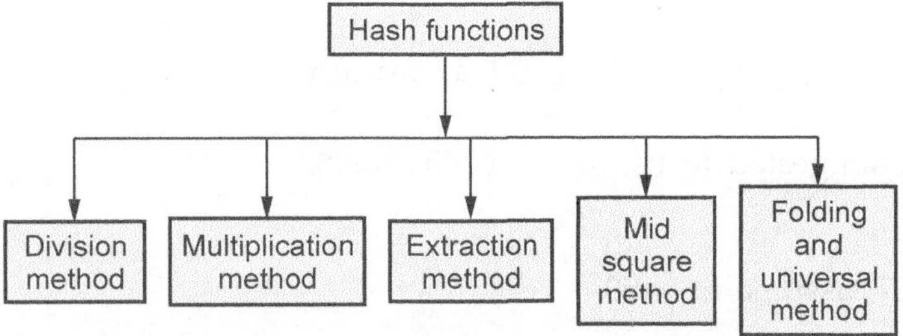

Fig. 3.2.1 Types of hash functions

3.2.1 Division Method

The hash function depends upon the remainder of division.

Typically the divisor is table length. For example :-

If the record 54, 72, 89, 37 is to be placed in the hash table and if the table size is 10 then

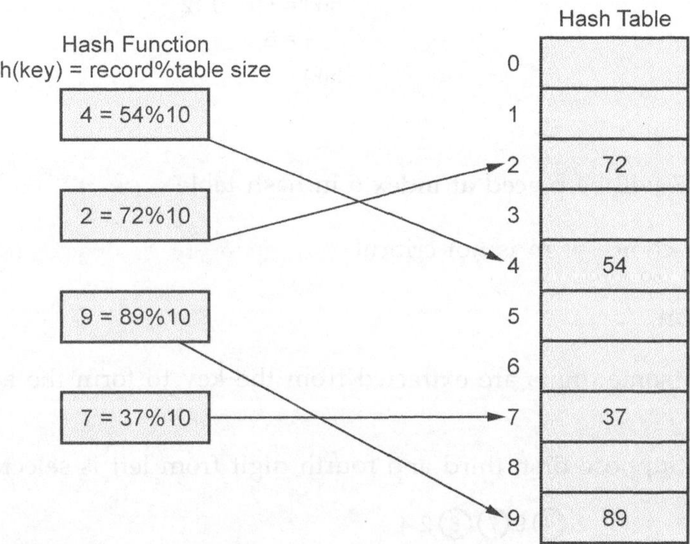

3.2.2 Multiplicative Hash Function

The multiplicative hash function works in following steps

1) Multiply the key 'k' by a constant A where A is in the range $0 < A < 1$. Then extract the fractional part of kA.

2) Multiply this fractional part by m and take the floor.

The above steps can be formulated as

$$h(k) = \lfloor m \{ kA \} \rfloor$$

Fractional part

Donald Knuth suggested to use A = 0.61803398987

Example :

Let key k = 107, assume m = 50.

A = 0.61803398987

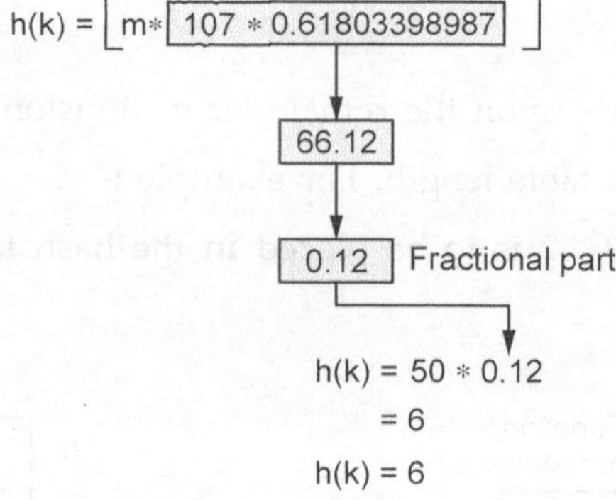

That means 107 will be placed at index 6 in hash table.

Advantage : The choice of m is not critical

3.2.3 Extraction

In this method some digits are extracted from the key to form the address location in hash table.

For example : Suppose first, third and fourth digit from left is selected for hash key.

4 9 7 8 2 4

478 → at 478 location in the hash table of size 1000 the key can be stored.

3.2.4 Mid Square

This method works in following steps

1) Square the key
2) Extract middle part of the result. This will indicate the location of the key element in the hash table.

Note that if the key element is a string then it has to be preprocessed to produce a number.

Let **key = 3111**

$$\therefore \quad (3111)^2$$

$$\downarrow$$

9 6 [7 8 3] 2 1

For the hash table of size of 1000

H(3111) = 783

3.2.5 Folding

There are two folding techniques

i) Fold shift ii) Fold boundary

i) **Fold shift :** In this method the key is divided into separate parts whose size matches with the size of required address. Then left and right parts are shifted and added with the middle part.

ii) **Fold boundary :** In this method the key is divided into separate parts. The leftmost and rightmost parts are folded on fixed boundary and added with the middle part.

For example

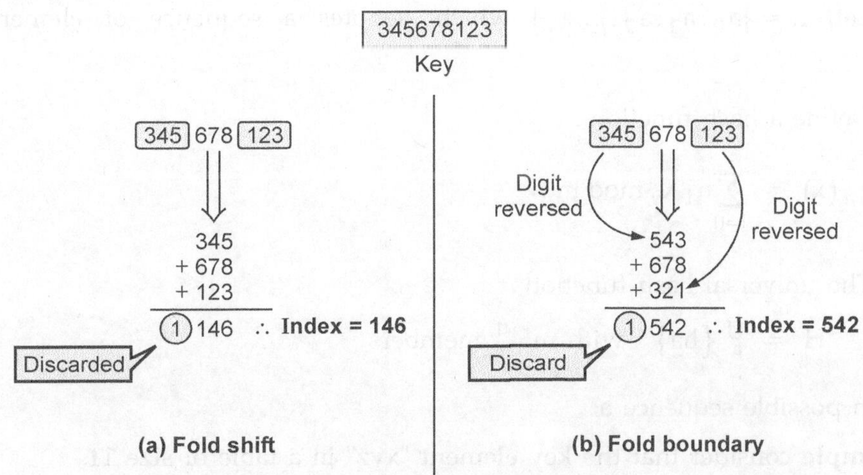

Fig. 3.2.2 Folding techniques

3.2.6 Universal Hashing

Universal hashing is a hashing technique in which randomized algorithm is used to select the hash function at random, from family of hash functions with the help of certain mathematical properties.

The universal hashing guarantees lower number of collisions.

Let

U be the set of universe keys

H be the finite collection of Hash functions mapping U into {0, 1,...., m−1}. Then H is called **universal** if, for x, y ∈ U (x ≠ y)

$$|\{h \in H : h(x) = h(y)\}| = \frac{|H|}{m}$$

That means, probability of a collision for two different keys x and y given a hash function randomly chosen from H is $\frac{1}{m}$.

Theorem : If h is chosen from a universal class of hash functions and is used to hash n keys into a table of size m, where n ≤ m, the expected number of collisions involving particular key x is less than 1.

Creation of set of universal Hash functions

Step 1 : Choose table size = m, where m is a prime number.

Step 2 : The key x can be divided into $\{x_0, x_1, \ldots x_r\}$ where maximal value of any x_i is less than m.

Step 3 : Let, $a = \{a_0, a_1, a_2, \ldots a_r\}$ which denotes a sequence of elements chosen randomly.

Step 4 : Define a hash function

$$h_a(x) = \sum_{i=0}^{r} a_i x_i \bmod m .$$

Step 5 : The universal hash function

$$H = \bigcup_{a} \{ha\} \text{ with } m^{r+1} \text{ members}$$

For each possible sequence a.

For example consider that the key element "xyz" in a table of size 11.

Let a = < 35, 100, 12>

Then $$h_a(K) = \left(\sum_{i=0}^{r} a_i K_i \right) \mathrm{mod\,size}$$

$$h(xyz) = (35 * 24 + 100 * 25 + 12 * 16) \% 11$$

$$h(xyz) = 0$$

That means **key = xyz** is stored at index 0 in Hash table.

3.3 Properties of Good Hash Function

SPPU : May-05, 10, 11, 12, 13, Dec.-07, 08, 12, 13, Marks 8

Rules for choosing good hash function

1. The hash function should be simple to compute.
2. Number of collisions should be less while placing the record in the hash table. Ideally no collision should occur. Such a function is called perfect hash function.
3. Hash function should produce such keys which will get distributed uniformly over an array.
4. The hash function should depend on every bit of the key. Thus the hash function that simply extracts the portion of a key is not suitable.

University Questions

1. *What is hashing function ? What are different ways to design a hash function ? Explain any one of the method in detail.* **SPPU : May-05, Dec.-07, Marks 8**
2. *What is a hashing function ? Explain any 4 types of hashing functions.* **SPPU : May-10, Marks 6, Dec.-12, Marks 8**
3. *What is hashing ? What are the characteristics of good hashing function ? Explain any two types of hash functions.* **SPPU : Dec.-08, Marks 8, May-11, Marks 6, May-13, Makrs 4**
4. *What is hash function ? Explain the following hash functions :*
   i) Mid square ii) Modulo division iii) Folding method iv) Digit analysis
   SPPU : May-12, Marks 8
5. *What is the use of hash tables ? Enlist the characteristics of good hash function.* **SPPU : Dec.-13, Marks 3**

3.4 Collision Resolution Strategies

SPPU : May-07, 08, 09, 14, Dec.-06, 07, 09, 10, 11, 13, Marks 12

Definition : If collisions occur then it should be handled by applying some techniques, such techniques are called **collision handling techniques.**

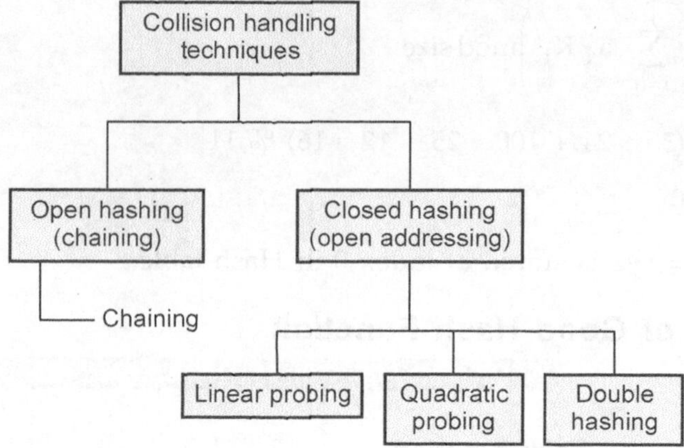

Fig. 3.4.1 Collision resolution techniques

3.4.1 Open and Closed Hashing

- The open hashing is also called as separate chaining and closed hashing is called open addressing.
- The difference between open hashing and closed hashing is that in **open hashing** the collisions are stored outside the table and in **closed hashing** the collisions are stored in the same table at some other slot.

3.4.2 Chaining

1. Chaining without replacement

In collision handling method chaining is a concept which introduces an additional field with data i.e. chain. A separate chain table is maintained for colliding data. When collision occurs we store the second colliding data by linear probing method. The address of this colliding data can be stored with the first colliding element in the chain table, without replacement.

For example consider elements,

131, 3, 4, 21, 61, 6, 71, 8, 9

Index	Data	Chain
0	–1	–1
1	131	2
2	21	5
3	3	–1
4	4	–1
5	61	7
6	6	–1
7	71	–1
8	8	–1
9	9	–1

Fig. 3.4.2 Chaining without replacement

From the example, you can see that the chain is maintained the number who demands for location 1. First number 131 comes we will place at index 1. Next comes 21 but collision occurs so by linear probing we will place 21 at index 2, and chain is maintained by writing 2 in chain table at index 1 similarly next comes 61 by linear probing we can place 61 at index 5 and chain will be maintained at index 2. Thus any element which gives hash key as 1 will be stored by linear probing at empty location but a chain is maintained so that traversing the hash table will be efficient.

The drawback of this method is in finding the next empty location. We are least bothered about the fact that when the element which actually belonging to that empty location cannot obtain its location. This means logic of hash function gets disturbed. Let us now see a program which implements chaining without replacement.

```
/*************************************************************************
Program to create hash table and to handle the collision using chianing
without replacement.In this program hash function is (number %10)
*************************************************************************/
#include<iostream.h>
#include<conio.h>
#include<stdlib.h>
#define MAX 10
class WO_chain
{
 private:
 int a[MAX][2];
 public:
 WO_chain();
 int create(int);
 void chain(int,int),display();
};
/*
------------------------------------------------------------------------
The constructor defined
------------------------------------------------------------------------
*/
WO_chain::WO_chain()
{
 int i;
 for(i=0;i<MAX;i++)
 {
  a[i][0]=-1;
  a[i][1]=-1;
 }
}

/*
------------------------------------------------------------------------
The create function is for generating the hash key
------------------------------------------------------------------------
*/
int WO_chain::create(int num)
```

```
{
 int key;
 key=num%10;
 return key;
}
/*
----------------------------------------------------------------------
The chain function handles the collision without replacement of numbers
----------------------------------------------------------------------
*/
void WO_chain::chain(int key,int num)
{
 int flag,i,count=0,ch;
 flag=0;
//checking full condition
  i=0;
  while(i<MAX)
  {
    if(a[i][0]!=-1)
    count++;
    i++;
  }
    if(count==MAX)
    {
     cout<<"\nHash Table Is Full";
     display();
     getch();
     exit(1);
        }
//placing number otherwise
 if(a[key][0]==-1)//no collision case
  a[key][0]=num;
 else //if collision occurs
  {
  ch=a[key][1];//taking the chain
  //If only one number in hash table with current obtained key
  if(ch==-1)
  {
        for(i=key+1;i<MAX;i++)//performing linear probing
        {
         if(a[i][0]==-1) //at immediate empty slot
         {
          a[i][0]=num;//placing number
          a[key][1]=i; //setting the chain
          flag=1;
          break;
         }
```

```
      }
  }
  //if many numbers are already in the hash table
  //we will find the next empty slot to place number
  else
  {
      while((a[ch][0]!=-1)&&(a[ch][1]!=-1))//traversing thro chain till empty slot is found*/
       ch=a[ch][1];
      for(i=ch+1;i<MAX;i++)
      {
       if(a[i][0]==-1)
       {
        a[i][0]=num;//placing the number
        a[ch][1]=i; //setting chain
        flag=1;
        break;
       }
      }
  }
//If the numbers are occupied somewhere from middle and are stored upto
//the MAX then we will search for the empty slot upper half of the array
if(flag!=1)
{
if(ch==-1)
  {
      for(i=0;i<key;i++)//performing linear probing
      {
       if(a[i][0]==-1) //at immediate empty slot
       {
        a[i][0]=num;//placing number
        a[key][1]=i; //setting the chain
        flag=1;
        break;
       }
      }
  }
  //if many numbers are already in the hash table
  //we will find the next empty slot to place number
  else
  {
      //traversing thro chain till empty slot is found
      while((a[ch][0]!=-1)&&(a[ch][1]!=-1))
       ch=a[ch][1];
      for(i=ch+1;i<key;i++)
      {
       if(a[i][0]==-1)
       {
```

```
        a[i][0]=num;//placing the number
        a[ch][1]=i; //setting chain
        flag=1;
        break;
       }
      }
 }
 }
}
}
/*
----------------------------------------------------------------------
The display function displays the hash table and chain table
----------------------------------------------------------------------
*/
void WO_chain::display()
{
 int i;
 cout<<"\n The Hash Table is...\n";
 for(i=0;i<MAX;i++)
        cout<<"\n  "<<i<<" "<<a[i][0]<<" "<<a[i][1];
}
/*
----------------------------------------------------------------------
The main function
----------------------------------------------------------------------
*/
void main()
{

 int num,key,i;
 char ans;
 WO_chain h;
 clrscr();
 cout<<"\nChaining Without Replacement";
 do
 {
  cout<<"\n Enter The Number";
  cin>>num;
  key=h.create(num);//returns hash key
  h.chain(key,num);//collision handled by chaining without replacement
  cout<<"\n Do U Wish To Continue?(y/n)";
  ans=getche();
 }while(ans=='y');
 h.display();//displays hash table
 getch();
}
```

Output

```
Chaining Without Replacement
Enter The Number 21

Do U Wish To Continue?(y/n)y
Enter The Number 31

Do U Wish To Continue?(y/n)y
Enter The Number 41

Do U Wish To Continue?(y/n)y
Enter The Number 2

Do U Wish To Continue?(y/n)y
Enter The Number 6

Do U Wish To Continue?(y/n)n
The Hash Table is...

0  -1  -1
1  21   2
2  31   3
3  41   4
4   2  -1
5  -1  -1
6   6  -1
7  -1  -1
8  -1  -1
9  -1  -1
```

2. Chaining with replacement

As previous method has a drawback of loosing the meaning of the hash function, to overcome this drawback the method known as changing with replacement is introduced. Let us discuss the example to understand the method. Suppose we have to store following elements :

131, 21, 31, 4, 5

0	– 1	– 1
1	131	2
2	21	3
3	31	– 1
4	4	– 1

5	5	– 1
6		
7		
8		
9		

Now next element is 2. As hash function will indicate hash key as 2 but already at index 2. We have stored element 21. But we also know that 21 is not of that position at which currently it is placed.

Hence we will replace 21 by 2 and accordingly chain table will be updated. See the table :

Index	Data	Chain
0	– 1	– 1
1	131	6
2	2	– 1
3	31	– 1
4	4	– 1
5	5	– 1
6	21	3
7	– 1	– 1
8	– 1	– 1
9	– 1	– 1

The value –1 in the hash table and chain table indicate the empty location.

The advantage of this method is that the meaning of hash function is preserved. But each time some logic is needed to test the element, whether it is at its proper position.

```
/**************************************************************************
Program to create hash table and to handle the collision using chaining
with replacement.In this program hash function is (number %10)
**************************************************************************/
#include<iostream.h>
#include<conio.h>
#include<stdlib.h>
#define MAX 10
class W_chain
{
 private:
  int a[MAX][2];
```

```
 public:
  W_chain();
  int create(int);
  void chain(int,int),display();
  int match(int,int);
  ~W_chain();
};
/*
----------------------------------------------------------------------
The constructor defined
----------------------------------------------------------------------
*/
W_chain::W_chain()
{
 int i;
 for(i=0;i<MAX;i++)
 {
  a[i][0]=-1;
  a[i][1]=-1;
 }
}
/*
----------------------------------------------------------------------
The destructor defined
----------------------------------------------------------------------
*/
W_chain::~W_chain()
{
 int i;
 for(i=0;i<MAX;i++)
 {
  a[i][0]=-1;
  a[i][1]=-1;
 }
}
/*
----------------------------------------------------------------------
The create function
----------------------------------------------------------------------
*/
int W_chain::create(int num)
{
 int key;
 key=num%10;
 return key;
}
```

```
/*
------------------------------------------------------------------
The match function
------------------------------------------------------------------
*/
int W_chain::match(int prev,int num)
{
 if(create(num)==create(prev))
       return 1;
 return 0;
}
/*
------------------------------------------------------------------
The chain function
------------------------------------------------------------------
*/
void W_chain::chain(int key,int num)
{
 int flag,i,count=0,ch,temp,j,prev_ch;
 flag=0;

//checking full condition
 i=0;
 while(i<MAX)
 {
       if(a[i][0]!=-1)
              count++;
       i++;
 }
       if(count==MAX)
       {
        cout<<"\nHash Table Is Full";
        display();
        getch();
        exit(1);
        }
//placing number otherwise
 if(a[key][0]==-1)//no collision case
  a[key][0]=num;
 else
 {
  ch=a[key][1];
  if(match(a[key][0],num))
  {
        if(ch==-1)//no chain
        {
         for(i=key+1;i<MAX;i++)
```

```
        if(a[i][0]==-1)
        {
         a[i][0]=num;
         a[key][1]=i;
         flag=1;
         break;
        }
   }
   else
   {
    while((a[ch][0]!=-1)&&(a[ch][1]!=-1))
    ch=a[ch][1];
   for(i=ch+1;i<MAX;i++)
   {
    if(a[i][0]==-1)
        {
         a[i][0]=num;
         a[ch][1]=i;
         flag=1;
         break;
        }
   }
  }
  }
  else                    //unmatched
  {
   if(ch==-1)
   {
    temp =a[key][0];
    for(i=key+1;i<MAX;i++)
        if(a[i][0]==-1)
        {
         a[key][0]=num;//replacement is done
         a[i][0]=temp;
         for(j=0;j<MAX;j++)
          if(key==a[j][1])
              a[j][1]=i;
              flag=1;
         break;
        }
   }
   else //chain exists
   {
    for(j=0;j<MAX;j++)
        if(key==a[j][1])
        prev_ch=j;
        temp=a[key][0];
```

```
        ch=key;
        while(a[ch][1]!=-1)     //traversal for continuous chain
        ch=a[ch][1];
        for(i=ch+1;i<MAX;i++)
         if(a[i][0]==-1)//actual replacement
          {
               a[i][0]=temp;
               a[ch][1]=i;
               a[key][0]=num;
               a[prev_ch][1]=a[key][1];
               a[key][1]=-1;
               flag=1;
               break;
          }
         }
    }
if(flag!=1)
{
    if(match(a[key][0],num))
    {
     if(ch==-1)//no chain
     {
      for(i=0;i<key;i++)
         if(a[i][0]==-1)
         {
          a[i][0]=num;
          a[key][1]=i;
          flag=1;
          break;
         }
     }
     else
     {
      while((a[ch][0]!=-1)&&(a[ch][1]!=-1))
      ch=a[ch][1];
     for(i=0;i<key;i++)
     {
      if(a[i][0]==-1)
         {
          a[i][0]=num;
          a[ch][1]=i;
          flag=1;
          break;
         }
     }
    }
    }
```

```
        else                    //unmatched
        {
         if(ch==-1)
         {
          temp =a[key][0];
          for(i=0;i<key;i++)
                if(a[i][0]==-1)
                {
                 a[key][0]=num;//replacement is done
                 a[i][0]=temp;
                 for(j=0;j<MAX;j++)
                  if(key==a[j][1])
                        a[j][1]=i;
                        flag=1;
                 break;
                }
         }
         else //chain exists
         {
          for(j=0;j<MAX;j++)
                if(key==a[j][1])
                prev_ch=j;
                temp=a[key][0];
                ch=key;
                while(a[ch][1]!=-1)   //traversal for continuous chain
                ch=a[ch][1];
                for(i=0;i<key;i++)
                 if(a[i][0]==-1)//actual replacement
                  {
                        a[i][0]=temp;
                        a[ch][1]=i;
                        a[key][0]=num;
                        a[prev_ch][1]=a[key][1];
                        a[key][1]=-1;
                        flag=1;
                        break;
                  }
                 }
         }
 }
 }
}
/*
---------------------------------------------------------------------
The display function
---------------------------------------------------------------------
*/
```

```
void W_chain::display()
{
 int i;
 cout<<"\n The Hash Table is...\n";
 for(i=0;i<MAX;i++)
        cout<<"\n "<<i<<"  "<<a[i][0]<<"  "<<a[i][1];
}
/*
------------------------------------------------------------------
The main function
------------------------------------------------------------------
*/
void main()
{
 int num,key;
 char ans;
 W_chain h;
 clrscr();
 cout<<"\nChaining With Replacement";
 do
 {
  cout<<"\n Enter The Number";
  cin>>num;
  key=h.create(num); //create hash key
  h.chain(key,num);
  cout<<"\n Do U Wish To Continue?(y/n)";
  ans=getche();
 }while(ans=='y');
 h.display();
 getch();
}
```

Output

```
Chaining With Replacement
 Enter The Number21

 Do U Wish To Continue?(y/n)y
 Enter The Number31

 Do U Wish To Continue?(y/n)y
 Enter The Number41

 Do U Wish To Continue?(y/n)y
 Enter The Number2

 Do U Wish To Continue?(y/n)y
```

```
Enter The Number5

Do U Wish To Continue?(y/n)

The Hash Table is...

0 -1 -1
1 21  3
2  2 -1
3 41  4
4 31 -1
5  5 -1
6 -1 -1
7 -1 -1
8 -1 -1
9 -1 -1
```

3.4.3 Open Addressing

Open addressing is a collision handling technique in which the entire hash table is searched in systematic way for empty cell to insert new item if collision occurs.

Various techniques used in open addressing are

1. Linear probing 2. Quadratic probing 3. Double hashing

1. Linear probing

When collision occurs i.e. when two records demand for the same location in the hash table, then the collision can be solved by placing second record linearly down wherever the empty location is found.

For example

Index	data
0	
1	131
2	21
3	31
4	4
5	5
6	61
7	7
8	8
9	

Fig. 3.4.3 Linear probing

In the hash table given in Fig. 3.4.3 the hash function used is number % 10. If the first number which is to be placed is 131 then 131 % 10 = 1 i.e. remainder is 1 so hash key = 1. That means we are supposed to place the record at index 1. Next number is 21 which gives hash key = 1 as 21 % 10 = 1. But already 131 is placed at index 1. That means collision is occurred. We will now apply linear probing. In this method, we will search the place for number 21 from location of 131. In this case we can place 21 at index 2. Then 31 at index 3. Similarly 61 can be stored at 6 because number 4 and 5 are stored before 61. Because of this technique, the searching becomes efficient, as we have to search only limited list to obtain the desired number.

```
/**********************************************************************
Program to create hash table and to handle the collision using linear
probing.In this Program hash function is (number%10)
**********************************************************************/
#include<iostream.h>
#include<conio.h>
#include<stdlib.h>
#define MAX 10
class Hash
{
 private:
  int a[MAX];
 public:
 Hash();
 int create(int);
 void linear_prob(int,int),display();
};
/*
-------------------------------------------------------------------
The constructor defined
-------------------------------------------------------------------
*/
Hash::Hash()
{
 int i;
 for(i=0;i<MAX;i++)
  a[i]=-1;
}

/*
-------------------------------------------------------------------
The create function is for generating the hash key
Input:the num means the number which we want to place in the hash table
Output:returns the hash key
Calls:none
Called By:main
```

```
----------------------------------------------------------------------
*/
int Hash::create(int num)
{
 int key;
 key=num%10;
 return key;
}
/*----------------------------------------------------------------------
The linear_prob function handles the collision
Input:the num,hash key and hash table by array a[]
Output:none
Calls:none
Called By:main
----------------------------------------------------------------------
*/
void Hash::linear_prob(int key,int num)
{
 int flag,i,count=0;
 flag=0;
 if(a[key]==-1)//if the location indicated by hash key is empty
  a[key]=num;//place the number in the hash table
 else
 {
  i=0;
  while(i<MAX)
  {
   if(a[i]!=-1)
          count++;
   i++;
  }
   if(count==MAX)        //checking for the hash full
   {
    cout<<"\nHash Table Is Full Hence "<<num<<" Can not Be Inserted";
    display();
    getch();
    exit(1);
   }
   for(i=key+1;i<MAX;i++)//moving linearly down
    if(a[i]==-1)    // searching for empty location
    {
     a[i]=num;  //placing the number at empty location
     flag=1;
     break;
    }
//From key position to the end of array we have searched empty location
//and now we want to check empty location in the upper part of the array
```

```
  for(i=0;i<key&&flag==0;i++)//array from 0th to keyth location will be scanned
   if(a[i]==-1)
   {
    a[i]=num;
    flag=1;
    break;
   }
 } //outer else
}//end

/*
--------------------------------------------------------------------
The display function displays the hash table
Output:none
Calls:none
Called By:main
--------------------------------------------------------------------
*/
void Hash::display()
{
 int i;
 cout<<"\n The Hash Table is..."<<endl;
 for(i=0;i<MAX;i++)
  cout<<"\n "<<i<<" "<<a[i];
}

/*
--------------------------------------------------------------------
The main function
Calls:create,linear_prob,display
Called By:O.S.
--------------------------------------------------------------------
*/
void main()
{
 int num,key;
 char ans;
 Hash h;
 clrscr();
 cout<<"\nCollision Handling By Linear Probing";
 do
 {
  cout<<"\n Enter The Number";
  cin>>num;
  key=h.create(num);//returns hash key
  h.linear_prob(key,num);//collision handled by linear probing
  cout<<"\n Do U Wish To Continue?(y/n)";
```

```
ans=getche();
}while(ans=='y');
h.display();//displays hash table
getch();
}
```

Output

```
Collision Handling By Linear Probing
Enter The Number 21

Do U Wish To Continue?(y/n)y
Enter The Number31

Do U Wish To Continue?(y/n)y
Enter The Number41

Do U Wish To Continue?(y/n)y
Enter The Number2

Do U Wish To Continue?(y/n)y
Enter The Number3

Do U Wish To Continue?(y/n)y
Enter The Number71

Do U Wish To Continue?(y/n)n
The Hash Table is...

0 -1
1 21
2 31
3 41
4 2
5 3
6 71
7 -1
8 -1
9 -1
```

Problem with linear probing

One major problem with linear probing is primary clustering. Primary clustering is a process in which a block of data is formed in the hash table when collision is resolved.

For example :

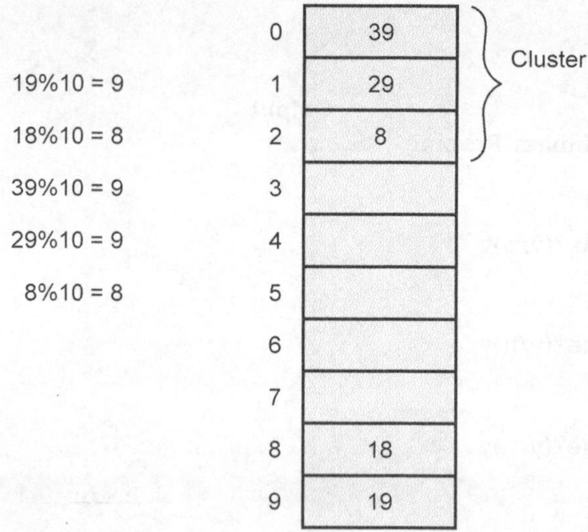

This clustering problem can be solved by quadratic probing.

2. Quadratic probing

Quadratic probing operates by taking the original hash value and adding successive values of an arbitrary quadratic polynomial to the starting value. This method uses following formula -

$$H_i(key) = (Hash(key)+i^2)\%m$$

where m can be a table size or any prime number.

For example : If we have to insert following elements in the hash table with table size 10 :

37, 90, 55, 22, 11, 17, 49, 87.

We will fill the hash table step by step

	Index	Value
	0	90
37%10 = 7	1	11
90%10 = 0	2	22
55%10 = 5	3	
22%10 = 2	4	
11%10 = 1	5	55
	6	

7	37
8	
9	

Now if we want to place 17 a collision will occur as 17%10=7 and bucket 7 has already an element 37. Hence we will apply quadratic probing to insert this record in the hash table.

$$H_i(\text{key}) = (\text{Hash}(\text{key})+i^2)\%m$$

we will choose value i = 0, 1, 2, ..., whichever is applicable.

Consider $i = 0$ then

$(17+0^2)\ \%10 = 7$

$(17+1^2)\ \%10 = 8$, when $i = 1$

The bucket 8 is empty hence we will place the element at index 8.

Then comes 49 which will be placed at index 9.

49%10 = 9

0	90
1	11
2	22
3	
4	
5	55
6	
7	37
8	17
9	49

Fig. 3.4.4

Now to place 87 we will use quadratic probing.

(87 + 0)%10 = 7

(87 + 1)%10 = 8 ... but already occupied

$(87 + 2^2)\%10 = 1$ ... already occupied

$(87 + 3^2)\%10 = 6$ ... this slot is free ∴ We place 87 at 6th index.

0	90
1	11
2	22
3	
4	
5	55
6	87
7	37
8	17
9	49

Fig. 3.4.5

It is observed that if we want to place all the necessary elements in the hash table the size of divisor (m) should be twice as large as total number of elements.

3. Double hashing

Double hashing is technique in which a second hash function is applied to the key when a collision occurs. By applying the second hash function we will get the number of positions from the point of collision to insert.

There are two important rules to be followed for the second function :

- It must never evaluate to zero.
- Must make sure that all cells can be probed.

The formula to be used for double hashing is

$$H_1(\text{key}) = \text{key mod tablesize}$$

$$H_2(\text{key}) = M - (\text{ key mod } M)$$

where M is a prime number smaller than the size of the table.

Consider the following elements to be placed in the hash table of size 10

37, 90, 45, 22, 17, 49, 55

Initially insert the elements using the formula for H_1(key).

Insert 37, 90, 45, 22.

$$H_1(37) = 37\%10 = 7$$
$$H_1(90) = 90\%10 = 0$$
$$H_1(45) = 45\%10 = 5$$
$$H_1(22) = 22\%10 = 2$$
$$H_1(49) = 49\%10 = 9$$

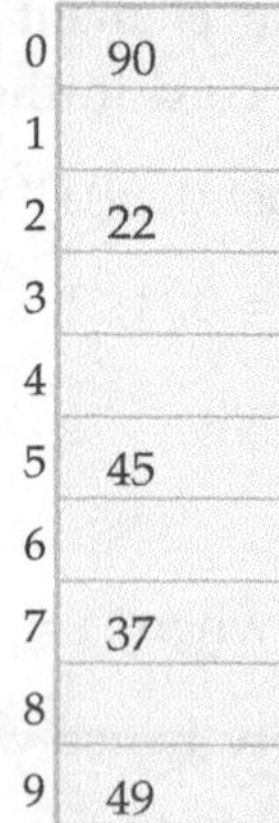

Now if 17 is to be inserted then

$$H_1(17) = 17\%10 = 7$$
$$H_2(key) = M - (key\%M)$$

Here M is a prime number smaller than the size of the table. Prime number smaller than table size 10 is 7.

Hence M = 7

$$H_2(17) = 7 - (17\%7) = 7 - 3 = 4$$

That means we have to insert the element 17 at 4 places from 37. In short we have to take 4 jumps. Therefore the 17 will be placed at index 1.

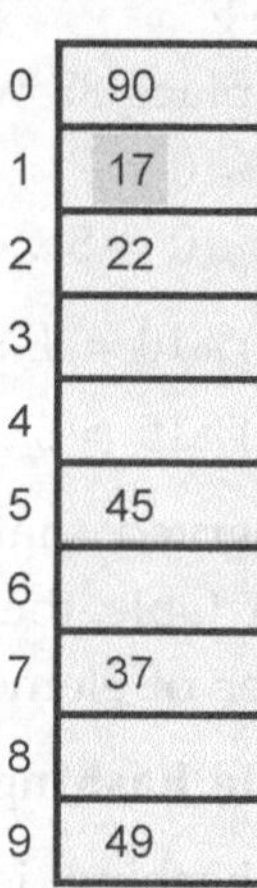

Fig. 3.4.6

Now to insert number 55.

$$H_1(55) = 55\%10 = 5 \ldots \text{collision}$$
$$H_2(55) = 7 - (55\%7) = 7 - 6 = 1$$

That means we have to take one jump from index 5 to place 55. Finally the hash table will be -

0	90
1	17
2	22
3	
4	
5	45

6	55
7	37
8	
9	49

Comparison of quadratic probing and double hashing

The double hashing requires another hash function whose probing efficiency is same as some another hash function required when handling random collision.

The double hashing is more complex to implement than quadratic probing. The quadratic probing is fast technique than double hashing.

4. Rehashing

Rehashing is a technique in which the table is resized, i.e., the size of table is doubled by creating a new table. It is preferable if the total size of table is a prime number. There are situations in which the rehashing is required-

- When table is completely full.
- With quadratic probing when the table is filled half.
- When insertions fail due to overflow.

In such situations, we have to transfer entries from old table to the new table by recomputing their positions using suitable hash functions.

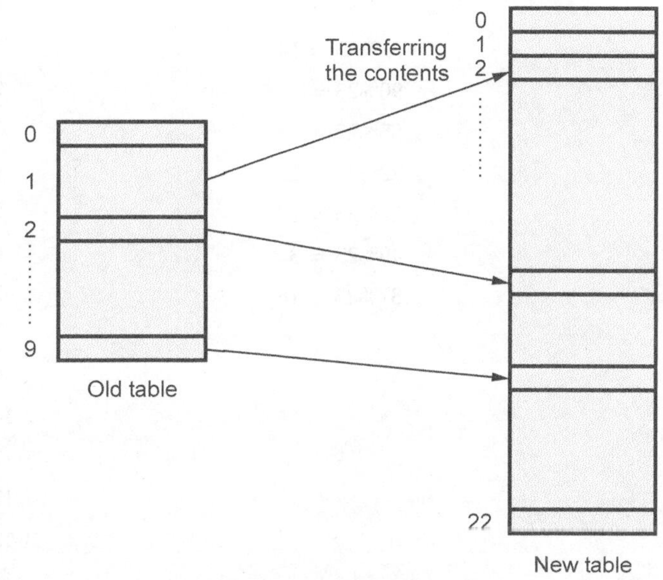

Fig. 3.4.7 Rehashing

Consider we have to insert the elements 37, 90, 55, 22, 17, 49 and 87. The table size is 10 and will use hash function,

H(key) = key mod tablesize

37%10 = 7

90%10 = 0

55%10 = 5

0	90
1	
2	22
3	

22%10 = 2

17%10 = 7 Collision solved by linear probing

49%10 = 9

4	
5	55
6	
7	37
8	17
9	49

Now this table is almost full and if we try to insert more elements collisions will occur and eventually further insertions will fail. Hence we will rehash by doubling the table size. The old table size is 10 then we should double this size for new table, that becomes 20. But 20 is not a prime number, we will prefer to make the table size as 23. And new hash function will be

H(key) = key mod 23

37%23 = 14

90%23 = 21

55%23 = 9

22%23 = 22

17%23 = 17

49%23 = 3

87%23 = 18

0	
1	
2	
3	49
4	
5	
6	
7	
8	
9	55
10	
11	
12	
13	
14	37
15	
16	
17	17
18	87
19	
20	
21	90
22	22

Now the hash table is sufficiently large to accommodate new insertions.

Advantages

1. This technique provides the programmer a flexibility to enlarge the table size if required.
2. Only the space gets doubled with simple hash function which avoids occurrence of collisions.

Example 3.4.1 *Give the input {4371, 1323, 6173, 4199, 4344, 9679, 1989} and hash function $h(X) = X(mod\ 10)$, show the results for the following :*

i) Open addressing hash table using linear probing

ii) Open addressing hash table using quadratic probing

iii)Open addressing hash table with second hash function $h^2(X) = 7 - (X\ mod\ 7)$.

SPPU : May-08, Marks 12

Solution : i) Open addressing hash table using linear probing :

We assume mod function as mod 10.

4371 mod 10 = 1

1323 mod 10 = 3

6173 mod 10 = 3 collision occurs

Hence by linear probing we will place 6173 at next empty location. That is, at location 4.

4199 mod 10 = 9

4344 mod 10 = 4 but location 4 is not empty.

Hence we will place 4344 at next empty location i.e. 5,

9679 mod 10 = 9 collision occurs so place at next location at 0. The hash table is of size 10. Hence we find the next empty location by rolling the table in forward direction.

1989 mod 10 – 9 collision occurs, so we find the next empty location at index 2.

The hash table will then be

Index	Keys
0	9679
1	4371
2	1989
3	1323
4	6173
5	4344
6	

7	
8	
9	4199

ii) Open addressing hash table using quadratic probing

In quadratic probing we consider the original hash key and then add an arbitrary polynomial. This sum is then considered for hash function. The hash function will be

$$H(Key) = (Key + i^2) \% m$$

where m can be a table size

If we assume m = 10, then the numbers can be inserted as follows -

Step 1 :

Index	Keys
0	
1	4371
2	
3	
4	
5	
6	
7	
8	
9	

4371 mod 10 = 1

Step 2 :

Index	Keys
0	
1	4371
2	
3	1323
4	
5	
6	
7	
8	
9	

1323 mod 10 = 3

Step 3 :

Index	Keys
0	
1	4371
2	
3	1323
4	6173
5	
6	
7	
8	
9	

6173 mod 10 = 3
As collision occurs we will apply quadratic probing.

$\therefore$ H(key) = $(H(key) + i^2) \% m$

Consider i = 0

$\therefore$ H (6173) = $(3 + 0^2) \% 10$
= 3 collision

Hence consider i = 1

H (6173) = $(3 + 1^2) \% 10$
= (3 + 1) % 10

H (6173) = 4

As index 4 is an empty slot, we will place 6173 at index 4.

Step 4 :

Index	Keys
0	
1	4371
2	
3	1323
4	6173
5	
6	
7	
8	
9	4199

4199 mod 10 = 9

As this slot is empty we will place 4199 at index 9

Step 5 :

Index	Keys
0	
1	4371
2	
3	1323
4	6173
5	4344
6	
7	
8	
9	4199

4344 mod 10 = 4
But index 4 shows an occupied slot. Hence collision occurs. Therefore we will place 4344 using quadratic probing.

$\therefore$ H(key) = $(H(key) + i^2)$ % m

H(key) = 4, i = 0, 1, 2, ...

m = 10

$\therefore$ H (key) = $(4 + 0^2)$ % 10 = 4 collision

H (key) = $(4 + 1^2)$ % 10 = 5

The index 5 is an empty slot. Hence we will place 4344 at index 5.

Step 6 :

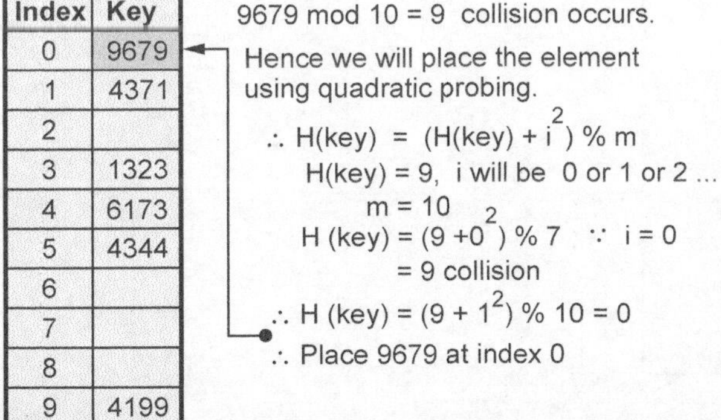

Index	Key
0	9679
1	4371
2	
3	1323
4	6173
5	4344
6	
7	
8	
9	4199

9679 mod 10 = 9 collision occurs.

Hence we will place the element using quadratic probing.

$\therefore$ H(key) = $(H(key) + i^2)$ % m

H(key) = 9, i will be 0 or 1 or 2 ...

m = 10

H (key) = $(9 + 0^2)$ % 7 $\because$ i = 0

= 9 collision

$\therefore$ H (key) = $(9 + 1^2)$ % 10 = 0

$\therefore$ Place 9679 at index 0

Step 7 :

Index	Key
0	9679
1	4371
2	
3	1323
4	6173
5	4344
6	
7	
8	1989
9	4199

1989 mod 10 = 9 collision occurs.

Hence we will place the element using quadratic probing.

$\therefore$ H(key) = (H(key) + i^2) % m.

H(key) = 9, hence

$\therefore$ H (key) = (9 + 0^2) % 10 $\because$ i = 0
= 9 collision

$\therefore$ H (key) = (9 + 1^2) % 10 $\because$ i = 1
= 0 collision

$\therefore$ H (key) = (9 + 2^2) % 10 $\because$ i = 2
= 3 collison

$\therefore$ H (key) = (9 + 3^2) % 10 $\because$ i = 3
= 8

Insert 1989 at index 8

iii) Open addressing hash table with second hash function

Step 1 :

Index	Key
0	
1	4371
2	
3	1323
4	
5	
6	
7	
8	
9	

4371 mod 10 = 1

1323 mod 10 = 3

Step 2 :

Index	Key
0	
1	4371
2	
3	1323
4	6173
5	
6	
7	
8	
9	

6173 mod 10 = 3 collision occurs. Hence we will apply second hash function.

$$h2(X) = 7 - (X \bmod 7)$$
$$h2(6173) = 7 - (6173 \bmod 7)$$
$$= 7 - 6$$
$$= 1$$

That means we have to take 1 jump from the index 3 (the place at which collision occurs). Hence we will place 6173 at index 4.

Step 3 :

Index	Key
0	
1	4371
2	
3	1323
4	6173
5	
6	
7	
8	
9	4199

4199 mod 10 = 9. As this slot is empty, we will place 4199 at index 9.

Step 4 :

Index	Key
0	
1	4371
2	
3	1323
4	6173
5	9679
6	
7	4344
8	
9	4199

4344 mod 10 = 4 collision occurs.
Hence
h(4344) = 7 – (4344 mod 7)
= 7 – 4
= 3

i.e. Take 3 jumps from index 4.
i.e. place 4344 at index 7.
Similarly element 9679 will be placed at index 5 using second hash function.

There is no place for 1989.

Example 3.4.2 *Explain linear probing with and without replacement using the following data : 12, 01, 04, 03, 07, 08, 10, 02, 05, 14, 06, 28*
Assume buckets from 0 to 9 and each bucket has one slot. Calculate average cost/number of comparison for both. **SPPU : May-09, Marks 10**

Solution : We assume hash function = key mod 10. As buckets are from 0 to 9 and each bucket has one slot, the keys can be inserted in the hash table using our hash function as follows -

Index	Key
0	10
1	01
2	12
3	03
4	04
5	02
6	05
7	07
8	08
9	14

12 % 10 = 2
01 % 10 = 1
04 % 10 = 4
03 % 10 = 3
07 % 10 = 7
08 % 10 = 8
10 % 10 = 0
02 % 10 = 2 collision occurs
∴ By linear probing place 02 at index 5.
05 % 10 = 5 collision occurs
∴ Place 05 at index 6
14 % 10 = 4 collision occurs
∴ Place 14 at index 9

Now as hash table is full we can not insert 06 and 28 keys in the hash table. Now if we want to search any key then following analysis is made

Key	12	01	04	03	07	08	10	02	05	14	06	28
Number of comparisons made for each key	1	1	1	1	1	1	1	4	2	6	10	10

Thus total number of comparisons made

$$= 1 + 1 + 1 + 1 + 1 + 1 + 1 + 4 + 2 + 6 + 10 + 10$$

= 39 buckets get examined.

That means average number of buckets that get examined per key

$$= \frac{\text{Total number of comparisons}}{\text{Number of keys}} = \frac{39}{12}$$

$$= 3.25$$

We must find loading density which denoted by α.

$$\alpha = \frac{n}{b} = \frac{\text{Number of keys}}{\text{Total number of buckets}} = \frac{12}{10}$$

$$\alpha = \mathbf{1.2}$$

The average number of key comparisons

$$= \frac{\text{Total number of comparisons}}{\text{Total number of buckets}} = \frac{39}{10} = 3.9$$

The average cost can be computed by calculating successful search (denoted by Sn) and unsuccessful search (denoted by U_n).

$$\therefore \quad Sn \approx \frac{1}{2}\left(1+\frac{1}{(1-\alpha)}\right)$$

$$\approx \frac{1}{2}\left(1+\frac{1}{(1-1.2)}\right)$$

$$\approx \frac{1}{2}\left(1+\frac{1}{(-0.2)}\right)$$

$$Sn \approx -2$$

$$Un \approx \frac{1}{2}\left(1+\frac{1}{(1-\alpha)^2}\right)$$

$$\approx \frac{1}{2}\left(1+\frac{1}{0.04}\right)$$

$$\approx 13$$

$$\text{Total cost} \approx \text{Sn} + \text{Un}$$

$$\approx -2 + 13$$

Total cost $\approx$ **11**

Example 3.4.3 *What do you understand by collision in hashing ? Represent the following keys in memory using linear probing with or without replacement. Use modulo (10) as your hashing function : (24, 13, 16, 15, 19, 20, 22, 14, 17, 26, 84, 96)*

SPPU : Dec.-09, Marks 8

Solution : Collision in hashing - Refer section 3.4.

i) Linear probing with replacement

We will consider the hash function as modulo (10) for the hash table size 12, that is from 0 to 11. In linear probing with replacement, we first find the probable position of the key element using hash function. If the location which we obtain from hash function is empty then place the corresponding key element at that location. If the location is not empty and the key element which is present at that location belongs to that location only then, move down in search of empty slot. Place the record at the empty slot.

If the location contains a record which does not belong to that location then replace that record by the current key element. Place the replaced record at some empty slot, which can be obtained by moving linearly down.

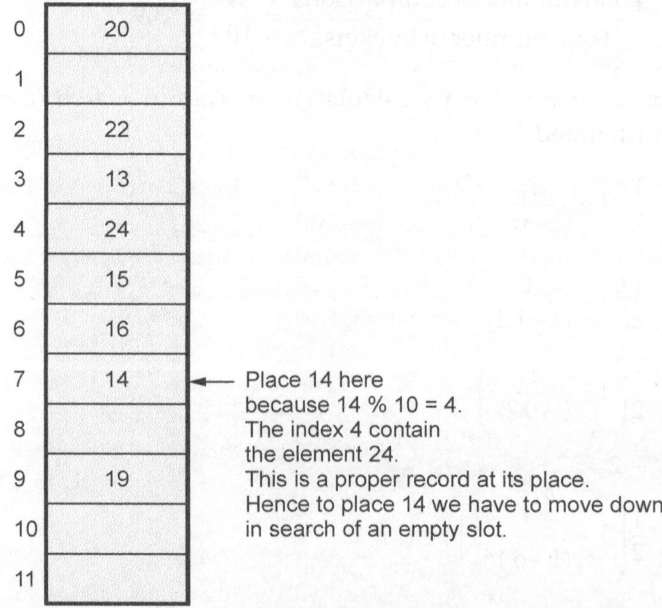

We get the empty location at index 7. Hence 14 is placed at index 7.

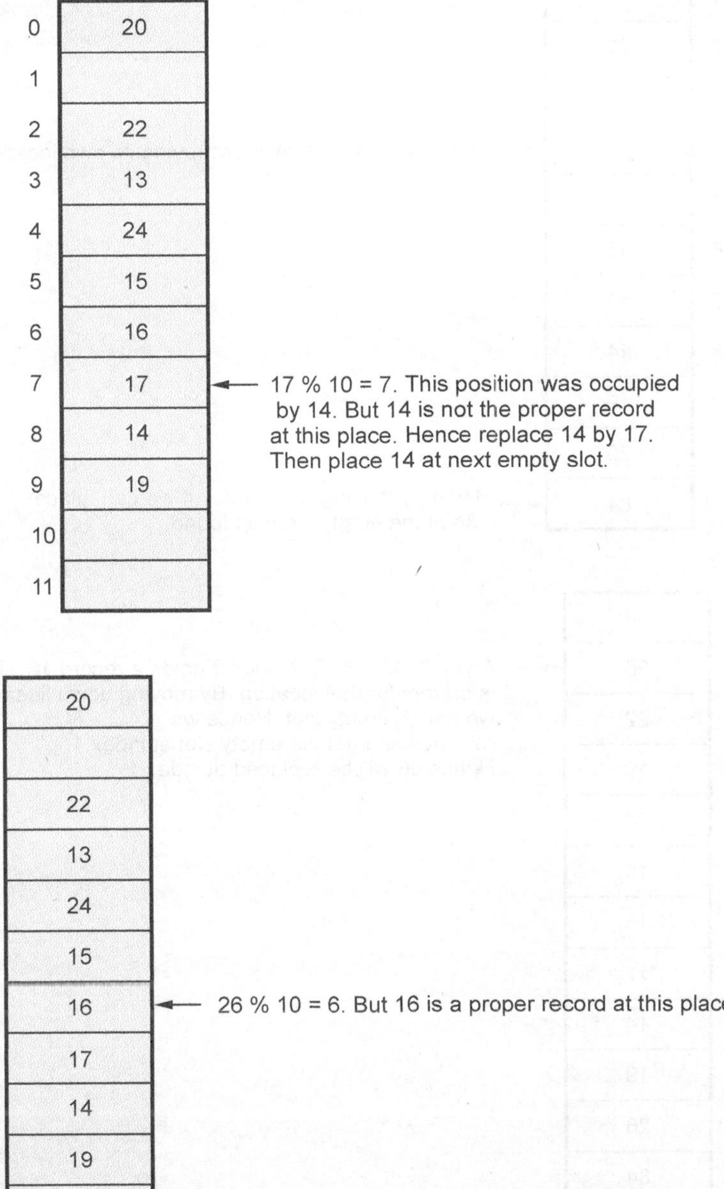

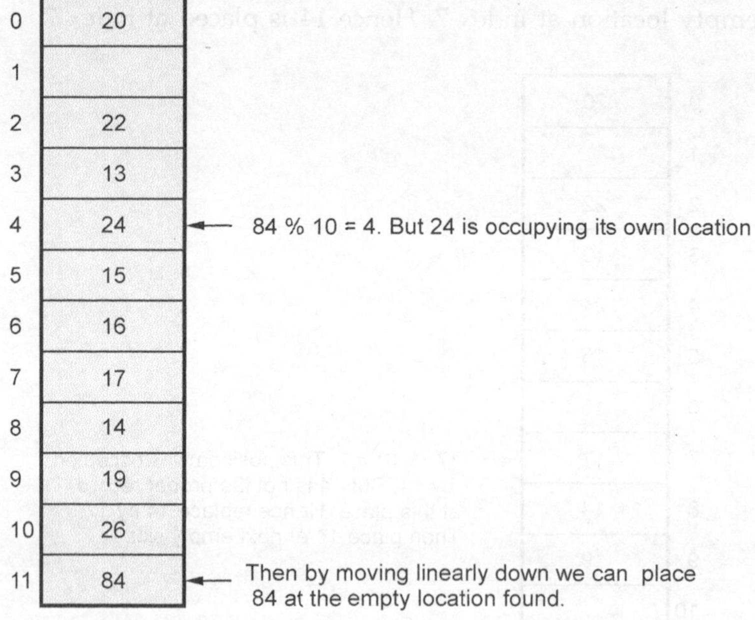

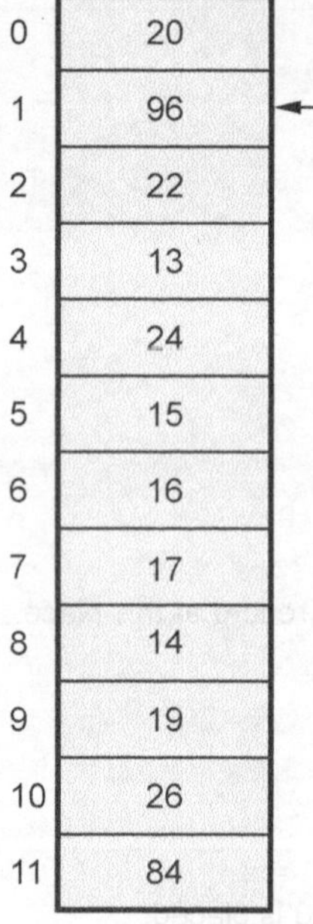

As 96 % 10 = 6. But index 6 holds a record 16 which is correct for that location. By moving down linearly we get no empty slot. Hence we roll back and get the empty slot at index 1. Hence 96 will be replaced at index 1.

ii) Linear probing without replacement

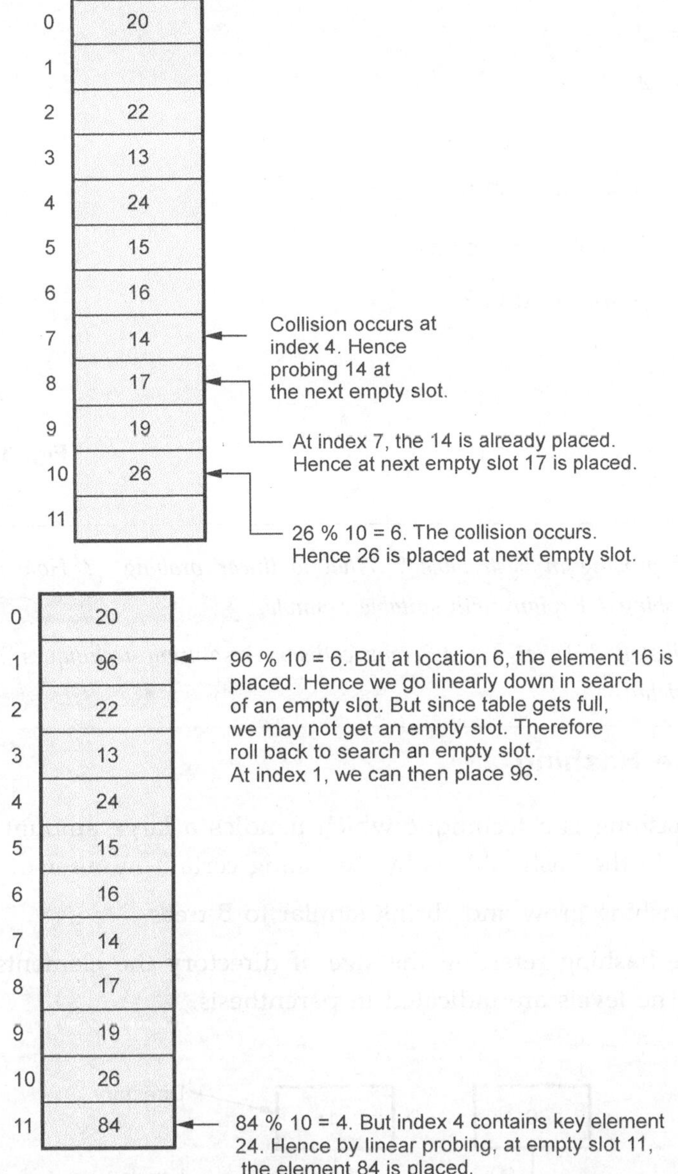

Example 3.4.4 *Assume the size of hash table as 8. The hash function to be used to calculate the hash value of the data X is X%8. Insert the following values in hash table : 10, 12, 20, 18, 15. Use linear probing without replacement for handling collision.*

SPPU : Dec.-13, Marks 3

Solution : Table size = 8

Hash function is x % 8

We will handle collision of the elements using linear probing without replacement.

10 % 8 = 2

12 % 8 = 4

20 % 8 = 4 - collision occurs

∴ place at 10 C 5.

18 % 8 = 2 - collision occurs

∴ place at 10 C 3.

15 % 8 = 7

0	
1	
2	10
3	18
4	12
5	20
6	
7	15

Fig. 3.4.8 Hash table

University Questions

1. *What is the probing in hash table ? What is linear probing ? How does it differs from quadratic probing ? Explain with suitable example.* **SPPU : Dec.-06,07, May-07, Marks 8**
2. *What is collision ? What are different collision resolution techniques ? Explain any two methods in detail.* **SPPU : Dec.-10, 11, May-14, Marks 8**

3.5 Extensible Hashing

- Extensible hashing is a technique which handles a large amount of data. The data to be placed in the hash table is by extracting certain **number of bits.**
- Extensible hashing grow and shrink similar to B-trees.
- In extensible hashing referring the size of directory the elements are to be placed in buckets. The levels are indicated in parenthesis.

For example :

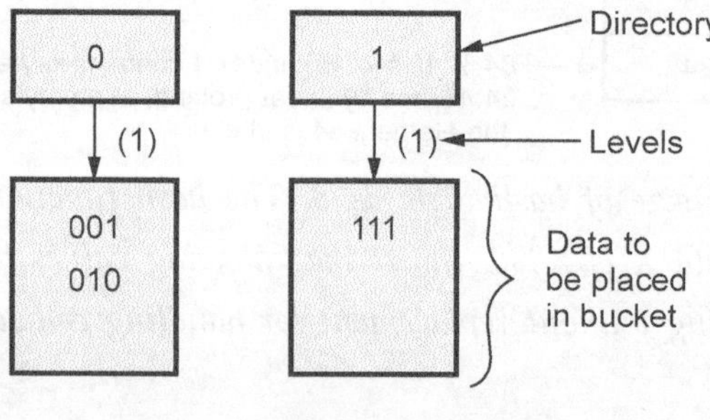

Fig. 3.5.1

- The bucket can hold the data of its global depth. If data in bucket is more than global depth then, split the bucket and double the directory.

Insertion Operation:

Consider an example for understanding the insertion operation

Consider we have to insert 1, 4, 5, 7, 8, 10. Assume each page can hold 2 data entries (2 is the depth).

Step 1 : Insert 1, 4.

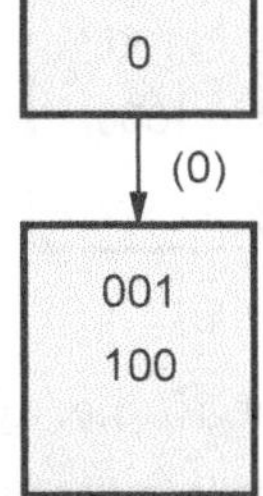

Fig. 3.5.2

1 = 001

4 = 100

We will examine last bit of data and insert the data in bucket.

Insert 5. The bucket is full. Hence double the directory.

1 = 001

4 = 100

5 = 101
↑

Based on last bit the data is inserted.

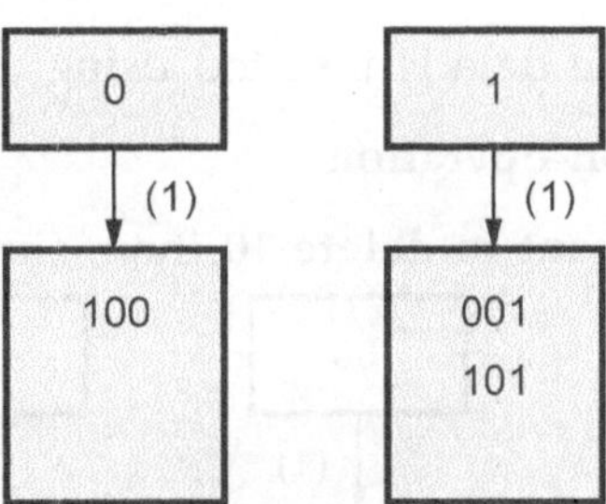

Fig. 3.5.3

Step 2 : Insert 7.

7 = 111

Insert 7 : But as depth is full we can not insert 7 here. Then double the directory and split the bucket.After insertion of 7. Now consider last two bits.

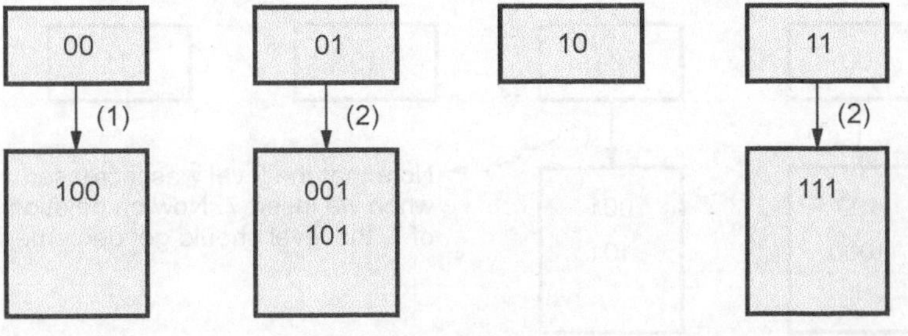

Fig. 3.5.4

Step 3 : Insert 8 i.e. 1000.

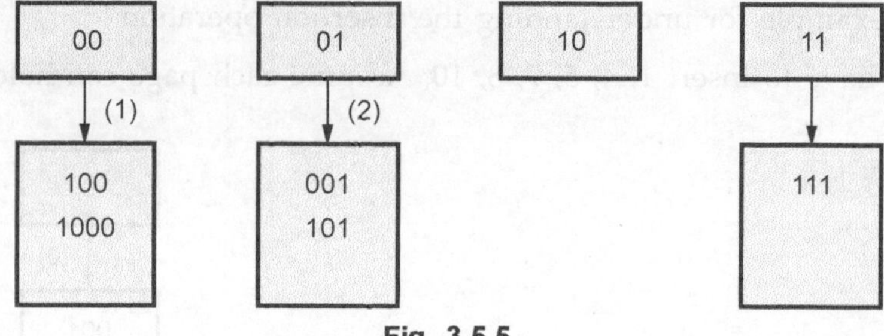

Fig. 3.5.5

Step 4 : Insert 10. i.e. 1010

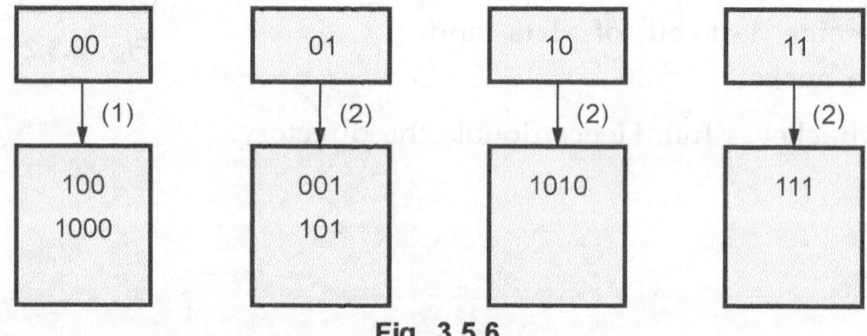

Fig. 3.5.6

Thus the data is inserted using extensible hashing.

Deletion operation

If we want to **delete 10** then, simply make the bucket of 10 empty.

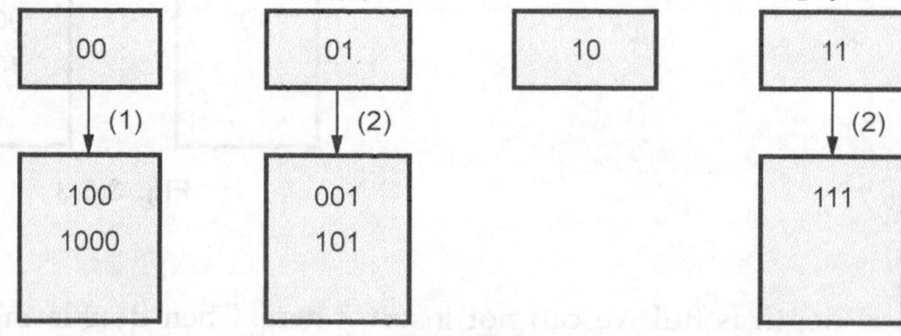

Fig. 3.5.7

Delete 7.

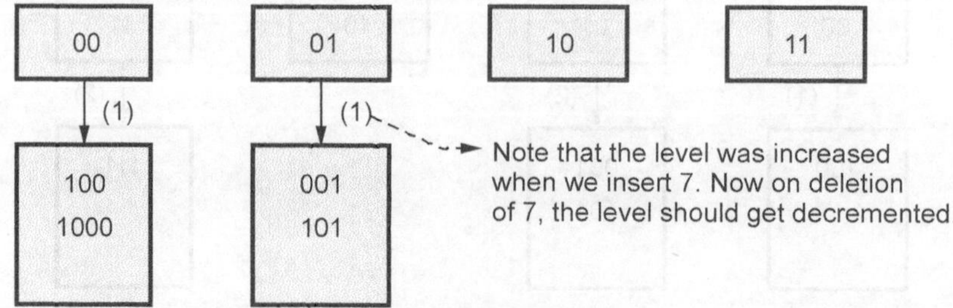

Fig. 3.5.8

Delete 8. Remove entry from directory 00.

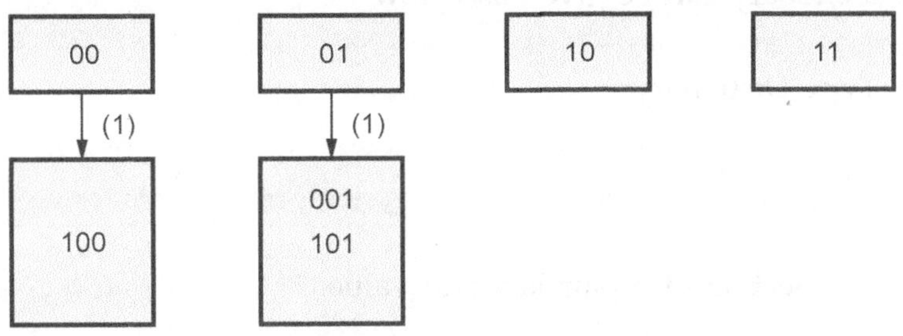

Fig. 3.5.9

3.6 Applications of Hashing

1. In compilers to keep **track of declared variables.**
2. For **online spelling checking** the hashing functions are used.
3. Hashing helps in **Game playing programs** to store the moves made.
4. For browser program while **caching the web pages, hashing** is used.

3.7 Dictionary

Definition : Dictionary is a collection of pairs of key and value where every value is associated with the corresponding key.

Basic **operations** that can be performed on dictionary are

1. Insertion of value in the dictionary.
2. Deletion of particular value from dictionary.
3. Searching of a specific value with the help of key.

For example : In the Library the book database is prepared which is actually a dictionary. When a book is issued to the student that book entry is deleted from the database and on returning of the book to the library the corresponding book entry is added in the book database. If a student demands for some specific book then its entry is searched in the book database.

Dictionary is a data structure using which these above mentioned operations can be performed efficiently.

3.7.1 ADT for Dictionary

The ADT for dictionary can be given as below -

AbstractDataType Dictionary

{

Instance :

Dictionary is a collection of a pair key and value.

Operations :

Size() - It returns the size of the dictionary if it returns 0 then the dictionary is supposed to be empty.

Insert() - The pair of key and value is inserted in the dictionary.

Delete() - The pair of key and value is deleted from the dictionary.

Search() - The desired value is searched in the dictionary by using key.

}

3.7.2 Representation of Dictionary

The dictionary can be represented as a linear list. The linear list is a collection of pair and value. There are two method of representing linear list.

1. **Sorted Array -** An array data structure is used to implement the dictionary.
2. **Sorted Chain A linked list data structure is used to implement the dictionary.**

The insert operation

Before any insertion of a node it is first checked if the node is already present in the dictionary or not. If it is not present then only the node is inserted in the list. There won't be any duplicate key in the dictionary.

The dictionary can be represented as given below -

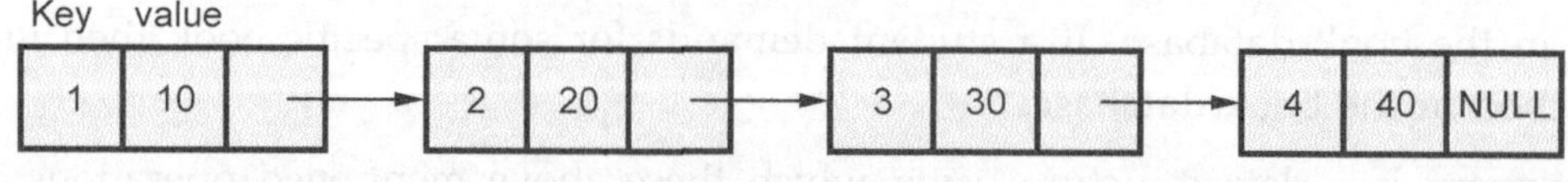

Fig. 3.7.1

The contents of dictionary are in the pair form. The pair is of key and value. The linear list is used to represent such a dictionary. Note that the contents of dictionary are always in sorted form.

Various operations on this linear list are -

1. Insertion of record in the list.
2. Deletion of any record from the list.
3. Finding length/size of the list.
4. Display of the list.

Structure of linear list for dictionary

The class definition for creating dictionary using linear list is as shown below -

```
Class sll
{
	private:
		struct node
		{
			int key;
			int value;
			struct node *next;
		}*head;
	Public:
	sll();//constructor
	void insert();
	void print();
	void del();
	int length();
	vsll();//destructor
};
```

Insertion of new node in the dictionary

Step 1 :

Consider that initially dictionary is empty then

head = NULL.

We will create a new node with some key and value contained in it. For instance we have created.

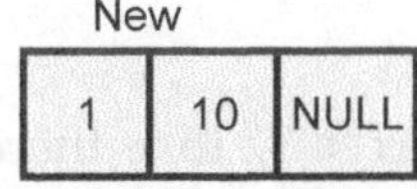

Fig. 3.7.2

Now as head is NULL, this new node becomes head. Hence the dictionary contains only one record.

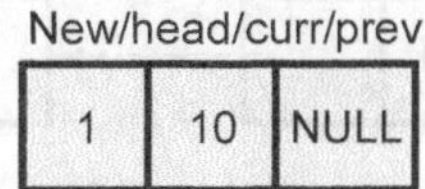

Fig. 3.7.3

This node will be 'curr' and 'prev' as well. The 'curr' node will always point to current visiting node and 'prev' will always point to the node previous to 'curr' node. As now there is only one node in the list we will mark 'curr' node as our 'prev' node.

Step 2 :

If we want to insert more record, say key = 4 and value 20, then we will create such a 'New' node.

Fig. 3.7.4

Then we will compare the key values of 'curr' and 'New' node.

If New → Key > Curr → Key then attach New node to 'curr' node.

curr → next = New

prev = curr

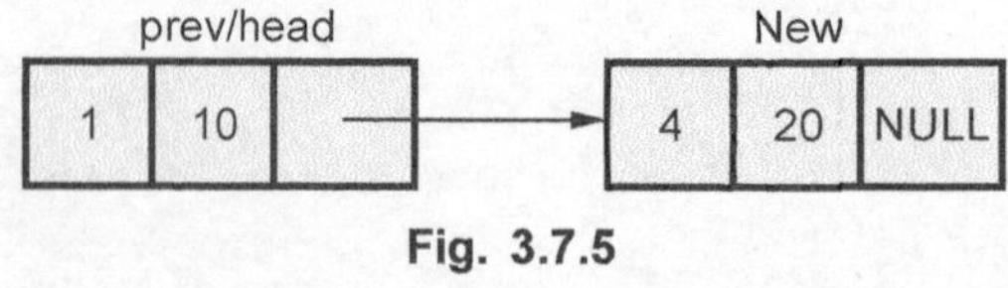

Fig. 3.7.5

Step 3 :

If we add again a new node < 7, 80 > then

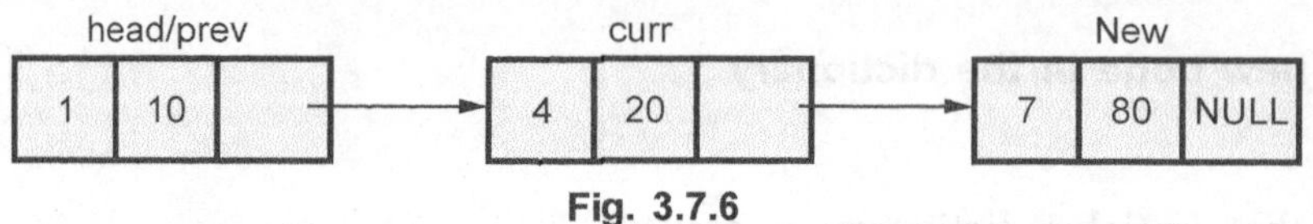

Fig. 3.7.6

Step 4 :

If we insert < 3, 15 > then we have to search for it proper position by comparing key value.

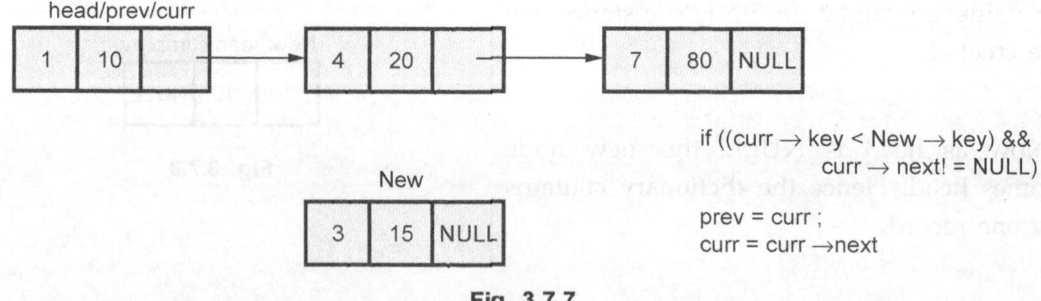

Fig. 3.7.7

Hence,

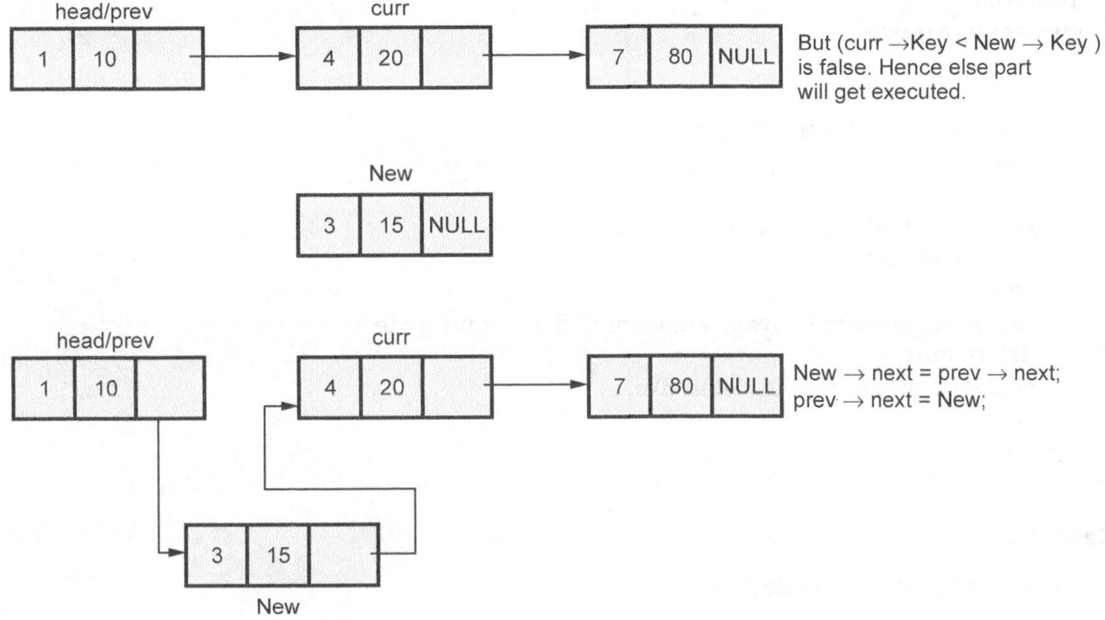

Fig. 3.7.8

Thus the dictionary becomes

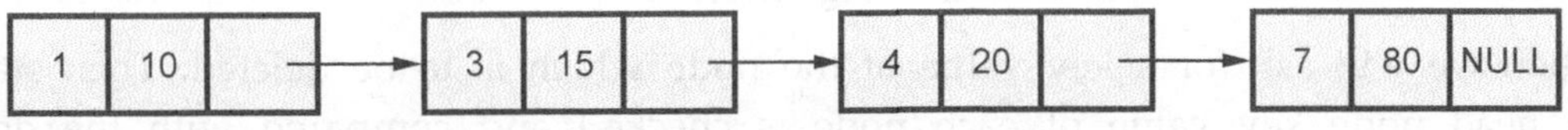

Fig. 3.7.9

Continuing in this fashion we can insert the new nodes in the dictionary.

The erase operation

```
void sll:: erase()
{
 node *curr, *prev ;
 int  k;
 curr=head;
 clrscr();
 cout<<"\nEnter the key value that you want to delete: ";
 cin>>k;
 while(curr!=NULL)
 {
```

```
if(curr->key==k)//traverse till required node to delete
            break;           //is found
   prev=curr;
  curr=curr->next;
 }
      if(curr==NULL)
      cout<<"\nNode not found";
      else
      {
       if(curr==head) //first node
       head=curr->next;
       else
        prev->next=curr->next; //intermediate or end node
       delete curr;
       cout<<"\nThe item is deleted\n";
        }
 getch();
}
```

Case 1 :

Consider the list is created as,

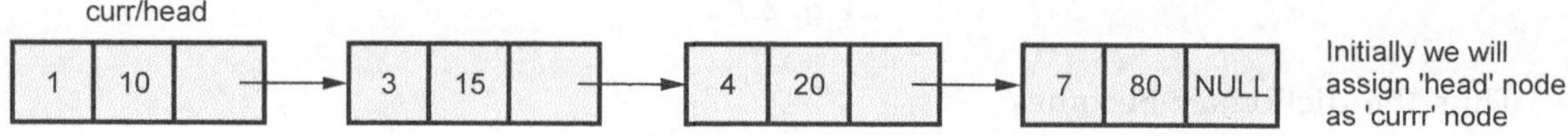

Fig. 3.7.10

Then we will ask for a key value of the node which is to be deleted. Then starting from head node key value of each node is checked and compared with the desired node's key value. We will get node which is to be deleted in variable 'curr'. The node given by variable 'prev' keeps track of previous node of 'curr' node. For instance if we want to delete node with key value 4 then,

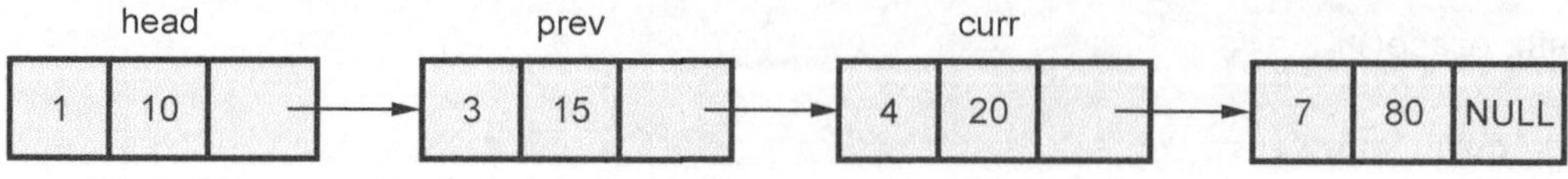

Fig. 3.7.11

To delete 'curr' node,

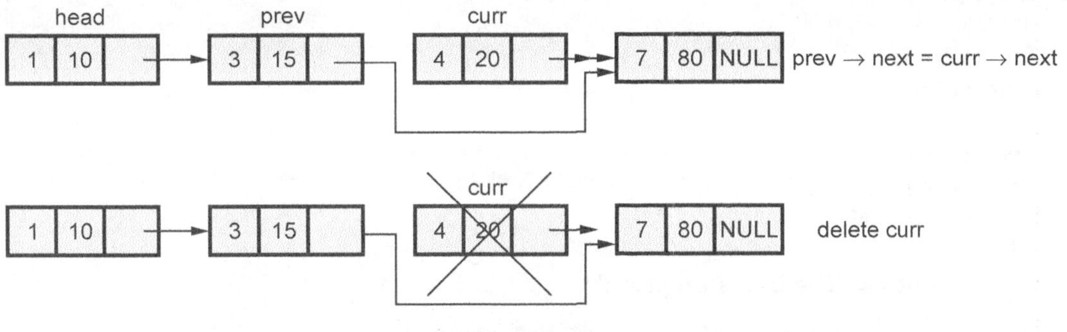

Fig. 3.7.12

Then the list will become,

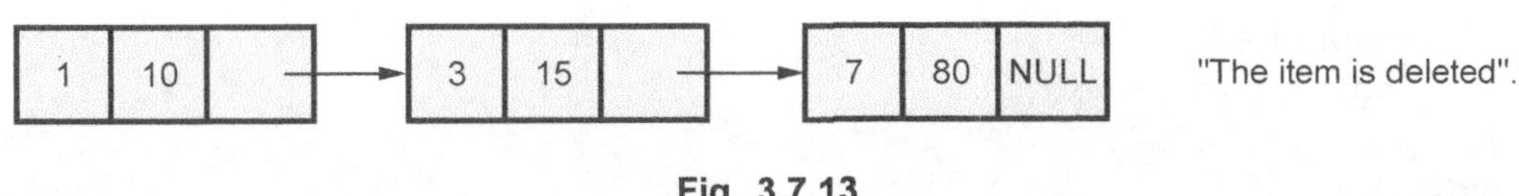

Fig. 3.7.13

Case 2 :

If the node to be deleted is a head node then consider following scenario.

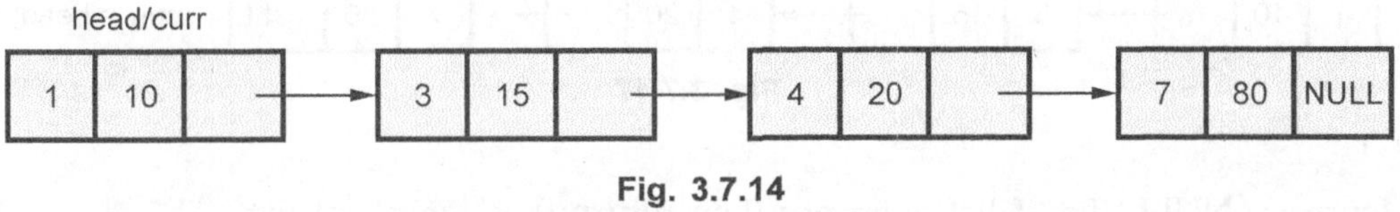

Fig. 3.7.14

We want to delete node with key value 1.

i.e. if (curr == head).

Then, we simply make 'head' node as next node and delete 'curr' node.

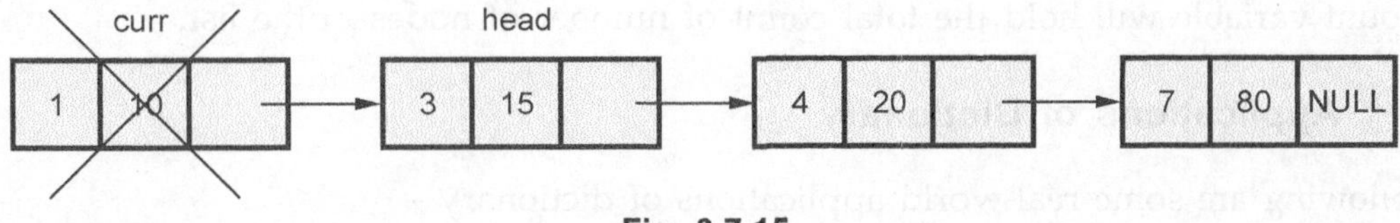

Fig. 3.7.15

Hence the list becomes

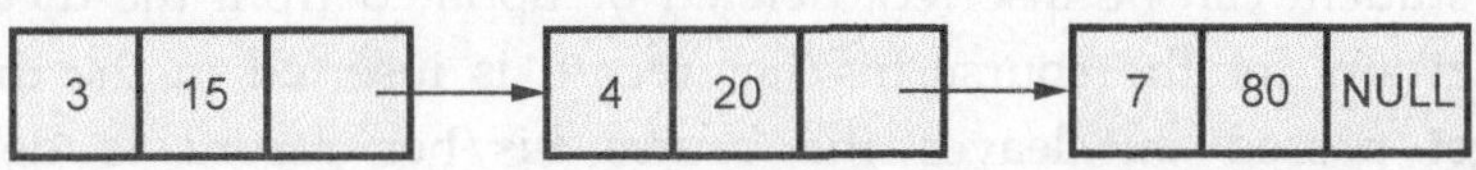

Fig. 3.7.16

The length operation

```
int sll ::length()
{
        node *curr ;
        int  count;

        count = 0;
        curr = head;
        if ( curr == NULL )
        {
                cout<<"The list is empty\n";
                getch();
                return 0;
        }
        while ( curr != NULL )
        {
                count++;
                curr = curr -> next;
        }
        getch();
        return count;
}
```

In length function the total length/size of linear list is obtained. Consider

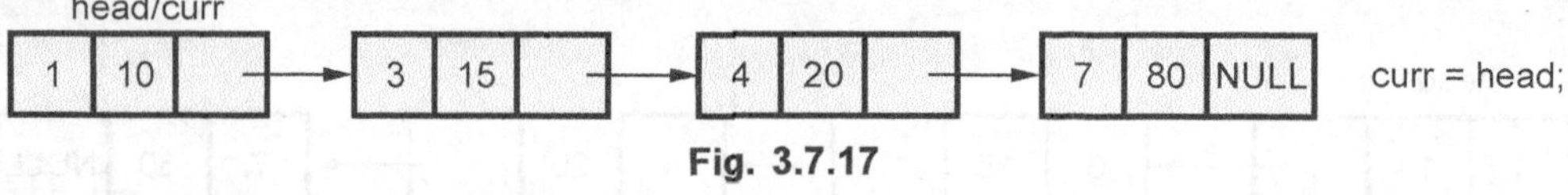

Fig. 3.7.17

Case 1 :

if (curr == NULL) i.e. if list is empty then return 0 as length of list.

Case 2 :

Otherwise initialize a variable 'count' by zero and as we traverse each node starting from 'head' node, we will increment count by 1. Hence after traversing the complete list the count variable will hold the total count of number of nodes in the list.

3.7.3 Applications of Dictionary

Following are some real-world applications of dictionary -

1. Student registration application

A record of student can be inserted, deleted or updated from the dictionary. When a new student registers for the course his/her record is inserted in the dictionary. When the students get passed out/leaves the course his/her record is deleted from the dictionary. An instructor can update the record for changing the assignment test score.

Every record in this dictionary is considered as a key value pair. For instance -

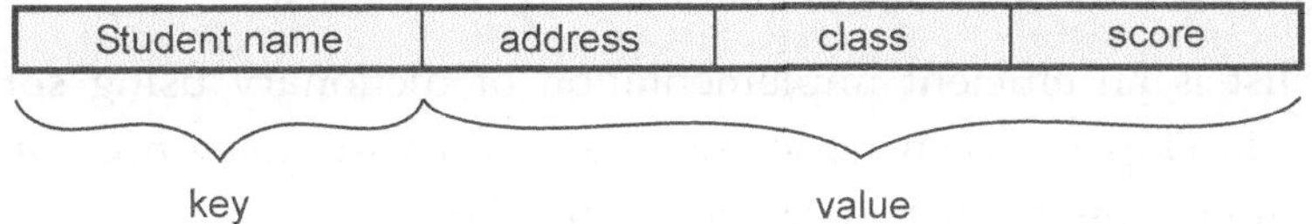

Fig. 3.7.18 Student record structure present in the dictionary

2. Telephone directory

This is an application of **dictionary with duplicates**. The dictionary with duplicates is similar to dictionary but it allows two or more pairs with same key. In the telephone directory the persons' surname acts as a **key** and his phone number, address and other information acts as **value**. These records are stored in alphabetical manner. Hence we can retrieve any desired phone number by searching the surname of corresponding person.

3. Word dictionary

This is an application of **dictionary with duplicates.** This is a typical example of dictionary data structure. The words are arranged in alphabetical manner. So spelling/meaning can be easily searched by going sequentially through a to z.

4. Symbol table used in compiler

Symbol table is a kind of buffer used in compiler for storing the identifiers and constants encountered in the source program(such as C, C++ and so on). The name of identifier acts as a **key** and the related information of identifier such as its value, scope(local/global), data type, memory address and so on acts as a **value**. Thus symbol table is a collection of key/value pairs. Compiler looks up the symbol table as soon as it encounters an identifier or a constant. If it is already defined in the symbol table then the compiler retrieves the values of corresponding identifier. If the identifier is not there in the symbol table then that corresponding entry of identifier is inserted in the symbol table.

3.8 Skip List

- Skip list is a variant list for the linked list.
- Skip lists are made up of a series of nodes connected one after the other. Each node contains a key and value pair as well as one or more references, or pointers, to nodes further along in the list.
- The number of references each node contains is determined randomly. The number of references a node contains is called its node level.

- There are two special nodes in the skip list one is **head node** which is the starting node of the list and **tail node** is the last node of the list.
- The skip list is an efficient implementation of dictionary using **sorted chain**. This is because in skip list each node consists of forward references of more than one node at a time. Following Figure shows the skip list.

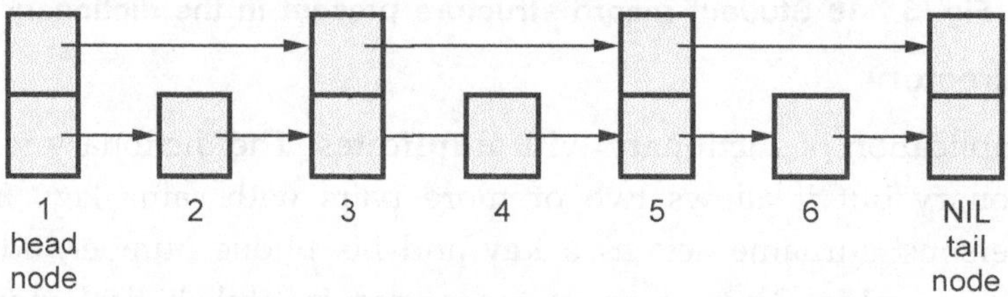

Fig. 3.8.1 Skip list

Consider a sorted chain as given below -

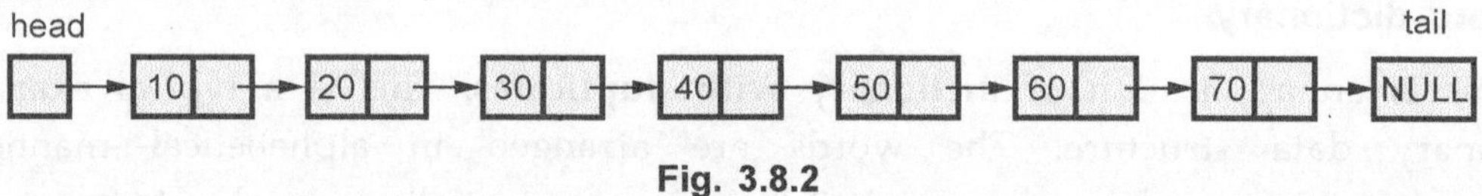

Fig. 3.8.2

Now to search any node from above given sorted chain we have to search the sorted chain from head node by visiting each node. But this searching time can be reduced if we **add one level in every alternate node**. This extra level contains the **forward pointer** of some node. That means in the sorted chain some nodes can hold pointers to more than one node. For example,

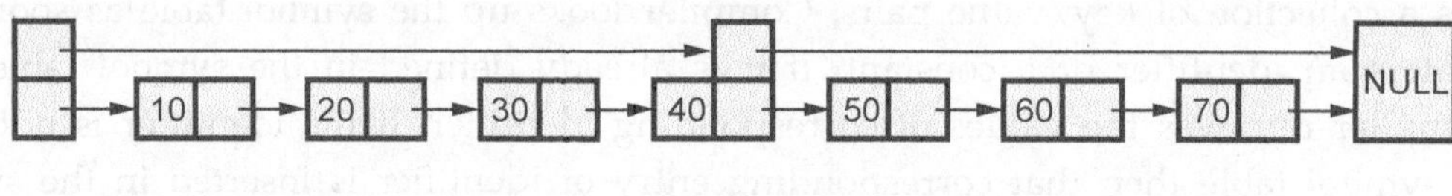

Fig. 3.8.3

If we want to search node 50 from above chain there we will require comparatively less time. This search again can be made efficient if we add few more pointers of forward references. For example,

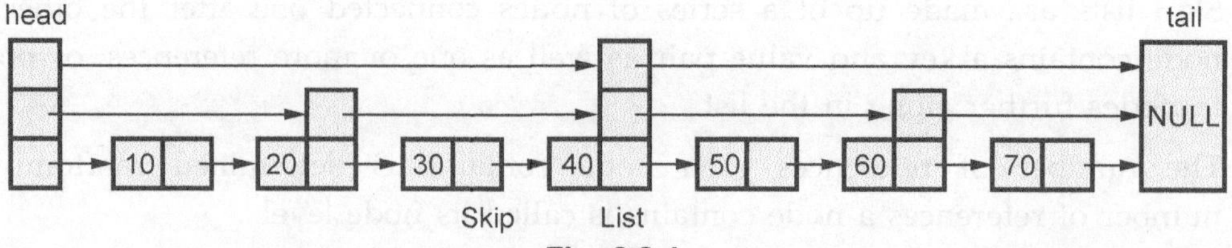

Fig. 3.8.4

In above sorted chain every second having one level of chain is added. For instance node 20 has two next chains one pointing to 30 and another pointing to node 40. This makes searching more efficient. In skip list the hierarchy of chains is maintained. The level 0 is a sorted chain of all pairs. The level i chain consists of a subset of pairs in every level i-1 chains.

Node structure of skip list

The head node contains maximum number of level chains of the skip list whereas the tail node contains simply NULL value and no pointer. Each node in the skip list consists of pair of key and value given by element and a next pointer which is basically an array of pointers.

```
template <class K, class E>
struct skipNode
{
  typedef pair<const K,E> pair_type;
  pair_type element;
  skipNode<K,E> **next;
  skipNode(const pair_type &New_pair,int MAX):element(New_pair)
 {
   next=new skipNode<K,E>*[MAX];
 }
};
```

The individual node will look like this -

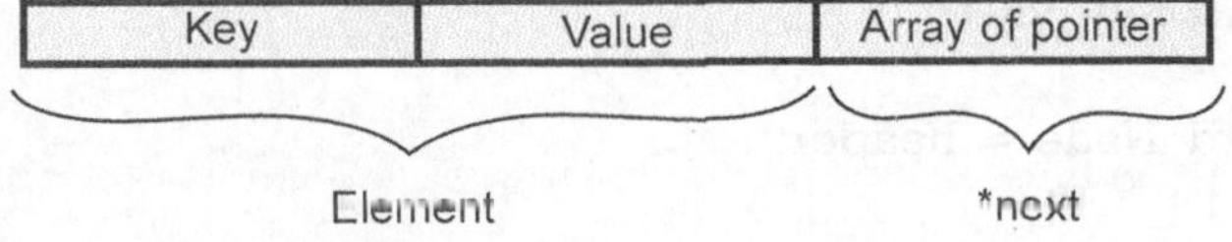

Fig. 3.8.5

3.8.1 Operations on Skip List

Various operations that can be performed on skip lists are

1. Searching a node from the skip list.
2. Insertion of a node from skip list.
3. Deletion of a node from skip list.

3.8.2 Searching of a Node

When we search for the 'key' node then follow these 3 rules -

1) If key = = current → key then the node is found.

2) If key < next → key, just go down one level.

3) If key ≥ next → key, go right along the link.

For example : Find 50 from the given skip list.

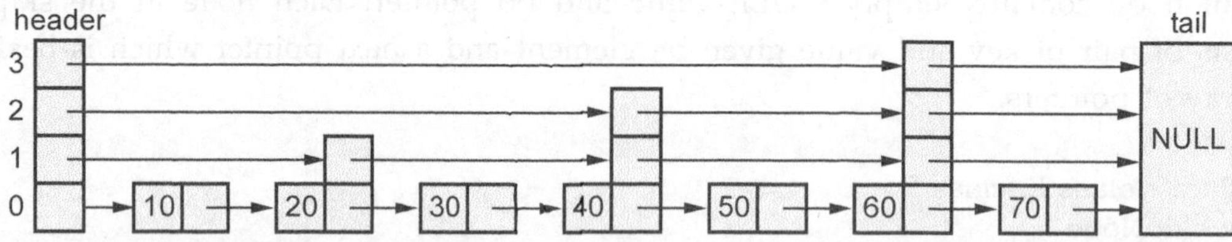

We will start search from level 3.

1) Key = 50, next → key = 60, just go down one level.

2) Now we are at level 2. Here next → key = 40 go right along the link. But this link indicates next → key = 60. Hence go down one more level.

3) Now we are at level 1. Here next → key = 60. Hence go down one more level.

4) Now we are at level 0. The next → key = key. Thus the node 50 is said to be present in the skip list.

The algorithm for the same is as given below -

```
Algorithm search(K& Key_val)
{
 skipNode  *Forward_Node = header;
  for (int i = levels; i >= 0; i--)
  {
    while (Forward_Node->next[i]->element.key < Key_val)
      Forward_Node = Forward_Node->next[i];
    last[i] = Forward_Node;
  }
  return Forward_Node->next[0];
}
```

The searching of a node takes O(logn) time.

3.8.3 Insertion of a Node

- While inserting a new node in the skip list, it is necessary to find its appropriate location in the skip lists. Note that after inserting a new node in the skip list, the sorted order need to be maintained.
- The level of the new node is determined randomly.

For example : Consider following skip list in which we want to insert 55.

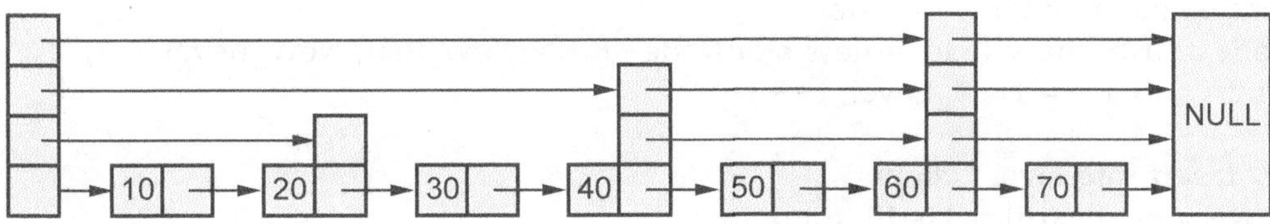

Before insertion of 55

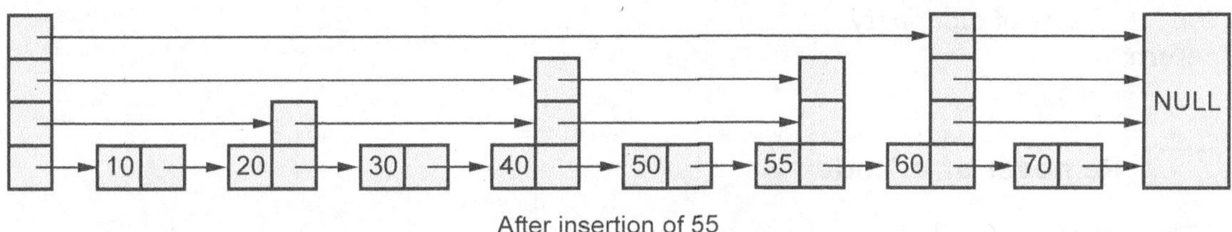

After insertion of 55

The algorithm for the same is as given below -

```
void insert(pair<K, E>& New_pair)
{// Insert New_pair in the skip list
  if (New_pair.key >= tailKey)
  {
        cout<<"Key is Too Large";
  }
  // if pair with the key value of New node
   // is already present
  skipNode<K,E>* temp = search(New_Pair.key);
  if (temp->element.key == New_Pair.key)
  {// update temp->element.value
    temp->element.value = New_pair.value;
    return;
  }

  // If the Key_val is not already present
 //then determine level for new node randomly
  int New_Level = randomlevel();
```

```
// level of retrieved for new node
  // Adjust New_Level to be <= levels + 1
  if (New_Level > levels)
  {
    New_Level = ++levels;
    last[New_Level] = header;
  }

  // get and insert new node just after node temp
//allocating memory for Newnode
skipNode<K,E> *newNode = new skipNode<K,E>(New_Pair, New_Level + 1);
  for (int i = 0; i <= New_Level; i++)
  {
     // insert into level i chain
    newNode->next[i] = last[i]->next[i];
    last[i]->next[i] = newNode;
  }
// number of pairs in the dictionary will be incremented by //1. As one node is inserted in
the dictionary
  len++; //size of dictionary
  return;
}
```

3.8.4 Removal of a Node

The deletion of a node works in two steps -

1) Search the node to be deleted from the skip list.

2) On obtaining the desired node, remove the node from the list and adjust the pointers.

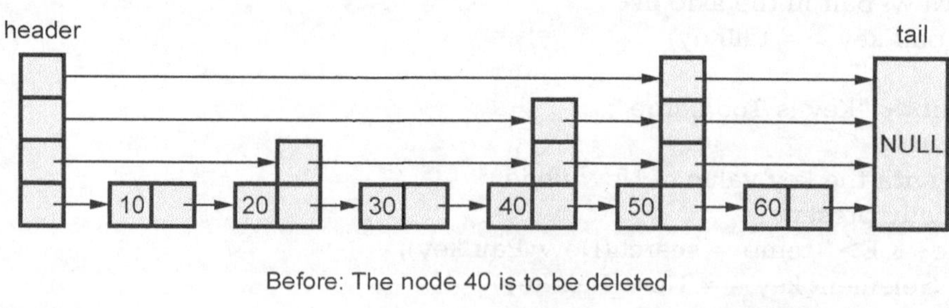

Before: The node 40 is to be deleted

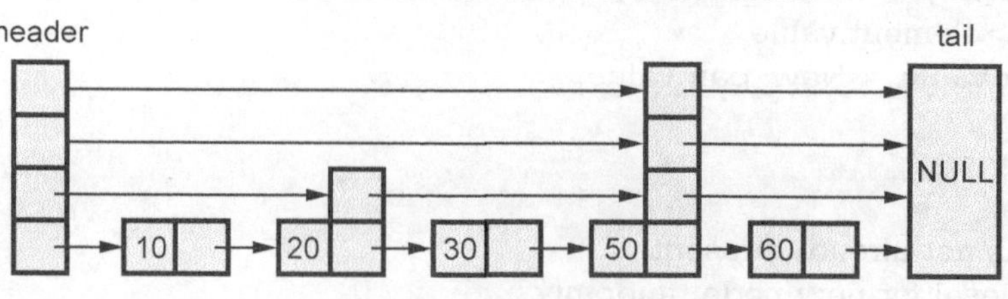

After: The node 40 is deleted

Fig. 3.8.6 Deletion operation

```
void delet(K& Key_val)
{
// Delete the pair, if any, whose key equals Key_val
  if (Key_val >= tailKey) // too large
    return;
  // see if matching pair present
  skipNode<K,E>* temp = search(Key_val);
  //temp node is to be deleted
  if (temp->element.key != Key_val) // node is not present
    return;
  // delete node from skip list
  for (int i = 0; i <= levels;i++)
  {
   if(last[i]->next[i] == temp)
     last[i]->next[i] = temp->next[i];
  }
  // update levels
  while (levels > 0 && header->next[levels] == tail)
   levels- -;
  delete temp;//free memory of the node to be deleted
    len- -;//the pair is removed from the dictionary
}
```

3.8.5 Features of Skip Lists

1) It is a randomized data structure.
2) This is a kind of linked list which works with levels.
3) It is ordered linked list which is called as sorted chain.
4) The bottommost list of the skip list contains all the nodes.
5) The expected time complexity for insertion, deletion and search operation is O(logn)

3.8.6 Comparison between Hashing and Skip Lists

Hashing	Skip List
This method is used to carry out dictionary operations using randomized processes.	Skip lists are used to implement dictionary operations using randomized processes.
It is based on hash function.	It does not require hash function.
If the sorted data is given then hashing is not an effective method to implement dictionary.	The sorted data improves the performance of skip list.

The space requirement in hashing is for hash table and a forward pointer is required per node.	The forward pointers are required for every level of skip list.
Hashing is an efficient method than skip lists.	The skip lists are not that much efficient.
Skip lists are more versatile than hash table.	Worst case space requirement is larger for skip list than hashing.

4 Search Trees

Syllabus

Symbol table - Representation of symbol tables - Static tree table and dynamic tree table, Introduction to dynamic programming, Weight balanced tree, Optimal Binary Search Tree (OBST), OBST as an example of dynamic programming, Height balanced tree - AVL tree.

Contents

4.1 Symbol Table - Representation

SPPU : Dec.-11, Marks 8

- **Definition**

The symbol table is defined as the set of **Name** and **Value** pairs.

For example

	Name	Value
0	a	10
1	b	0
2	c	0
3		
4		
5		
6		

Fig. 4.1.1 Symbol table storing 3 identifiers

- **Use of Symbol Table**

The symbol tables are typically used in **compilers**. Basically compiler is a program which scans the application program (for instance : your C program) and produces machine code. During this scan compiler stores the identifiers of that application program in the symbol table. These identifiers are stored in the form of name, value address, type. Here the name represents the name of identifier, value represents the value stored in an identifier, the address represents memory location of that identifier and type represents the data type of identifier. Thus compiler can keep track of all the identifiers with all the necessary information.

- **Types of Symbol Tables**

There are two types of symbol tables.

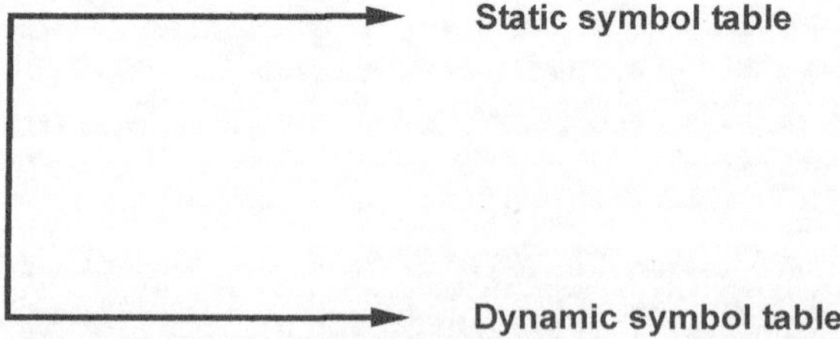

The static symbol table stores the fixed amount of information whereas dynamic symbol table stores the dynamic information.

These symbol tables are normally used to implement static and dynamic data structures. Hence there can be static tree tables or dynamic tree tables, which are implemented using static and dynamic symbol tables respectively.

Examples of static symbol table : Optimal Binary Search Tree (OBST), Huffman's coding can be implemented using static symbol table.

Example of dynamic symbol table : An AVL tree is implemented using dynamic symbol table.

- **Advantages of using Symbol Tables**

Following are some advantages of using symbol tables. As symbol table is normally used in compiler, these advantages are relevant to compilers -

1. During compilation of source program, **fast look up** for the required identifiers is possible due to use of symbol table.
2. The runtime allocation for the identifiers is managed using symbol tables.
3. Use of symbol table allows to handle certain issues like scope of identifiers, and implicit declarations.

- **Operations on Symbol Table**

Following operations can be performed on symbol table -

1. Insertion of an item in the symbol table.
2. Deletion of any item from the symbol table.
3. Searching of desired item from symbol table.

University Question

1. *What is symbol table ? What are operations on symbol table ? Give complete specification of symbol table ADT.* **SPPU : Dec.-11, Marks 8**

4.2 Static Tree Table

Symbol tables are used to store identifiers or to implement some data structures. For example binary search tree can be stored in the symbol table and when we want to search any node from binary search tree, then actually a symbol table is searched. The arrangement of nodes in binary search tree affects the searching time. Hence in order to obtain any node quickly from symbol table, we must arrange binary search tree in some specific manner. Therefore before understanding the concept of static tree we will discuss "how to arrange BST in order to have efficient search of any node?" Consider, that there are 3 nodes say A, B and C. We can draw binary search trees in 6 different ways, out of that following are two different BSTs.

From above two BSTs if we want to search a node A then, we have to compare key value A with 3 nodes, in case of Tree 1. But for Tree 2, to search node A will require 2 comparisons only. This shows that arrangement of nodes is an important factor in **searching.** It is therefore necessary to compute the **cost of a tree**. The formula for computing the cost of a tree is -

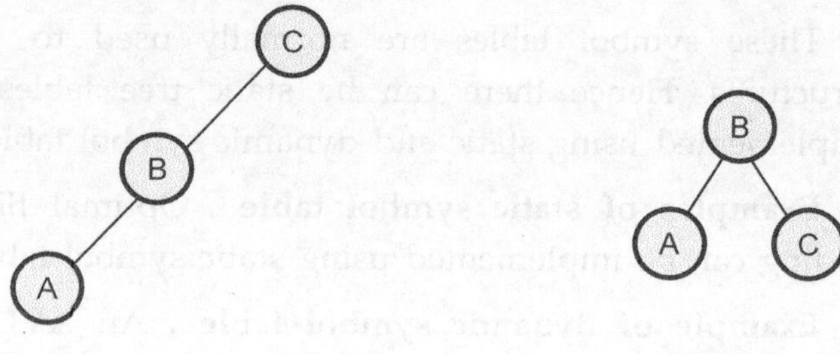

Fig. 4.2.1 Two different arrangements of BSTs for nodes A, B and C.

$$\text{Cost of a tree} = \frac{\sum(\text{Number of nodes} \times \text{Number of comparisons})}{\text{Total number of nodes present in the tree}}$$

Let us now compute the cost of above drawn two trees.

Tree 1 cost computation

Node	Number of comparisons
A	3
B	2
C	1

$$\text{Cost of tree} = \frac{\sum(\text{Number of nodes} \times \text{Comparisons made})}{\text{Total number of nodes}} = \frac{(1\times3)+(1\times2)+(1\times1)}{3}$$

Cost of Tree1 = 2

Tree 2 cost computation

Node	Number of comparisions
A, C	2
B	1

$$\text{Cost of tree} = \frac{\sum(\text{Number of nodes} \times \text{Comparisons made})}{\text{Total number of nodes}} = \frac{(2\times2)+(1\times1)}{3}$$

Cost of Tree 2 = 1.66

The above computations clearly show that the cost of second tree is less than that of first tree. That means we can search any desired node more quickly in Tree 2 than in Tree 1.

But in above searching we have considered successful searches only. In order to obtain the total cost of searching we must consider the **failure nodes**. Hence a concept of extended binary tree has come up. The **extended binary tree** is a kind of binary tree in which every null link is replaced by a special node called **failure node**.

For example

Here the square nodes are the special nodes called failure nodes.

Now we can compute the cost of a tree by considering **successful** and **unsuccessful searches**. Hence following formula is used to compute the total cost of binary tree -

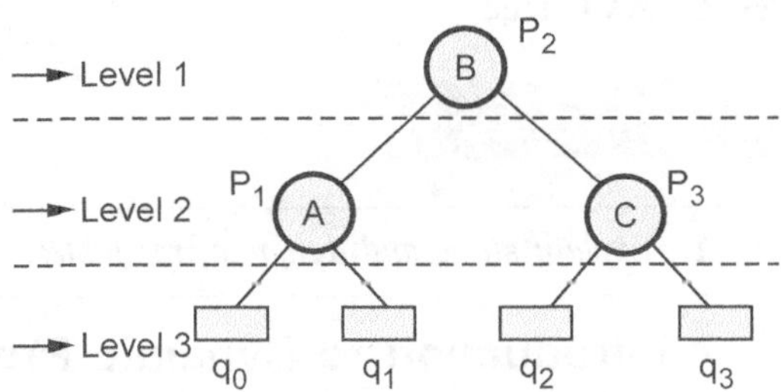

Fig. 4.2.2 Extended binary tree

$$\text{Total cost} = \left[\sum_{i=1}^{n} p_i \text{ (Level of } i^{th} \text{ node)}\right] + \left[\sum_{i=1}^{n} q_i \text{ (Level of failure node i)} - 1\right]$$

where p_i and q_i represent the probabilities of success and failure respectively.

Computing the cost of the tree in Fig. 4.2.2.

Let us assume,

$p_i = q_i = 1/7$, Here we have assumed equal probabilities.

Then,

$$\text{Total cost} = \left[\frac{1}{7}*1+\frac{1}{7}*2+\frac{1}{7}*2\right]+\left[\frac{1}{7}*2+\frac{1}{7}*2+\frac{1}{7}*2+\frac{1}{7}*2\right] = \left[\frac{1}{7}+\frac{4}{7}\right]+\left[\frac{8}{7}\right]$$

$$\text{Total cost} = \frac{13}{7}$$

Static symbol table is a symbol table in which there are fixed number of entries. There is **no insertion** and **deletion of** any entry. Only fixed set is considered for building the symbol table.

Optimal Binary Search Tree (OBST) is a data structure which is used to implement the static symbol table. In OBST there is fixed set of identifiers, from which a tree with minimum cost is built.

4.3 Dynamic Tree Table

SPPU : Dec.-10, Marks 4

Dynamic symbol table is a kind of symbol table in which entries are constantly changing. That means there can be frequent insertion and deletion operations that can be carried out on the data structure. For example if there exists a tree in which frequent insertion of nodes or frequent deletions are done then such a tree needs to change its structure more often. For implementing such a dynamic tree structure, a dynamic symbol table is used. Let us understand the concept of dynamic tree by **height-balance tree** or **AVL tree**.

University Question

1. *Explain static and dynamic tree tables.* SPPU : Dec.-10, Marks 4

4.4 Introduction to Dynamic Programming

- **Dynamic programming** is a method in which the solution to a problem is obtained by making sequence of decisions. The optimal solution to the given problem is obtained from the sequence of all possible solutions being generated.
- This technique is invented by a U.S. Mathematician Richard Bellman in 1950.
- In the word dynamic **programming** the word programming stands for **planning** and it does not mean by computer programming.
- The dynamic programming works on **principle of optimality** to solve the problems.

General method

Dynamic programming is typically applied to optimization problems.

For a given problem we may get any number of solutions. From all those solutions we seek for optimum solution (minimum value or maximum value solution). And such an optimal solution becomes the solution to the given problem.

4.4.1 Problems that can be Solved using Dynamic Programming

Various problems those can be solved using dynamic programming are,

i) For computing n^{th} Fibonacci number.

ii) Computing binomial coefficient.

iii) Warshall's algorithm.

iv) Floyd's algorithm.

v) Optimal binary search trees.

4.4.2 Principle of Optimality

The dynamic programming makes use of principle of optimality when finding solution to given problem. The principle of optimality states that "in an optimal sequence of choices or decisions, each subsequence must also be optimal."

When it is not possible to apply principle of optimality, it is almost impossible to obtain the solution using dynamic programming approach.

For example : While constructing optimal binary search tree we always select the value of k which is obtained from minimum cost. Thus it follows principle of optimality.

The Optimal Binary Search Tree (OBST) is an example of dynamic programming. We will discuss it in section 4.6.

4.5 Weight-Balance Tree

- The weight balance tree (WBT) is a binary search tree, whose balance is based on the sizes of the subtrees, in each node.
- These trees were introduced by Nievergelt and Reingold in 1970 as trees of bounded balance or BB[α] trees.
- A weight balance tree is a binary tree in which the number of nodes in the left subtree is at least half and at most twice the number of nodes in right subtree.
- The balance factor at each node = $\dfrac{\text{number of external nodes of left subtree}}{\text{total number of external nodes of tree}}$
- **Example**

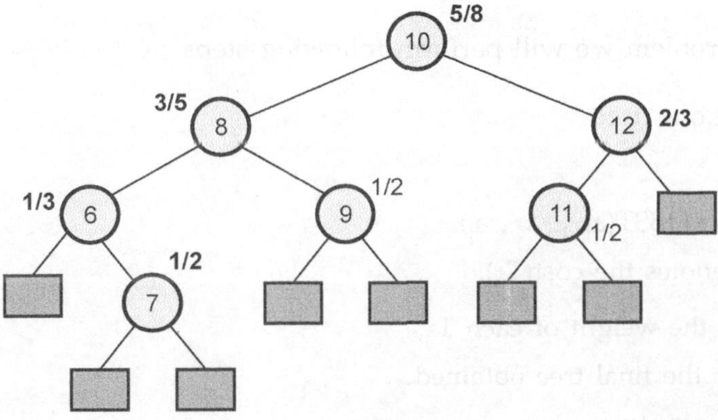

Fig. 4.5.1

- The depth of weight balance tree is O(logn).

4.6 Optimal Binary Search Tree (OBST)

SPPU : Dec.-09, 13, May-10, Marks 10

Suppose we are searching a word from a dictionary. And for every required word, we are looking in the dictionary then it becomes a time consuming process. To perform this lookup more efficiently we can build the binary search trees of common words as key elements. Again we can make this binary search tree efficient by arranging frequently used words nearer to the root and less frequently used words away from the root. Such an arrangement of binary search tree makes our task of searching the desired word more simplified, as well as efficient. Now with this approach only optimal binary search technique is invented. The element having more probability of appearance should be placed nearer to the root of binary search tree and the element which appears for least number of times, i.e. the element with lesser probability should be placed away from the root. The binary search tree created with such kind of arrangement is called Optimal Binary Search Tree (OBST). Now let us define "What is optimal binary search tree ?"

Problem Description

Let $\{a_1, a_2, \ldots a_n\}$ be a set of identifiers such that $a_1 < a_2 < a_3$. Let p(i) be the probability with which we can search for a_i and $q_{(i)}$ be the probability of searching element x such that $a_i < x < a_{i+1}$ and $0 \le i \le n$. In other words $p_{(i)}$ is the probability of successful search and q(i) be the probability of unsuccessful search. Also $\sum_{1 \le i \le n} p_{(i)} + \sum_{1 \le i \le n} q_{(i)}$ then obtain a tree with minimum cost. Such a tree with optimum cost is called **optimal binary search tree.**

To solve this problem we will perform following steps.

Step 1 : Notations used

Let,

$T_{ij} = \text{OBST}(a_{i+1}, \ldots, a_j)$

C_{ij} denotes the cost(T_{ij}).

W_{ij} is the weight of each T_{ij}.

T_{0n} is the final tree obtained.

T_{00} is empty.

$T_{i,i+1}$ is a single-node tree that has element a_{i+1}.

During the computations the root values are computed and r_{ij} stores the **root value** of T_{ij}.

Step 2 : We will apply following formula for computing each sequence.

$$C(i, j) = \min_{i< k \leq j} \{C(i, k-1) + C(k, j)\} + W(i, j)\}$$

$$W(i, j) = W[i, j-1] + p[j] + q[j];$$

$$r[i, j] = k$$

Example : Consider n = 4 and (q_1, q_2, q_3, q_4) = (do, if, int, while). The values for p's and q's are given as p(1 : 4) = (3, 3, 1, 1) and q(0 : 4) = (2, 3, 1, 1, 1). Construct the optimal binary search tree. We will apply following formulae for the computation of W, C and r.

$W_{i, i} = q_i, r_{i, i} = 0, C_{i, i} = 0$

$$W_{i, i+1} = q_i + q_{(i+1)} + p_{(i+1)}$$

$$r_{i, i+1} = i + 1$$

$$C_{i, i+1} = q_i + q_{(i+1)} + p_{(i+1)}$$

$$W_{i, j} = W_{i, j-1} + p_j + q_j$$

$$r_{i, j} = k$$

$$C_{i, j} = \min_{i< k \leq j} \{C_{(i, k-1)} + C_{k, j}\} + W_{i, j}$$

We will construct tables for values of W, C and r.

Let $i = 0$

$$W_{00} = q_0 = 2$$

When i = 1

$$W_{11} = 3$$

When i = 2

$$W_{22} = 1$$

When i = 3

$$W_{33} = 1$$

When i = 4

$$W_{44} = q_4 = 1$$

When i = 0 and j – i = 1 then

$$W_{01} = q_0 + q_1 + p_1 = 2 + 3 + 3$$

$$W_{01} = 8$$

When i =1 and j – i = 1

$$W_{12} = q_1 + q_2 + p_2 = 3 + 1 + 3$$

$$W_{12} = 7$$

When i = 2 and j – i = 1

$$W_{23} = q_2 + q_3 + p_3 = 1 + 1 + 1$$

$$W_{23} = 3$$

When i = 3 and j – i = 1

$$W_{34} = q_3 + q_4 + p_4 = 1 + 1 + 1$$

$$W_{34} = 3$$

Now, when i = 0 and j – i = 2

$$W_{ij} = W_{i,\, j-1} + p_j + q_j$$

$$W_{02} = W_{01} + p_2 + q_2 = 8 + 3 + 1$$

$$W_{02} = 12$$

When i =1 and j – i = 2

$$W_{13} = W_{12} + p_3 + q_3 = 7 + 1 + 1$$

$$W_{13} = 9$$

When i = 2 and j – i = 2 then

$$W_{24} = W_{23} + p_4 + q_4 = 3 + 1 + 1$$

$$W_{24} = 5$$

Now, when i = 0 and j – i = 3 then

$$W_{03} = W_{02} + p_3 + q_3 = 12 + 1 + 1$$

$$W_{03} = 14$$

When i = 1 and j – i = 3 then

$$W_{14} = W_{13} + q_4 + p_4 = 9 + 1 + 1$$

$$W_{14} = 11$$

When i = 0 and j – i = 4 then

$$W_{04} = W_{03} + q_4 + p_4 = 14 + 1 + 1$$

$$W_{04} = 16$$

The table for W can be represented as

j − i ↓ / i →	0	1	2	3	4
0	$W_{00} = 2$	$W_{11} = 3$	$W_{22} = 1$	$W_{33} = 1$	$W_{44} = 1$
1	$W_{01} = 8$	$W_{12} = 7$	$W_{12} = 3$	$W_{34} = 3$	
2	$W_{02} = 12$	$W_{13} = 9$	$W_{24} = 5$		
3	$W_{03} = 14$	$W_{14} = 11$			
4	$W_{04} = 16$				

We will now compute for C and r.

As $C_{i,\,i} = 0$ and $r_{i,\,i} = 0$

$C_{00} = 0 \quad C_{11} = 0 \quad C_{22} = 0 \quad C_{33} = 0 \quad C_{44} = 0$

$r_{00} = 0 \quad r_{11} = 0 \quad r_{22} = 0 \quad r_{33} = 0 \quad r_{44} = 0$

Similarly, $C_{i,\,i+1} = q_i + q_{(i+1)} + p_{(i+1)}$ and $r_{i,\,i+1} = i+1$

$\therefore$ When $i = 0$

$$C_{01} = q_0 + q_1 + p_1 = 2 + 3 + 3$$

$$C_{01} = 8$$

$$r_{01} = 1$$

When $i = 1$

$$C_{12} = q_1 + q_2 + p_2 = 3 + 1 + 3$$

$C_{12} = 7$ and $r_{12} = 2$

When $i = 2$

$$C_{23} = q_2 + q_3 + p_3 = 1 + 1 + 1$$

$C_{23} = 3$ and $r_{23} = 3$

When $i = 3$

$$C_{34} = q_3 + q_4 + p_4 = 1 + 1 + 1$$

$C_{34} = 3$ and $r_{34} = 4$

Now we will compute C_{ij} and r_{ij} for $j - 1 \geq 2$.

As $$C_{i,j} = \min_{i < k \leq j} \{C_{(i, k-1)} + C_{k, j}\} + W_{i, j}$$

Hence we will find k.

For C_{02} we have i = 0 and j = 2. Value of K will be between i and j i.e. between 0 and 2. For $r_{i, j-1}$ to $r_{i+1, j}$ i.e. for r_{01} to $r_{1, 2}$. We will compute minimum value of $C_{i\,j}$.

Let $r_{01} = 1$ and $r_{12} = 2$. Then we will assume value of k =1 and will compute C_{ij}. Similarly with k = 2 we will compute C_{ij} and will pick up minimum value of C_{ij} only.

Let us compute C_{ij} with following formula,

$$C_{ij} = C_{i, k-1} + C_{kj}$$

For **k = 1, i = 0, j = 2.**

$$C_{02} = C_{00} + C_{12} = 0 + 7$$

$$C_{02} = 7 \qquad \text{...(1)}$$

For **k = 2, i = 0, j = 2**

$$C_{02} = C_{01} + C_{22} = 8 + 0$$

$$C_{02} = 8 \qquad \text{...(2)}$$

From equations (1) and (2) we can select minimum value of C_{02} is 7. That means **k = 1** gives us minimum value of $C_{i,\,j}$.

Hence $\mathbf{r_{ij} = r_{02} = k = 1}$

Now

$$C_{02} = \min\{C_{(i,k-1)} + C_{kj}\} + W_{ij}$$

$$= 7 + W_{02}$$

$$= 7 + 12$$

$$C_{02} = 19$$

Continuing in this fashion we can compute C_{ij} and r_{ij}. It is as given below.

j − i \ i →	0	1	2	3	4
0	$C_{00} = 0$ $r_{00} = 0$	$C_{11} = 0$ $r_{11} = 0$	$C_{22} = 0$ $r_{22} = 0$	$C_{33} = 0$ $r_{33} = 0$	$C_{44} = 0$ $r_{44} = 0$
1	$C_{01} = 8$ $r_{01} = 1$	$C_{12} = 7$ $r_{12} = 2$	$C_{23} = 3$ $r_{23} = 3$	$C_{34} = 3$ $r_{34} = 4$	
2	$C_{02} = 19$ $r_{02} = 1$	$C_{13} = 12$ $r_{13} = 2$	$C_{24} = 8$ $r_{24} = 3$		
3	$C_{03} = 25$ $r_{03} = 2$	$C_{14} = 19$ $r_{14} = 2$			
4	$C_{04} = 32$ $r_{04} = 2$	} T_{04}			

Therefore T_{04} has a root r_{04}. The value of r_{04} is 2. From (a_1, a_2, a_3, a_4) = (do, if, int, while) a_2 becomes the root node. Hence root is **if**.

$$r_{ij} = k$$

$$r_{04} = 2$$

Then r_{ik-1} becomes left child and r_{kj} becomes the right child. In other words r_{01} becomes the left child and r_{24} becomes right child of r_{ij}. Here $r_{01} = 1$ so a_1 becomes left child of a_2 and $r_{24} = 3$ so a_3 becomes right child of a_2.

For the node r_{24} $i = 2$, $j = 4$ and $k = 3$. Hence left child of it is $r_{ik-1} = r_{22} = 0$. That means left child of $r_{24} = a_3$ is empty. The right child of r_{24} is $r_{34} = 4$. Hence a_4 becomes right child of a_3. Thus all $n = 4$ nodes are used to build a tree. The optimal binary search tree is

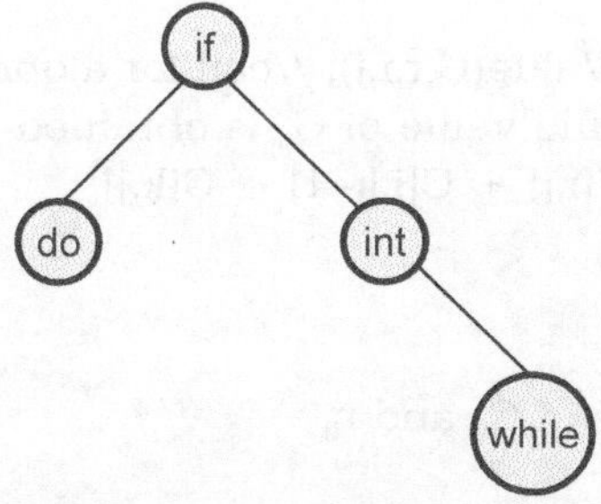

Fig. 4.6.1 OBST

4.6.1 Algorithm

```
Algorithm Wt(p,q,W,n)
//p is an input array [1..n]
//q is an input array [0..n]
// W[i,j] will be output for this function such that W[0..n,0..n]
{
  for i←1 to n do
    W[i,i] ← q[i]; // initialize
  for m←1 to n do
  {
   for I←0 to n–m do
    {
      k ← i+m;
      W[i,k]←W[i,k–1] + p[k] + q[k];
    }
  }
write(W[0:n]);//print the values of W
}
```

- For computing C_{ij}, r_{ij} following algorithm is used.

```
Algorithm OBST(p,q,W,C,r)
{
  //computation of first two rows
for i=0 to n do
{
          C[i,i] ← 0;
                r[i,i] ← 0;
               C[i,i+1] ← q[i]+q[i+1]+p[i+1];
                r[i,i+1]←i+1;
          }
          for m ← 2 to n do
          {
                for ← 0 to n–m do
                {
                      j←i+m;
                      k←Min_Value(C,r,i,j); //call for algorithm Min_Value
                      // minimum value of Cij is obtained for deciding value of k
                      C[i,j]←W[i,j] + C[i,k–1] + C[k,j];
                      r[i,j]←k;
}
}
write(C[0:n],r[0:n]);//print values of Cij and rij
}

Algorithm Min_Value(C,r,i,j)
{
      minimum← ∞;
```

```
// finding the range of k
      for (m←r[i,j–1] to r[i+1,j]) do
      {
            if(C[i,m–1]+C[m,j])< minimum then
            {
                  minimum ← C[i,m–1]+C[m,j];
                  k←m;
            }
            return k;//This k gives minimum value of C
      }
}
```

Following algorithm is used for creating the tree T_{ij}.

```
Algorithm build_tree(r,a,i,j)
{
   T ← new(node); //allocate memory for a new node
   k ← r[i,j];
   T –> data ← a[k];
   if (j==i+1)
      return;
   T–>left=build_tree(r,a,i,k–1);
   T–>right=build_tree(r,a,k,j);
}
```

In order to obtain the optimal binary search tree we will follow :

1. Compute the weight using Wt function.
2. Compute C_{ij} and r_{ij} using OBST.
3. Build the tree using build_tree function.

Example 4.6.1 *How many binary search trees(BSTs) can be constructed for given 'n' identifiers? i) Construct all possible Binary Search Trees for the identifier set* (q_1, q_2, q_3) = *(do, if, while)*

ii) Compute the total cost of each BST constructed by you assuming equal probabilities for successful and unsuccessful search i.e.

$(p_1, p_2, p_3) = (1/7, 1/7, 1/7)$ *for successful search and* $(q_0, q_1, q_2, q_3) = (1/7, 1/7, 1/7, 1/7)$ *for unsuccessful search. Which BST is an optimal binary search tree ?*

iii) Compute the total cost of each BST constructed by you assuming probabilities for successful and unsuccessful search as :

$(p_1, p_2, p_3) = (0.5, 0.1, 0.05)$ *for successful search and* $(q_0, q_1, q_2, q_3) = (0.15, 0.1, 0.05, 0.05)$ *for unsuccessful search. Which BST is an optimal binary search tree?*

SPPU : Dec.-09, Marks 10

Solution : i) All possible binary search tree for (do, if, while) are -

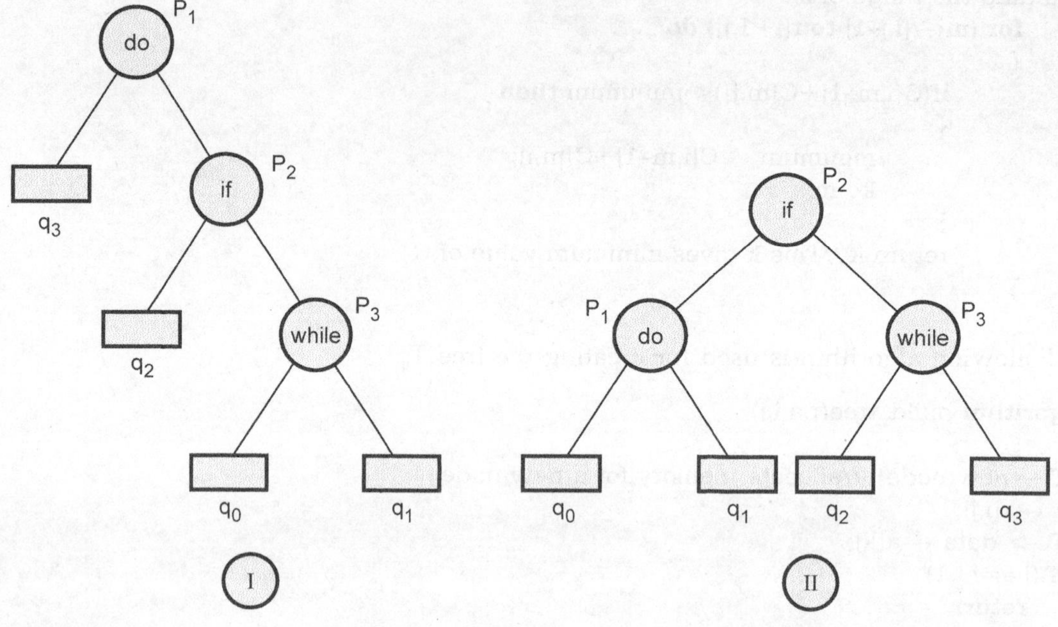
do
P1
if
P2
q3
q2
while
P3
q0
q1
I
if
P2
do
P1
while
P3
q0
q1
q2
q3
II

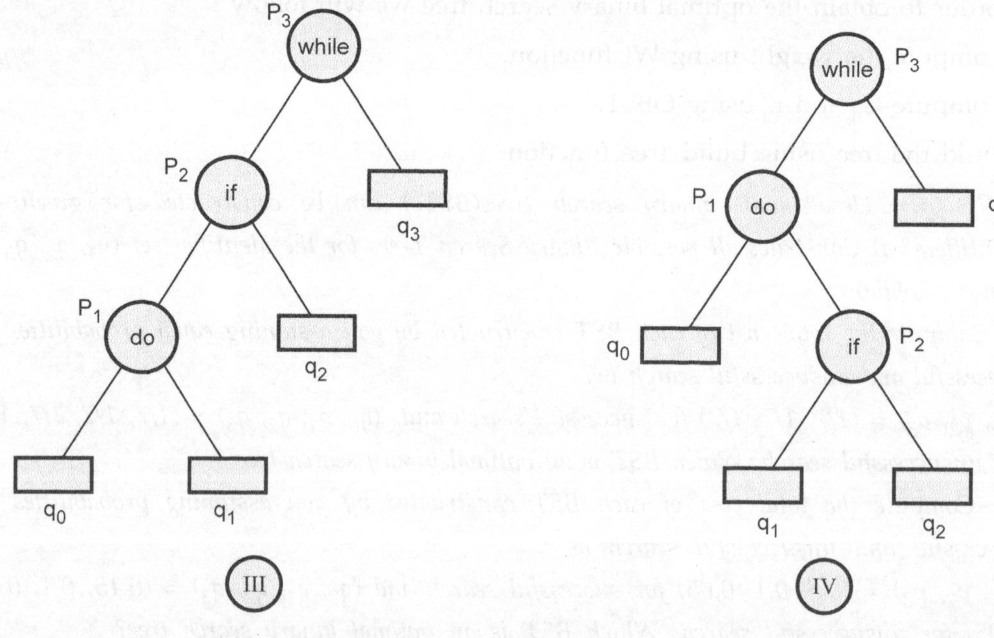
while
P3
if
P2
q3
do
P1
q2
q0
q1
III
while
P3
do
P1
q3
q0
if
P2
q1
q2
IV

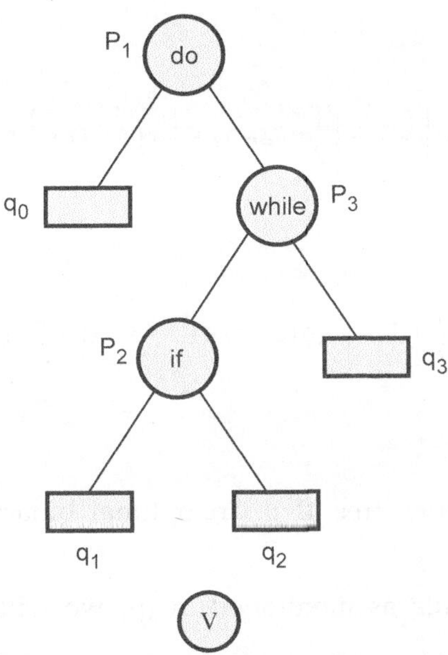

Fig. 4.6.2 All possible BSTs for 3 nodes

Thus there are 5 possible BSTs for 3 identifiers. Let a_i be a node then the cost can be computed by following formula -

ii) Cost (tree) = $\sum_{1 \le i \le n} P(i) * \text{level}(a_i) + \sum_{0 \le i \le n} q(i) * (\text{level}(E_i) - 1)$

where E_i represents the equivalence class for all the identifiers a_i.

$$\text{Cost(tree I)} = \left[\frac{1}{7} * 3 + \frac{1}{7} * 2 + \frac{1}{7} * 1\right] + \left[\frac{1}{7} * (4-1) + \frac{1}{7} * (4-1) + \frac{1}{7} * (3-1) + \frac{1}{7} * (2-1)\right] = \frac{6}{7} + \frac{9}{7}$$

successful nodes (such as do, if, while) | (unsuccessful nodes denoted by square)

Cost (tree I) = $\frac{15}{7}$

$$\text{Cost(treeII)} = \left[\left(\frac{1}{7} * 1\right) + \left(2 * \frac{1}{7} + 2 * \frac{1}{7}\right)\right] + \left[\frac{1}{7} * (3-1) + \frac{1}{7} * (3-1) + \frac{1}{7} * (3-1) + \frac{1}{7} * (3-1)\right] = \frac{5}{7} + \frac{8}{7}$$

Cost(tree II) = $\frac{13}{7}$

$$\text{Cost(tree III)} = \left[\frac{1}{7} * 1 + \frac{1}{7} * 2 + \frac{1}{7} * 3\right] + \left[\frac{1}{7} * (2-1) + \frac{1}{7} * (3-1) + \frac{1}{7} * 2 * (4-1)\right] = \frac{6}{7} + \frac{9}{7}$$

Cost (tree III) = $\frac{15}{7}$

Cost (tree IV) = $\left[\frac{1}{7}*1+\frac{1}{7}*2+\frac{1}{7}*3\right]+\left[\frac{1}{7}*(2-1)+\frac{1}{7}*(3-1)+\frac{1}{7}*(4-1)+\frac{1}{7}*(4-1)\right]=\frac{6}{7}+\frac{9}{7}$

Cost (tree IV) = $\frac{15}{7}$

Cost (tree V) = $\left[\frac{1}{7}*1+\frac{1}{7}*2+\frac{1}{7}*3\right]+\left[\frac{1}{7}*(2-1)+\frac{1}{7}*(3-1)+\frac{1}{7}*(4-1)+\frac{1}{7}*(4-1)\right]$

Cost (tree V) = $\frac{15}{7}$

From all these computations tree II is an optimal binary search tree because it has least cost.

iii) Using the same formula as mentioned in (ii) we will compute the cost of all the trees shown in Fig. 4.6.2.

Cost (tree I) = [(0.5∗ 1 + 0.1∗ 2 + 0.05∗ 3)]+[0.05∗ 1 + 0.05∗ 2 + 0.15∗ 3 + 0.1∗ 3]

= [0.5 + 0.2 + 0.15] + [0.90]

= 0.80 + 0.90

Cost(tree I) = 1.70

Cost (tree II)= $[P_2*1+P_1*2+P_3*2]+[q_0*2+q_1*2+q_2*2+q_3*2]$

= [0.1∗ 1 + 0.5∗ 2 + 0.05∗ 2]+[0.15∗ 2 + 0.1∗ 2 + 0.05∗ 2 + 0.05∗ 2]

Cost (tree II)= 1.90

Cost (tree III) = $[P_1*3+P_2*2+P_3*1]+[3*(q_0+q_1)+2*(q_2)+1*q_3]$

= [05∗3+0.1∗2+0.05∗1]+[3∗(0.15+0.1)+2∗0.05+0.05]

Cost (tree III) = 1.30

Cost (tree IV) = $[P_1*2+P_2*3+P_3*1]+[2*q_0+3*(q_1+q_2)+1*q_3]$

= [0.5∗ 2 + 0.1∗ 3 + 0.05∗ 1]+[2∗ 0.15 + 3∗(0.1 + 0.05) + 0.05]

Cost (tree IV) = 1.25

Cost (tree V) = $[P_1*1+P_2*3+P_3*2]+[1*q_0+3*q_1+3*q_2+2*q_3]$

= [0.5∗ 1 + 0.1∗ 3 + 0.05∗ 2]+[1∗ 0.15 +3∗ 0.1 ∗ 3∗ 0.05 + 2∗ 0.05]

Cost (tree V) = 1.60

All these computations show that tree IV is optimal binary search tree.

University Questions

1. *What is an optimal binary search tree ? What is its use ?* **SPPU : May-10, Marks 4**
2. *Enlist the names of static tree tables with suitable example.* **SPPU : Dec.-13, Marks 2**

4.7 Height Balance Tree(AVL)

SPPU : Dec.-05, 07, 10, 11, 12, 13, 14, May-10, 11, 12, 13, 14, Marks 10

Adelsion **Velski** and **Lendis** in 1962 introduced binary tree structure that is balanced with respect to **height of subtrees**. The tree can be made balanced and because of this retrieval of any node can be done in **O(logn) times,** where n is total number of nodes. From the name of these scientists the tree is called **AVL tree**.

Definition

An empty tree is height balanced if T is a non empty binary tree with T_L and T_R as its left and right subtrees. The T is height balanced if and only if

i) T_L and T_R are height balanced.

ii) $h_L - h_R <= 1$ where h_L and h_R are heights of T_L and T_R.

The idea of balancing a tree is obtained by calculating the balance factor of a tree.

Definition of Balance Factor

The balance factor BF(T) of a node in binary tree is defined to be $\mathbf{h_L - h_R}$ where h_L and h_R are heights of left and right subtrees of T.

For any node in AVL tree the balance factor i.e. BF(T) is **–1, 0 or +1.**

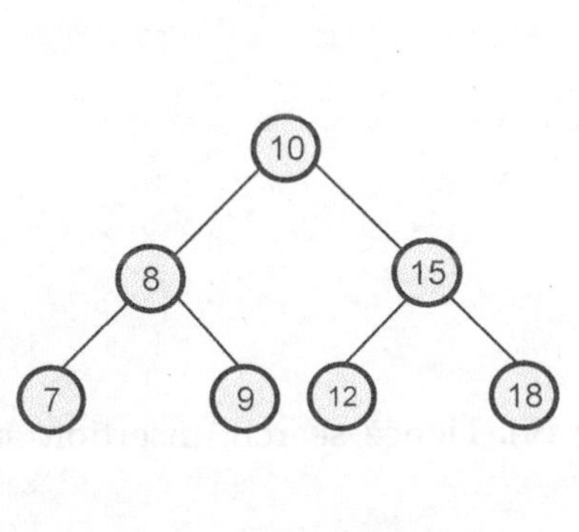

Fig. 4.7.1 AVL tree

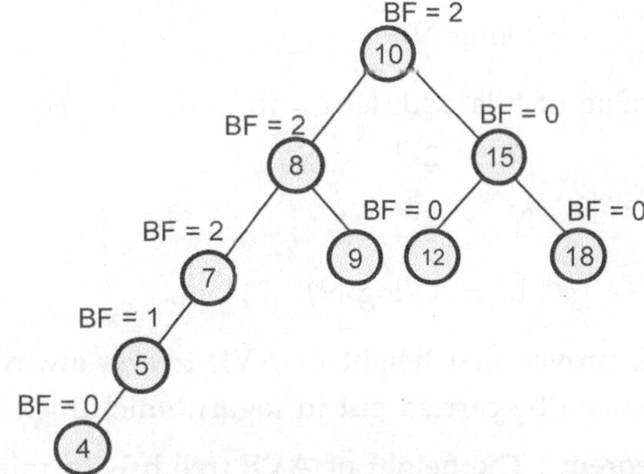

Fig. 4.7.2 Not an AVL tree

4.7.1 Height of AVL Tree

Theorem : The height of AVL tree with n elements (nodes) is O(logN).

Proof : Let an AVL tree with N nodes in it. N_h be the minimum number of nodes in an AVL tree of height h.

In worst case, one subtree may have height h–1 and other subtree may have height h–2. And both these subtrees are AVL trees. Since for every node in AVL tree the height of left and right subtrees differ by at most 1. Hence,

$$N_h = N_{h-1} + N_{h-2} + 1$$

where N_h denotes the minimum number of nodes in an AVL tree of height h.

$\therefore \quad N_0 = 0 \qquad N_1 = 2$

We can also write it as

$$\begin{aligned} N > N_h &= N_{h-1} + N_{h-2} + 1 \\ &> 2N_{h-2} \\ &> 4N_{h-4} \\ &\vdots \\ &> 2^i N_{h-2i} \end{aligned}$$

If value of h is even, let $i = \frac{h}{2-1}$

Then equation becomes,

$$N > 2^{h/2-1} N_2$$

$$= N > 2^{h/2-1} \times 4 \quad \because N_2 = 4$$

$$= O(\log N)$$

If value of h is odd, let i = (h – 1)/2 then equation becomes.

$$N > 2^{(h-1)/2} N_1$$

$$N > 2^{(h-1)/2} \times 1 \quad \because N_1 = 1$$

$$\therefore \quad h = O(\log N)$$

This proves that height of AVL tree is always O(log N). Hence search, insertion and deletion can be carried out in logarithmic time.

Theorem : The height of AVL tree h with minimum number of nodes n is 1.44 logn.

Proof : Let F_h be the AVL tree with height h having minimum number of nodes. The tree can be shown as below.

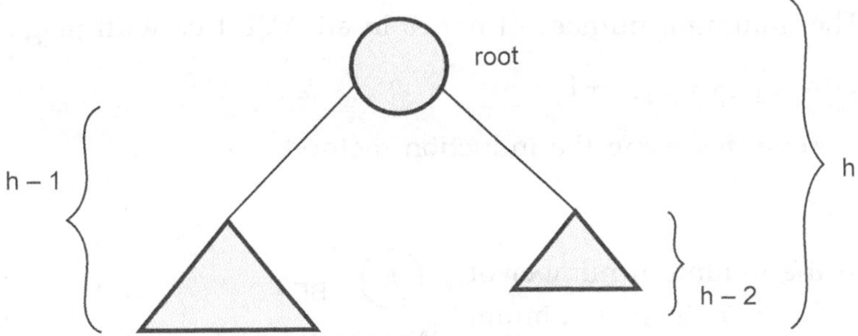

Fig. 4.7.3 AVL tree F_h

Hence minimum number of nodes in AVL tree is

$$= \text{Length of left subtree} + \text{Length of right subtree} + 1$$

$$|F_h| = |F_{h-1}| + |F_{h-2}| + 1$$

Also $|F_0| = 1$ and $|F_1| = 2$

This denotes the Fibonacci tree.

Adding 1 to both sides.

$$|F_h| + 1 = (|F_{h-1}| + 1) + (|F_{h-2}| + 1)$$

Thus the numbers $|F_h| + 1$ are Fibonacci numbers. Using approximate formula for Fibonacci numbers, we will get an approximate value as :

$$|F_h| + 1 \approx \frac{1}{\sqrt{5}} \left(\frac{1+\sqrt{5}}{2} \right)^{h+3}$$

Taking logarithm

$$= h \approx 1.44 \log |F_h|$$

Hence the worst case height of an AVL tree with n nodes is 1.44 log n.

The Fibonacci trees are as shown below.

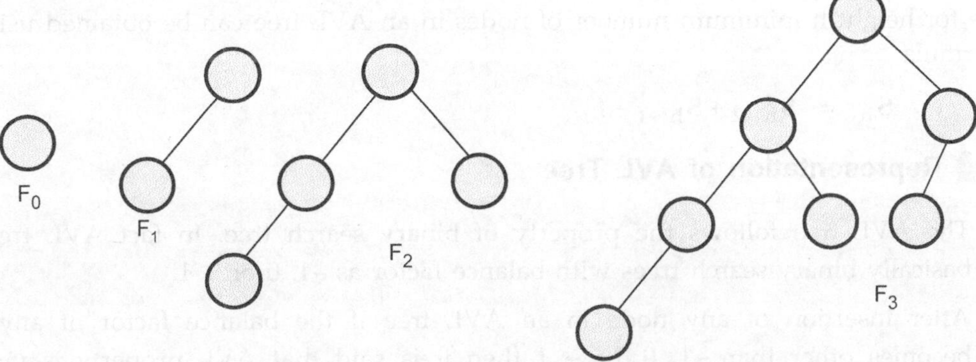

Fig. 4.7.4

Theorem : The minimum number of nodes in an AVL tree with height h is

$$S_h = S_{h-2} + S_{h-1} + 1$$

Proof : We can prove this using the induction method.

Basis of induction

If **h = 0** then the minimum number of nodes is 1. If **h = 1** then minimum number of nodes are **2**.

Fig. 4.7.5 AVL trees

This proves that

$$S_h = S_{h-2} + S_{h-1} + 1$$

Induction Hypothesis :

We assume that $S_m = S_{m-2} + S_{m-1} + 1$ is true.

Induction step : Now consider that we can obtain minimum number of nodes for an AVL tree with height k + 1, using following formula

$$S_{k+1} = S_{k+1-2} + S_{k+1-1} + 1$$

$$S_{k+1} = S_{k-1} + S_k + 1 \quad \text{... (1)}$$

If we assume m = k + 1 then equation (1) becomes

$$S_m = S_{m-2} + S_{m-1} + 1$$

This statement is true ∵ Induction hypothesis.

Hence

$$S_{k+1} = S_{k-1} + S_k + 1 \text{ is also true.}$$

Thus it is true that

$$S_k = S_{k-2} + S_k + 1$$

Hence for height h minimum number of nodes in an AVL tree can be obtained using the formula

$$S_h = S_{h-2} + S_{h-1} + 1$$

4.7.2 Representation of AVL Tree

- The AVL tree follows the property of binary search tree. In fact AVL trees are basically binary search trees with balance factor as –1, 0 or + 1.
- After insertion of any node in an AVL tree if the balance factor of any node becomes other than –1, 0, or + 1 then it is said that AVL property is violated.

Then we have to restore the destroyed balance condition. The balance factor is denoted at right top corner inside the node.

For example :

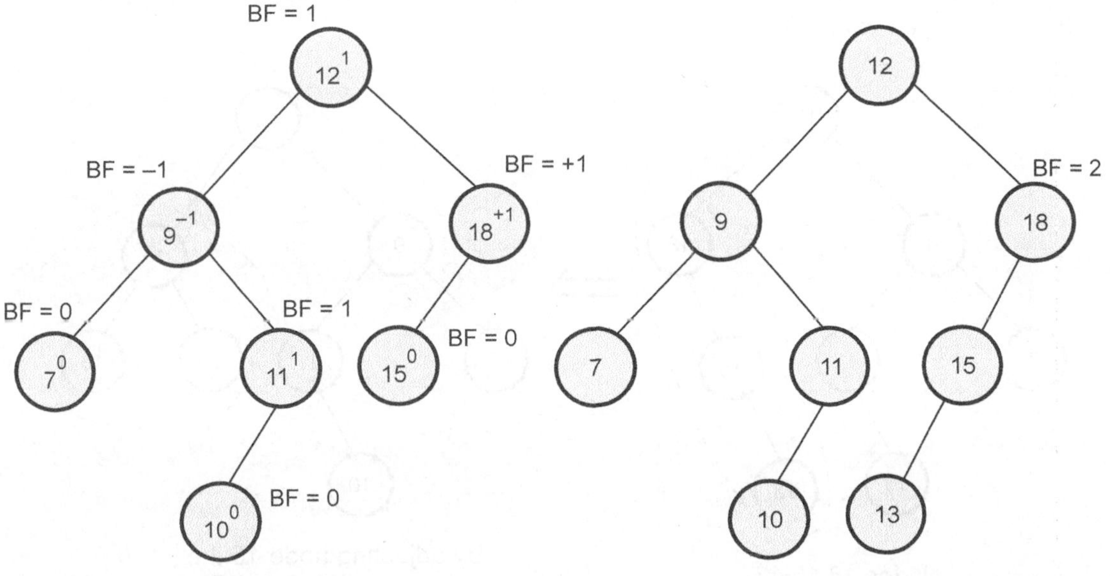

Original AVL tree

Insert 13 property violated

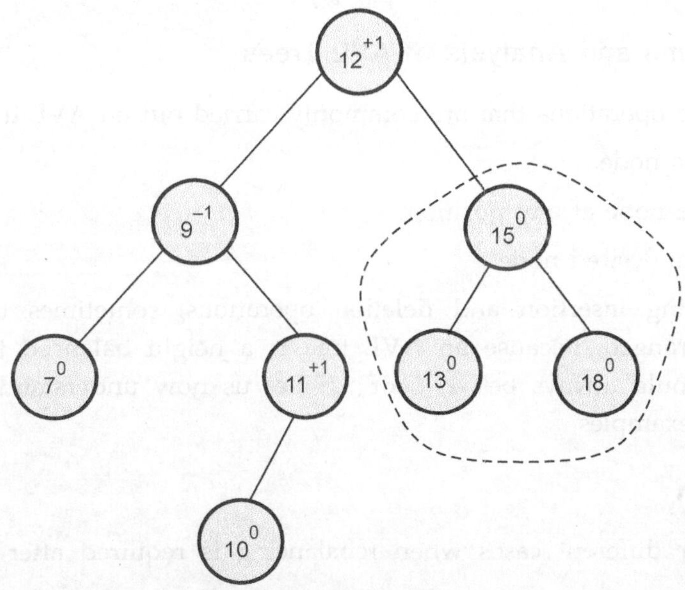

Restore AVL property

Fig. 4.7.6 Restoring AVL property

- After an insertion of a new node if balance condition gets destroyed, then the nodes on that path (new node insertion point to root) needs to be readjusted. That means only the affected subtree is to be rebalanced.
- The rebalancing should be such that entire tree should satisfy AVL property.

In above given example -

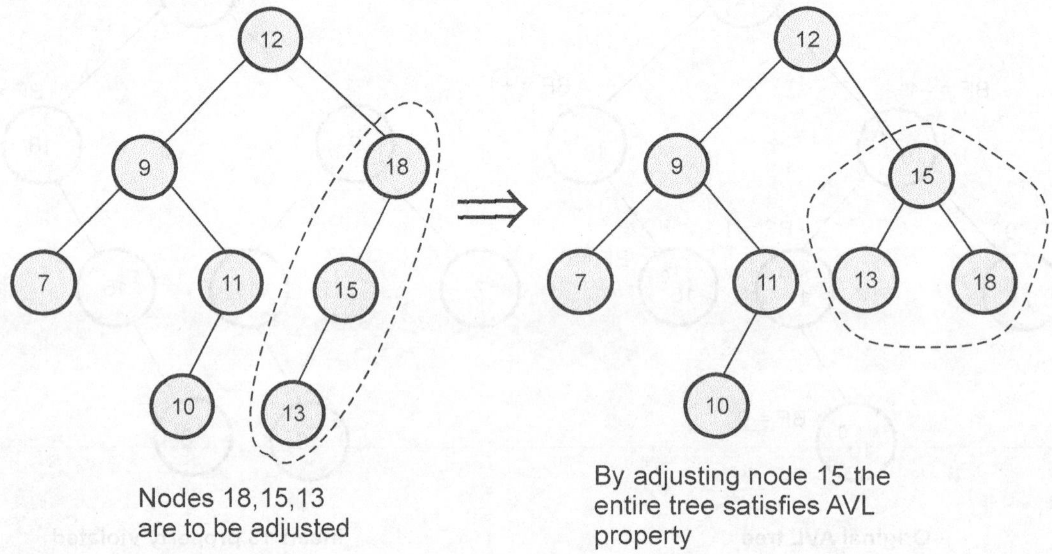

Fig. 4.7.7

4.7.3 Algorithms and Analysis of AVL Trees

There are three operations that are commonly carried out on AVL tree. And those are

1. Insertion of a node.
2. Deletion of a node at any position.
3. Searching the desired node.

After performing insertion and deletion operations, sometimes the tree structure needs to be rearranged, because an AVL tree is a height balanced tree in which the balance factor should always be –1, 0 or +1. Let us now understand these operations with the help of examples.

4.7.4 Insertion

There are four different cases when rebalancing is required after insertion of new node.

1. An insertion of new node into left subtree of left child (LL).
2. An insertion of new node into right subtree of left child (LR).

3. An insertion of new node into left subtree of right child (RL).
4. An insertion of new node into right subtree of right child (RR).

There is a symmetry between case 1 and 4. Similarly symmetry exists between case 2 and 3.

Some modifications done on AVL tree in order to rebalance it is called rotations of AVL tree.

There are two types of rotations.

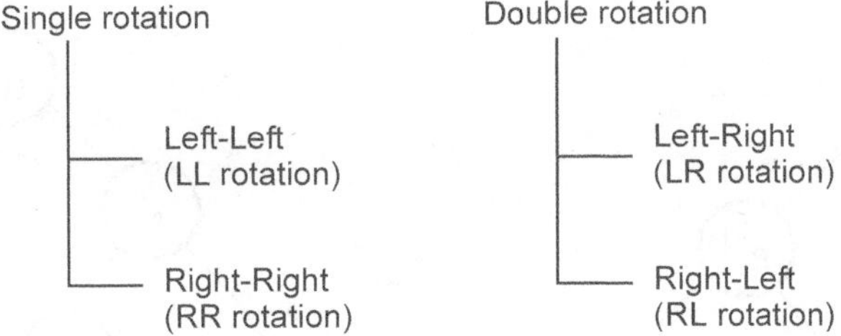

Insertion algorithm

1. Insert a new node as new leaf just as in ordinary binary search tree.
2. Now trace the path from insertion point (new node inserted as leaf) towards root. For each node 'n' encountered, check if heights of left (n) and right (n) differ by at most 1.
   a) If yes, move towards parent (n).
   b) Otherwise restructure by doing either a single rotation or a double rotation.

Thus once we perform a rotation at node 'n' we do not require to perform any rotation at any ancestor on 'n'.

Different rotations in AVL tree

1. LL rotation

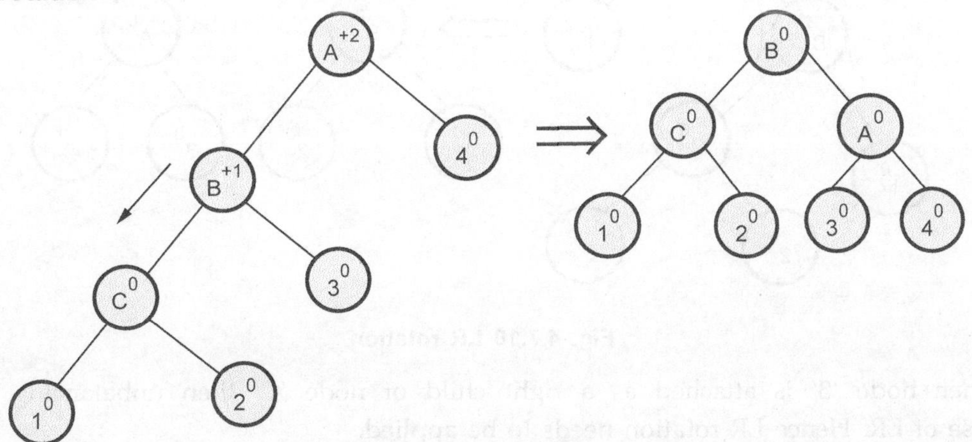

Fig. 4.7.8 LL rotation

When node '1' gets inserted as a left child of node 'C' then AVL property gets destroyed i.e. node A has balance factor + 2.

The LL rotation has to be applied to rebalance the nodes.

2. RR rotation

When node '4' gets attached as right child of node 'C' then node 'A' gets unbalanced. The rotation which needs to be applied is RR rotation as shown in Fig. 4.7.9

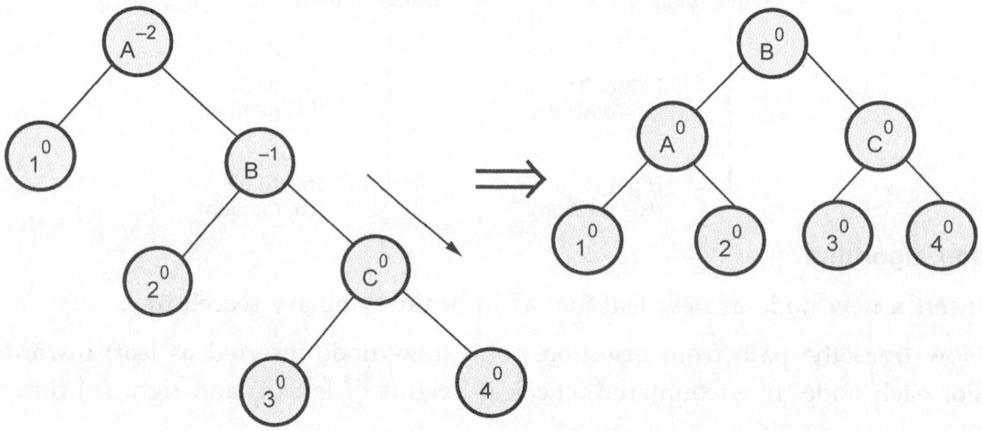

Fig. 4.7.9 RR rotation

3. LR rotation

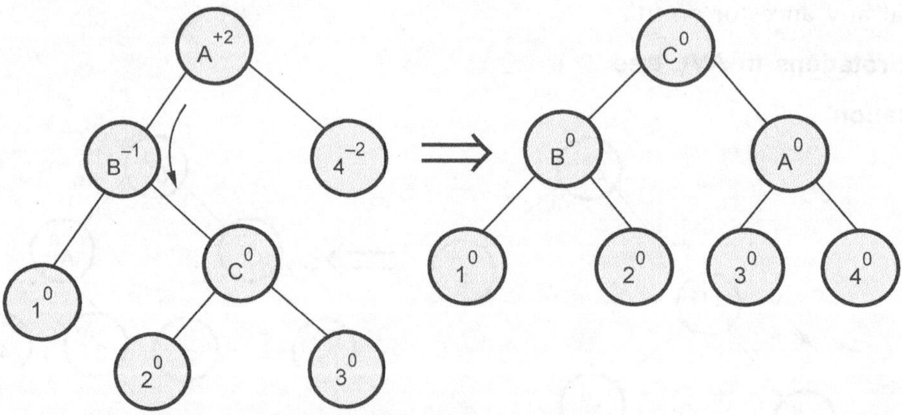

Fig. 4.7.10 LR rotation

When node '3' is attached as a right child of node 'C' then unbalancing occurs because of LR. Hence LR rotation needs to be applied.

4. RL rotation

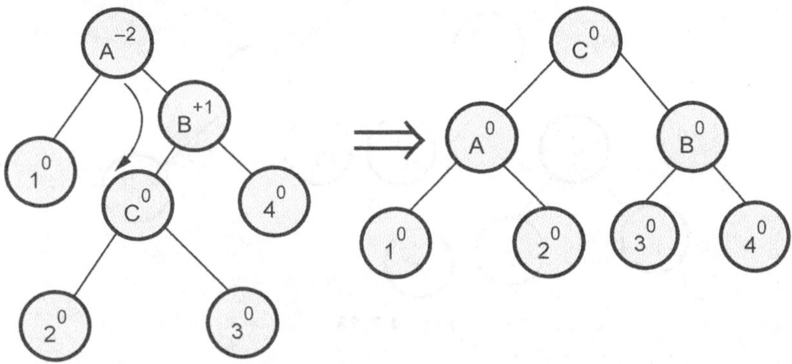

Fig. 4.7.11 RL rotation

When node '2' is attached as a left child of node 'C' then node 'A' gets unbalanced as its balance factor becomes – 2. Then RL rotation needs to be applied to rebalance the AVL tree.

Example 4.7.1 *Consider an AVL tree as given below.*
to insert 1, 25, 28, 12 in this tree.

Solution :

Insert 1

To insert node '1' we have to attach it as a left child of '2'. This will unbalance the tree as follows. We will apply LL rotation to preserve AVL property of it.

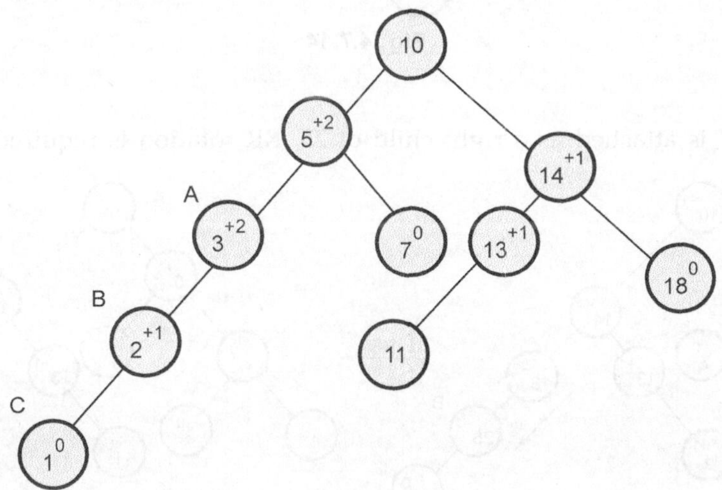

Fig. 4.7.12

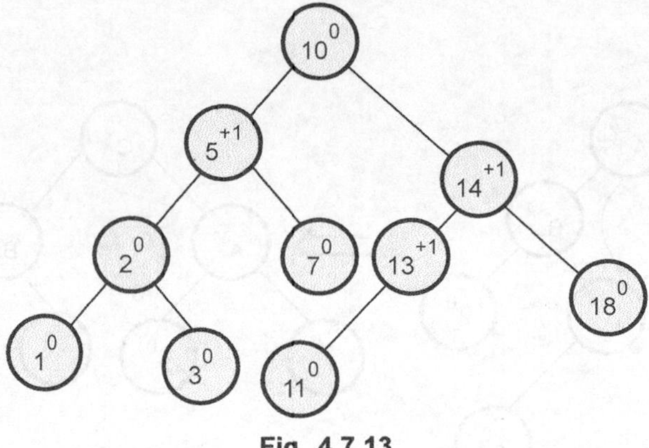

Fig. 4.7.13

Insert 25

We will attach 25 as a right child of 18. No balancing is required as entire tree preserves the AVL property.

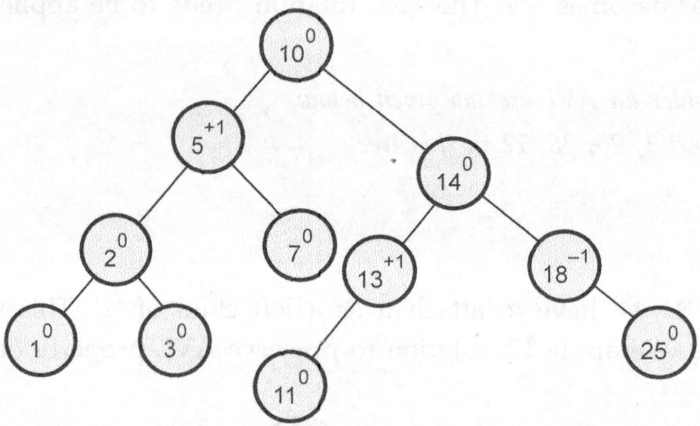

Fig. 4.7.14

Insert 28

The node '28' is attached as a right child of 25. RR rotation is required to rebalance.

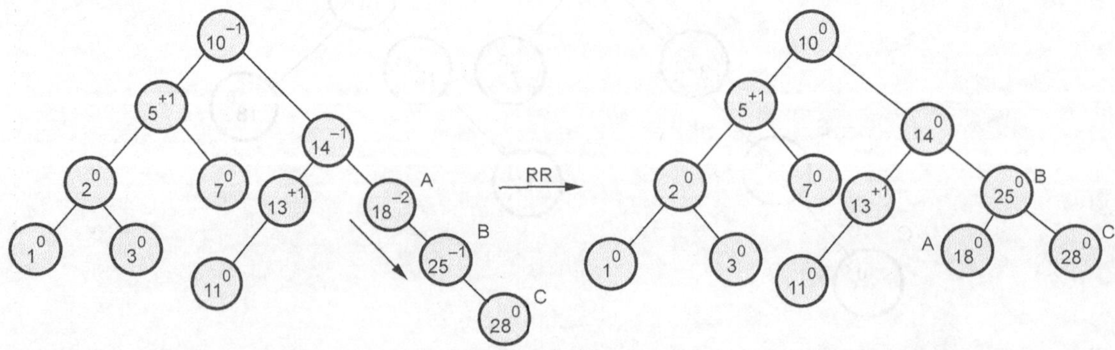

Fig. 4.7.15

Now we will insert 12.

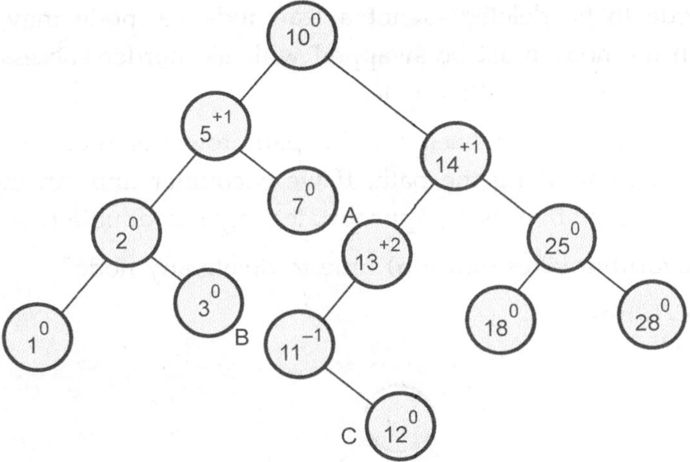

Fig. 4.7.16

To rebalance the tree we have to apply LR rotation

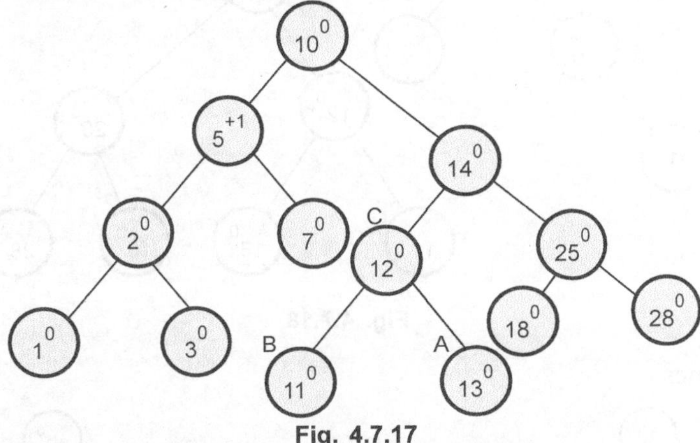

Fig. 4.7.17

Thus by applying various rotations depending upon direction of insertion of new node the AVL tree can be restructured.

4.7.5 Deletion

Even after deletion of any particular node from AVL tree, the tree has to be restructured in order to preserve AVL property. And thereby various rotations need to be applied.

Algorithm for deletion

The deletion algorithm is more complex than insertion algorithm.

1. Search the node which is to be deleted.

2. a) If the node to be deleted is a leaf node then simply make it NULL to remove.

   b) If the node to be deleted is not a leaf node i.e. node may have one or two children, then the node must be swapped with its inorder successor. Once the node is swapped, we can remove this node.

3. Now we have to traverse back up the path towards root, checking the balance factor of every node along the path. If we encounter unbalancing in some subtree then balance that subtree using appropriate single or double rotations.

The deletion algorithm takes **O(log n)** time to delete any node.

Consider an AVL tree.

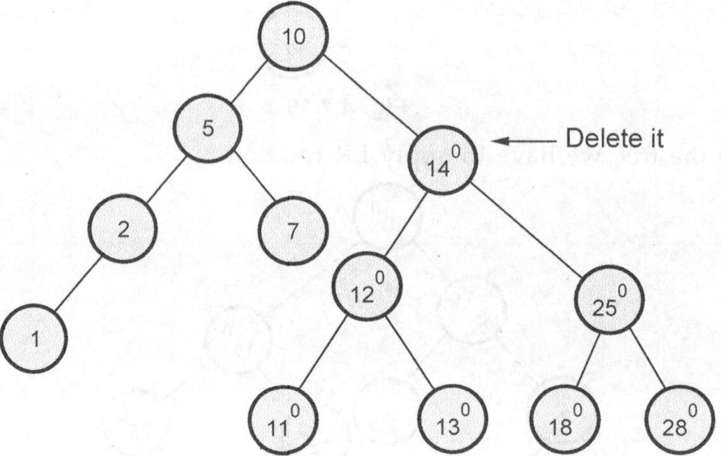

Fig. 4.7.18

The tree becomes

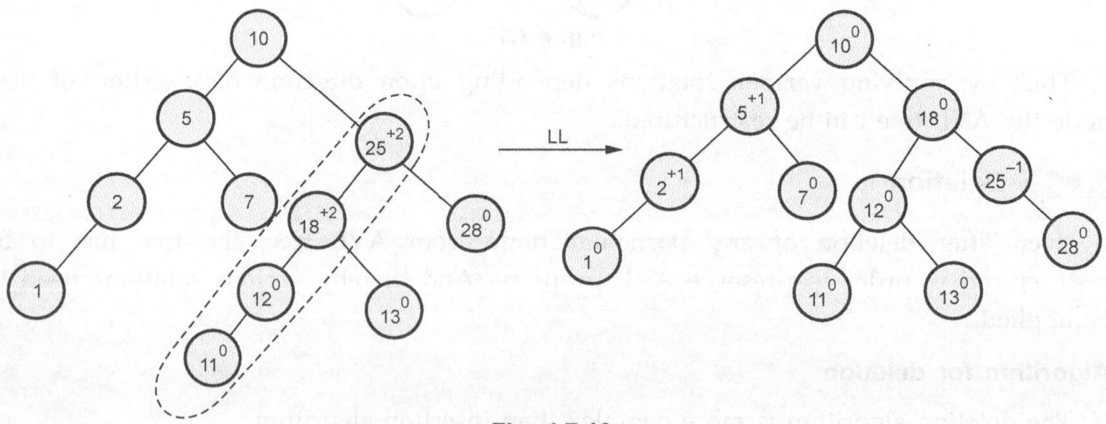

Fig. 4.7.19

Thus the node 14 gets deleted from AVL tree.

4.7.6 Searching

The searching of a node in an AVL tree is very simple. As AVL tree is basically binary search tree, the algorithm used for searching a node from binary search tree is used for searching a node from AVL tree.

Algorithm for searching

1. Consider the node to be searched as **'Key'** node.
2. Compare **key** with **root** node. If key < root then go to the left node and call this left node as current node. If key > root then go to the right node and call this right node as current node otherwise the desired node is the root node.
3. Compare **key** with **current** node. If key < current node then go to left node and call this left node as current node. If key > current node then go to right node and call this right node as current node. Otherwise if key = current node then desired node is present in an AVL tree. Thus repeat step 3 until the desired node is found or visiting the entire tree is not over.

For example :

Consider an AVL tree as given below -

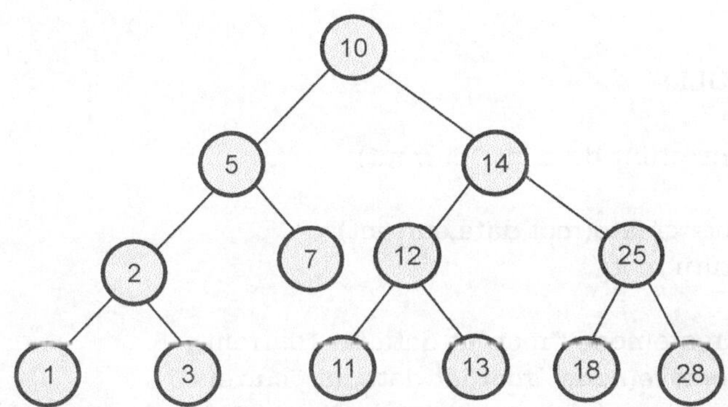

Now if we want to search for node 18 then we will follow the following steps -

1. Compare 18 with root node 10. As 18 > 10 we will move on right sub-branch.
2. Compare 18 with 14. As 18 > 14, we will move on right sub-branch.
3. Compare 18 with 25. As 18 < 25, we will move on left sub-branch.
4. Compare 18 with 18. As the match is found, we will declare that "the desired node is present in an AVL tree."

The searching of a node from AVL tree takes **O(logn)** time.

4.7.7 AVL Tree Implementation

C++ Program

```
#include<iostream.h>
#include<stdlib.h>
#define FALSE 0
#define TRUE 1

//Tree node


        typedef struct Node
                {
                        int data;
                        int BF;
                        struct Node *left;
                        struct Node *right;
                }node;

class AVL
{
        node *root;
        public:
                AVL()
                {
                root=NULL;
                }
                node *insert(int data,int *current)
                {
                        root=create(root,data,current);
                        return root;
                }
                node *create(node *root,int data,int *current);
                node *remove(node *root,int data,int *current);
                node *find_succ(node *temp,node *root,int *current);
                node *right_rotation(node *root,int *current);
                node *left_rotation(node *root,int *current);
                void display(node *root);
};
node *AVL::create(struct Node *root,int data,int *current)
{
 node *temp1,*temp2;
 if(root==NULL)//initial node
 {
        root= new node;
        root->data=data;
        root->left=NULL;
```

```
        root->right=NULL;
        root->BF=0;
        *current=TRUE;
        return(root);
}
if(data<root->data)
{
        root->left=create(root->left,data,current);
        // adjusting left subtree
        if(*current)
        {
         switch(root->BF)
         {
                case 1:temp1=root->left;
                                if(temp1->BF==1)
                                {
                                        cout<<"\n single rotation: LL rotation";
                                        root->left=temp1->right;
                                        temp1->right=root;
                                        root->BF=0;
                                        root=temp1;
                                }
                                else
                                {
                                        cout<<"\n Double roation:LR rotation";
                                        temp2=temp1->right;
                                        temp1->right=temp2->left;
                                        temp2->left=temp1;
                                        root->left=temp2->right;
                                        temp2->right=root;
                                        if(temp2->BF==1)
                                         root->BF=-1;
                                        else
                                         root->BF=0;
                                        if(temp2->BF==-1)
                                         temp1->BF=1;
                                        else
                                         temp1->BF=0;
                                        root=temp2;
                                }
                                root->BF=0;
                                *current=FALSE;
                                break;
                case 0:
                                root->BF=1;
                                break;
                case -1:
```

```
                        root->BF=0;
                        *current=FALSE;
    }
  }
}
if(data> root->data)
{
 root->right=create(root->right,data,current);
 //adjusting the right subtree
 if(*current!=NULL)
 {
    switch(root->BF)
    {
     case 1:
                        root->BF=0;
                        *current=FALSE;
                        break;
     case 0:
                        root->BF=-1;
                        break;
     case -1:
                        temp1=root->right;
                        if(temp1->BF==-1)
                        {
                            cout<<"\n single rotation:RR rotation";
                            root->right=temp1->left;
                            temp1->left=root;
                            root->BF=0;
                            root=temp1;
                        }
                        else
                        {
                            cout<<"\n Double rotation:RL rotation";
                            temp2=temp1->left;
                            temp1->left=temp2->right;
                            temp2->right=temp1;
                            root->right=temp2->left;
                            temp2->left=root;
                            if(temp2->BF==-1)
                             root->BF=1;
                            else
                             root->BF=0;
                            if(temp2->BF==1)
                             temp1->BF=-1;
                            else
                             temp1->BF=0;
                            root=temp2;
```

```
                                    }
                                    root->BF=0;
                                    *current=FALSE;
                        }
                  }
            }
            return(root);
}
/*

            Display of Tree in inorder fashion
*/
void AVL::display(node *root)
{
 if(root!=NULL)
 {
      display(root->left);
      cout<<root->data<<"  ";
      display(root->right);
 }
}
/*

 Deletion of desired node the tree

*/
node *AVL::remove(node *root,int data,int *current)
{
 node *temp;
 if(root->data==13)
      cout<<root->data;
 if(root==NULL)
 {
      cout<<"\n No such data";
      return (root);
 }
 else
 {
      if(data<root->data)
      {
       root->left=remove(root->left,data,current);
       if(*current)
            root=right_rotation(root,current);
      }
      else
      {
       if(data>root->data)
```

```
        {
                root->right=remove(root->right,data,current);
                if(*current)
                 root=left_rotation(root,current);
        }
        else
        {
                temp=root;
                if(temp->right==NULL)
                {
                 root=temp->left;
                 *current=TRUE;
                 delete(temp);
                }
                else
                {
                 if(temp->left==NULL)
                 {
                        root=temp->right;
                        *current=TRUE;
                        delete(temp);
                 }
                 else
                 {
                        temp->right=find_succ(temp->right,temp,current);
                        if(*current)
                         root=left_rotation(root,current);
                 }
                }
        }
       }
 }
 return (root);
}
node *AVL::find_succ(node *succ,node *temp,int *current)
{
 node *temp1=succ;
 if(succ->left!=NULL)
 {
       succ->left=find_succ(succ->left,temp,current);
       if(*current)
        succ=right_rotation(succ,current);
 }
 else
 {
       temp1=succ;
       temp->data=succ->data;
```

```
        succc=succ->right;
        delete temp1;
        *current=TRUE;
 }
 return (succ);
}
node *AVL::right_rotation(node *root,int *current)
{
 node *temp1,*temp2;
 switch(root->BF)
 {
        case 1:
                                root->BF=0;
                                break;
        case 0:
                                root->BF=-1;
                                *current=FALSE;
                                break;
        case -1:
                                temp1=root->right;
                                if(temp1->BF<=0)
                                {
                                        cout<<"\n single rotation: RR rotation";
                                        root->right=temp1->left;
                                        temp1->left=root;

                                        if(temp1->BF==0)
                                        {
                                         root->BF=-1;
                                         temp1->BF=1;
                                         *current=FALSE;
                                        }
                                        else
                                        {
                                         root->BF=temp1->BF=0;
                                        }
                                        root=temp1;
                                }
                                else
                                {
                                 cout<<"\n Double Rotation:RL rotation";
                                 temp2=temp1->left;
                                 temp1->left=temp2->right;
                                 temp2->right=temp1;
                                 root->right=temp2->left;
                                 temp2->left=root;
```

```
                        if(temp2->BF==-1)
                            root->BF=1;
                        else
                            root->BF=0;
                        if(temp2->BF==1)
                            temp1->BF=-1;
                        else
                            temp1->BF=0;
                        root=temp2;
                        temp2->BF=0;
                    }
            }
            return (root);
    }
node* AVL::left_rotation(node *root,int *current)
{
 node *temp1,*temp2;
 switch(root->BF)
 {
    case -1:
                            root->BF=0;
                            break;
    case 0:
                            root->BF=1;
                            *current=FALSE;
                            break;
    case 1:
                            temp1=root->left;
                            if(temp1->BF>=0)
                            {
                             cout<<"\nsingle rotation LL rotation";
                             root->left=temp1->right;
                             temp1->right=root;
                             if(temp1->BF==0)
                             {
                                 root->BF=1;
                                 temp1->BF=-1;
                                 *current=FALSE;
                             }
                             else
                             {
                                 root->BF=temp1->BF=0;
                             }
                             root=temp1;
                            }
                            else
                            {
```

```
                              cout<<"\nDouble rotation:LR rotation";
                              temp2=temp1->right;
                              temp1->right=temp2->left;
                              temp2->left=temp1;
                              root->left=temp2->right;
                              temp2->right=root;

                              if(temp2->BF==1)
                                   root->BF=-1;
                              else
                                   root->BF=0;

                              if(temp2->BF==-1)
                               temp1->BF=1;
                              else
                               temp1->BF=0;
                              root=temp2;
                              temp2->BF=0;
                         }
               }
 return root;
}

void main()
{
 AVL obj;
 node *root=NULL;
 int current;
  root=obj.insert(40,&current);
 root=obj.insert(50,&current);
 root=obj.insert(70,&current);
 cout<<endl;
 obj.display(root);
 cout<<endl;
 root=obj.insert(30,&current);
 cout<<endl;
 obj.display(root);
  root=obj.insert(20,&current);
 cout<<endl;
 obj.display(root);
 root=obj.insert(45,&current);
 cout<<endl;
 obj.display(root);
  root=obj.insert(25,&current);
 cout<<endl;
 obj.display(root);
 root=obj.insert(10,&current);
```

```
cout<<endl;
obj.display(root);
 root=obj.insert(5,&current);
cout<<endl;
obj.display(root);
root=obj.insert(22,&current);
cout<<endl;
obj.display(root);
root=obj.insert(1,&current);
cout<<endl;
obj.display(root);
 root=obj.insert(35,&current);
 cout<<"\n\nFinal AVL tree is: \n";
obj.display(root);
root=obj.remove(root,20,&current);
root=obj.remove(root,45,&current);
cout<<"\n\n AVL tree after deletion of a node: \n";
obj.display(root);
cout<<"\n";
}
```

Output

```
 single rotation:RR rotation
40  50  70

30  40  50  70
 single rotation: LL rotation
20  30  40  50  70
 Double rotation:LR rotation
20  30  40  45  50  70
 Double rotation:LR rotation
20  25  30  40  45  50  70
10  20  25  30  40  45  50  70
 single rotation: LL rotation
5  10  20  25  30  40  45  50  70
 Double rotation:LR rotation
5  10  20  22  25  30  40  45  50  70
 single rotation: LL rotation
1  5  10  20  22  25  30  40  45  50  70
 Double rotation:LR rotation

Final AVL tree is:
1  5  10  20  22  25  30  35  40  45  50  70
single rotation LL rotation

 AVL tree after deletion of a node:
1  5  10  22  25  30  35  40  50  70
```

4.7.8 Comparison between BST, OBST and AVL Tree

Binary Search Tree : This is binary tree in which nodes can be inserted or deleted based on their values. In binary search tree left node is less than parent node. The right node is greater than parent node. Binary search tree can be implemented using arrays or linked data structures.

Optimal Binary Search Tree (OBST)

The optimal binary search tree is basically a binary search tree with optimum cost. There is a fixed set of identifiers from which OBST is built. The static symbol table is used to implement OBST.

Height Balanced Search Tree

The height balanced tree is basically a binary search tree which is constructed using balance factor. Its implementation is a dynamic implementation.

Example 4.7.2 *Draw a diagram to show different stages during the building of AVL tree for the following sequence of keys : A, Z, B, Y, C, X, D, E, V, F, M, R. In each case show the balance factor of all the nodes and name the type of rotation used for balancing.*

SPPU : Dec.-05, Marks 6

Solution :

Step 1 : Insert A **Step 2 :** Insert Z

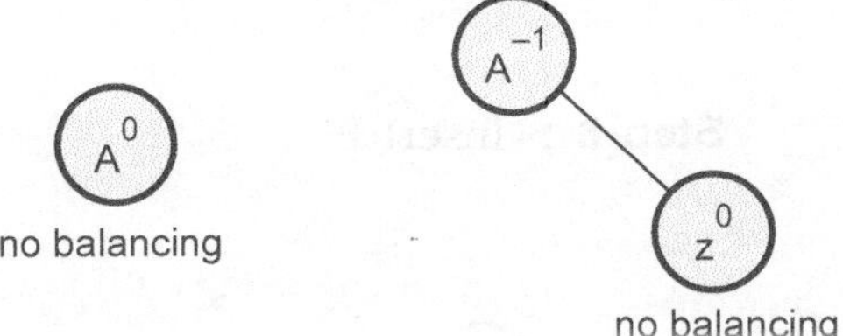

Step 3 : Insert B **Step 4 :** Insert Y

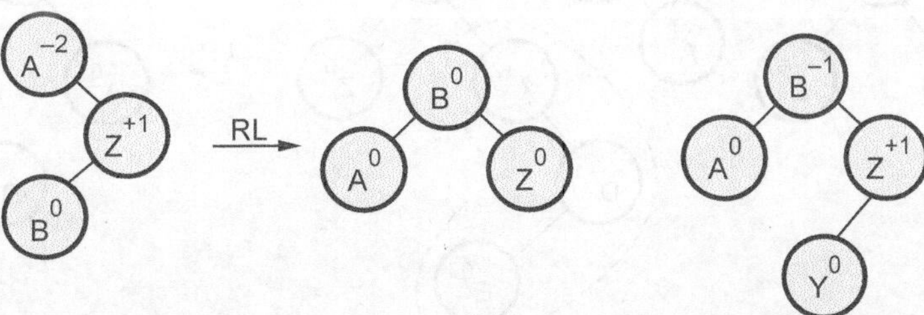

Step 5 : Insert C

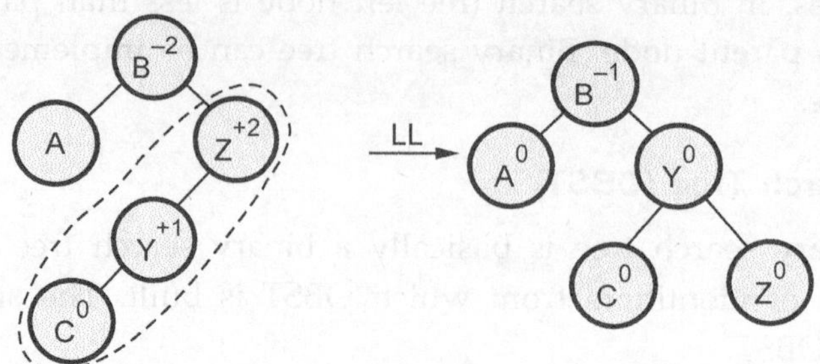

Step 6 : Insert X

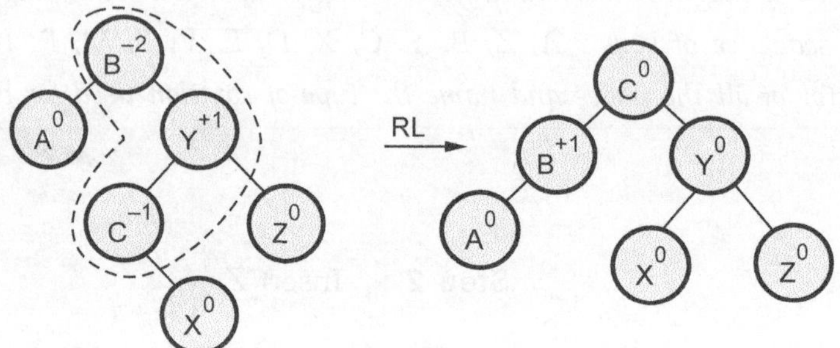

Step 7 : Insert D **Step 8 :** Insert E

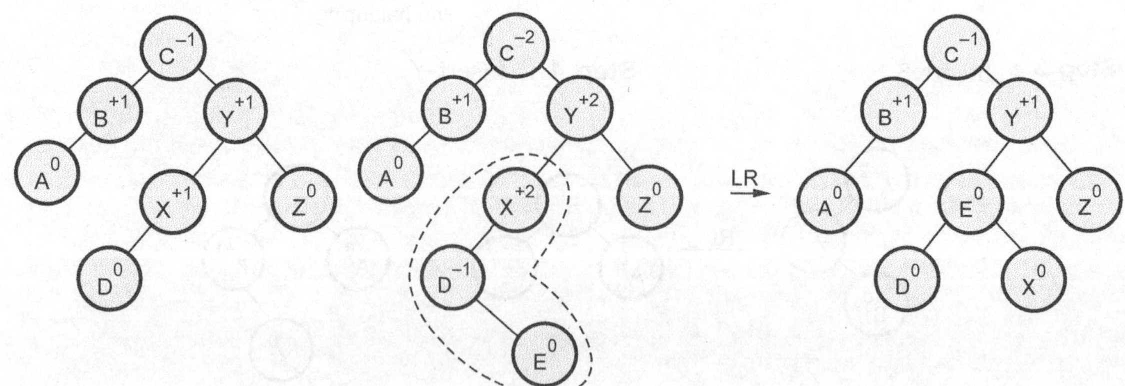

Step 9 : Insert V

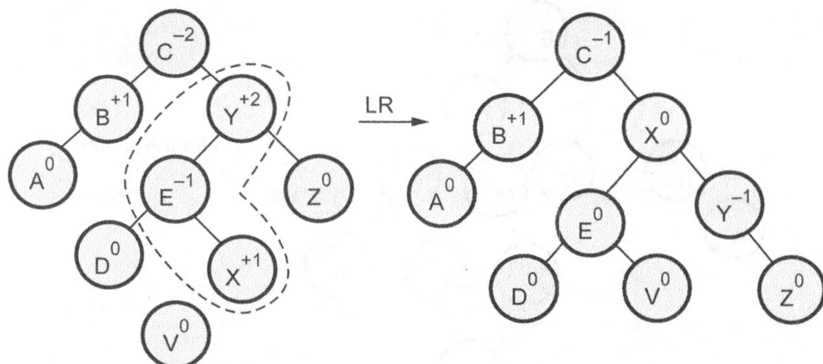

Step 10 : Insert F

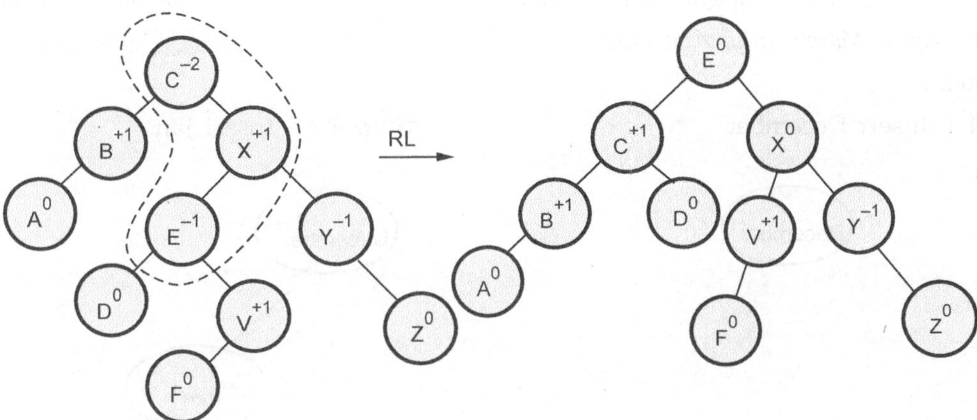

Step 11 : Insert M

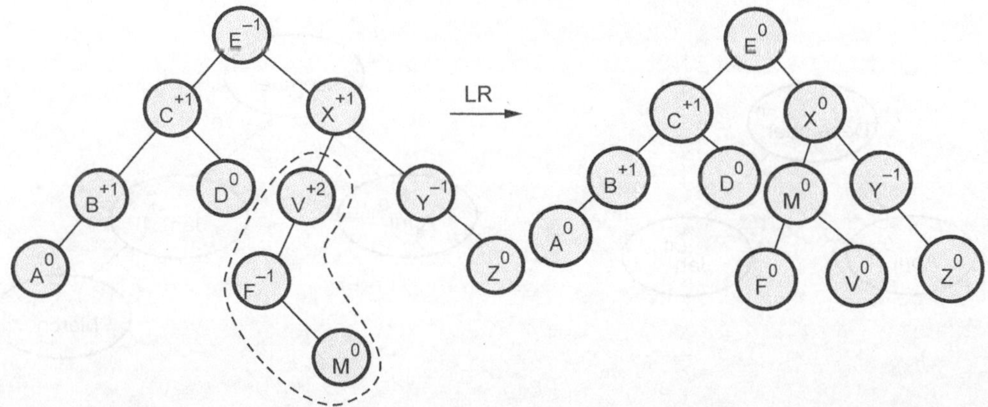

Step 12 : Insert R

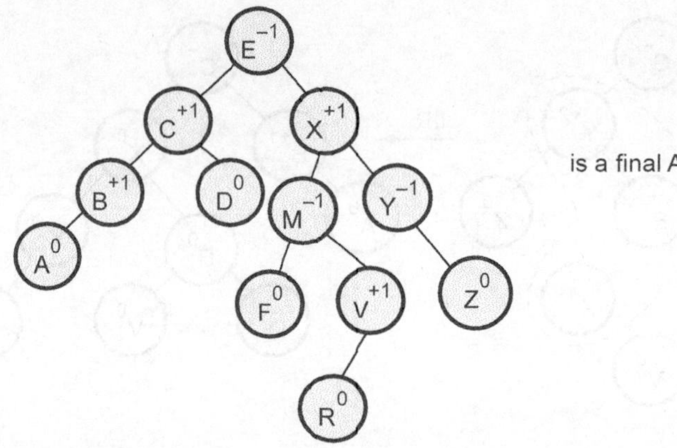

is a final AVL tree.

Example 4.7.3 *Obtain height balanced tree for the following sequence of data : December, Jan., April, March, July, Aug., Oct., Nov., May, June.* **SPPU : Dec.-07, May-10, Marks 8**

Solution. :

Step 1 : Insert December

Step 2 : Insert Jan.

Step 3 : Insert April

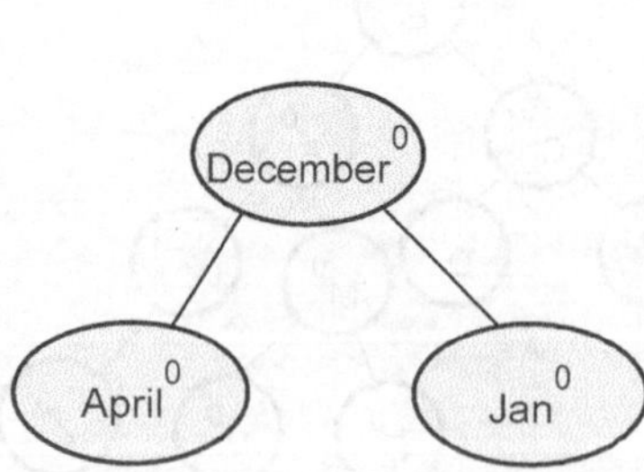

Step 4 : Insert March

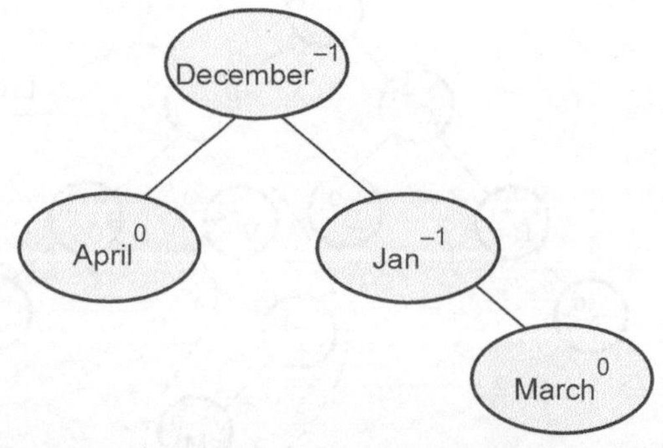

Step 5 : Insert July

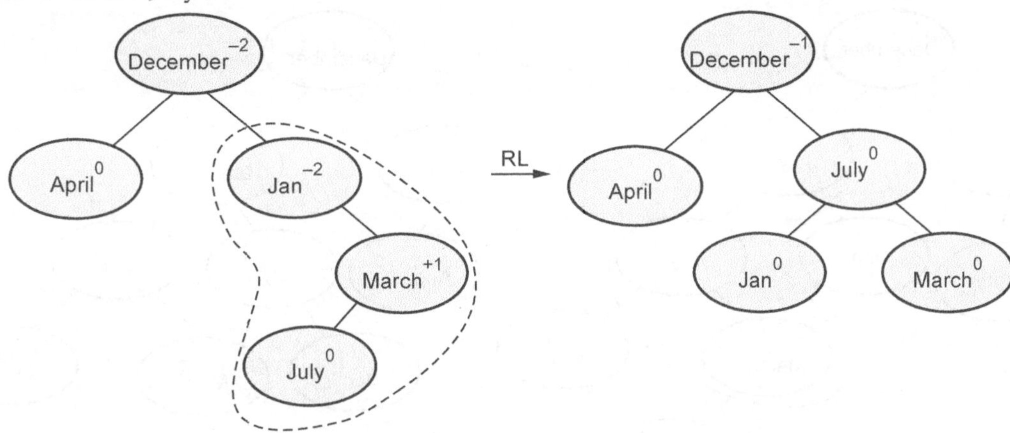

Step 6 : Insert August

Step 7 : Insert Oct.

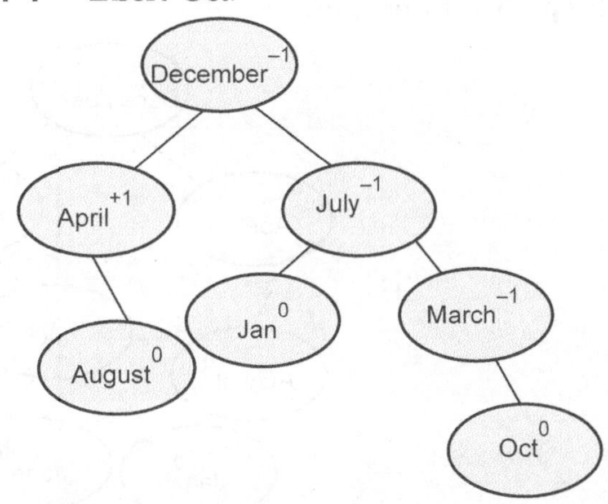

Step 8 : Insert Nov.

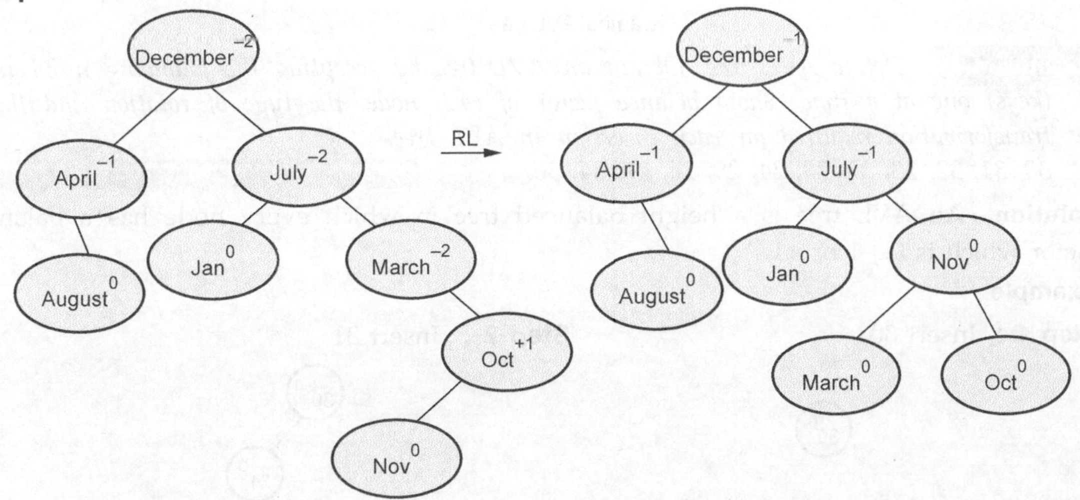

Step 9 : Insert May

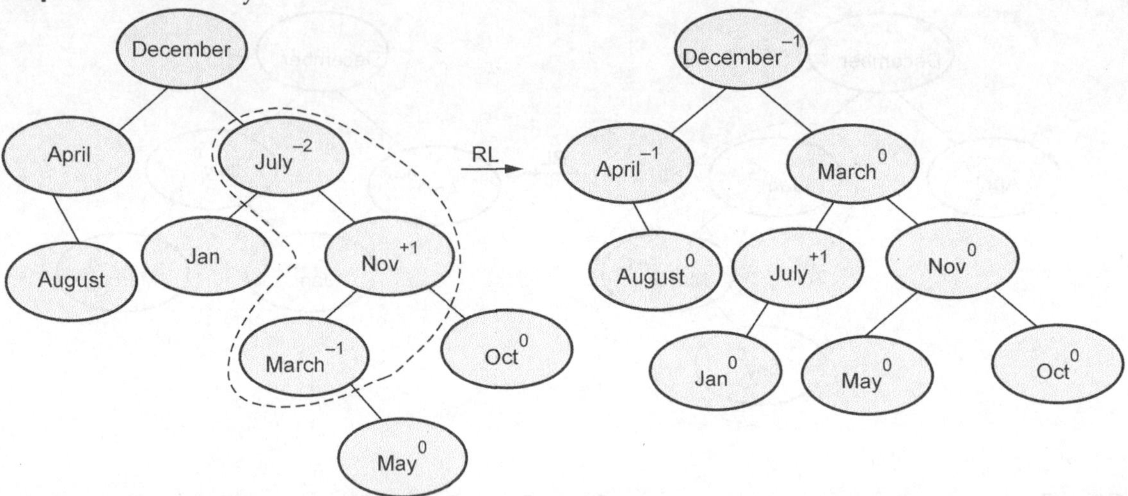

Step 10 : Insert June

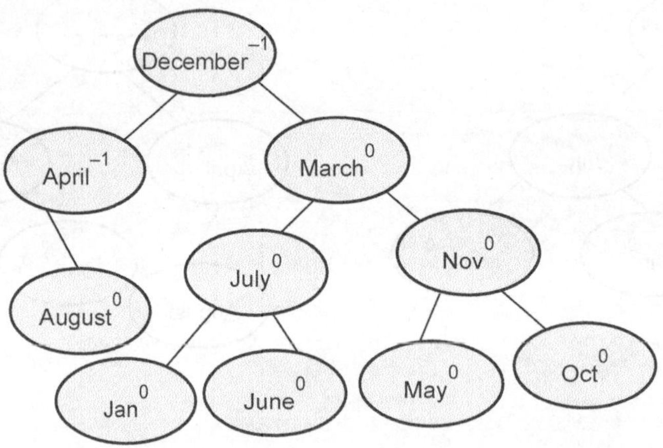

is a final AVL tree.

Example 4.7.4 *Define AVL tree. Obtain an AVL tree by accepting the following numbers (keys) one at a time. Show balance factor of each node, the type of rotation and the transformation required for each insertion in AVL tree.*
30, 31, 32, 23, 22, 28, 24, 29, 26, 27, 34, 36. **SPPU : Dec.-08, May-10, Marks 10**

Solution. : An AVL tree is a height balanced tree in which every node has a balance factor which is 0, –1 or +1.

Example

Step 1 : Insert 30 **Step 2 :** Insert 31

Step 3 : Insert 32

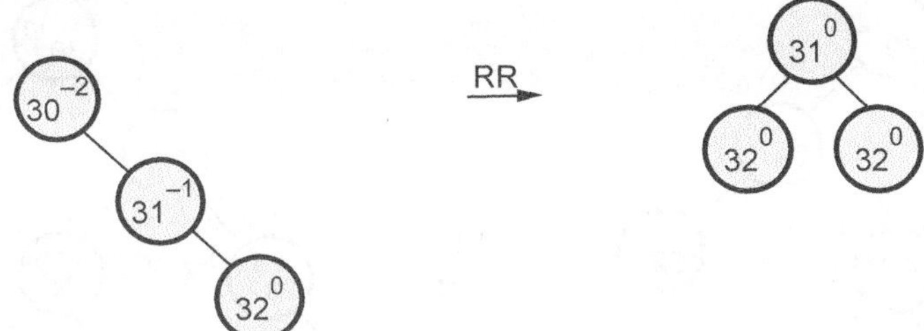

Step 4 : Insert 23

Step 5 : Insert 22

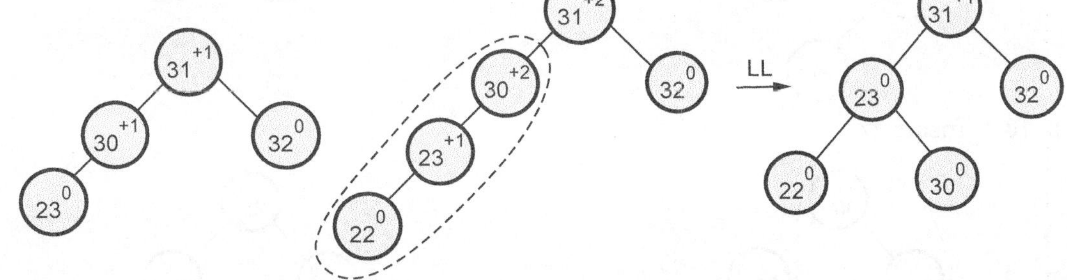

Step 6 : Insert 28

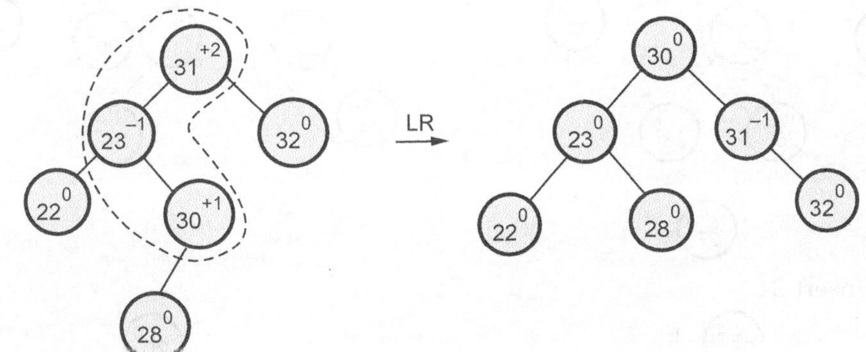

Step 7 : Insert 24

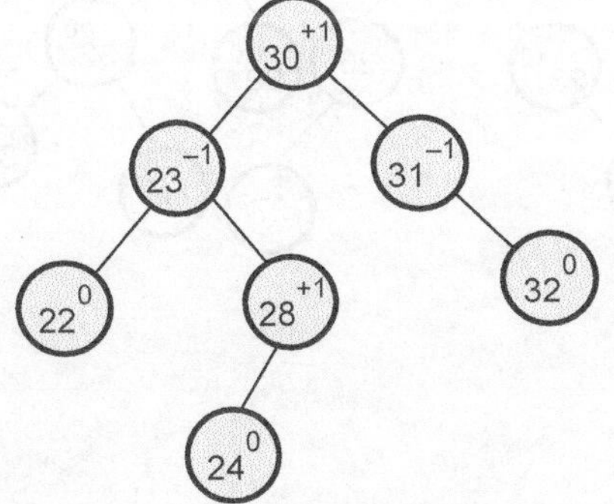

Step 8 : Insert 29

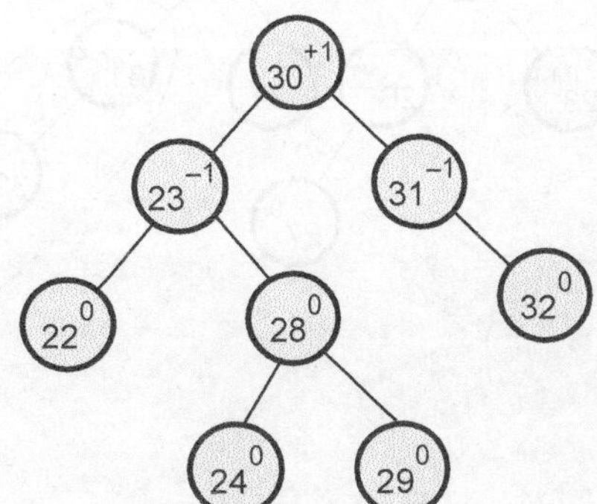

Step 9 : Insert 26

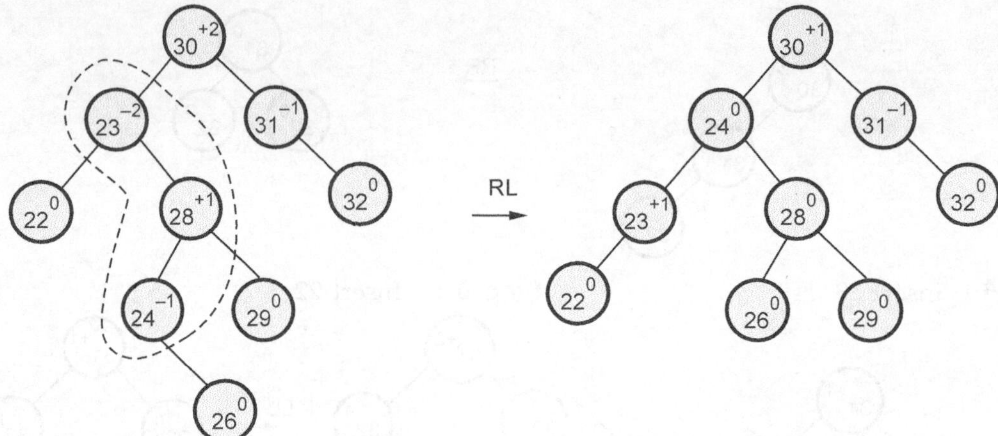

Step 10 : Insert 27

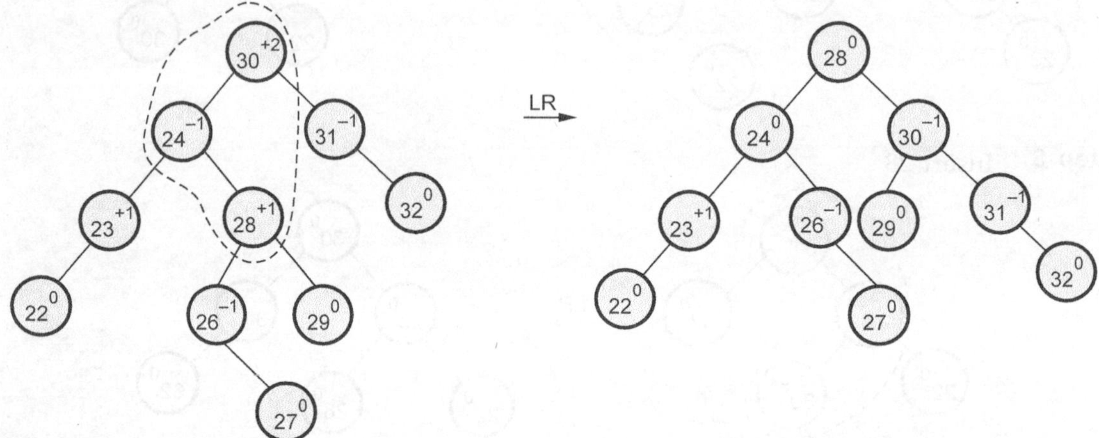

Step 11 : Insert 34

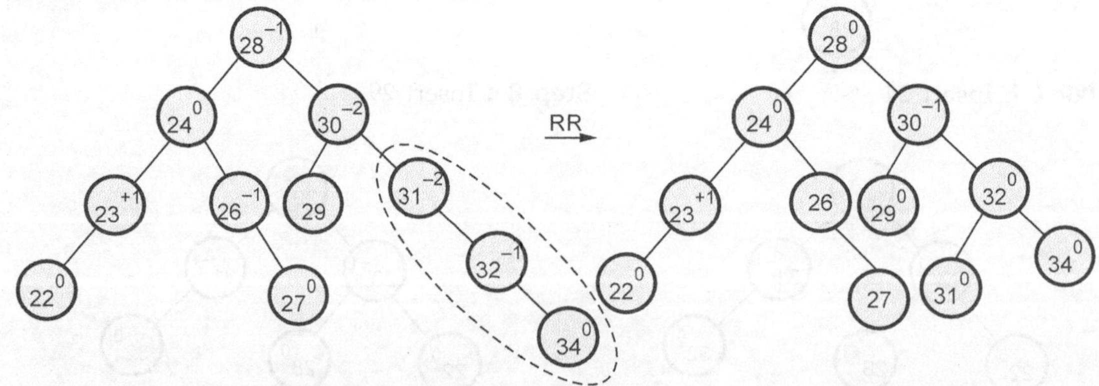

Step 12 : Insert 36

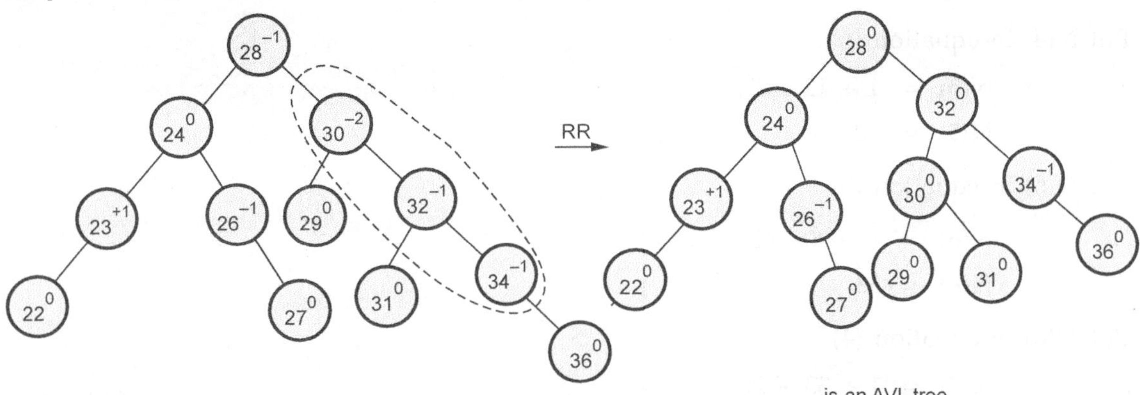

Example 4.7.5 *What is the size of the smallest AVL tree with height 8 ?*

SPPU : Dec.-05, Marks 4

Solution. : If h is the height of an AVL tree then minimum number of nodes can be obtained for such AVL tree using the following formula.

$$N(h) = 1 + N(h-1) + N(h-2) \quad ...(1)$$

If there is only one node then h = 0, for 2 nodes the h = 1. We can formulate and say

$$N(0) = 1, \quad N(1) = 2 \quad ...(2)$$

Hence using equation (1) we can obtain minimum number of nodes for height 8.

$$N(8) = 1 + N(7) + N(6) \quad ...(3)$$

$$N(7) = 1 + N(6) + N(5) \quad ...(4)$$

$$N(6) = 1 + N(5) + N(4) \quad ...(5)$$

$$N(5) = 1 + N(4) + N(3) \quad ...(6)$$

$$N(4) = 1 + N(3) + N(2) \quad ...(7)$$

$$N(3) = 1 + N(2) + N(1) \quad ...(8)$$

$$N(2) = 1 + N(1) + N(0)$$

$\therefore$ $N(2) = 1 + 2 + 1$ $\quad \because$ From equation (2)

$$\mathbf{N(2) = 4}$$

Put N(2) in equation (8)

$\therefore$ $N(3) = 1 + 4 + 2$

$$\mathbf{N(3) = 7}$$

Put N(3) in equation (7)

$\therefore$ $N(4) = 1 + 7 + 4$

N(4) = 12

Put N(4) in equation (6)

∴ N(5) = 1 + 12 + 7

N(5) = 20

Put N(5) in equation (5)

∴ N(6) = 1 + 20+ 12

N(6) = 33

Put N(6) in equation (4)

∴ N(7) = 1 + 33 + 20

N(7) = 54

Put N(7) in equation (3)

∴ N(8) = 1 + 54 + 33

N(8) = 88

That means minimum number of nodes are 88 for an AVL tree of height 8.

Example 4.7.6 *Construct an AVL tree for given sequence of data. In each case show the balance factor of all nodes and name the type of rotation used for balancing the tree 40, 60, 80, 50, 45, 47, 44, 42, 75, 46, 41.* **SPPU : May-11, Marks 10**

Solution :

Step 1 : **Step 2 : Insert 60** **Step 3 : Insert 80**

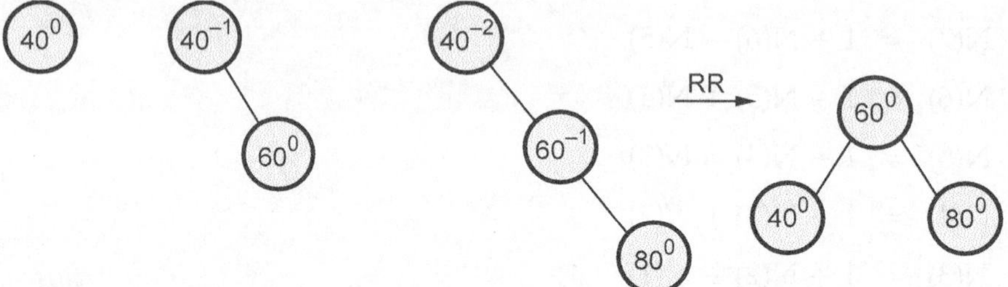

Step 4 : Insert 50 **Step 5 : Insert 45**

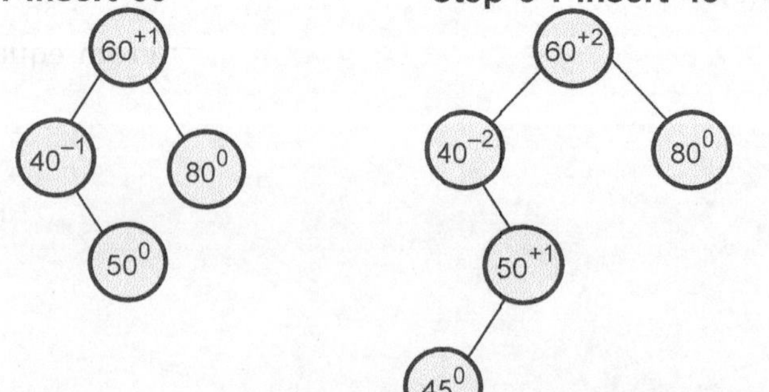

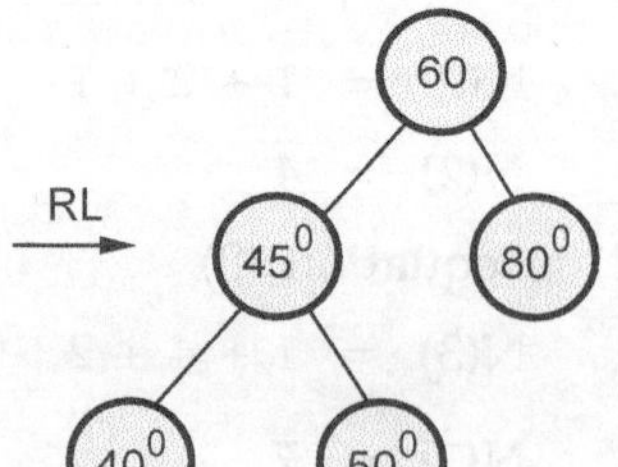

Step 6: insert 47

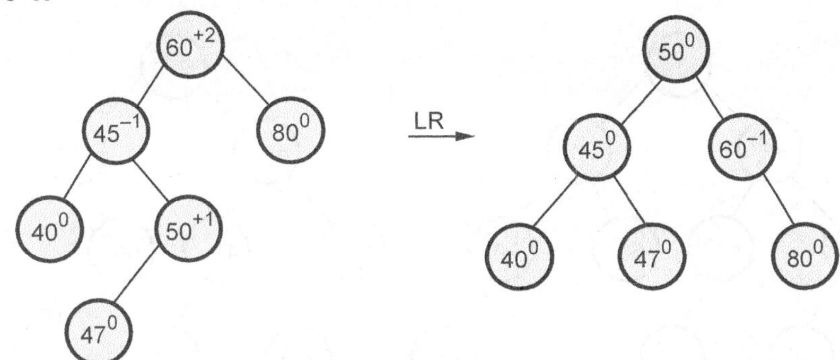

Step 7 : Insert 44 **Step 8 : Insert 42**

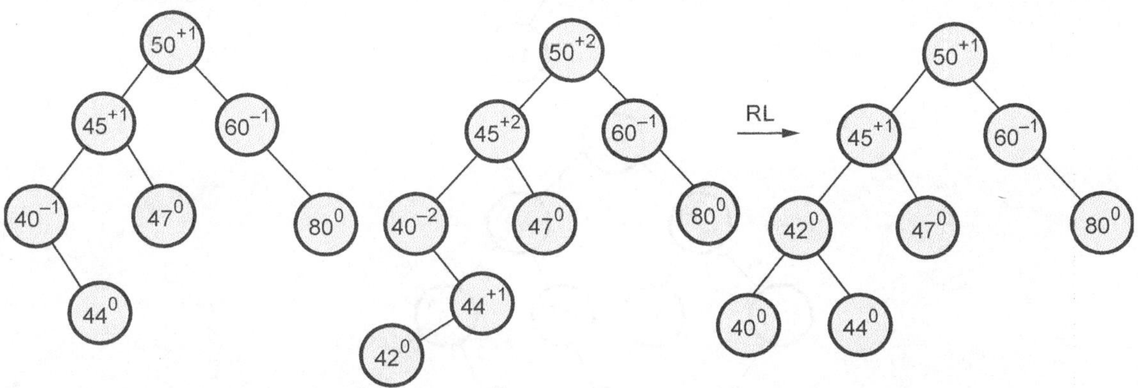

Step 9 : Insert 75

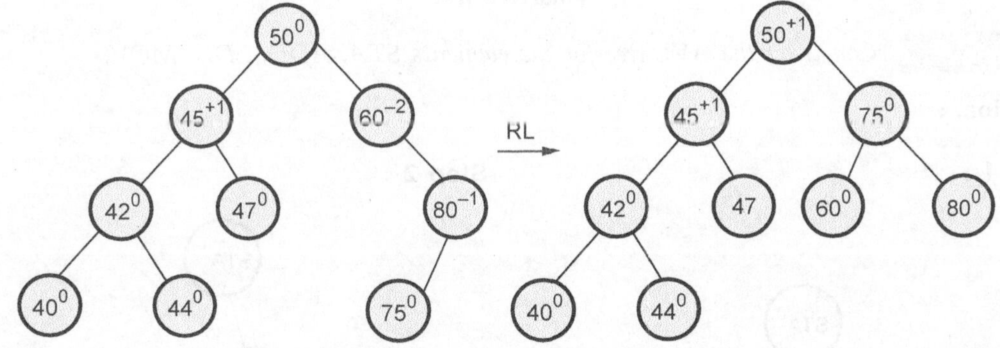

Step 10 : Insert 48

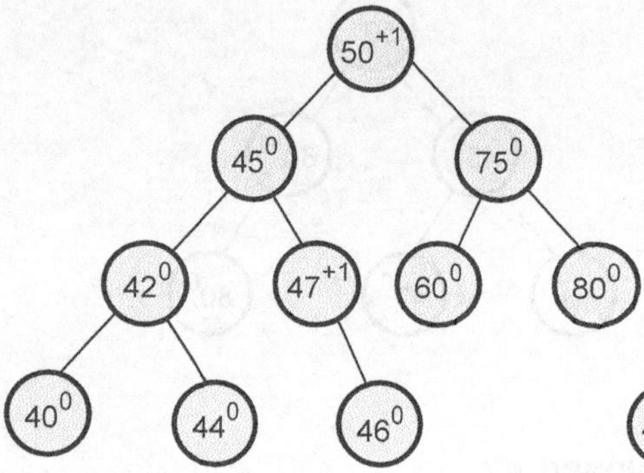

Step 11 : Insert 41

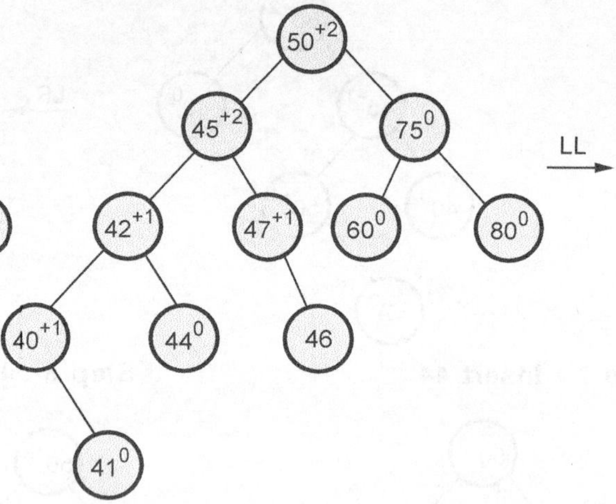

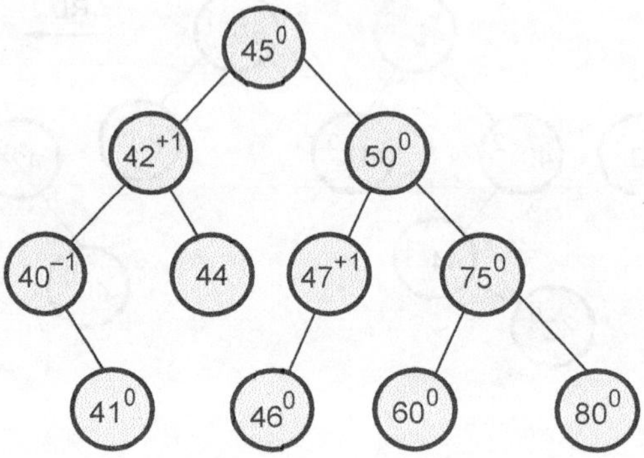

Final AVL Tree

Example 4.7.7 *Construct the AVL tree for the elements STA, ADD, LDA, MOV.*

Solution. :

Step 1 :

Step 2 :

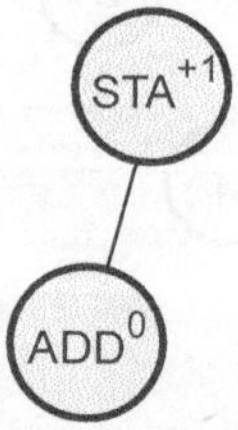

Step 3 :

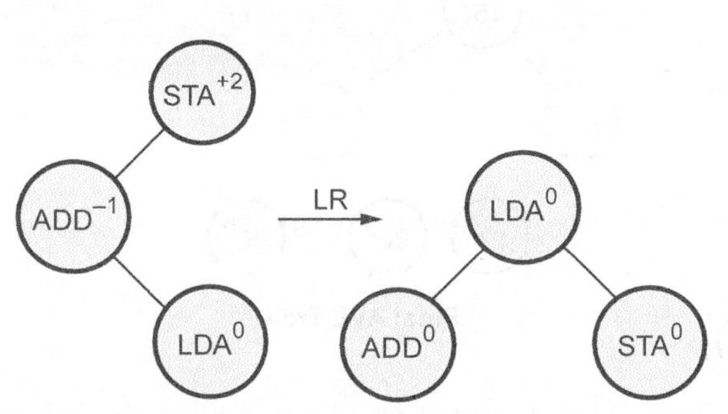

Step 4 :

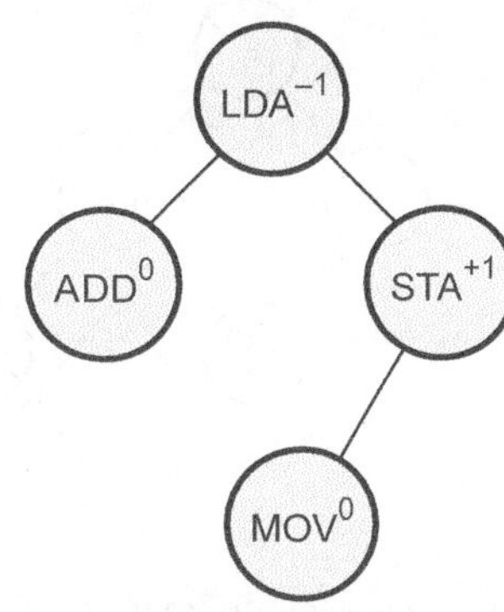

This is final AVL tree

Example 4.7.8 *Create an AVL tree for the following data by inserting it in an order one at a time:*

10, 20, 15, 12, 25, 30.

SPPU : Dec.-13, Marks 4

Solution :

Step 1 : Insert 10

Step 2 : Insert 20

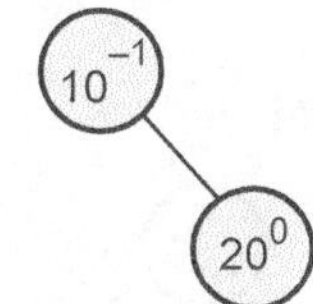

Step 3 : Insert 15

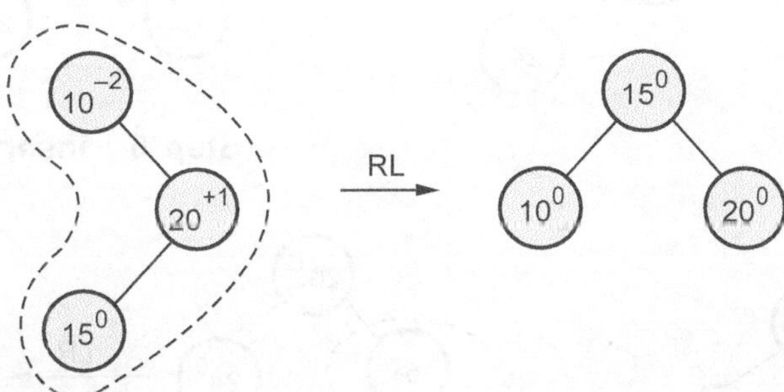

Step 4 : Insert 12

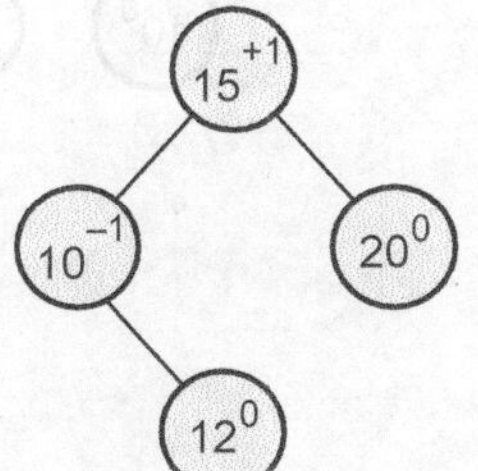

Step 5 : Insert 25

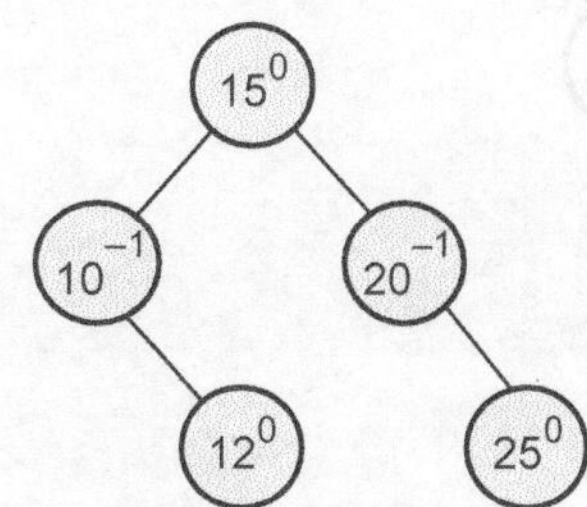

Step 6 : Insert 30

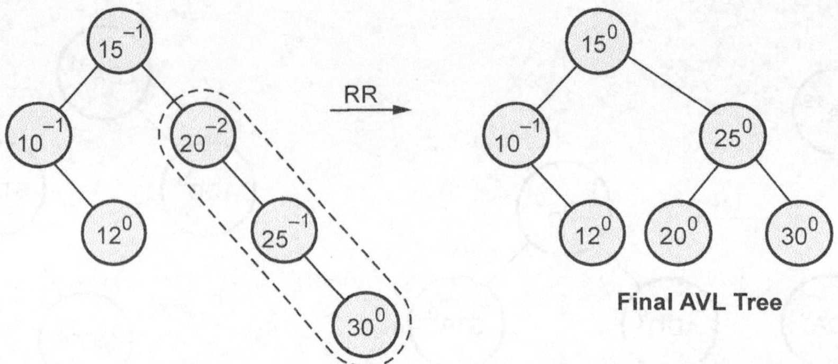

Example 4.7.9 *Construct AVL tree for the following data by inserting each data item one at a time. 15, 20, 24, 10, 13, 7, 30, 36, 25.* **SPPU : May-14, Marks 6**

Solution :

Step 1 : Insert 15 **Step 2 : Insert 20**

Step 3 : Insert 24

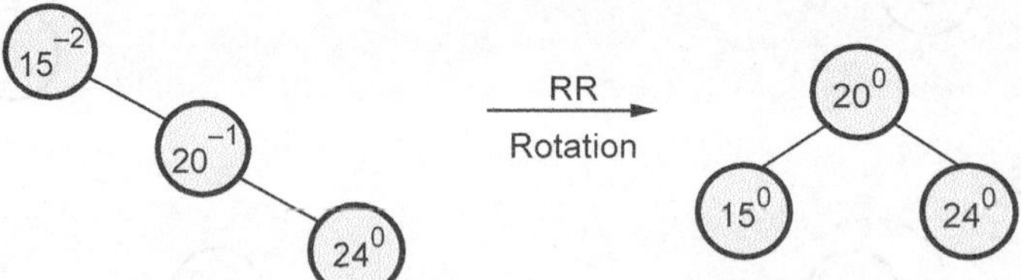

Step 4 : Insert 10 **Step 5 : Insert 13**

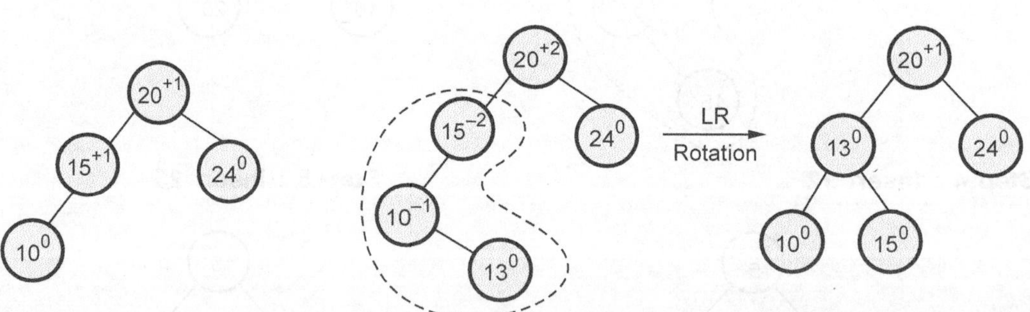

Step 6 : Insert 7

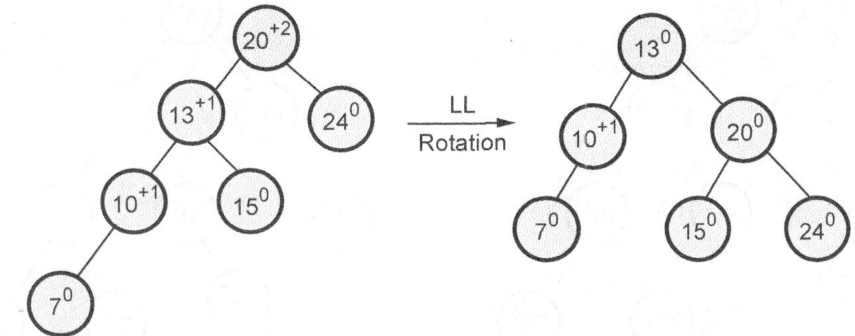

Step 7 : Insert 30

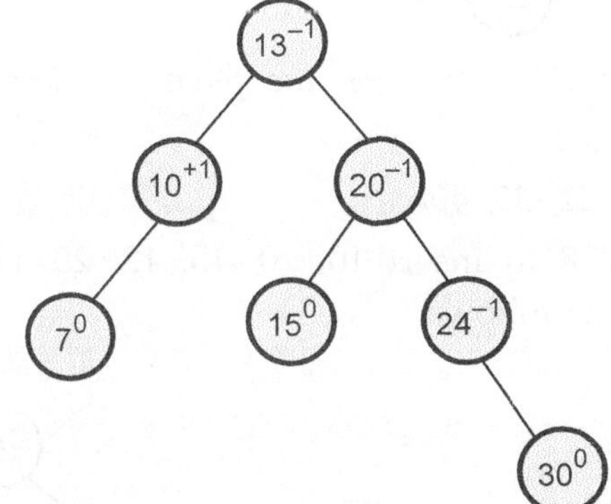

Step 8 : Insert 36

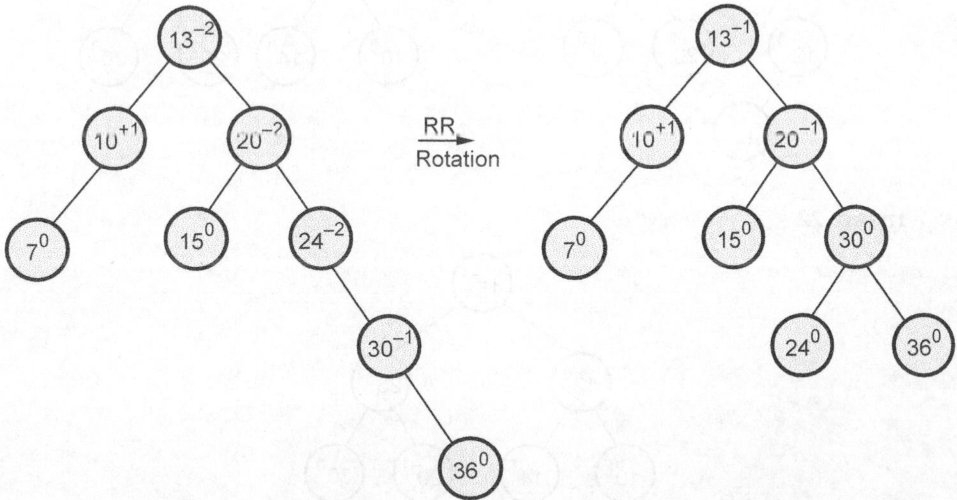

Step 9 : Insert 25

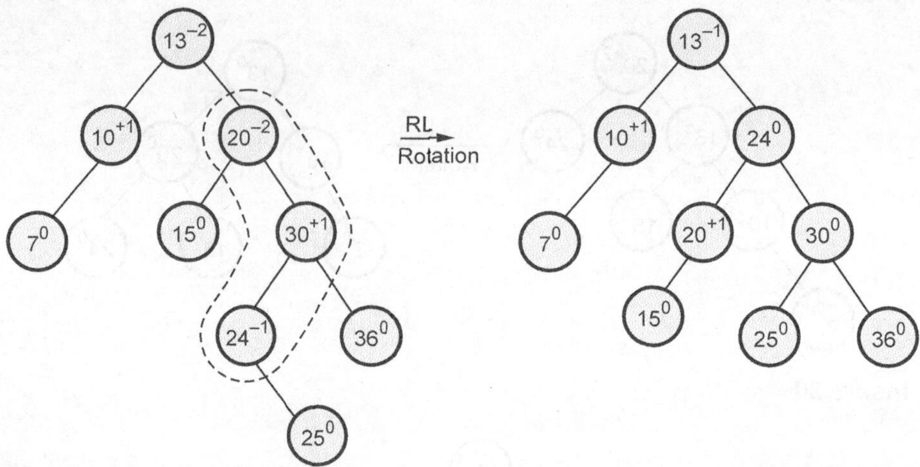

Example 4.7.10 *Construct the AVL tree for the following data by inserting each of the following data item one at a time :*

10, 20, 15, 12, 25, 30, 14, 22, 35, 40. **SPPU : Dec.-14, Marks 5**

Solution : Refer example 4.7.8 to insert 10, 20, 15, 12, 25 and 30. Further insertion of elements in the AVL tree is as follows

Step 1 : Insert 14

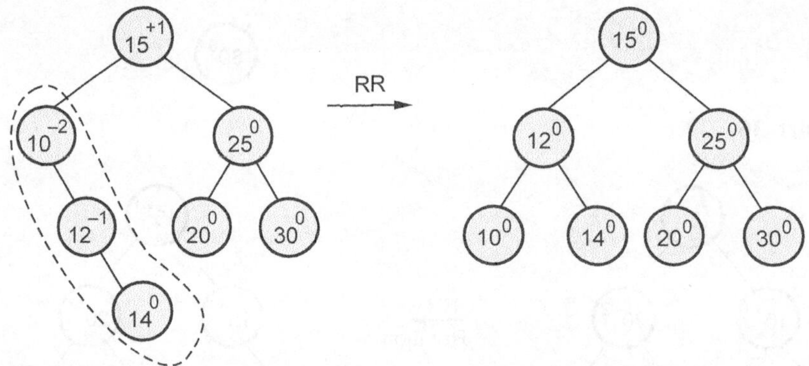

Step 2 : Insert 22

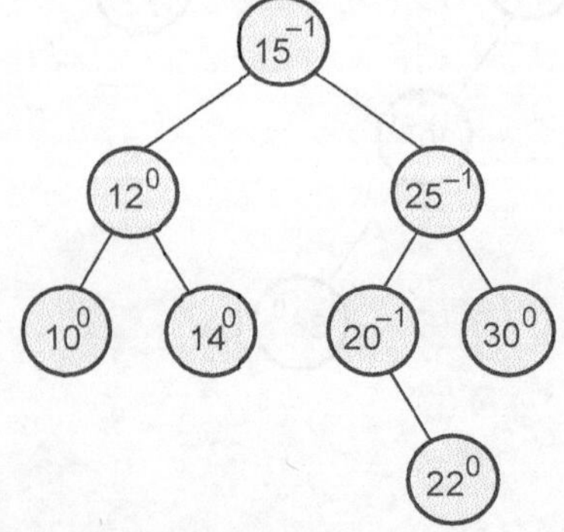

Step 3 : **Insert 35**

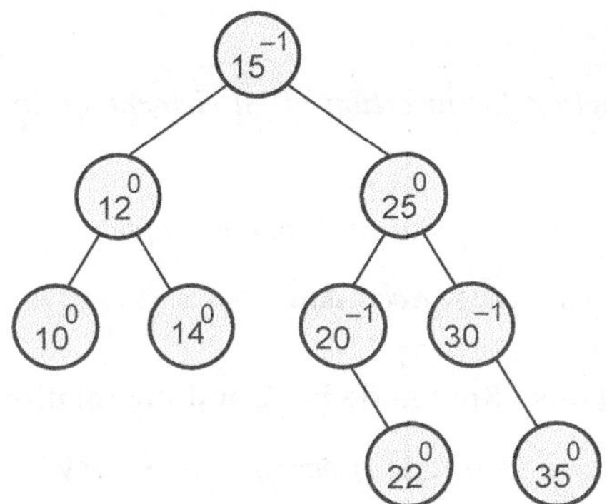

Step 4 : **Insert 40**

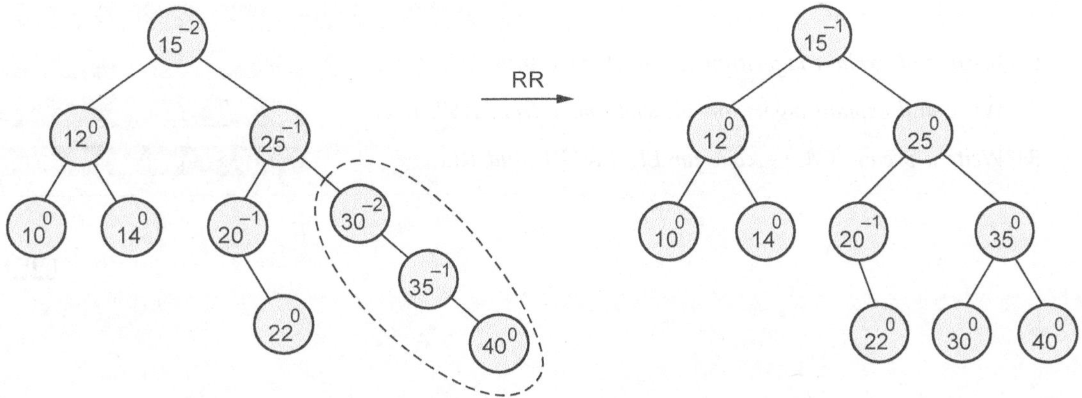

AVL tree

4.7.9 Comparison of AVL Tree with Binary Search Tree

Sr. No.	AVL tree	Binary search tree
1.	An AVL tree is an height balanced search tree.	Binary search tree is not a balanced tree.
2.	There is a requirement of computation of balanced factor for each node in an AVL tree.	There is no concept of balance factor.
3.	Searching of any desired node is faster due to balancing of height.	Searching is not efficient when there are large number of nodes in the tree.
4.	Complex to implement.	Simple to implement.

University Questions

1. *Write nonrecurrsive function for insertion of an element in an AVL tree.*

   SPPU : May-10, Marks 4

2. *What is height balance tree ? Explain with one example.* **SPPU : Dec.-10, Marks 4**

3. *Create AVL tree for the following given data*

   65, 85, 95, 30, 06, 71, 23, 99, 44, 21. **SPPU : Dec.-10, Marks 8**

   [Ans : Root node is 65, and the rotations required are RR, LL, LR, RL]

4. *Write a program C/C++ for word/text processing using AVL tree implementation.*

   SPPU : Dec.-11, Marks 8

5. *Explain with examples LL, LR, RR an RL rotations for AVL tree.*

   SPPU : May-11, Marks 6, May-12, Marks 8

6. *Write and explain algorithm to insert node into AVL tree.* **SPPU : May-10,12, Marks 8**

7. *Write and explain algorithm to delete node from AVL tree.* **SPPU : Dec.-12, Marks 8**

8. *Write a pseudo C/C++ code for LL, LR, RR and RL.* **SPPU : May-13, Marks 8**

❑❑❑

5 Indexing and Multiway Tree

Syllabus

***Indexing and multiway trees** - Indexing, Indexing techniques, Types of search tree - Multiway search tree, B-Tree, B+Tree, Trie tree, Splay tree, Red-black tree, K-dimensional tree, AA tree. **Set**-set ADT, Realization of set and operations. **Heap**-basic concepts, Realization of heap and operations, Heap as a priority queue, Heap sort.*

Contents

5.1 Indexing

- Data is stored in the form of records. Every record has a key field, which helps to recognize that particular record uniquely.
- **Indexing** is a technique of efficiently retrieving the records from the database files based on the fields of the record on which the indexing has been done.
- **Definition of Index :** The index is a collection of pairs of the form (key value, address).
- **Example :** Consider following sample student file

Roll No.	Name	Std.
100	AAA	IX
200	BBB	VI
300	CCC	V
400	DDD	IV
500	EEE	X

If these records are stored at addresses a_1, a_2, a_3, ... and so on. on disk then indexing can be indexing.

Name	disk Address
AAA	a_1
BBB	a_2
CCC	a_3
DDD	a_4
EEE	a_5

Advantages of Indexing

1) Indexing is useful in managing large data.
2) It provides faster access.
3) Any record can be searched easily.
4) Indexing helps to reduce unwanted memory access.
5) There is proper memory allocation due to indexing.

5.2 Indexing Techniques

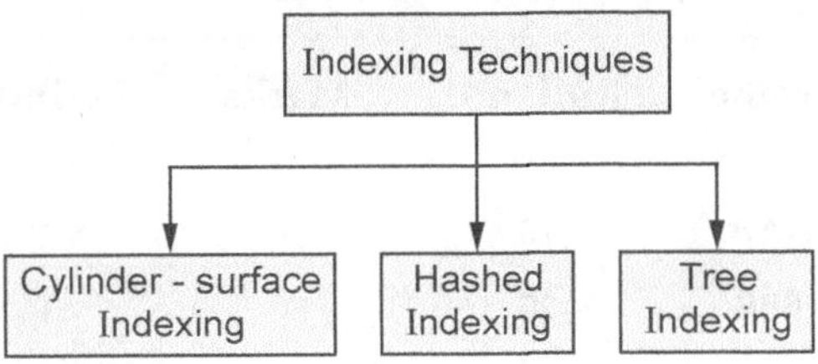

Fig. 5.2.1 Indexing Techniques

1) Cylinder - Surface Indexing

Cylinder - surface indexing is normally done on sequential file organization. Such a file is placed on the hard disk. For locating position of any record on the hard disk the cylinders and surfaces are used. The hard disk layout showing cylinder surfaces and tracks is shown below.

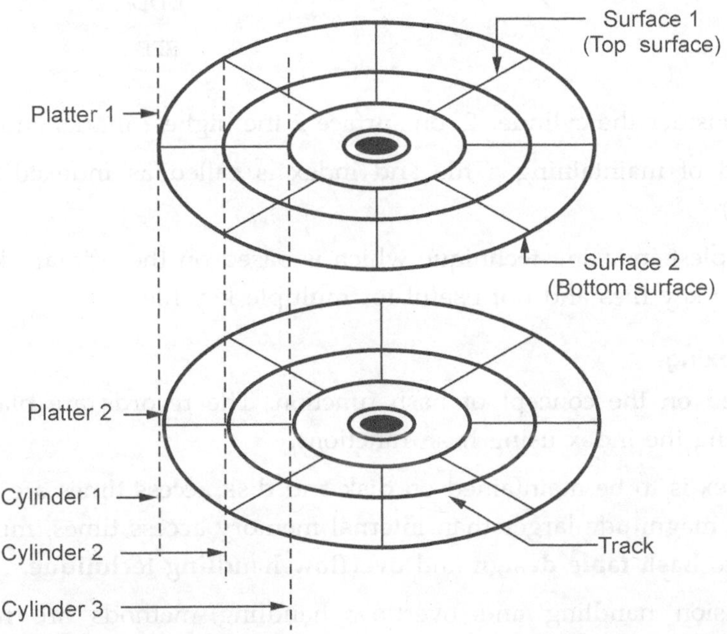

A cylinder is basically the set of all the tracks that all the heads are currently located at. The tracks are the concentric rings on the hard-disk and sectors are the pie shaped portion on the each track. The read/write head is for reading or writing record at particular location. These locations can be accessed with the help of cylinder-surface index. Each cylinder has two surfaces.

For example :

Consider a student database, stored on the cylinder -

Record Number	Name	Roll_no.	Marks	Cylinder	Surface
1	AAA	10	70	1	1
2	BBB	20	80	1	2
3	CCC	30	90	2	1
4	DDD	40	95	2	2
5	EEE	50	55	3	1

The highest Marks value can be retrieved as follows -

Cylinder	Student with Highest Marks
1	BBB
2	DDD
3	EEE

Similarly Consider the cylinder 2, on surface 2 the highest marks entry is made.

This method of maintaining a file and index is called as Indexed Squential Access Method (ISMA)

It is the simplest indexing technique which is based on the primary key. This method works for single key files and not useful for multiple key files.

2) Hashed Indexing

- It is based on the concept of hash function. The records are placed on disks by maintaining the index using hash functions.
- Since index is to be maintained on disk and disk access times are generally several orders of magnitude larger than internal memory access times, much consideration is given to **hash table design** and **overflow handling technique.**
- The collision handling and overflow handling methods are required for this hashed indexing which are -

  i) Rehashing ii) Open addressing iii) Chaining.

3) Tree Indexing

- In this technique, for searching a record from a database, then records are arranged in a tree like manner. Then using AVL tree search technique the desired record present on disk can be accessed.

- The entire AVL tree resides on disk.
- This is worse indexing technique as compared to cylinder surface indexing.

5.3 Types of Search Tree

Definition of Search Tree : The search tree is a tree data structure which is used for locating specific key from the given set of data.

The advantage of search trees is that it becomes efficient to search a node from the tree.

Various types of search trees are -

1. Binary Search Tree
2. Height Balanced Trees such as AVL tree
3. Multiway Search Trees such as B- Tree, B+ Trees
4. Red Black Trees
5. Splay Tree
6. Trie Tree
7. K dimensional Tree
8. AA Tree

Let us discuss various types of search trees in detail -

5.4 Multiway Search Tree

A multiway search tree of order m is an ordered tree where each node has at the most m children. If there are n number of children in a node then (n – 1) is the number of keys in the node.

For example :

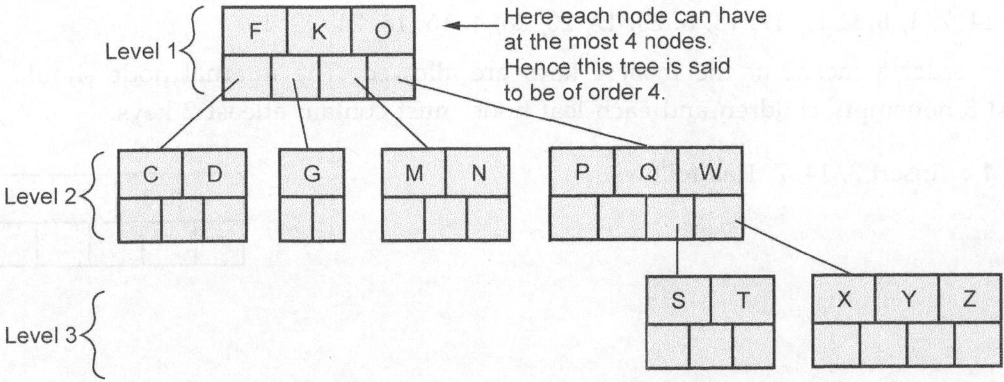

Fig. 5.4.1 Multiway tree of order 4

Following is a tree of order 4.

From above tree following observations can be made -

1. The node which has n children possess (n – 1) keys.
2. The keys in each node are in ascending order.
3. For every node Node.child [0] has only keys which are less than Node.key [0] similarly, Node.child [1] has only keys which are greater than Node.key [0].

In other words, the node at level 1 has F, K and O as keys. At level 2 the node containing keys C and D are arranged as child of key F (the cell before F). Similarly the node containing key G will be child of F but should be attached after F and before K, as G is between F and K. Here the alphabets F, K, O are called keys and branches are called children. The B-tree of order m should be constructed such that -

Rule 1 : All the leaf nodes are on the bottom level.

Rule 2 : The root node should have atleast two children.

Rule 3 : All the internal nodes except root node have atleast ceil (m/2) non-empty children. The ceil is a function such that ceil (3.4) = 4, ceil (9.3) = 10, ceil (2.98) = 3 ceil (7) = 7.

Rule 4 : Each leaf node must contain atleast ceil (m/2) – 1 keys.

5.5 B Tree

SPPU : May-05, 07, 11, 12, 13, 14, Dec.-05, 07,09, 10,12, 13, Marks 8

B-tree is a specialized multiway tree used to store the records in a disk. There are number of subtrees to each node. So that the height of the tree is relatively small. So that only small number of nodes must be read from disk to retrieve an item. The goal of B-trees is to get fast access of the data.

5.5.1 Insertion

We will consruct a B-tree of order 5 following numbers.

3, 14, 7, 1, 8, 5, 11, 17, 13, 6, 23, 12, 20, 26, 4, 16, 18, 24, 25, 19.

The order 5 means at the most 4 keys are allowed. The internal node should have atleast 3 nonempty children and each leaf node must contain atleast 2 keys.

Step 1 : Insert 3, 14, 7, 1 as follows.

1	3	7	14

Step 2 : If we insert 8 then we need to split the node 1, 3, 7, 8, 14 at medium. Hence

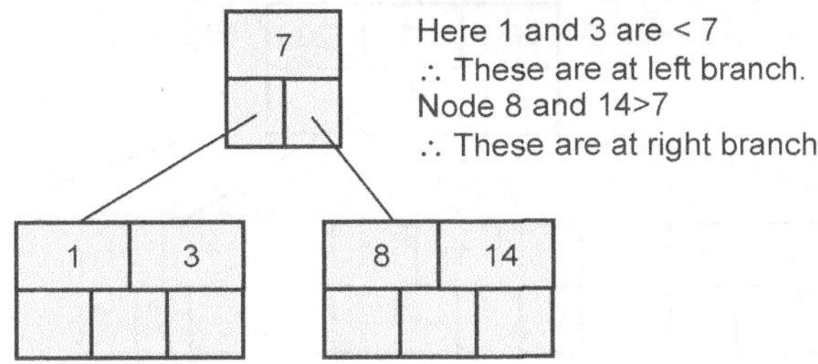

Step 3 : Insert 5, 11, 17 which can be easily inserted in a B-tree.

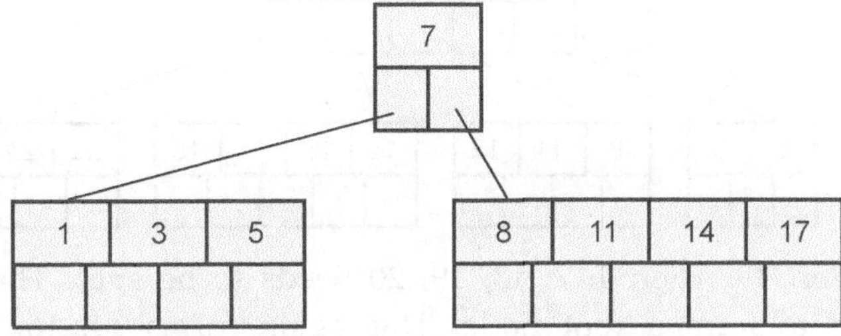

Step 4 : Now insert 13. But if we insert 13 then the leaf node will have 5 keys which is not allowed. Hence 8, 11, 13, 14, 17 is split and medium node 13 is moved up.

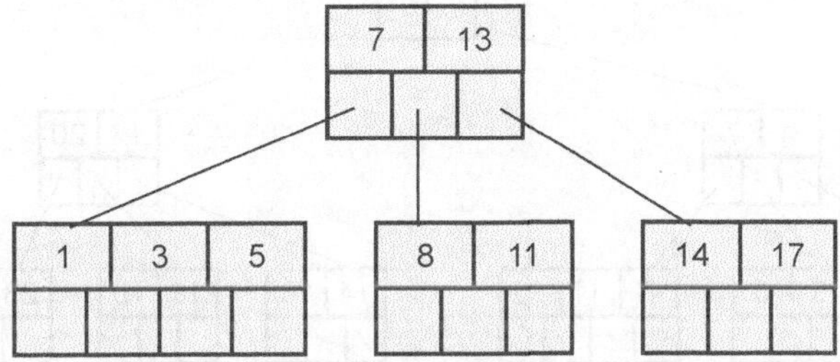

Step 5 : Now insert 6, 23, 12, 20 without any split.

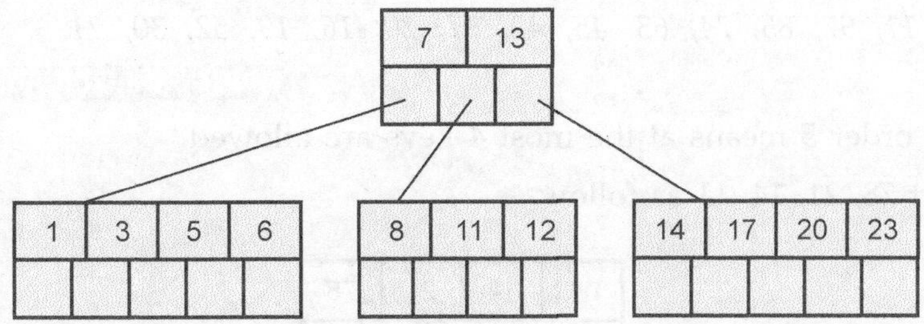

Step 6 : The 26 is inserted to the rightmost leaf node which cause key to be 6. Hence 14, 17, 20, 23, 26 the node is split and 20 will be moved up.

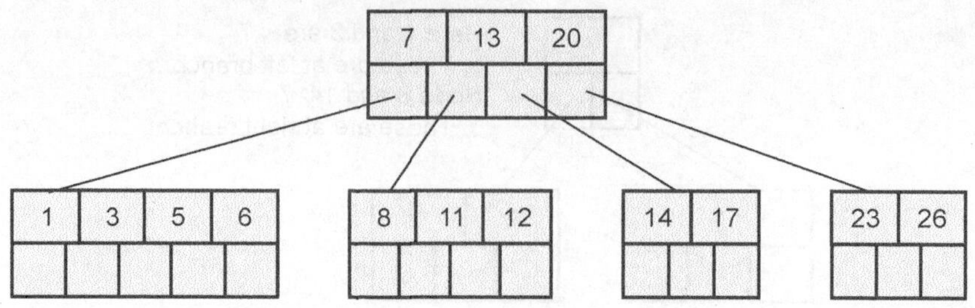

Step 7 : Insertion of node 4 causes leftmost node to split. The 1, 3, 4, 5, 6 causes key 4 to move up. Then insert 16, 18, 24, 25.

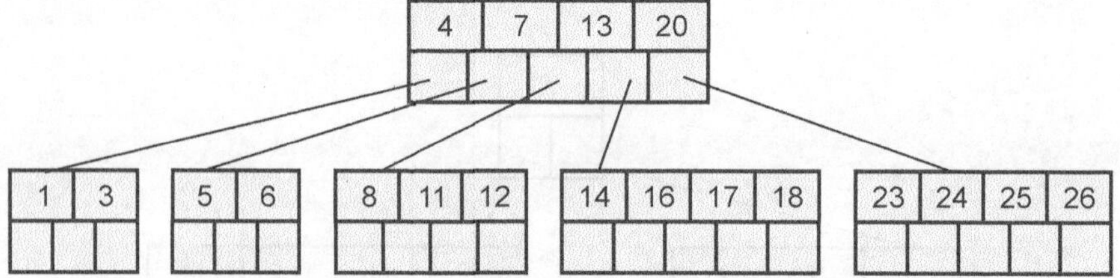

Step 8 : Finally insert 19. Then 4, 7, 13, 19, 20 needs to be split. The median 13 will be moved up to form a root node. This again forms 14, 16, 17, 18, 19 which is again divided and the mid element 17 is moved up.

The tree then will be -

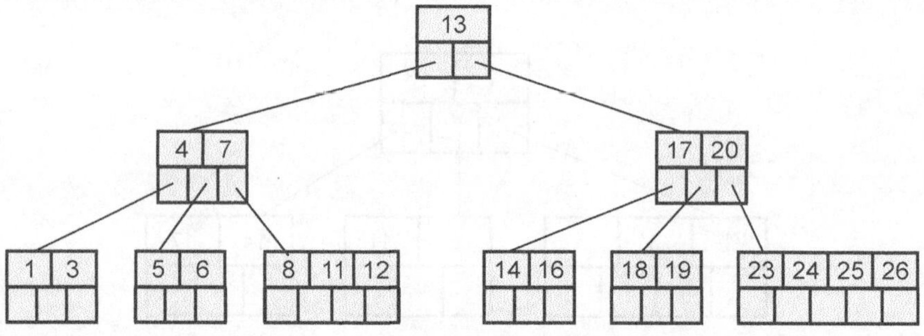

Thus the B-tree is constructed.

Example 5.5.1 *Explain the steps to built a B-tree of order 5 for following data :*

78, 21, 14, 11, 97, 85, 74, 63, 45, 42, 57, 20, 16, 19, 52, 30, 21.

SPPU : Dec.-05, May-07, Marks 6

Solution : The order 5 means at the most 4 keys are allowed.

Step 1 : Insert 78, 21, 14, 11 as follows -

11	14	21	78

Step 2 : If we insert 97 then the sequence becomes 11 14 21 78 97. Then, the sequence will split, 21 will go up. The partial tree will be -

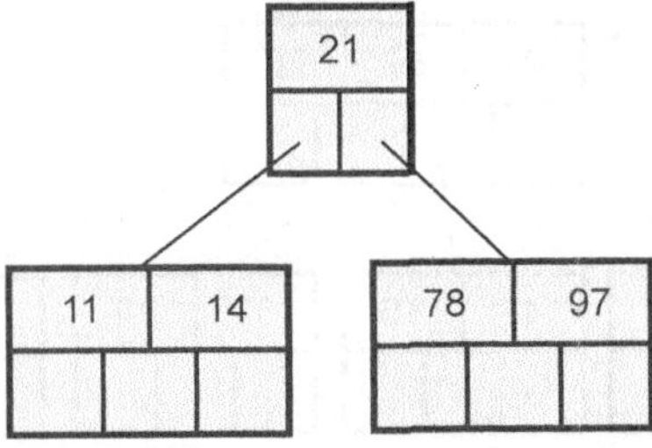

Step 3 : Now insert 85, 74. Then the tree will be -

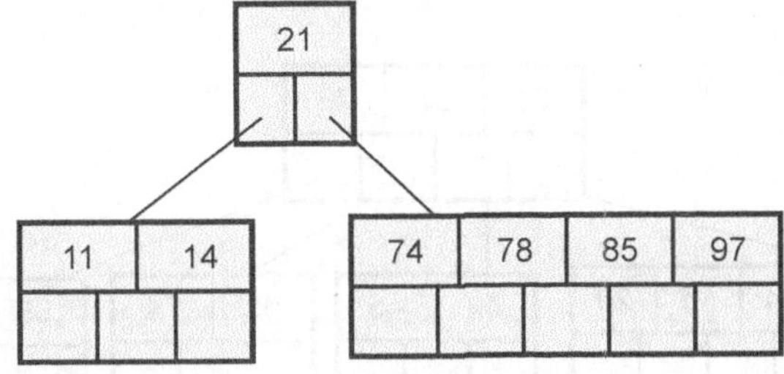

Step 4 : Insert 63. The sequence will then be 63 74 78 85 97. This sequence will then split, 78 will go up. The partial tree will be -

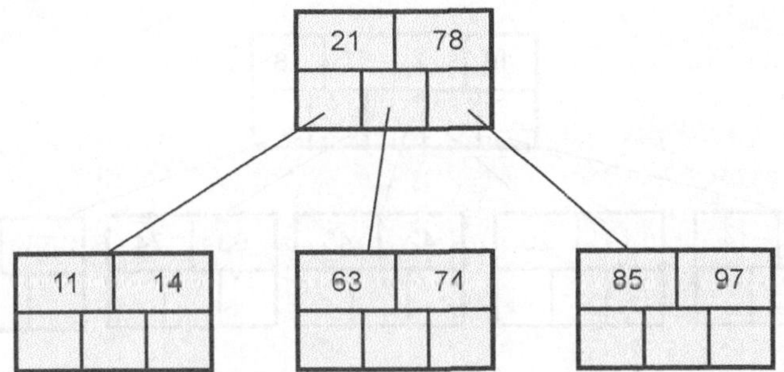

Step 5 : Insert 42, 45.

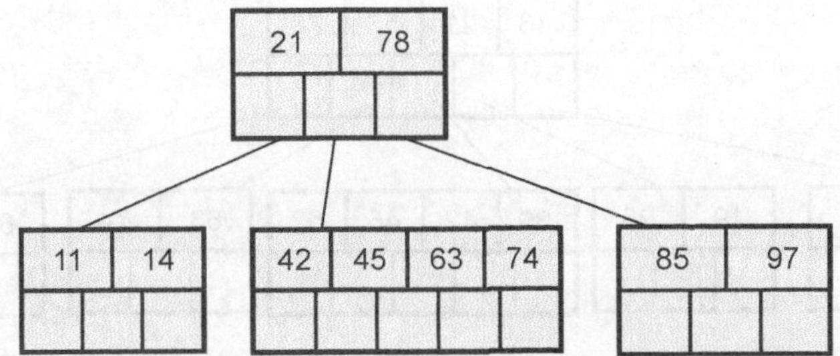

Step 6 : If we insert 57, then the sequence will be 42 45 57 63 74. Then this sequence will split and 57 will go up.

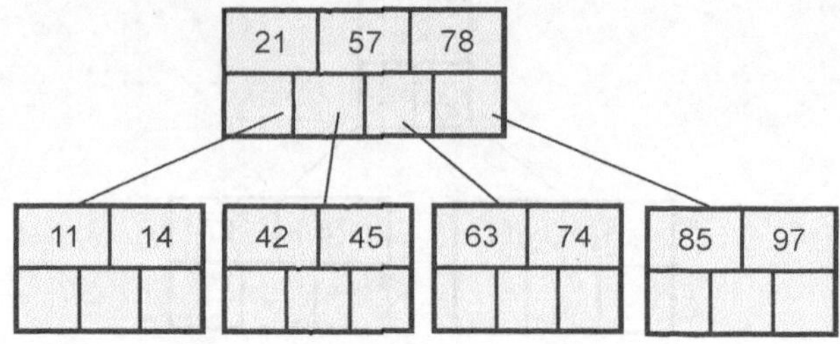

Step 7 : Insert 20, 16. The tree will be -

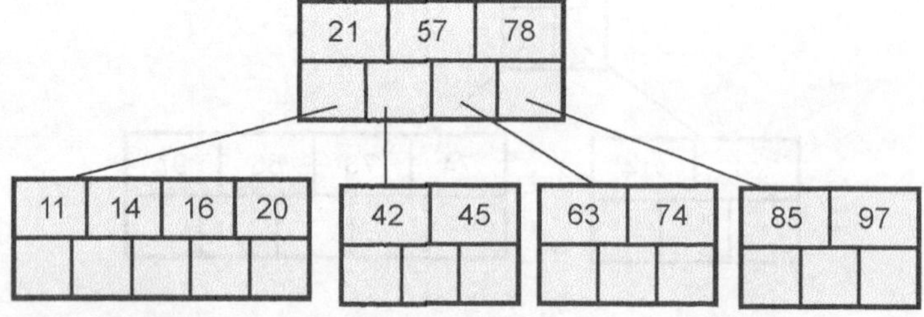

Step 8 : If we insert 19, then the sequence will be 11 14 16 19 20. It will split and 16 will go up.

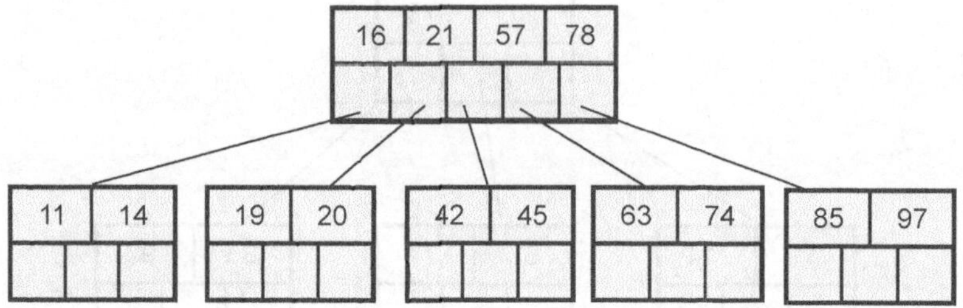

Step 9 : Insert 52, 30.

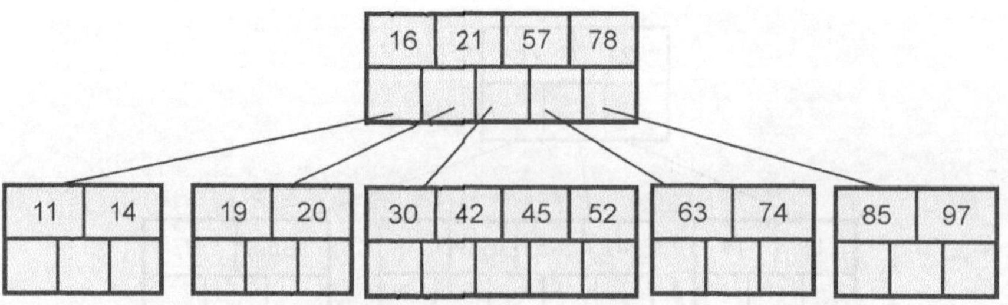

Step 10 : Insert 21. The sequence will becomes 21 30 42 45 52. Then 42 will go up. But now the sequence at root level becomes 16 21 42 57 78. Again 42 will be the middle element and it will go up.

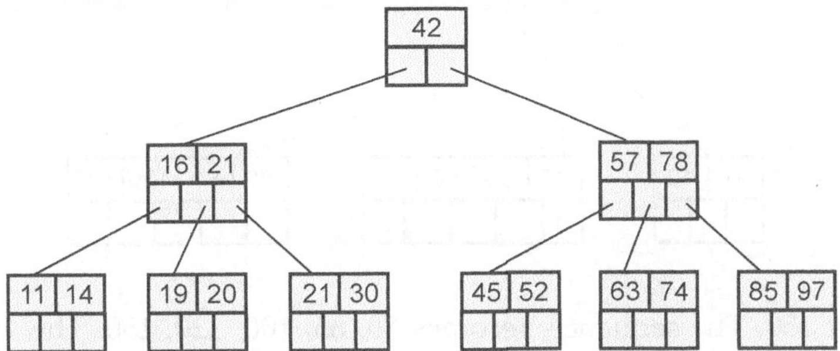

This is the required B-tree.

Example 5.5.2 *What is B tree ? Generate a B tree of order 5 for given data 50, 85, 12, 10, 6, 60, 70, 80, 37, 100, 120, 65, 150, 62, 30, 17, 15, 28, 75, 78.*

SPPU : May-11,12, Dec.-12, Marks 10

Solution : B-tree : B-tree is a specialized multiway tree used to store the records in a disk. There are number of subtrees to each node. So that the height of the tree is relatively small. So that only small number of nodes must be read from disk to retrieve an item.

The order 5 means, 4 keys are allowed, in each node.

Step 1 : Insert 50, 85, 12, 10.

Step 2 : Insert 6. The sequence becomes 6, 10, 12, 50 85. Then the 12 will go up

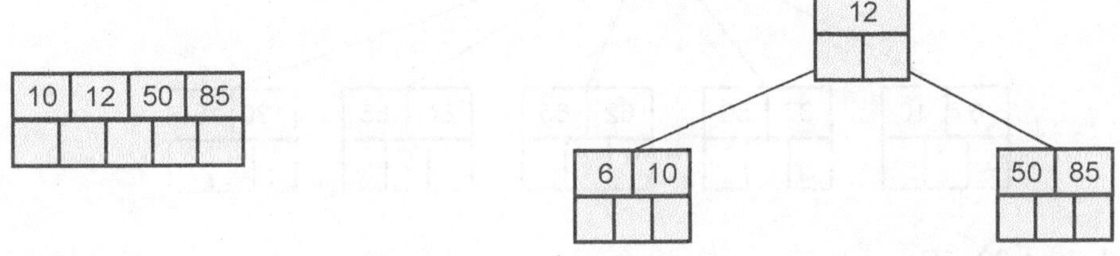

Step 3 : Insert 60, 70

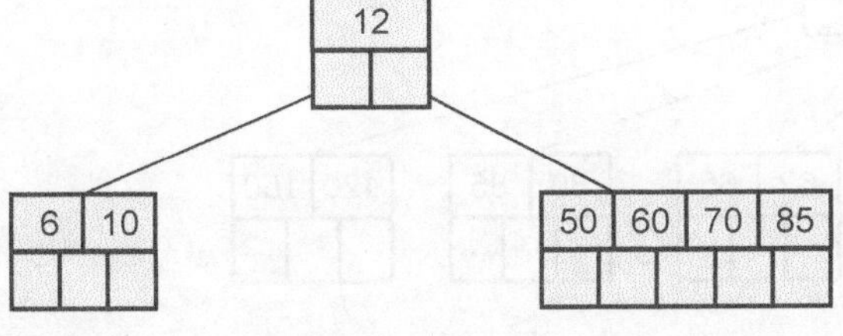

Step 4 : Insert 80. The sequence becomes 50, 60, 70, 80, 85. The 70 will go up.

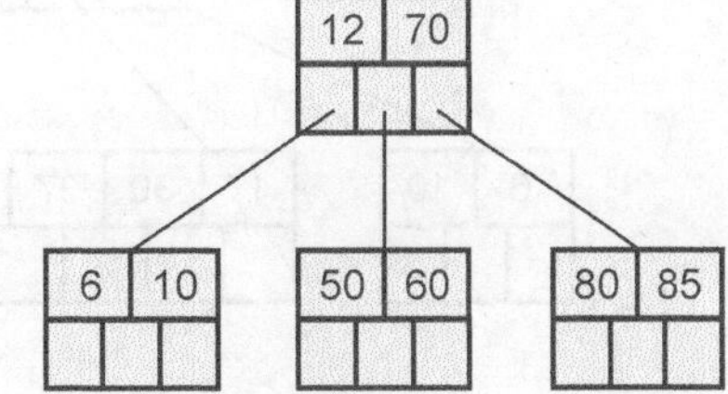

Step 5 : Insert 37, 100, 120, 65

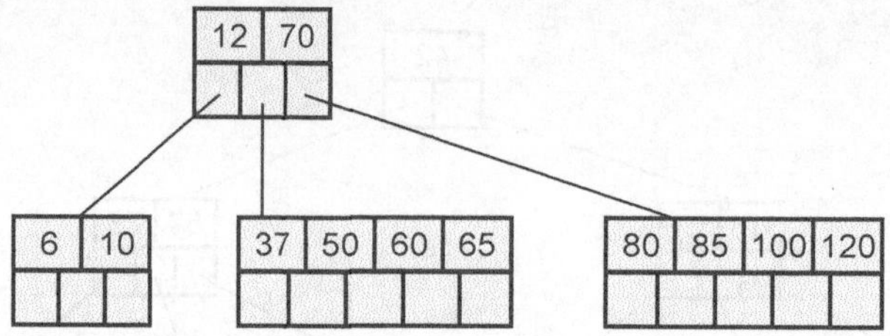

Step 6 : Insert 150. The sequence becomes 80, 85, 100, 120, 150. The 100 will go up.

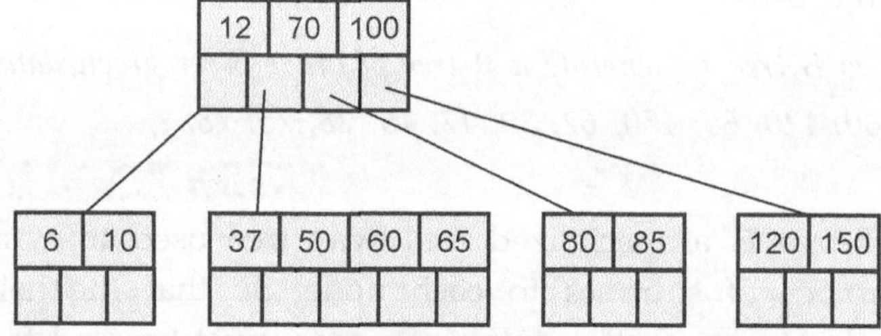

Step 7 : Insert 62. The sequence becomes 37, 50, 60, 62, 65. The 60 will go up.

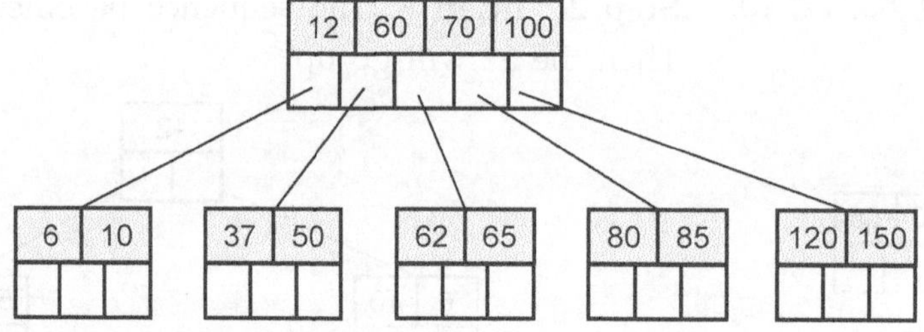

Step 8 : Insert 30, 17.

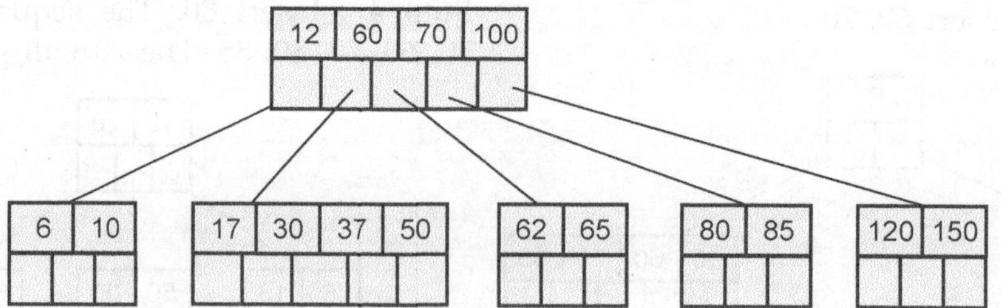

Step 9 : Insert 15. The sequence becomes 15, 17, 30, 37, 50. The 30 will go up. But at root level the sequence becomes 12, 30, 60, 70, 100. Again the 60 will go up.

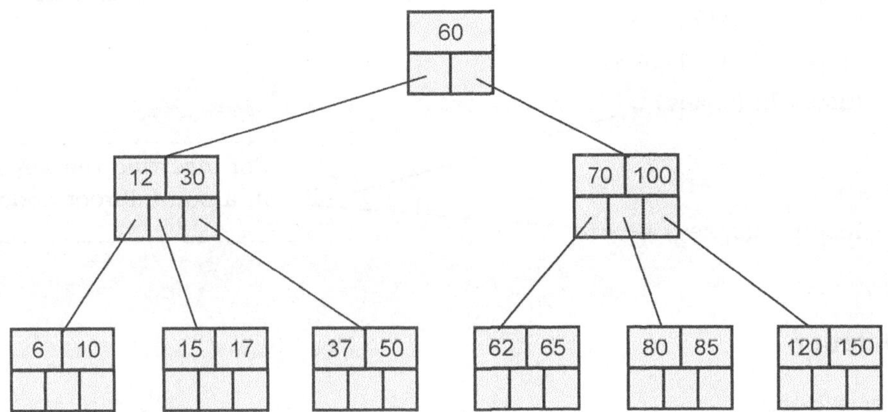

Step 10 : Insert 28, 75, 78.

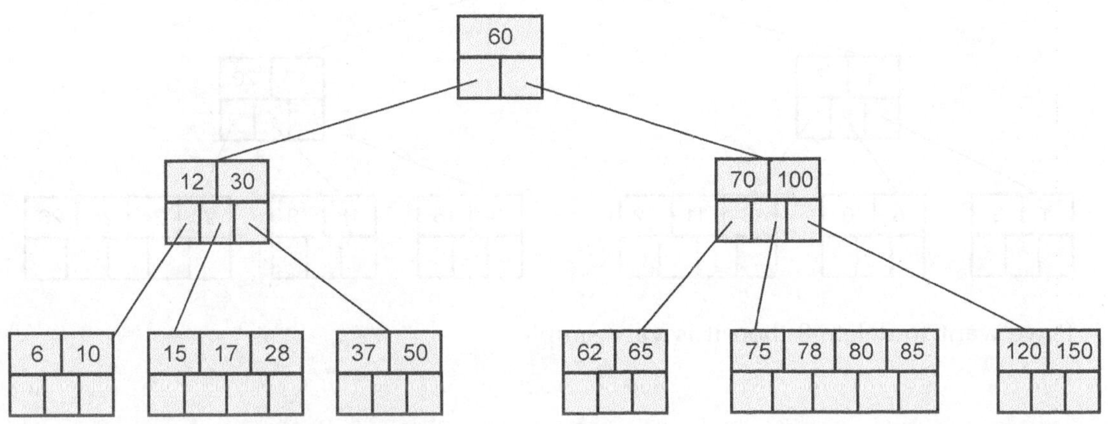

Algorithm for insertion in B-tree

```
Algorithm insert (root, key)
{
    // Problem Description: This algorithm is for
    // inserting key node in B-tree.
    temp ← root
    if (n[temp] = 2t – 1) then        Insertion is needed if
                                      (2t – 1) key are there.
        s ← get_node( ) // memory is allocated.
    {
```

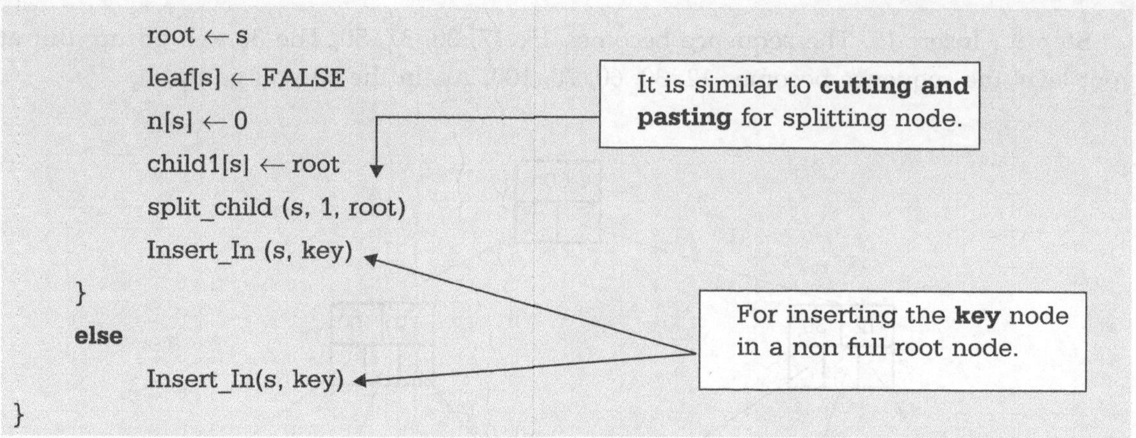

```
        root ← s
        leaf[s] ← FALSE
        n[s] ← 0
        child1[s] ← root
        split_child (s, 1, root)
        Insert_In (s, key)
    }
    else
        Insert_In(s, key)
}
```


5.5.2 Deletion

Consider a B-tree.

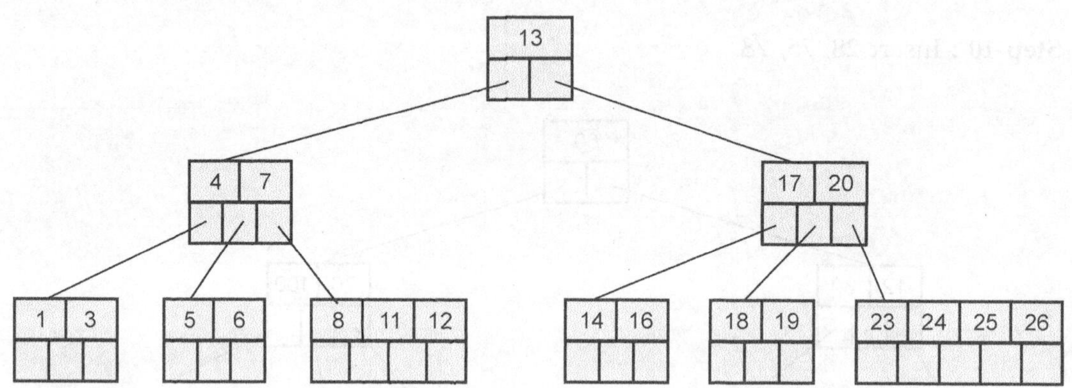

If we want to delete 8 then it is very simple.

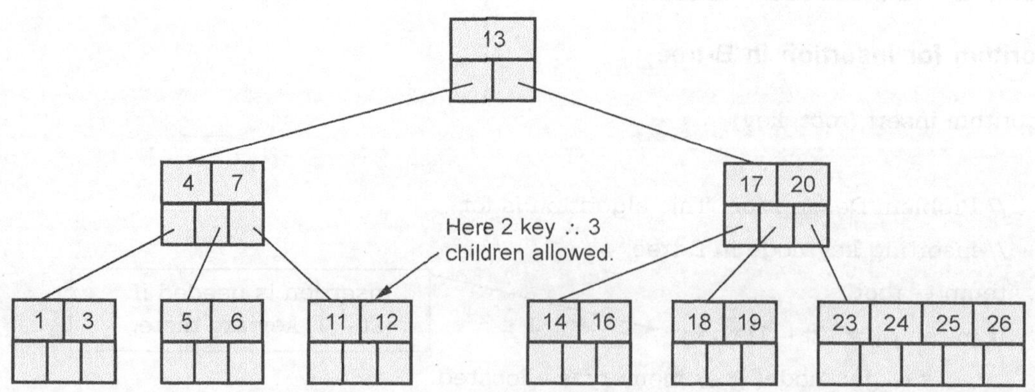

Now we will delete 20, the 20 is not in a leaf node so we will find its successor which is 23. Hence 23 will be moved up to replace 20.

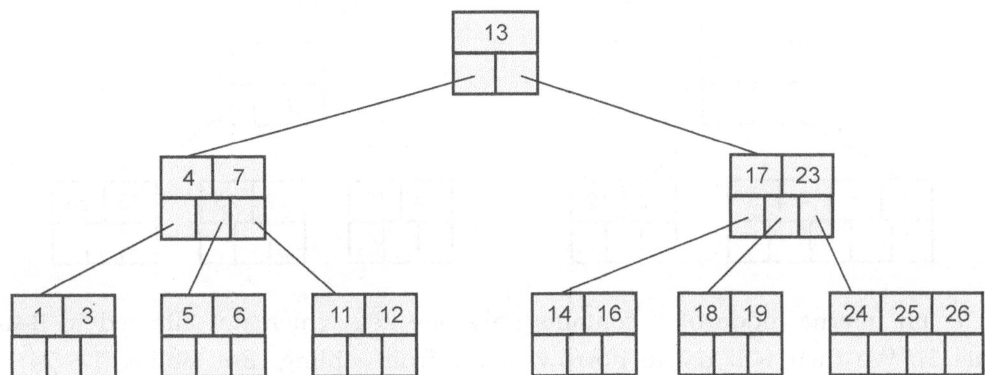

Next we will delete 18. Deletion of 18 from the corresponding node causes the node with only one key, which is not desired (as per rule 4) in B-tree of order 5. The sibling node to immediate right has an extra key. In such a case we can borrow a key from parent and move spare key of sibling to up. See the following figure.

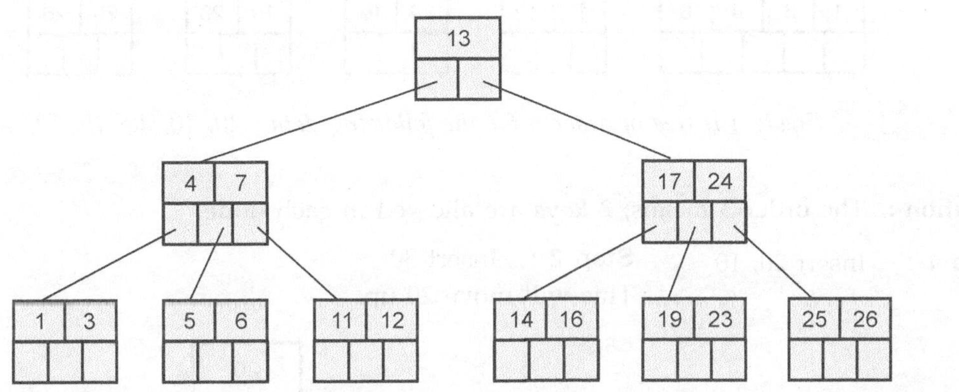

Now delete 5. But deletion of 5 is not easy. The first thing is 5 is from leaf node. Secondly this leaf node has no extra keys. In such a situation we can combine this node with one of the siblings. That means remove 5 and combine 6 with the nodes 1, 3. To make the tree balanced we have to move parent's key down. Hence we will move 4 down as 4 is between 1, 3 and 6. The tree will be -

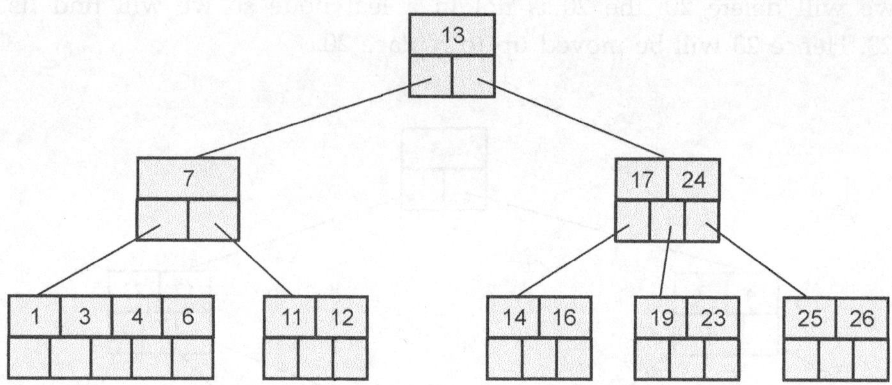

But again internal node of 7 contains only one key which not allowed in B-tree (as per rule 3). We then will try to borrow a key from sibling. But sibling 17, 24 has no spare key. Hence what we can do is that, combine 7 with 13 and 17, 24. Hence the B-tree will be

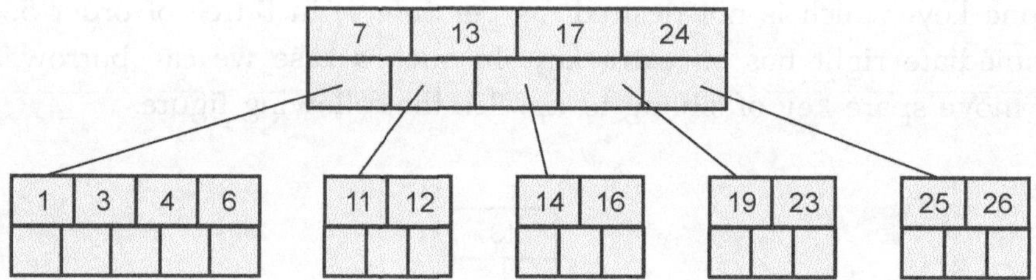

Example 5.5.3 *Create a B tree of order 3 for the following data : 20, 10, 30, 15, 12, 40, 50*

SPPU : Dec.-13, Marks 4

Solution : The order 3 means, 2 keys are allowed in each node.

Step 1 : Insert 20, 10

Step 2 : Insert 30

This will move 20 up.

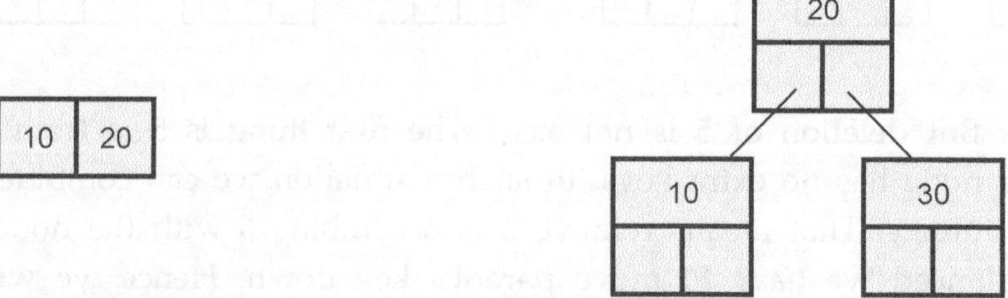

Step 3 : Insert 15

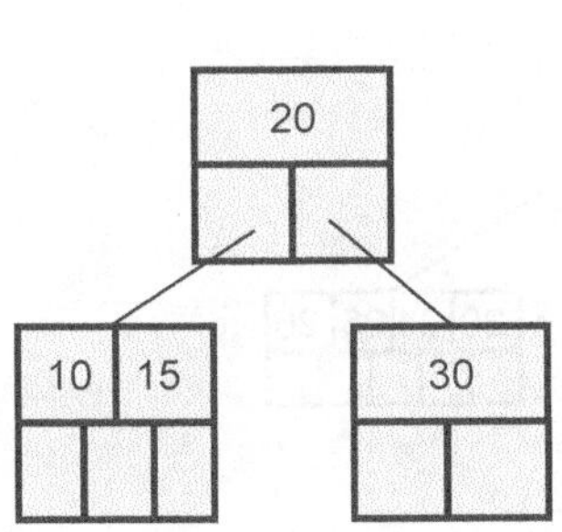

Step 4 : Insert 12.

This will make the list as 10, 12, 15. The 12 will group and join the 20.

Step 5 : Insert 40

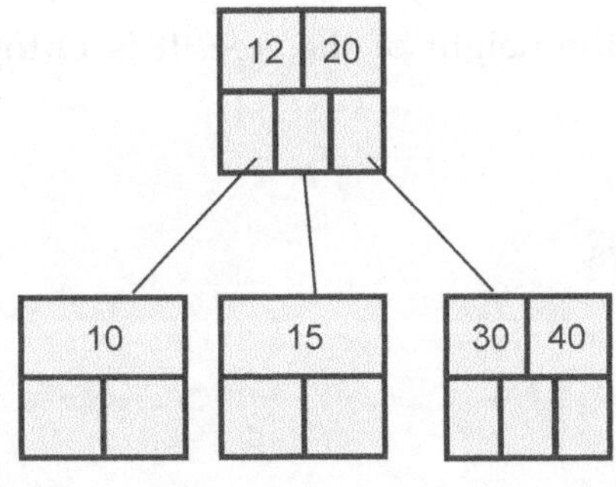

Step 6 : Insert 70

This will make the sequence as 30, 40, 70. Due to which 40 will go up. But again the sequence 12, 20, 40 need to get split. The 20 will go up.

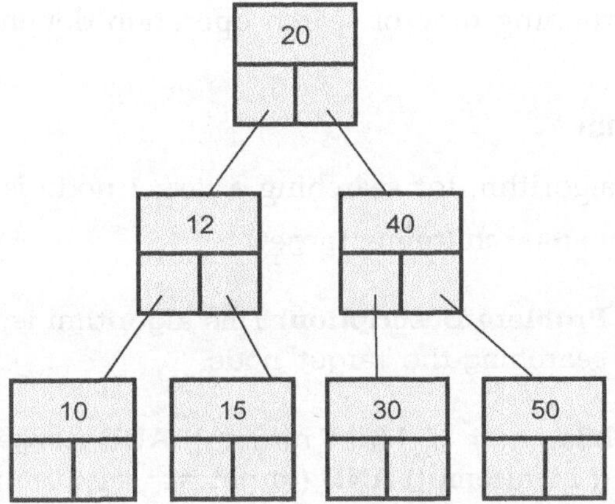

5.5.3 Searching

The search operation on B-tree is similar to a search on binary search tree. Instead of choosing between a left and right child as in binary tree, B-tree makes an m-way choice. Consider a B-tree as given below -

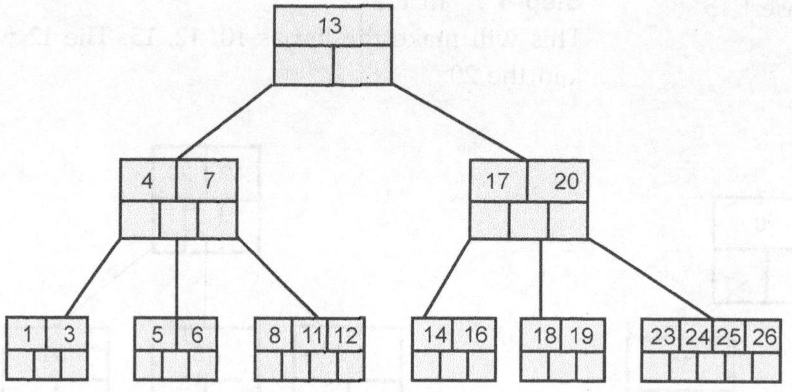

If we want to search node 11 then

i) 11 < 13 : Hence search left node.

ii) 11 > 7 : Hence rightmost node.

iii) 11 > 8 , move in second block.

iv) Node 11 is found.

The running time of search operation depends upon the height of the tree. It is **O(log n)**.

Algorithm

The algorithm for searching a target node is as follows.

```
Algorithm Search (temp, target)
{
    // Problem Description: This algorithm is for
    // searching the 'target' node
        i ← 1
    while i ← i + 1 (( i ≤ n[temp]) AND (target > key_i [temp]))
    if (( i ≤ n[temp]) AND (target == key_i[temp]))
        return (temp, i)
    if (leaf [temp] == TRUE) then
        return NULL
    else READ ( C_i[temp] )
        return search ((C_i [temp], target)
}
```

Desired node is present.

The **search** operation on B-tree is similar to a search operation on a binary tree. The desired child is chosen by performing linear search of values in the node. The running time of this algorithm is O(log n).

5.5.4 Height of B-Trees

The maximum height of B-tree gives an upper bound on number of disk access. The minimum number of keys in a B-tree of order 2m and depth h is

$$1 + 2m + 2m(m + 1) + 2m\,(m+1)^2 + \ldots + 2m\,(m+1)^{h-1}$$

$$= 1 + \sum_{i=1}^{h} 2m\,(m+1)^{i-1}$$

The maximum height of B-tree with n keys

$$\log_{m+1} \frac{n}{2m} = \mathbf{O(\log n)}$$

5.5.5 Variants of B-Trees

There are two variants of B-trees - B+ trees and B* trees.

The B+ tree is a B-tree in which the data is stored only in the leaf nodes due to which the efficient data access is possible.

The B* tree is a B-tree in which each node except root node is at least 2/3 full rather than just half full.

5.5.6 Implementation of B-Trees

C++ Code

```
/*********************************************************************
Implementation of various operations of  B-tree
*********************************************************************/
#include<iostream.h>
#include <stdio.h>
#include <string.h>
#include<conio.h>
#include <stdlib.h>
#define MAX 4 //maximum order m
#define MIN 2 //minimum allowed elements

typedef char Type[10];
typedef struct Btree
{
      Type  key;
} BT;

typedef struct treenode
{
            int count;
```

```
            BT entry[MAX+1];
            treenode *branch[MAX+1];
}node;
class B
{
 private:
 node *root;
 public:
 int LT(char *,char *);
 int EQ(char *,char *);
 node *Search(Type target,node *root,int *targetpos);
 int SearchNode(Type target,node *current,int *pos);
 node *Insert(BT New,node *root);
 int MoveDown(BT New,node *current,BT *med,node **medright);
 void InsertIn(BT med,node *medright,node *current,int pos);
 void Split(BT med,node *medright,node *current,int pos,BT *newmedian, node
**newright);
 void Delete(Type target, node **root);
 void Del_node(Type target, node *current);
 void Remove(node *current, int pos);
 void Successor(node *current, int pos);
 void Adjust(node *current, int pos);
 void MoveRight(node *current, int pos);
 void MoveLeft(node *current, int pos);
 void Combine(node *current, int pos);
 void InOrder(node *root);
};

int B::LT(char *a,char *b)
{
 if((strcmp(a,b)) < (0))
      return 1;
 else
      return 0;
}
int B::EQ(char *a,char *b)
{
 if((strcmp(a,b)) == (0))
      return 1;
 else
 return 0;
}
/*
Search: traverse B-tree in search of desired node
*/

node* B::Search(Type target, node *root, int *targetpos)
```

```
{
 if (root==NULL)
  return NULL;
 else if (SearchNode(target, root, targetpos))
  return root;
 else
  return Search(target, root->branch[*targetpos], targetpos);
}
/*
SearchNode: searches keys in node for target.
*/
int B::SearchNode(Type target,node *current, int *pos)
{
 if (LT(target, current->entry[1].key))
 {  /* searching the leftmost branch. */
  *pos = 0;
  return 0;
 }
 else
 { /* searching through the keys.    */
  for(*pos = current->count;
   LT(target, current->entry[*pos].key) && *pos > 1; (*pos)--);
  return EQ(target, current->entry[*pos].key);
 }
}
/*
Insert: inserts entry into the B-tree.
*/
node *B::Insert(BT newentry,node *root)
{
 BT medentry; // node to be inserted as new root
 node *medright; // subtree on right of medentry
 node *New;  // required when the height of the tree increases
 if (MoveDown(newentry, root, &medentry, &medright))
 {
     New = new node;
     New->count = 1;
     New->entry[1] = medentry;
     New->branch[0] = root;
     New->branch[1] = medright;
     return New;
 }
 return root;
}
/*
MoveDown: recursively move down tree searching for newentry.
*/
```

```
int B::MoveDown(BT New,node *current,BT *med,node **medright)
{
 int pos;
 if (current == NULL)
 {
  *med = New;/*new node*/
  *medright = NULL;
  return 1;
 }
 else
 {                /* Search the current node.    */
   if(SearchNode(New.key, current, &pos))
     cout<<"Duplicate key !!";
   if(MoveDown(New, current->branch[pos], med, medright))
     if (current->count < MAX)
      {
          //insertion of median key.
          InsertIn(*med, *medright, current, pos);
          return 0;
      }
     else
      {
      Split(*med, *medright, current, pos, med, medright);
      return 1;
     }
    return 0;
 }
}

/*
 InsertIn: inserts a key into a node
 */
void B::InsertIn(BT med,node *medright,node *current, int pos)

{
 /* index to move keys to make room for medentry   */
 int i;
 for (i = current->count; i > pos; i--)
 {
  /* Shift all the keys and branches to the right    */
  current->entry[i+1] = current->entry[i];
  current->branch[i+1] = current->branch[i];
 }
 current->entry[pos+1] = med;
 current->branch[pos+1] = medright;
 current->count++;
```

```
}
/*
 Split: splits a full node.
*/

void B::Split(BT med,node *medright,node *current, int pos,
                                        BT *newmedian,node **newright)
{
 int i;      /* used for copying from *current to new node   */
 int median; /* median position in the combined, overfull node   */
 if (pos <= MIN) /* Determine if new key goes to left or right half. */
   median = MIN;
 else
   median = MIN + 1;
 /* Get a new node and put it on the right.  */
  *newright = new node;
  for (i = median+1; i <= MAX; i++)
   { /* Move half the keys.  */
     (*newright)->entry[i - median] = current->entry[i];
     (*newright)->branch[i - median] = current->branch[i];
   }
   (*newright)->count = MAX - median;
   current->count = median;
   if (pos <= MIN)      /* Pushing in the new key. */
     InsertIn(med, medright, current, pos);
   else
     InsertIn(med, medright, *newright, pos - median);
   *newmedian = current->entry[current->count];
   (*newright)->branch[0] = current->branch[current->count];
   current->count--;
}

/*
 Delete: deletes target from the B-tree.
*/

void B::Delete(Type target, node **root)
{
  node *Prev;
  Del_node(target,*root);
  if ((*root)->count == 0)//empty root
  {
        Prev = *root;
        *root = (*root)->branch[0];
        free(Prev);
  }
}
```

```
/*
Del_node: look for target to delete.
*/

void B::Del_node(Type target,node *current)
{
 int pos;   /* location of target or of branch on which to search   */
 if (!current)
 {
  cout<"Item not in the B-tree.";
  return;
 }
 else
 {
  if (SearchNode(target, current, &pos))
    if (current->branch[pos-1])
     {
      Successor(current, pos);
      /* replaces entry[pos] by its successor */
                                     Del_node(current->entry[pos].key,current->branch[pos]);
     }
     else
      Remove(current, pos);
     /* removes key from pos of *current   */
  else
 /* Target was not found in the current node.*/
     Del_node(target, current->branch[pos]);
  if (current->branch[pos])
   if (current->branch[pos]->count < MIN)
     Adjust(current, pos);
 }
}

/*
Remove: delete an entry and the branch to its right.
*/

void B::Remove(node *current, int pos)
{
 int i;     /* index for moving entries */
 for (i = pos+1; i <= current->count; i++)
 {
  current->entry[i-1] = current->entry[i];
  current->branch[i-1] = current->branch[i];
 }
```

```
 current->count- -;
}
/*
Successor: finds and replaces an entry by its immediate successor.
*/
void B::Successor(node *current, int pos)
{
 node *leaf;     /* used to move down the tree to a leaf */
 /* Move to leftmost    */
 for (leaf=current->branch[pos];leaf->branch[0];
 leaf = leaf->branch[0]);
   current->entry[pos] = leaf->entry[1];
}

/*
Adjust: Adjusts the minimum number of entries.
*/

void B::Adjust(node *current, int pos)
{

  if (pos == 0)   /*  leftmost key  */
   if (current->branch[1]->count > MIN)
     MoveLeft(current, 1);
   else
     Combine(current, 1);
  else if (pos == current->count) /*  rightmost key */
   if (current->branch[pos-1]->count > MIN)
      MoveRight(current, pos);
   else
      Combine(current, pos);
  else if (current->branch[pos-1]->count > MIN)
      MoveRight(current, pos);
  else if (current->branch[pos+1]->count > MIN)
      MoveLeft(current, pos+1);
  else
      Combine(current, pos);
}

/*
 MoveRight: move a key to the right.
*/
void B::MoveRight(node *current, int pos)
{
          int i;
          node *t;
```

```
        t = current->branch[pos];
        for (i = t->count;i > 0;i - -)
        {
        /* Shift all keys in the right node one position.  */
                t->entry[i+1] = t->entry[i];
                t->branch[i+1] = t->branch[i];
        }
         /* Move key from parent to right node.  */
        t->branch[1] = t->branch[0];
        t->count++;
        t->entry[1] = current->entry[pos];
        /* Move last key of left node into parent  */
        t = current->branch[pos-1];
        current->entry[pos] = t->entry[t->count];
        current->branch[pos]->branch[0] = t->branch[t->count];
        t->count--;
}

/*
 MoveLeft: move a key to the left.

 */
void B::MoveLeft(node *current, int pos)
{
        int c;
        node *t;
        t = current->branch[pos-1]; /* Move key from parent into left node. */
        t->count++;
        t->entry[t->count] = current->entry[pos];
        t->branch[t->count] = current->branch[pos]->branch[0];

        t = current->branch[pos];  /* Move key from right node into parent. */
        current->entry[pos] = t->entry[1];
        t->branch[0] = t->branch[1];
        t->count- -;
        for (c = 1; c <= t->count; c++) {
                /* Shift all keys in right node one position leftward.  */
                t->entry[c] = t->entry[c+1];
                t->branch[c] = t->branch[c+1];
        }
}

/*
Combine: combine adjacent nodes.
*/

void B::Combine(node *current, int pos)
```

```
{
        int c;
        node *right;
        node *left;

        right = current->branch[pos];
        left = current->branch[pos-1];      /* left node. */
        left->count++;              /* Insert the key from the parent. */
        left->entry[left->count] = current->entry[pos];
        left->branch[left->count] = right->branch[0];

        for (c = 1; c <= right->count; c++)
    { /* Insert all keys from right node. */
          left->count++;
          left->entry[left->count] = right->entry[c];
          left->branch[left->count] = right->branch[c];
        }

        for (c = pos; c < current->count; c++)
        { /* Delete key from parent node. */
          current->entry[c] = current->entry[c+1];
          current->branch[c] = current->branch[c+1];
        }
        current->count--;
        free(right);    /* free the right node. */
}

/*
InOrder: inorder traversal of the B-Tree.
*/

void B::InOrder(node *root)
{
        int pos;

        if (root)
        {
                InOrder(root->branch[0]);
                for (pos = 1; pos <= root->count; pos++)
                {
                        cout<<" "<<root->entry[pos].key;
                        InOrder(root->branch[pos]);
                }
        }
}
```

```
void main()
{
 int choice,targetpos;
 Type inKey;
 BT New;
 B obj;
 node *root, *target;
 root = NULL;
 while(1)
 {
  cout<<"\n\t\t Implementation of B-tree";
  cout<<"\n 1.Insert \n 2.Delete \n 3.Search \n 4.Display";
  cout<<"\n Enter Your choice";
  cin>>choice;
  switch(choice)
  {
   case 1:cout<<"Enter the Key to be inserted :";
          flushall();
          gets(New.key);
          root = obj.Insert(New, root);
          break;
   case 2:cout<<"Enter the Key to be deleted :";
          flushall();
               gets(New.key);
          cout<<"\n Deleting the desired item..."<<endl;
          obj.Delete(New.key, &root);
          break;
   case 3:cout<<"Enter the Key to be searched for :";
          flushall();
          gets(New.key);
          target = obj.Search(New.key, root, &targetpos);
          if (target)
          cout<<"The Searched Item: "<<target->entry[targetpos].key<<endl;
          else
          printf("Item is not present\n");
               break;
   case 4:cout<<"\n\nInOrder Traversal :\n";
          obj.InOrder(root);
               break;
   case 5:exit(0);
  }
 }
}
```

Output

```
                Implementation of B-tree
1.Insert
2.Delete
3.Search
4.Display
Enter Your choice1
Enter the Key to be inserted :13
                Implementation of B-tree
1.Insert
2.Delete
3.Search
4.Display
Enter Your choice1
Enter the Key to be inserted :21

                Implementation of B-tree
1.Insert
2.Delete
3.Search
4.Display
Enter Your choice1
Enter the Key to be inserted :25

                Implementation of B-tree
1.Insert
2.Delete
3.Search
4.Display
Enter Your choice1
Enter the Key to be inserted :45

                Implementation of B-tree
1.Insert
2.Delete
3.Search
4.Display
Enter Your choice1
Enter the Key to be inserted :32

                Implementation of B-tree
1.Insert
2.Delete
3.Search
4.Display
Enter Your choice1
```

```
Enter the Key to be inserted :40

              Implementation of B-tree
1.Insert
2.Delete
3.Search
4.Display
Enter Your choice1
Enter the Key to be inserted :51

              Implementation of B-tree
1.Insert
2.Delete
3.Search
4.Display
Enter Your choice4
InOrder Traversal :
 13  21  25  32  40  45  51
              Implementation of B-tree
1.Insert
2.Delete
3.Search
4.Display
              Implementation of B-tree
1.Insert
2.Delete
3.Search
4.Display
Enter Your choice3
Enter the Key to be searched for :25
The Searched Item: 25

              Implementation of B-tree
1.Insert
2.Delete
3.Search
4.Display
Enter Your choice2
Enter the Key to be deleted :40

Deleting the desired item...

              Implementation of B-tree
1.Insert
2.Delete
3.Search
4.Display
```

```
Enter Your choice4

InOrder Traversal :
 13 21 25 32 45 51
            Implementation of B-tree
1.Insert
2.Delete
3.Search
4.Display
Enter Your choice
```

University Questions

1. *Write short note on B-tree.* **SPPU : Dec.-09, Marks 4**
2. *What is B-tree? Write a pseudo C algorithm for deleting a node from B-tree.* **SPPU : May-05,11,13, Dec.-07,10,12, Marks 8**
3. *Write a pseudo C/C++ code to search the data stored in a B tree.* **SPPU : Dec.-13, Marks 6**
4. *Write an algorithm to search an element in a B Tree.* **SPPU : May-14, Marks 4**

5.6 B+ Tree

SPPU : May-09, 10, 14, Dec.-10, 11, Marks 10

In B-trees the traversing of the nodes is done in inorder manner which is time consuming. We want such a data structure of B-tree which will allow us to access data sequentially, instead of inorder traversing.

In B+ trees from leaf nodes reference to any other node can be possible. The leaves in B+tree form a linked list which is useful in scanning the nodes sequentially. The insertion and deletion operations are similar to B-trees.

Consider following B+tree.

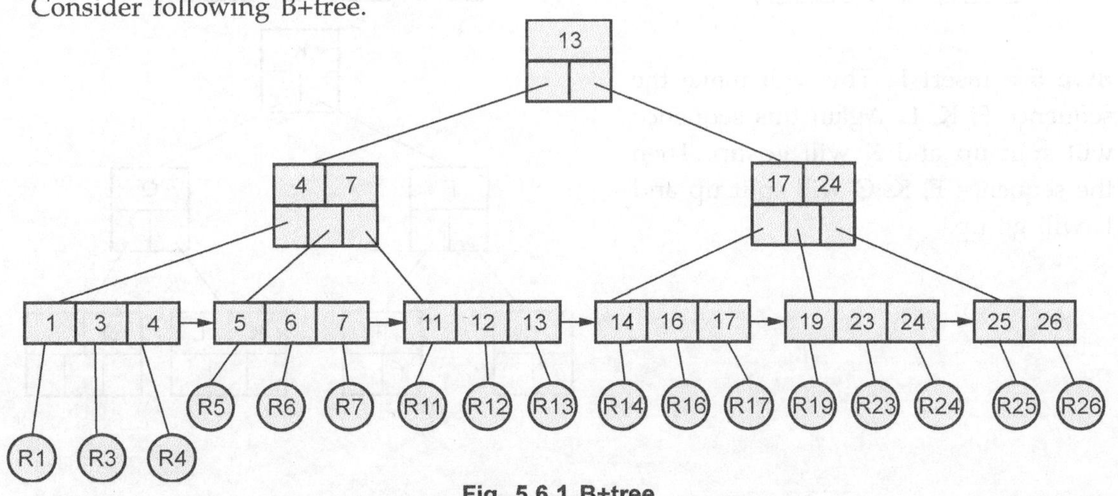

Fig. 5.6.1 B+tree

From leaf node only any key can be accessed of entire tree. There is no need to traverse the tree in inorder fashion. Thus B+tree gives faster access to any key.

Example 5.6.1 *Construct a B+tree for F, S, Q, K, C, L, H, T, V, W, M, R.*

SPPU : Dec.-10, Marks 8

Solution : The method for constructing B+tree is similar to the building of B tree but the only difference here is that, the parent nodes also appear in the leaf nodes. We will build B+tree for order 5.

The order 3 means at the most 2 keys are allowed.

Step 1 : Insert F and S

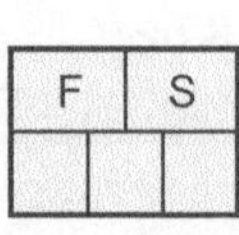

Step 2 : If we insert Q then the sequence will be F, Q, S. The Q will go up.

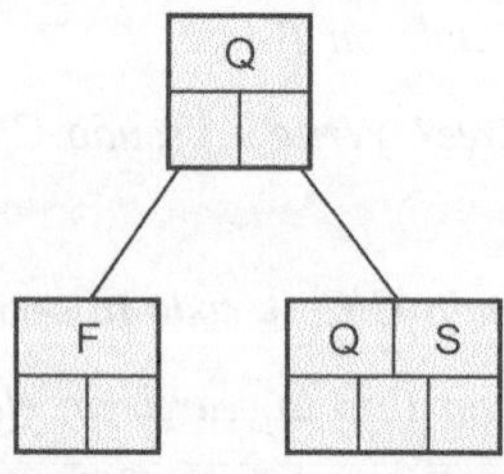

Step 3 : Insert K.

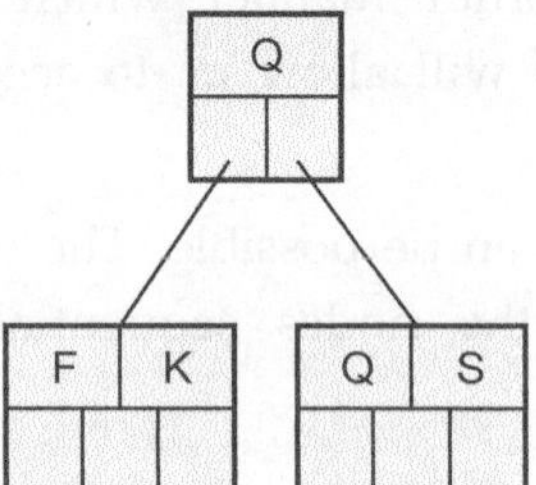

Step 4 : Insert C. But this will create a sequence C, F, K. This will split and F will go up.

F Q

C | F K | Q S

Step 5 : Insert L. This will make the sequence F, K, L. Again this sequence will split up and K will go up. Then the sequence F, K, Q will split up and K will go up.

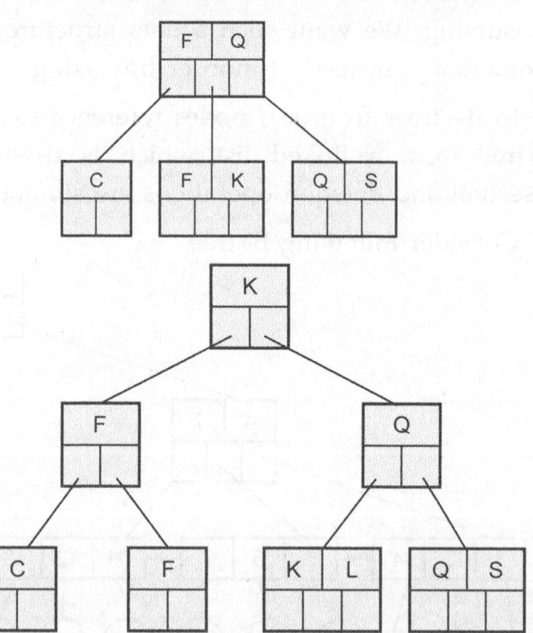

Step 6 : Insert H. This will make the sequence F, H, K. The sequence will split up and H will go up.

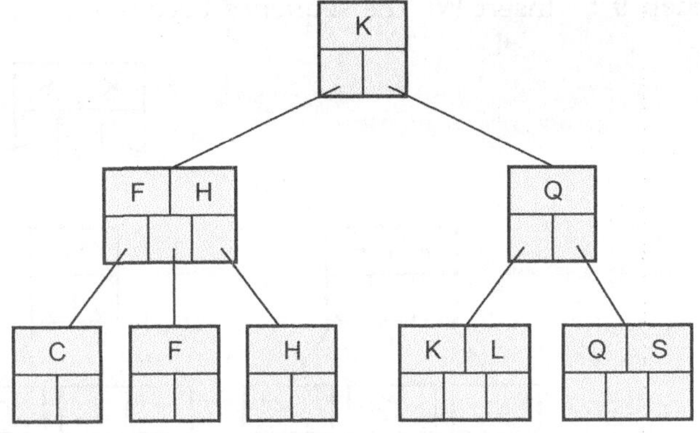

Step 7 : Insert T. The sequence Q, S, T will split up. The S will go up.

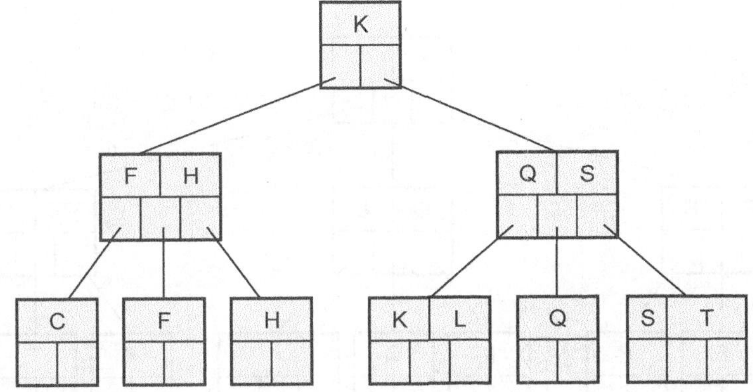

Step 8 : Insert V. The sequence S, T, V will - split - up. T will go up. But again the sequence Q, S, T will split up and S will go up.

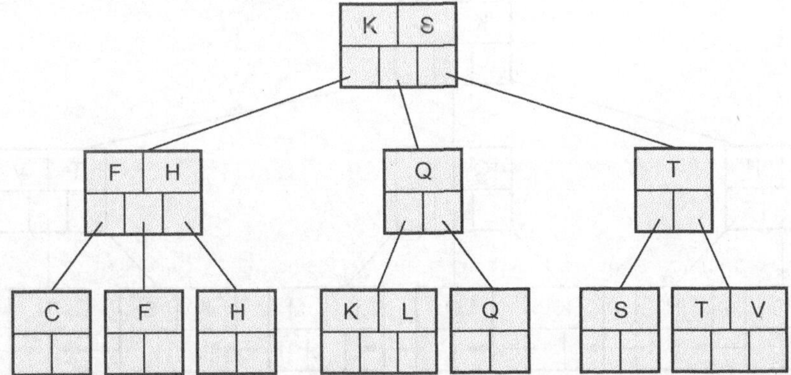

Step 9 : Insert W. The sequence becomes T, V, W. The V goes up.

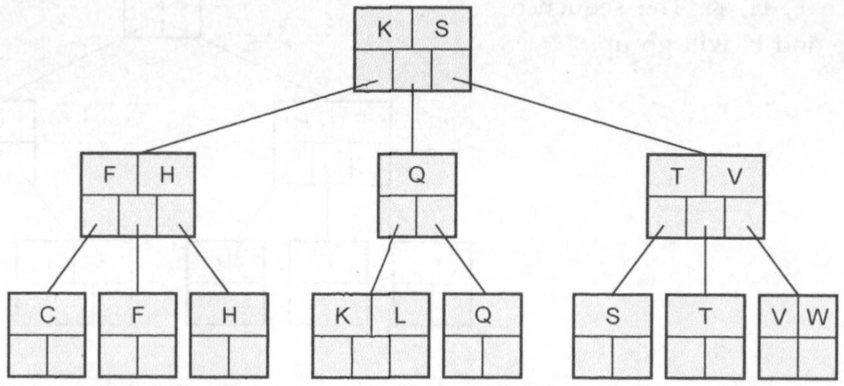

Step 10 : Insert M. The sequence K, L, M will split up. The L will go up.

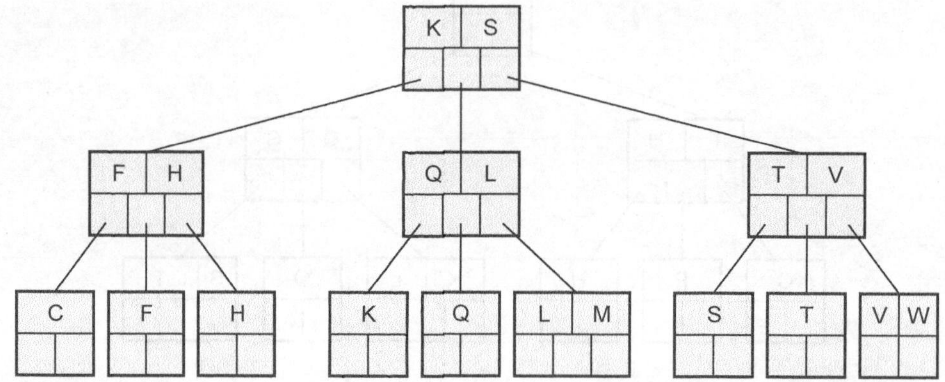

Step 11 : Insert R.

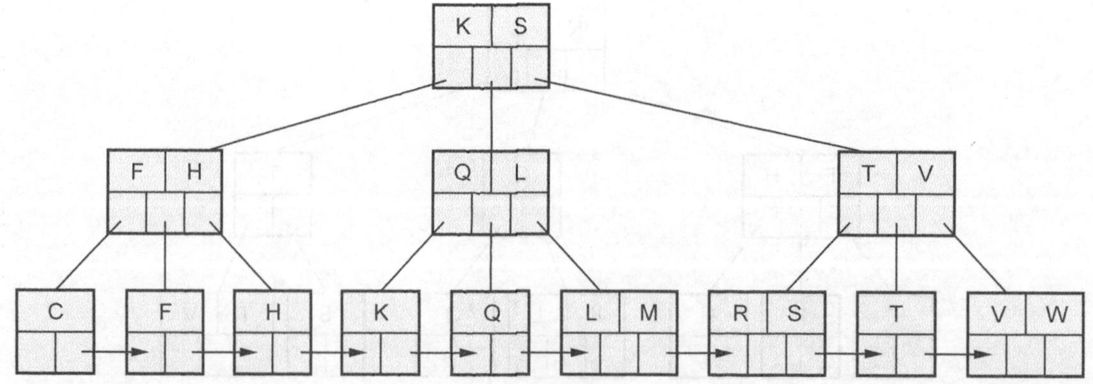

Fig. 5.6.2

Example 5.6.2 *Construct B+ tree for the following data :*

30, 31, 23, 32, 22, 28, 24, 29, 15, 26, 27, 34, 39, 36.

SPPU : May-09, Marks 6, Dec.-11, Marks 10

Solution : We will assume B+tree of order 5. That means maximum 4 keys are allowed in each node.

Step 1 : Insert 30, 31, 23, 32.

23	30	31	32

Step 2 : Insert 22. The sequence becomes 22 23 30 31 32. Then the 30 will go up.

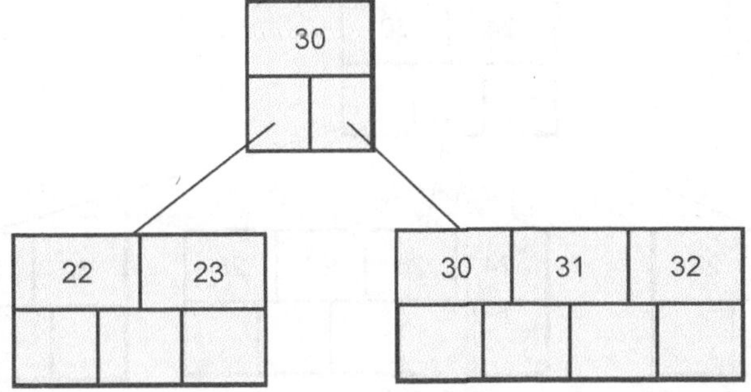

Step 3 : Insert 28, 24.

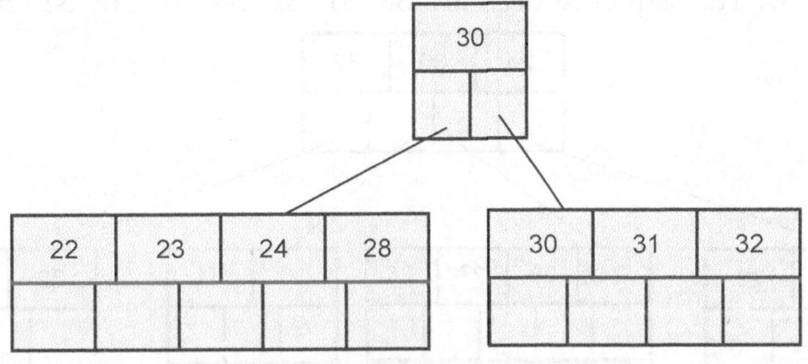

Step 4 : Insert 29. Then the sequence becomes 22 23 24 28 29. Hence 24 will go up.

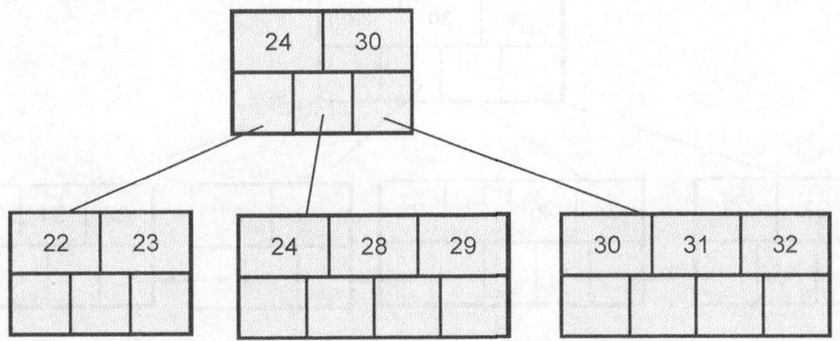

Step 5 : Insert 15, 26, 27.

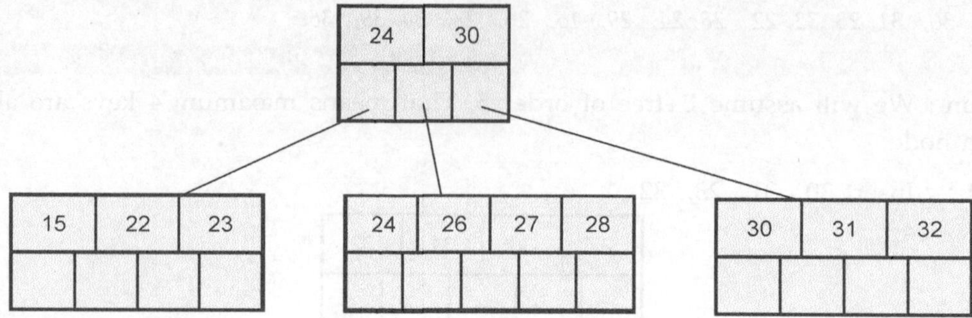

Step 6 : Insert 34.

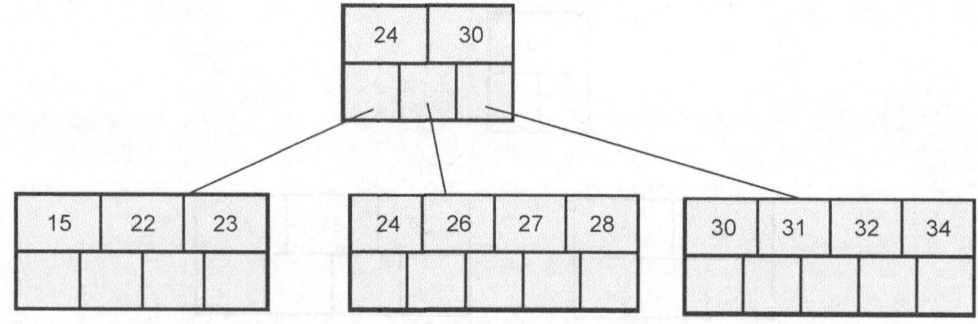

Step 7 : Insert 39. The sequence becomes 30 31 32 34 39. The 32 will go up.

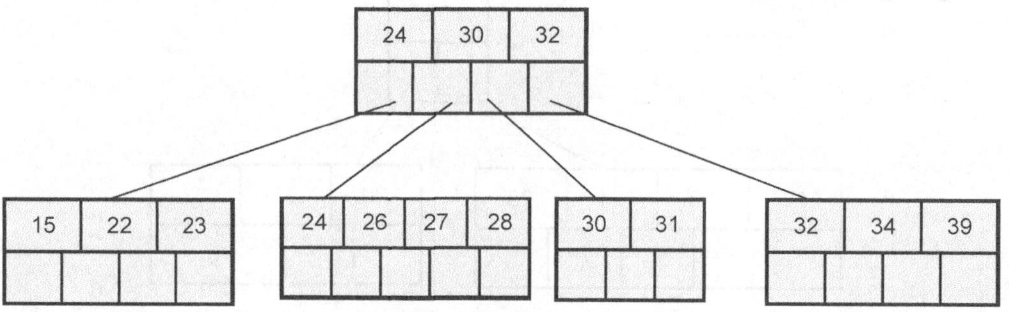

Step 8 : Insert 36.

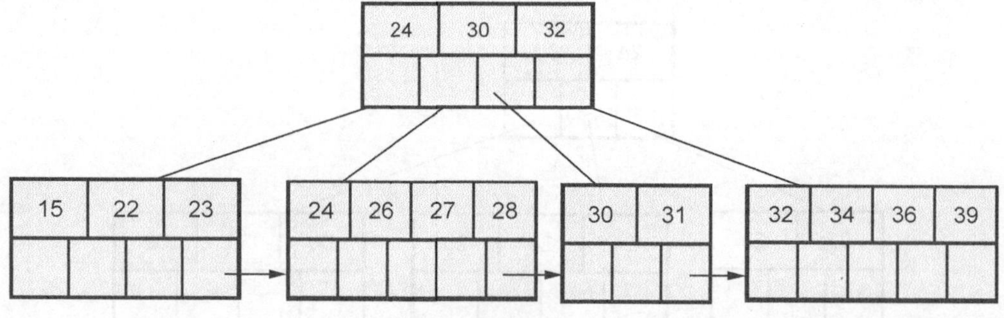

is required B+ tree.

University Questions

1. *What is a B+ tree? Give structure of its internal node. What are the variations of B and B+ trees. Give any two variations.* **SPPU : May-10, Marks 6**
2. *What is B+tree ? Give structure of its internal node. What are the order of B+ tree and characteristics of B+ tree.* **SPPU : May-14, Marks 7**

5.7 Trie Tree

Definition : A trie (derived from retrieval) is a multiway tree data structure used for storing strings over an alphabet. It is used to store a large amount of strings. The pattern matching can be done efficiently using tries. Following figure represents the trie.

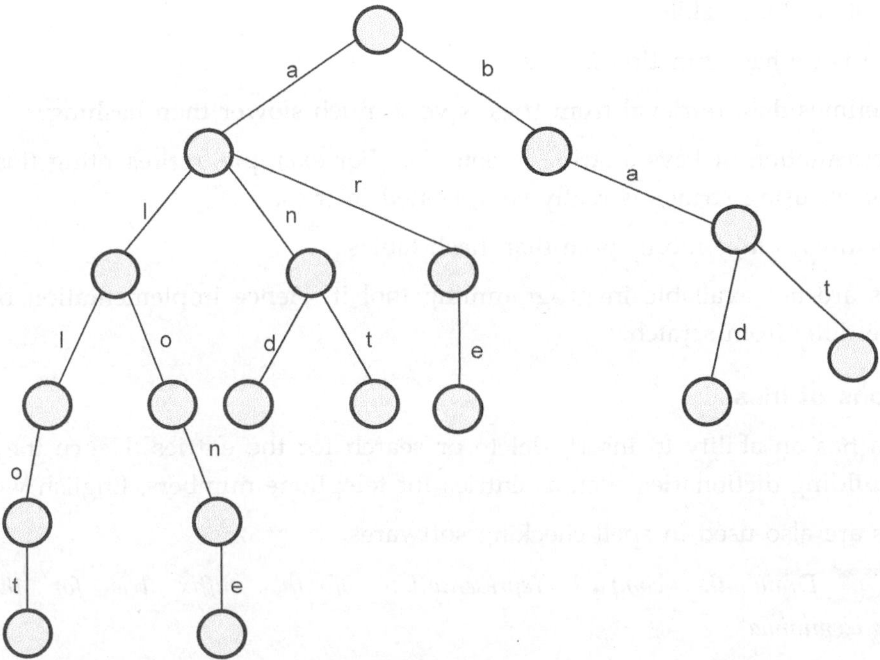

Fig. 5.7.1 Trie

The trie shows words like allot, alone, ant, and, are, bat, bad. The idea is that all strings sharing common prefix should come from a common node. The tries are used in spell checking programs.

- Preprocessing pattern improves the performance of pattern matching algorithm. But if a text is very large then it is better to preprocess text instead of pattern for efficient search.
- A trie is a data structure that supports pattern matching queries in time proportional to the pattern size

Advantages of tries

1. In tries the keys are searched using common prefixes. Hence it is faster. The lookup of keys depends upon the height in case of binary search tree.
2. Tries take less space when they contain a large number of short strings. As nodes are shared between the keys.
3. Tries help with longest prefix matching, when we want to find the key.

Comparison of tries with hash table

1. Looking up data in a trie is faster in worst case as compared to imperfect hash table.
2. There are no collisions of different keys in a trie.
3. In trie if single key is associated with more than one value then it resembles buckets in hash table.
4. There is no hash function in trie.
5. Sometimes data retrieval from tries is very much slower than hashing.
6. Representation of keys a string is complex. For example, representing floating point numbers using strings is really complicated in tries.
7. Tries always take more space than hash tables.
8. Tries are not available in programming tool it. Hence implementation of tries has to be done from scratch.

Applications of tries

1. Tries has an ability to insert, delete or search for the entries. Hence they are used in building dictionaries such as entries for telephone numbers, English words.
2. Tries are also used in spell-checking softwares.

Example 5.7.1 *Draw the compact representation of the suffix trie for the string "minimizeminima"*

Solution : Let us store the string in an array.

m	i	n	i	m	i	z	e	m	i	n	i	m	a
0	1	2	3	4	5	6	7	8	9	10	11	12	13

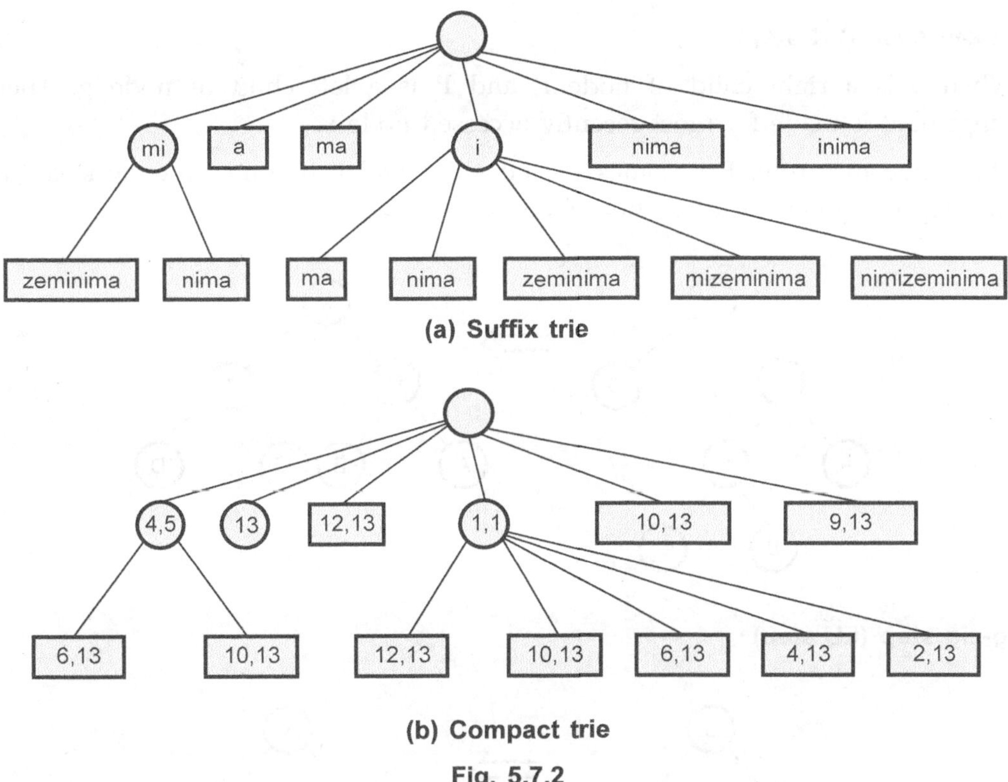

(a) Suffix trie

(b) Compact trie

Fig. 5.7.2

5.8 Splay Tree

- A splay tree is a self balancing binary search tree with no explicit balance condition. The splay tree has a **property** that recently accessed elements can be accessed quickly.
- All normal operations that are performed on binary search tree are performed on splay tree. But there is a special operation called **splaying** is performed on splay tree.
- Splaying means arranging the elements of a tree in such a way that the most recently accessed node will be placed as root of the tree.

Cases of Splaying

Various cases that arise are

1. Zig-zag step
2. Zig-zig step
3. Zig step.

These are basically rotations applied for the node x. Zig means left and zag means right. Let 'P' be the parent node of 'x' and 'g' be the grandparent of x.

1. Zig-zag case (LR step)

When x is a right child of node P and P is a left child of node g. Then the rearrangement is made for most recently accessed node x.

The x becomes root, P becomes its left child and g becomes the right child. The zig-zag step is equivalent to rotation about x.

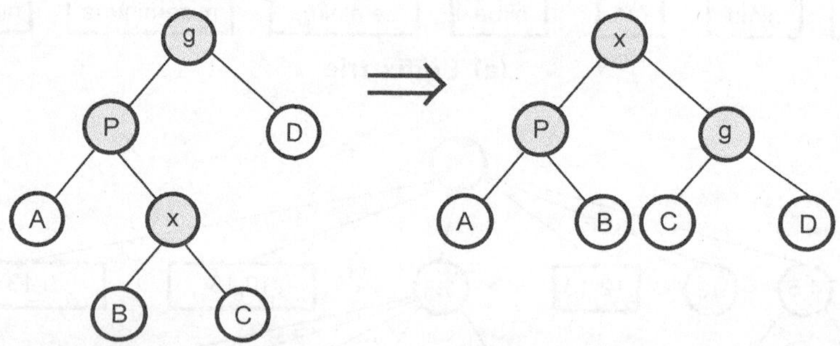

2. Zig-zig step (LL step)

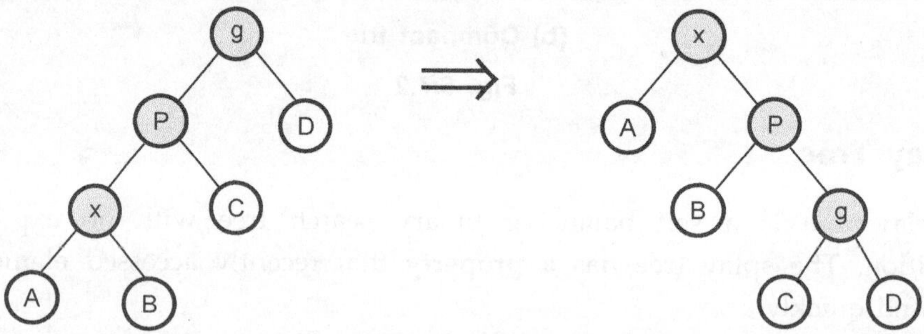

The P node becomes right child of x and g becomes right child of P, when elements get rearranged in zig-zig step.

3. Zig step (L step)

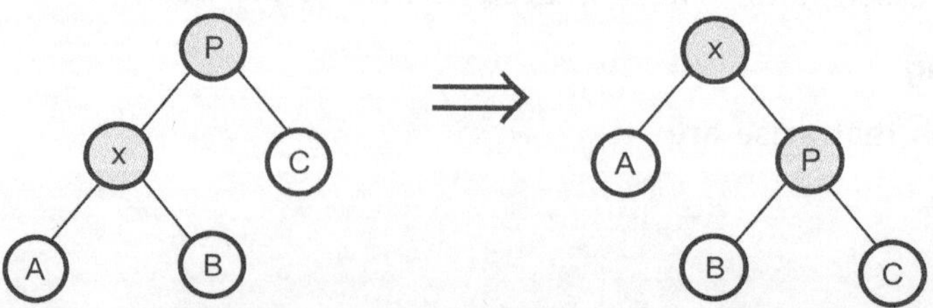

When x is attached as a left child of P node then the rearrangement that is needed is of zig type. In such a rearrangement P becomes right child of x node.

5.8.1 Splay Operations

Various operations supported by splay tree are

1. Splay
2. Find
3. Insert
4. Delete

The splay operation starts at splay node. The splay node is basically root of the binary search tree.

During splay operation the splay node that is been selected is at the deepest level. To move this node at root the sequence of splay steps are performed. When splay node reaches to root position the sequence of splay step is empty. The splay steps involve various rotations such as zig-zag, zig, zig-zig.

Search Operation

For searching the desired element from the given tree, the splaying operations are applied. If the node is present in the tree then, after performing spalying, the key node will be at root position. Let us understand this with the help of examples -

Example 5.8.1 *Search the element 3 from the given tree using splaying operations.*

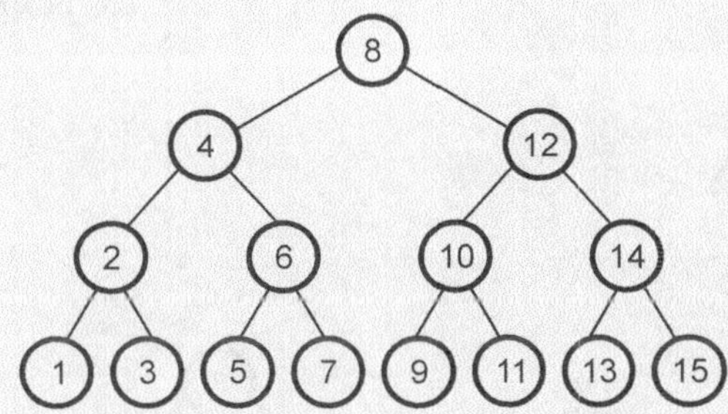

Solution : Now if want to find node '3'. Then focus of splay operation consists of node being splayed its parent and its grandparent.

The nodes involved in splay operation indicate zig-zag or LR rotation.

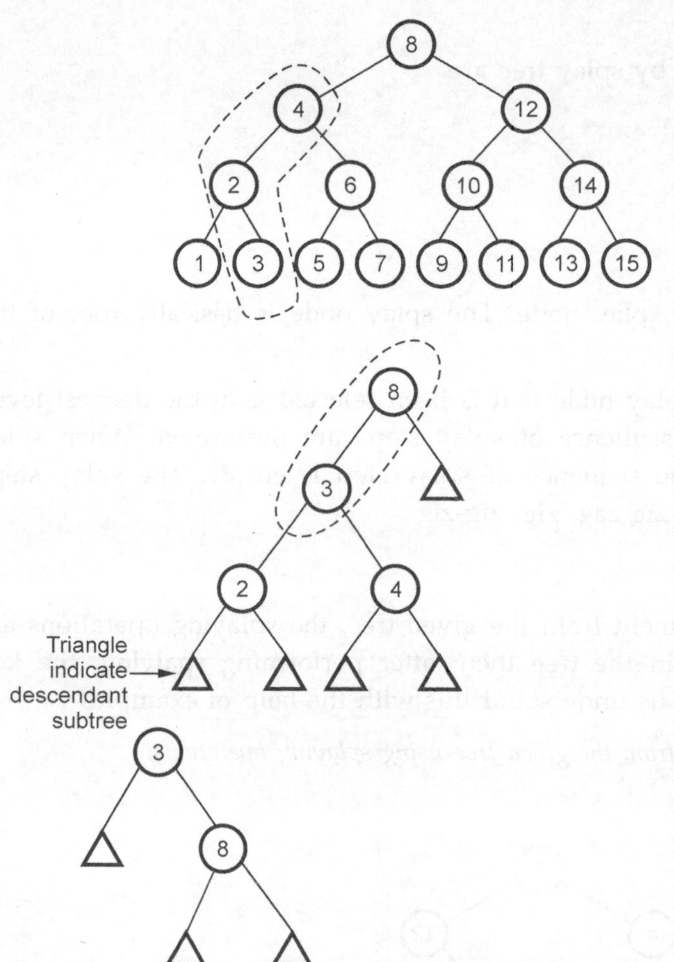

Now if we will apply zig-zag (LR) rotation.

After performing zig-zag rotation we get this tree. But again node '3' is not at root's position. Focusing on '3' we get the indication to apply zig(L) rotation.

After applying zig rotation we get such a tree. Note that '3' is at root's postion.

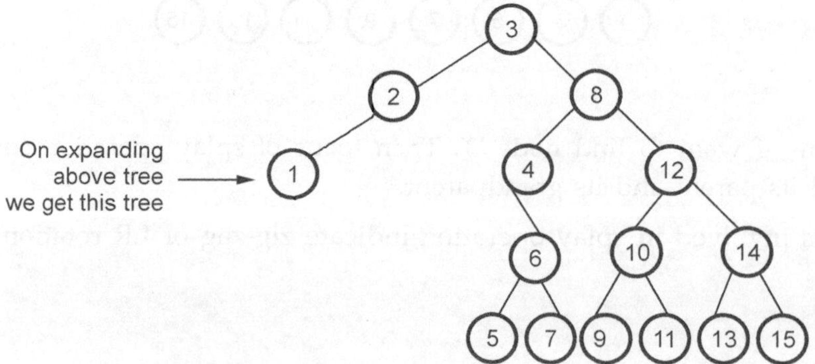

Example 5.8.2 *Search the node 8 from the given tree using splaying*

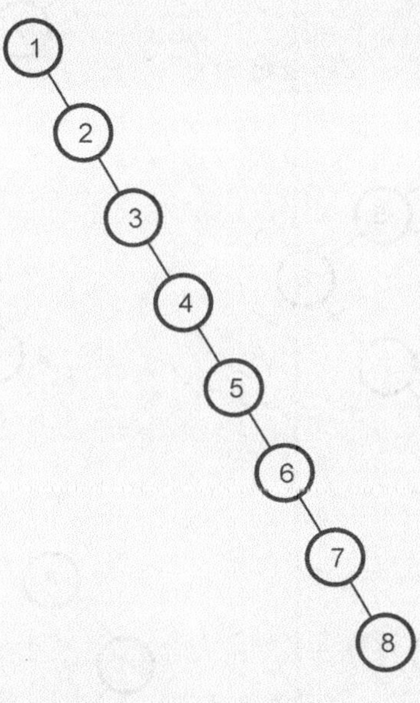

Solution : Now if splay node is 8 then the sequence of operations performed are -

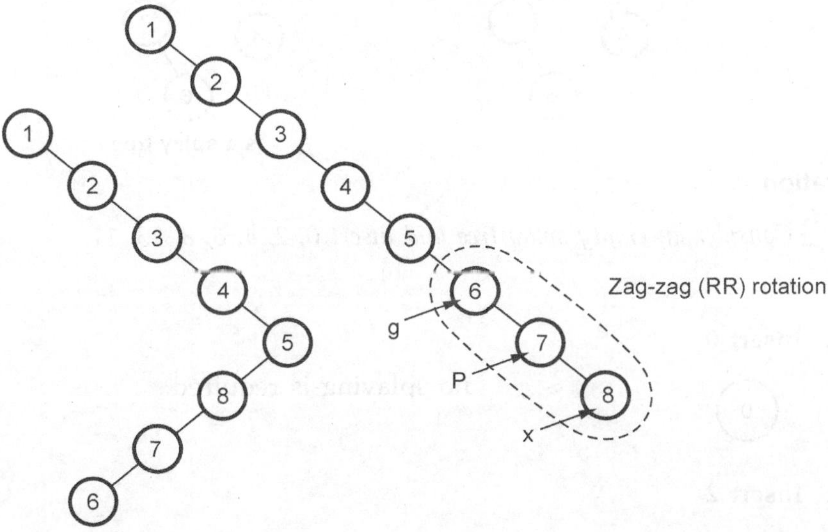

This is called zag-zag or RR operation which is mirror operation of LL or zig-zig. Now focusing on node '8' we get zag-zag operation.

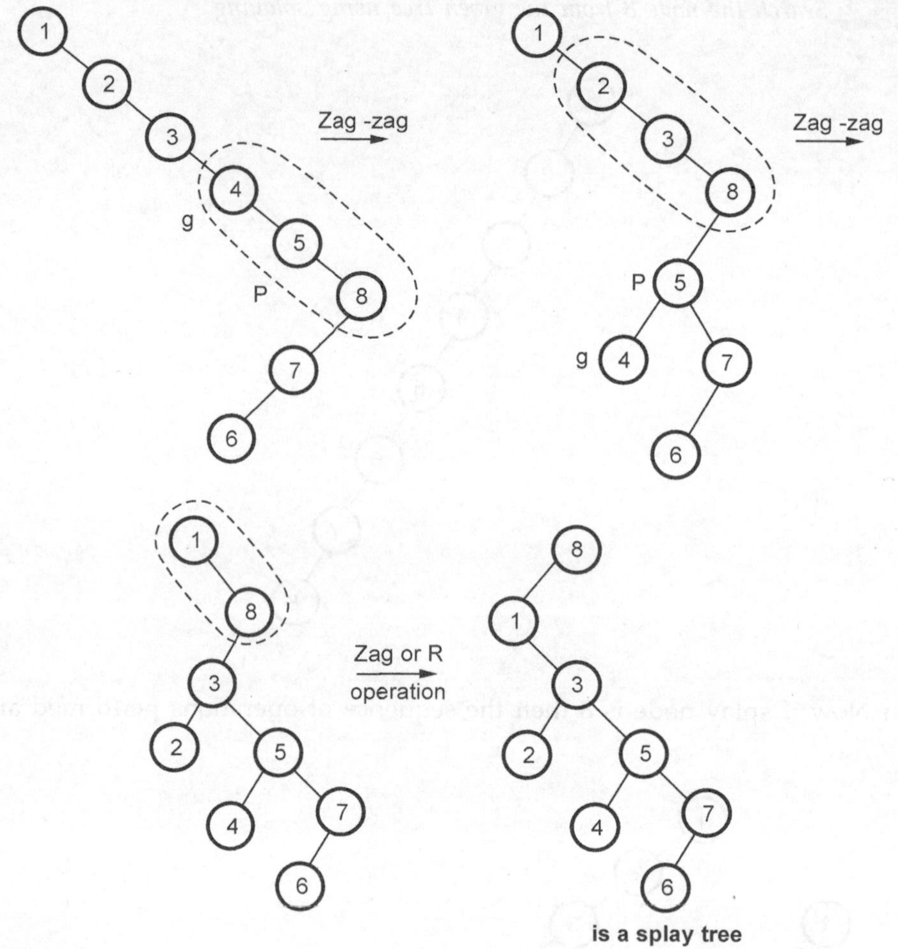

Insert Operation

Example 5.8.3 *Consider an empty splay tree and insert 0, 2, 4, 6, 8, 13, 11.*

Solution :

Step 1 : Insert 0

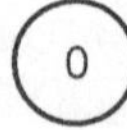

no splaying is required.

Step 2 : Insert 2

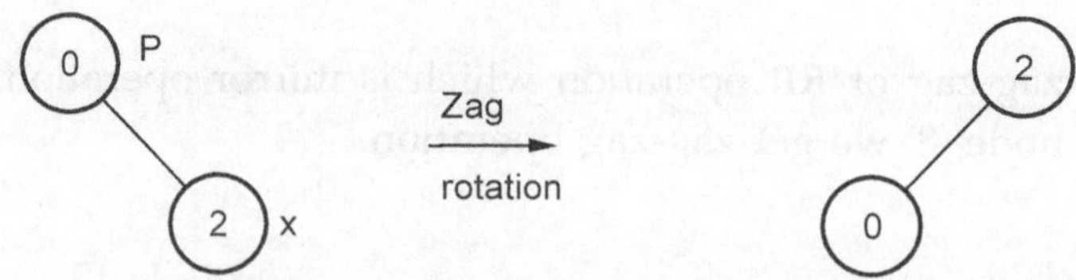

Step 3 : Insert 4

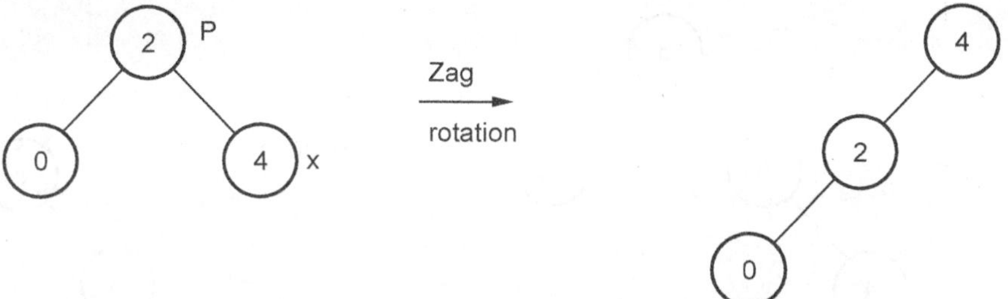

Step 4 : Insert 6

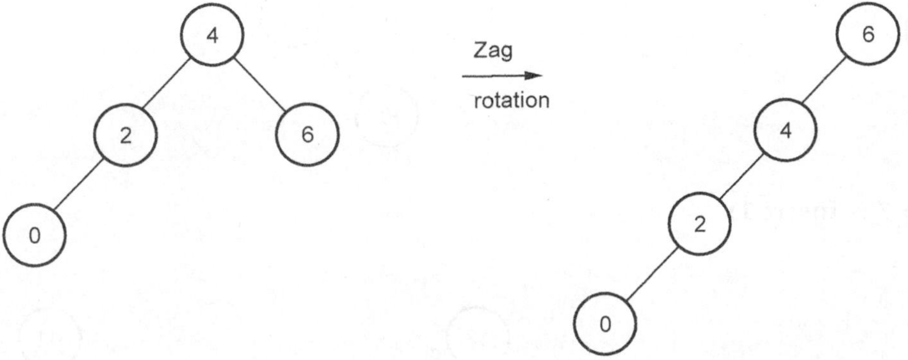

Step 5 : Insert 8

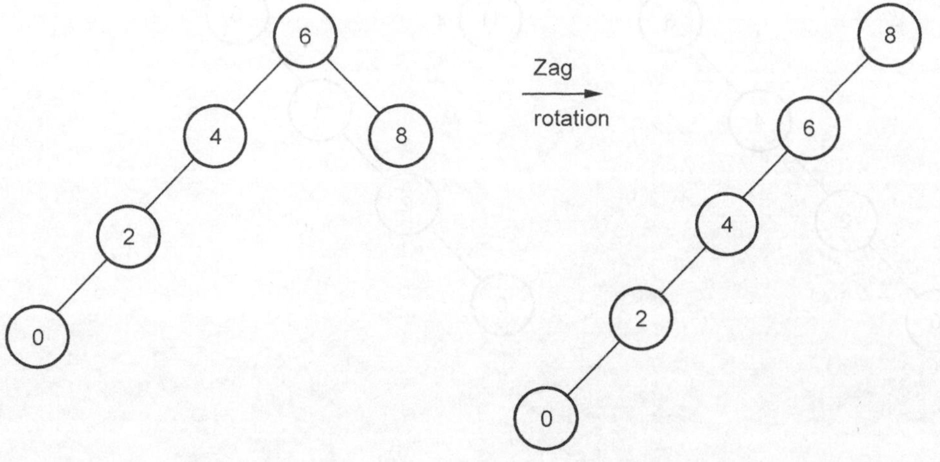

Step 6 : Insert 13

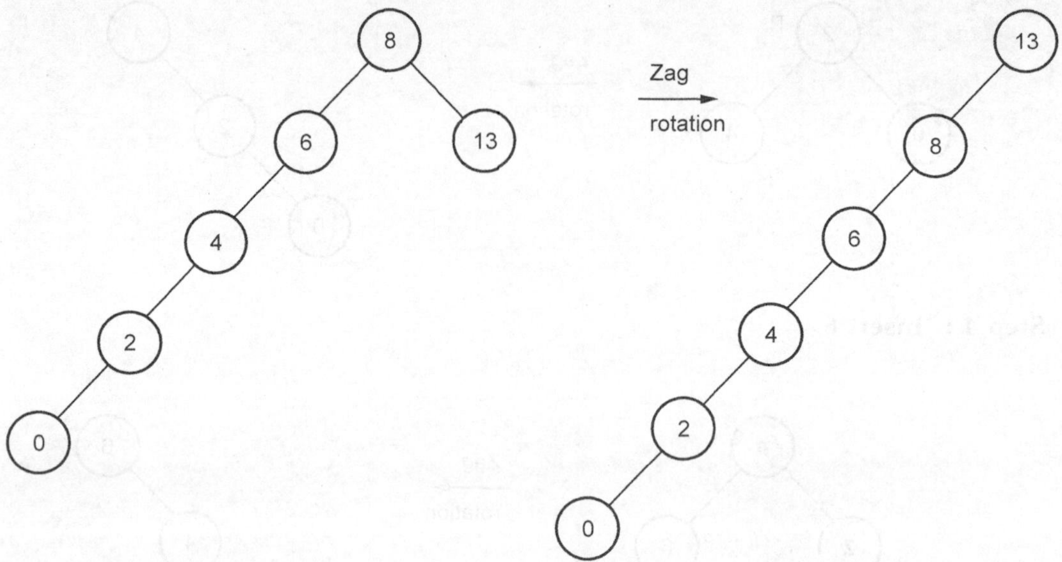

Step 7 : Insert 11

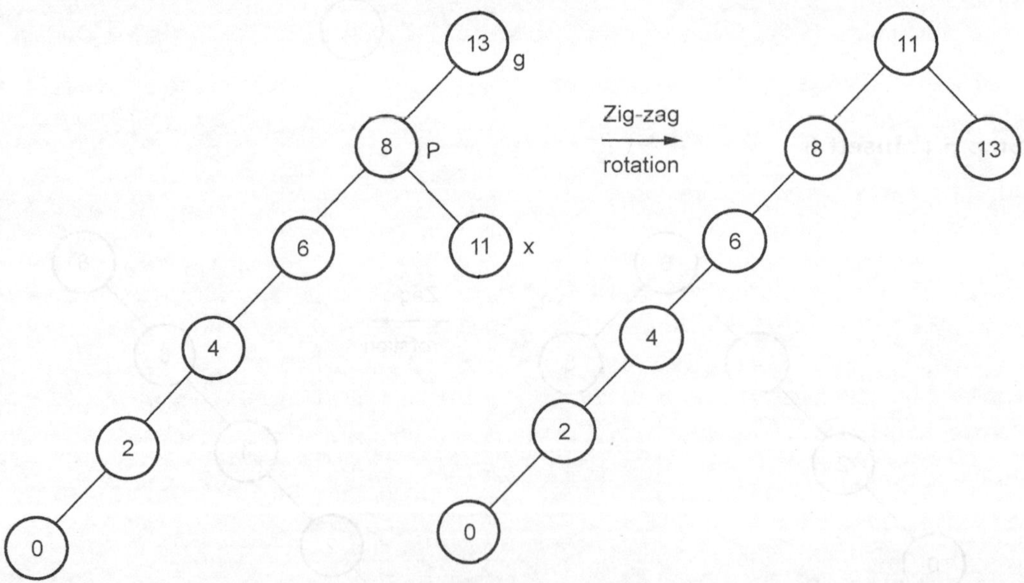

Delete Operation

Consider a tree

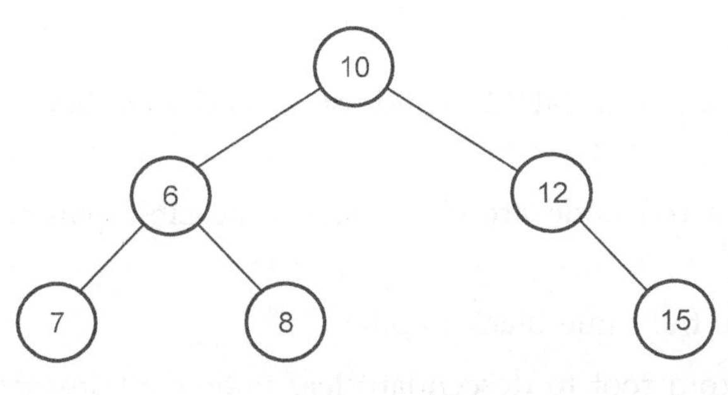

Deletion of 6

If we want to delete a node 8, then just copy inorder successor of node 8. As there is no inorder successor of 8, We will delete 8. Then the parent node of deleted node that is node 6 becomes root node, by applying zig operation.

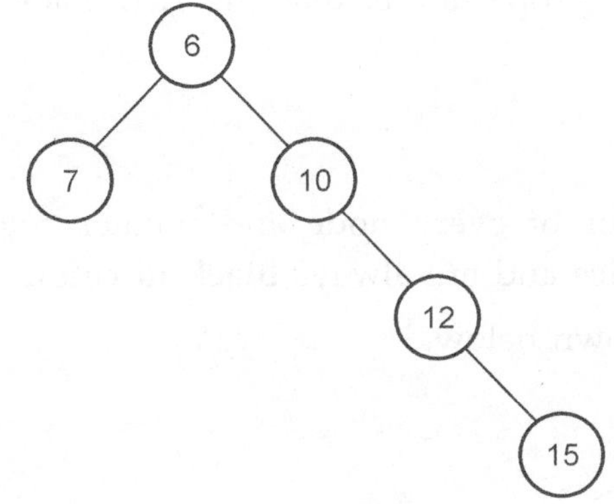

Deletion of 12

Now if we delete 12 then, just copy '15' at the '12' s place. And then allow 10 (i.e. parent of 12) to be the root node. Then we get -

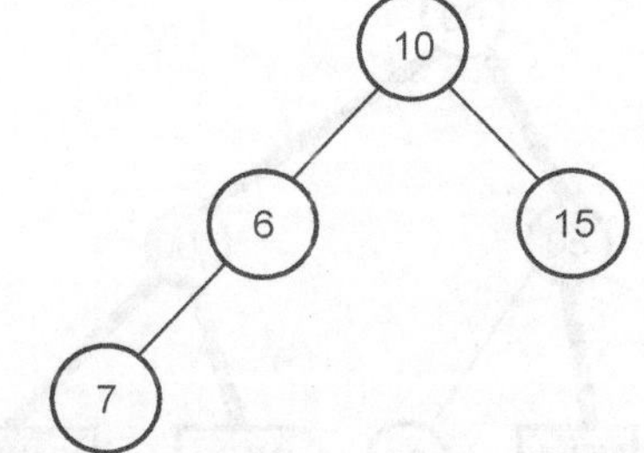

This is the required splay tree.

5.9 Red Black Tree

Red-Black tree is a binary search tree in which every node is colored with either **red** or **black**. It is a type of self balancing binary search tree. It has a good efficient worst case running time complexity.

5.9.1 Properties of Red Black Tree

The Red-Black tree satisfies all the properties of binary search tree in addition to that it satisfies following additional properties -

1. **Root property :** The root is black.
2. **External property :** Every leaf (Leaf is a NULL child of a node) is black in Red-Black tree.
3. **Internal property :** The children of a red node are black. Hence possible parent of red node is a black node.
4. **Depth property :** All the leaves have the same black depth.
5. **Path property :** Every simple path from root to descendant leaf node contains same number of black nodes.

The result of all these above mentioned properties is that the Red-Black tree is roughly balanced.

5.9.2 Representation

While representing a Red-Black tree color of every node and pointer colors are shown. The **leaf nodes** are simply NULL nodes and are always **black in color.**

As an example a Red-Black tree is as shown below.

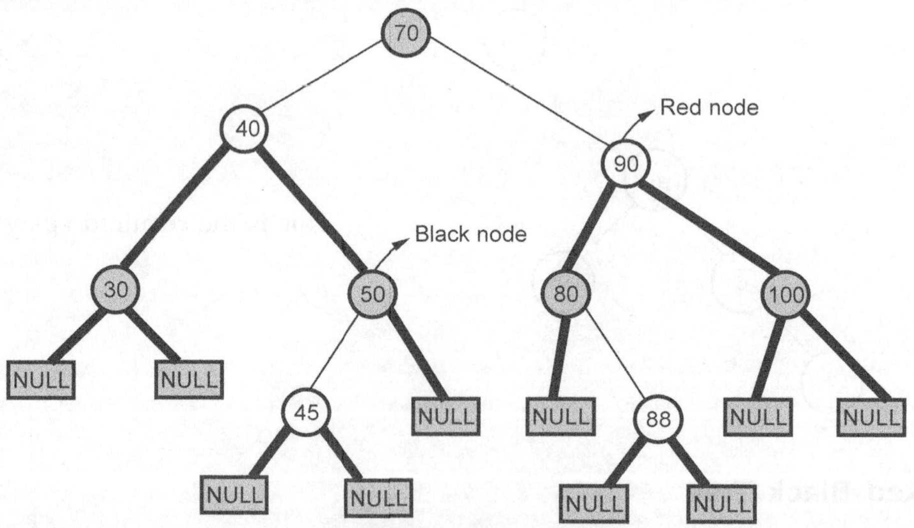

Fig. 5.9.1 Red-Black tree

The Red-Black tree shown in above given figure has black nodes that are shaded in black and unshaded nodes are red nodes. Similarly the leaves are black and all are NULL pointers only. The pointers to black node are black pointers which are shown by thick lines remaining are red pointers. But in practice, we explicitly mention the color of nodes. The above given Red-Black tree follows all the **properties of Red-Black tree** -

1. It is a **binary search tree**.
2. The **root** node is **black**.
3. The **children of red node are black**.
4. No root - to external node path has two consecutive red nodes (e.g. 70-90-80-88-NULL).
5. All the root to external node paths contain same number of black nodes (including root and external node).

For e.g. : Consider path 70-40-30-NULL and 70-90-80-88-NULL in both these paths 3 black nodes are there. Similarly other paths can be checked.

5.9.3 Insertion in Red Black Tree

- Every new node which is to be inserted is marked red.
- Not every insertion causes imbalancing but if imbalancing occurs then that can be removed depending upon the configuration of tree before new insertion made.
- In Red black tree during insertion of a node two operations need to be performed for balancing the tree.

i) Recoloring

ii) Rotation

Let, if x is a newly inserted node then there exists two cases -

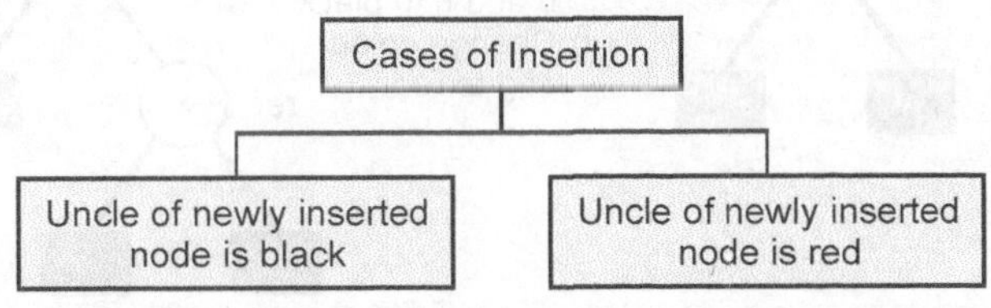

Fig. 5.9.2

Let us understand insertion operation in Red black tree.

Step 1 : Perform insertion of node x same like insertion in binary search tree.

Step 2 : The color of newly inserted node is red.

Step 3 : If x is a root node, change color of x to **black**.

Step 4 : If newly inserted node x is red and its parent is also red then only balancing is needed.

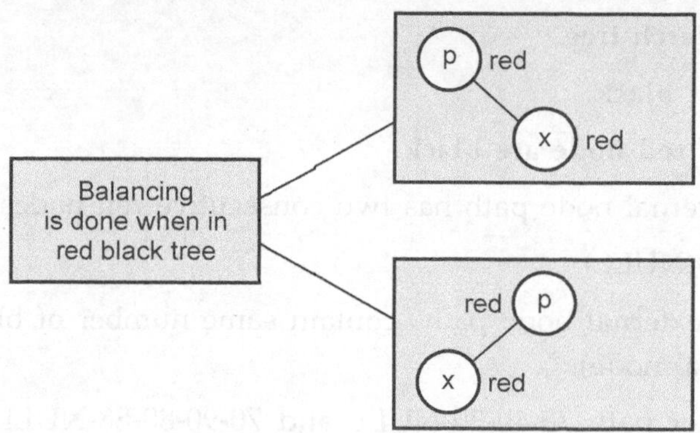

Fig. 5.9.3

Step 5 : As discussed earlier, there are two cases.

I) If x's uncle is **RED** then

i) Change color of parent and uncle as **black.**

ii) Change color of grand parent as red

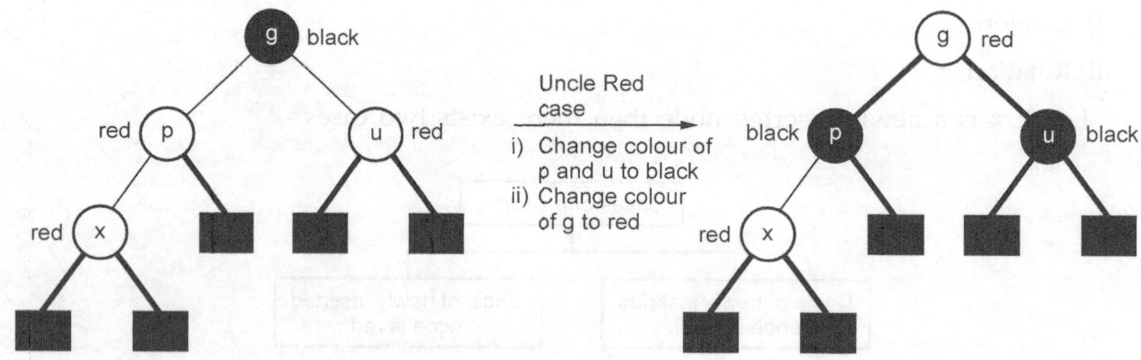

Fig. 5.9.4

II) If x's uncle is **black** then there are four configurations just similar to AVL tree. These configurations are LL, LR, RR and RL case. Let us understand them in detail.

i) Left left case :

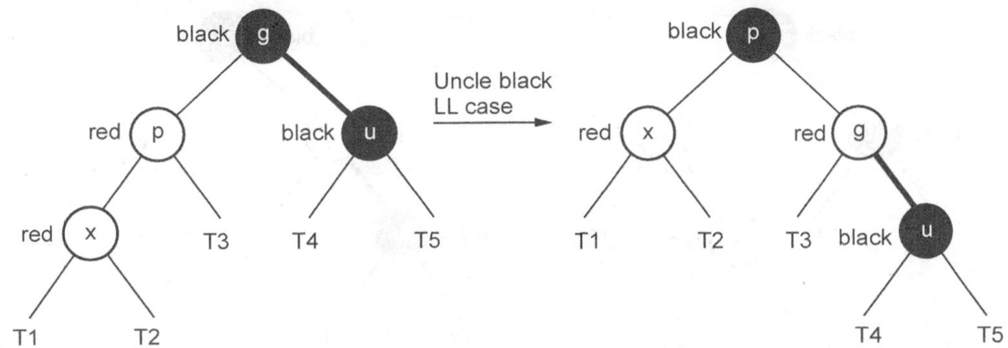

Fig. 5.9.5

ii) Left right case

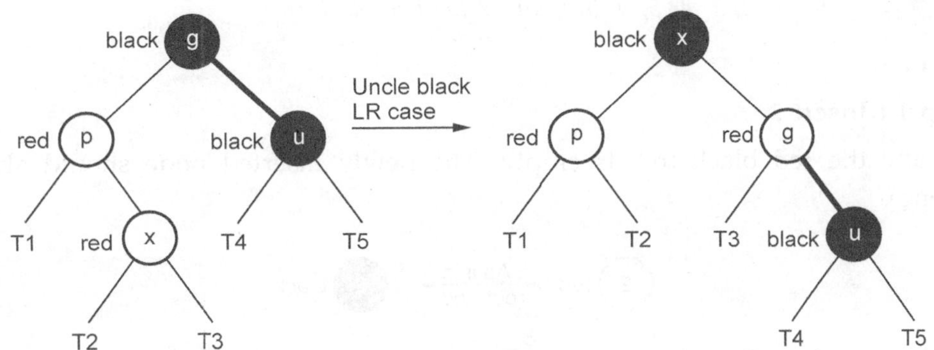

Fig. 5.9.6

iii) Right right case :

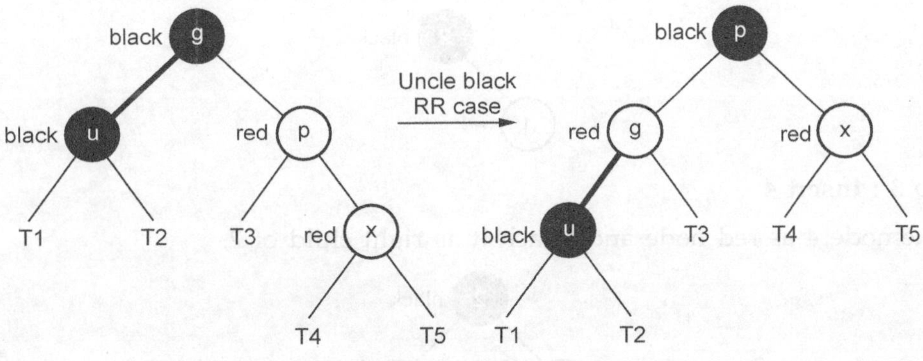

Fig. 5.9.7

iv) Right left case :

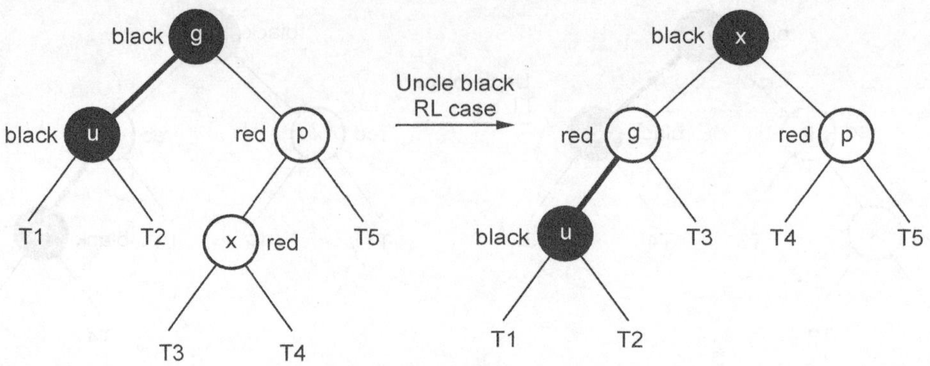

Fig. 5.9.8

Let us understand how to use these configurations with the help of example.

Example 5.9.1 *Insert 2, 1, 4, 5, 9, 3, 6 and 7 for Red black tree.*

Solution :

Step 1 : Insert 2

Initially the red black tree is empty. The newly inserted node should always be red. Hence.

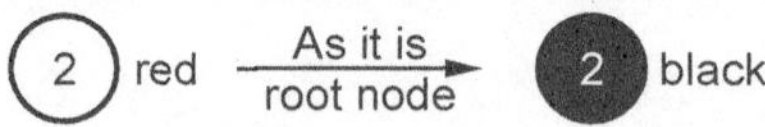

Step 2 : Insert 1

Make node for value 1 and it should be red as it is newly inserted node. Since 1 < 2, attach this red node as left child of 2.

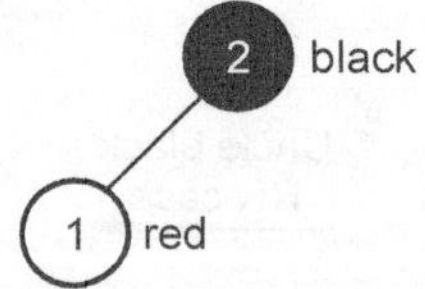

Step 3 : Insert 4

Make node 4 as red node and attach it as right child of 2.

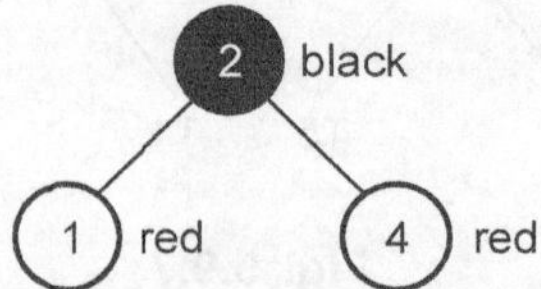

Step 4 : Insert 5

Here node 5 is a red node attached as right child of red node 4.

But there should not be red child of red node. Hence we need to make adjustments.

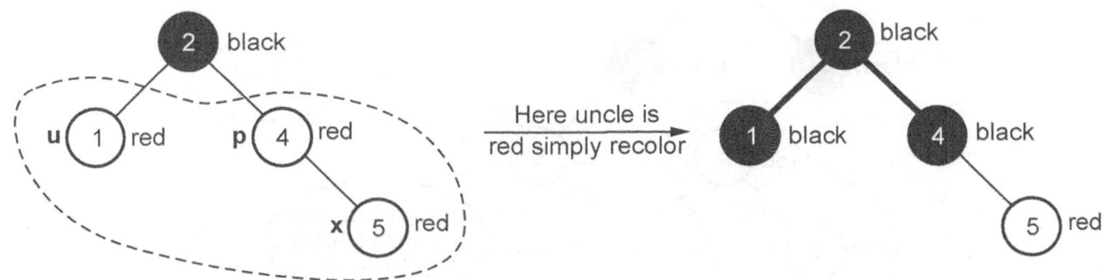

Step 5 : Insert node 9

Insert node 9 as a right child of 5. Naturally the node 9 is red initially.

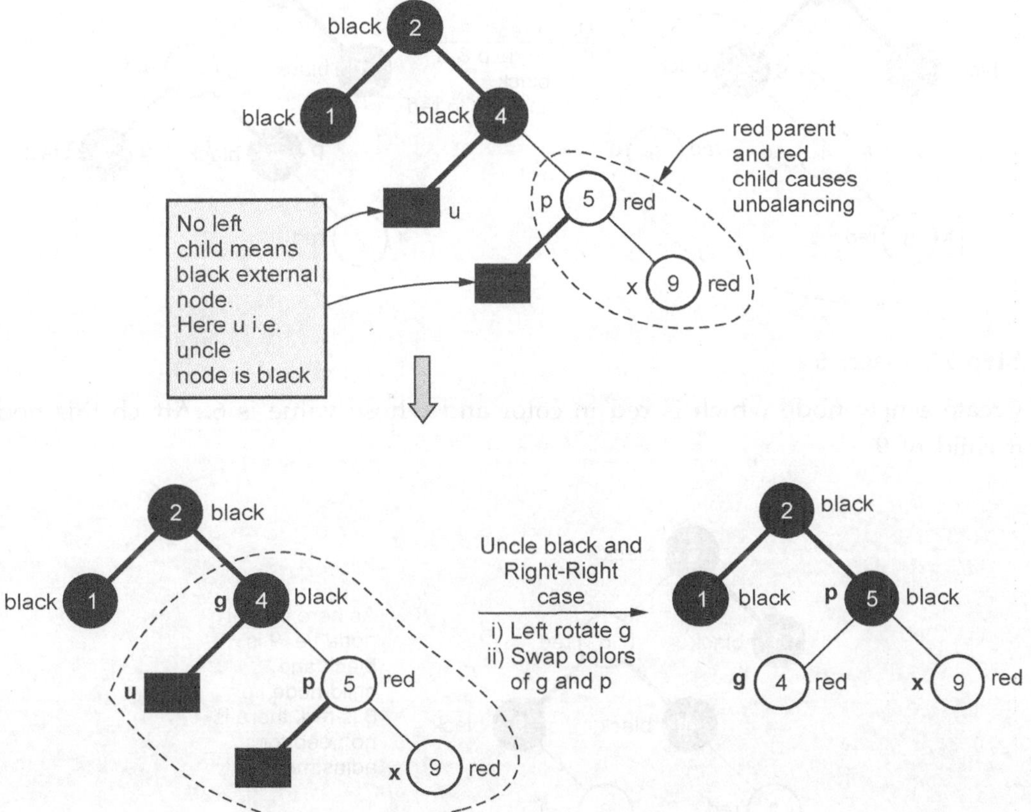

Step 6 : Insert 3

Create a new node which is red in color and whose value is 3. Attach it as left child of 4.

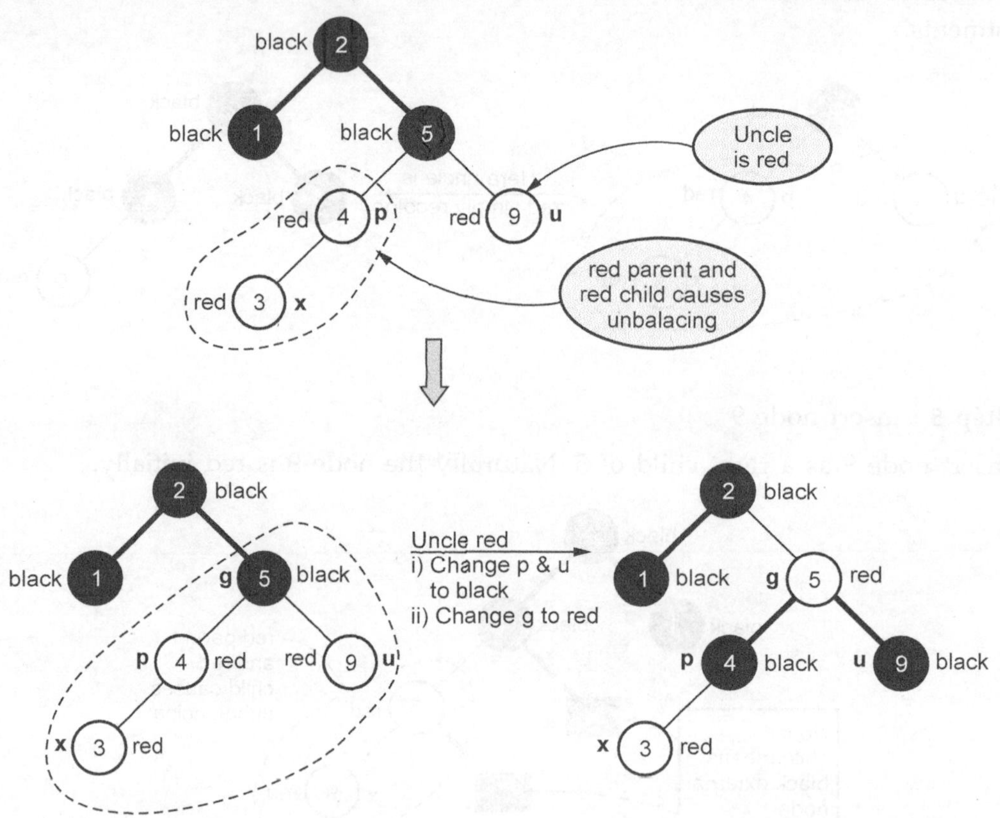

Step 7 : Insert 6

Create a new node which is red in color and whose value is 6. Attach this node as a left child of 9.

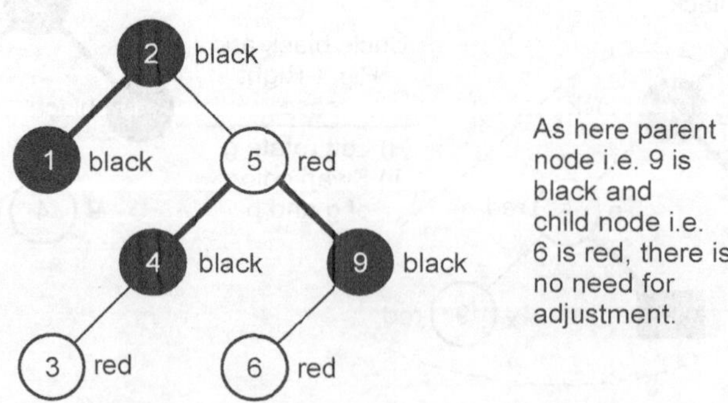

Step 8 : Insert 7

Create a new node which is red in color and whose value is red. Attach this node as right child of node 6.

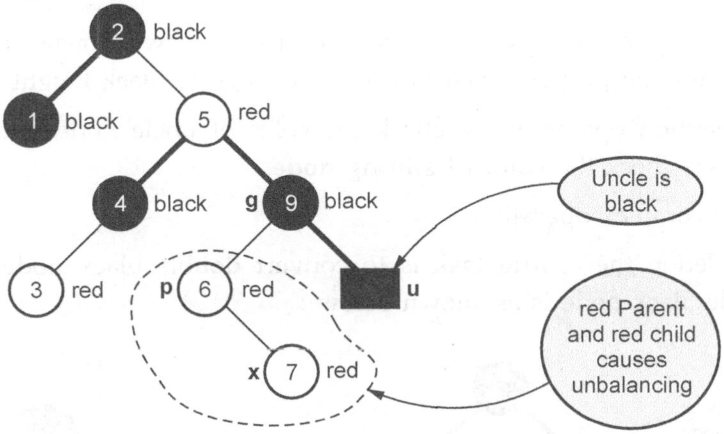

Uncle is black

red Parent and red child causes unbalancing

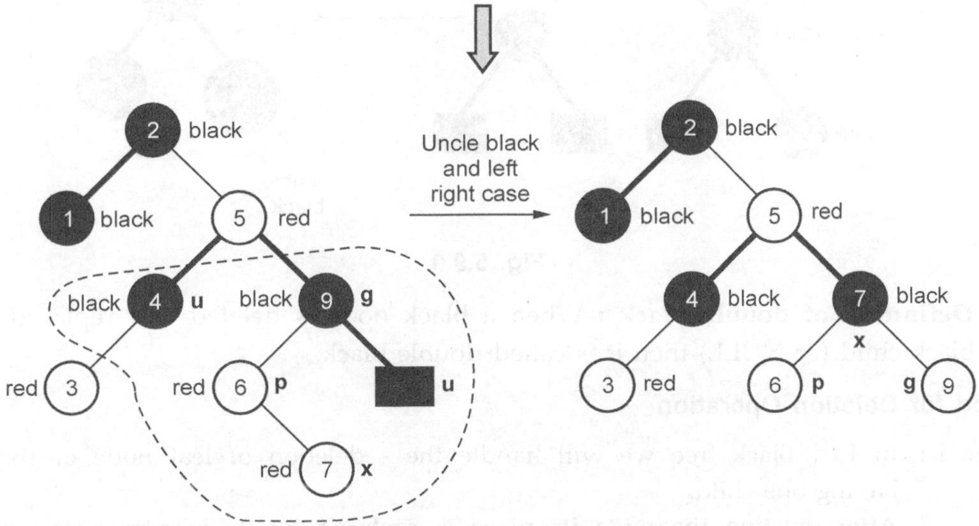

Uncle black and left right case

Thus finally we get, following Red black tree.

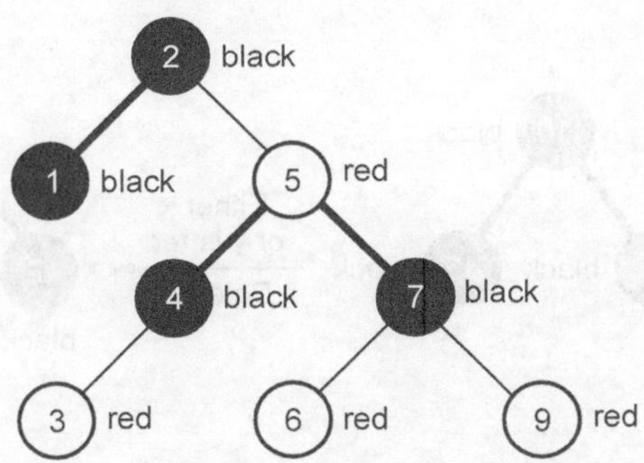

5.9.4 Deletion Operation

- During deletion operation, we have to perform two operations - i) Recoloring and ii) Rotation.
- The main property that violates after insertion is two consecutive reds. But in deletion, the main property that violates is change of black height in subtrees.
- During insertion operation we check the color of uncle node but during deletion operation we check the **color of sibling node.**
- Deletion is complex operation.
- During deletion the central task is to convert double black node to single black. The double black node is as shown below :

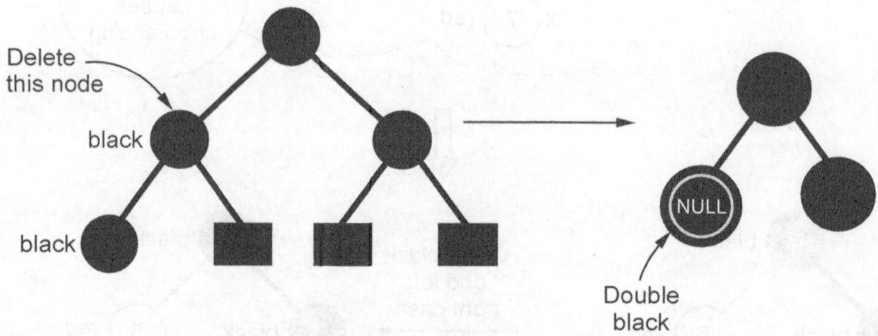

Fig. 5.9.9

- **Definition of double black :** When a black node is deleted and replaced by its black child (or NULL) then it is called double black.

Method for Deletion Operation

Step 1 : In Red Black tree we will handle the - deletion of leaf node or the node having one child.
After deleting the node its place is replaced by its inorder successor (just similar to deletion operation in BST).

Step 2 : **Case 1 :** The node to be deleted is red or the node to be deleted has a red child.

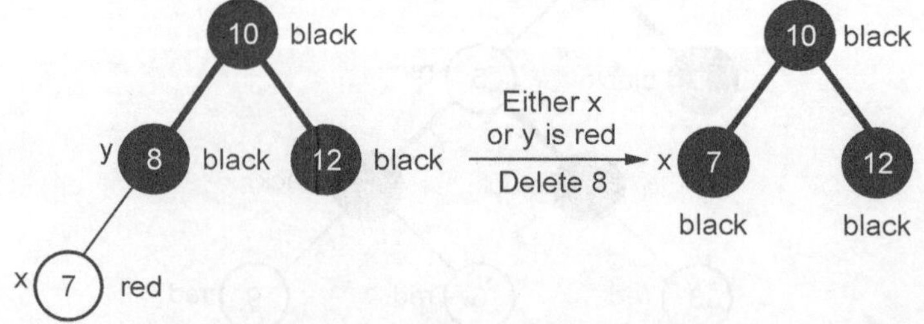

Step 3 : Case 2 : If Both x and y are black.

i) Delete node y and make the node x as double black.

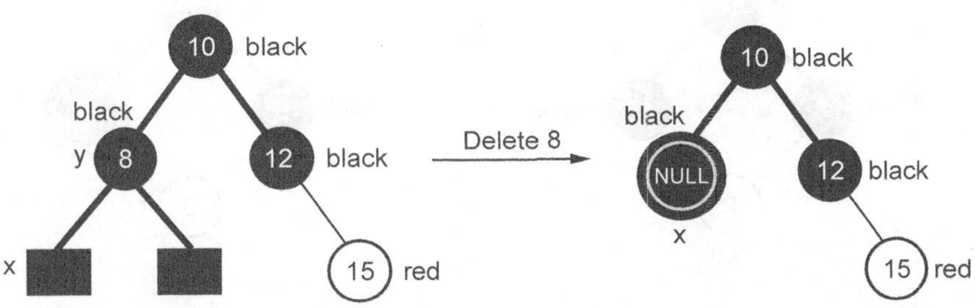

ii) Now current node x is a double black node and we have to convert it to single black. Now this conversion is based on sibling.

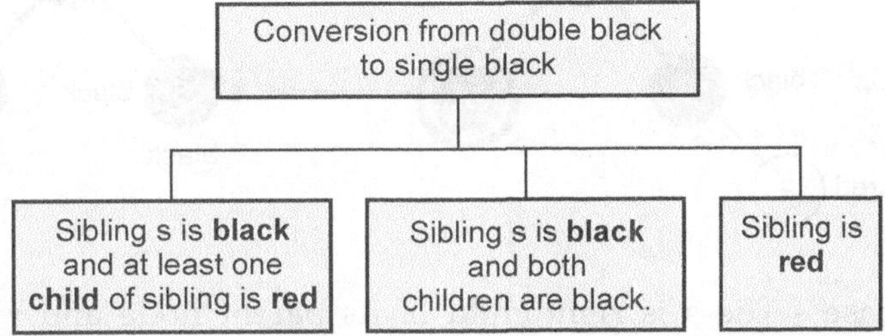

The above shown cases can be handled as follows -

Case A : If Sibling s is black and at least one child of it is red.

i) Left left case - The s is left child of parent and r is left child.

For example - Delete 12

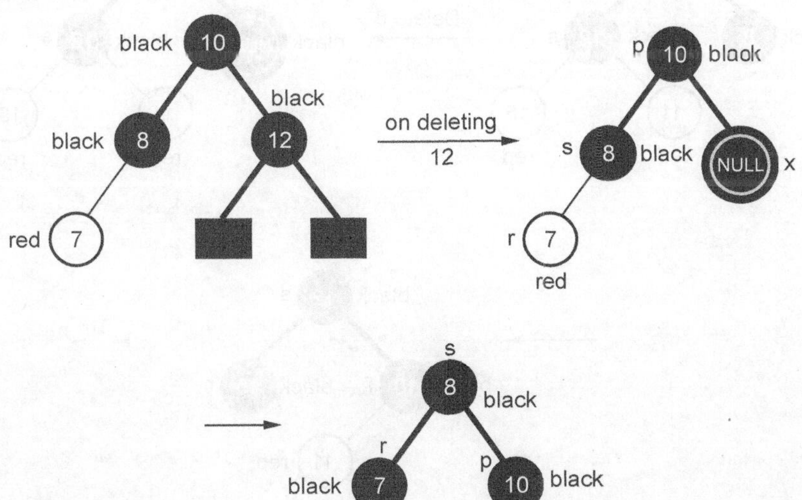

ii) Left right case - The s is a left child of its parent and r is a right child.

For example :

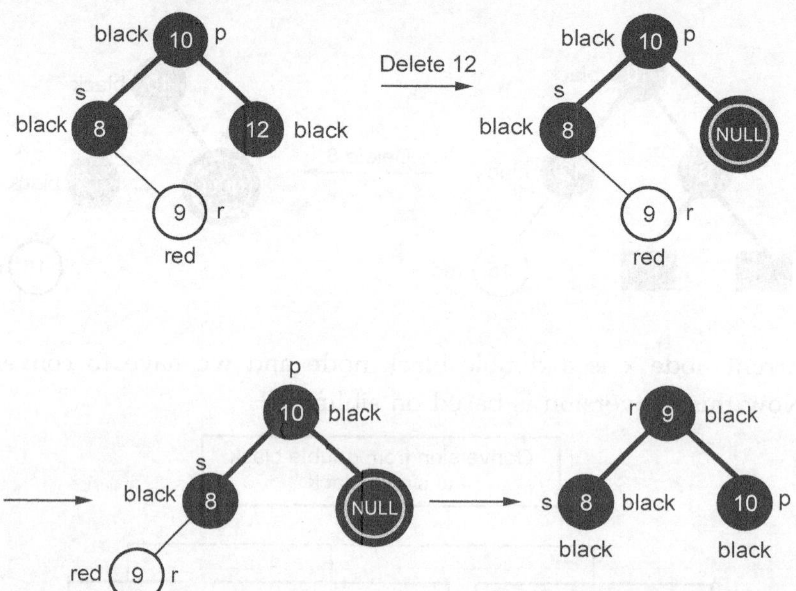

iii) Right right case - The s is right child of its parent node and r is right child of s. Both the children of s are red.

For example :

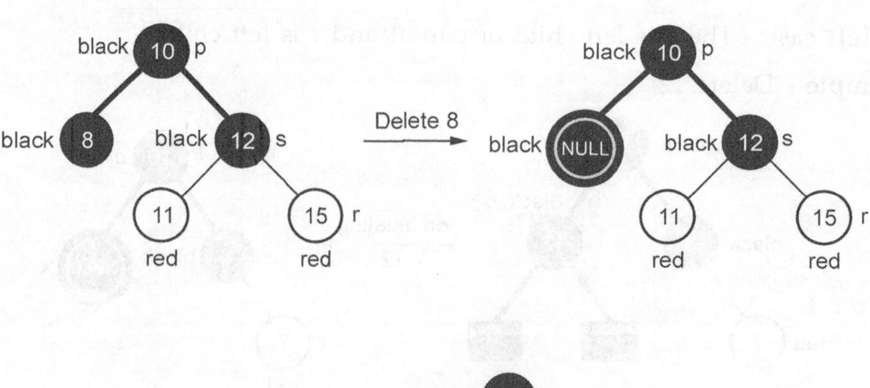

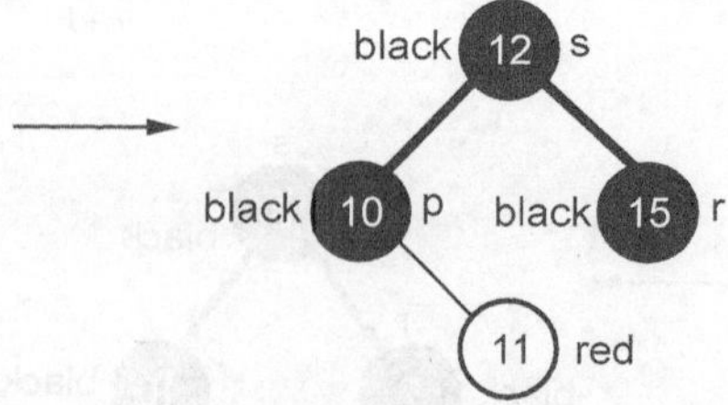

iv) Right left case - The S is right child of its parent and r is left child of s.

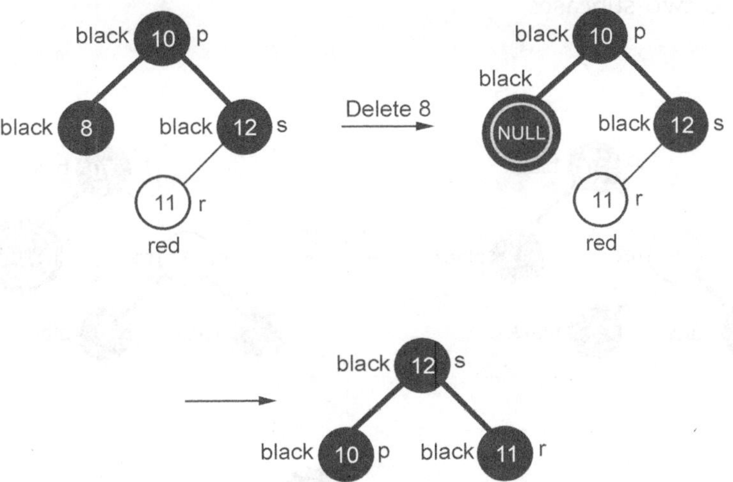

Case B : If sibling is black and both of its children are black. In this case after removing the desired node, the recoloring is performed. And then to remove double black parent, the case matching from A, B and C is reapplied.

For example :

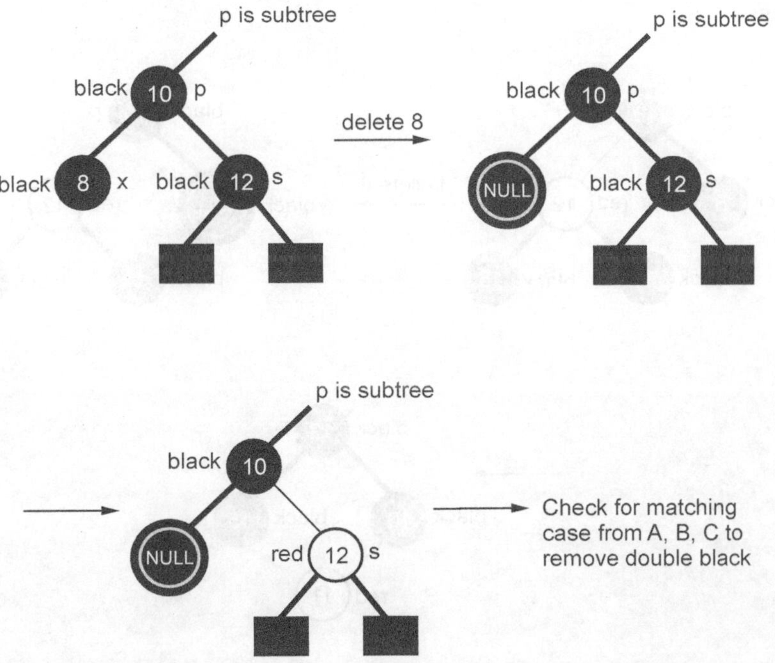

Case C : If sibling is red.

This case has two subcases

i) Left case

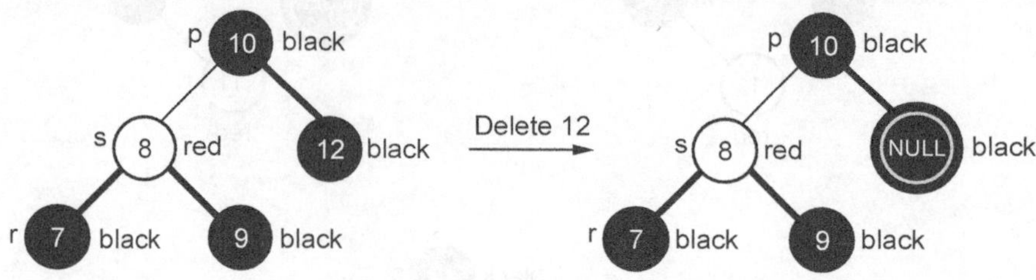

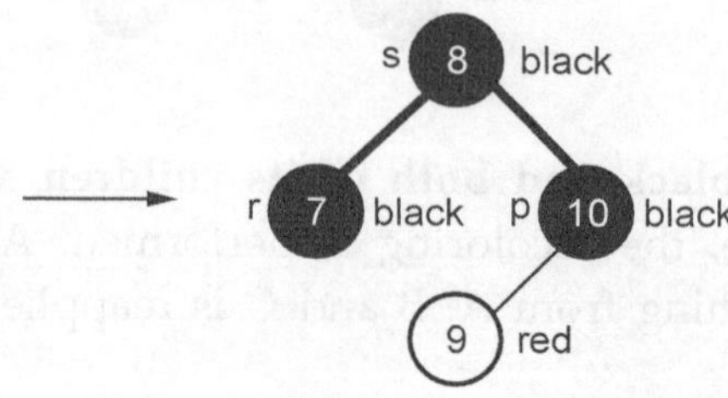

ii) Right case

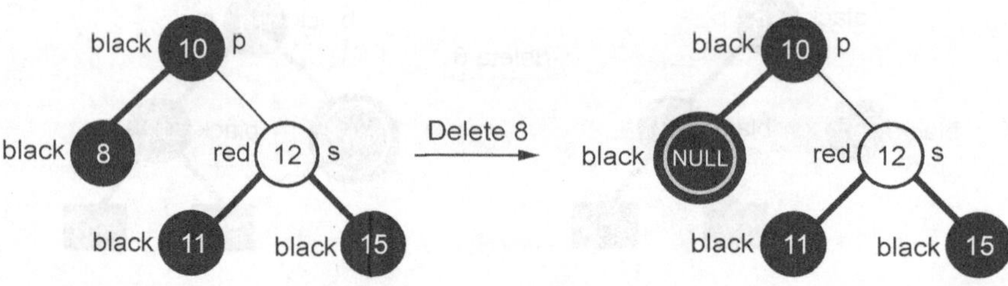

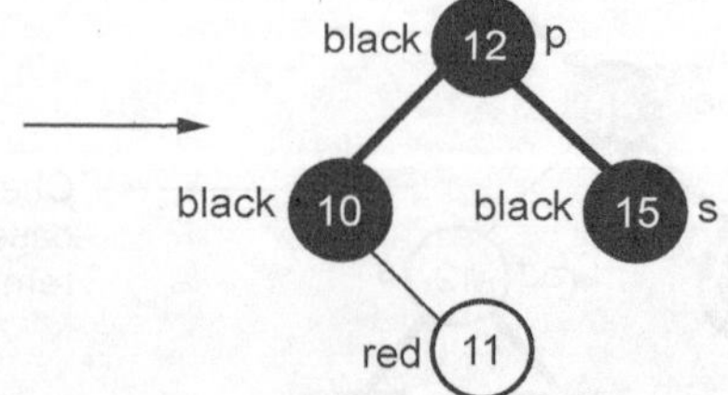

Example 5.9.2 *Following is a Red-Black tree.*

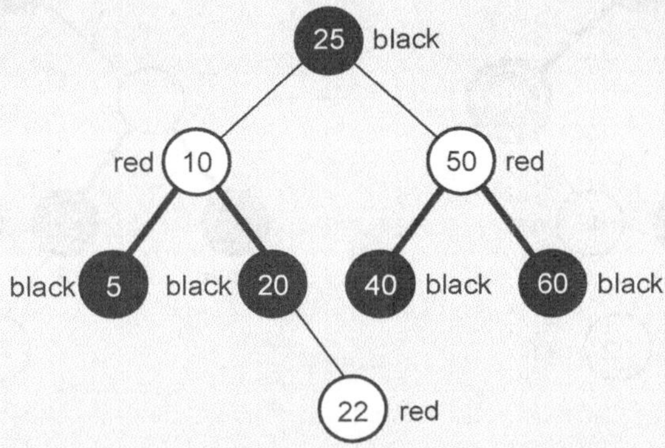

Delete 60, then 50 and finally 40 from the above tree. Show clearly the balancing done after each deletion.

Solution :

Step 1 : Delete 60

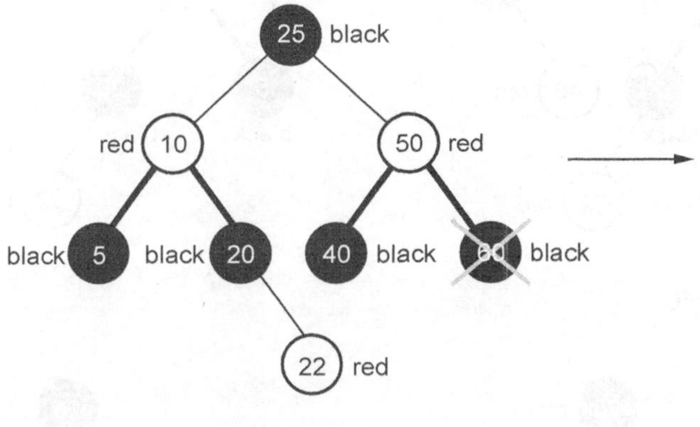

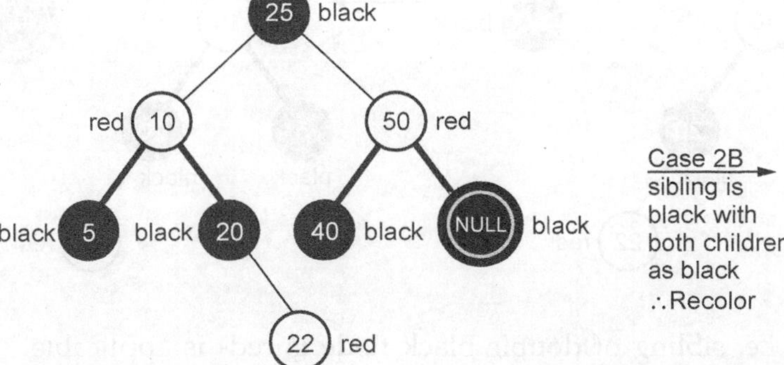

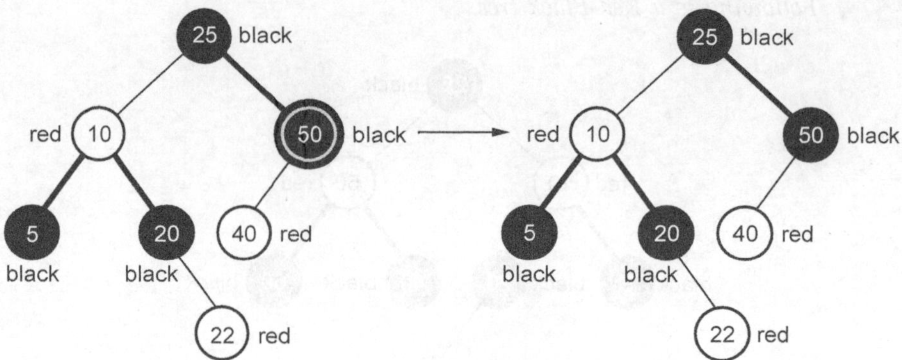

Step 2 : Delete 50

This is case 1 in which the node to be deleted has one red child.

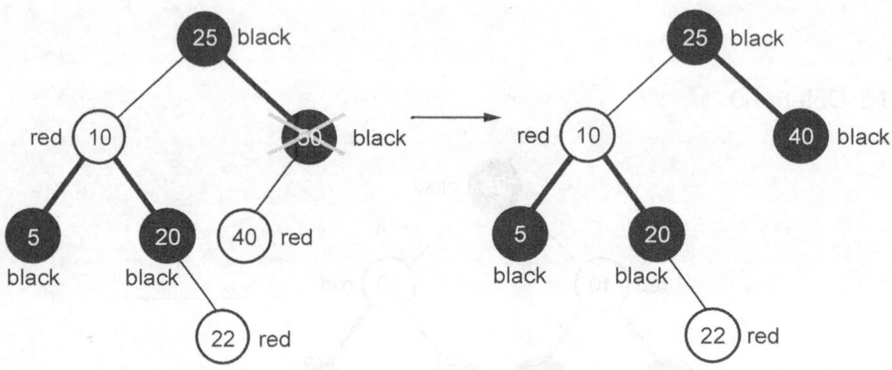

Step 3 : Delete 40

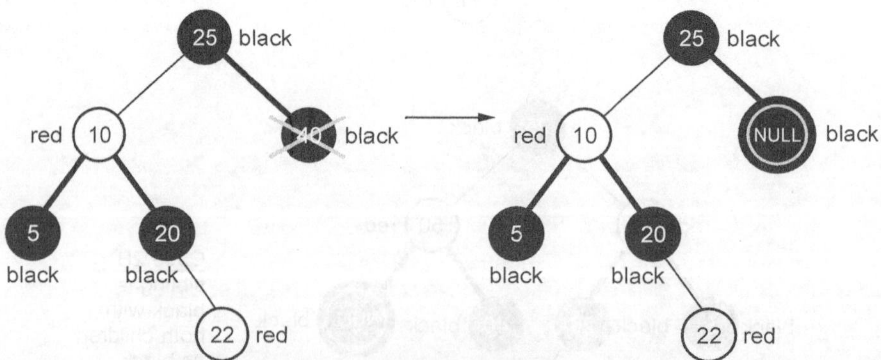

Here case C i.e. sibling of double black node is red- is applicable.

The left case is applicable and we rotate in such a way that 10 becomes the root node.

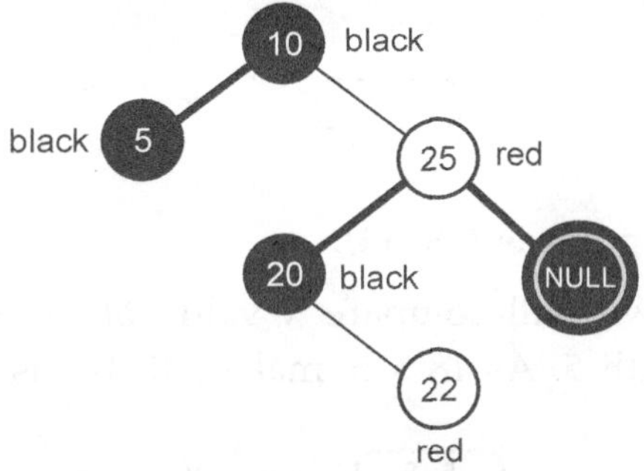

Now apply case A (ii) as sibling is black with red child. Hence apply LR rotation to get.

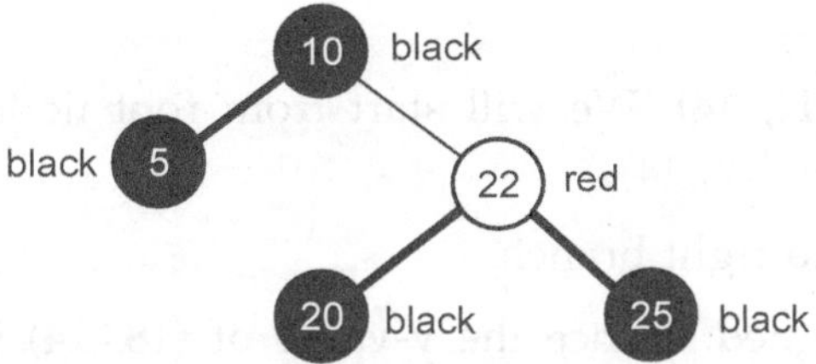

Thus we get balanced Red. Black tree after deletions.

5.10 K-dimensional Tree

- The K-dimensional tree is also known as **KD tree.**
- It is a data structure used in Computer science for organizing some number of points in a space with K dimensions.
- It is basically a **binary search tree** with some constraints.
- The points are arranged in a space which is called as **K-Dimensional space.**
- The points left side in the space represents the left subtree and the points in the right represent the right subtree.
- The K represents the dimensions. That means a tree with 2 dimension, 3 dimension and so on can be drawn. We will understand this concept for 2-D tree.

Example 5.10.1 *Draw a K-Dimensional tree for following points.*
(5,8), (18, 14), (12, 14), (8, 11), (10, 2), (3,6), (11, 20).

Solution :

Step 1 : We will read the point **(5,8)** make it as root node. The root is said to be x-aligned.

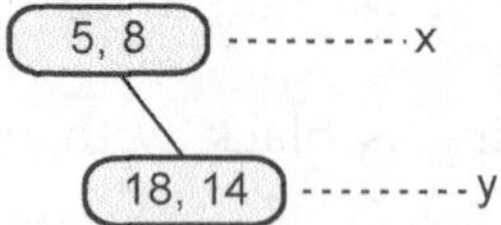

Step 2 : Now the next point is **(18, 14).**

As root is x aligned, we will compare x value of (5, 8) with x value of (18, 14). That means compare 18 with 5. As 18 > 5, make (18, 14) as right child of (5, 8).

This node is y-aligned.

Step 3 : Now read **(12, 14).** We will start from root node. The x-value of (5, 8) is compared with x-value of (12, 14).

As 12 > 5, move on to right branch.

Here (18, 14) is y-aligned. Hence the y-value of (18, 14) is compared with y-value of (12-14). As 14 = 14 move on to right branch and attach (12, 14) as right child of (18,14).

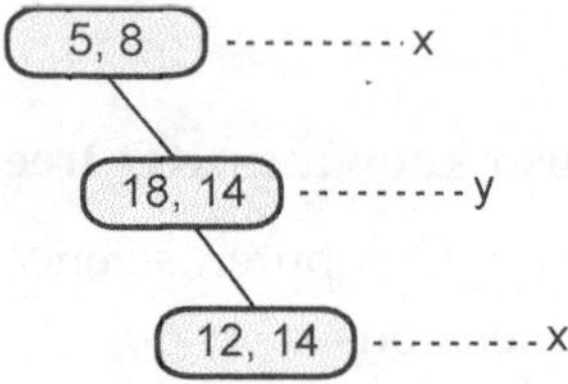

Step 4 : The next point is **(8,11).** Starting from root we will compare x and y values of (8, 11) alternatively and attach (8, 11) as left child of (18, 14). The partial construction is as follows -

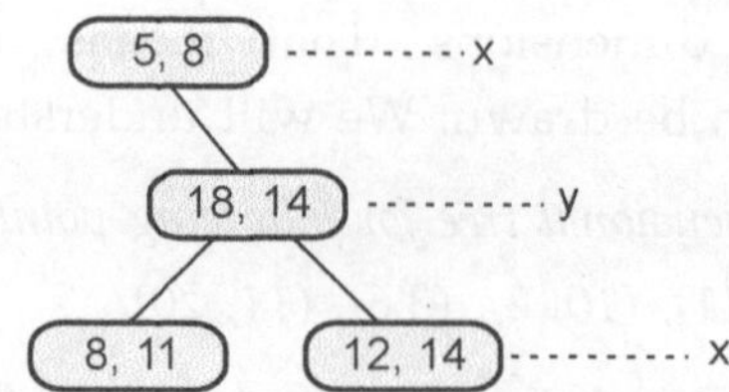

Step 5 : Next point is **(10, 2).**

10 > 5 (From 5, 8)), 10 < 14 (from (18, 14)),

10 > 8 (from 8, 11)). Hence attach (10, 2) as a right child of (8, 11).

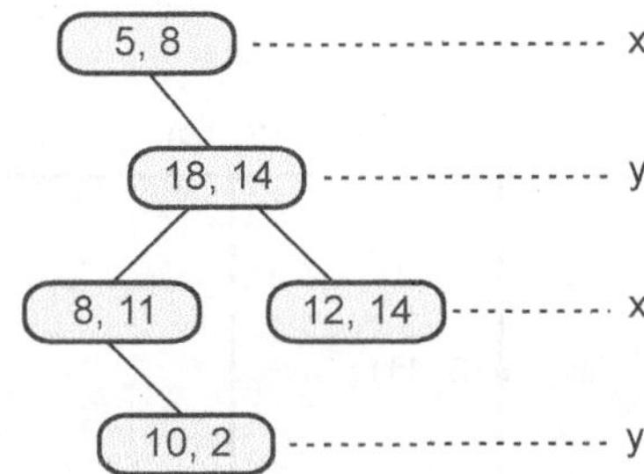

Continuing in this fashion, we get following tree -

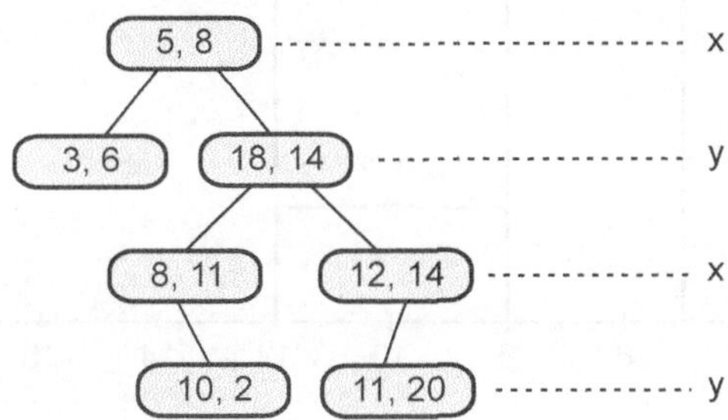

Step 6 : These points can be plotted on X-Y plane.

i) For point (5, 8), X = 5. Hence draw a vertical line at x = 5.

ii) For point (3, 6), Y = 6. Hence draw a horizontal line at Y = 6. But as (3, 6) is a left child of (5, 8), draw this line at the left of x = 5 line.

In this way, the lines X and Y can be drawn to divide the space. The K-D space spotting is as shown below -

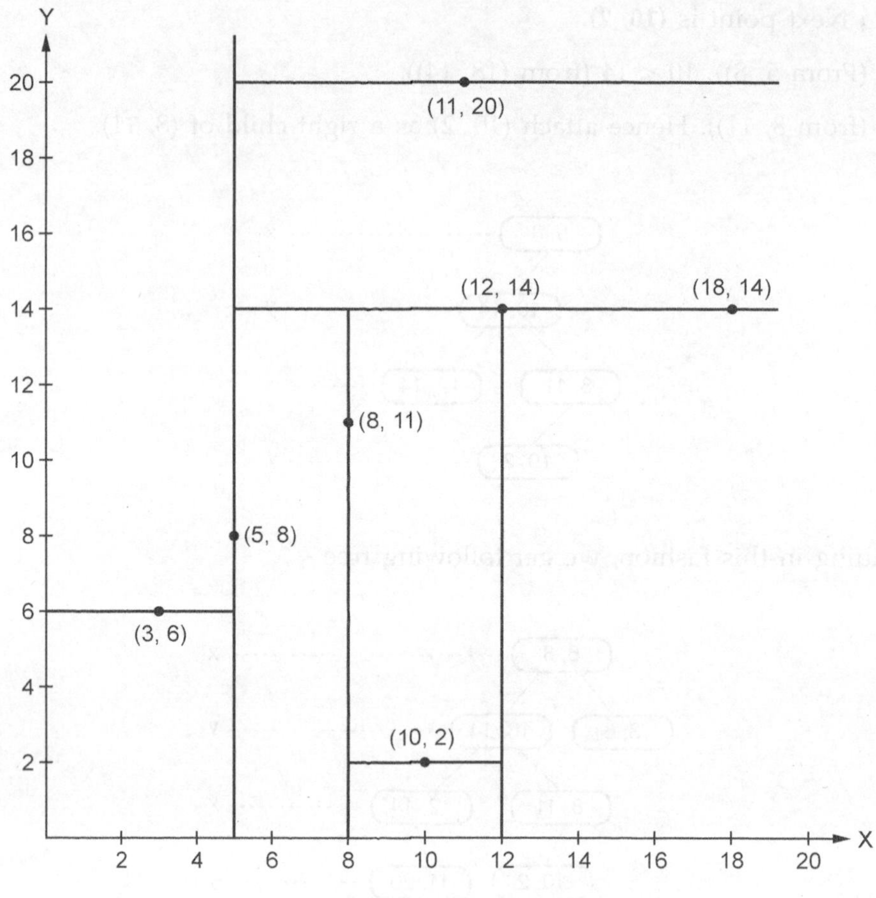

Fig. 5.10.1 K-D space

Applications of K-D Tree

Following are some applications of KD tress -

1. **Nearest neighbor search :** For finding the nearest police station for reporting the crime, the nearest neighbor search is conducted with the help of K-D tree.
2. **Database queries :** For the implementation of complex queries, which involves multidimensional search key, the query problem is converted geometrical problem in order to get the answer.

5.11 AA Tree

- The AA tree is named after its inventor Arne Anderson.
- The AA tree is created from the idea of Red Black tree, but contains fewer rotations and less complex.
- The time complexity for operations of AA tree is **O(log n).**

Properties of AA trees

- The ordering properties of AA trees are same as that of Red-Black trees with some additional property.
- The properties are as follows -

1) Every node is colored either red or black.
2) The root node is always black.
3) All the external nodes are black.
4) If node is red then its children must be black.
5) All path from any node to a descendant leaf must contain the same number of black nodes.
6) The left child may not be red.

For example

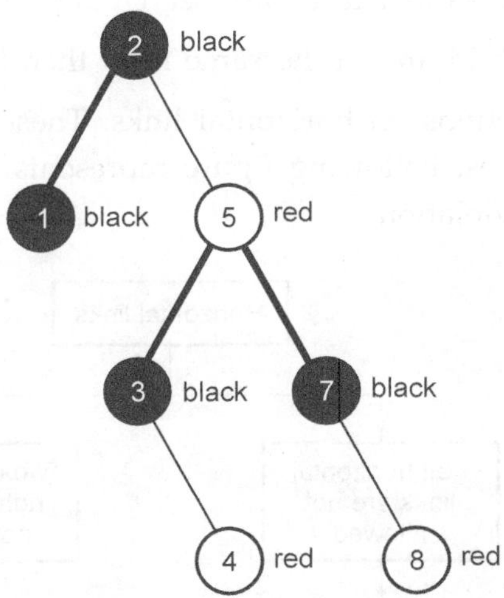

Fig. 5.11.1 AA tree

Advantages of AA Trees

1) The AA tree eliminates half the restructuring cases of Red Black trees.
2) It simplifies deletion by removing complex cases in Red Black tree.

Representing the Balance Information

- There is a concept of **level** in AA trees. Each node stores the information about the level.
- **Definition of Level -** The level can be defined using following properties -

i) If a node is a leaf node then it must be present at level 1.

ii) If a node is red, then its level is level of its parent.

iii) If a node is black, then its level is one less than the level of its parent.

AA Tree Invariants

AA tree must always satisfy following invariants

1) The level of a leaf node is 1.

2) The level of a left child is strictly less than that of its parent.

3) The level of a right child is less than or equal to that of its parent.

4) The level of right grand child is strictly less than that of its grandparent.

5) Every node of level greater than one must have two children.

5.11.1 Insertion Operation

- The nodes are inserted similar to binary search algorithm.
- If the parent and its child are on the same level then horizontal links are possible.
- There are some restrictions on horizontal links. These restrictions are for avoiding unbalancing in AA trees. Following figure represents the restrictions on horizontal links and remedy on violation.

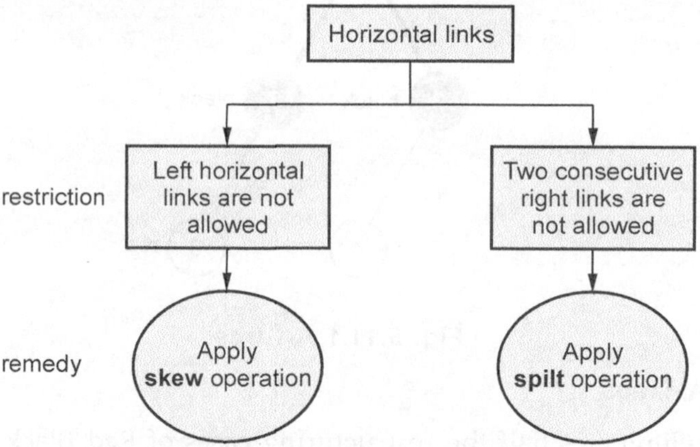

Fig. 5.11.2 Insertion in AA tree

- Let us understand the **skew** and **split** operations.

1) Skew operation

- The skew operation is a single right rotation when an insertion creates horizontal link.

i) In this operation, the left horizontal link is removed.

ii) It may create consecutive right horizontal links in process.

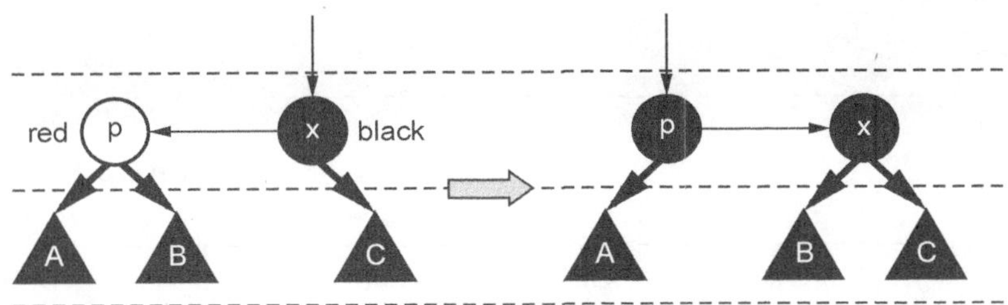

Fig. 5.11.3

2) Split operation

The split operation is single left rotation when insertion creates **two horizontal links.**

i) In this operation, two consecutive right horizontal links are removed.

ii) It causes level of middle node to be increased by one.

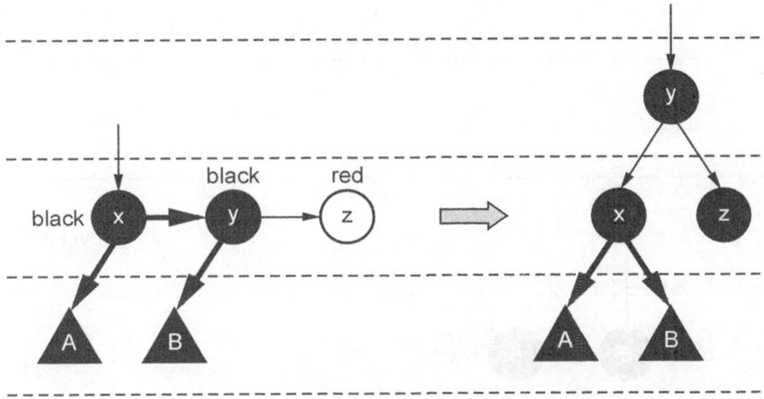

Fig. 5.11.4

Example 5.11.1 *Insert the elements 8, 3, 10, 18, 12, 2 in AA tree.*

Solution : We will insert the elements one by one. We will apply skew and split operations when horizontal links cause unbalancing in the tree.

Step 1 : Insert 8

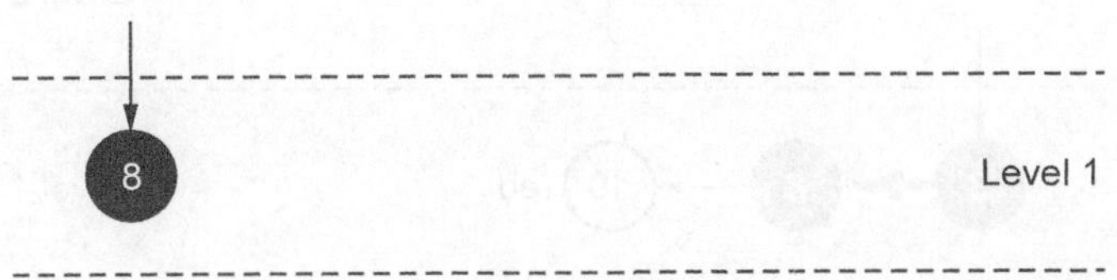

Step 2 : Insert 3

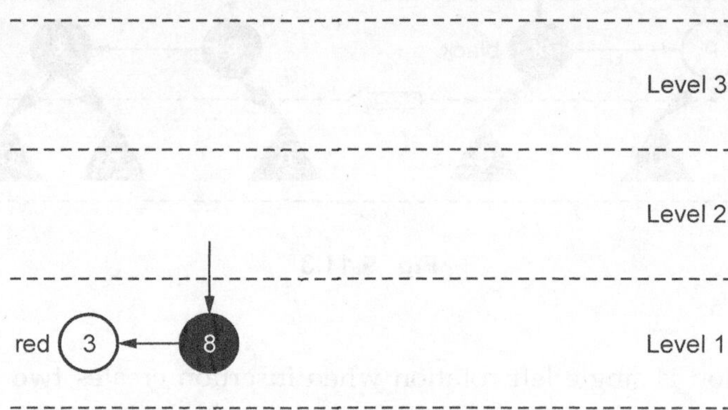

But since right left child is not allowed in AA tree, we will apply **skew** operation, to balance the AA tree

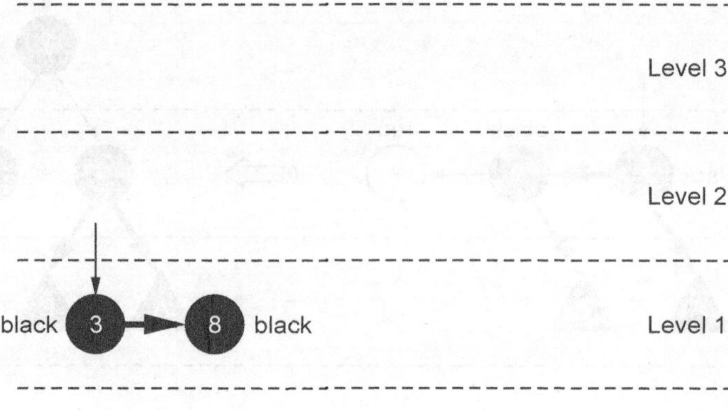

Step 3 : Insert 10

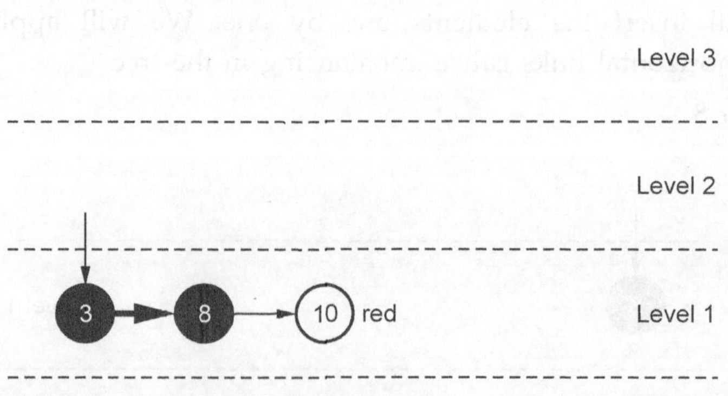

Here two consecutive horizontal links occur. This is not allowed. Hence we will apply **split** operation. The resultant tree will be -

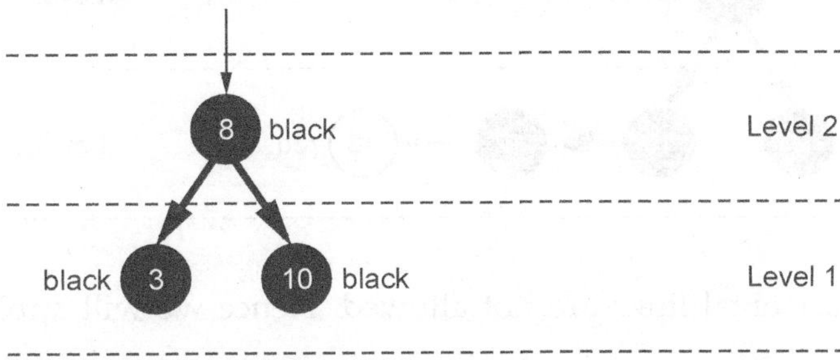

Step 4 : Insert 18

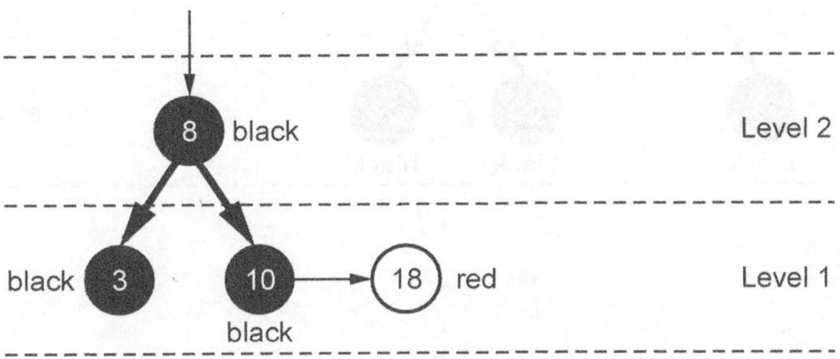

Step 5 : Insert 12

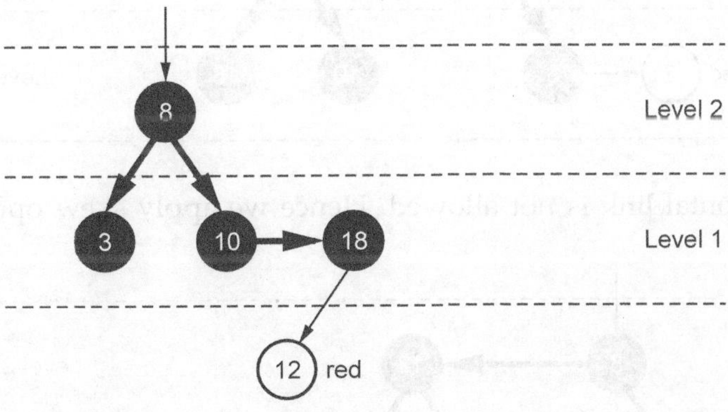

Again left link from 18 to 12 is not allowed. Hence we apply skew operation. The balanced AA tree will then be,

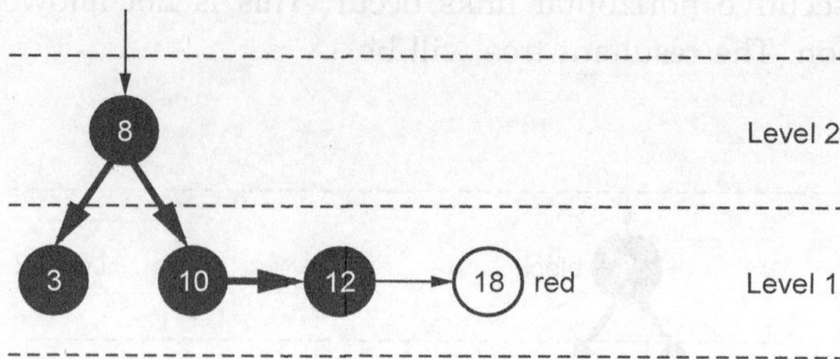

But still two horizontal links are not allowed. Hence we will apply split operation.

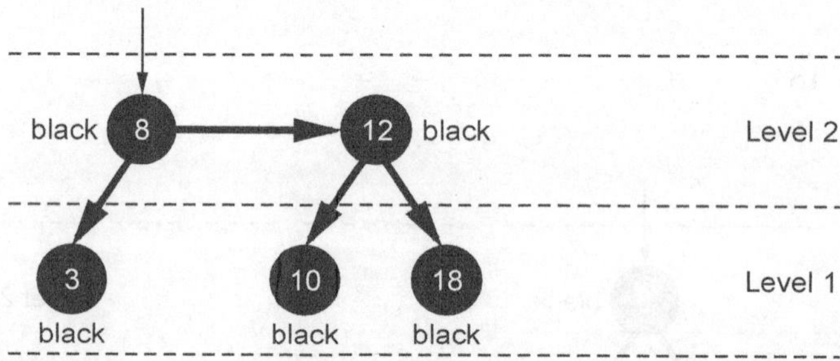

Step 6 : Insert 2

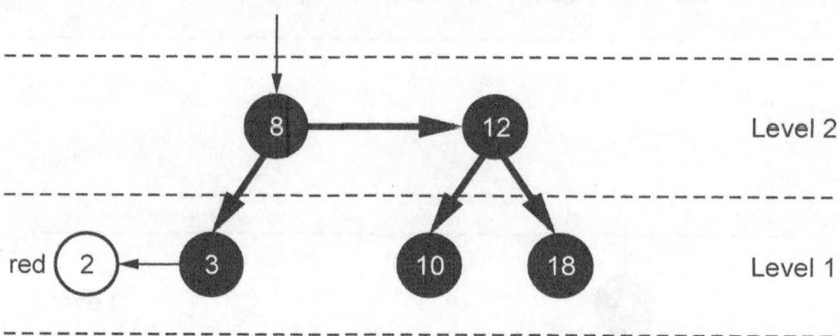

The left horizontal link is not allowed. Hence we apply skew operation.

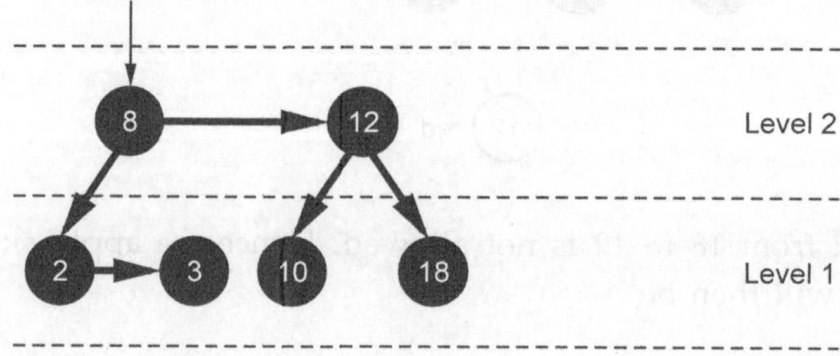

Thus, the AA tree is created.

5.11.2 Deletion Operation

- The node is deleted similar to binary search tree.

i) To delete a leaf node with no children, simply remove the node.

ii) To delete node with one child, replace node with its child.

iii) To delete an internal node, replace that node with either its successor or predecessor.

This deletion may cause unbalancing in AA tree which can be rebalanced with the help of skip and skew operations.

Following are the rules that can be applied to rebalance the AA tree.

Rule 1 : Decrease the level of the node when

i) If the child node is more than one level down.

ii) A node is right horizontal child of another node whose level was decreased.

Rule 2 : Skew the level of the node whose level was decreased.

i) Skew the subtree from the root node, where the decremented node is root.

ii) Skew the root node's right child.

iii) Skew the root node's right-right child.

Rule 3 : Split the level of the node whose level was decreased.

i) Split the root node of the subtree.

ii) Split the root node's right child.

Let us understand deletion operation with the help of example -

Example 5.11.2 *Delete 4 from the following AA tree.*

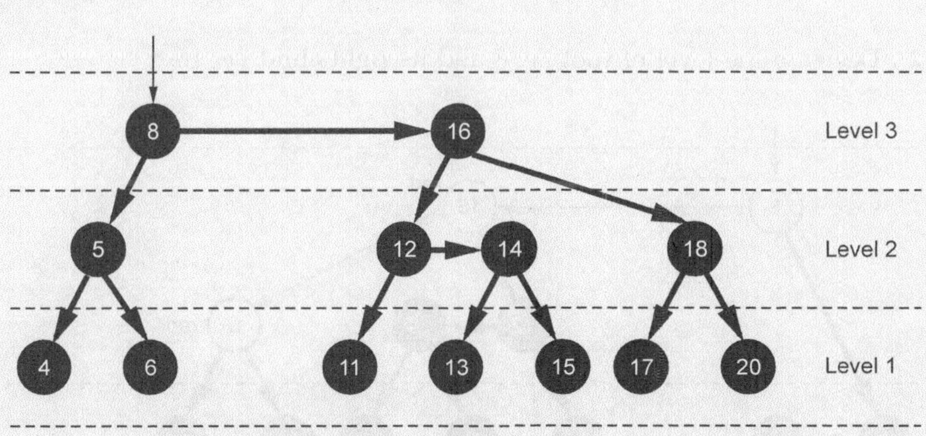

Fig. 5.11.5

Solution :

Step 1 : Delete node 4.

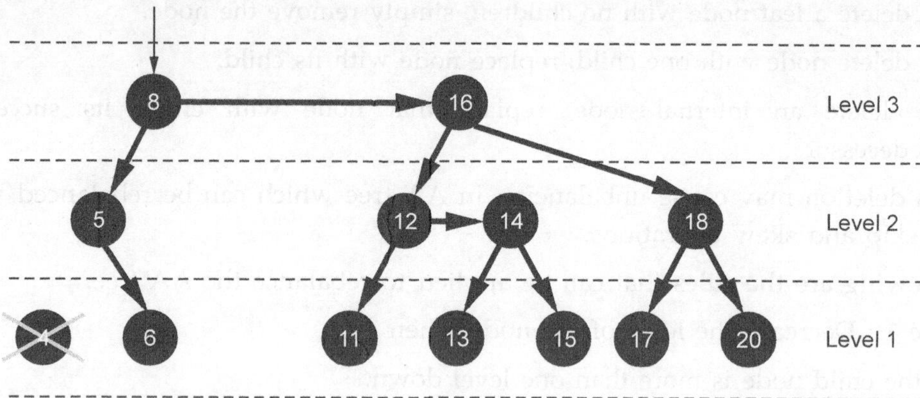

It can also be represented as follows :

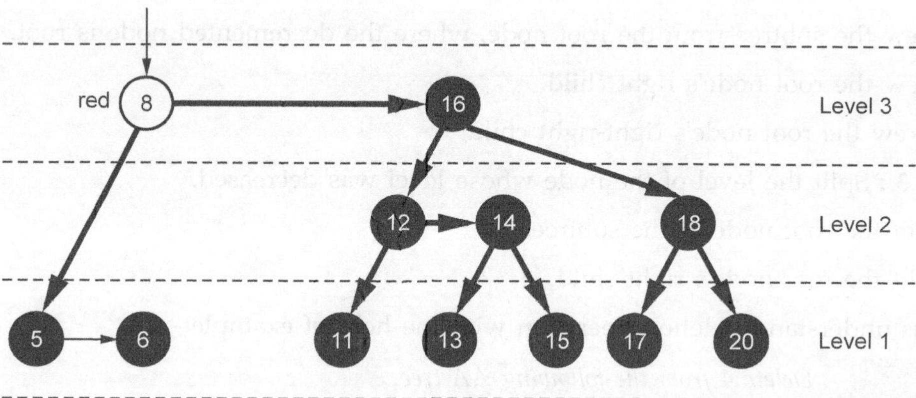

Step 2 : Decrease the level of root i.e. 8 and its right child i.e. 16.

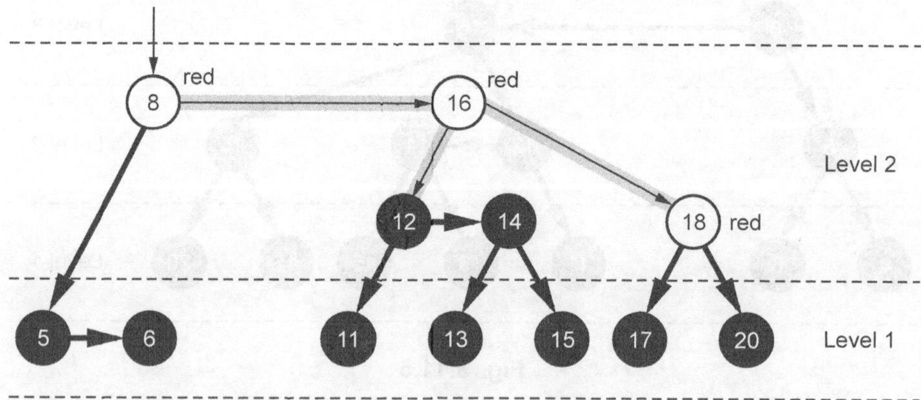

Step 3 : Skew for right child of 8.

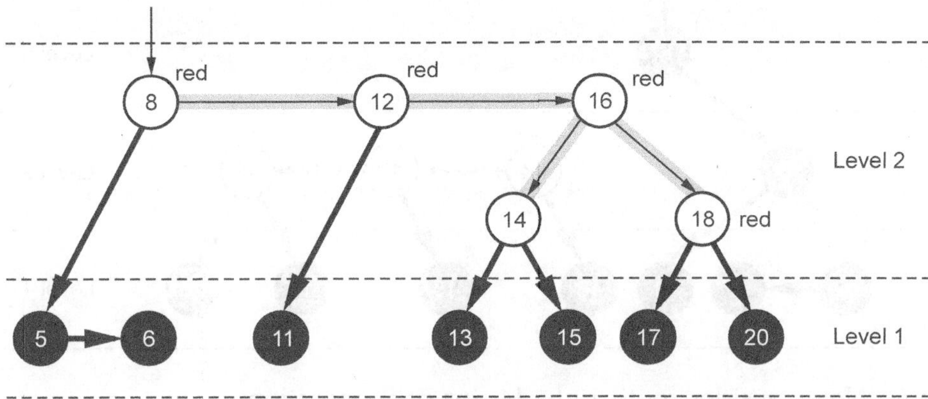

That means make 8 as parent of 12 and 12 as parent of 16. Attach 14 as left child of 16.

Step 4 : Skew at root's right right. That means focus node 16.

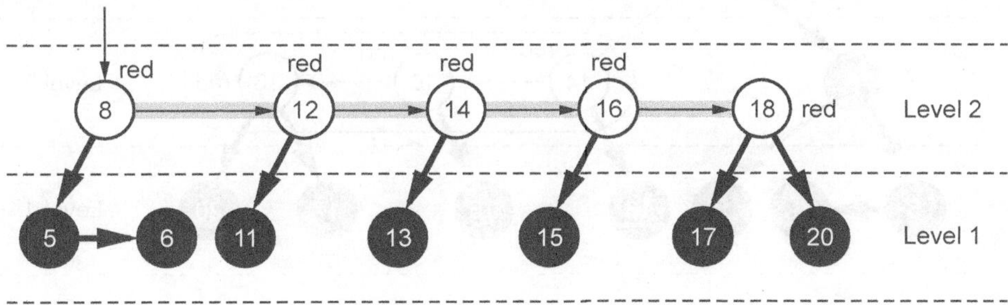

In this skew operation 14 becomes parent of 16. And the right child of 14 which was actually 15 becomes left child of 16.

Step 5 : Now we get consecutive horizontal red links. To balance such AA tree, we will perform split operation.

First split will be at root.

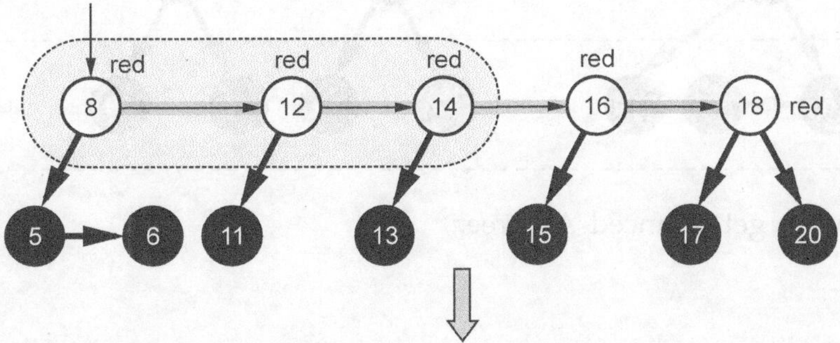

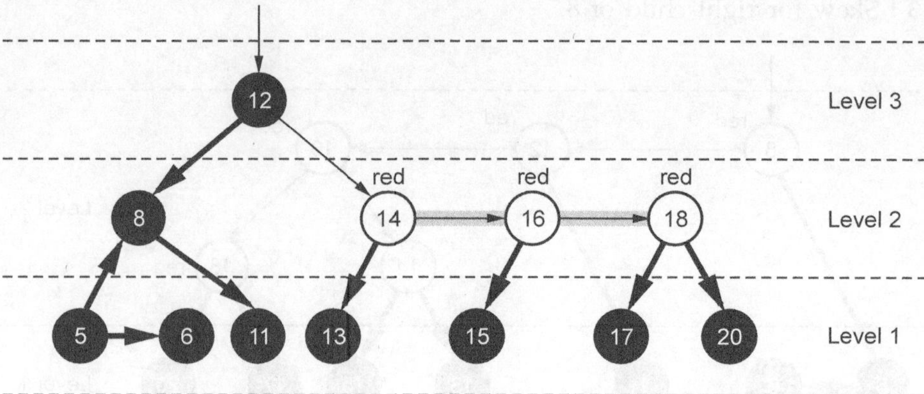

Step 6 : Now consider root's right 14, for split operation.

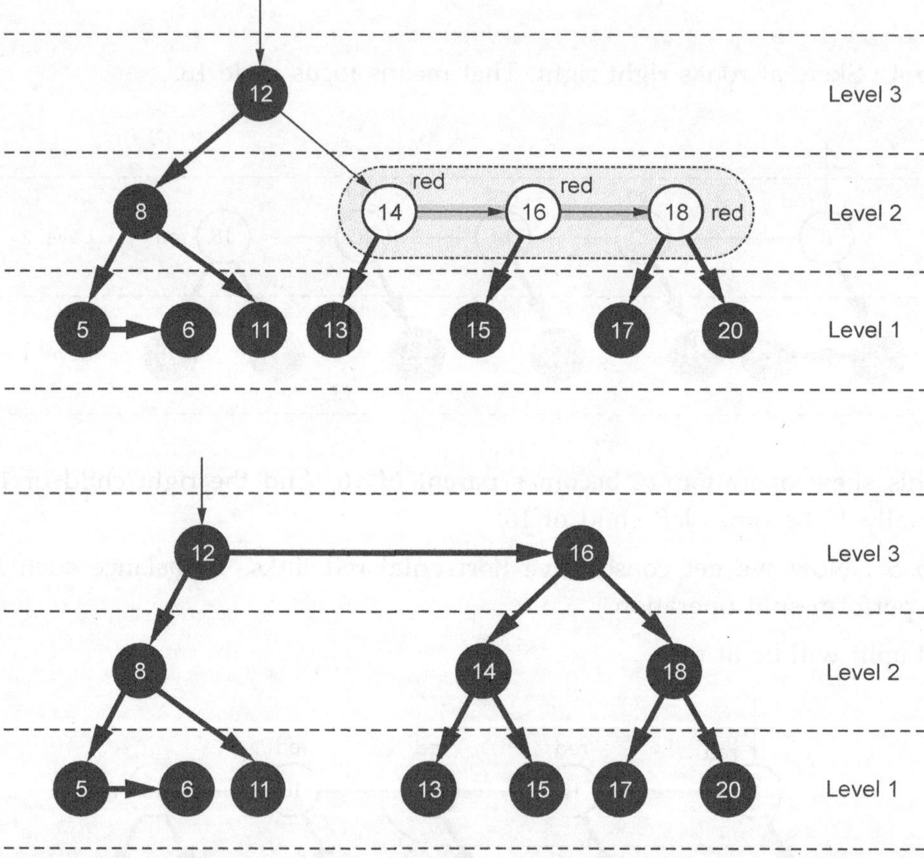

Thus, now we get balanced AA tree.

5.12 Set

5.12.1 Set ADT

Set is defined as **collection of objects**. These objects are called **elements of the set.** All the elements are enclosed within curly brackets '{' and '}' and every element is separated by commas. If 'a' is an element of set A then we say that $a \in A$ and if 'a' is not an element of A then we say that $a \notin A$.

Typically set is denoted by a **capital letter**. The set can be represented using three methods.

1) Listing method

The elements are listed in the set.

For example : A set of element which are less than 5. Then,

$$A = \{0,1, 2, 3, 4\}$$

2) Describing properties

The properties of elements of a set define the set.

For example : A set of vowels. Hence here vowel is a property of the set which defines the set as :

$$A = \{a, e, i, o, u\}$$

3) Recursion method

The recursion occurs to define the elements of the set.

For example : $A = \{ x | x \text{ is square of n} \}$ where $n \leq 10$.

This defines the set as :

$$A = \{0,1, 4, 9, 16,........ 100\}$$

Subset : The subset A is called subset of set B if every element of set A is present in set B but reverse is not true. It is denoted by $A \subseteq B$. For example $A = \{1, 2, 3\}$ and $B = \{1, 2, 3, 4, 5\}$ then $A \subseteq B$.

Empty set : The set having no element in it is called empty set. It is denoted by $A = \{ \}$ and it can be written as ϕ (phi).

Null string : The null element is denoted by ε or $\wedge$ character. Null element means no value character. But ε does mean ϕ.

Power set : The power set is a set of all the subsets of its elements.

For example : A = {1, 2, 3}

Then power set : Q = {ϕ, {1}, {2}, {3}, {1,2}, {1,3}, {3,2}, {2,3}, {1,2,3} }

The number of elements are always equal to 2^n where n is number of elements in original set. As in set A there are 3 elements. Therefore in power set Q there are 2^3 = 8 elements.

Equal set : The two sets are said to be equal (A = B) if $A \subseteq B$ and $B \subseteq A$ i.e. every element of set A is an element of B and every element of B is an element of A.

For example :

A = {1, 2, 3} and B = {1, 2, 3} then A = B.

|A| denotes the length of set A. i.e. number of elements in set A.

For example : if

A = {1, 2, 3, 4, 5} then

|A| = 5

Abstract DataType Set

{

Definition : Set is defined as **collection of objects**. These objects are called **elements of the set**. All the elements are enclosed within curly brackets '{' and '}' and every element is separated by commas.

Operations :

1. **union :** It is a combination of two sets.
2. **Intersection :** The set of common elements from two sets.
3. **Difference :** The set of elements which is present in A but abscent in set B.

}

5.12.2 Realization of Set and Operations on Set

Various operations that can be carried out on set are -

i) Union

ii) Intersection

iii) Difference

iv) Complement

i) $A \cup B$ is union operation - If

A = {1, 2, 3} B = {1, 2, 4} then

$A \cup B$ = {1, 2, 3, 4} i.e. combination of both the sets.

ii) $A \cap B$ is intersection operation - If

$$A = \{1, 2, 3\} \quad \text{and} \quad B = \{2, 3, 4\} \quad \text{then}$$

$A \cap B = \{2, 3\}$ i.e. collection of common elements from both the sets.

iii) $A - B$ is the difference operation - If

$$A = \{1, 2, 3\} \quad \text{and} \quad B = \{2, 3, 4\} \quad \text{then}$$

$A - B = \{1\}$ i.e. elements which are there in set A but not in set B.

iv) $\overline{A}$ is a complement operation - If

$\overline{A} = U - A$ where U is a universal set.

For example :

if $U = \{10, 20, 30, 40, 50\}$

$A = \{10, 20\}$

then $\overline{A} = U - A$

$= \{30, 40, 50\}$

C Functions for Set operations

1. Union Operation

```
void Union(int a[],int b[],int term1,int term2)
{
 int c[MAX];
 int i,j,k,n,flag;
 k=0;
 flag=0;
 for(i=0;i<3;i++)
 {
        c[k++]=a[i];
 }
 for(j=0;j<3;j++)
 {
        flag=0;
        for(i=0;i<3;i++)
        {
               if(a[i]==b[j])
                      flag=1;
        }
        if(flag==0)
               c[k++]=b[j];
 }
 n=k;
```

```
        printf("\n The A union B={");
        for(k=0;k<n;k++)
         printf(" %d",c[k]);
        printf(" }");

}
```

2. Intersection Operation

```
void Intersection(int a[MAX],int b[MAX],int term1,int term2)
{
 int c[MAX];
 int i,j,k,n,flag;
 k=0;
 flag=0;
 for(i=0;i<3;i++)
 {
        flag=1;
        for(j=0;j<3;j++)
        {
                if(a[i]==b[j])
                        flag=0;
        }
        if(flag==0)
                c[k++]=a[i];
 }
 n=k;
        printf("\n The A intersection B={");
        for(k=0;k<n;k++)
         printf(" %d",c[k]);
        printf(" }");

}
```

3. Difference

```
void difference(int a[],int b[],int term1,int term2)
{
 int c[MAX];
 int i,j,k,n,flag;
 k=0;
 flag=0;
 for(i=0;i<3;i++)
 {
        flag=1;
        for(j=0;j<3;j++)
        {
                if(a[i]==b[j])
                {
```

```
                        flag=0;
                        break;
                }
        }
        if(flag==1)
                c[k++]=a[i];
}
n=k;
        printf("\n The A difference B={");
        for(k=0;k<n;k++)
         printf(" %d",c[k]);
        printf(" }");

}
```

4. Symmetric Difference

```
void symm_difference(int a[MAX],int b[MAX],int term1,int term2)
{
 int c[MAX],d[MAX],e[MAX];
 int i,j,k,n,m,p,flag;
 int term3,term4;
++ k=0;  //finding union
        //of A and B
 flag=0;
 for(i=0;i<3;i++)
 {
        c[k++]=a[i];
 }
 for(j=0;j<3;j++)
 {
        flag=0;

        for(i−0;i<3;i++)
        {
                if(a[i]==b[j])
                        flag=1;
        }
        if(flag==0)
                c[k++]=b[j];
 }
 term3=k;
 m=0;            //finding intersection of A and B
 flag=0;
 for(i=0;i<3;i++)
 {
        flag=1;
        for(j=0;j<3;j++)
```

Symmetric difference is a set elements which are present in one set and is not present in another set.

```
        {
                if(a[i]==b[j])
                                flag=0;
        }
        if(flag==0)
                d[m++]=a[i];
}
term4=m;
p=0;//finding difference of A and B
flag=0;
for(i=0;i<term3;i++)
{
        flag=1;
        for(j=0;j<term4;j++)
        {
                if(c[i]==d[j])
                {
                        flag=0;
                        break;
                }
        }
        if(flag==1)
                e[p++]=c[i];
}
n=p;
printf("\n The Symmetric difference is={");
for(i=0;i<n;i++)
        printf(" %d",e[i]);
printf(" }");
}
```

5.13 Heap - Basic Concept

SPPU : Dec.-07, May-10, Marks 4

In this section we will learn *"What is heap?"* and *"How to construct heap?"*

Definition : Heap is a **complete binary tree** or a almost complete binary tree in which every **parent node** be either **greater** or **lesser than** its child nodes.

Heap can be **min heap** or **max heap.**

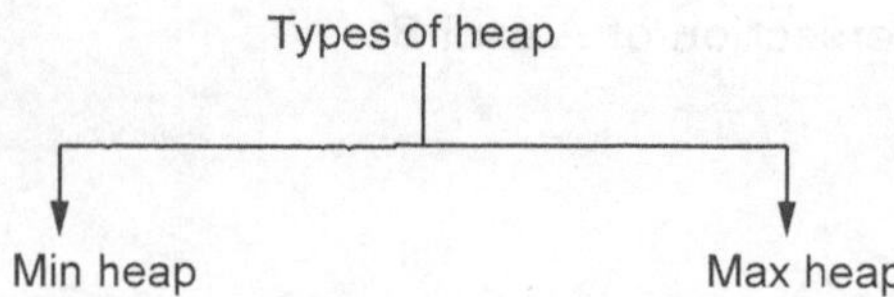

A **Max heap** is a tree in which value of each node is greater than or equal to the value of its children nodes.

For example :

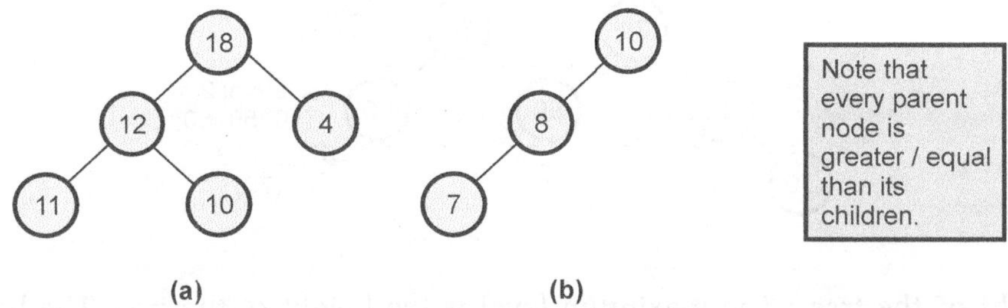

Fig. 5.13.1 Max heap

A **Min heap** is a tree in which value of each node is less than or equal to value of its children nodes.

For example :

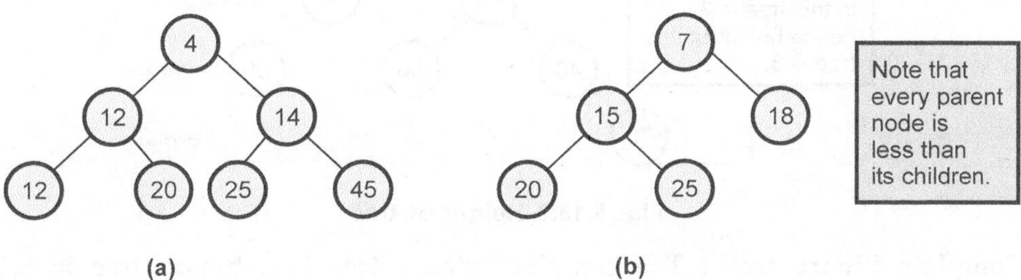

Fig. 5.13.2 Min heap

Parent being greater or lesser in heap is called **parental property**. Thus heap has two important properties.

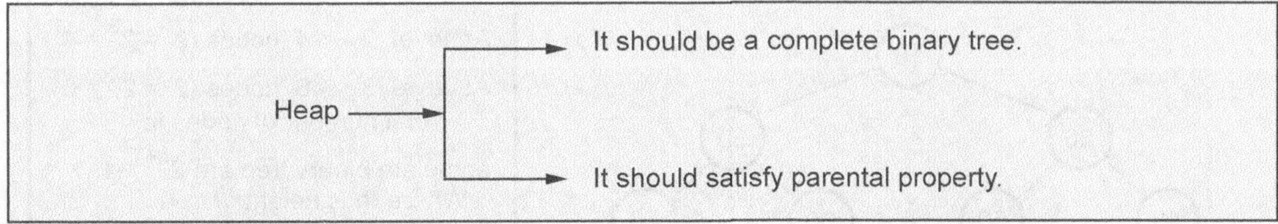

Before understanding the construction of heap let us learn/revise few basics that are required while constructing heap.

- **Level of binary tree :** The root of the tree is always at level 0. Any node is always at a level one more than its parent nodes level.

For example :

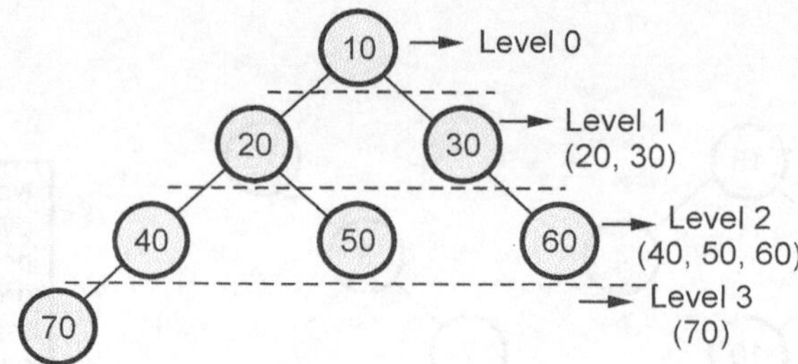

- **Height of the tree :** The maximum level is the height of the tree. The height of the tree is also called **depth** of the tree.

For example :

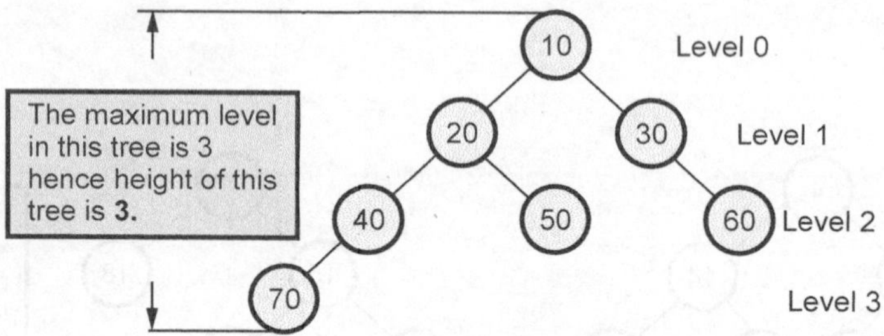

Fig. 5.13.3 Height of tree

- **Complete binary tree :** The complete binary tree is a binary tree in which all leaves are at the same depth or total number of nodes at each level i are 2^i.

For example :

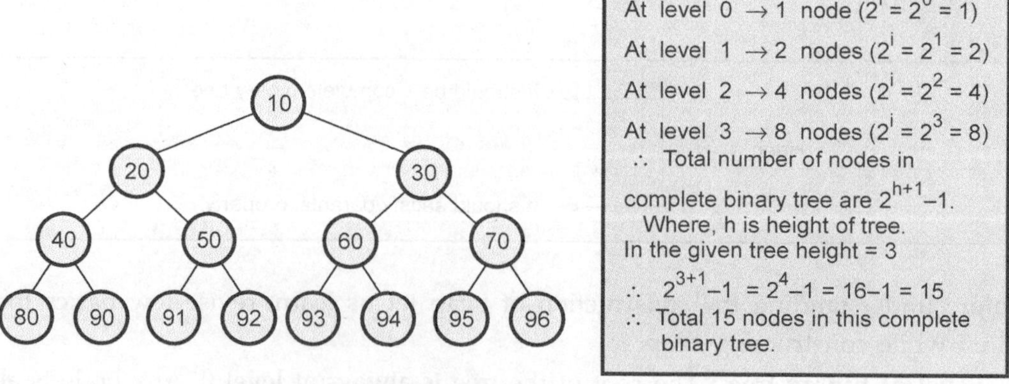

Fig. 5.13.4 Complete binary tree

- **Almost complete binary tree :** The almost complete binary tree is a tree in which -
  - i) Each node has a left child whenever it has a right child. That means there is always a left child, but for a left child there may not be a right child.
  - ii) The leaf in a tree must be present at height h or h–1. That means all the leaves are on two adjacent levels.

For example :

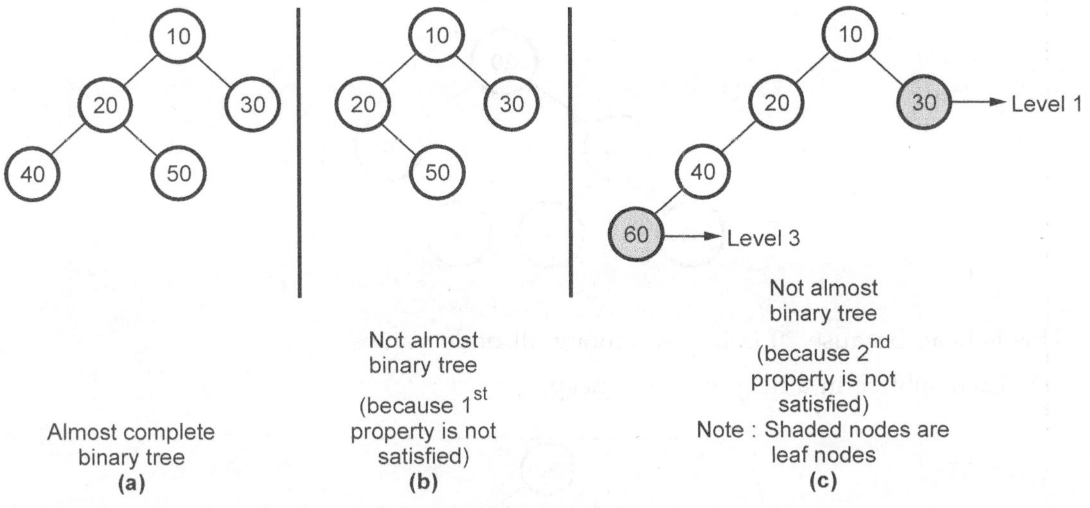

Fig. 5.13.5

In Fig. 5.13.5 (a) the given binary tree is satisfying both the properties. That is all the leaves are at either level 2 or level 1 and when right child is present left child is always present.

In Fig. 5.13.5 (b), the given binary tree is not satisfying the first property; that is the right child is present for node 20 but it has no left child. Hence it is not almost complete binary tree.

In Fig. 5.13.5 (c), the given binary tree is not satisfying the second property; that is the leaves are at level 3 and level 1 and not at adjacent levels. Hence it is not almost complete binary tree.

5.13.1 Heaps using Priority Queues

There are some important properties that should be followed by heap.

1. There should be either "complete binary tree" or "almost complete binary tree".

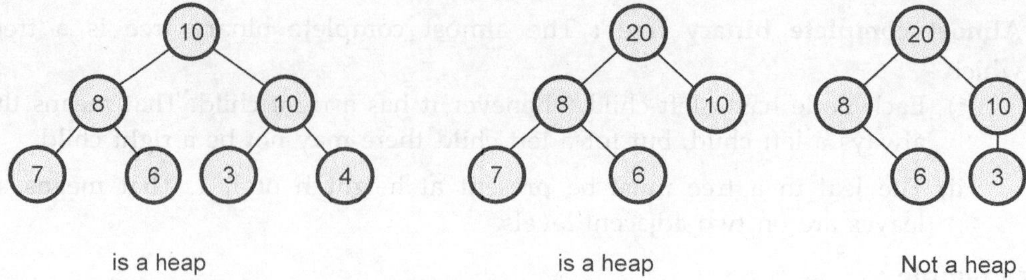

is a heap   is a heap   Not a heap

2. The root of a heap always contains its largest element.

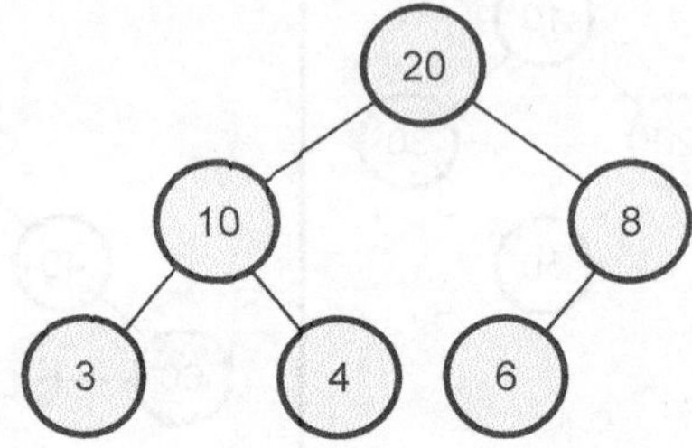

This is heap because 20 is largest among all node values.

3. Each subtree in a heap is also a heap.

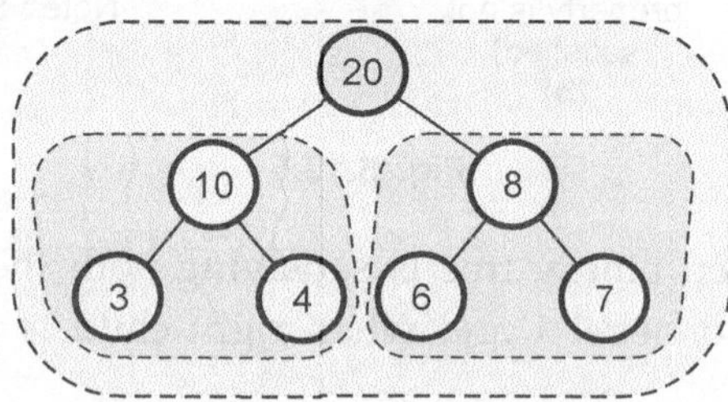

The tree and subtrees are shown by dotted lines. Each tree/subtree itself is a heap.

4. Heap can be implemented as **array** by recording its elements in the top-down and left to right fashion.

For example :

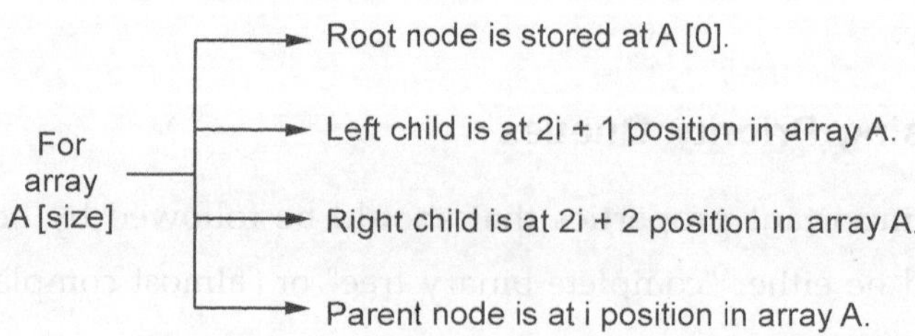

Consider heap as shown below.

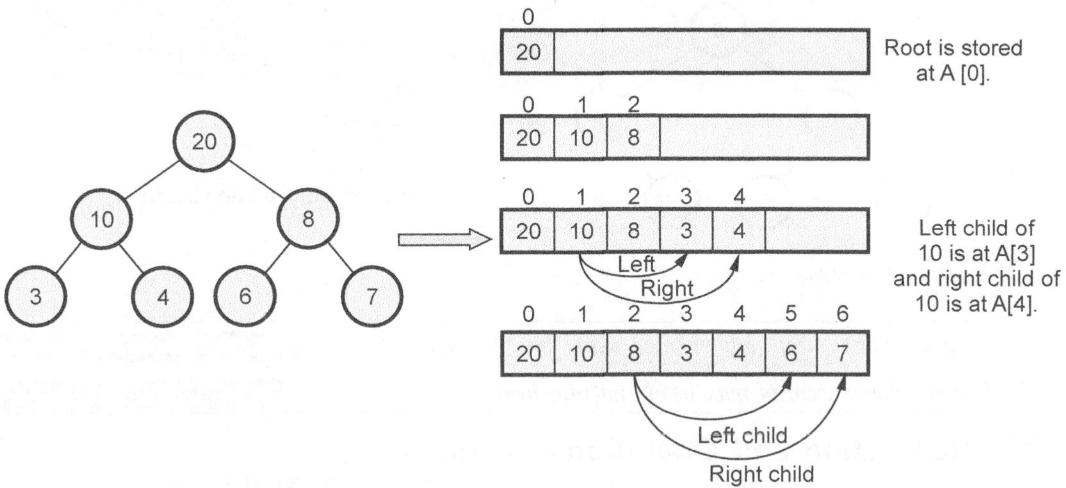

Thus array can represent complete heap.

Example 5.13.1 *For a given heap, give the array representation of it.*

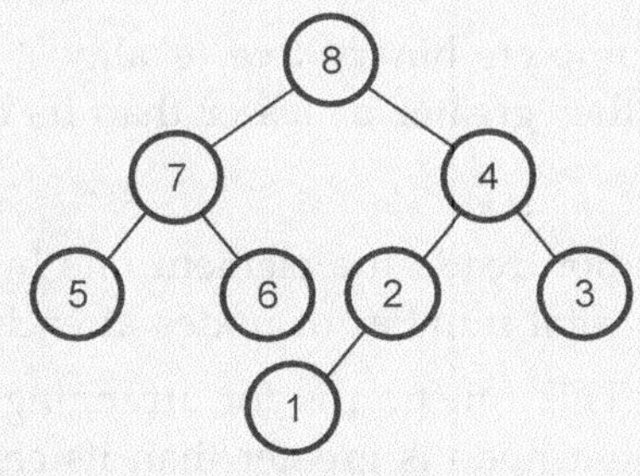

Solution : Root node is stored at 0th index. For each parent node i we will store left node at (2i + 1) and right node at (2i + 2) positions in array.

The array will then be -

0	1	2	3	4	5	6	7	8	9	10	11
8	7	4	5	6	2	3					1

Example 5.13.2 *Draw a tree for given heap represented by an array.*

0	1	2	3	4	5
9	6	8	2	5	7

Solution :

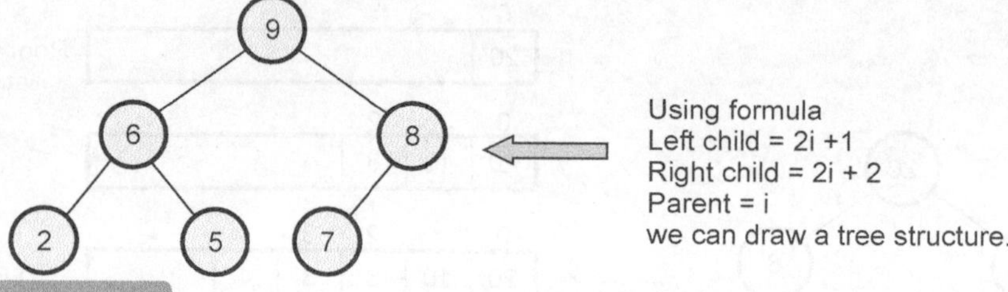

University Questions

1. *How is priority heap implemented using binary heap ?* **SPPU : Dec.-07, Marks 4**
2. *Explain the concept of max heap and min heap.* **SPPU : May-10, Marks 4**

5.14 Realization and Operations on Heap

SPPU : May-05, 08, 09, 10, 11, 12, 13, Dec.-05, 07, 10, 11, Marks 12

AbstractDataType Heap

{

Instances : Heap is a complete binary tree or almost complete binary tree in which every parent node is either greater or lesser than its child nodes.

Operations :

1. **Create-tree :** This operation reads the element one by one and creates the complete binary tree. In this tree total number of nodes at each level i are 2^i.
2. **ParentDominance ( ) :** This function is for arranging each node in the tree in such a manner that each parent node is greater than its child nodes.

}

5.14.1 Insertion of Element in the Heap

The algorithm for inserting an element in the heap can be as given below -

Algorithm for insertion of element :

1. Insert element at the last position in heap.
2. Compare with its parent, swap the two nodes if parental dominance condition gets violeted.

   [Parental dominance = Parent is greater than its children]
3. Continue comparing the new element with nodes up, each time by satisfying parental dominance condition.

For example

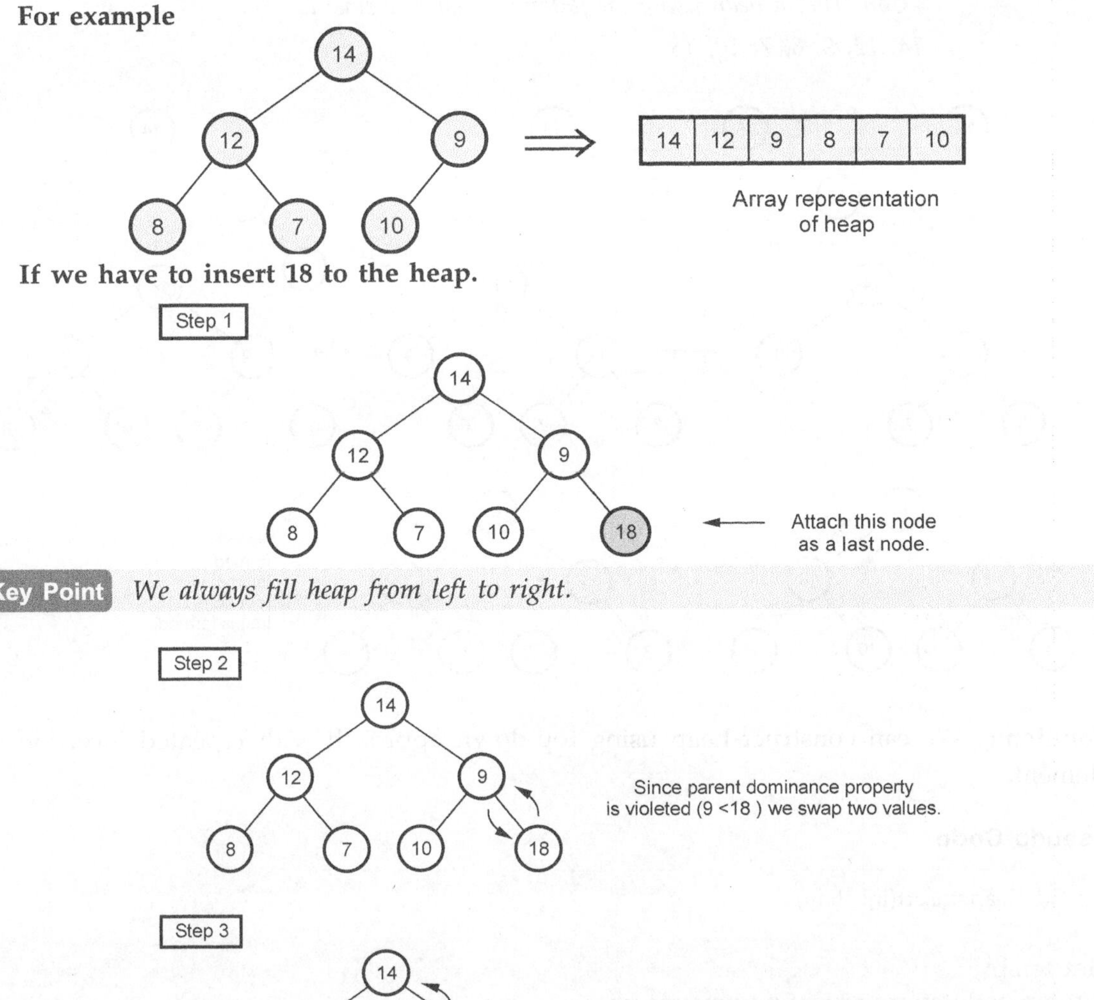

If we have to insert 18 to the heap.

Key Point *We always fill heap from left to right.*

Step 4

18
12
14
8
7
10
9

Thus we get a heap by inserting element.

In top-down approach the heap is constructed from top to bottom scanning of a tree, each time checking parent dominace property.

Example 5.14.1 *Construct a heap using for following list of elements.*
14, 12, 9, 8, 7, 10, 18

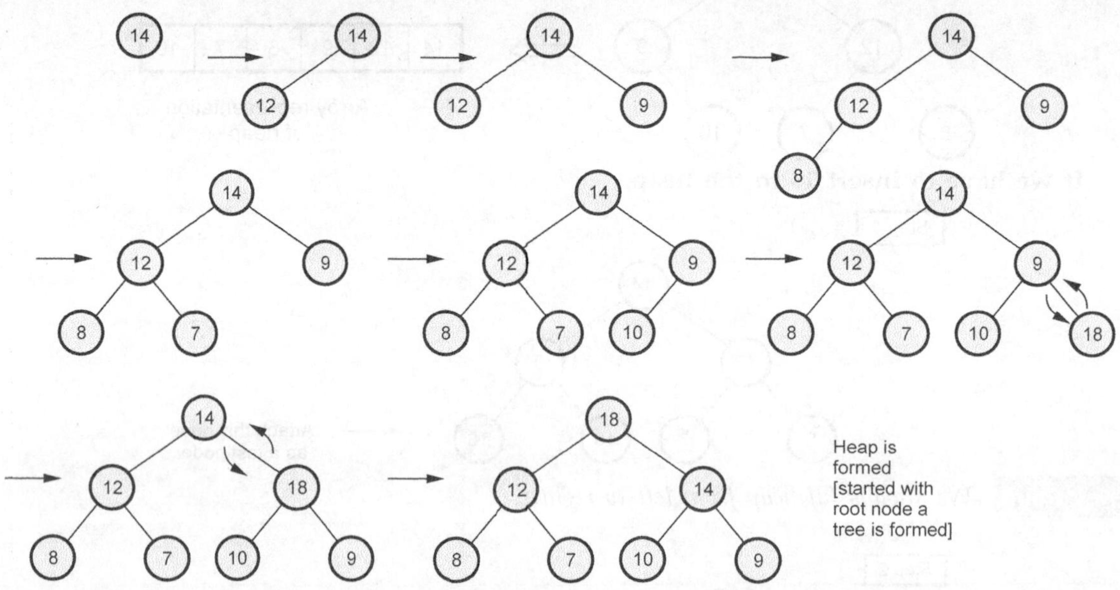

Solution : We can construct heap using top-down approach with repeated insertion of element.

Pseudo Code

```
void Heap::insert(int item)
{
 int temp;
//temp node starts at leaf and moves up
 temp=++size;
 while(temp!=1 && heap[temp/2]<item)
 {
// the element cannot be placed in array H
  H[temp]=H[temp/2];//moving element down
   temp=temp/2;//finding the parent
 }
 H[temp]=item;//placing the element at its position
 }
```

5.14.2 Deletion of Element From the Heap

Algorithm for deletion of element from heap :

The root of a heap can be deleted and the heap fixed up can be as follows :

1. Exchange the root with the last leaf.
2. Decrease the heap's size by 1.
3. Heapify the smaller tree using bottom-up construction algorithm.

While constructing heap nodes are attached like this,

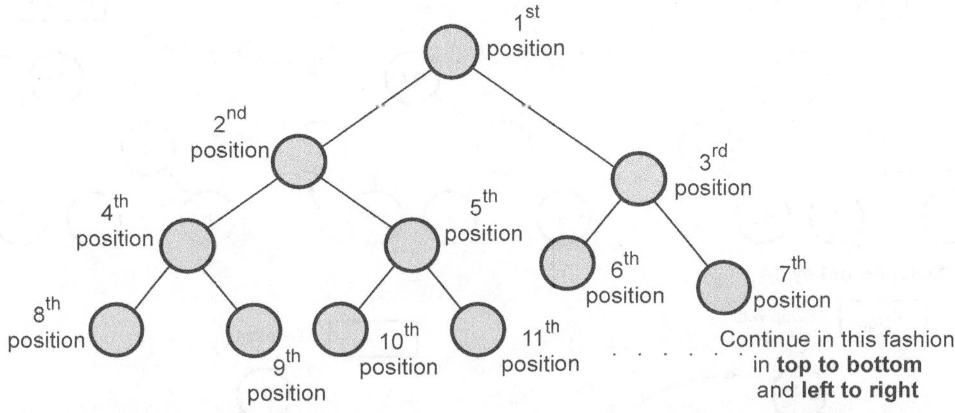

Understanding of positions in a tree or a heap is necessary for performing delete operation. Because the key to be deleted is always swapped with last node and the last node is always deleted from heap. Also each time we have to maintain heap property (i.e. parent dominance - parent being greater). Let us understand this delete operation with the help of some examples.

Perform deletion on following heap.

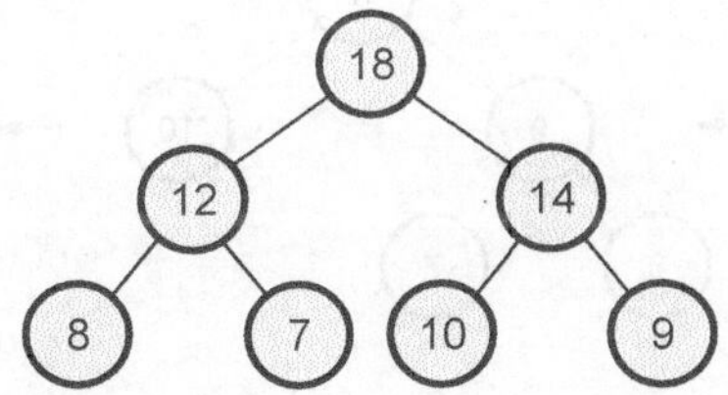

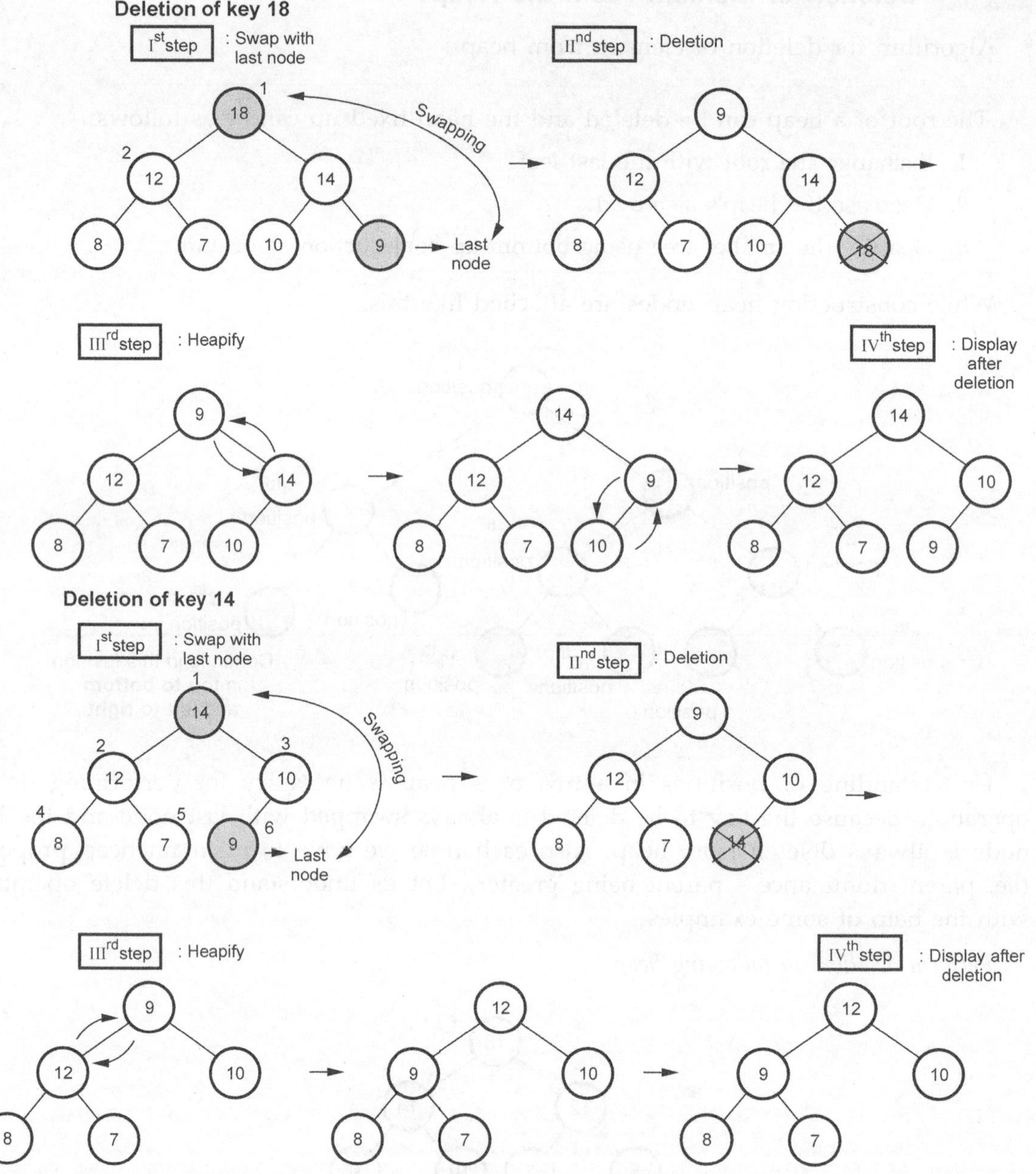

Continuing in this fashion we can perform deletion operation on given heap.

Key Point *Always root's key has to be deleted from a heap.*

Analysis

The basic operation in deletion algorithm is the key comparison that should be made to "heapify" the tree after the swap has been made. Each time, after deletion the size of the tree is decreased by 1. It requires less number of key comparisons than twice the heap's height. Therefore time complexity of deletion of **O(log n).**

Example 5.14.2 *Consider the heap in the following Fig. 5.14.1.*

i) Apply deleet operation to the heap. Repair heap after deletion.

ii) Insert 38 into the heap. Repair heap after insertion.

SPPU : Dec.-05,07, Marks 6

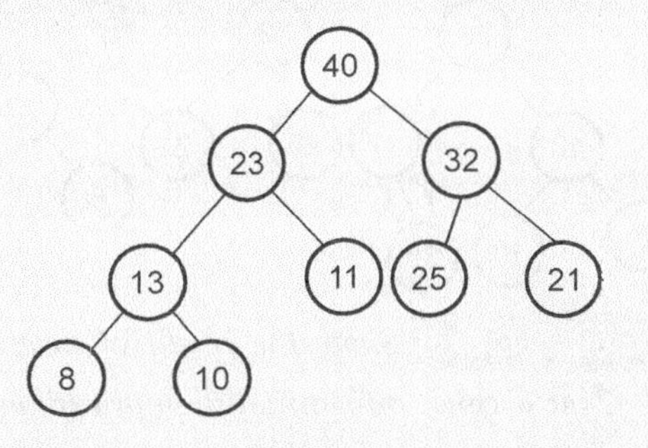

Fig. 5.14.1

Solution : i) For delete operation we will choose node 40 because this node is of highest priority.

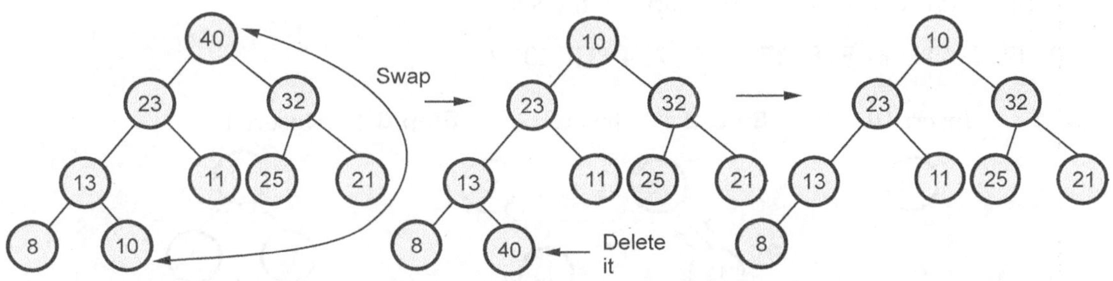

After deleting the node 40, we need to heapify the tree

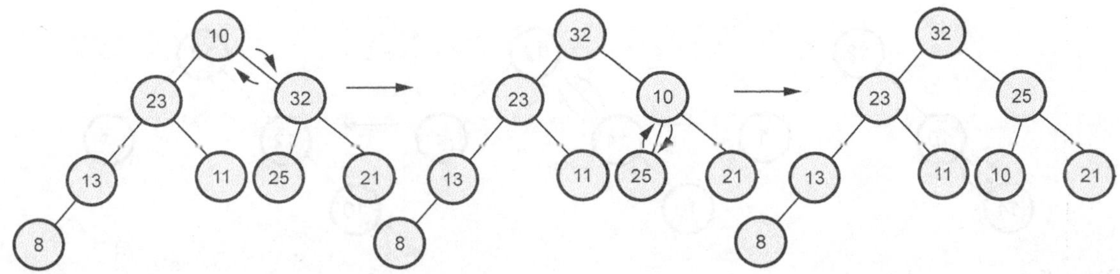

ii) Insert 38 : Consider the given heap.

After inserting 38, we need to heapify the tree. That means we have to maintain the heap property i.e. **parent node must be greater than the child nodes.**

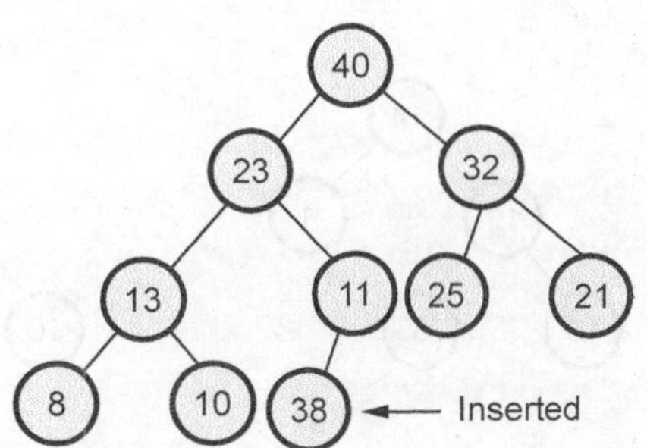

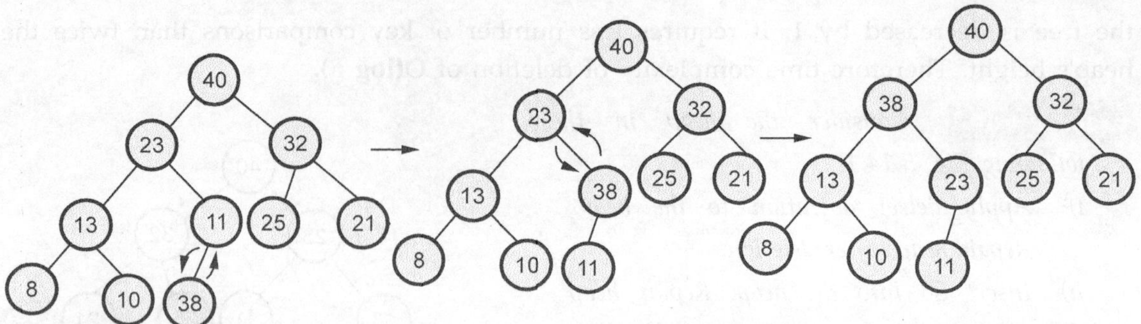

Example 5.14.3 *Show the result of inserting 10, 12, 1, 14, 6, 5, 8, 15, 3, 9, 7, 4, 11, 13 and 2 at a time, into initially empty binary heap. After creating such heap delete the element 8 from heap, how do you repair the heap? Then insert the element in the heap and show the final result (insertion should be at other than lead node).*

SPPU : May-08, Marks 12 , Dec.-10, Marks 10

Solution : We will create max heap for the set

10 12 1 14 6 5 8 15 3 9 7 4 11 13 2

Step 1 : Insert 10. **Step 2 :** Insert 12. **Step 3 :** Insert 1.

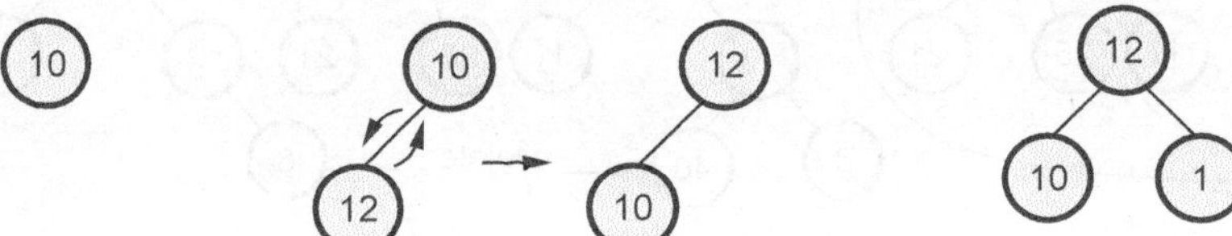

Step 4 : Insert 14.

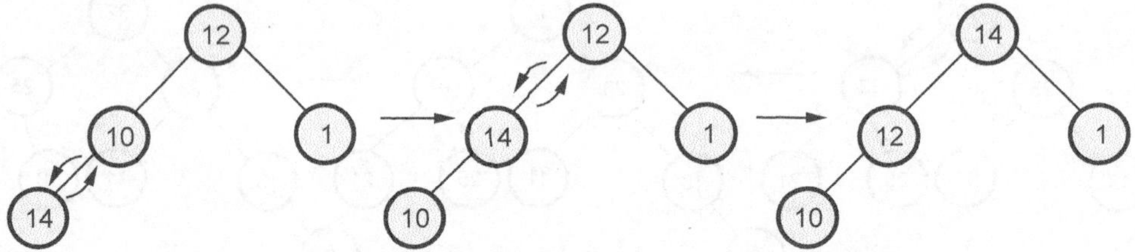

Step 5 : Insert 6. **Step 6 :** Insert 5. **Step 7 :** Insert 8.

14

12 1

10 6

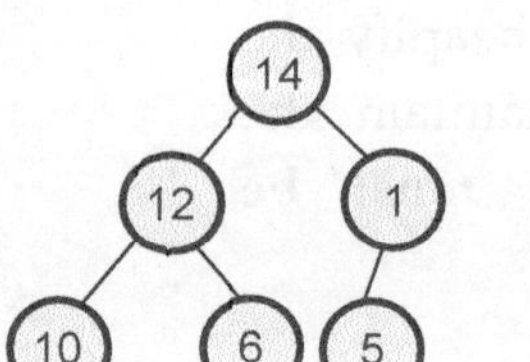

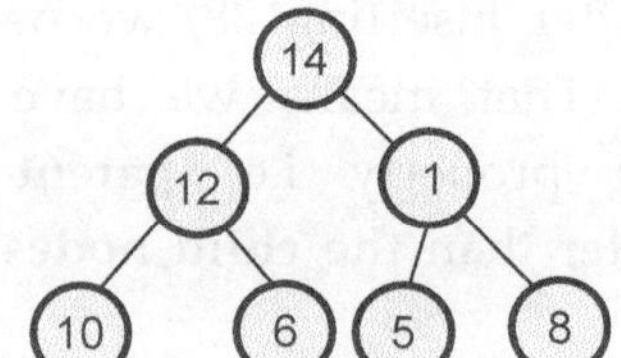

Step 8 : Insert 15

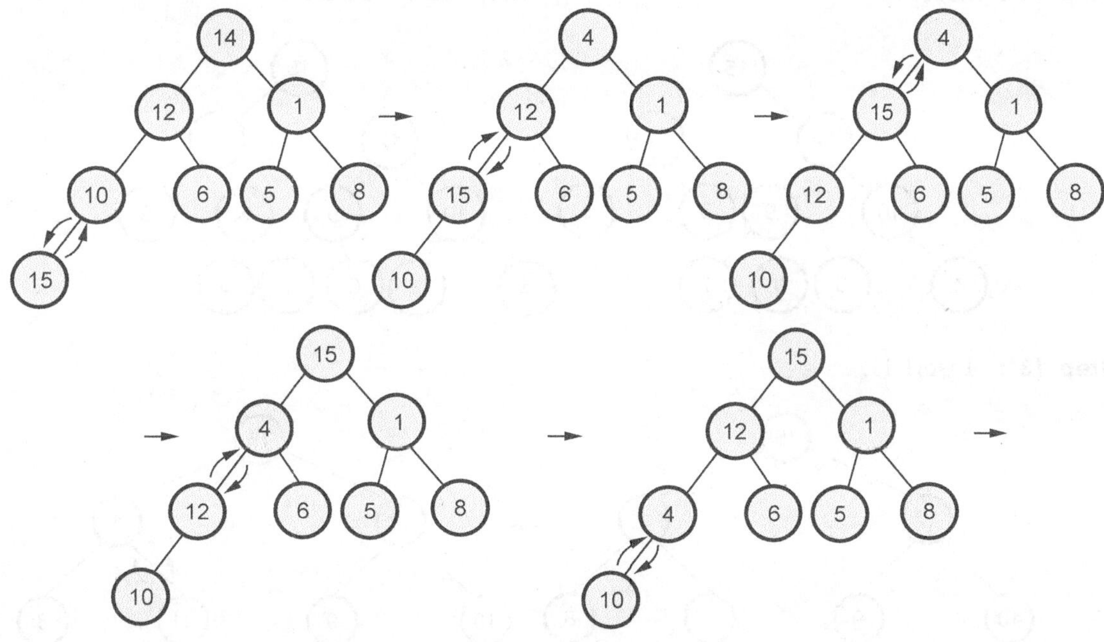

Step 9 : Insert 3.

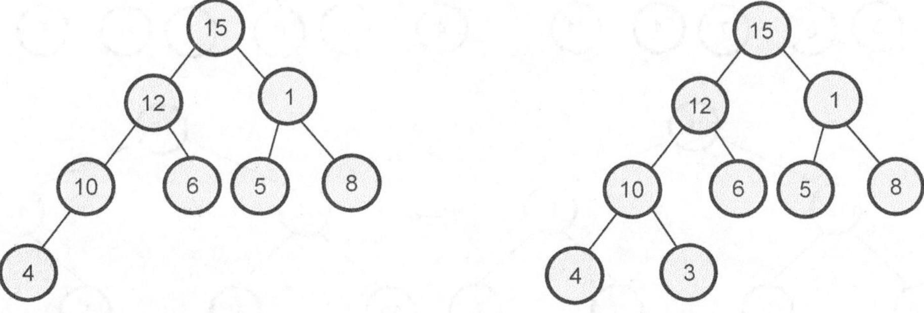

Step 10 : Insert 9.

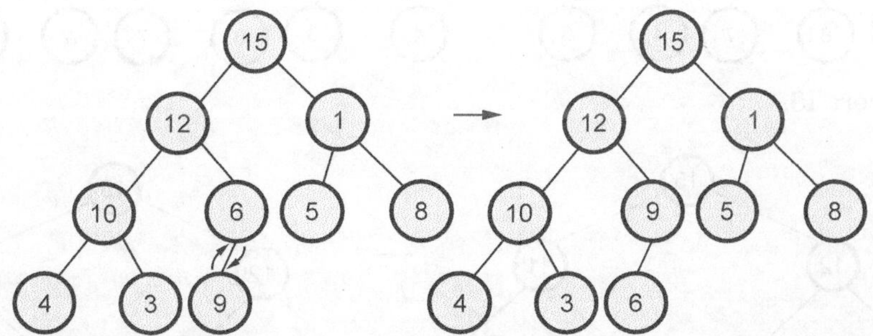

Step 11 : Insert 7. **Step 12 :** Insert 4.

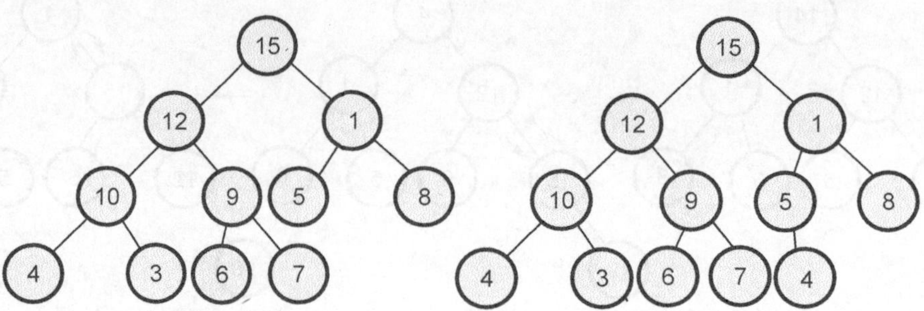

Step 13 : Insert 11.

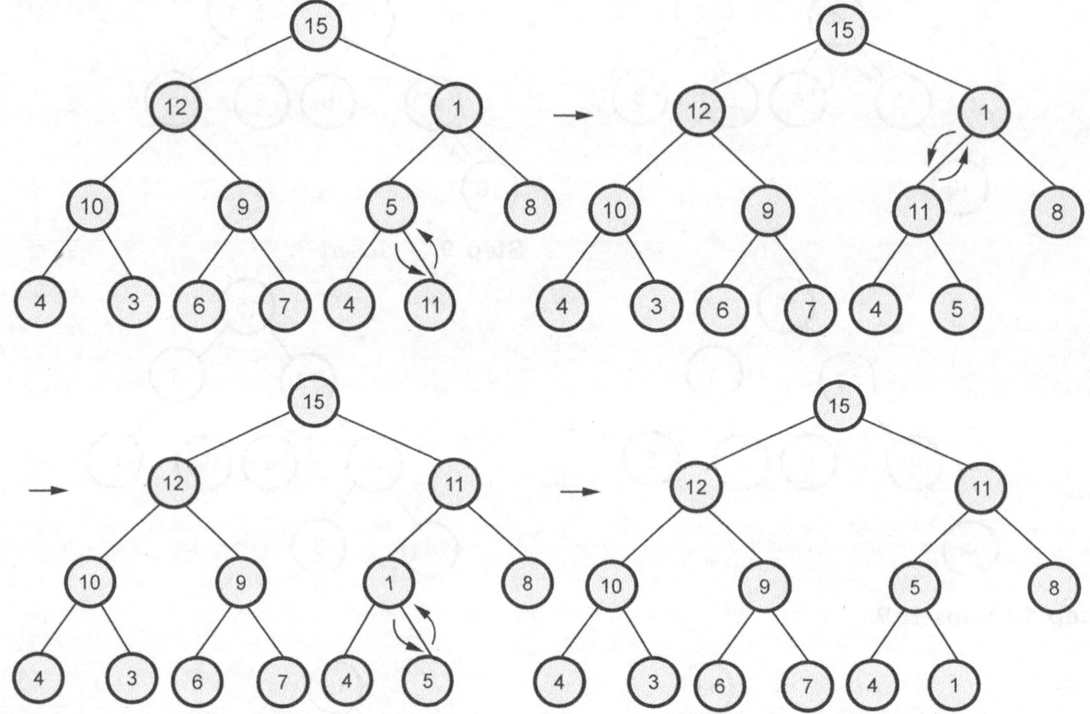

Step 14 : Insert 13.

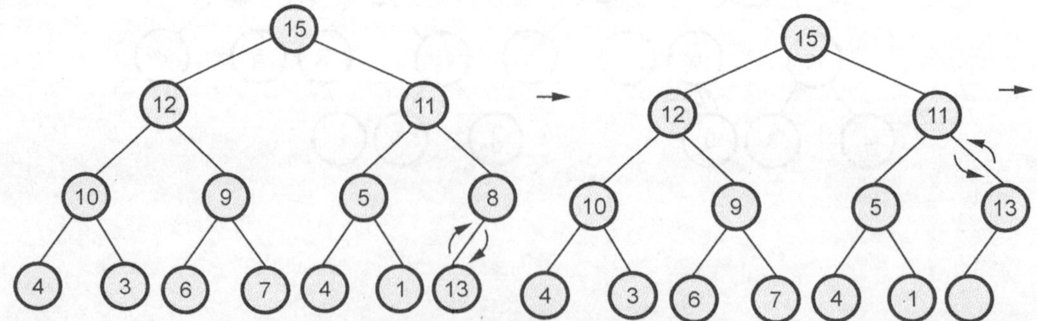

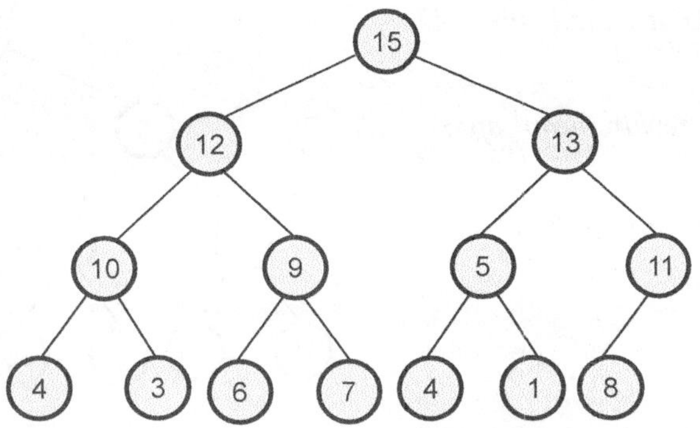

Step 15 : Insert 2

Deletion of 8

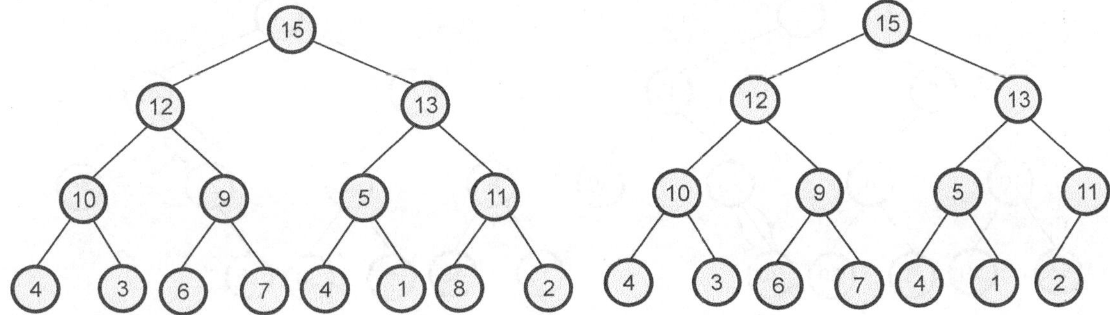

Insertion of node

If we insert node 20 then,

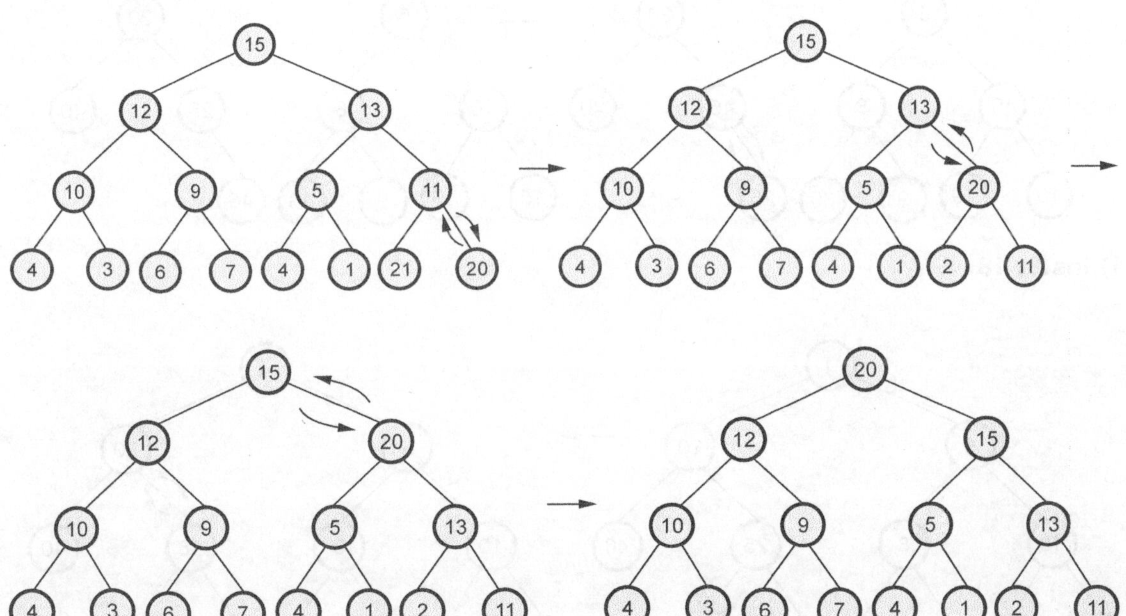

Example 5.14.4 *Consider the following D Heap :*

1) *Insert 18 and repair heap after insertion.*
2) *Delete min element and repair heap after deletion*

SPPU : May-09, Marks 6

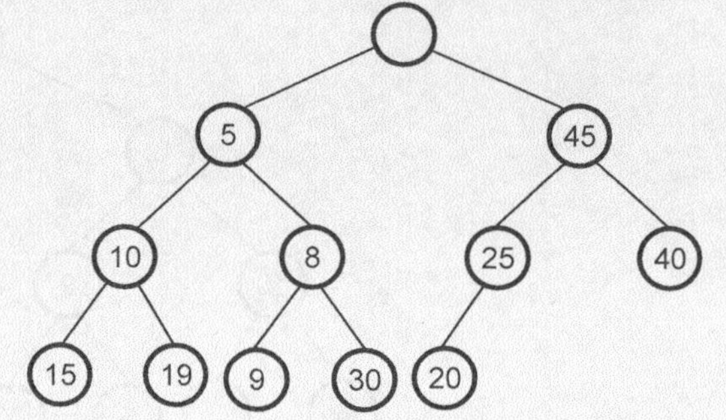

Solution : Assume the data at root node is 1.

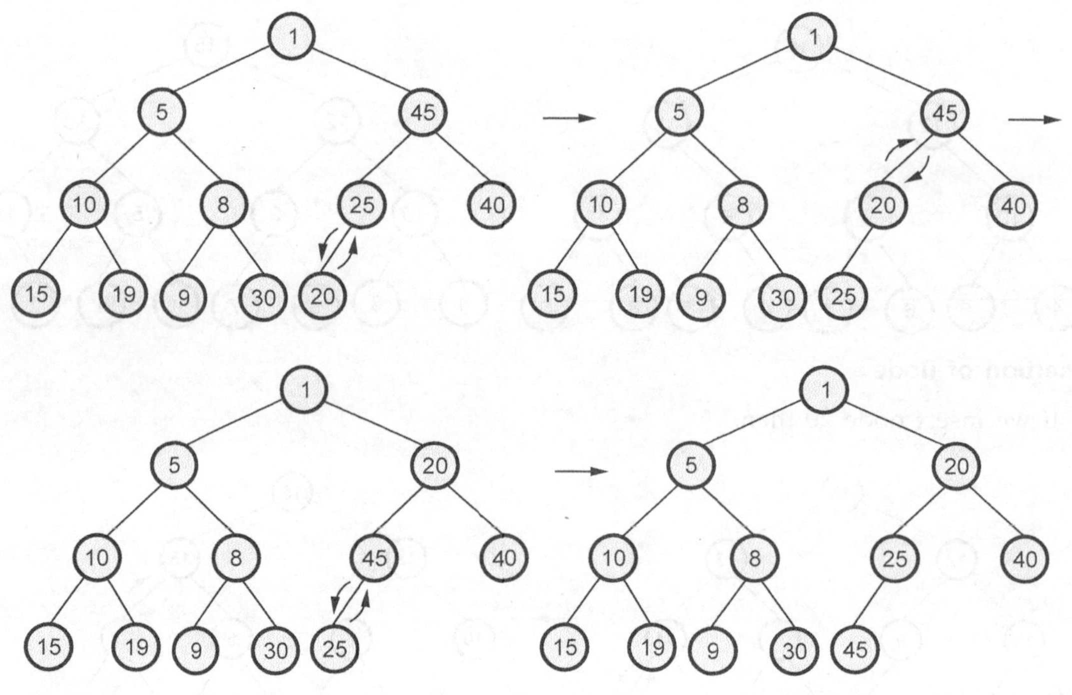

1) Insert 18

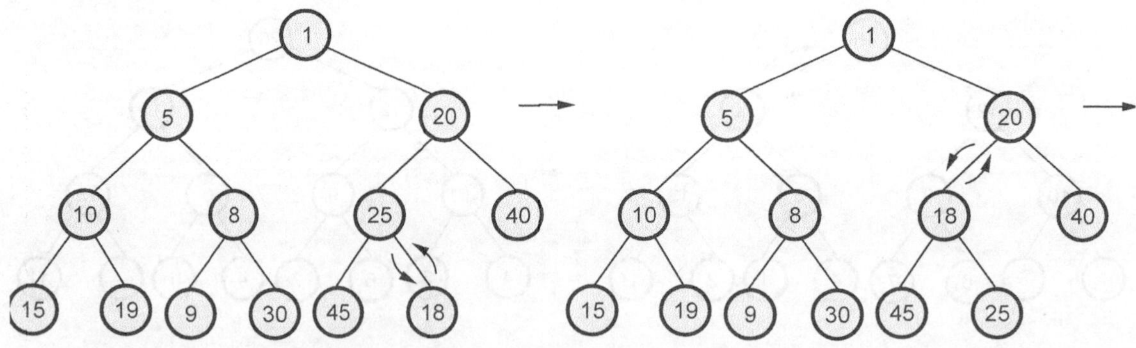

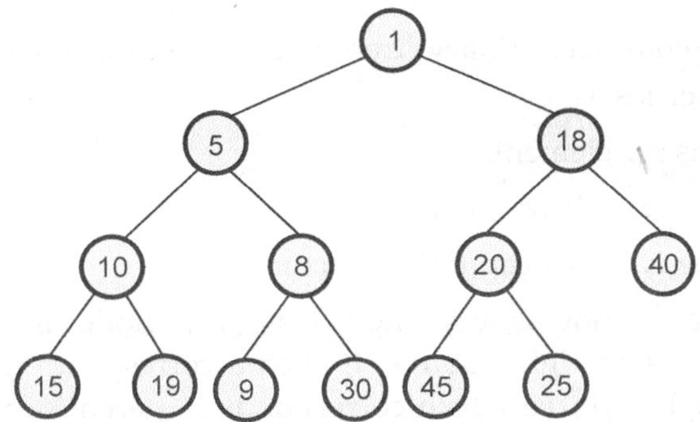

2) Deletion of min element i.e. 1.

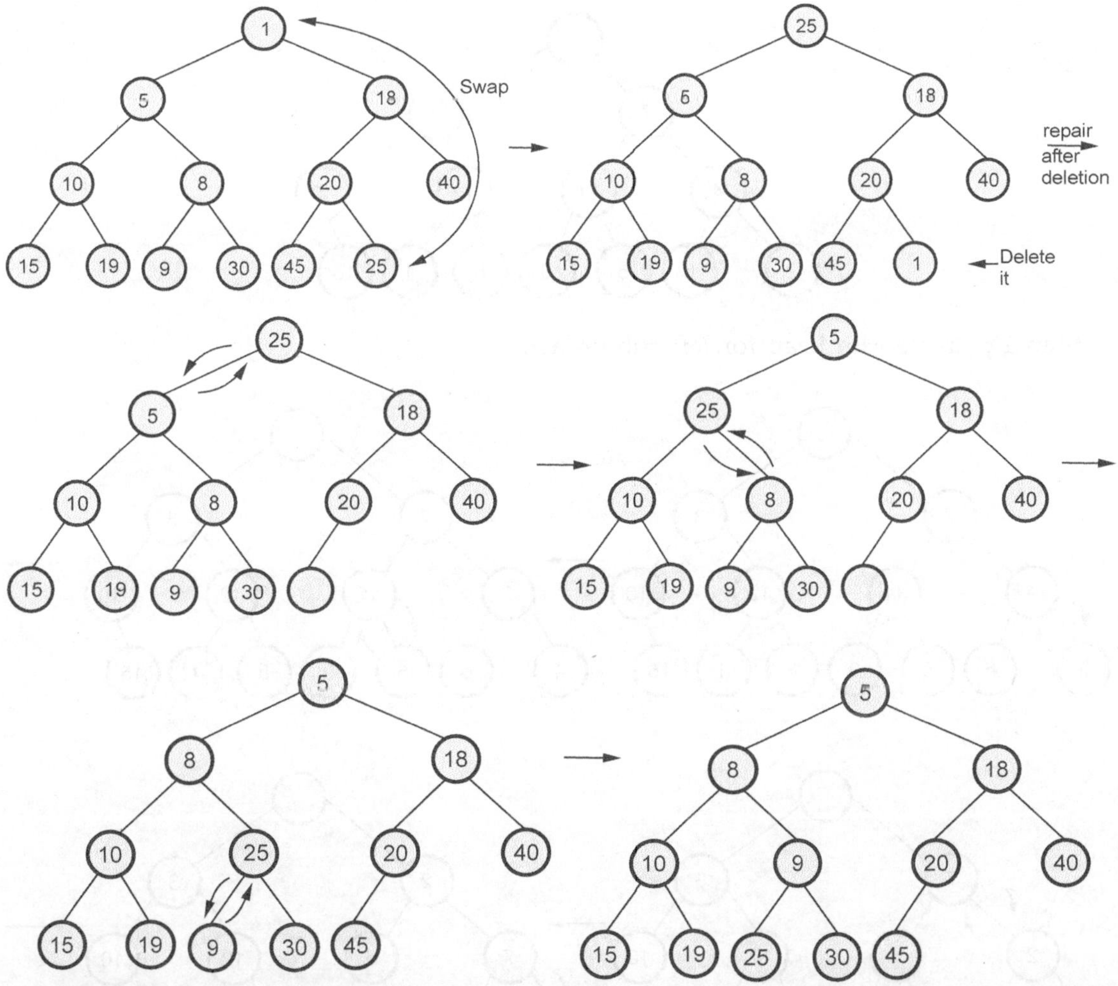

Swap

repair after deletion

Delete it

Example 5.14.5 *Define double ended heap. Construct a DEAP for given data 7, 3, 4, 11, 12, 10, 2, 6, 5, 9, 8, 1, 15. After deleting max element from DEAP, what will be the resultant DEAP ?* **SPPU : May-11, Marks 10**

Solution : DEAP is a complete binary tree data structure which is either empty or satisfies following properties -

1) The root contains no element.
2) The left subtree is min-heap data structure.
3) The right subtree is max heap data structure.
4) If right subtree is not empty then i is any node in left subtree and j is corresponding node in right subtree. If such a corresponding j does not exist then j is the node in right subtree which corresponds to parent of i.

DEAP construction

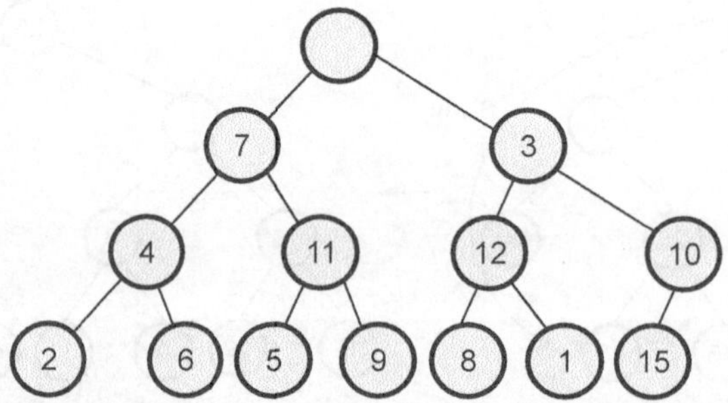

Step 1 : Create Min heap for left sub-branch.

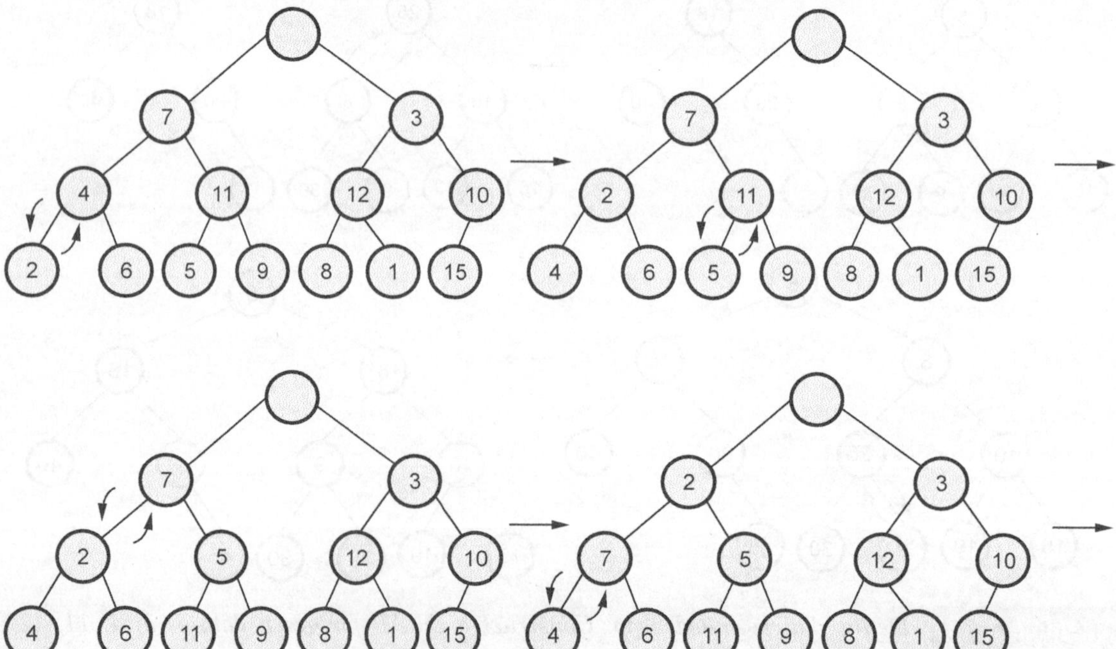

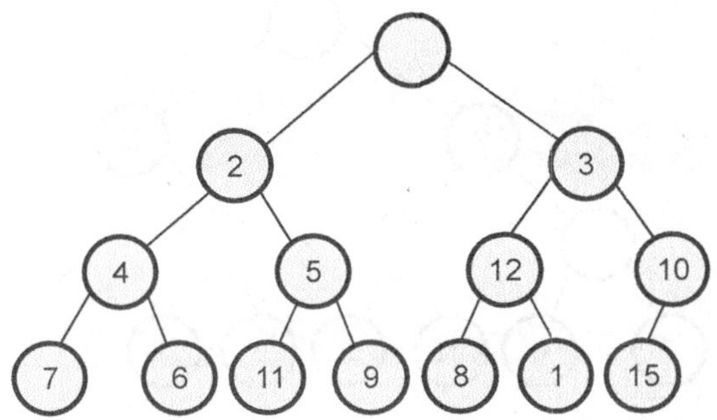

Step 2 : Now we will create Max heap for right subbranch.

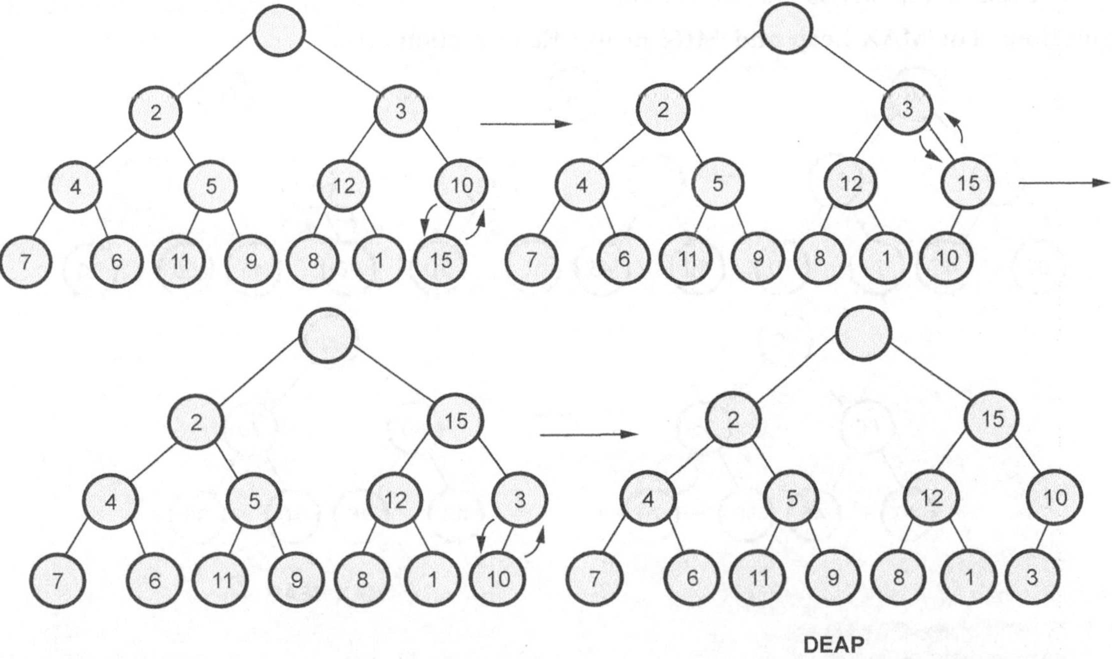

Deletion of maximum element from DEAP

The element 15 is deleted.

The last element is placed at the position of 15.

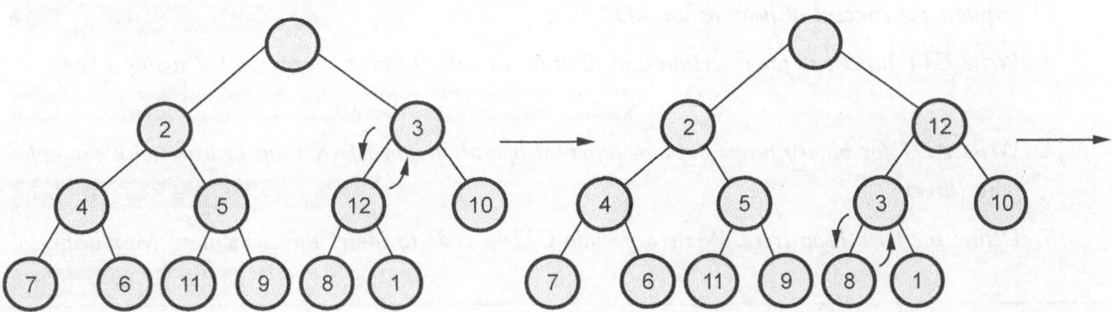

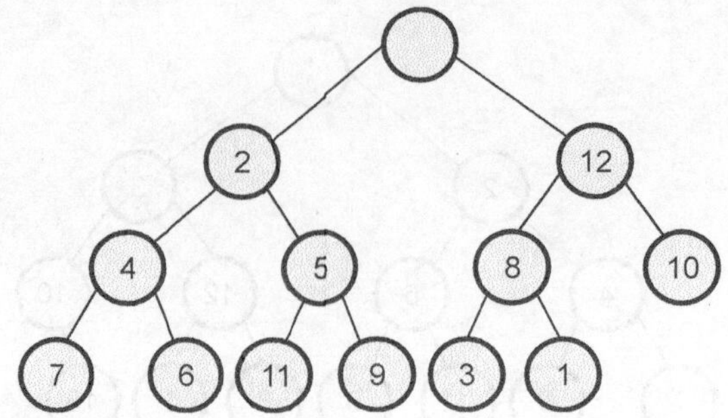

Example 5.14.6 *Explain in brief MAX heap and MIN heap. Draw MAX heap for given list of elements {40, 80, 35, 90, 45, 50, 70}.* **SPPU : Dec.-11, Marks 10**

Solution: For MAX heap and MIN heap : Refer section 5.14.

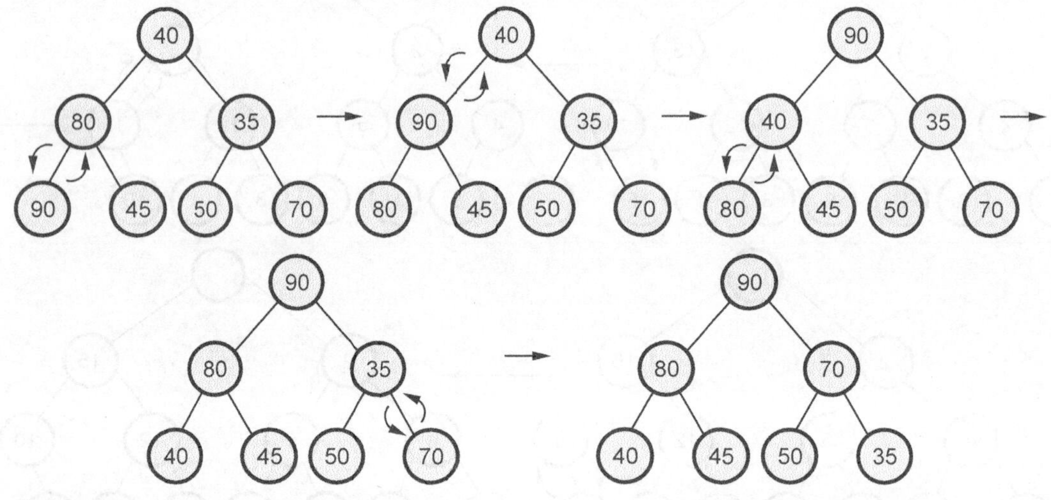

MAX HEAP

University Questions

1. *Write an algorithm to take N-elements and do the following :*
   i) Insert them into heap one by one.
   ii)Build heap in linear time. **SPPU : May-05, Marks 8**
2. *Explain the concept of heap as an ADT.* **SPPU : May-10, Marks 4**
3. *Write C++ functions for insertion and deletion in priority queue, represented using a heap.* **SPPU : Dec.-07, May-10, Marks 8, Dec.-10, Marks 8**
4. *Write ADT for binary heap. Explain different operations on MAX heap in brief with examples (any three).* **SPPU : May-12, Marks 10**
5. *Define the term heap trees. Write a pseudo C/C++ code to insert the element in Max heap.* **SPPU : May-13, Marks 8**

5.15 Heap Sort

SPPU : Dec.-05, 11, 12, 13, May-12, 14, Marks 8

Heap sort is a sorting method discovered by J. W. J. Williams. It works in two stages.

1. **Heap construction :** First construct a heap for given numbers.

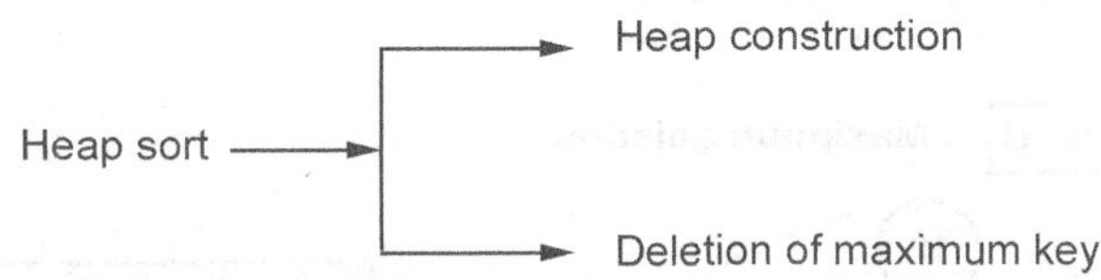

2. **Deletion of maximum key :** Delete root key always for (n – 1) times to remaining heap. Hence we will get the elements in decreasing order. For an array implementation of heap, delete the element from heap and put the deleted element in the last position in array. Thus after deleting all the elements one by one, if we collect these deleted elements in an array starting from last index of array.

We get a list of elements in a ascending order.

Let us understand this technique with the help of some examples.

Sort the following elements using heap sort.

14, 12, 9, 8, 7, 10, 18.

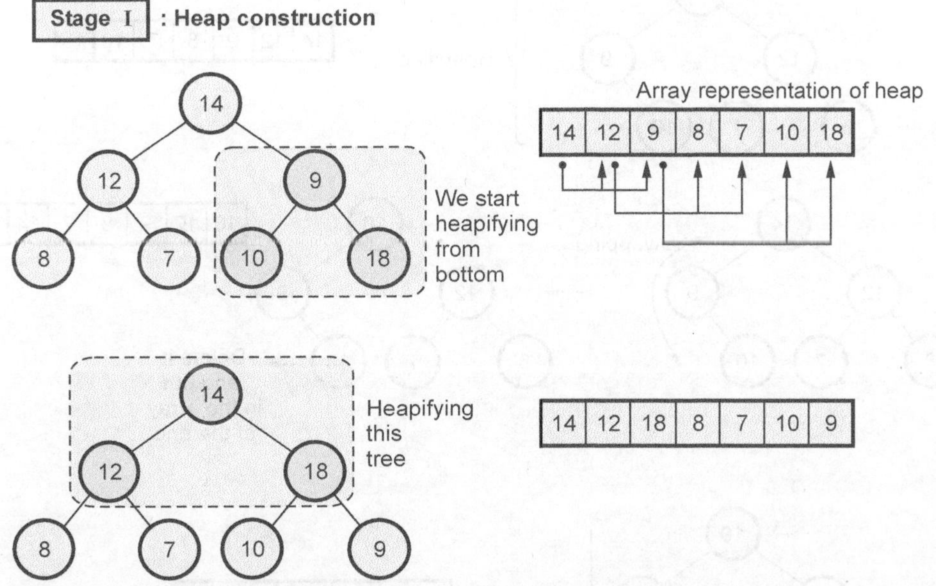

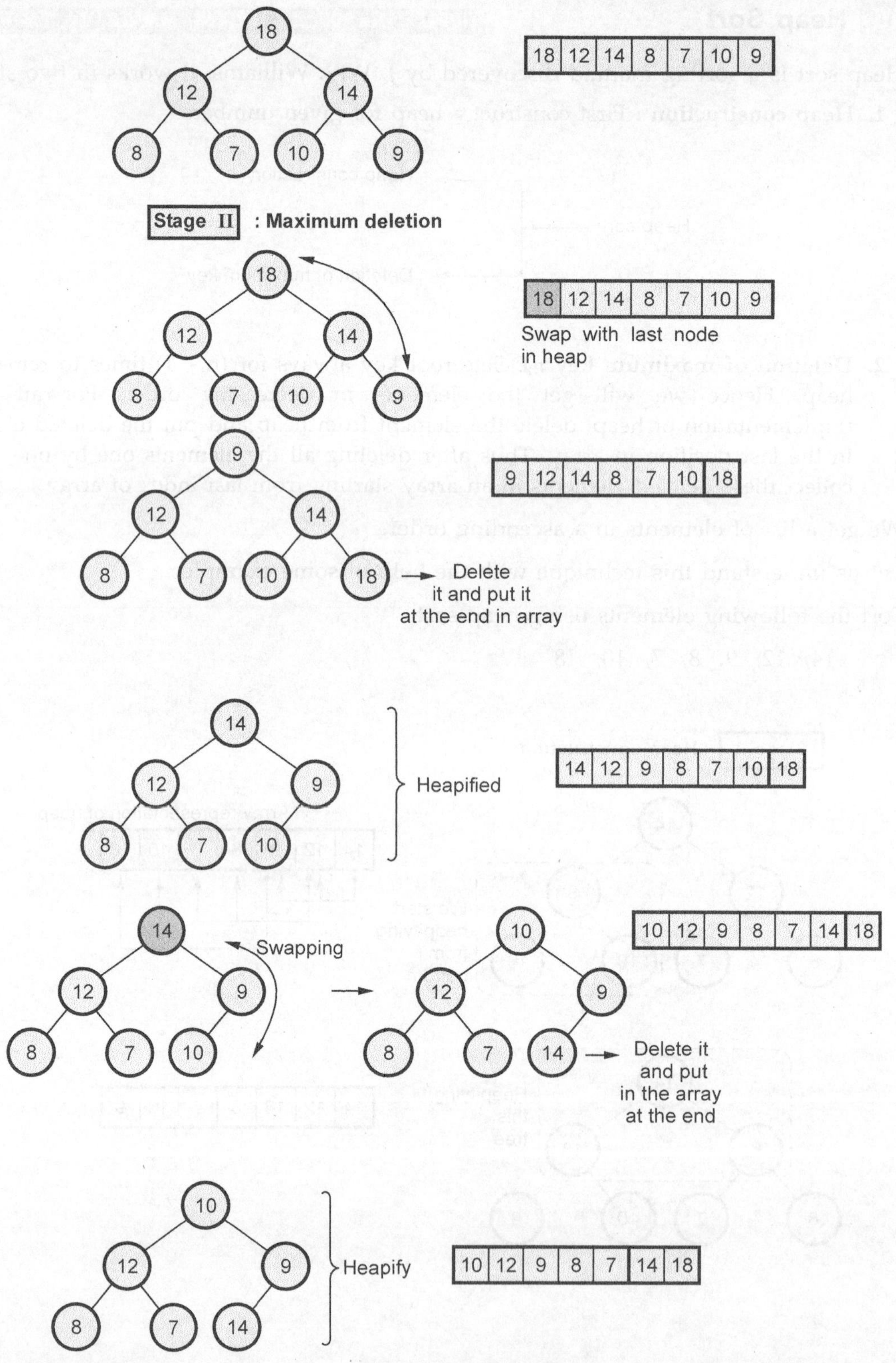

18 12 14 8 7 10 9
Stage II : Maximum deletion
18 12 14 8 7 10 9
Swap with last node in heap
9 12 14 8 7 10 18
Delete it and put it at the end in array
Heapified
14 12 9 8 7 10 18
Swapping
10 12 9 8 7 14 18
Delete it and put in the array at the end
Heapify
10 12 9 8 7 14 18

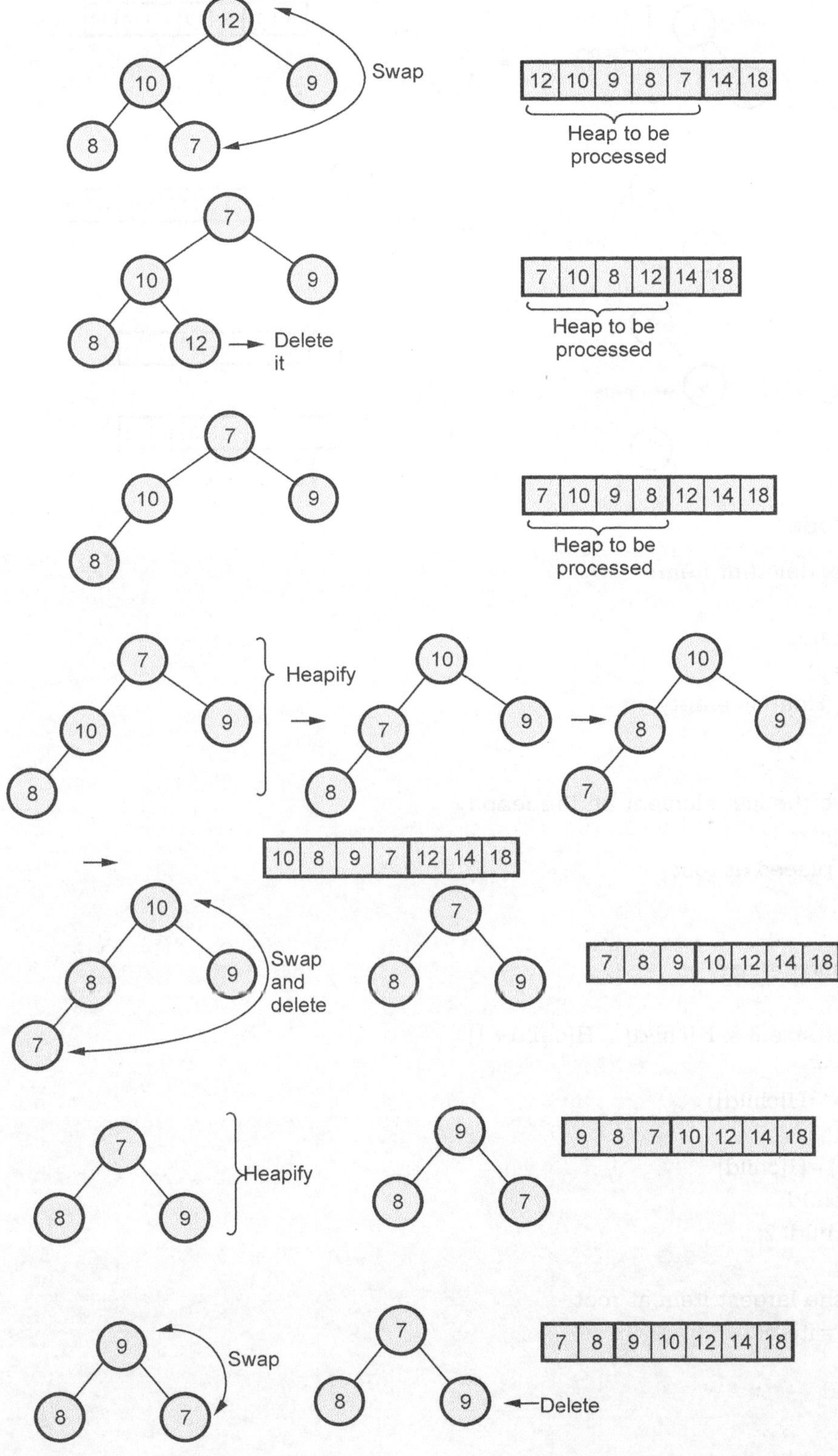
Swap
12 10 9 8 7 14 18
Heap to be processed
Delete it
7 10 8 12 14 18
Heap to be processed
7 10 9 8 12 14 18
Heap to be processed
Heapify
10 8 9 7 12 14 18
Swap and delete
7 8 9 10 12 14 18
Heapify
9 8 7 10 12 14 18
Swap
7 8 9 10 12 14 18
Delete

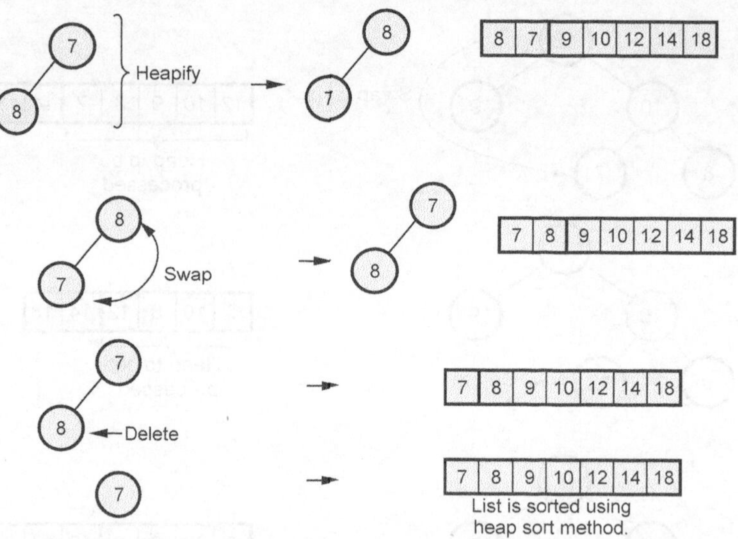

Pseudo Code

```
void Heap::delet(int item)
{
 int item,temp;
 if(size==0)
  cout<<"Heap is empty";
 else
 {
   //remove the last element and reheapify
  item=H[size--];
 //item is placed at root
  temp=1;
  child=2
  while(child<=size)
  {
    if(child<size && H[child]< H[child+1]
     child++;
   if(item>=H[child])
    break;
   H[temp]=H[child]
   temp=child;
   child=child*2;
  }
  //place the largest item at root
  H[temp]=item;
 }
}
```

Analysis

As this algorithm works in two stages, we get the running time.

Running time for heap sort = Running time required by heap construction + Running time required by deletion of root key

$$C(n) = C_1(n) + C_2(n) \quad \text{... (5.15.1)}$$

As the heap construction requires O(n) time,

$$C_1(n) = O(n) \quad \text{... (5.15.2)}$$

Now let us compute time required by second stage (Maximum deletion stage).

Let, number of key comparisons needed for eliminating root keys from heap are for size from n to 2. Then we can establish following relation.

$$C_2(n) \le 2\lfloor \log_2 (n-1) \rfloor + 2\lfloor \log_2 (n-2) \rfloor + \ldots + 2\lfloor \log_2 1 \rfloor$$

$$\le \underbrace{2\sum_{i=1}^{n-1} \log_2 i}_{2(n-1)\log_2(n-1)}$$

Because a formula is

$$\sum_{i=1}^{n} \log_2 i \approx n \log_2 n$$

$$\therefore \sum_{i=1}^{n-1} \log_2 i = (n-1)\log_2 (n-2)$$

But

$$2(n-1)\log_2(n-1) = (2n-2)\log_2(n-1)$$

$$= 2n\log_2(n-1) - 2\log_2(n-1)$$

$\therefore$ $C_2(n) \le 2n\log_2 n$ we get,

$$C_2(n) = O(n \log_2 n) \quad \text{... (5.15.3)}$$

Now, put equations (5.15.2) and (5.15.3) in equation (5.15.1), we get,

$$C(n) = O(n) + O(n \log_2 n)$$

$$C(n) = O(n \log_2 n)$$

Time complexity of heap sort is Θ **(n log n)** in both worst and average case.

Features of heap sort

1. The time complexity of heap sort is Θ (n log n).
2. This is an in-place sorting algorithm. That means it does not require extra storage space while sorting the elements.

3. For random input it works slower than quick sort.
4. Heap sort is not a stable sorting method.
5. The space complexity of heap sort is O(1). As it does not require any extra storage to sort.

5.15.1 Implementation

```
#include<iostream.h>
#include<stdlib.h>
#include<conio.h>
#define MAX 10
class Heap
{
	private:
		int arr[MAX];
		int n;
	public:
		Heap();
		void insert(int num);
		void makeheap();
		void heapsort();
		void display();
};
Heap::Heap()
{
	n=0;
	for(int i=0;i<MAX;i++)
		arr[i]=0;
}

void Heap::insert(int num)
{
	if(n<MAX)
	{
		arr[n]=num;
		n++;
	}
	else
		cout<<"\n Array is full";
}

void Heap::makeheap()
{
	for(int i=1;i<n;i++)
	{
		int val=arr[i];
```

```
            int j=i;
            int f=(j-1)/2;
            while(j>0&&arr[f]<val)//creating a MAX heap
            {
                    arr[j]=arr[f];
                    j=f;
                    f=(j-1)/2;
            }
            arr[j]=val;
        }
}
void Heap::heapsort()
{
        for(int i=n-1;i>0;i- -)
        {
            int temp=arr[i];
            arr[i]=arr[0];
            int k=0;
            int j;
            if(i==1)
                    j=-1;
            else
                    j=1;
            if(i>2&&arr[2]>arr[1])
                    j=2;
            while(j>=0&& temp <arr[j])
            {
                    arr[k]=arr[j];
                    k=j;
                    j=2*k+1;
                    if(j+1<=i-1&&arr[j]<arr[j+1])
                                        j++;
                    if(j>i-1)
                                        j=-1;
            }
            arr[k]=temp;
        }
}
void Heap::display()
{
        for(int i=0;i<n;i++)
                            cout<<"\n"<<arr[i];
        cout<<"\n";
}
void main()
{
        Heap obj;
```

```
    obj.insert(14);
    obj.insert(12);
    obj.insert(9);
    obj.insert(8);
    obj.insert(7);
    obj.insert(10);
    obj.insert(18);
    cout<<"\n The Elements are ..."<<endl;
    obj.display();
    obj.makeheap();
    cout<<"\n Heapified"<<endl;
    obj.display();
    obj.heapsort();
    getch();
}
```

Output

```
 The Elements are ...

14
12
9
8
7
10
18
```

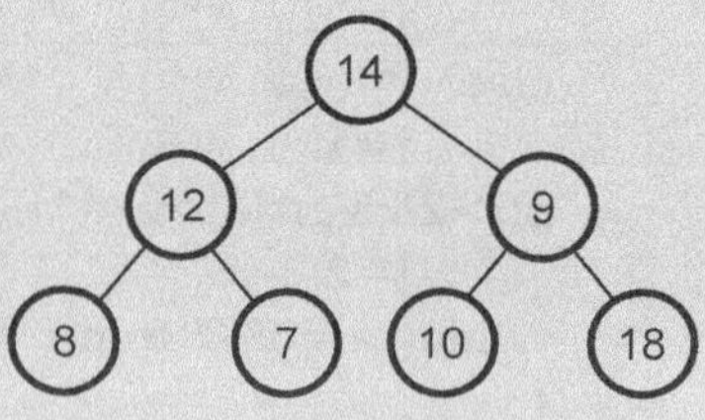

```
 Heapified

18
12
14
8
7
9
10
```

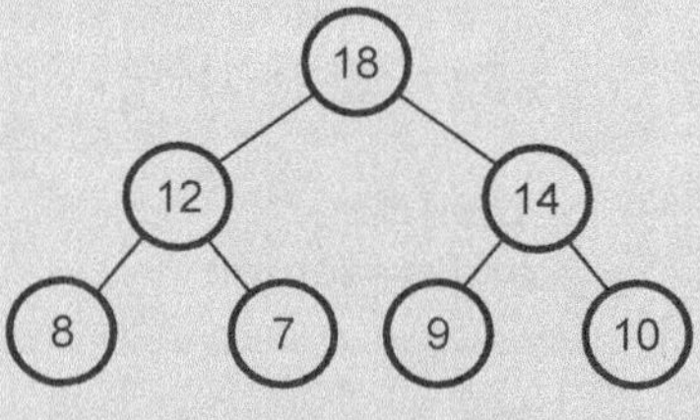

```
Elements sorted by Heap sort...
7
8
9
10
12
14
18
```

Example 5.15.1 *State algorithm to sort elements of a given array in ascending order using heap sort. Sort the following numbers using heap sort : 48, 0, –1, 82, 108, 72, 54.*

SPPU : Dec.-11, May-12, Marks 8

Solution :Algorithm :

Step 1 : Construct the min heap from given set of elements.

Step 2 : Swap the root key with the last node key of the heap.

Step 3 : Delete the last node and store its key in priority queue.

Step 4 : Heapify the remaining heap structure.

Step 5 : Repeat step 2 to 4 until the last remaining node.

Step 6 : Delete the last node and store it in priority queue.

Step 7 : Print all the elements of the priority queue from front to rear. This will display the elements in sorted order.

Consider, 48, 0, – 1, 82, 108, 72, 54.

Step 1 : We will create a complete binary tree for given elements.

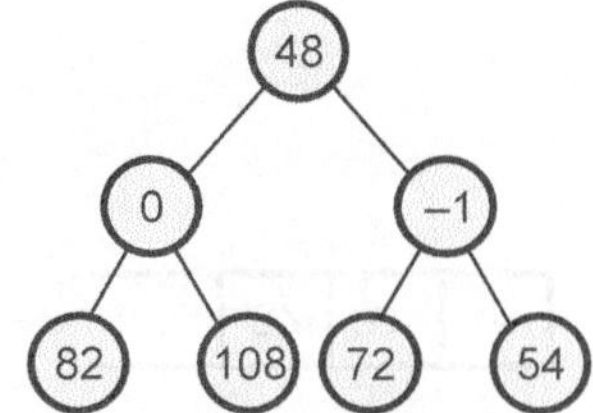

Step 2 : Now, we will build the min heap from the binary tree.

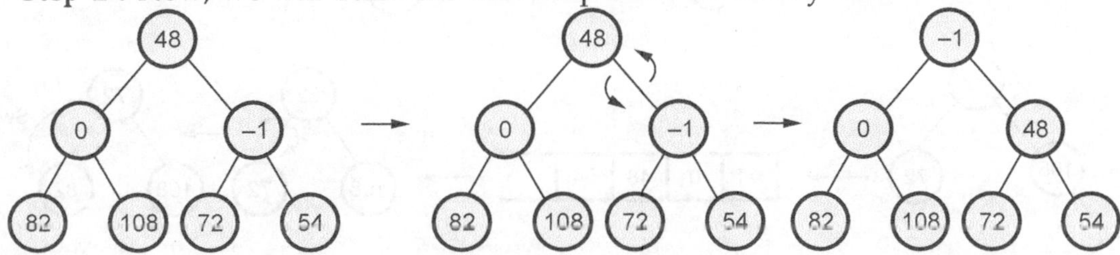

Step 3 : Now delete each element from the heap.

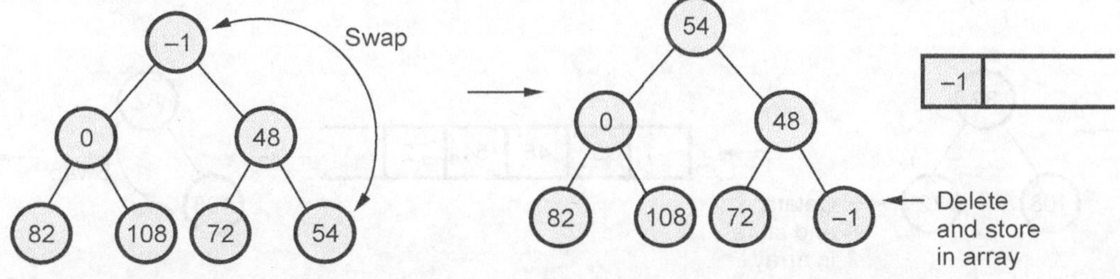

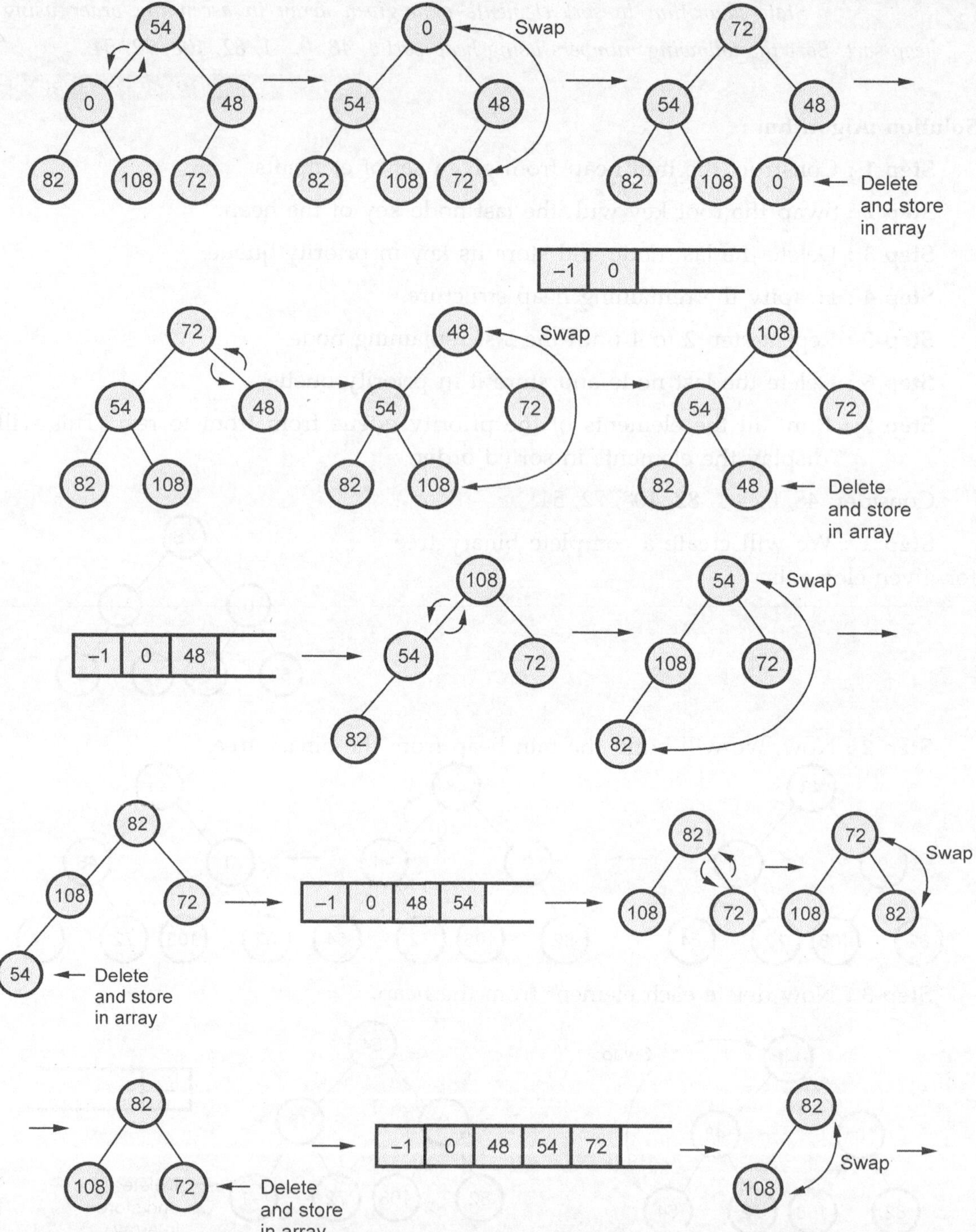

Swap
Delete and store in array
–1 0
Swap
Delete and store in array
–1 0 48
Swap
Delete and store in array
–1 0 48 54
Swap
Delete and store in array
–1 0 48 54 72
Swap

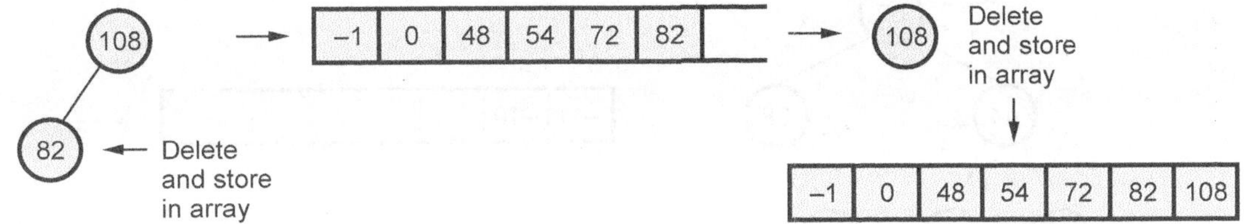

Sorted Array

Example 5.15.2 *State algorithm to sort elements of a given array in ascending order using heapsort. Sort the following numbers using heapsort in ascending order :*
38, – 10, – 11, 72, 98, 62, 44. **SPPU : Dec.-12, Marks 10**

Solution :

Step - I

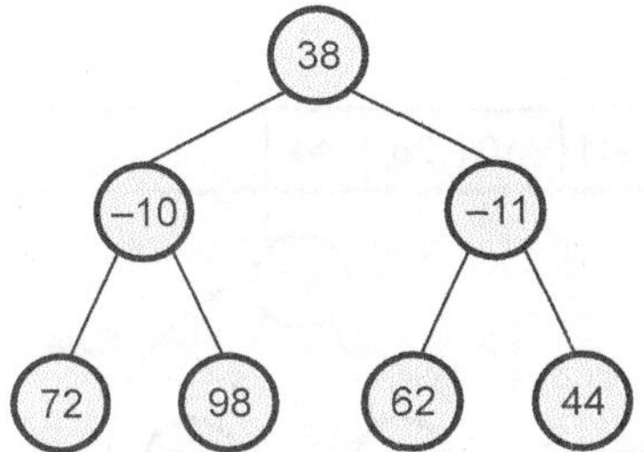

Step - II

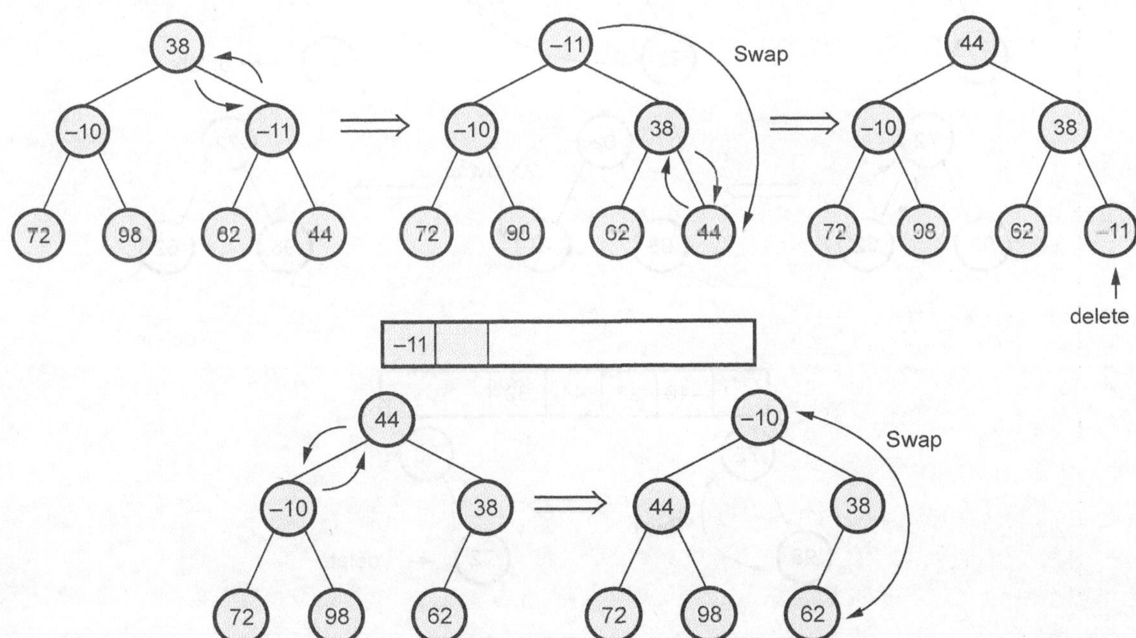

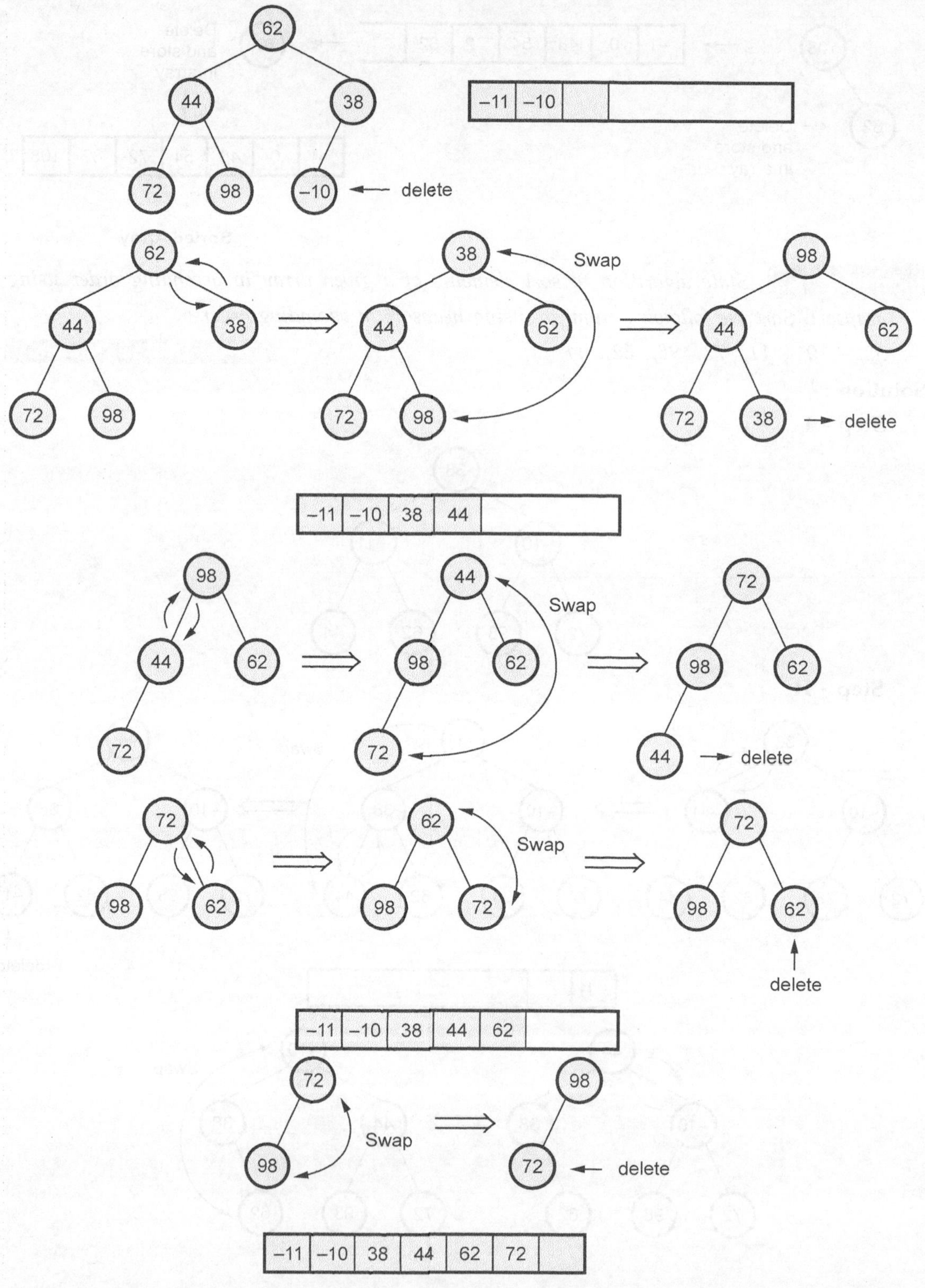

62
44
38
72
98
–10
delete
–11
–10
62
44
38
72
98
38
44
62
72
98
Swap
98
44
62
72
38
delete
–11
–10
38
44
98
44
62
72
44
98
62
72
Swap
72
98
62
44
delete
72
98
62
62
98
72
Swap
72
98
62
delete
–11
–10
38
44
62
72
98
Swap
98
72
delete
–11
–10
38
44
62
72

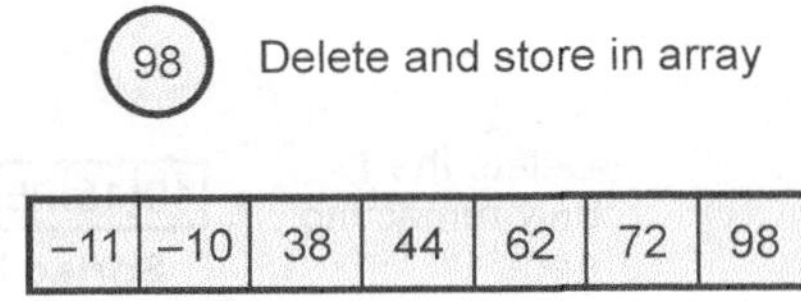

Sorted array

Example 5.15.3 *Sort the following data in ascending order using heap sort 15, 10, 40, 25.*

SPPU : Dec.-13, Marks 4

Solution :

Step 1 : We will build the complete binary tree.

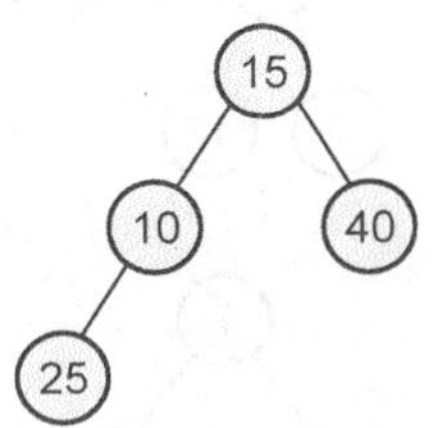

Step 2 : We will build the min-heap structure. That means parent node must be less than child nodes.

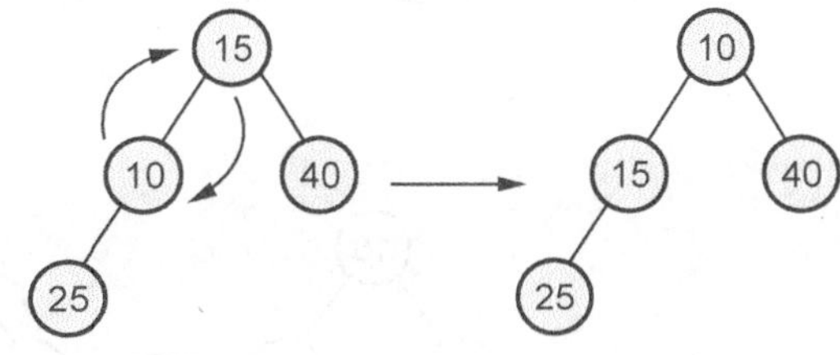

Step 3 : We will delete root node by swapping it with last node.

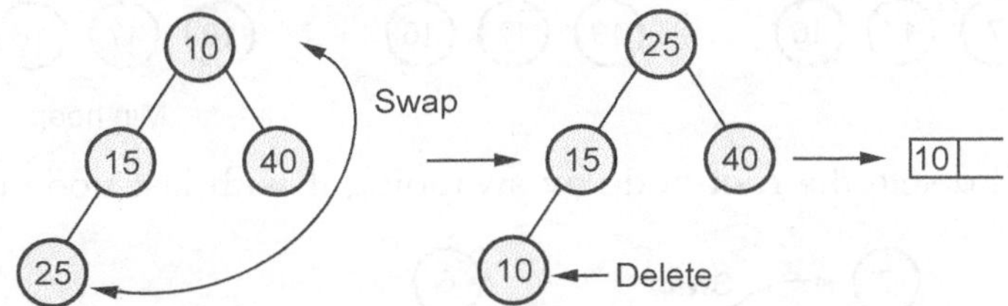

Step 4 :

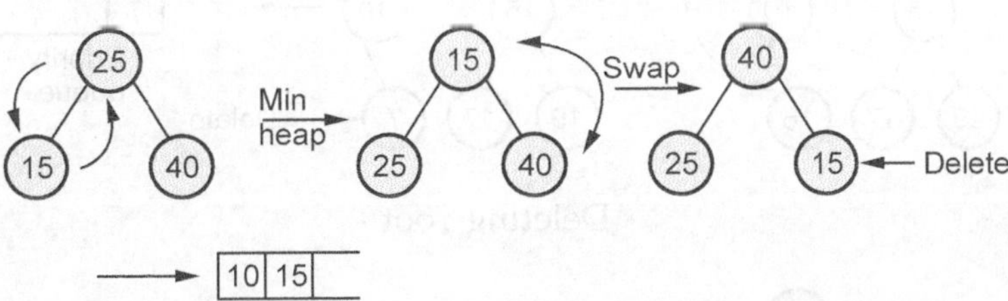

Step 5 :

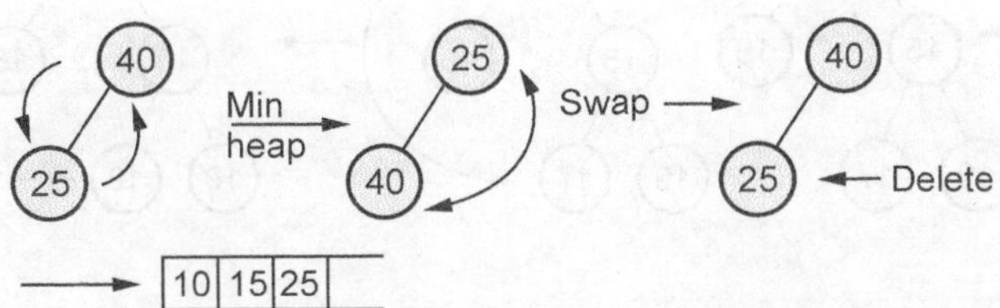

Step 6 :

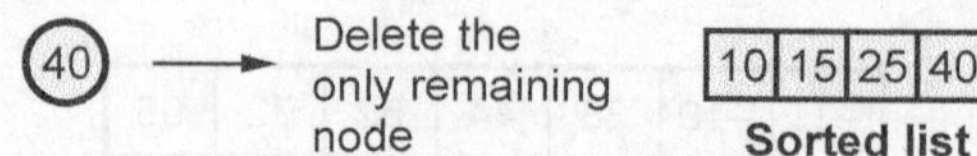

Example 5.15.4 *Sort the following data in ascending order using heap sort 15, 19, 10, 7, 17, 16.*

SPPU : May-14, Marks 6

Solution :

Stage I We will construct min heap i.e. parent minimum.

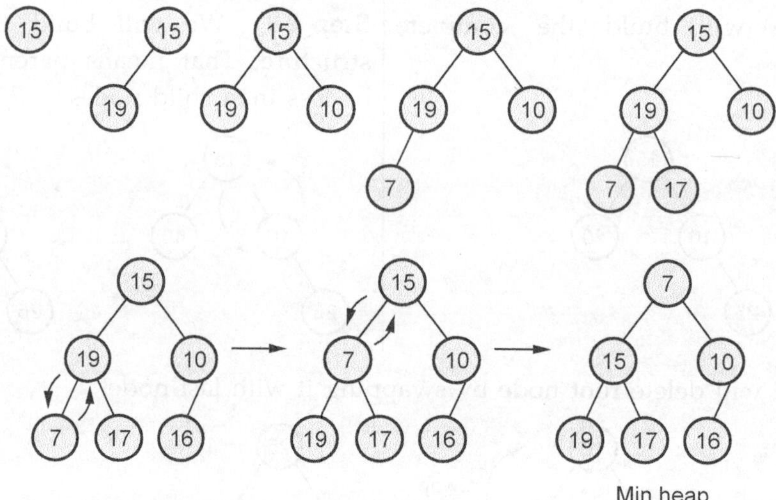

Stage II We will delete the root node by swapping it with last node of heap.

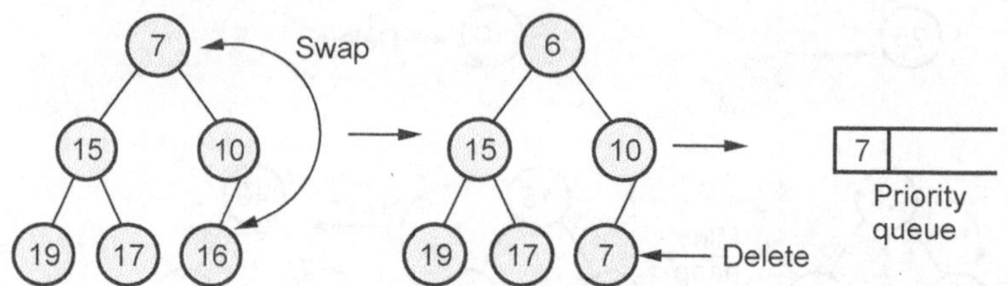

Heapifying - Deleting root -

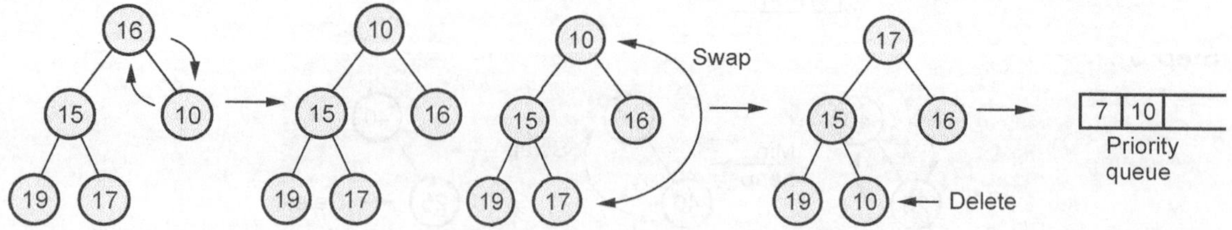

Heapifying -

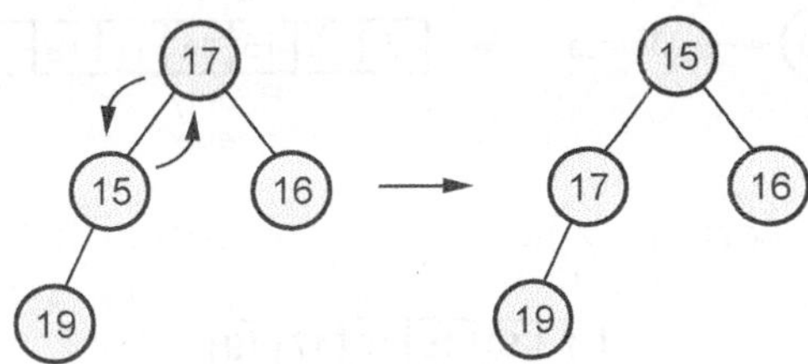

Deleting root

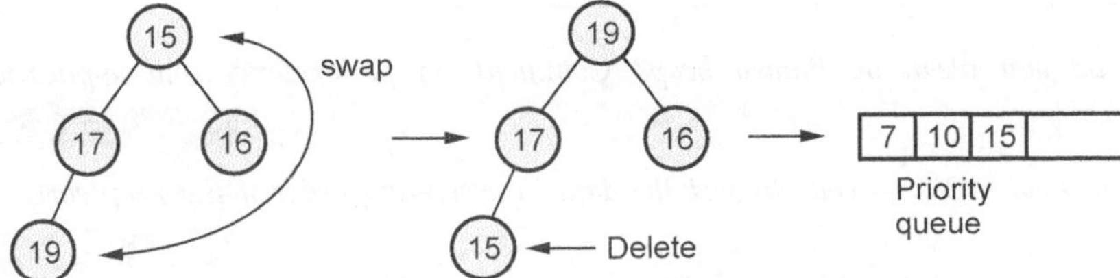

Heapifying

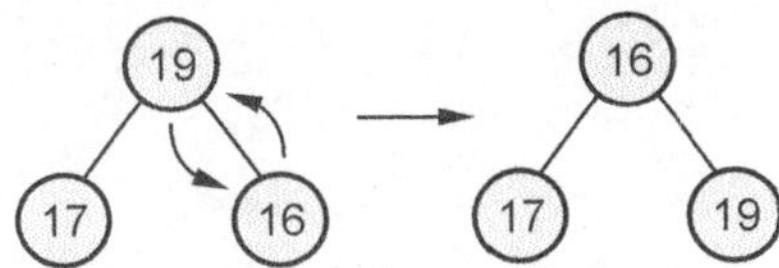

Deleting root

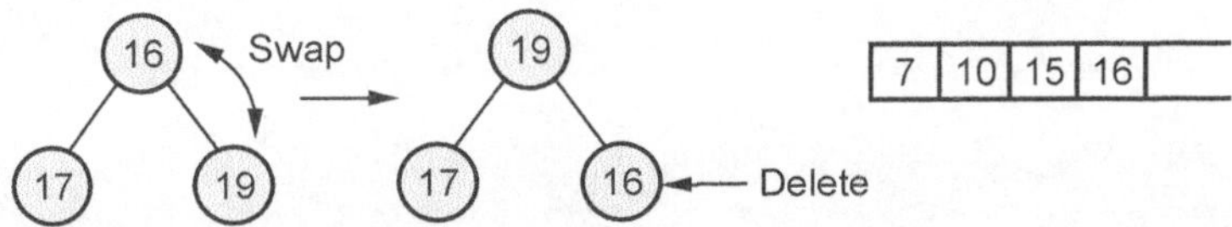

Heapifying

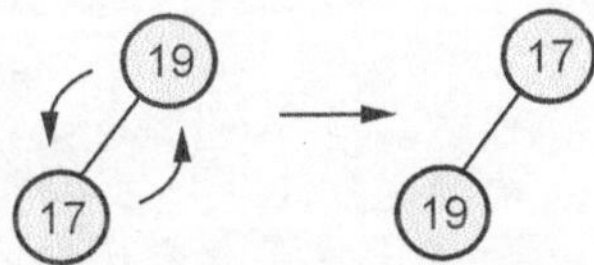

Deleting root

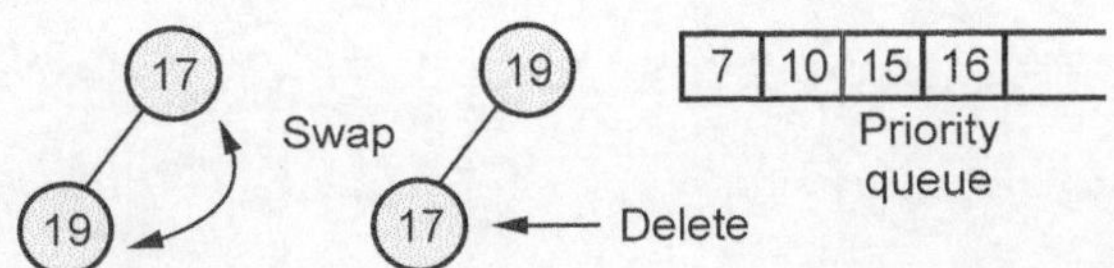

Heapifying and deleting root node

19 ← Delete → | 7 | 10 | 15 | 16 | 17 | 19 |

Priority queue

Thus the elements are sorted by heap sort. The sorted list is

7	10	15	16	17	19

University Questions

1. *What do you mean by binary heap? Comment on performance and application of binary heaps.* **SPPU : Dec.-05, Marks 6**
2. *Write a pseudo C/C++ code to sort the data in ascending order using heap sort.* **SPPU : Dec.-13, Marks 6**

❑❑❑

6 File Organization

Syllabus

***Sequential file organization** - Concept and primitive operations, **Direct access file** - Concepts and primitive operations, **Indexed sequential file organization** - Concept, Types of indices, Structure of index sequential file, **Linked organization** - Multi list files, Coral rings, Inverted files and cellular partitions. **External sort** - Consequential processing and merging two lists, Multiday merging - A k way merge algorithm.*

Contents

6.1 File Definition and Concept

File can be defined as the collection of records in which each record consists of one or more fields.

For example

Roll Number	Name	Marks	Address
10	AAA	90	MG Road
20	BBB	88	Shivaji Nagar
30	CCC	76	S.K.Marg
.	.	.	.
.	.	.	.
.	.	.	.

Fig. 6.1.1 Sample File containing student record

- **Various operations that can be performed on the file are -**

  1. Insertion of record into the file
  2. Deletion of record
  3. Updation of record
  4. Retrieval of record.

- **Query**

Query is basically a string which consists of combination of key values specified for retrieval of desired record.

For example :

```
SELECT * FROM DEPT WHERE EMP_ID >10
```

This query will retrieve all the records from the DEPT table where employee ID is greater than 10.

- **Fixed length record file**

The file in which all the records are of same length or of fixed length is called fixed length record file.

For example

Consider a file which consists of -

Exam_No	Name	Marks
137	Archana	89
455	Lekhana	83
342	Jayashree	67

872	Rahul	55

The field length can be

Exam_no : 5
Name : 10
Marks : 3

Thus each record can be 18 bytes long

The first record then can be stored like this -

1	3	7			A	r	c	h	a	n	a		
	8	9											

Advantages

If the record size is fixed then there is fast access to any desired record. Because, the starting address and ending address of each record is known.

Disadvantage

If the record is too large there are chances of loosing some information. Similarly if record is too short then there may be wastage of some memory.

- **Variable length record**

The file in which the records can be of different length is called variable length record file.

For example

Exam_No	Name	Marks
137	Archana	89
455	Lekhana	83
342	Jayashree	67
872	Rahul	55

For storing these records we use the terminators. The # is used to indicate end of each field and $ is used to indicate the end of the file.

Maximum 17 bytes can be required for each individual record to get stored. Because, the following record **342 Jayashree 67** takes maximum space

The first record then can be stored like this -

1	3	7	#	A	r	c	h	a	n	a	#	8	9
$													

Advantages

1. If the record size is smaller then less space will be required to store and there will not be any wastage of space.
2. Storing of the records will be faster.

Disadvantage

1. Searching a particular record is slower because the starting and ending addresses of each record are not known.

6.2 File Handling in C++

SPPU : Dec.-13, Marks 3

C++ provides following classes to perform input and output of characters to and from the files.

ofstream	This stream class is used to write on files.
ifstream	This stream class is used to read from files.
fstream	This stream class is used for both read and write from/to files.

To perform file I/O, we need to include **<fstream.h>** in the program. It defines several classes, including **ifstream, ofstream** and **fstream**. These classes are derived from **ios**, so **ifstream, ofstream** and **fstream** have access to all operations defined by **ios**. While using file I/O we need to do following tasks -

1. To create an input stream, declare an object of type **ifstream**.
2. To create an output stream, declare an object of type **ofstream**.
3. To create an input/output stream, declare an object of type **fstream**.

Let us write a simple program.

```
#include <iostream.h>
#include <fstream.h>
void main()
{
  ofstream fobj; //creating object
  fobj.open ("output.txt"); //opening the file using object
  fobj << "Writing...Tested OK!!!\n";//writing to the file
  fobj.close();//closing the file
}
```

The above program basically creates a file called **output.txt** and writes the message "Writing...Tested OK!!!" in that file. At the end of the program the file is closed.

Open file operation

The file operations are associated with the object of one of the classes : *ifstream, ofstream* or *fstream*. Hence we need to create an object of the corresponding class.

The file can be opened by the function called *open()*. The syntax of file open is

```
Open(filename,mode)
```

The *filename* is a null terminated string that represents the name of the file that is to be opened. The **mode** is optional parameter and is used with the flags as given below -

Modes in which file can be opened

ios::in	Open for input operation.
ios::out	Open for output operation.
ios::binary	Open for binary operations.
ios::ate	If this flag is set then initial position is set at the end of the file otherwise initial position is at the beginning of the file.
ios::app	The output operations are appended to the file. This is an appending mode. That means contents are inserted at the end of the file.
ios::trunc	The contents of pre existing file get destroyed and it is replaced by new one.

We can use open() function using the above given syntax as -

```
ofstream obj;
obj.open("sample.bin".ios::out|ios::binary)
```

That means the file sample.bin is opened for output operation in binary mode. Thus we can combine the flags using OR operator (|).

The *is_open()* is a boolean function that can be used to check whether the file is open or not.

For example

```
if(obj.is_open())
{
 cout<<"File is Successfully opened for operations";
}
```

Close file operation

To close the file the member function *close()* is used. The *close* function takes no parameter and returns no value.

For example

```
        obj.close();
```

You can detect when the end of an input file has been reached by using the *eof( )* member function of *ios*. It returns true when the end of the file has been encountered and false otherwise.

Handling multiple files

We can open more than one files and can write the contents to them. In the following program we have created two different files namely: **emp.dat** and **dept.dat**. Through our C++ program we are writing some contents to them. Later on reading those contents and displaying them on the console. The program is

C++ Program

```
#include<iostream.h>
#include<fstream.h>
#include<conio.h>
#include<stdlib.h>
void main()
{
    ofstream out_obj;
    //creating the file for writing purpose
    out_obj.open("emp.dat");
    //writing the data to the file
    out_obj<<"Rahul\n";
    out_obj<<"Lekhana\n";
    out_obj<<"Nandan\n";
     out_obj<<"Archana\n";
    out_obj<<"Yogesh\n";
    //closing the file
    out_obj.close();
    out_obj.open("dept.dat");
    //writing the data to the file
    out_obj<<"Accounts\n";
    out_obj<<"Proof\n";
    out_obj<<"Marketing\n";
    out_obj<<"DTP\n";
     out_obj<<"Graphics Design\n";
    out_obj.close();
    //Reading from the files
    char Data[80];
    ifstream in_obj;
```

```
    in_obj.open("emp.dat");
    cout<<"\n Following are the contents of emp.dat file...\n";
    while(in_obj)
    {
        in_obj.getline(Data,80);
        cout<<"\n"<<Data;
    }
    in_obj.close();
    in_obj.open("dept.dat");
    cout<<"\n Following are the contents of dept.dat file...\n";
    while(in_obj)
    {
        in_obj.getline(Data,80);
        cout<<"\n"<<Data;
    }
    in_obj.close();
    getch();
}
```

Output

```
Following are the contents of emp.dat file...

Rahul
Lekhana
Nandan
Archana
Yogesh

Following are the contents of dept.dat file...

Accounts
Proof
Marketing
DTP
Graphics Design
```

emp.dat

Rahul
Lekhana
Nandan
Archana
Yogesh

dept.dat

Accounts
Proof
Marketing
DTP
Graphics Design

Handling Binary files

We can make use of two functions namely: **read** and **write** for handling the binary file format.

The syntax of read and write functions will be -

input_obj.read((char *) &*variable*, sizeof(*variable*));

memory block size of block

output_obj. write ((char*) & variable, size of (variable));

The memory block must be type cast to pointer to character type This block acts as a buffer in which read contents can be stored or the data to be written in the file can be stored.

Following is a simple program in which we have some data in array **a**. We will be writing the contents of array **a** to the file **"input.dat"**. Then we will read the file and retrieve the contents in another array **b.** Finally the array **b** will be displayed on the console.

C++ Program

```
#include<iostream.h>
#include<fstream.h>
#include<conio.h>
#include<stdlib.h>
void main()
{

        ofstream out_obj;
        int a[5]={10,20,30,40,50};
        int b[5];
        out_obj.open("input.dat");
        out_obj.write((char *)&a,sizeof(a));
        out_obj.close();
        ifstream in_obj;
        in_obj.open("input.dat");
        in_obj.read((char *)&b,sizeof(b));
        cout<<"\n The contents of input.dat file are...\n";
        for(int i=0;i<5;i++)
        {
                cout<<"\n"<<b[i];
        }
        in_obj.close();
}
```

Output

```
The contents of input.dat file are...

10
20
30
40
50
```

Finding end of the file

For finding end of the file we use **eof()** function. This function is a member function of **ios** class. If end of file is encountered then it returns a non-zero value.

For example

```
if (seqfile. eof () ! = 0)
{
    cout << " You are at the end of the file";
}
```

Positioning the pointer in the file

While performing file operations, we must be able to reach at any desired position inside the file. For this purpose there are two commonly used functions -

1) seek

The seek operation is using two functions seekg and seekp.

- **seekg** means get pointer of specific location for reading of record.
- **seekp** means get pointer of specific location for writing of record.

The syntax of **seek** is

seekg (offset, reference - position);

seekp (offset, reference - position);

where, **offset** is any constant specifying the location.

reference - position is for specifying beginning, end or current position. It can be specified as,

ios : : beg	for beginning location
ios : : end	for end of file
ios : : cur	for current location

2) tell

This function tells us the current position.

For example

seqfile. tellg ()	-	gives current position of get pointer (for reading the record).
seqfile. tellp ()	-	gives current position of put pointer (for writing the record).

University Question

1. *Explain the various modes of opening the file in C or C++.* **SPPU : Dec.-13, Marks 3**

6.3 File Organization

Definition : File organization deals with representation or arrangement of data on external storage.

- The method by which records can be retrieved or updated from the file is called **access method.**
- The records can be organized in a way file in various ways. These ways are represented by following figure.

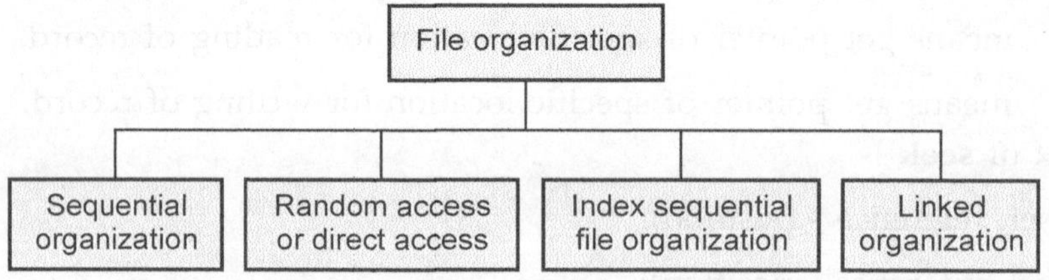

Fig. 6.3.1 Types of file organization

Let us discuss each type of file organization one by one.

6.4 Sequential Organization

- This type of file organization makes use of ISMA scheme.
- The ISMA scheme i.e. **I**ndex **S**equential **M**emory **A**ccess scheme is a kind of file organization in which record can be arranged using cylinder and surfaces.

For example

Consider the arrangement of students' record in which cylinders and surfaces are used.

Record number	Name	Roll_number	Marks	Cylinder	Surface
1	AAA	10	70	1	1
2	BBB	20	90	1	2
3	CCC	30	80	2	1
4	DDD	40	55	2	2
5	EEE	50	78	3	1

Now if we want to find record of Roll_number 40 then we can search it based on the cylinder. That is we will first search for the cylinder number 2, then we will make the search based on the surface. When we reach at the surface 2 of cylinder 2 then the desired record can be obtained within the track.

Advantages of sequential organization

1. The sequential file organization is simple to implement.
2. It is suitable for the small database applications.

Disadvantages of sequential organization

1. If database is very huge then it turns out to be a non efficient technique for retrieval of record.
2. If the number of tracks are more on the surfaces then multiple disk access may be required to obtain the desired record.

Basic operations that can be performed on sequential file organization are

1. Create
2. Display
3. Delete
4. Update
5. Append
6. Search

Following is C++ program which implements the sequential file.

```
/******************************************************************************
Program for performing various operations on Sequential File organization.
******************************************************************************/
#include<iostream.h>
#include<iomanip.h>
#include<fstream.h>
#include<string.h>
#include<conio.h>
#include<stdlib.h>
class EMP_CLASS
{
 typedef struct EMPLOYEE
 {
       char name[10];
       int emp_id;
       int salary;
 }Rec;
 Rec Records;
```

This record structure is for the sequential file
For example

name	emp_id	salary
AAA	10	1000
BBB	20	2000
CCC	30	3000

```
        public:
        void Create();
        void Display();
        void Update();
        void Delete();
        void Append();
        int Search();
};
void EMP_CLASS::Create()
{
    char ch='y';
    fstream seqfile;
    seqfile.open("EMP.DAT",ios::in|ios::out|ios::binary);
    do
    {
        cout<<"\n Enter Name: ";
        cin>>Records.name;
        cout<<"\n Enter Emp_ID: ";
        cin>>Records.emp_id;
        cout<<"\n Enter Salary: ";
        cin>>Records.salary;
        //then write the record containing this data in the file
        seqfile.write((char*)&Records,sizeof(Records));
        cout<<"\nDo you want to add more records?";
        cin>>ch;
     }while(ch=='y');
     seqfile.close();
}
void EMP_CLASS::Display()
{
    fstream seqfile;
    int n,m,i;
    seqfile.open("EMP.DAT",ios::in|ios::out|ios::binary);
    //positioning the pointer in the file at the beginning
    seqfile.seekg(0,ios::beg);
    cout<<"\n The Contents of file are ..."<<endl;
    //read the records sequentially
    while(seqfile.read((char *)&Records,sizeof(Records)))
    {
        if(Records.emp_id!=-1)
        {
            cout<<"\nName: "<<Records.name;
            cout<<"\nEmp_ID: "<<Records.emp_id;
            cout<<"\nSalary: "<<Records.salary;
            cout<<"\n";
        }
 }
```

User must enter the desired data in the members of the structure **Records**

```
 int last_rec=seqfile.tellg();//last record position
//formula for computing total number of  objects in the file
 n=last_rec/(sizeof(Rec));
 cout<<"\n\n Total number of objects are "<<n<<"(considering logical deletion)";
 seqfile.close();
}
void EMP_CLASS::Update()
{
      int pos;
      cout<<"\n For updation,";
      fstream seqfile;
      seqfile.open("EMP.DAT",ios::in|ios::out|ios::binary);
      seqfile.seekg(0,ios::beg);
//obtaining the position of desired record in the file
      pos=Search();
      if(pos==-1)
      {
       cout<<"\n The record is not present in the file";
       return;
      }
//calculate the actual offset of the desired record in the file
      int offset=pos*sizeof(Rec);
      seqfile.seekp(offset);//seeking the desired record for modification
      cout<<"\n Enter the values for updation...";
      cout<<"\n Name: ";cin>>Records.name;            New values for the
      cout<<"\n Emp_Id: ";cin>>Records.emp_id;        updation of record
      cout<<"\n Salary: ";cin>>Records.salary;
      seqfile.write((char*)&Records,sizeof(Records))<<flush;
      seqfile.seekg(0);
      seqfile.close();
      cout<<"\n The record is updated!!!";
}
void EMP_CLASS::Delete()
{
      int id,pos;
      cout<<"\n For deletion,";
      fstream seqfile;
      seqfile.open("EMP.DAT",ios::in|ios::out|ios::binary);
      seqfile.seekg(0,ios::beg);//seeking for reading purpose
      pos=Search();//finding pos. for the record to be deleted
      if(pos==-1)
      {
       cout<<"\n The record is not present in the file";
       return;
      }
//calculate offset to locate the desired record in the file
      int offset=pos*sizeof(Rec);
```

```
        seqfile.seekp(offset);//seeking the desired record for deletion
        strcpy(Records.name,"");
        Records.emp_id=-1;                 It's a logical deletion
        Records.salary=-1;
        seqfile.write((char*)&Records,sizeof(Records))<<flush;
        seqfile.seekg(0);
        seqfile.close();
        cout<<"\n The record is Deleted!!!";
}
void EMP_CLASS::Append()
{
        fstream seqfile;
        seqfile.open("EMP.DAT",ios::ate|ios::in|ios::out|ios::binary);
        seqfile.seekg(0,ios::beg);
        int i=0;
        while(seqfile.read((char *)&Records,sizeof(Records)))
        {
                i++;//going through all the records
                        // for reaching at the end of the file
        }
        //instead of above while loop
        //we can also use seqfile.seekg(0,ios::end)
        //for reaching at the end of the file
        seqfile.clear();//turning off EOF flag
        cout<<"\n Enter the record for appending";
        cout<<"\nName: ";cin>>Records.name;
        cout<<"\nEmp_ID: ";cin>>Records.emp_id;
        cout<<"\nSalary: ";cin>>Records.salary;
        seqfile.write((char*)&Records,sizeof(Records));
        seqfile.seekg(0);//reposition to start(optional)
        seqfile.close();
        cout<<"\n The record is Appended!!!";
}
int EMP_CLASS::Search()
{
        fstream seqfile;
        int id,pos;
        cout<<"\n Enter the Emp_ID for searching the record ";
        cin>>id;
        seqfile.open("EMP.DAT",ios::ate|ios::in|ios::out|ios::binary);
        seqfile.seekg(0,ios::beg);
        pos=-1;
        int i=0;
        while(seqfile.read((char *)&Records,sizeof(Records)))
        {
                if(id==Records.emp_id)
                {
```

```
                    pos=i;
                    break;
            }
            i++;
        }
        return pos;
}
void main()
{
        EMP_CLASS List;
        char ans='y';
        int choice,key;
        clrscr();
        do
        {
         cout<<"\n              Main Menu              "<<endl;
         cout<<"\n 1.Create";
         cout<<"\n 2.Display";
         cout<<"\n 3.Update";
         cout<<"\n 4.Delete";
         cout<<"\n 5.Append";
         cout<<"\n 6.Search";
         cout<<"\n 7.Exit";
         cout<<"\n Enter your choice ";
         cin>>choice;
         switch(choice)
         {
                case 1:List.Create();
                                        break;
                case 2:List.Display();
                                        break;
                case 3:List.Update();
                                        break;
                case 4:List.Delete();
                                        break;
                case 5:List.Append();
                                        break;
                case 6:key=List.Search();
                        if(key<0)
                                        cout<<"\n Record is not present in the file";
                        else
                                        cout<<"\n Record is present in the file";
                                        break;
                case 7:exit(0);
         }
        cout<<"\n\t Do you want to go back to Main Menu?";
        cin>>ans;
```

```
    }while(ans=='y');
}
```

Output

```
        Main Menu

1.Create
2.Display
3.Update
4.Delete
5.Append
6.Search
7.Exit
Enter your choice 1

Enter Name: AAA

Enter Emp_ID: 10

Enter Salary: 1000

Do you want to add more records?y

Enter Name: BBB

Enter Emp_ID: 20

Enter Salary: 2000

Do you want to add more records?y

Enter Name: CCC

Enter Emp_ID: 30

Enter Salary: 3000

Do you want to add more records?n

    Do you want to go back to Main Menu?y

        Main Menu

1.Create
2.Display
3.Update
4.Delete
```

```
5.Append
6.Search
7.Exit
Enter your choice 2
The Contents of file are ...

Name: AAA
Emp_ID: 10
Salary: 1000

Name: BBB
Emp_ID: 20
Salary: 2000

Name: CCC
Emp_ID: 30
Salary: 3000


Total number of objects are 3(considering logical deletion)
    Do you want to go back to Main Menu?y

        Main Menu
1.Create
2.Display
3.Update
4.Delete
5.Append
6.Search
7.Exit
Enter your choice 3

For updation,
Enter the Emp_ID for searching the record 20

Enter the values for updation...
Name: XXX

Emp_Id: 30

Salary: 10000

The record is updated!!!
    Do you want to go back to Main Menu?n
```

6.5 Direct Access File

Random organization is a kind of file organization in which records are stored at random locations on the disks.

There are three techniques used in random organization and those are given in following Fig. 6.5.1.

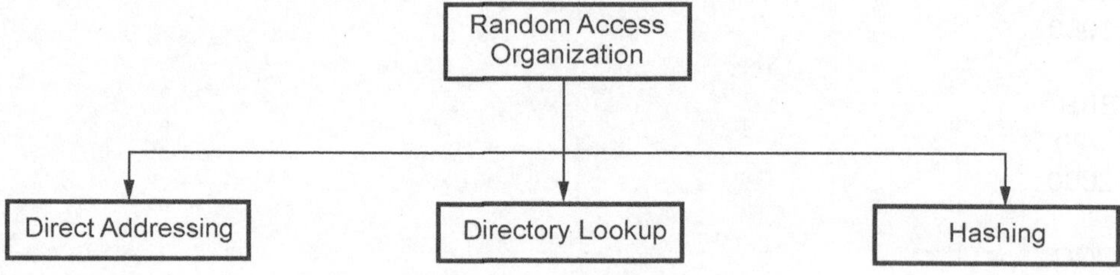

Fig. 6.5.1 Random access organization

Let us discuss each of them -

1. Direct Addressing

- In direct addressing two types of records are handled: fixed length record and variable length record.
- For storing the fixed length records the disk space is divided into the nodes. These nodes are large enough to hold individual record.
- Every fixed length record is stored in node number # which is equal to the primary key value. For example: If a primary key value is 185 then the record must be present in the node number 185.

For example

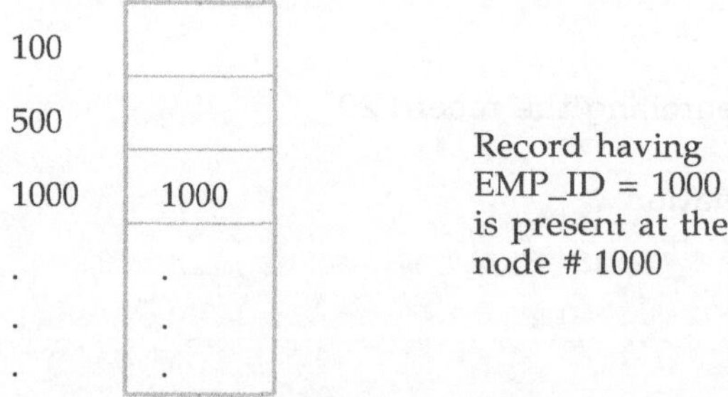

Fig. 6.5.2 Storing of fixed length record

- If we consider that the records are stored on the external storage devices then **deletion** and **searching** of the record requires one disk access. If we want to **update** a record then it requires two disk access, one for reading the record and one for writing the updated data back to the disk.

- For storing the **variable length records** on the disk, the address (pointer) of each individual record is stored in the file at specific index. We can locate the variable length record using the index of the pointer. This pointer will point to desired record which is present on the disk.

Variable length records make the storage management more **complex**.

2. Directory Lookup

- In this scheme the index for the pointers to the records is maintained.
- For retrieving the desired record first of all the index for the record address is searched and then using this record address the actual record is accessed.
- The **drawback** of this method is that it requires more disk access than direct address method.
- **Advantage** of this method is that effective disk space utilization in it as compared to direct addressing method.

3. Hashing

- Hashing is a technique in which hash key is obtained using some suitable **hash function** and record is placed in the hash table with the help of this **hash key**.
- Thus in this random organization, the record can be quickly searched with the help of hash function being used.
- For creation of hash table the available file space is divided into **buckets** and **slots**.
- Some file space is left aside for handling the overflow situation.

The total number of slots per bucket is equal to the total number of records each bucket can hold.

Operations on Direct Access File

Various operations that can be performed on direct access file are

1. Create
2. Insert a record into a file
3. Delete a record from a file
4. Update a record.

Let us see the C++ implementation of it.

The C++ implementation of direct access file organization is as follows -

```
/*********************************************************************
Program for implementing Direct Access File using the hashing technique.
Collision handling is performed using linear probing and
chaining without replacement.
            [hash function=(record_id mod 10)]
*********************************************************************/
```

```
#include<iostream.h>
#include<iomanip.h>
#include<fstream.h>
#include<string.h>
#include<conio.h>
#include<stdlib.h>
class EMP_CLASS
{
 typedef struct EMPLOYEE
 {
      char name[10];
      int emp_id;
      int salary;
      int link;
      int loc;
 }Rec;
 Rec Records;
      public:
            int size;
            int Chain_tab[10][10];
            EMP_CLASS();
            void Insert();
            void init();
            void Display();
            void Search();
            void chain_wo_repl();
            friend int Hash(int);
};
EMP_CLASS::EMP_CLASS()
            {
             strcpy(Records.name,"");
             Records.emp_id=-1;
             Records.salary=-1;
             Records.link=-1;
            }
void EMP_CLASS::init()
{
 fstream seqfile;
 seqfile.open("EMP.DAT",ios::out|ios::binary);
 cout<<"\n Enter the Hash table size ";
 cin>>size;
 for(int i=0;i<size;i++)
 {
  strcpy(Records.name,"");
  Records.emp_id=-1;
  Records.salary=-1;
  Records.link=-1;
```

```
 Records.link=i;
       seqfile.write((char*)&Records,sizeof(Records));
 for(int i=0;i<size;i++)
 for(int j=0;j<size;j++)
 Chain_tab[i][j]=-1;
 }
 cout<<"\n\n Hash table is initialised...";
 cout<<"\n Now, insert the records in the hash table";
 seqfile.close();
}
int Hash(int num)
{
 int key;
 key=num%10;
 return key;
}
void EMP_CLASS::chain_wo_repl()
{
 fstream seqfile;
 int i,j,h,offset;
 seqfile.open("EMP.DAT",ios::in|ios::out|ios::binary);
 for(i=0;i<size;i++)
       {
            h=i;
            for(j=0;j<size;j++)
            {
                  if(Chain_tab[i][j]==1)
                  {
                   offset=h*sizeof(Records);
                   seqfile.seekg(offset);
                   seqfile.read((char*)&Records,sizeof(Records));
                   seqfile.seekp(offset);
                   Records.link=j;
                   seqfile.write((char*)&Records,sizeof(Records));
                   h=j;
                  }
            }
       }
       seqfile.close();
}
void EMP_CLASS::Insert()
{
       int i,h;
       char ch='y';
       char new_name[10];
       int new_emp_id;
       int new_salary;
```

```
fstream seqfile;
init();//initialising the hash table
seqfile.open("EMP.DAT",ios::in|ios::out|ios::binary);
do
{
        cout<<"\n Enter Name: ";
        cin>>new_name;
        cout<<"\n Enter Emp_ID: ";
        cin>>new_emp_id;
        cout<<"\n Enter Salary: ";
        cin>>new_salary;
        h=Hash(new_emp_id);
        int offset;
        offset=h*sizeof(Records);

        //seeking for reading record
        seqfile.seekg(offset);
        seqfile.read((char*)&Records,sizeof(Records));
        //seeking for writing record
        seqfile.seekp(offset);
        if(Records.emp_id==-1)
        {
          strcpy(Records.name,new_name);
          Records.emp_id=new_emp_id;
          Records.salary=new_salary;
          Records.link=-1;
          Records.loc=h;//h is used for marking the loc.
          seqfile.write((char*)&Records,sizeof(Records))<<flush;
         //thus rec. is inserted at the hashed position in file
        }
        else//collision occurs
        {
        int flag=0;
        int prev_link=Records.loc;
        do      //handling collision
        {
         h++;//searching down for empty loc.in the file
         if(h>size+1)
         {
                cout<<"\n The hash table is Full, Can't insert record!!!";
                return;

         }
         offset=h*sizeof(Records);
         seqfile.seekg(offset);
         seqfile.read((char*)&Records,sizeof(Records));
         if(Records.emp_id==-1) //finding empty loc. using linear probing
```

Calling Hash function to get the direct location for the record in the file. Function returns a hash key in variable **h**

Using **h** for getting actual position in the file. Hence offset is calculated

```
            {
                seqfile.seekp(offset);//seeking the empty slot in the file
                strcpy(Records.name,new_name);//for placing the record
                Records.emp_id=new_emp_id;
                Records.salary=new_salary;
                Records.link=-1;
                Records.loc=h;//setting the location for colliding record
                seqfile.write((char*)&Records,sizeof(Records))<<flush;
               //collinding record is placed in the file at proper pos.
               //chain table is maintained for keeping track of all the colliding
entries.
                Chain_tab[prev_link][h]=1;
                flag=1;//indicates colliding record is inserted
            }//end of if
           }while(flag==0);//collision handled
           }//end of else
           cout<<"\nDo you want to add more records?";
           cin>>ch;
           chain_wo_repl();//setting the chain to handle collision
       }while(ch=='y');
       seqfile.close();
}
void EMP_CLASS::Display()
{
       fstream seqfile;
       seqfile.open("EMP.DAT",ios::in|ios::out|ios::binary);
       seqfile.seekg(0,ios::beg);
       cout<<"\n The Contents of file are ..."<<endl;
       cout<<"\nLoc.      Name        Emp_ID     Salary       Link    ";
       while(seqfile.read((char *)&Records,sizeof(Records)))
       {

               if(strcmp(Records.name,"")!=0)//not displaying empty slots
               {
               cout<<"\n-------------------------------------------------\n";
       cout<<Records.loc<<"    "<<Records.name<<<flush<<"    "<<Records.emp_id;
       cout<<"        "<<Records.salary<<"         "<<Records.link;

              }
       }
 seqfile.close();
}
void EMP_CLASS::Search()
{
       fstream seqfile;
       int key,h,offset,flag=0;
       cout<<"\n Enter the Emp_ID for searching the record ";
```

```
        cin>>key;
        seqfile.open("EMP.DAT",ios::in|ios::binary);
        h=Hash(key);//obtaining the location of rec.using hash function
        while(seqfile.eof()==0)
        {       //h is a hash key
                offset=h*sizeof(Records);
                //using h for getting actual position in the file
                //hence offset is calculated
                seqfile.seekg(offset,ios::beg);//seeking rec.of that offset
                seqfile.read((char *)&Records,sizeof(Records));//reading that rec.
                if(key==Records.emp_id)//checking if it is required rec.
                {
                        cout<<"\n The Record is present in the file and it is...";
                        cout<<"\n Name: "<<Records.name;
                        cout<<"\n Emp_ID: "<<Records.emp_id;
                        cout<<"\n Salary: "<<Records.salary;
                        flag=1;//means desired reocrd is obtained
                        return;
                }
                else//following link for colliding record
                {
                 h=Records.link;//moving along the chain
                }
        }//endof while
         if(flag==0)
         cout<<"\n The Record is not present in the file";
         seqfile.close();
}
void main()
{
        EMP_CLASS List;
        char ans='y';
        int choice,key;
        clrscr();
        do
        {
         cout<<"\n              Main Menu               "<<endl;
         cout<<"\n 1.Insert";
         cout<<"\n 2.Display";
         cout<<"\n 3.Search";
         cout<<"\n 4.Exit";
         cout<<"\n Enter your choice: ";
         cin>>choice;
         switch(choice)
         {
                case 1:List.Insert();
                                        break;
```

```
            case 2:List.Display();
                                        break;
            case 3:List.Search();
                                        break;
            case 4:exit(0);
        }
        cout<<"\n\t Do you want to go back to Main Menu?";
        cin>>ans;
        }while(ans=='y');
}
```

Output

```
        Main Menu

 1.Insert
 2.Display
 3.Search
 4.Exit
 Enter your choice: 1

 Enter the Hash table size 8


 Hash table is initialised...
 Now, insert the records in the hash table
  Enter Name: AAA

 Enter Emp_ID: 10

 Enter Salary: 1000

Do you want to add more records?y

 Enter Name: FFF

 Enter Emp_ID: 55

 Enter Salary: 5000

Do you want to add more records?y

 Enter Name: BBB

 Enter Emp_ID: 11

 Enter Salary: 1111
```

```
Do you want to add more records?y
 Enter Name: CCC
 Enter Emp_ID: 22
 Enter Salary: 2000

Do you want to add more records?y
 Enter Name: DDD
 Enter Emp_ID: 33
 Enter Salary: 3000
Do you want to add more records?y
 Enter Name: EEE
 Enter Emp_ID: 42
 Enter Salary: 4200
Do you want to add more records?y
 Enter Name: GGG
 Enter Emp_ID: 03
 Enter Salary: 3333
Do you want to add more records?y
 Enter Name: HHH
 Enter Emp_ID: 32
 Enter Salary: 7000
Do you want to add more records?y
 Enter Name: III
 Enter Emp_ID: 62
```

```
Enter Salary: 8000

The hash table is Full, Can't insert record!!!
        Do you want to go back to Main Menu?y

            Main Menu

1.Insert
2.Display
3.Search
4.Exit
Enter your choice: 2
The Contents of file are ...
Loc.    Name    Emp_ID  Salary  Link
--------------------------------------------
0       AAA     10      1000    -1
--------------------------------------------
1       BBB     11      1111    -1
--------------------------------------------
2       CCC     22      2000    4
--------------------------------------------
3       DDD     33      3000    6
--------------------------------------------
4       EEE     42      4200    7
--------------------------------------------
5       FFF     55      5000    -1
--------------------------------------------
6       GGG     3       3333    -1
--------------------------------------------
7       HHH     32      7000    -1

            Main Menu

1.Insert
2.Display
3.Search
4.Exit

Enter your choice: 3

Enter the Emp_ID for searching the record 32

The Record is present in the file and it is...
Name: HHH
Emp_ID: 32
```

```
Salary: 7000
          Main Menu

1.Insert
2.Display
3.Search
4.Exit
Enter your choice: 4
```

6.6 Index Sequential File Organization

- The main drawback of sequential file is that searching operation is not efficient. Because in sequential organization primary key of every record is compared with searching key. To optimize this operation concept of index sequential file is introduced.
- In index sequential file organization, a separate file for storing indexes of every record is maintained along with the master file.

For example

There are two files "IND.DAT" and "EMP.DAT".

Using the positions field of "IND.DAT" file we can quickly retrieved the desired record.

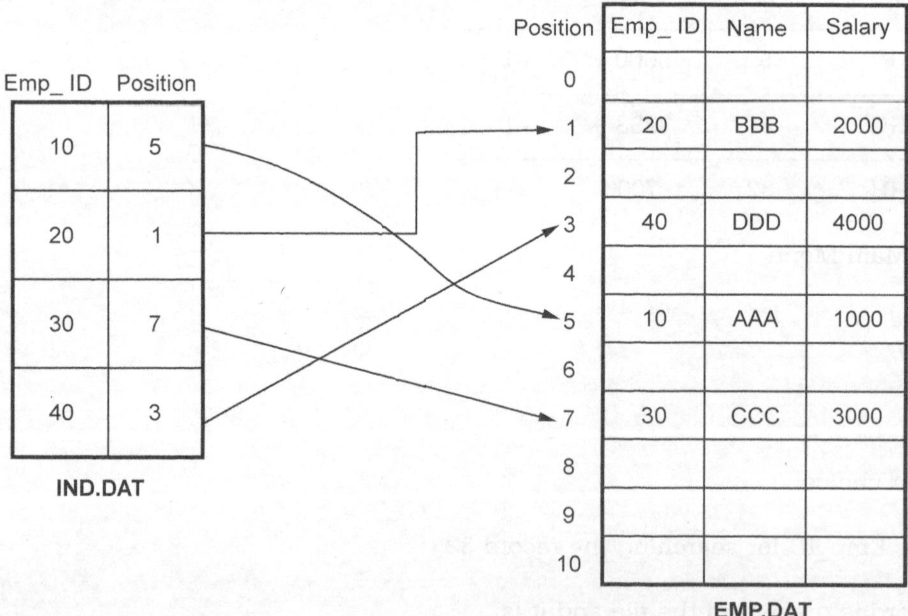

Fig. 6.6.1 Structure of index sequential file

- The index sequential organization, accelerates the retrieval of any desired record. In this case, we need not have to scan the entire memory block of record. Instead of that using primary key (such as EMP_ID) and position we can access the record from master file.

Advantages

1. Desired record can be accessed efficiently by using index which is maintained in separate file.
2. Variable length records can also be handled using index sequential file.

Disadvantages

1. At least two files need to be maintained : One master file and another index file. Hence extra amount of memory is required in order to maintain index file.
2. While performing insertion and deletion index manipulation is required.

6.6.1 Types of Indices

i) **Primary indexes :** A file can be made ordered using a key. This key index is called primary key index. For example -

10	AAA	217	
20	BBB	101	
30	CCC	117	
40	DDD	301	
50	EEE	313	
60	EEE	410	
70	FFF	570	

ii) **Clustering index :** If records of a file are ordered on a non-key field that does not have distinct values for each record, then same disk block occupies certain number of records. All the tuples with identical key value are stored next to each other.For example

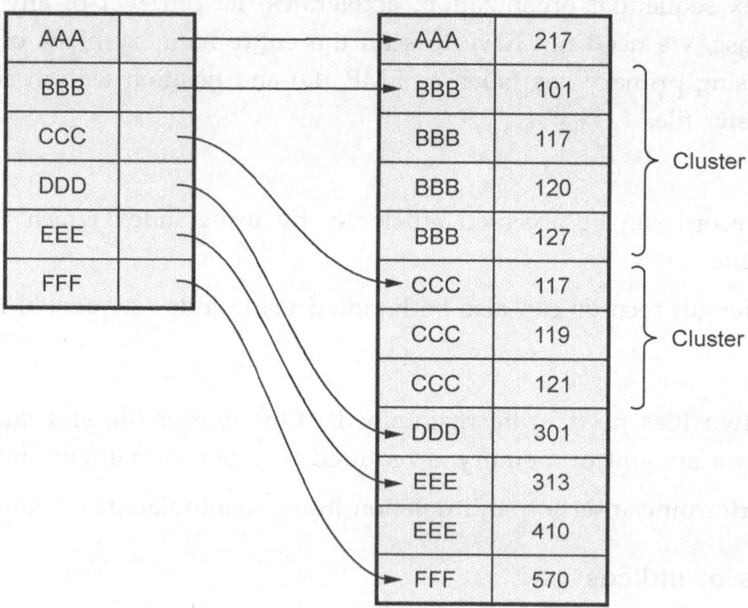

iii) Secondary indexes : Secondary index is a key which is other than a primary key is used for indexing. When certain fields other than the defined key fields are used frequently then in order to improve the performance secondary index is used.

AAA	
BBB	
CCC	
DDD	
EEE	
FFF	

10	AAA	
11	AAA	
12	AAA	
20	BBB	
21	BBB	
30	CCC	
40	DDD	
41	DDD	
42	DDD	
43	DDD	
50	EEE	

For example primary index could be for roll number of the student and secondary index could be for name of the student.

Using secondary index searching data becomes efficient.

Following is C++ program which implements index sequential file organization.

```
/***************************************************************************
Program for performing various operations on
Index Sequential File organization.
***************************************************************************/
#include<iostream.h>
#include<iomanip.h>
#include<fstream.h>
#include<string.h>
#include<conio.h>
#include<stdlib.h>
class EMP_CLASS
{
 typedef struct EMPLOYEE
 {
     char name[10];
     int emp_id;
     int salary;
 }Rec;

 typedef struct INDEX
 {
     int emp_id;
     int position;
 }Ind_Rec;
 Rec Records;
 Ind_Rec Ind_Records;
     public:
         EMP_CLASS();
         void Create();
         void Display();
         void Update();
         void Delete();
         void Append();
         void Search();
};
EMP_CLASS::EMP_CLASS()//constructor
         {
          strcpy(Records.name,"");
         }
void EMP_CLASS::Create()
{
     int i,j;
     char ch='y';
     fstream seqfile;
```

This record structure is for the sequential file
For example

name	emp_id	salary
AAA	10	1000
BBB	20	2000
CCC	30	3000

This record structure is for the index file
For example -

emp_id	salary
10	0
20	1
30	2

```
	fstream indexfile;
	i=0;
	indexfile.open("IND.DAT",ios::in|ios::out|ios::binary);
	seqfile.open("EMP.DAT",ios::in|ios::out|ios::binary);
	do
	{
		cout<<"\n Enter Name: ";
		cin>>Records.name;
		cout<<"\n Enter Emp_ID: ";
		cin>>Records.emp_id;
		cout<<"\n Enter Salary: ";
		cin>>Records.salary;
		seqfile.write((char*)&Records,sizeof(Records))<<flush;
		Ind_Records.emp_id=Records.emp_id;
		Ind_Records.position=i;
		indexfile.write((char*)&Ind_Records,sizeof(Ind_Records))<<flush;
		i++;
		cout<<"\nDo you want to add more records?";
		cin>>ch;
	}while(ch=='y');
	seqfile.close();
	indexfile.close();
}
void EMP_CLASS::Display()
{
	fstream seqfile;
	fstream indexfile;
	int n,i,j;
	seqfile.open("EMP.DAT",ios::in|ios::out|ios::binary);
	indexfile.open("IND.DAT",ios::in|ios::out|ios::binary);
	indexfile.seekg(0,ios::beg);
	seqfile.seekg(0,ios::beg);
	cout<<"\n The Contents of file are ..."<<endl;
	i=0;
	while(indexfile.read((char *)&Ind_Records,sizeof(Ind_Records)))
	{

			i=Ind_Records.position*sizeof(Rec);//getting pos from index file
			seqfile.seekg(i,ios::beg);//seeking record of that pos from seq.file
			seqfile.read((char *)&Records,sizeof(Records));//reading record
			if(Records.emp_id!=-1)//if rec. is not deleted logically
			{	//then display it
			cout<<"\nName: "<<Records.name<<flush;
			cout<<"\nEmp_ID: "<<Records.emp_id;
			cout<<"\nSalary: "<<Records.salary;
			cout<<"\n";
			}
```

Opening both the files for reading and writing purpose

User must enter some records to store them first in the sequential file.

Records for index file are created from seq.file and writing them to ind.file

This while loop will read the record from index file and using the index position the record from sequential file is retrieved.

```
     }
 seqfile.close();
 indexfile.close();
}
void EMP_CLASS::Update()
{
        int pos,id;
        char New_name[10];
        int New_emp_id;
        int New_salary;
        cout<<"\n For updation,";
        cout<<"\n Enter the Emp_ID for for searching ";
        cin>>id;
        fstream seqfile;
        fstream indexfile;
        seqfile.open("EMP.DAT",ios::in|ios::out|ios::binary);
        indexfile.open("IND.DAT",ios::in|ios::out|ios::binary);
        indexfile.seekg(0,ios::beg);

        pos=-1;
        //reading index file for getting the index
        while(indexfile.read((char *)&Ind_Records,sizeof(Ind_Records)))
        {
                if(id==Ind_Records.emp_id)//the desired record is found
                {
                        pos=Ind_Records.position;//getting the position
                        break;
                }
        }
        if(pos==-1)
        {
         cout<<"\n The record is not present in the file";
         return;
        }
        else
        {
                cout<<"\n Enter the values for updation...";
                cout<<"\n Name: ";cin>>New_name;
                cout<<"\n Salary: ";cin>>New_salary;
//calculating the position of record in seq. file using the pos of ind. file
                int offset=pos*sizeof(Rec);
                seqfile.seekp(offset);//seeking the desired record for modification
                strcpy(Records.name,New_name);//can be updated
                Records.emp_id=id;//It's unique id,so don't change
                Records.salary=New_salary;//can be updated
                seqfile.write((char*)&Records,sizeof(Records))<<flush;
```

```
            cout<<"\n The record is updated!!!";
        }
        seqfile.close();
        indexfile.close();

}
void EMP_CLASS::Delete()
{
        int id,pos;
        cout<<"\n For deletion,";
        cout<<"\n Enter the Emp_ID for for searching ";
        cin>>id;
        fstream seqfile;
        fstream indexfile;
        seqfile.open("EMP.DAT",ios::in|ios::out|ios::binary);
        indexfile.open("IND.DAT",ios::in|ios::out|ios::binary);
        seqfile.seekg(0,ios::beg);
        indexfile.seekg(0,ios::beg);
        pos=-1;
        //reading index file for getting the index
        while(indexfile.read((char *)&Ind_Records,sizeof(Ind_Records)))
        {
            if(id==Ind_Records.emp_id) //desired record is found
            {
                pos=Ind_Records.position;
                Ind_Records.emp_id=-1;
                break;
            }
        }
        if(pos==-1)
        {
         cout<<"\n The record is not present in the file";
         return;
        }
        //calculating the position of record in seq. file using the pos of ind. file
        int offset=pos*sizeof(Rec);
        seqfile.seekp(offset);//seeking the desired record for deletion
        strcpy(Records.name,"");
        Records.emp_id=-1; //logical deletion
        Records.salary=-1; //logical deletion
        seqfile.write((char*)&Records,sizeof(Records))<<flush;//writing deleted status
    //From index file also the desired record gets deleted as follows
        offset=pos*sizeof(Ind_Rec);//getting position in index file
        indexfile.seekp(offset); //seeking that record
        Ind_Records.emp_id=-1; //logical deletion of emp_id
        Ind_Records.position=pos;//position remain unchanged
        indexfile.write((char*)&Ind_Records,sizeof(Ind_Records))<<flush;
```

Marking this record as deleted in index file b'coz this is the desired record which we wish to delete from seq. file

```
        seqfile.seekg(0);
        indexfile.close();
        seqfile.close();
        cout<<"\n The record is Deleted!!!";
}
void EMP_CLASS::Append()
{
        fstream seqfile;
        fstream indexfile;
        int pos;
        indexfile.open("IND.DAT",ios::in|ios::binary);
        indexfile.seekg(0,ios::end);
        pos=indexfile.tellg()/sizeof(Ind_Records);
        indexfile.close();

        indexfile.open("IND.DAT",ios::app|ios::binary);
        seqfile.open("EMP.DAT",ios::app|ios::binary);

        cout<<"\n Enter the record for appending";
        cout<<"\nName: ";cin>>Records.name;
        cout<<"\nEmp_ID: ";cin>>Records.emp_id;
        cout<<"\nSalary: ";cin>>Records.salary;
        seqfile.write((char*)&Records,sizeof(Records));//inserting rec at end in seq. file
        Ind_Records.emp_id=Records.emp_id;          //inserting rec at end in ind. file
        Ind_Records.position=pos;                   //at calculated pos
        indexfile.write((char*)&Ind_Records,sizeof(Ind_Records))<<flush;
        seqfile.close();
        indexfile.close();
        cout<<"\n The record is Appended!!!";
}
void EMP_CLASS::Search()
{
        fstream seqfile;
        fstream indexfile;
        int id,pos,offset;
        cout<<"\n Enter the Emp_ID for searching the record ";
        cin>>id;
        indexfile.open("IND.DAT",ios::in|ios::binary);
        pos=-1;
        //reading index file to obtain the index of desired record
        while(indexfile.read((char *)&Ind_Records,sizeof(Ind_Records)))
        {
                if(id==Ind_Records.emp_id)//desired record found
                {
                        pos=Ind_Records.position;//seeking the position
                        break;
                }
```

Current position/size of individual record = position of record in ind. file

```
        }
        if(pos==-1)
        {
                cout<<"\n Record is not present in the file";
                return;
        }
//calculate offset using position obtained from ind. file
        offset=pos*sizeof(Records);
        seqfile.open("EMP.DAT",ios::in|ios::binary);
//seeking the record from seq. file using calculated offset
        seqfile.seekg(offset,ios::beg);//seeking for reading purpose
        seqfile.read((char *)&Records,sizeof(Records));
        if(Records.emp_id==-1)
        {
                cout<<"\n Record is not present in the file";
                return;
        }
        else //emp_id=desired record's id
        {
                cout<<"\n The Record is present in the file and it is...";
                cout<<"\n Name: "<<Records.name;
                cout<<"\n Emp_ID: "<<Records.emp_id;
                cout<<"\n Salary: "<<Records.salary;
        }
        seqfile.close();
        indexfile.close();
}
void main()
{
        EMP_CLASS List;
        char ans='y';
        int choice,key;
        clrscr();
        do
        {
         cout<<"\n              Main Menu              "<<endl;
         cout<<"\n 1.Create";
         cout<<"\n 2.Display";
         cout<<"\n 3.Update";
         cout<<"\n 4.Delete";
         cout<<"\n 5.Append";
         cout<<"\n 6.Search";
         cout<<"\n 7.Exit";
         cout<<"\n Enter your choice: ";
         cin>>choice;
         switch(choice)
         {
```

```
            case 1:List.Create();
                                        break;
            case 2:List.Display();
                                        break;
            case 3:List.Update();
                                        break;
            case 4:List.Delete();
                                        break;
            case 5:List.Append();
                                        break;
            case 6:List.Search();
                                        break;
            case 7:exit(0);
        }
    cout<<"\n\t Do you want to go back to Main Menu?";
    cin>>ans;
    }while(ans=='y');
}
```

Output

```
        Main Menu

 1.Create
 2.Display
 3.Update
 4.Delete
 5.Append
 6.Search
 7.Exit
 Enter your choice: 1

 Enter Name: AAA

 Enter Emp_ID: 10

 Enter Salary: 1000
Do you want to add more records?y

 Enter Name: BBB

 Enter Emp_ID: 20

 Enter Salary: 2000
Do you want to add more records?y

 Enter Name: CCC
```

```
Enter Emp_ID: 30

Enter Salary: 3000

Do you want to add more records?n

        Do you want to go back to Main Menu?y


            Main Menu

1.Create
2.Display
3.Update
4.Delete
5.Append
6.Search
7.Exit
Enter your choice: 2

The Contents of file are ...

Name: AAA
Emp_ID: 10
Salary: 1000

Name: BBB
Emp_ID: 20
Salary: 2000

Name: CCC
Emp_ID: 30
Salary: 3000

        Do you want to go back to Main Menu?y
            Main Menu

1.Create
2.Display
3.Update
4.Delete
5.Append
6.Search
7.Exit
Enter your choice: 3
```

```
For updation,
Enter the Emp_ID for for searching 20

Enter the values for updation...
Name: MMM

Salary: 2222

The record is updated!!!
        Do you want to go back to Main Menu?y
           Main Menu

1.Create
2.Display
3.Update
4.Delete
5.Append
6.Search
7.Exit
Enter your choice: 2

The Contents of file are ...

Name: AAA
Emp_ID: 10
Salary: 1000

Name: MMM
Emp_ID: 20
Salary: 2222

Name: CCC
Emp_ID: 30
Salary: 3000

        Do you want to go back to Main Menu?y
           Main Menu

1.Create
2.Display
3.Update
4.Delete
5.Append
6.Search
7.Exit
Enter your choice: 4
```

```
For deletion,
 Enter the Emp_ID for for searching 30

 The record is Deleted!!!
        Do you want to go back to Main Menu?y

            Main Menu

 1.Create
 2.Display
 3.Update
 4.Delete
 5.Append
 6.Search
 7.Exit
 Enter your choice: 2

 The Contents of file are ...

Name: AAA
Emp_ID: 10
Salary: 1000

Name: MMM
Emp_ID: 20
Salary: 2222

        Do you want to go back to Main Menu?y
            Main Menu

 1.Create
 2.Display
 3.Update
 4.Delete
 5.Append
 6.Search
 7.Exit
 Enter your choice: 5

 Enter the record for appending
Name: KKK

Emp_ID: 40

Salary: 4000
```

```
The record is Appended!!!
      Do you want to go back to Main Menu?y
         Main Menu

1.Create
2.Display
3.Update
4.Delete
5.Append
6.Search
7.Exit
Enter your choice: 7
```

6.7 Linked Organization

- In linked organization the logical sequence of the records is different than the physical sequence. In any sequential organization if we are accessing n^{th} node at Loc_i then $(n+1)^{th}$ record may be located at (Loc_i+c) where c is the constant which represents the length of the record or it may be some inter-record spacing.
- In linked organization we can access next logical record by following the **link-value** pair. The link-value pair denotes each individual record.
- The typical structure of every record is as follows -

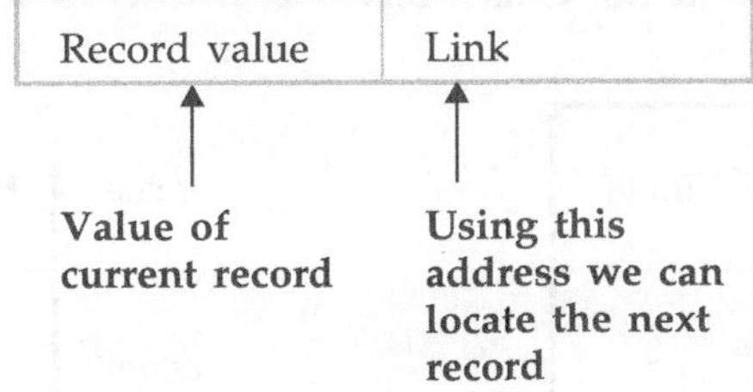

Thus records in the linked organization can be stored as follows -

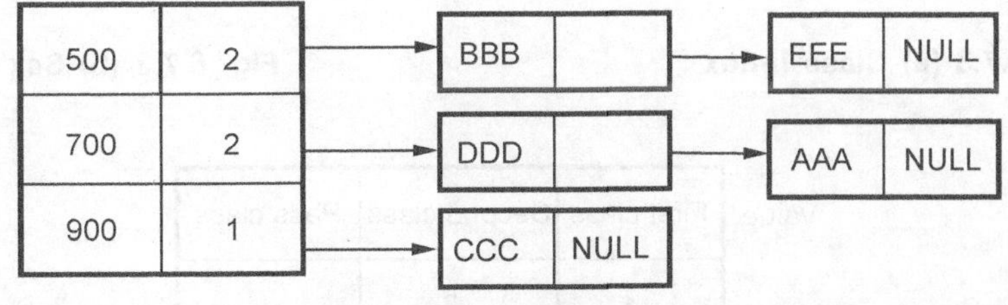

Fig. 6.7.1 Roll_No index

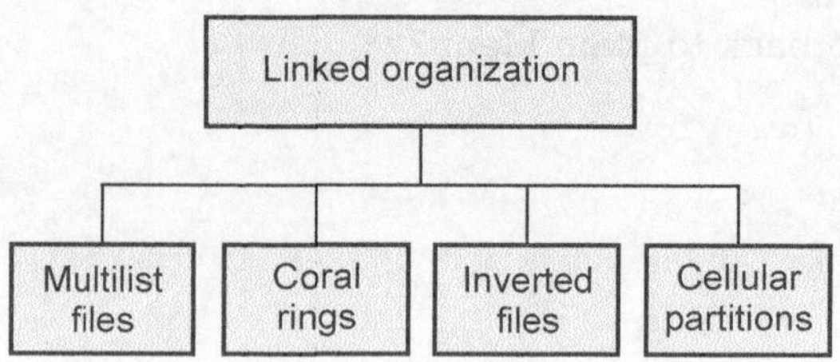

Fig. 6.7.2 Linked organization

1. Multi-list Files

- In linked organization the searching of record is possible by using primary as well as secondary keys. Hence several indices for each corresponding keys must be maintained. This leads to **multi-list structure** for linked file organization.
- **Example**

Consider a **multi-list** structure for student database -

Each individual record looks like this

Roll_No	Class	Sex	Marks

Individual record

The index for each key field i.e. Class, Sex and Marks is as follows -

Value	Fifth	Tenth
Length	2	3
Pointer to first record	BBB	EEE

Fig. 6.7.3 (a) Class index

Value	Female	Male
Length	3	2
Pointer to first record	BBB	EEE

Fig. 6.7.3 (b) Sex index

Value	First class	Second class	Pass class
Length	1	3	1
Pointer to first record	EEE	AAA	BBB

Fig. 6.7.3 (c) Marks index

The index on the primary key Roll_no is maintained using multi-list structure which is as shown below -

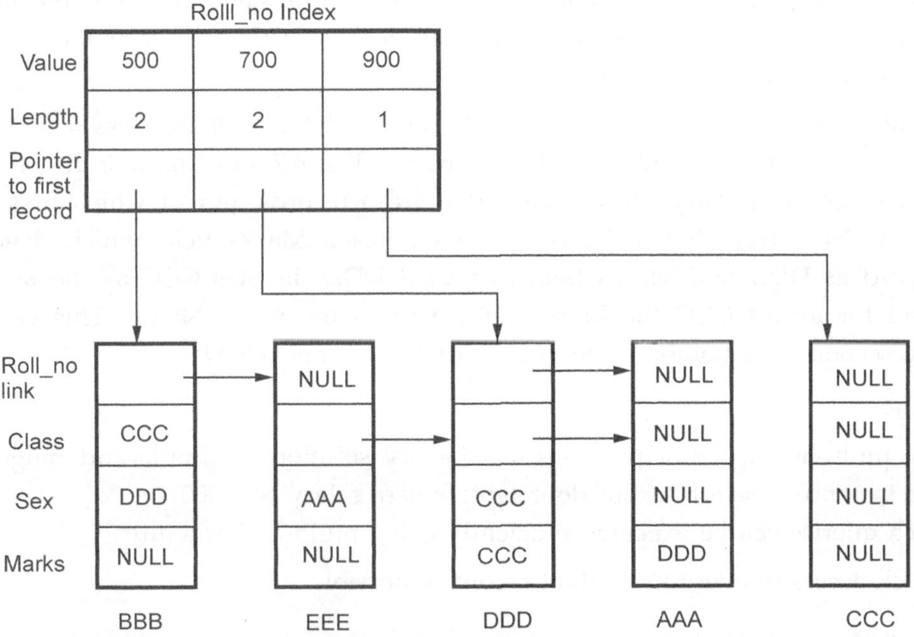

Fig. 6.7.4 Multi-list structure

- **In the Roll_no record structure, there are 3 fields - value, length and pointer to the first record.**
  - The value field indicates the upper bound value for the Roll_no. For instance : If the roll number of particular student is 437 then it lies between 0 to 500. Note that here upper bound is 500. Hence the record of that student must be associated with value 500. Similarly if roll_number of particular student is 689 then it must be associated with the value 700. The length field denotes total number of records.
  - From above Fig. 6.7.4 length 2 in the value of 500 means there are 2 records whose Roll_no lie between 0 to 500. Similarly length 2 for value 700 means there are 2 records who have Roll_no that lie between 500 to 700.
  - The third field is the pointer or a link field which points to the first record. For instance in above Fig. 6.7.4 For **value 500** the pointer field points to record BBB and in the record BBB there is a field Roll_no link which points to record EEE. Thus there are total 2 records BBB and EEE with value 500.
- Similarly for **value 700** there are 2 records the pointer field points to the first record DDD. The record DDD shows the next record of it by pointing to AAA (Refer the Roll_no link of record DDD).

- And for **value 900** there is only one record i.e. CCC which is pointed by pointer field. The index for each key field is maintained which is useful for executing any query. Observe Fig. 6.7.4 of class index. This figure tells us that there are two records for fifth standard and 3 records for tenth standard. The first student of fifth standard class is BBB and second student is CCC. (Just refer the class field of record BBB from Fig. 6.7.4)
- Thus we can solve the query "select * from stud_table where class = fifth" and the answer will be BBB and CCC. If we observe Fig. 6.7.4 of Marks index, the column of **second class** value shows that there are 3 records, out of which first record is AAA. Now from Fig. 6.7.4 record AAA has a Marks field which denotes next record as DDD and Marks field of record DDD denotes CCC as the next record. And for record CCC the Marks field denotes the value NULL. This all indicates the second class holder students are AAA, CCC and DDD.

Advantages

1) The multi-list structure provides satisfactory solution to simple and range queries. For instance : "Select * from dept_table where salary > 10000"
   Such queries can be executed efficiently using multi-list structure.
2) Quick access to every individual record is possible.

Disadvantage

1) Some amount of memory gets consumed in maintaining the link or address field.

2. Coral Ring

Coral ring is a file organization in which doubly linked multi-list structure is maintained. Each list is a circular list. Thus coral ring structure is a kind of structure in which **circular doubly** linked list is maintained for connecting the records together.

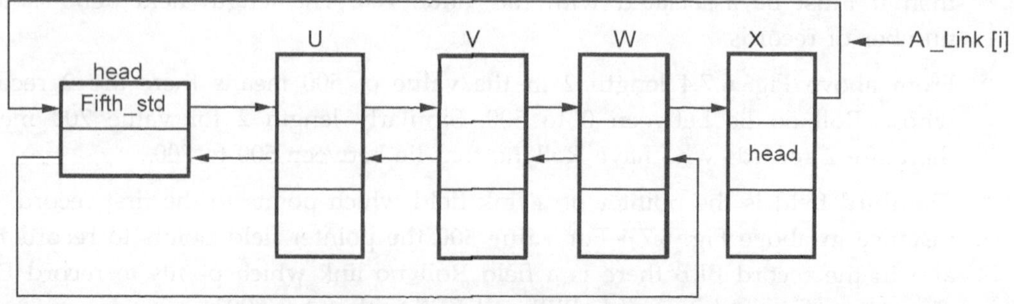

The forward circular list contains nodes head U, V, W, X.

The reverse circular list contains nodes head W, V, U.

Fig. 6.7.5 Coral ring structure

Associated with each record there are two link fields i.e. forward link and back link. Thus records get associated with each other by circular linked list.

3. Inverted Files

- Inverted files are similar to multi-lists.
- The difference between multi-list and inverted files is that in multi-lists records with the same key value are linked together along with the **link information** being kept in **individual record**. But in case of inverted files this **link information** is kept in the **index itself**.

For example

437	BBB
488	EEE
689	DDD
695	AAA
778	CCC

Fig. 6.7.6 (a) Roll_No index

Fifth	BBB, CCC
Tenth	EEE, DDD, AAA

Fig. 6.7.6 (b) Class index

Female	BBB, DDD, CCC
Male	EEE, AAA

Fig. 6.7.6 (c) Sex index

First class	EEE
Second class	AAA, DDD, CCC
Pass class	BBB

Fig. 6.7.6 (d) Marks index

Consider Fig. 6.7.6 (a) of Roll-no index which shows records BBB, EEE, DDD, AAA and CCC. In Fig. 6.7.6 (b) of class index two class are there fifth and tenth and we can observe that in the link information is stored in the index itself. Hence for fifth class records are BBB and CCC. And for tenth class records are EEE, DDD and AAA .

Similarly from sex index Fig. 6.7.6 (c), it is clear that BBB, DDD and CCC are females and EEE and AAA are males.

- The above index structure is a dense index structure **Dense Indexing**. The dense index is a kind of indexing in which record appers for every search key value in the file.

- Thus in inverted files the index entries is of variable length. Hence inverted files structure is **more complex** than multi-list file structure.
- Following are the two steps that are adopted while searching a record from inverted files -

  i) Index of required record is searched first of all.

  ii) Then actual record is retrieved.
- In inverted files the index structure is important. The records can be arranged sequentially, randomly or linked depending on primary key.
- The number of disk accesses required = Number of records being retrieved + Processing for indexes.

Advantages

1) Inverted files are space saving as compared to other file structures when record retrieval does not require retrieval does not require retrieval of key fields.

Disadvantages

1) Insertion and deletion of records is complex because it requires the ability to insert and delete within indexes.

2) Index maintainance is complicated as compared to multi-list.

4. Cellular Partitions

- For reducing the searching time during file operations, the storage media (e.g. secondary memory, magnetic disk, magnetic tape etc.) may be divided into cells.
- The cells can be of two types -

  i) Entire disk pack can be a cell

  ii) A cylinder can be a cell.
- A list of records can occupy either entire disk pack or it may lie on particular cylinder.
- If all the records lie on the same cylinder then without moving the read/write head the records can be accessed.
- If the cell is nothing but entire disk pack then the disk is partitioned into different partitions. Such partitions are called **cellular partitions**. Then these different cells can be searched in parallel.

Advantages of cellular partitions

1) Various read operations can be performed parallely in order to reduce the search time.

2) Faster execution of any query.

Disadvantage

1) If multiple records lie in the same cell then reading a single cell becomes a time consuming process.

6.8 External Sort

- In external sorting, the **data stored on secondary memory** is part by part loaded into main memory, sorting can be done over there.
- The sorted data can be then stored in the intermediate files. Finally these intermediate files can be merged repeatedly to get sorted data.
- Thus **huge amount** of data can be sorted using this technique.

6.8.1 Consequential Processing and Merging Two Lists

The external merge sort is a technique in which the data is loaded in intermediate files. Each intermediate file is sorted independently and then combined or merged to get the sorted data.

For example :

Consider that there are 10,000 records that has to be sorted. Clearly we need to apply external sorting method. Suppose main memory has a capacity to store 500 records in blocks, with each block size of 100 records.

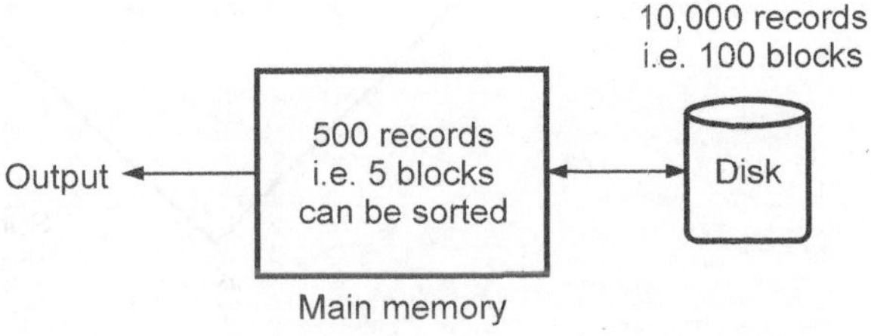

Fig. 6.8.1

The sorted 5 blocks (i.e. 500 records) are stored in intermediate file. This process will be repeated 20 times to get all the records sorted in chunks.

In the second step, we start merging a pair of intermediate files in the main memory to get output file.

For example -

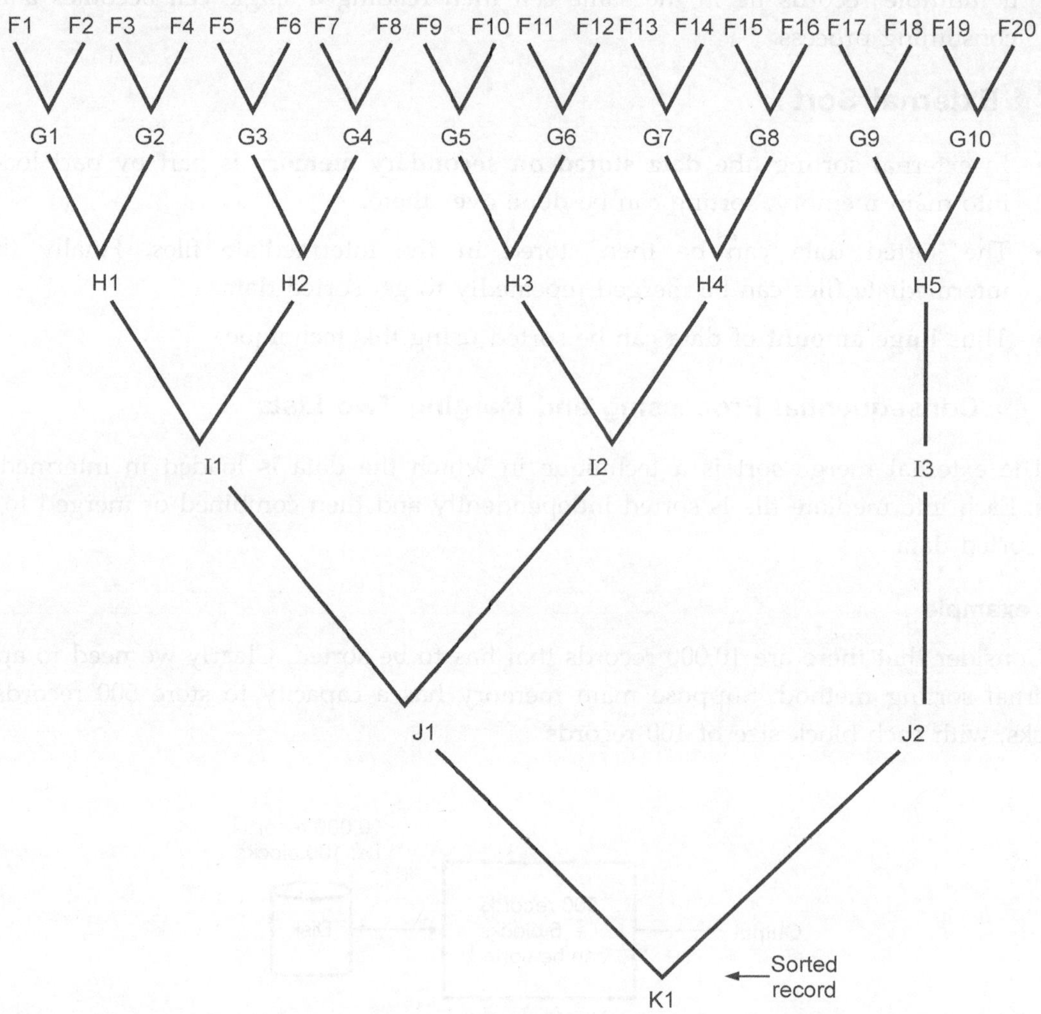

Fig. 6.8.2

6.8.2 Multiway Merge

- Multiway merge sort is a technique of merging 'm' sorted lists into single sorted list. The **two-way** merge is a special case of multiway merge sort.
- The two way merge sort makes use of two input tapes and two output tapes for sorting the records.

- It works in two stages -

  Stage 1 : Break the records into block. Sort individual record with the help of two input tapes.

  Stage 2 : Merge the sorted blocks and create a single sorted file with the help of two output tapes.

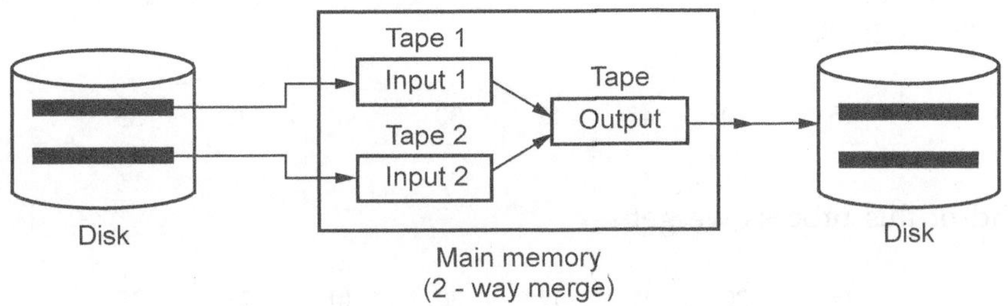

Fig. 6.8.3 Two-way merge

Let us understand it with the help of an example.

Example 6.8.1 *Sort the following list of elements using two way merge sort with M = 3.*
20, 47, 15, 8, 9, 4, 40, 30, 12, 17, 11, 56, 28, 35

Solution :

As M = 3, we will break the records in the group of 3 and sort them. Then we will store them on tape. We will store data on alternate tapes.

Stage I : Sorting Phase

1) 20, 47, 15. We arrange in sorted order → 15, 20, 47

Tb1 :	15	20	47

2) Read next three records sort them and store them on Tape Tb2

8, 9, 4 → 4, 8, 9

Tb2 :	4	8	9

3) Read next three records, sort them and store on tape Tb1.

40, 30, 12 → 12, 30, 40

Tb1 :	15	20	47	12	30	40

4) Read next three records, sort them and store on tape Tb2.

17, 11, 56 → 11, 17, 56

Tb2 :	4	8	9	11	17	56

5) Read next two remaining records, sort them and store on Tape Tb1

28, 35, → 28, 35

Tb1 :	15	20	47	12	30	40	28	35

At the end of this process we get

Tb1 :	15	20	47	12	30	40	28	35

Tb2 :	4	8	9	11	17	56

Stage II : Merging of runs

The input tapes Tb1 and Tb2 will use two more output tapes Ta1 and Ta2, for sorting. Finally the sorted data will be on tape Ta1.

Tb1 :	15	20	47	12	30	40	28	35

Tb2 :	4	8	9	11	17	56

We will read the elements from both the tapes Tb1 and Tb2, compare them, and store on Ta1 in sorted order.

Ta1 :	4	8	9	15	20	47

Now we will read second blocks from Tb1 and Tb2. Sort the elements and store on Ta2.

Ta2 :	11	12	17	30	40	56

Finally read the third block from Tb1 and store in sorted manner on Ta1. We will not compare this block with Ta2 as there is no third block. Hence we will get

Ta1 :

4	8	9	15	20	47	28	35

Ta2 :

11	12	17	30	40	56

Now compare first blocks of Ta1 and Ta2 and store sorted elements on Tb1.

Tb1 :

4	8	9	11	12	15	17	20	30	40	47	56

Tb2 :

28	35

Now both Tb1 and Tb2 contains only single block each. Sort the elements from both the blocks and store the result on Ta1.

Ta1 :

4	8	9	11	12	15	17	20	28	30	35	40	47	56

Thus we get **sorted list.**

Algorithm

Step 1 : Divide the elements into the blocks of size M. Sort each block and write runs on disk.

Step 2 : Merge two runs

i) Read first value on each of two runs

ii) Compare and sort

iii) Write on output tape.

Step 3 : Repeat the step 2 and get longer and longer runs on alternate tapes. Finally we will get single sorted list.

Analysis : The algorithm requires **log(N/M) Passes** plus initial run construction pass.

- Initially

  1st tape contains N records = M records * N/M runs.

  After storing the runs on two tapes, each contains half of the runs

  Two tapes * M_records per run * $\frac{1}{2}$(N/M) runs = N records

- After merge 1st pass - double the length of runs, halve the number of runs

  Two tapes * 2M_records per run * $\frac{1}{2} * \frac{1}{2}$ * (N/M) runs = N records

- After merge 2nd pass

  Two tapes $*$ 4 M_records per run $* \frac{1}{4} * \frac{1}{2} * (N/M)$ runs = N records

- After merge S-th pass

  Two tapes $*$ 2^SM records per run $* (1/2^S)(1/2)(N/M)$ runs = N records

After the last merge, there will be only one run equal to whole file.

$$2^S M = N$$

$$2^S = N/M$$

$$S = \log(N/M)$$

Hence at each pass the N records are processed and we get the time complexity as O(N log (N/M)).

6.8.3 K way Merge Algorithm

In this method instead of two tapes the k tapes. The basic two way merge algorithm is used. The representation of multiway merge technique is as shown in Fig. 6.8.4.

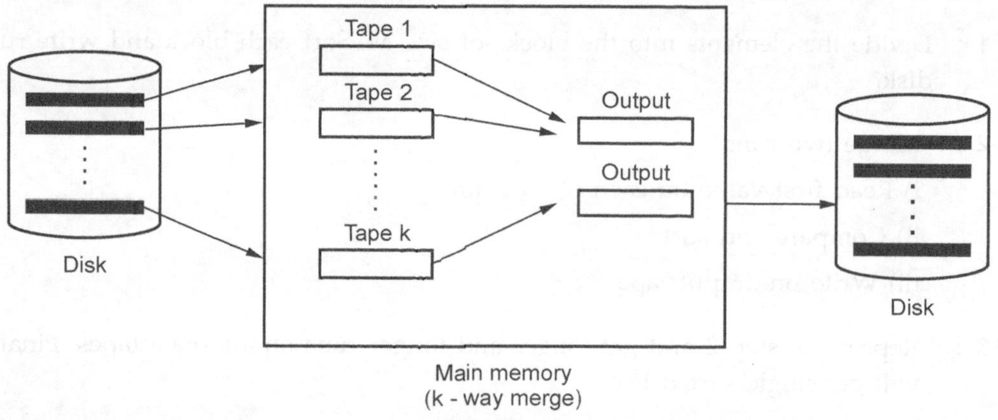

Fig. 6.8.4

Let us understand this technique with the help of illustrative example.

Example 6.8.2 *Sort the following list of elements using k way merge sort with k = 3.*

20, 47, 15, 8, 9, 4, 40, 30, 12, 17, 11, 56, 28, 35

Solution : We will read three records in the memory, sort them and store on tape Tb1, them read next three records, sort them and store on tape Tb2, similarly store next three sorted records on Tb3.

20, 47, 15 → 15, 20, 47

8, 9, 4 → 4, 8, 9

40, 30, 12 → 12, 30, 40

Tb1 :	15	20	47
Tb2 :	4	8	9
Tb3 :	12	30	40

1) Now read next 3 records (i.e. 17, 11, 56), sort them and store on Tb1.

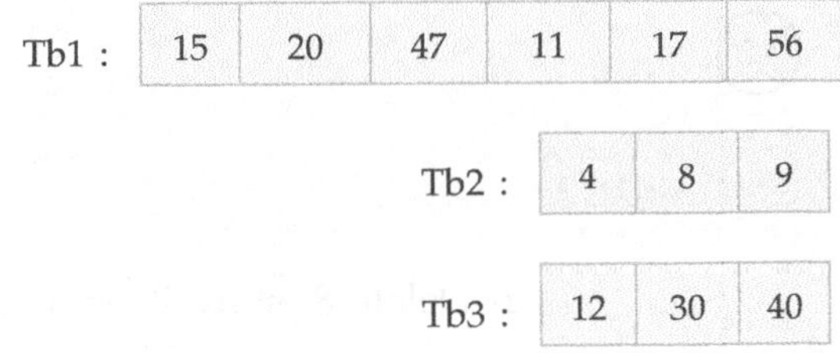

2) Read next records (i.e. 28, 35) and sort them store on tape Tb2.

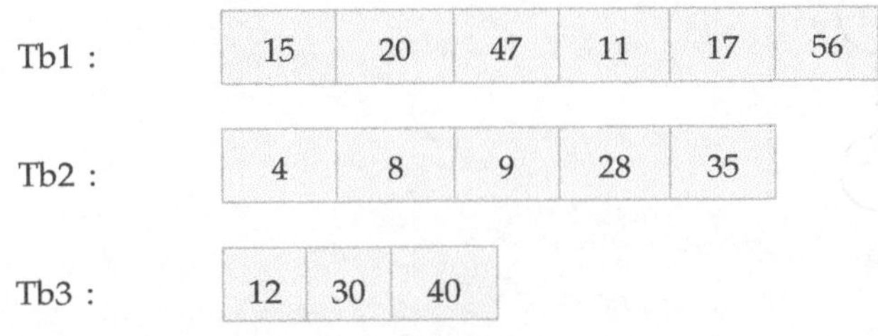

Nothing will be stored on Tb3. Thus we get

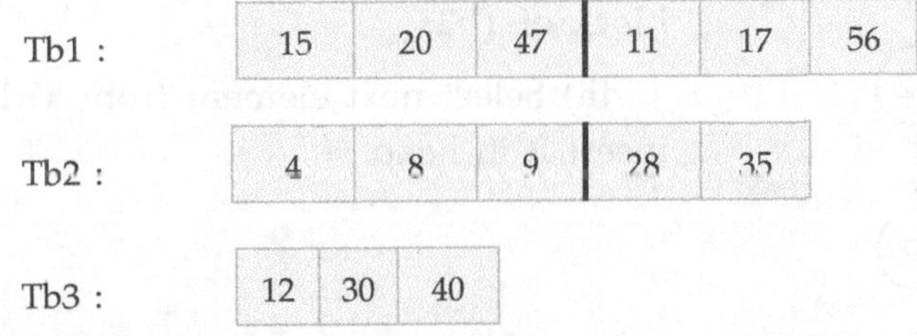

Stage 2 : Merging

In this stage, we will build heap for the first elements of first block elements of Tb1, Tb2 and Tb3 (i.e. 15, 4, 12). Then perform **deleteMin** operation and store the elements on Ta1.

Step 1 : 1) Build heap for 15, 4, 12

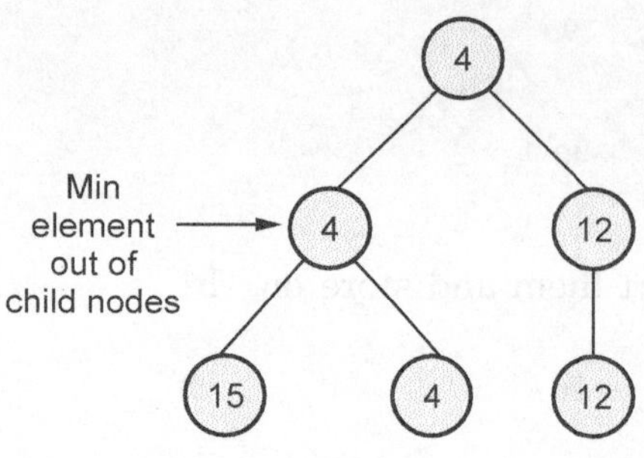

i) Delete 4, store it on Ta1.

ii) As 4 is from Tb2, insert next element of Tb2 i.e. 8 in heap.

2) Build heap for 15, 8, 12

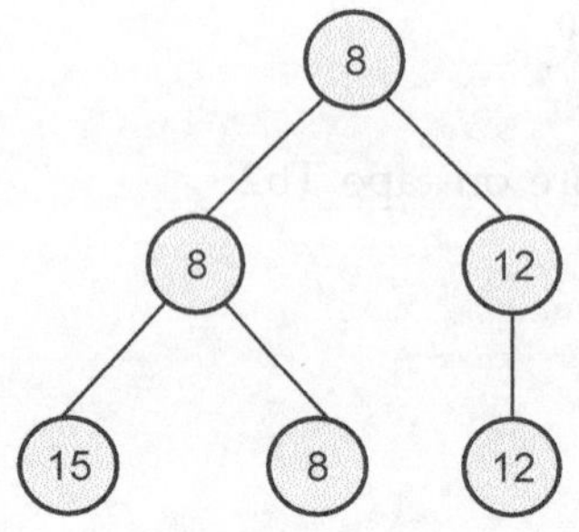

i) Delete 8, store it on Ta1.

ii) As 8 is from Tb2, insert next element i.e. 9 in heap.

3)

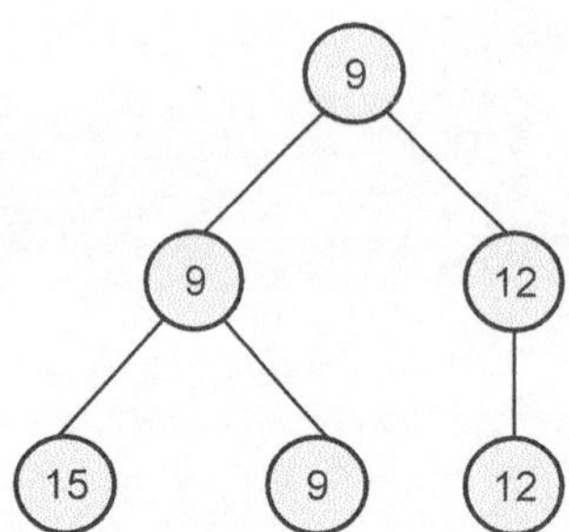

i) Delete 9, store it on Ta1.

ii) There is no next record from first block of Tb2.

iii) Select next element from Tb1, i.e. 20 insert it in heap.

4)

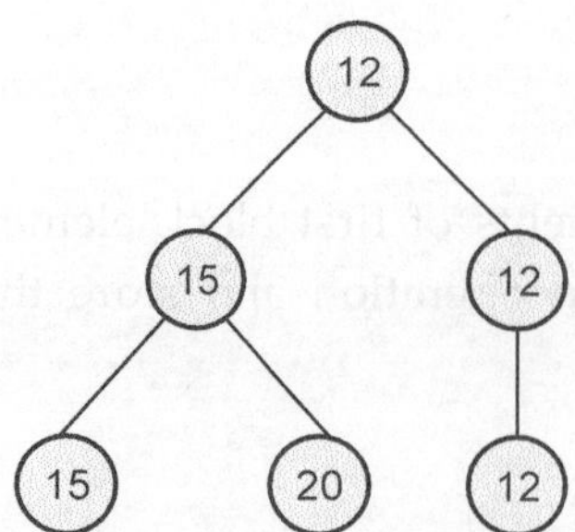

i) Delete 12, store it on Ta1.

ii) As 12 is from Tb3, select next element of 12 i.e. 30 and insert it in heap.

5)

Proceeding in this way, we get

Ta1 :	4	8	9	12	15	20	30	40	47

Step 2 : Similarly by constructing heap for second block of elements, performing **deleteMin** we get

Ta2 :	11	17	28	35	56

Step 3 : Now we have two tapes Ta1 and Ta2. We will now build heap for 4 and 11 (i.e. first elements of Ta1 and Ta2).

1)

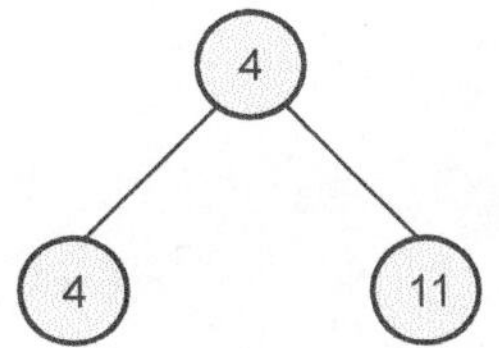

i) Delete 4, insert it in Tb1.

ii) As 4 is from Ta1, we will delete 4 from heap and insert next element i.e. 8 in heap.

2)

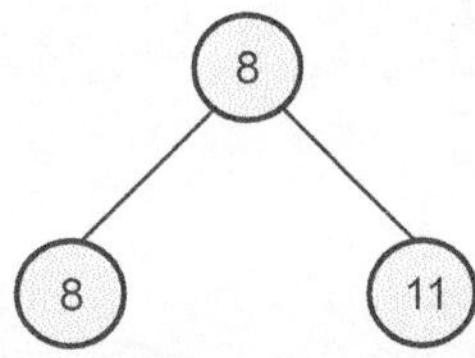

i) Delete 8, store on Tb1.

ii) Next element of 8 is 9. So insert it in the heap.

3)

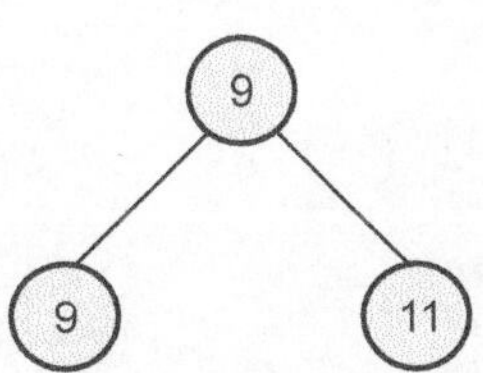

4) Proceeding in this manner we get sorted list on Tb1 as

Tb1 :	4	8	9	11	12	15	17	20	28	30	35	40	47	56

This is the sorted list

Algorithm :

1) Read M values at a time into internal memory, sort, write on disk.

2) Merge k runs

   2a) Read first value on each of k runs, and build min heap.

   2b) Remove minimum from heap and write to disk.

   2c) Read next value from disk and insert that value on heap.

3) Repeat step 2 until all first k runs are processed.

4) Finally merge all the runs into single run to get sorted list.

Analysis :

The number of passes for multiway merging is $\log_k(N/M)$

❑❑❑

May - 2017 **Advanced Data Structures** S.E. (Computer) Semester - II (Course - 2015)	**SPPU** **Solved Paper** **[5152]-568**

Time : Two Hours] **[Maximum Marks : 50**

N.B. : - *i) Answer four questions in all.*

ii) Neat diagrams must be drawn wherever necessary.

iii) Figures to the right indicate full marks.

iv) Assume suitable data, if necessary.

Q.1 A) *Write a non-recursive pseudo for post order traversal of binary tree.* **(Refer section 1.6.1)** **[5]**

B) *Consider the given graph and find the shortest path by using Dijkstra's algorithm from 'a' to 'g'.* **[7]**

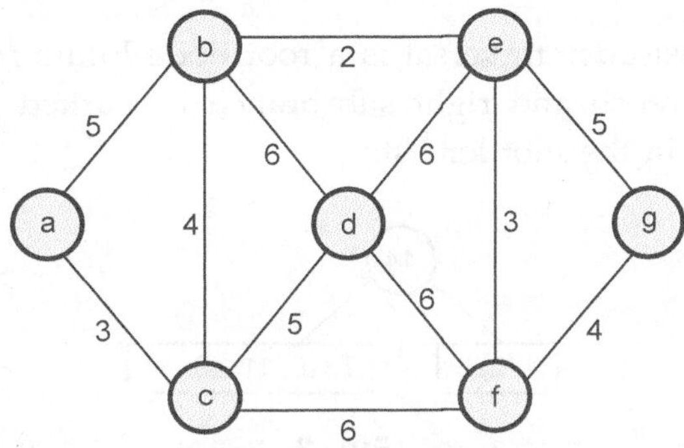

Fig. 1

Ans. :

Selected tree	Distance towards other vertices
a	d(a, b) = 6, d(a, c) = 3 d(a, d) = ∞, d(a, e) = ∞ d(a, f) = ∞, d(a, g) = ∞
a-c	d(a, b) = 5, d(c, d) = 8 d(c, e) = ∞ d(c, f) = 9 d(c, g) = ∞
a-b	d(c, d) = 8, d(b, e) = 7 d(c, f) = 9, d(c, g) = ∞
a-b-e	d(c, d) = 8, d(c, f) = 9 d(e, f) = 12

a-c-d	d(c, f) = 9 d(e, g) = 12
a-c-d-f	d(e, g) = 12
a-b-e-g	Shortest distance = 12

Thus shortest path from a to g is a-b-e-g with path length 12.

OR

Q.2 A) *Construct a binary tree from given two traversals :* **[6]**

Inorder traversal - 1 2 3 14 7 10 11 40 30

Postorder traversal - 1 3 2 7 10 40 30 11 14

Ans. : Let

Step 1 :

Inorder	1	2	3	14	7	10	11	40	30
Postorder	1	3	2	7	10	40	30	11	14

The last node in postorder traversal is a root node locate root node in the inorder sequence. The left-subbranch and right sub branch is marked using left sub-sequence and right sub-sequence in the inorder list.

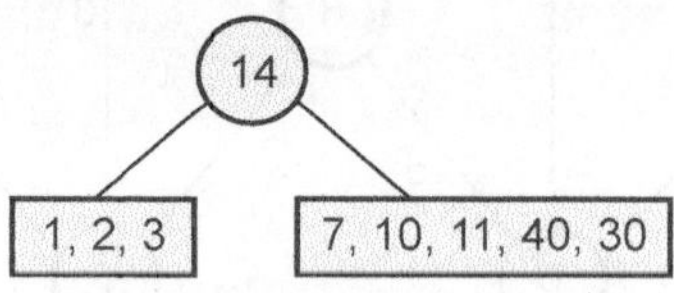

Fig. 2

Step 2 : We will handle two subbranches i.e. left sub-branch and right sub-branch as follows

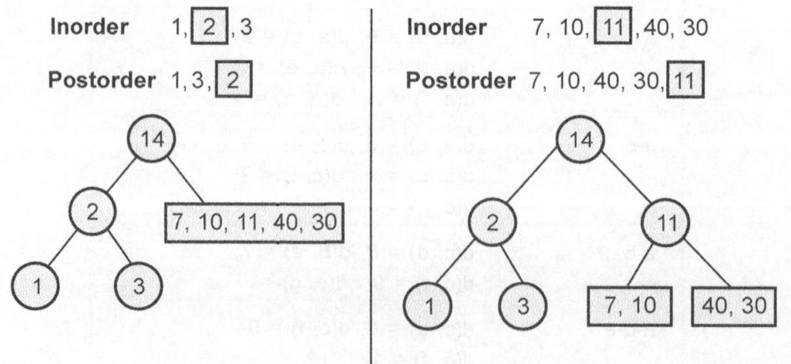

Fig. 3

Step 3 :

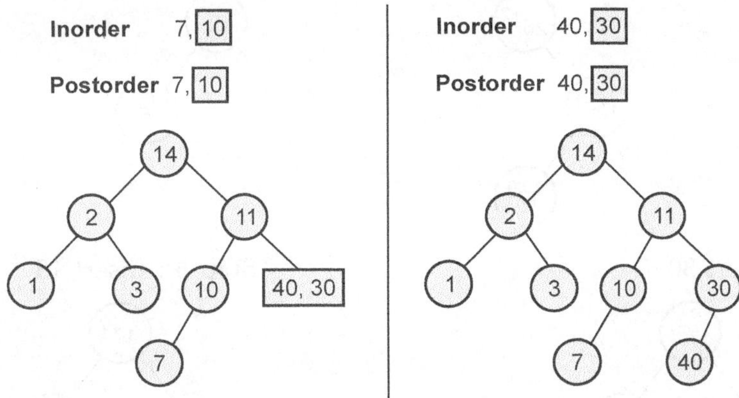

Fig. 4

Thus we get the binary tree as

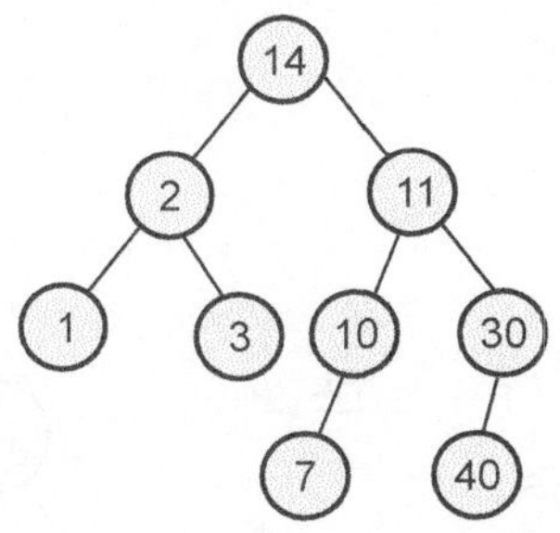

Fig. 5

B) *Write a short note on topological sorting.* **(Refer section 2.9)** **[6]**

Q.3 A) *Write short note on skip list.* **(Refer section 3.8)** **[6]**

B) *Build the AVL tree for the following data. Show the step by step construction 25, 12, 17, 30, 15, 14, 37, 27, 40, 29, 28.* **[6]**

Ans. :

Step 1 : Insert 25

Step 2 : Insert 12

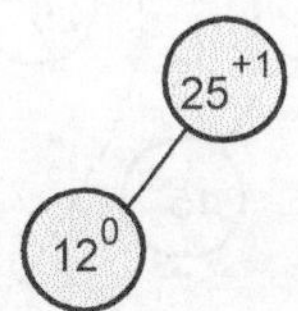

Step 3 : Insert 17

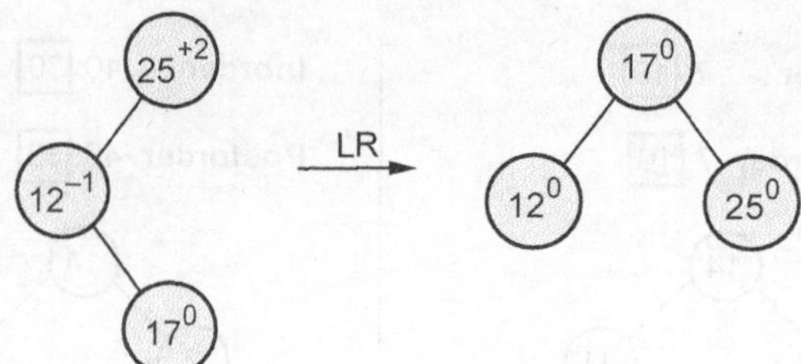

Step 4 : Insert 30

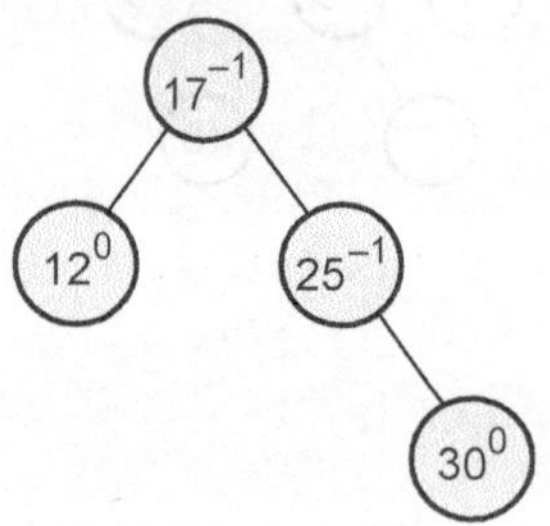

Step 5 : Insert 15

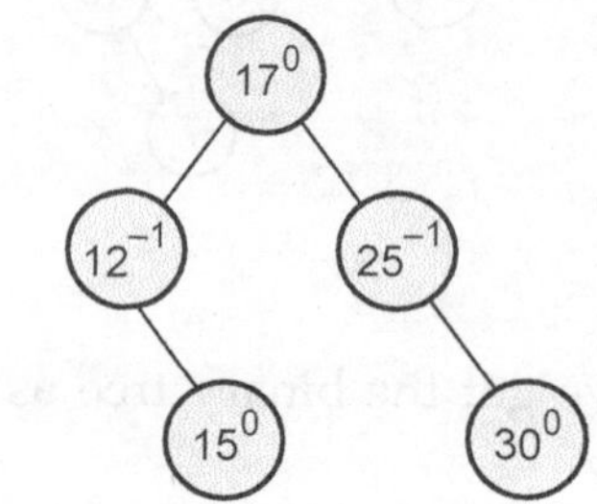

Step 6 : Insert 14

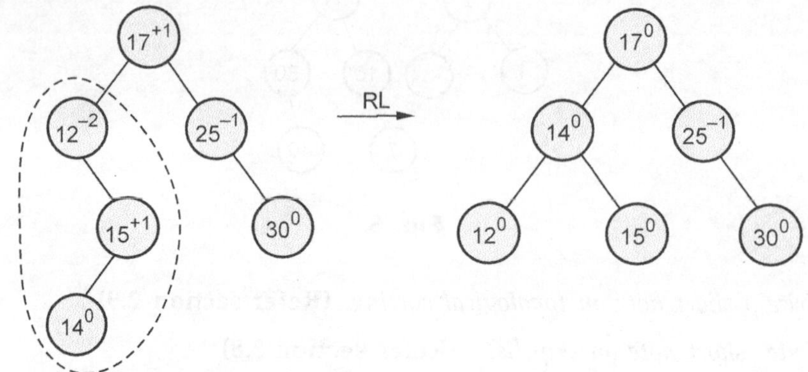

Step 7 : Insert 37

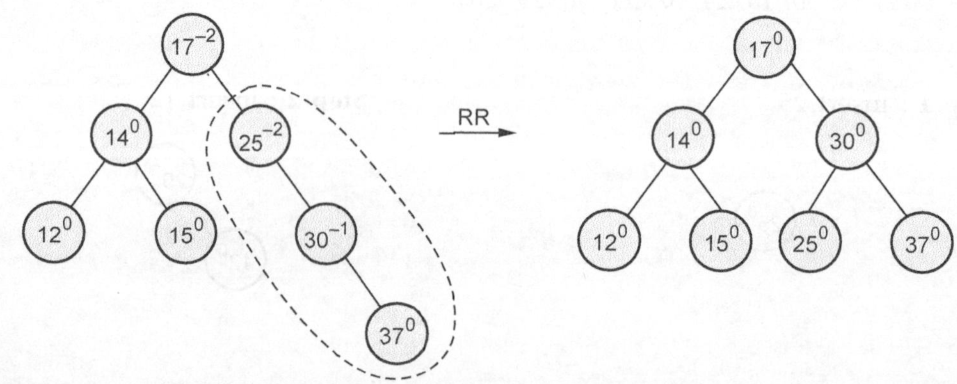

Step 8 : Insert 27

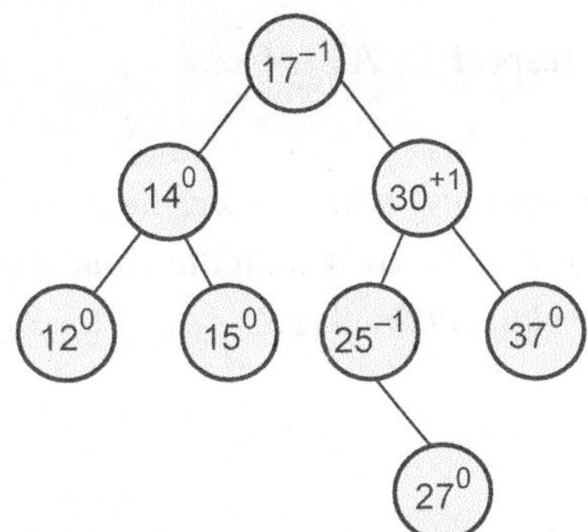

Step 9 : Insert 40

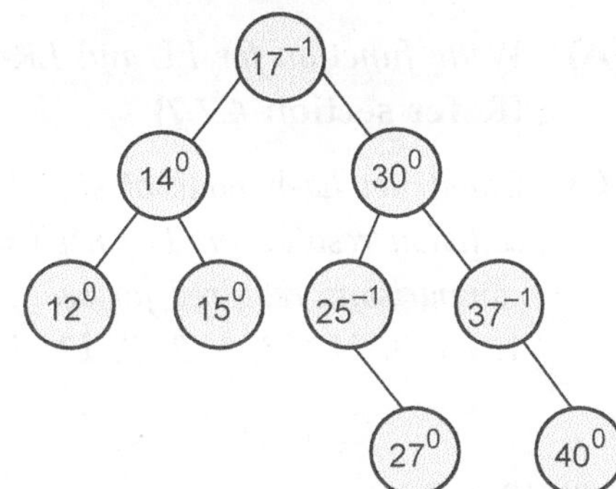

Step 10 : Insert 29

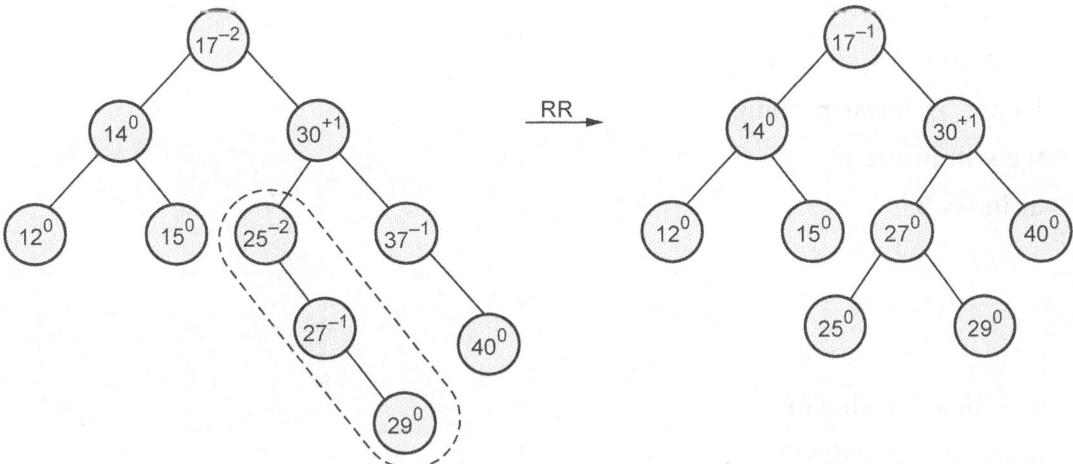

Step 11 : Insert 28

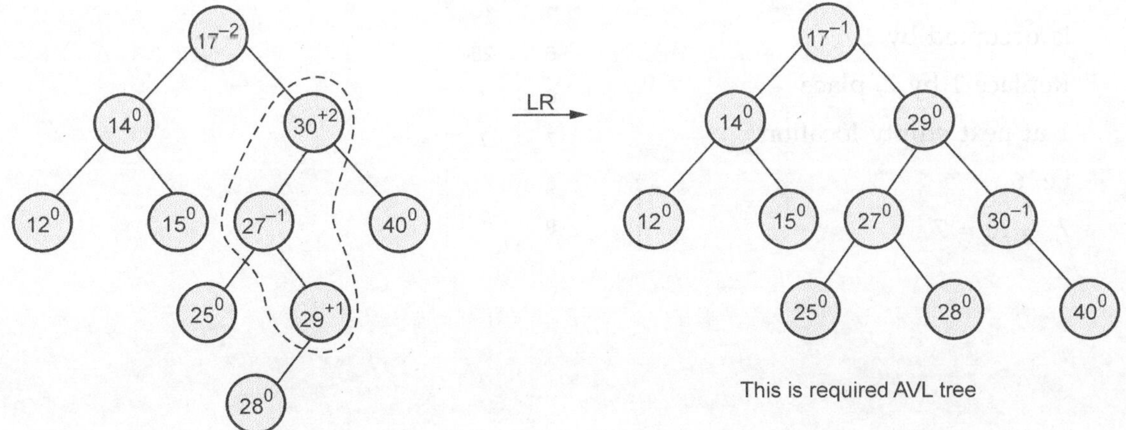

This is required AVL tree

OR

Q.4 A) *Write function for LL and LR rotation with respect to AVL tree.*
(Refer section 4.7.7) **[6]**

B) *Construct hash table of size 10 using linear probing with replacement strategy for collision resolution. The hash function is h(x) = x % 10. Calculate total numbers of comparisons required for searching. Consider slot per bucket is*
1, 25, 3, 21, 13, 1, 2, 7, 12, 4, 8 **[6]**

Ans. :

25 % 10 = 5

3 % 10 = 3

21 % 10 = 1

13 % 10 = 3 Collision

Hence by linear probing we will insert 13 at index 3.

Index	Value
0	
1	21
2	
3	3
4	13
5	25
6	
7	
8	
9	

1 % 10 = 1 collission

∴ Insert 1 at index 2

2 % 10 = 2. But index 2 is not empty it is occupied by 1.

Replace 1 by 2, place 1 at next empty location i.e. 6

7 % 10 = 7

Index	Value
0	
1	21
2	2
3	3
4	13
5	25
6	1
7	7
8	
9	

12 % 10 = 2 Again collision occurs. Hence place 12 at next empty location i.e. 8

Index	Value
0	
1	21
2	2
3	3
4	13
5	25
6	1
7	7
8	12
9	

4 % 10 = 4. But index 4 is occupied by 13. We will replace it by 4 and probe 13 at next empty location i.e. 9.

Index	Value
0	
1	21
2	2
3	3
4	4
5	25
6	1
7	7
8	12
9	13

8 % 10 = 8. But index 8 is already occuppied by element 12. Hence replace 12 by 8. Then probe 8 at next empty location

Index	Value
0	12
1	21
2	2
3	3
4	4
5	25
6	1
7	7
8	8
9	13

Q.5 A) *Construct a B tree of order 3 for the following data : 50, 30, 21, 90, 10, 13, 20, 70, 25, 92, 80.* **[7]**

Ans. : The order 3 means, 2 keys are allowed in each node.

Step 1 : Insert 50, 30

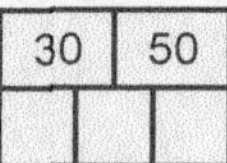

Step 2 : Insert 21. The sequence will become 21, (30), 50. Hence 30 will go up.

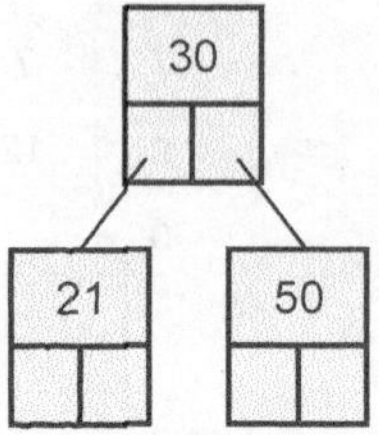

Step 3 : Insert 90, 10

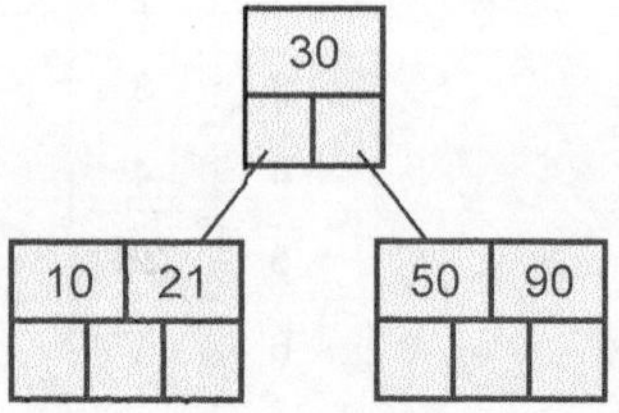

Step 4 : Insert 13. The sequence will become 10, (13), 21. The 13 will go up. The B-tree will be

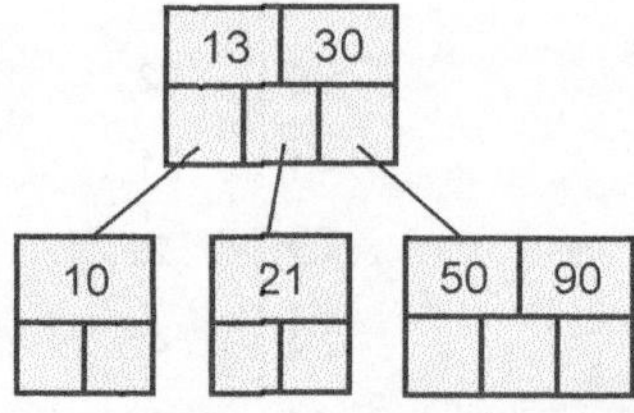

Step 5 : Insert 20

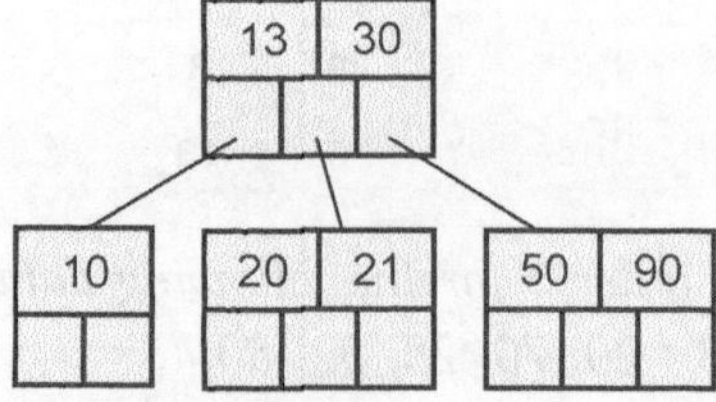

Step 6 : Insert 70. The sequence will become 50, (70), 90. The 70 will go up. Then the sequence will be 13, (30), 70. The 30 will go up.

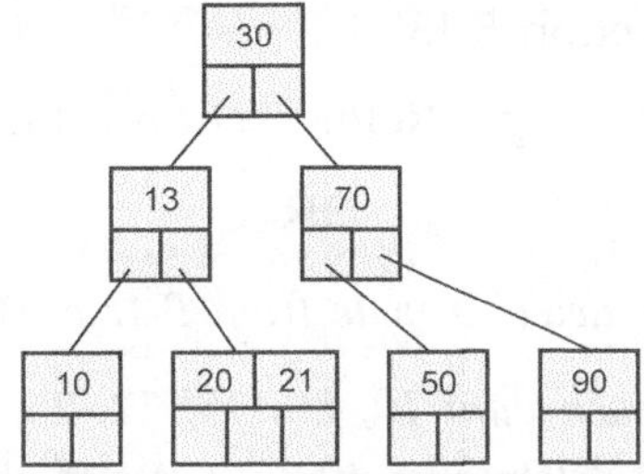

Step 7 : Insert 25. The sequence will become 20, (21), 25. The 21 will go up.

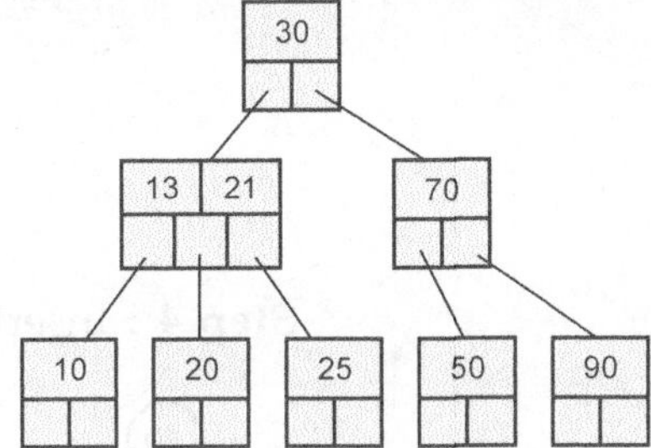

Step 8 : Insert 92.

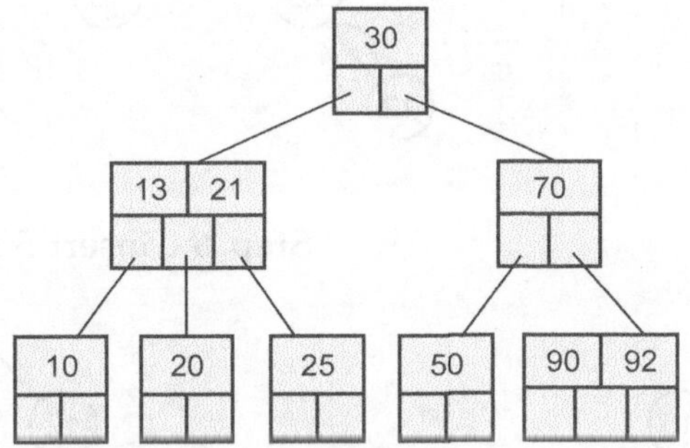

Step 9 : Insert 80. The sequence in the node will be 80, (90), 92. The 90 will go up. Finally the B-tree will be

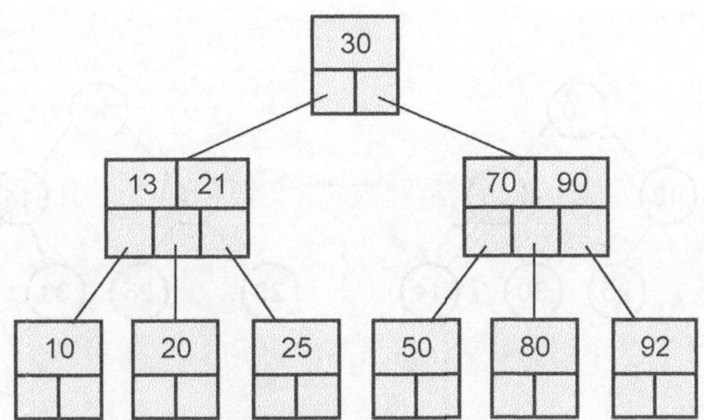

B) *What is max heap ? Write a function to insert an element in max heap. What is the time complexity of inserting an element in max heap ?* **[7]**

Ans. : **Max heap :** Refer section 5.13.

Insertion of an element in heap - Refer section 5.14.1

OR

Q.6 A) *Write an algorithm to delete a node from B-tree.* **(Refer section 5.5.6)** **[7]**

B) *Create min heap of given data 10, 20, 15, 12, 25, 30, 14, 2, 5, 4. After creation of min heap perform one delete operation on it and show the final min heap.* **[7]**

Ans. : **Step 1 :** Insert 10.

Step 2 : Insert 20

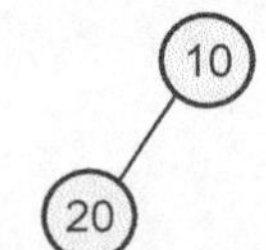

Step 3 : Insert 15.

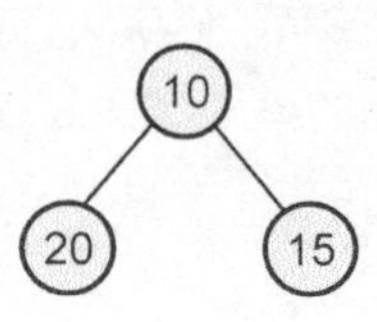

Step 4 : Insert 12

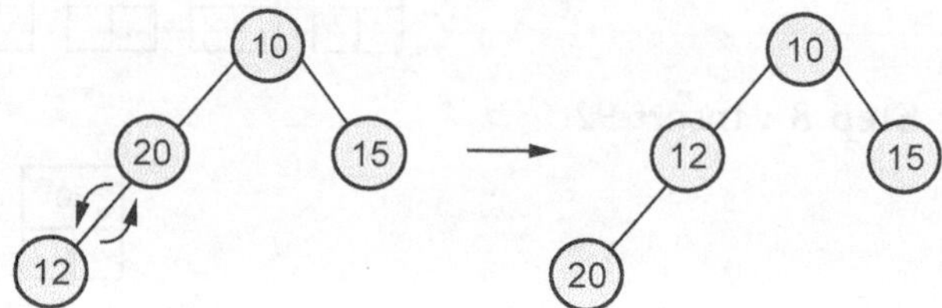

Step 5 : Insert 25.

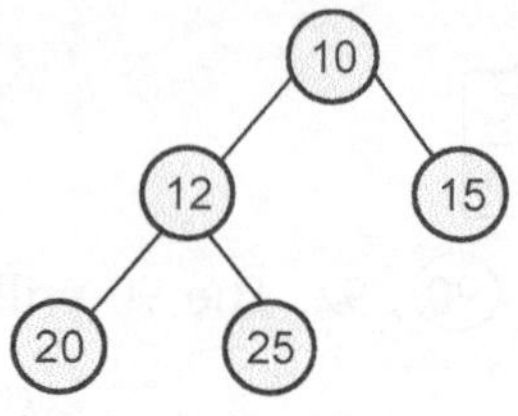

Step 6 : Insert 30

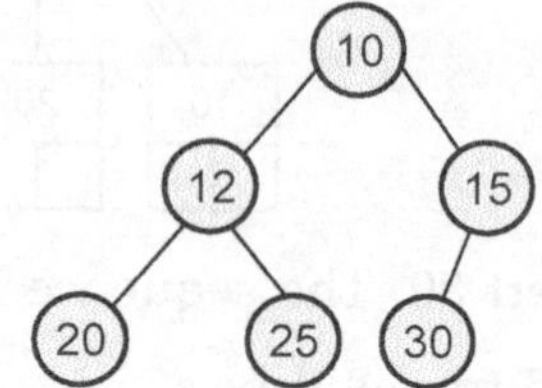

Step 7 : Insert 14.

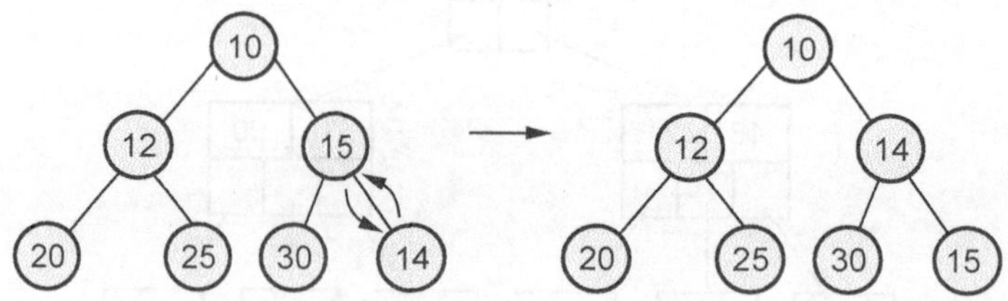

Step 8 : Insert 2

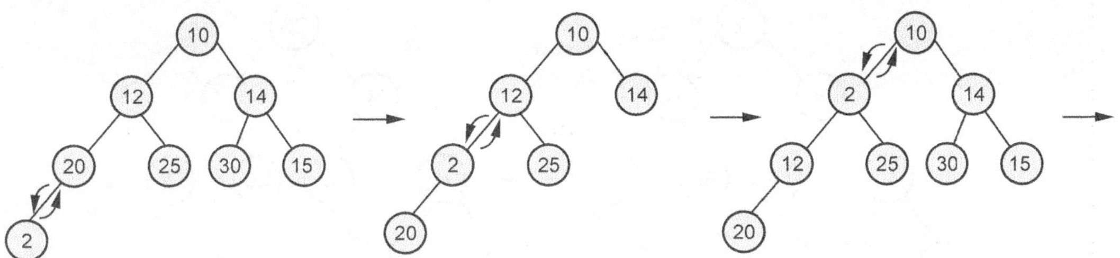

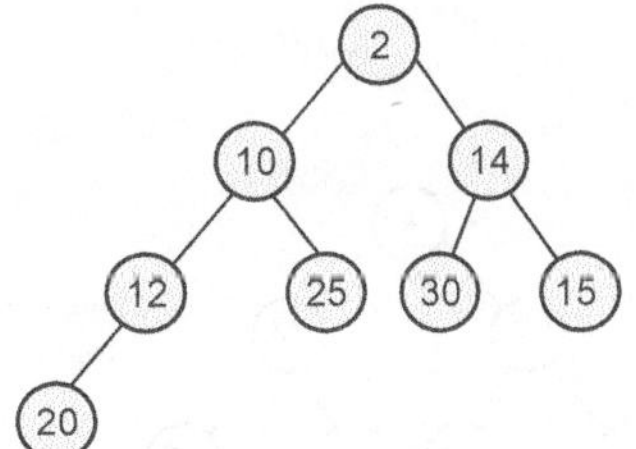

Step 9 : Insert 5

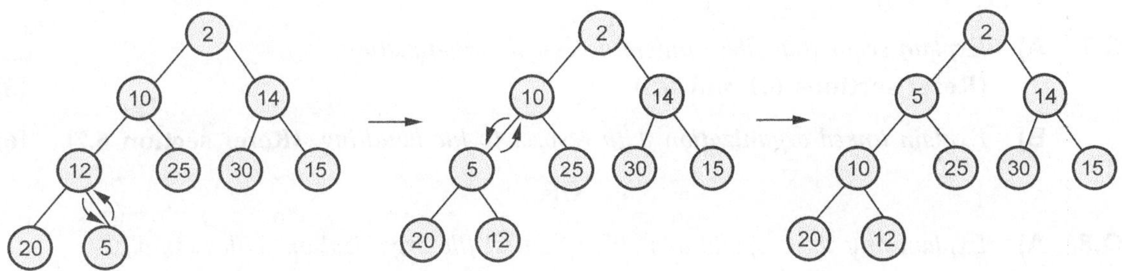

Step 10 : Insert 4.

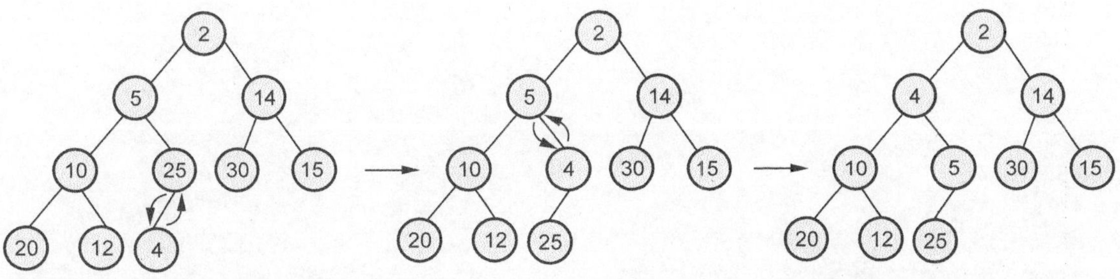

This is required min heap

Step 11 : One Deletion : The root node will be deleted.

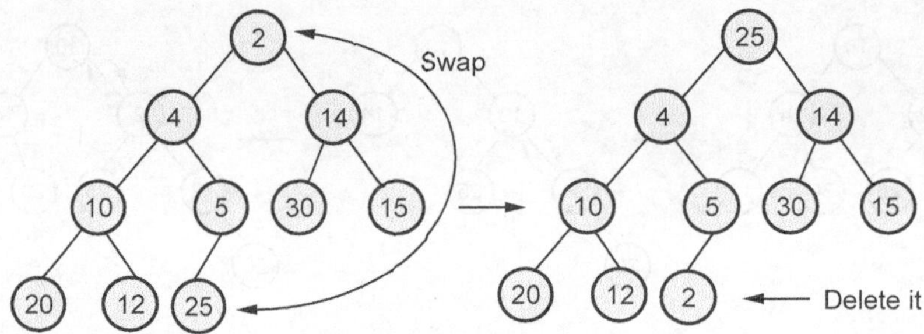

Step 12 : Now heapify to maintain min heap.

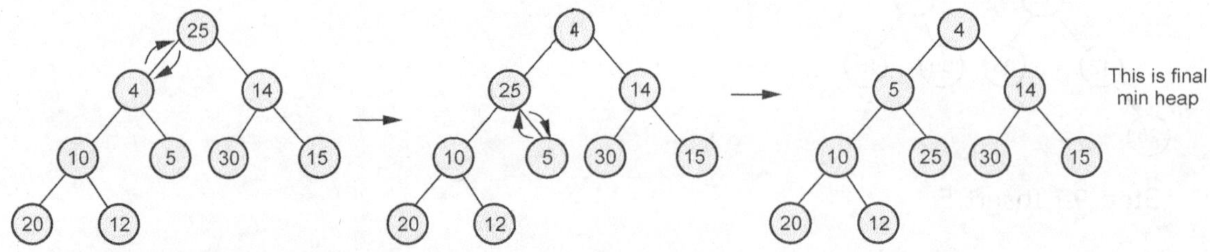

Q.7 A) *Explain sequential file, random access file organization.*
(Refer sections 6.4 and 6.5) **[6]**

B) *Explain linked organization with respect to file handling.* **(Refer section 6.7)** **[6]**

OR

Q.8 A) *Explain any three operations on sequential file organization with example.*
(Refer section 6.2) **[6]**

B) *Write a short note on external sort.* **(Refer section 6.8)** **[6]**

❑❑❑

December - 2017 **Advanced Data Structures** S.E. (Computer) Semester - II (Course - 2015)	**SPPU** **Solved Paper** **[5252]-568**

Time : Two Hours] **[Maximum Marks : 50**

N.B. :

i) Answer four questions.

ii) Figures to the right indicate full marks.

iii) Assume suitable data, if necessary.

Q.1 a) *From the given traversals construct the binary tree.* **[4]**

Pre-order : G, B, Q, A, C, K, F, P, D, E, R, H

In-order : Q, B, K, C, F, A, G, P, E, D, H, R

Ans. : Step 1 : The first element in preorder sequence is root or parent node. We will locate this element in inorder sequence. Here the first pre-order element is G. Now, in the inorder sequence the list left to G forms left subbranch and the sequence right to G forms the right sub branch.

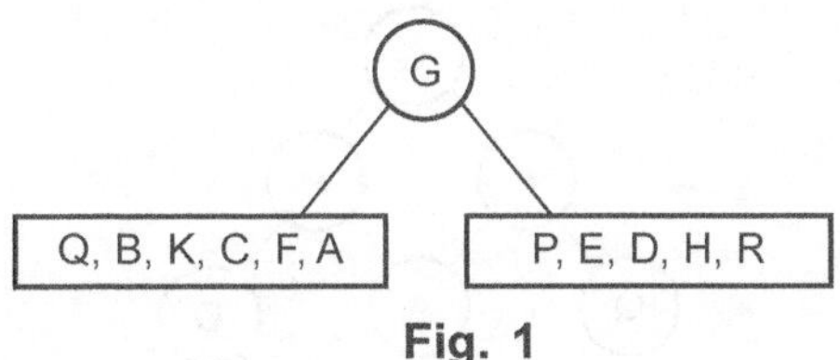

Fig. 1

We will repeat the above procedure for each sub-branch.

Step 2 :

Preorder : B, Q, A, C, K, F,

Inorder : Q, B, K, C, F A

G

B

Q

K, C, F, A

Preorder : P, D, E, R, H,

Inorder : P, E, D, H, R,

G

P

E, D, H,R

Step 3 :

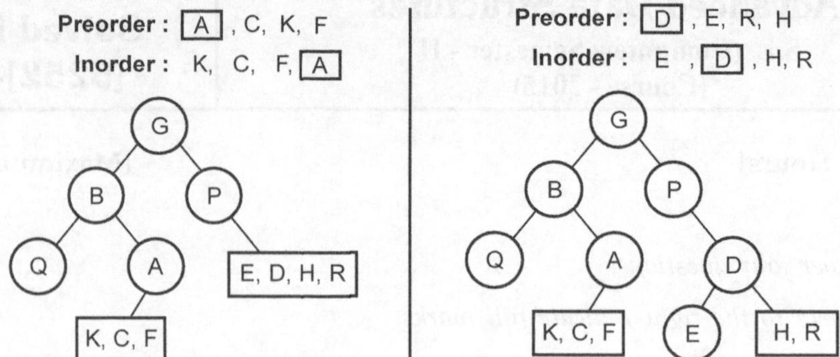

Step 4 :

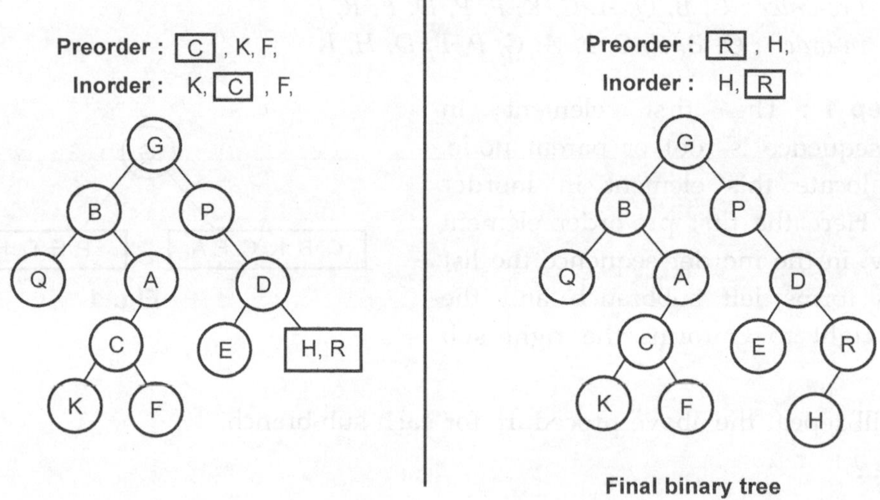

Final binary tree

b) *Find the MST for the graph given using Kruskals Algorithm and show all the steps.* **[4]**

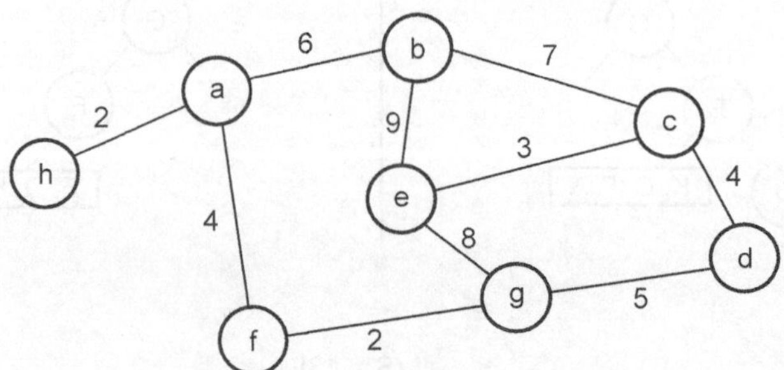

Fig. 2

Ans. :

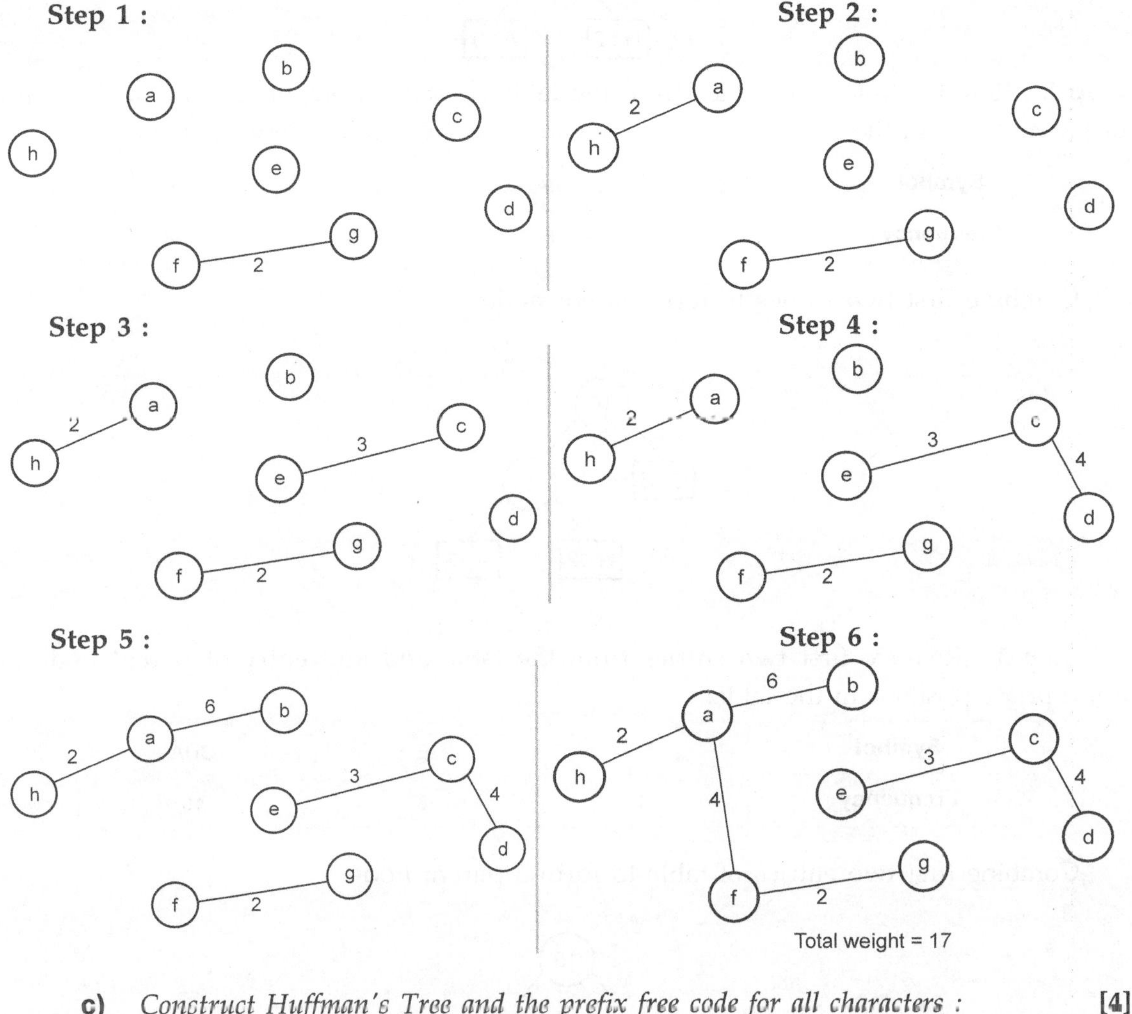

c) *Construct Huffman's Tree and the prefix free code for all characters :* **[4]**

Symbol	A	C	E	H	I
Frequency	3	5	8	2	7

Ans. : We will arrange the data in ascending order of **frequency.**

Step 1 : Now combine first two least values from table and create a parent node.

Symbol	H	A	C	I	E
Frequency	2	3	5	7	8

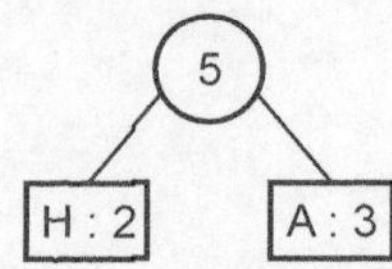

Step 2 : Remove first two entries from the table present in Step 1. Then add the entry of parent node in the table to maintain sorting order of the elements in table.

Symbol	C	HA	I	E
Frequency	5	5	7	8

Combine first two values to form parent node.

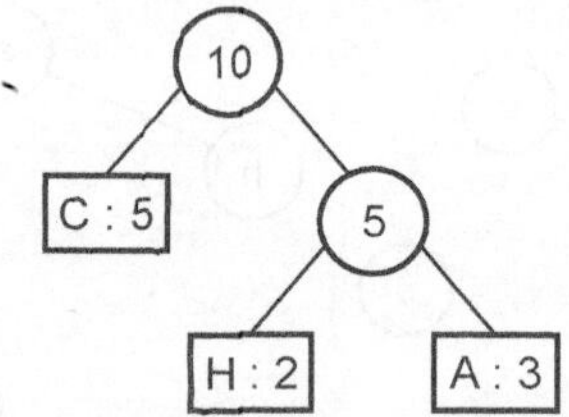

Step 3 : Remove first two entries from the table and add entry of parent node at appropriate position in the table.

Symbol	I	E	CHA
Frequency	7	8	10

Combine first two entries of table to form a parent node.

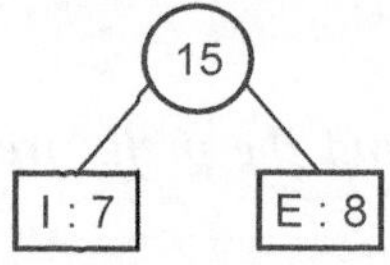

Step 4 : Remove first two entries from the table and add entry of parent node at appropriate position in the table.

Symbol	CHA	IE
Frequency	10	15

Combine two entries of the table to form parent node.

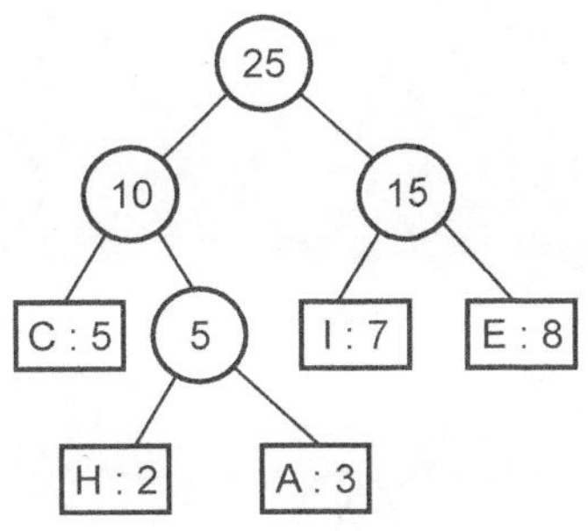

This is Huffman's tree

For encoding, the left branch is encoded as 0 and right branch as 1.

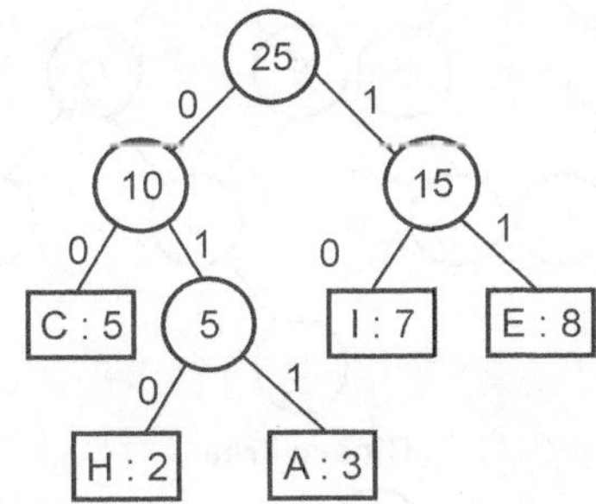

Symbol	A	C	E	H	I
Prefix Code	011	00	11	010	00

OR

Q.2 a) *For the binary tree represented as an array, perform in-order threading on the tree :* **[4]**

1	2	3	4	5	6	7	8	9	10	11	12	13	14	15	16	17	18	19	20	21	22	23	24	25	26	27	28
A	B	C	D	E	F	G		H	I				J	K													L

Ans. : The root node is placed at index 1.

The formula for obtaining left and right child are

$$\text{Left (n)} = 2n$$

$$\text{Right (n)} = 2n + 1$$

$\therefore$ Left (1) i.e. left child of A = $2 \times 1 = 2$ i.e. B

Right (1) i.e. right child of A = $2 \times 1 + 1 = 3$ i.e. C

In this way we could build the tree.

Continuing in this way

Continuing in this way

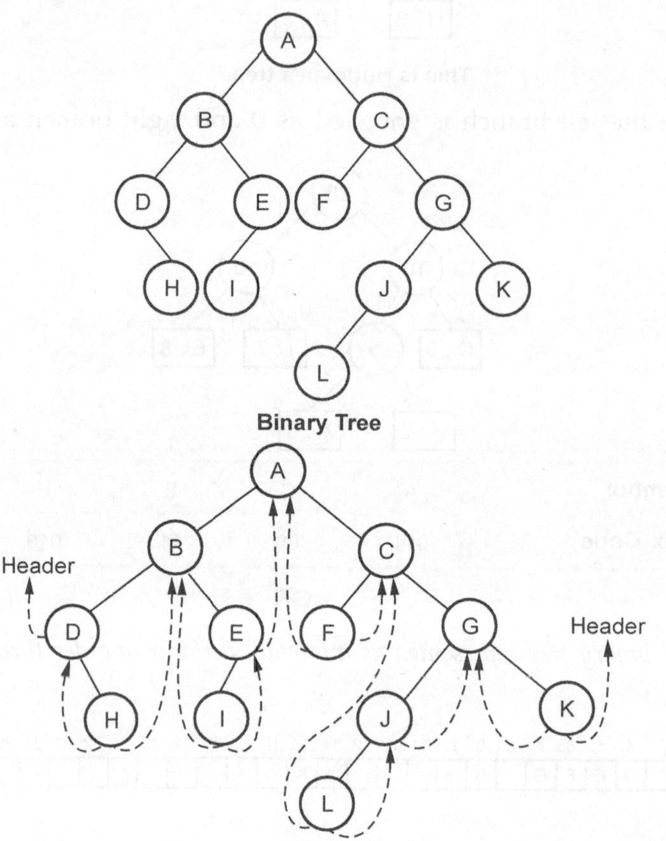

In- order threading on the tree

b) *Define DFS and BFS for a graph. Show BFS and DFS for the following graph with starting vertex as 1.* **[4]**

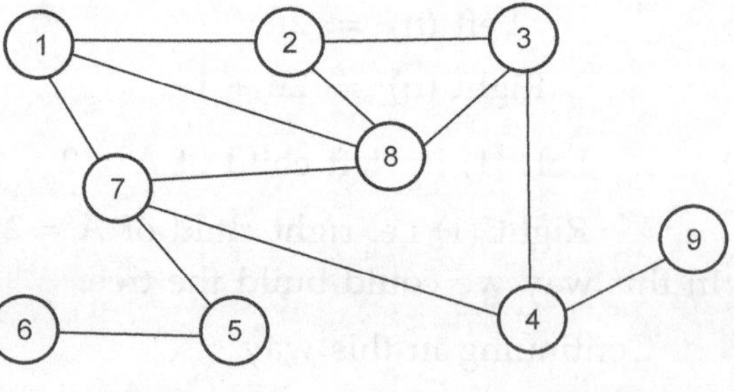

Fig. 3

Ans. : **BFS** : In BFS we start from some vertex and find all the adjacent vertices of it. This process will be repeated for all the vertices so that the vertices lying on same breadth get printed.

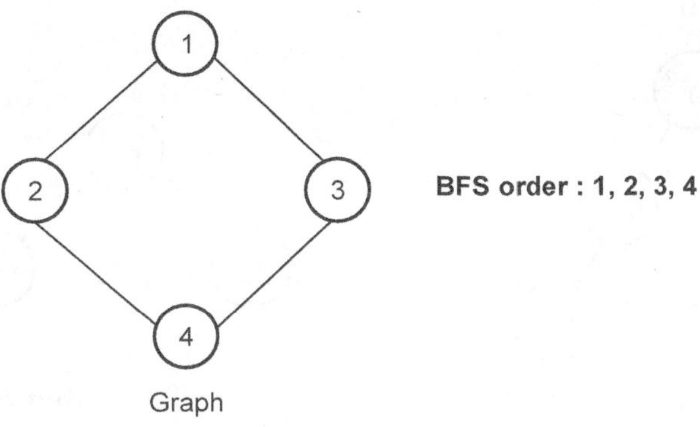

BFS order : 1, 2, 3, 4

Fig. 4

DFS : • In depth first search traversal we start from one vertex and traverse the path as deeply as we can go. When there is no vertex further, we traverse back and search for unvisited vertex.

- The DFS will be (if we start from vertex 0) 0 - 1 - 2 - 3 - 4
- The DFS will be (if we start from vertex 3) 3 - 4 - 0 - 1 - 2

For example

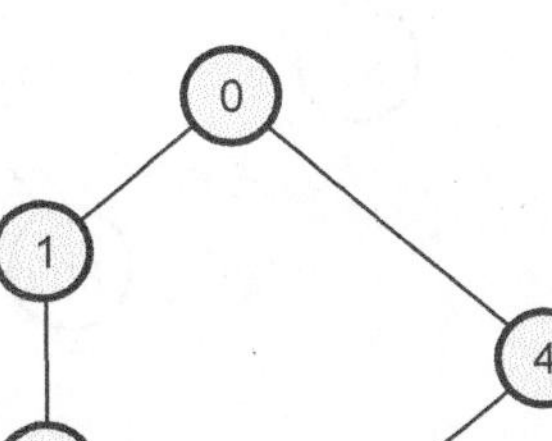

For example -

BFS sequence for given example :

1, 2, 7, 8, 3, 4, 5, 9, 6

DFS sequence for given example :

1, 2, 3, 4, 7, 5, 6, 9, 8

c) *Write pseudo-code for performing level order traversal of a binary tree.* **(Refer section 1.7.2)** **[4]**

Q.3 a) *Obtain AVL trees for the following data :* **[6]**

30, 50, 110, 80, 40, 10, 120, 60, 20, 70, 100, 90

Ans. :

Step 1 :

Step 2 :

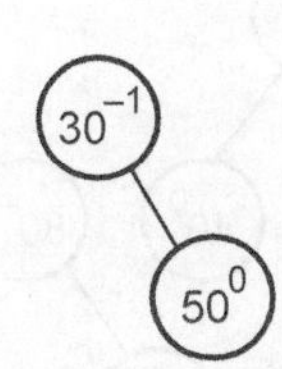

Step 3 : Insert 110

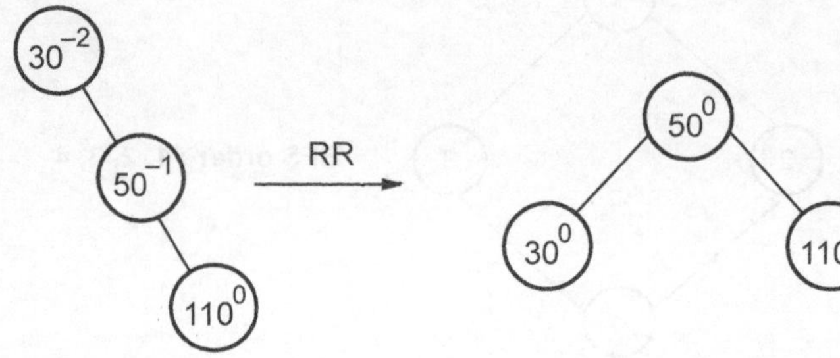

Step 4 : Insert 80

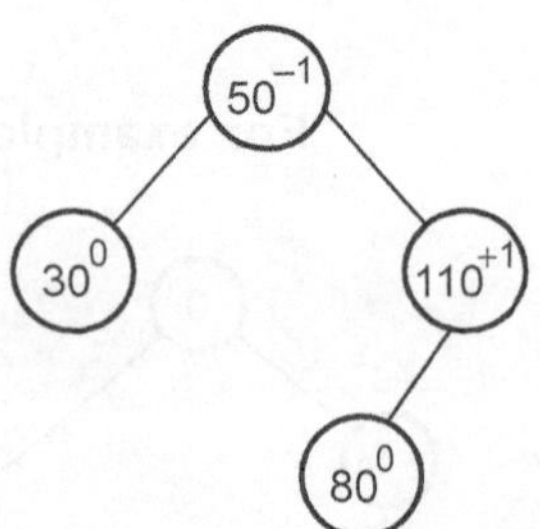

Step 5 : Insert 40

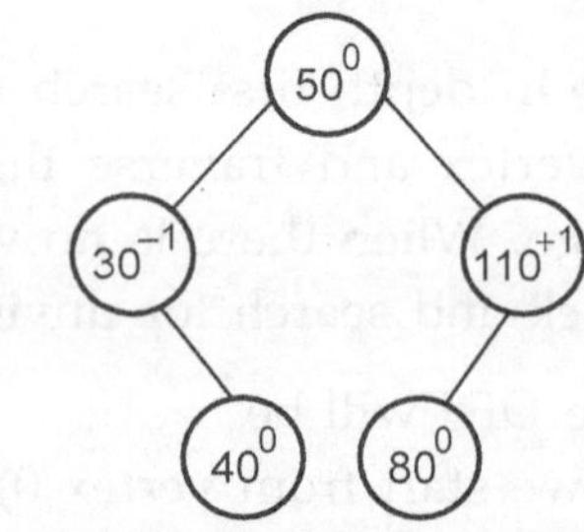

Step 6 : Insert 10

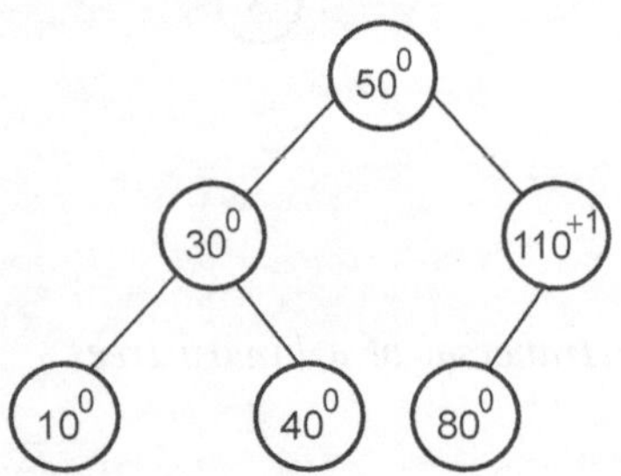

Step 7 : Insert 120

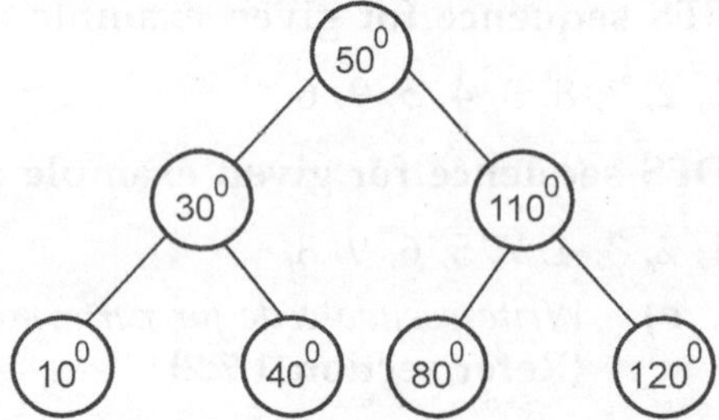

Step 8 : Insert 60

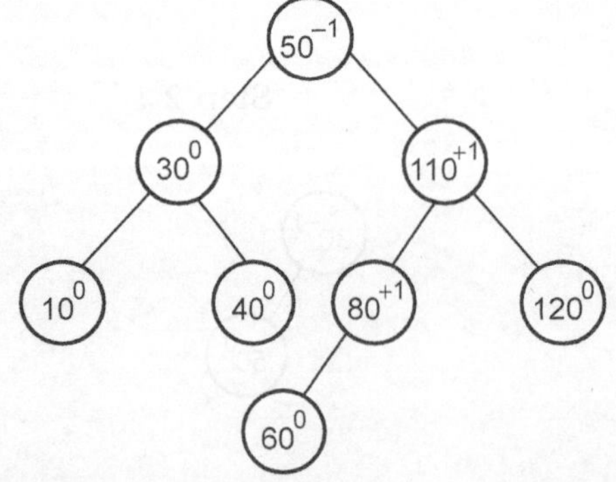

Step 9 : Insert 20

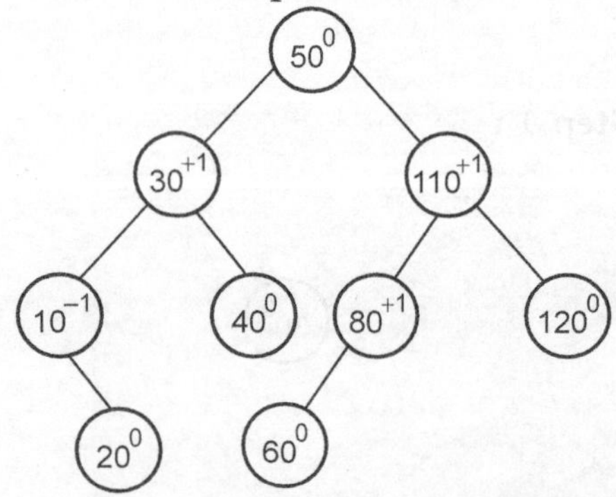

Step 10 : Insert 70

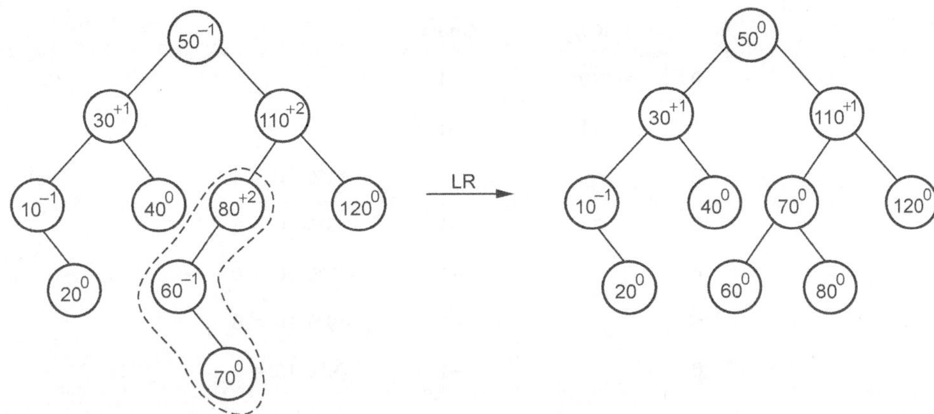

Step 11 : Insert 100

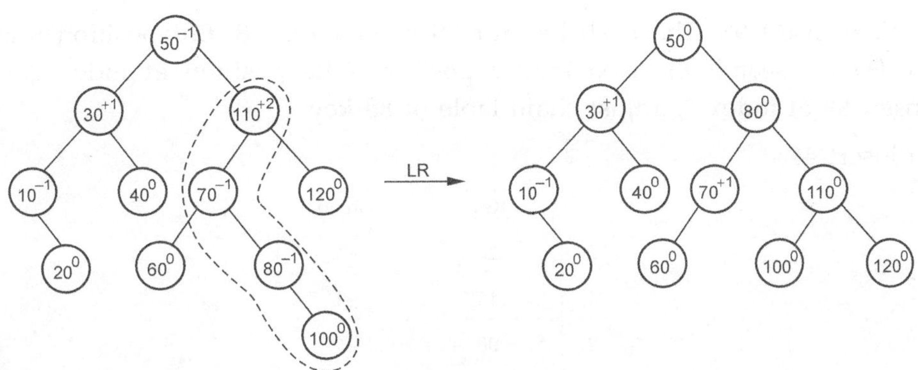

Step 12 : Insert 90

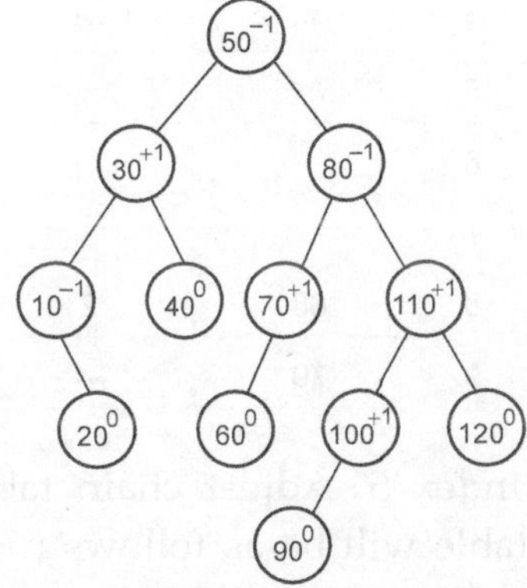

This is required AVL Tree

b) *For the given set of values.* **[6]**

11, 33, 20, 88, 79, 98, 44, 68, 66, 22 Create a hash table with size 10 and resolve collision using chaining with replacement and without replacement. Use the modulus Hash function. (key % size).

Ans. : **Step 1 :** Without replacement

	Key	Chain	
0	20	–1	
1	11	–1	
2		–1	11% 10 = 1
3	33	–1	33% 10 = 3
4		–1	20% 10 = 0
5		–1	88% 10 = 8
6		–1	79% 10 = 9
7		–1	

Step 2 : Now insert 98. The hash key for 98 is 98% 10 = 8. But position 8 is already occupied. So we search for next empty position. The position at index 2 is empty. Hence insert 98 at index 2, adjust chain table of 88 key.

Then insert 44.

	Key	Chain
0	20	–1
1	11	–1
2	98	–1
3	33	–1
4	44	–1
5		
6		
7		
8	88	2
9	79	–1

Step 3 : Insert 68 at position index 5. Adjust chain table. Insert 66 at index 6. Now insert 22 at index 7. The hash table will be as follows :

0	20	–1
1	11	–1
2	98	5
3	33	–1

4	44	–1
5	68	7
6	66	–1
7	22	–1
8	88	2
9	79	–1

Chaining with replacement : In this technique we place the actual element to its belonging position. If the position of element is occupied by an element which does not belong to that corresponding location then we make replacement.

Step 1 : Insert 11, 33, 20, 88, 79

	Key	Chain
0	20	–1
1	11	–1
2		
3	33	–1
4		
5		
6		
7		
8	88	–1
9	79	–1

Step 2 : Now to insert 98, the collision occurs. 98 % 10 = 8. At index 8 we have stored element 88 which deserves that place, hence we cannot replace 88 by 98. Hence by linear probing. we can insert 98 at location 2. Then insert 44, and 68, 66. Adjust the chain table accordingly.

	Key	Chain
0	20	–1
1	11	–1
2	98	5
3	33	–1
4	44	–1

5	68	–1
6	66	–1
7		–1
8	88	2
9	79	–1

Step 3 : Now to insert 22 we get 22 % 10 = 2. At the index 2 element 98 is stored which does not belong to location 2. Hence replace it by 22 and adjust chain table appropriately.

	Key	Chain
0	20	–1
1	11	–1
2	22	–1
3	33	–1
4	44	–1
5	68	–1
6	66	–1
7	98	5
8	88	7
9	79	–1

OR

Q.4 a) *Find the Optimal Binary Search Tree for the :* **[6]**

Identifier set {a1, a2, a3} = {do, if, while}

where n = 3 and probabilities of successful search as {p1, p2, p3} = {0.5, 0.1, 0.05} and probability of unsuccessful search as {q0, q1, q2, q3} = {0.15, 0.1, 0.05, 0.05}.

(Refer example 4.6.1)

b) *What is hash function ? What are characteristics of good hash function? Explain the different types of hash functions ?*

(Refer sections 3.2 and 3.3) **[6]**

Q.5 a) *Insert the following keys to a 5-ways B-tree :* **[6]**

3, 7, 9, 23, 45, 1, 5, 14, 25, 24, 13, 11, 8, 19, 4, 31, 35, 56

Ans. : The order 5 means at the most 4 keys are allowed.

Step 1 : Insert 3, 7, 9, 23

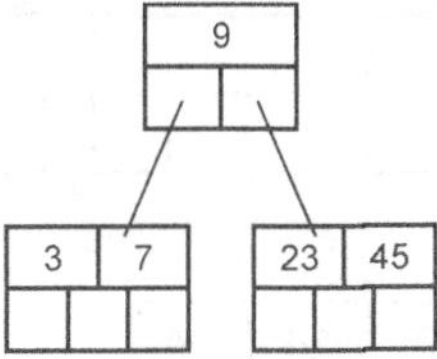

Step 2 : If we insert 45 then the sequence becomes 3, 7, (9), 23, 45. The 9 will go up

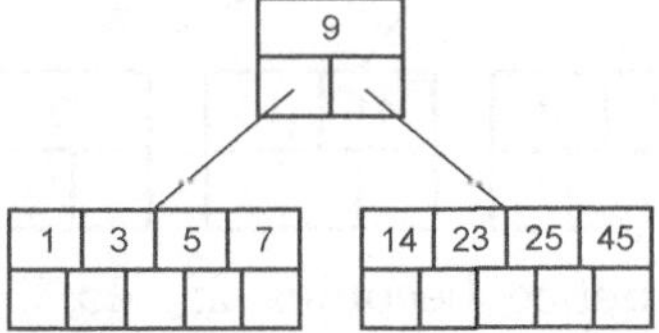

Step 3 : Insert 1, 5, 14, 25.

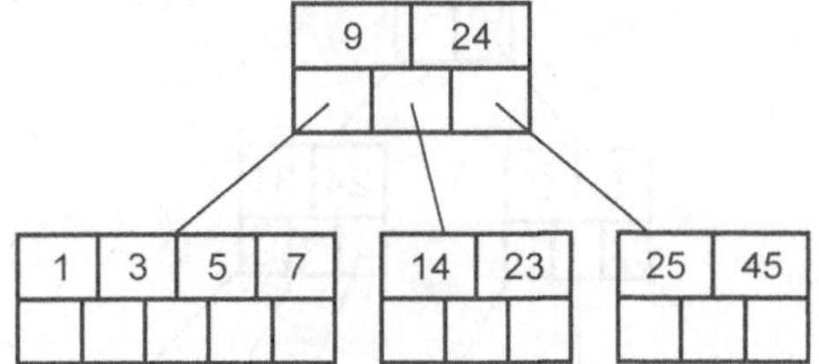

Step 4 : If we insert 24, then the sequence becomes 14, 23, (24), 25, 45.

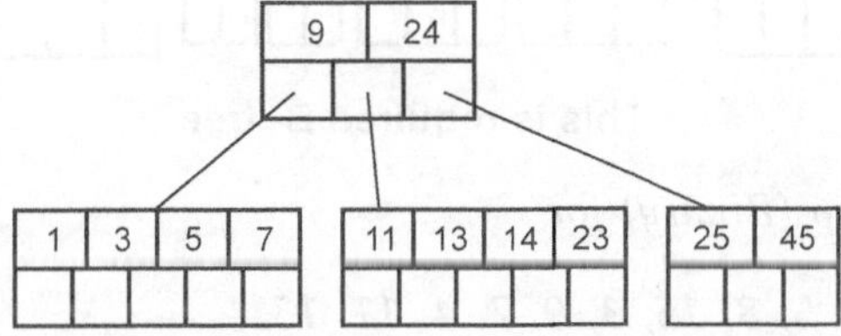

Step 5 : Insert 13, 11.

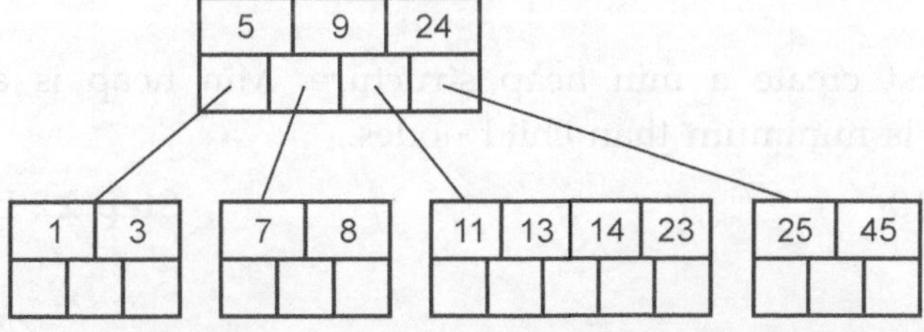

Step 6 : Insert 8. The sequence becomes 1, 3, (5), 7, 8. The 5 will go up.

Step 7 : Insert 19. The sequence will be 11, 13, (14), 19, 23. The 14 will go up.

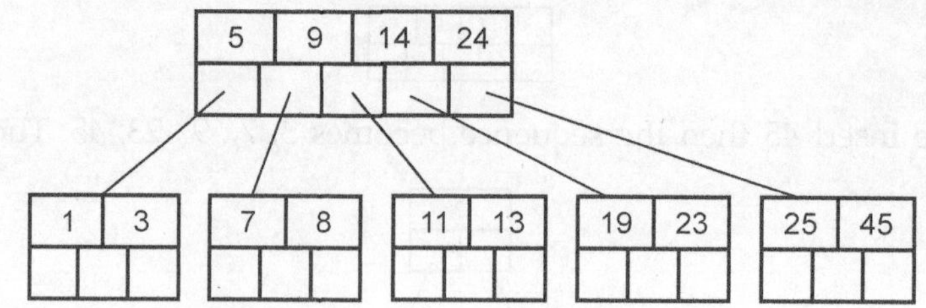

Step 8 : Insert 4, 31 and 35.

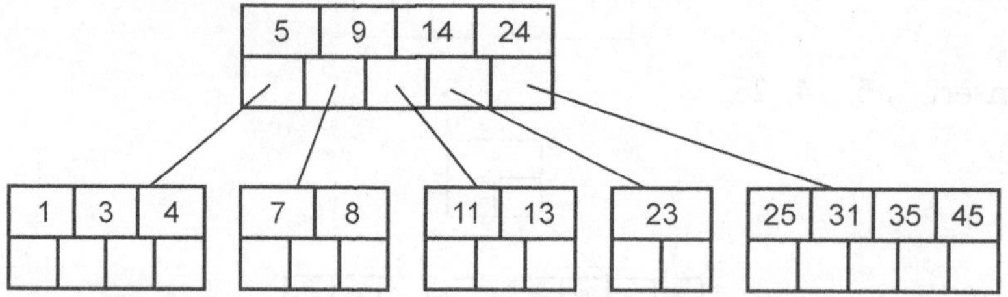

Step 9 : Insert 56. The sequence becomes 25, 45, (31) , 35, 56. The 31 will go up. Then the sequence **becomes** 5, 9, (14), 24, 31. The 14 will go up. Finally B-tree will be

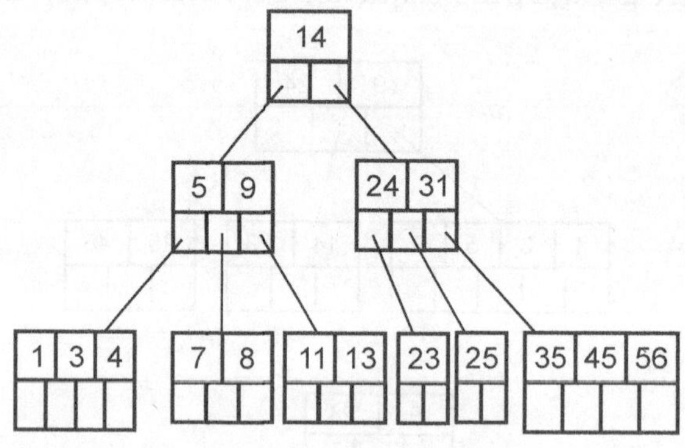

This is required B- tree

b) *Create Min Heap (Binary) for* **[6]**

10, 12, 1, 14, 6, 5, 8, 15, 3, 9, 7, 4, 11, 13

After creating Min Heap delete element 1 from Heap and repair it.

Then insert element 20 and show final result.

Ans. : We will first create a min heap structure. Min heap is a heap structure in which parent node is minimum than child nodes.

Step 1 : Insert 10

Step 2 : Insert 12

Step 3 : Insert 1

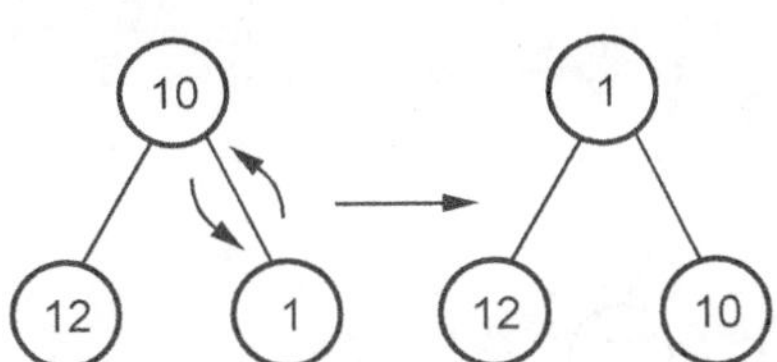

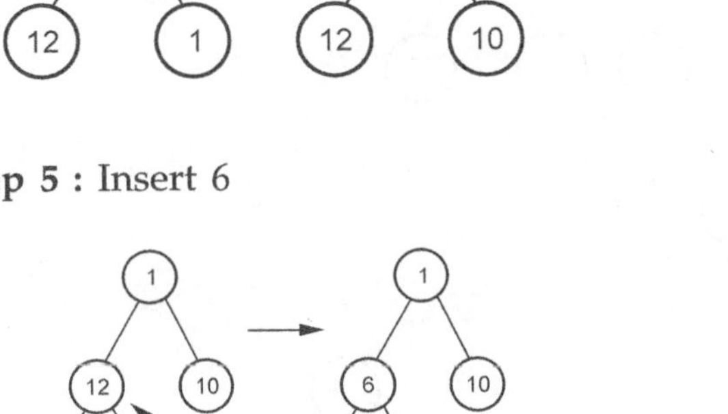

Step 4 : Insert 14

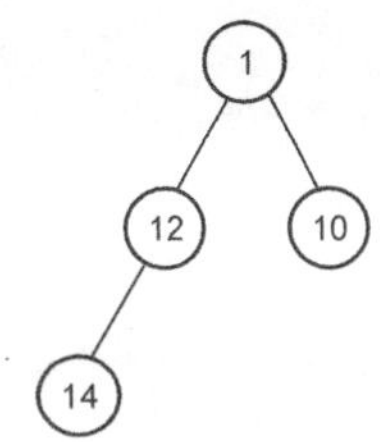

Step 5 : Insert 6

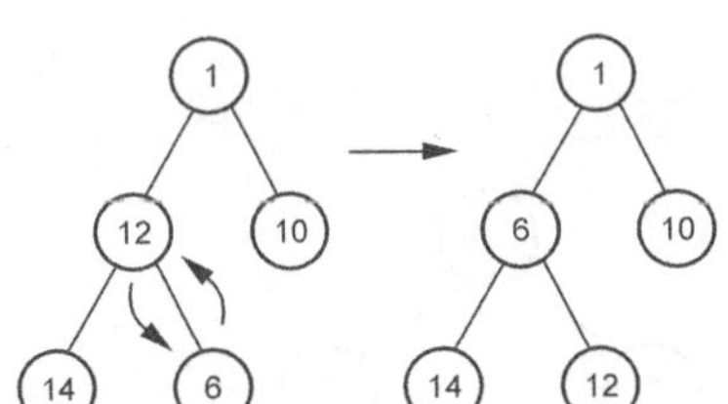

Step 6 : Insert 5

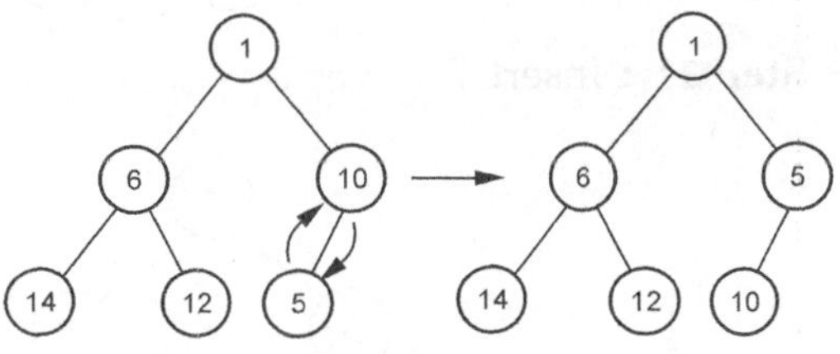

Step 7 : Insert 8

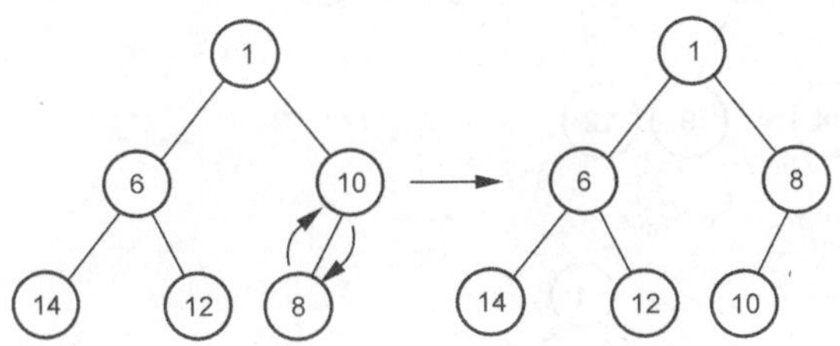

Step 8 : Insert 15

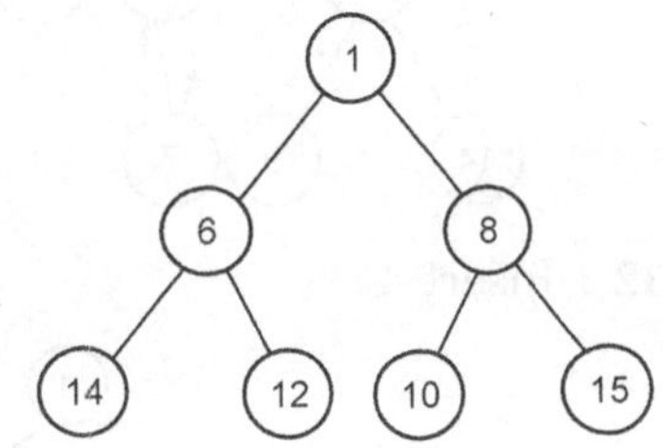

Step 9 : Insert 3

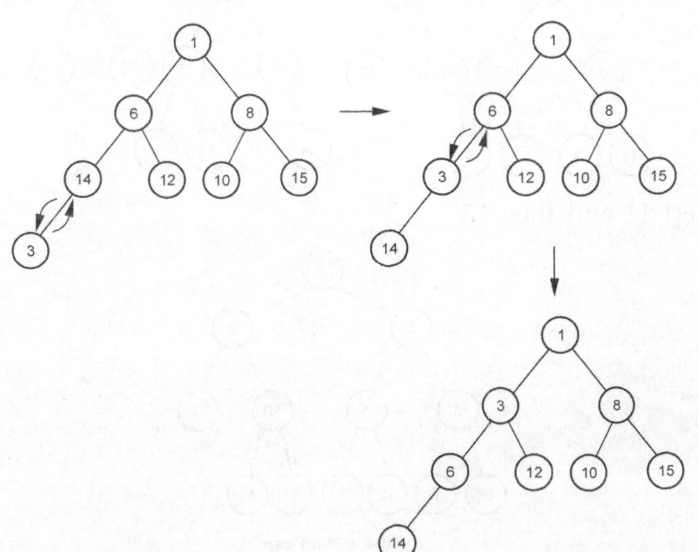

Step 10 : Insert 9

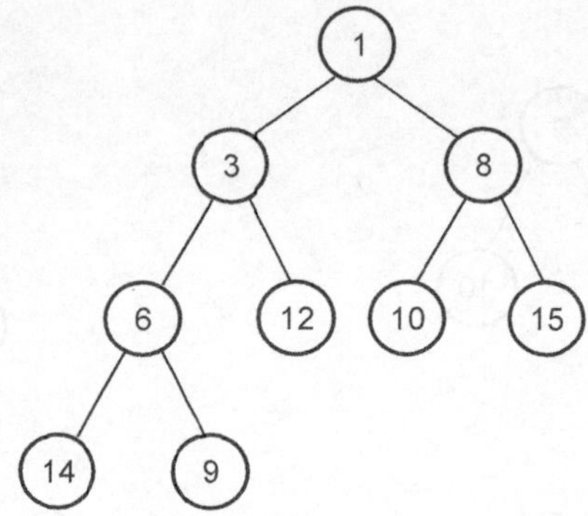

Step 11 : Insert 7

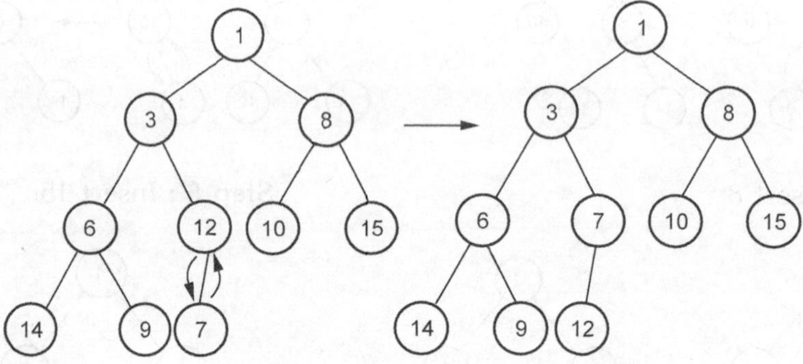

Step 12 : Insert 4

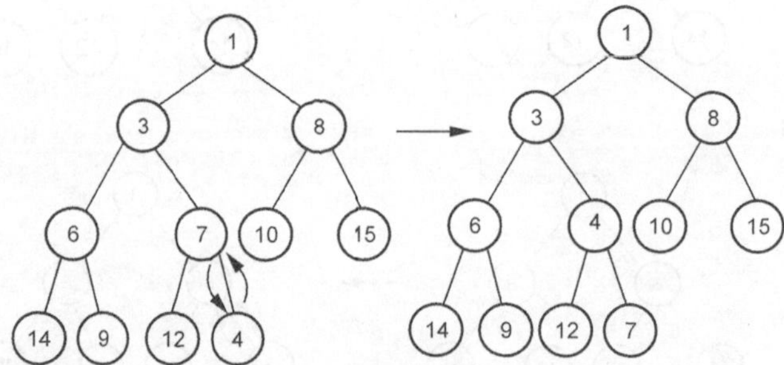

Step 13 : Insert 11 and then 13

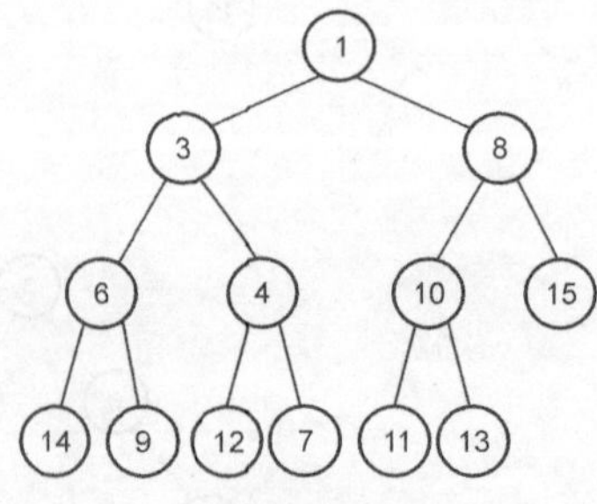

This is Min Heap

Step 14 : Delete 1 from heap

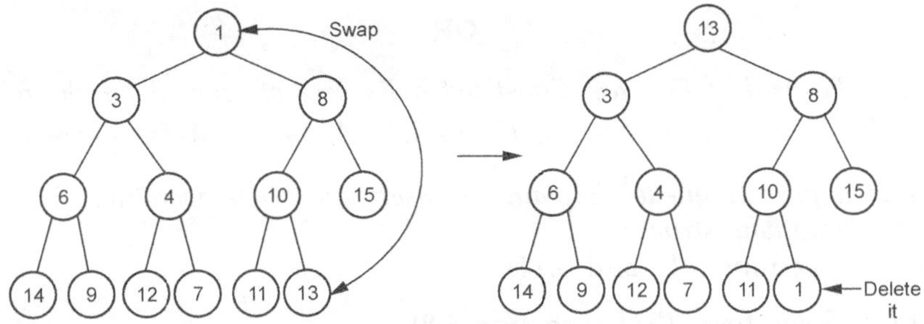

After deleting 1 we need to heapify the tree.

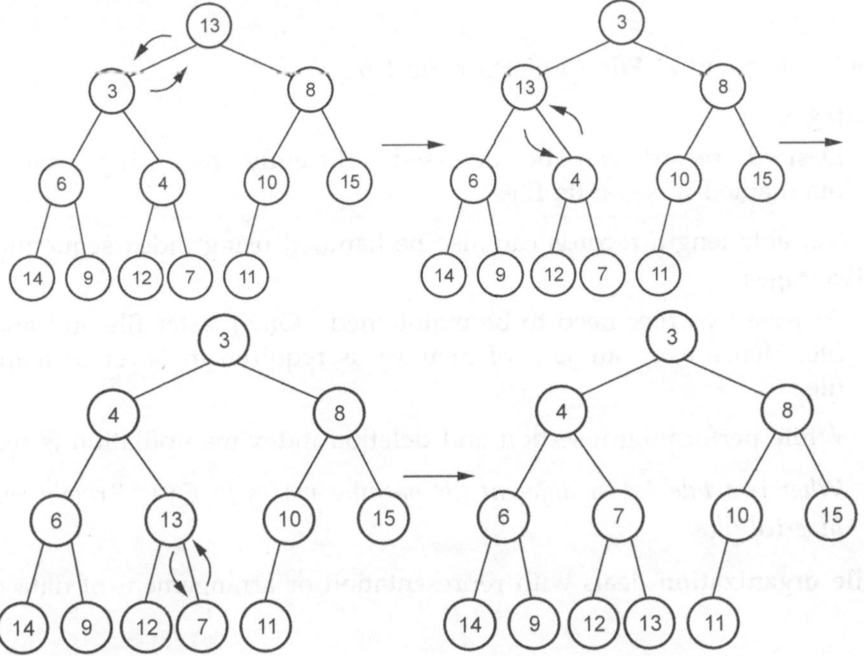

Step 15 : Insert 20

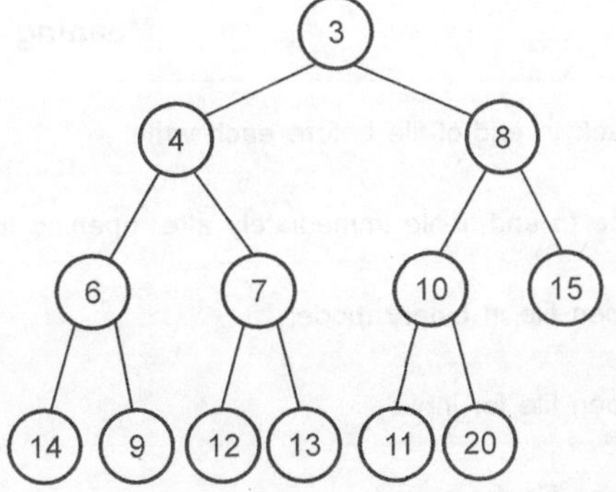

Final Heap

c) *Define Red-Black Trees.* **(Refer section 5.9)** **[2]**

OR

Q.6 a) *State the need of B+ tree. Construct a B+ tree of order 5 for the following data : 30, 31, 23, 32, 22, 28, 24, 29, 15, 26, 27, 34, 39, 36* **(Refer example 5.6.2)** **[6]**

b) *What is priority queue? Explain the insert and delete operations for priority queues using heap data structure.*
(Refer sections 5.13 and 5.14) **[6]**

c) *Define Splay trees.* **(Refer section 5.8)** **[2]**

Q.7 a) *What is index sequential file organization? State its advantages and disadvantages.* **[6]**

Ans. : Index Sequential File : Refer section 6.6

Advantages

1. Desired record can be accessed efficiently by using index which is maintained in separate file.
2. Variable length records can also be handled using index sequential file.

Disadvantages

1. At least two files need to be maintained : One master file and another index file. Hence extra amount of memory is required in order to maintain index file.
2. While performing insertion and deletion index manipulation is required.

b) *What is a File ? List different file opening modes in C++. Explain the concept of inverted files.* **[6]**

Ans. : File organization deals with representation or arrangement of data on external storage.

Various modes in C++

Mode	Meaning
ios::app	Seek to end-of-file before each write.
ios::ate	See to end-of-file immediately after opening file.
ios::binary	Open file in binary mode.
ios::in	Open file for input
ios::out	Open file for output

Inverted File : Refer section 6.7 (3)

OR

Q.8 a) *Write a C++ program to create a file. Insert records in the file by opening file in append mode. Search for a specific record entered by user.* **[6]**

Ans. :

C++ Program :

```
#include<iostream.h>
#include<iomanip.h>
#include<fstream.h>
#include<string.h>
#include<conio.h>
#include<stdlib.h>
class EMP_CLASS
{
 typedef struct EMPLOYEE
 {
        char name[10];
        int emp_id;
        int salary;
 }Rec;
 Rec Records;
            public:
            void Create();
            void Display();
            void Update();
            void Delete();
            void Append();
            int Search();
};
void EMP_CLASS::Create()
{
        char ch='y';
        fstream seqfile;
        seqfile.open("EMP.DAT",ios::in|ios::out|ios::binary);
        do
        {
            cout<<"\n Enter Name: ";
            cin>>Records.name;
```

```
            cout<<"\n Enter Emp_ID: ";
            cin>>Records.emp_id;
            cout<<"\n Enter Salary: ";
            cin>>Records.salary;
            //then write the record containing this data in the file
            seqfile.write((char*)&Records,sizeof(Records));
            cout<<"\nDo you want to add more records?";
            cin>>ch;
        }while(ch=='y');
        seqfile.close();
}
void EMP_CLASS::Append()
{
        fstream seqfile;
        seqfile.open("EMP.DAT",ios::ate|ios::in|ios::out|ios::binary);
        seqfile.seekg(0,ios::beg);
        int i=0;
        while(seqfile.read((char *)&Records,sizeof(Records)))
        {
                i++;//going through all the records
                        // for reaching at the end of the file
        }
        //instead of above while loop
        //we can also use seqfile.seekg(0,ios::end)
        //for reaching at the end of the file
        seqfile.clear();//turning off EOF flag
        cout<<"\n Enter the record for appending";
        cout<<"\nName: ";cin>>Records.name;
        cout<<"\nEmp_ID: ";cin>>Records.emp_id;
        cout<<"\nSalary: ";cin>>Records.salary;
        seqfile.write((char*)&Records,sizeof(Records));
        seqfile.seekg(0);//reposition to start(optional)
        seqfile.close();
        cout<<"\n The record is Appended!!!";
}
int EMP_CLASS::Search()
{
        fstream seqfile;
        int id,pos;
```

```
	cout<<"\n Enter the Emp_ID for searching the record ";
	cin>>id;
	seqfile.open("EMP.DAT",ios::ate|ios::in|ios::out|ios::binary);
	seqfile.seekg(0,ios::beg);
	pos=-1;
	int i=0;
	while(seqfile.read((char *)&Records,sizeof(Records)))
	{
		if(id==Records.emp_id)
		{
			pos=i;
			break;
		}
		i++;
	}
	return pos;
}
```

b) *Compare index sequential and direct access files.* **[6]**

Ans. :

Sr. No.	Index Sequential File	Direct Access File
1.	Desired record can be obtained using the index which is maintained in a separate file.	Desired record can be obtained using the hash key. This hash key is returned by some hash function.
2.	Insertion and deletion operations can be performed by simple index manipulation.	On insertion or deletion of records, collision may occur. Hence collision handling techniques are required.
3.	Variable length records are allowed.	Record length must be fixed.
4.	Index key is obtained using primary key of the record.	Hash key is obtained by passing primary key of record to hash function.
5.	Records are arranged sequentially in the master file.	Records can be arranged randomly. This arrangement is influenced by hash key.
6.	It is less efficient.	It is more efficient

May - 2018 **Advanced Data Structures** **S.E. (Computer) Semester - II** **(Course - 2015)**	**SPPU** **Solved Paper** **[5352]-568**

Time : Two Hours] **[Maximum Marks : 50**

N.B. : - *i) Answer to the questions (Q. No. 1 or Q. No. 2, Q. No. 3 or Q. No. 4, Q. No. 5 or Q. No. 6, Q. No. 7 or Q. No. 8).*

ii) Assume suitable data, if necessary.

iii) Draw neat labeled diagram whenever necessary.

iv) Figures to the right indicate full marks.

Q.1 a) *Write an algorithm to delete node from BST.* **(Refer section 1.10)** **[6]**

b) *Write an algorithm for preorder traversal of binary tree and give suitable example.* **(Refer section 1.6)** **[6]**

OR

Q.2 a) *Draw any directed graph with minimum 6 it nodes and represent graph using adjacency matrix, adjacency list, adjacency multilist and inverse adjacency list.* **[6]**

Ans. : The required directed graph is as shown below.

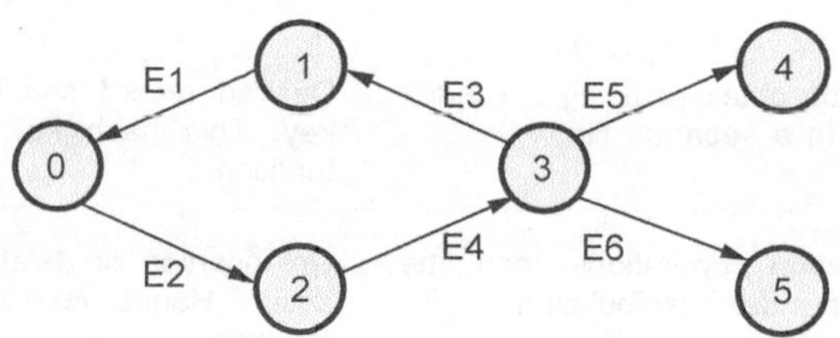

Fig. 1

i) The Adjacency matrix is

	0	1	2	3	4	5
0	0	0	1	0	0	0
1	1	0	0	0	0	0
2	0	0	0	1	0	0
3	0	1	0	0	1	1
4	0	0	0	0	0	0
5	0	0	0	0	0	0

ii) The Adjacency list is

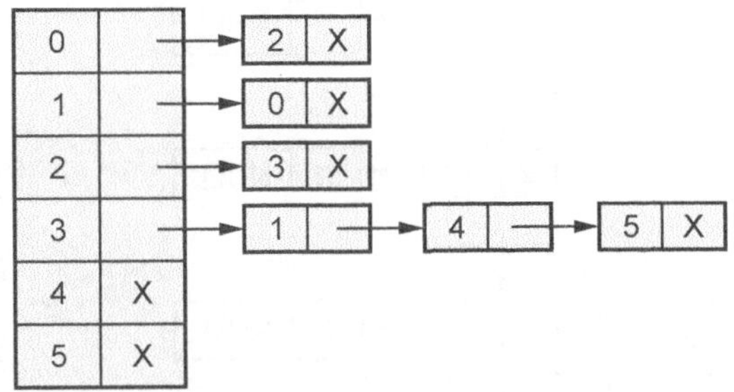

Edge 1		1	0	Edge 3	NULL	edge (0, 1)
Edge 2		0	2	NULL	NULL	edge (0, 2)
Edge 3		3	1	Edge 4	NULL	edge (3, 1)
Edge 4		2	3	NULL	NULL	edge (2, 3)
Edge 5		3	4	NULL	NULL	edge (3, 4)
Edge 6		3	5	NULL	NULL	edge (3, 5)

Fig. 2 Adjacency multilist

In above multilist various edges are represented. In the node of edge 1 the edge (1,0) is represented. For vertex 1, the incident edge is E3. Hence, we enter 'Edge 3' in the fourth field. For vertex 0, the incident edge is E1 itself. So we need not have to mention this self defining edge. So we enter NULL in fifth field.

Again for Edge 2, for vertex 0 the incident edge is 1 - 0 (Edge 1) but this edge is already defined. Hence, we mention NULL in 4th field of Edge 2.

The inverse adjacency list is a list in which only incoming edge to a vertex is represented.

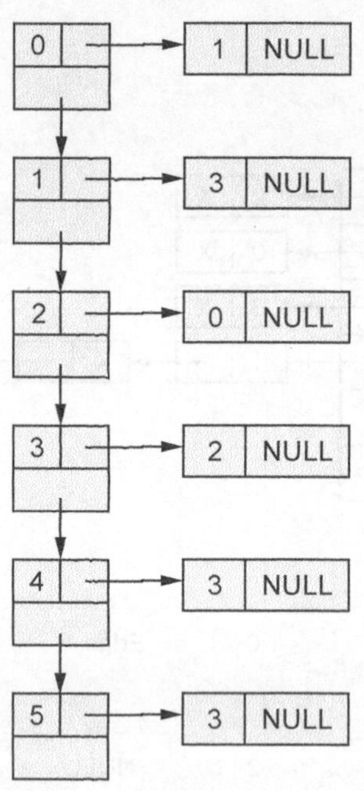

Fig. 3

b) *Consider the graph represented by following adjacency matrix.*

	1	2	3	4	5	6
1	0	3	1	6	0	0
2	3	0	5	0	3	0
3	1	5	0	5	6	4
4	6	0	5	0	0	2
5	0	3	6	0	0	6
6	0	0	2	2	6	0

And find minimum spanning tree of this graph using Prim's algorithm. **[6]**

Ans. : The graph can be drawn as follows :

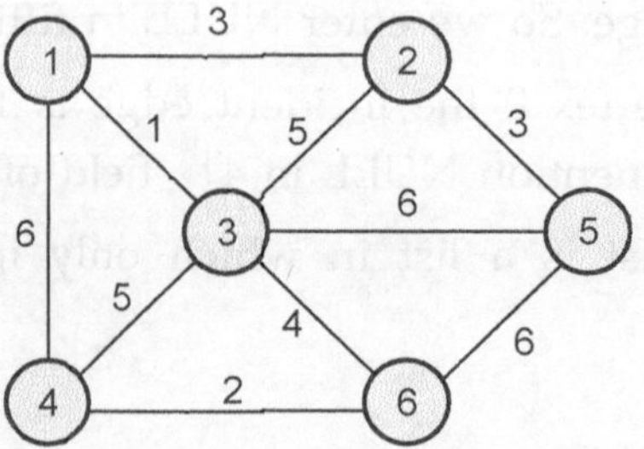

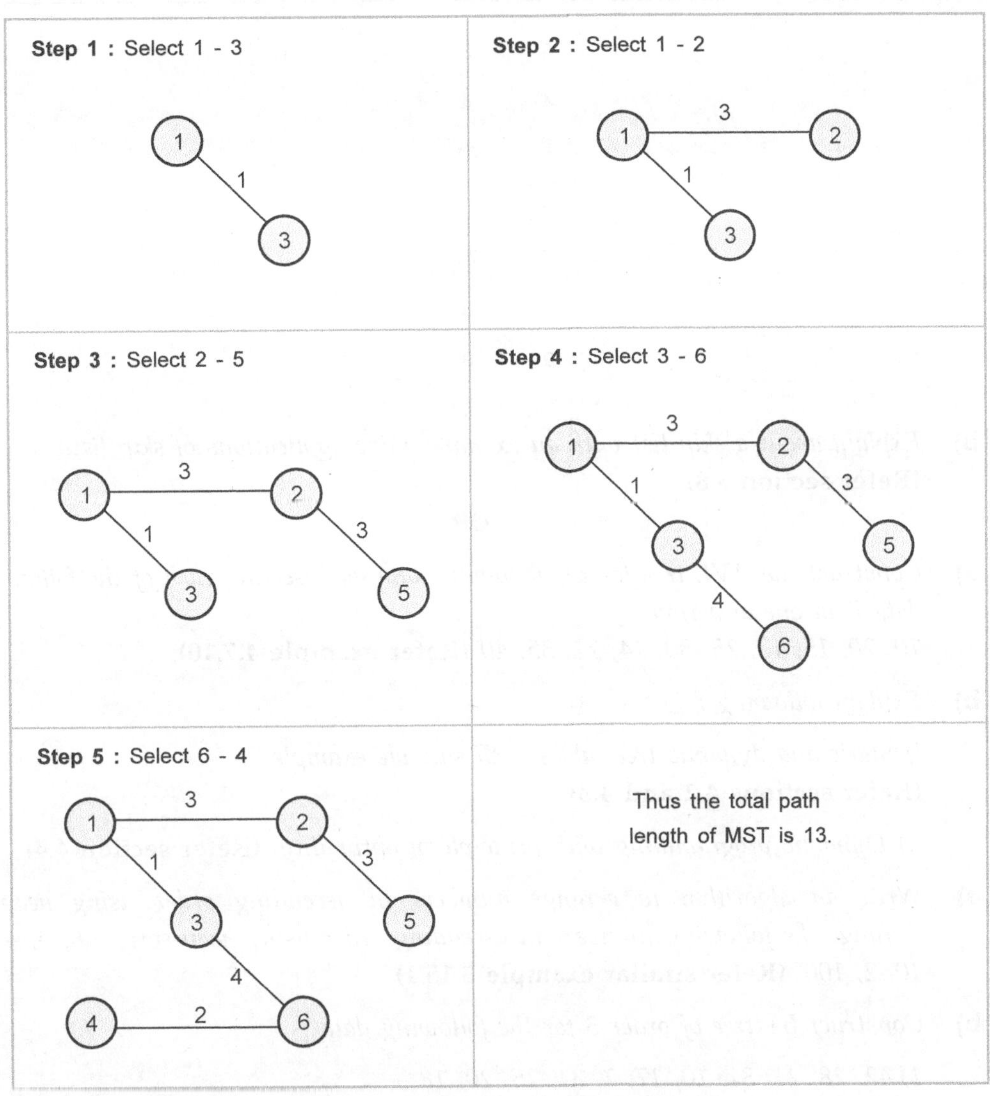

Q.3 a) *Construct hash table of size 10 using linear probing without replacement strategy for collision resolution. The hash function is h(x) = x % 10. Consider slot per bucket is 1.*

31, 3, 4, 21, 61, 6, 71, 8, 9, 25 **[6]**

Ans. : The hash table after inserting elements using linear probing without replacement.

0	25
1	31
2	21

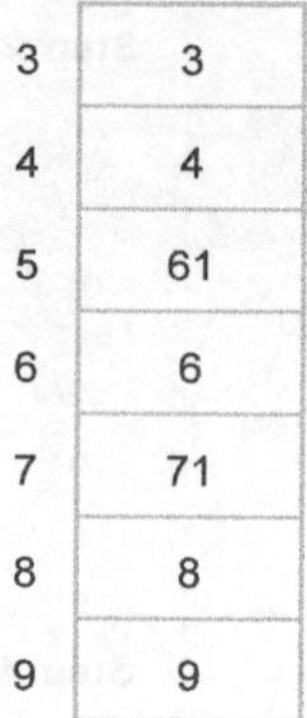

3	3
4	4
5	61
6	6
7	71
8	8
9	9

b) *Explain about a skip list with an example. Give applications of skip list.* **(Refer section 3.8)** **[6]**

OR

Q.4 a) *Construct the AVL tree for the following data by inserting each of the following data item one at a time*

10, 20, 15, 12, 25, 30, 14, 22, 35, 40 **(Refer example 4.7.10)** **[6]**

b) *Explain following :*

i) Static and dynamic tree tables with suitable example. **(Refer sections 4.2 and 4.3)** **[3]**

ii) Dynamic programming with principle of optimality. **(Refer section 4.4)** **[3]**

Q.5 a) *Write an algorithm to arrange numbers in ascending order using heap sort. Arrange the following numbers in ascending order using heap sort : 48, 0, – 1, 82, 10, 2, 100.* **(Refer similar example 5.15.1)** **[7]**

b) *Construct B+ tree of order 3 for the following data :* **[7]**

1, 42, 28, 21, 31, 10, 17, 7, 31, 25, 20, 18

Ans. : The B + tree of order 3 means at the most 2 key values are allowed in a tree.

Step 1 : Insert 1, 42

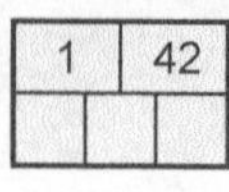

Step 2 : Insert 28. The sequence becomes 1, (28), 42. The 28 will go up.

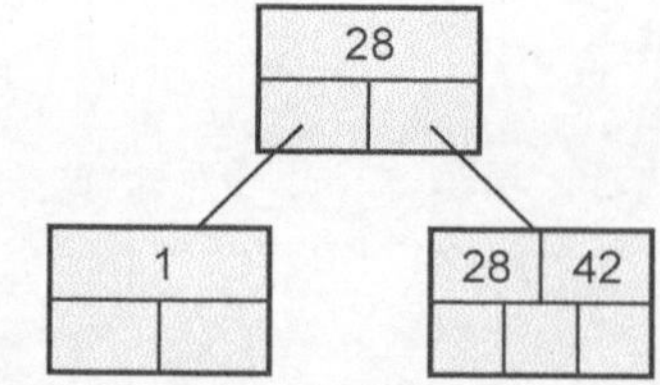

Step 3 : Insert 21.

Step 4 : Insert 31. The sequence becomes 28, (31), 42. The 31 will go up.

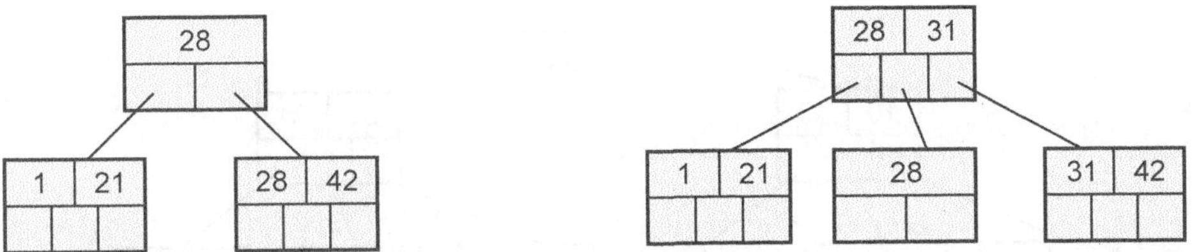

Step 5 : Insert 10. The sequence becomes 1, (10), 21. The 10 will go up. Now the sequence becomes 10, (28), 31. The 28 will go up.

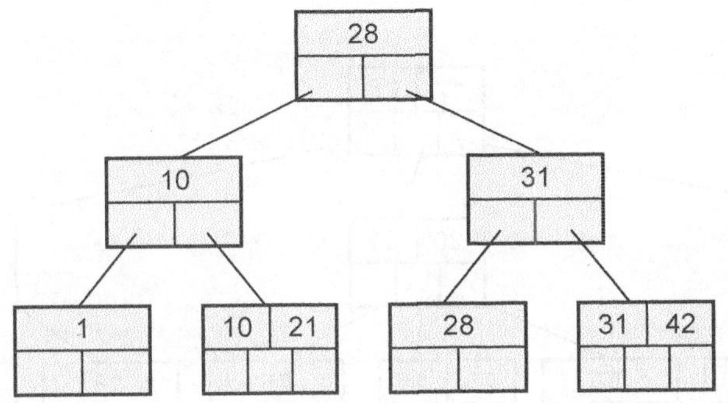

Step 6 : Insert 17. The sequence becomes 10, (17), 21. The 17 will go up.

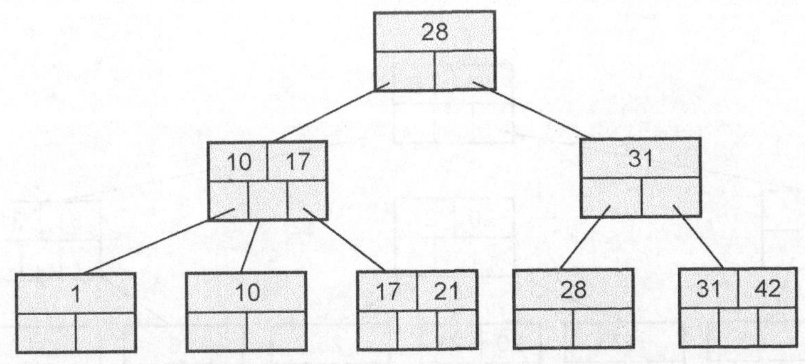

Step 7 : Insert 7. Insert 31. The sequence becomes 31, (31), 42. The 31 will go up.

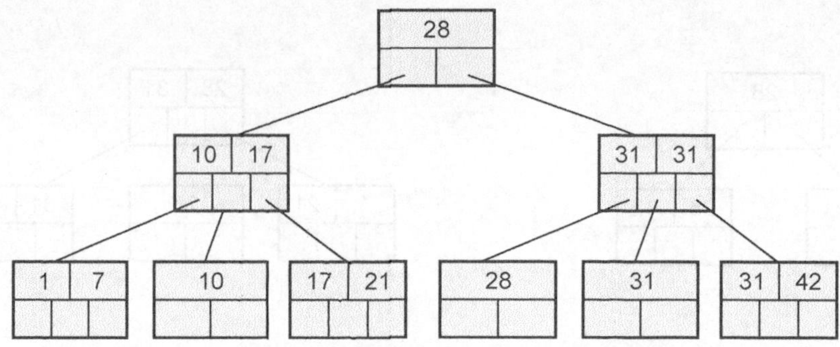

Step 8 : Insert 25. The sequence becomes 17, (21), 25. The 21 will go up. The sequence becomes 10, 17, 21. Now 17 will go up.

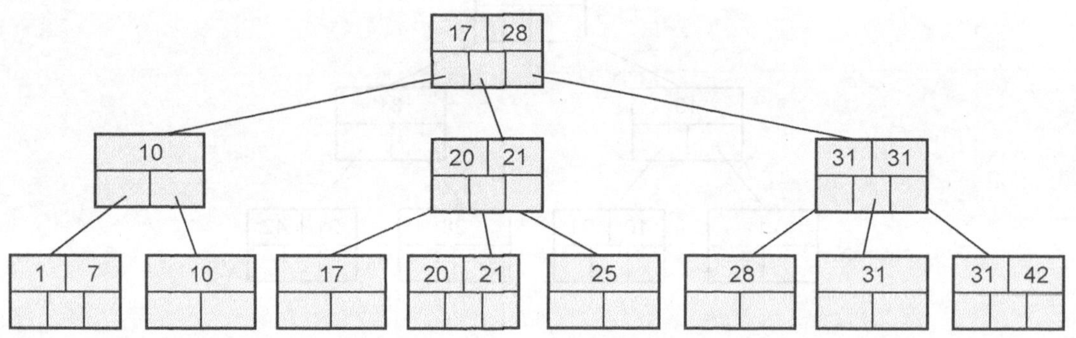

Step 9 : Insert 20. The sequence becomes 17, (20), 21. The 20 will go up.

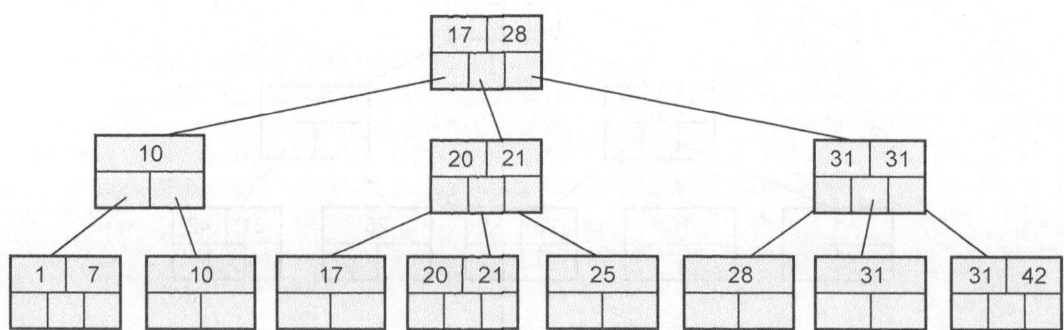

Step 10 : Insert 18

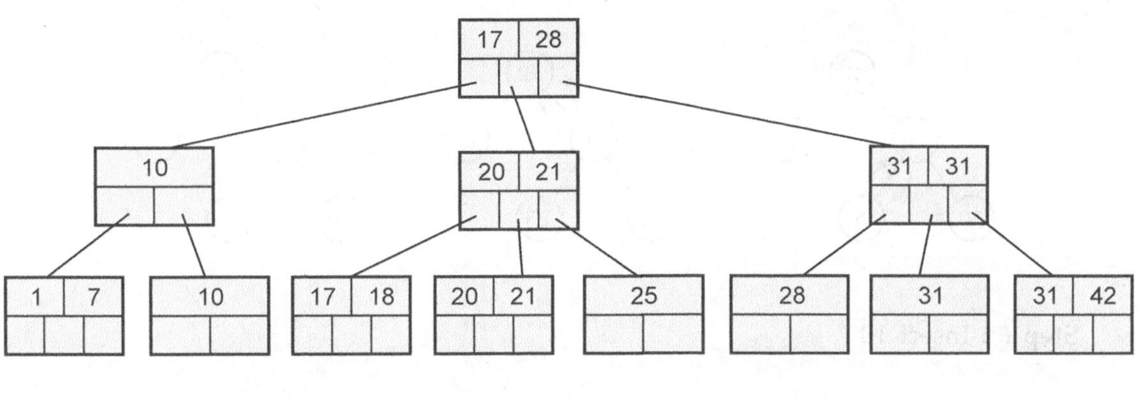

OR

Q.6 a) *Build the min-heap for the following data :* **[8]**

25, 12, 27, 30, 5, 10, 17, 29, 40, 35

After creation of min-heap perform one delete operation on it and show the final min-heap.

Ans. :

Step 1 : Insert 25.

Step 2 : Insert 12

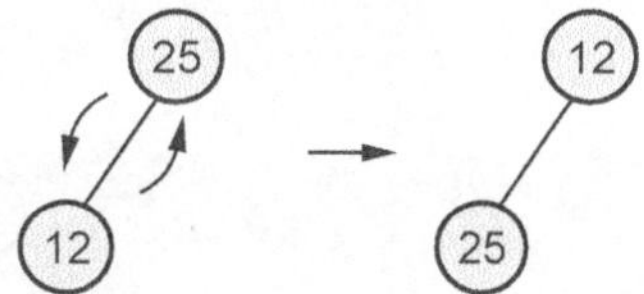

Step 3 : Insert 27

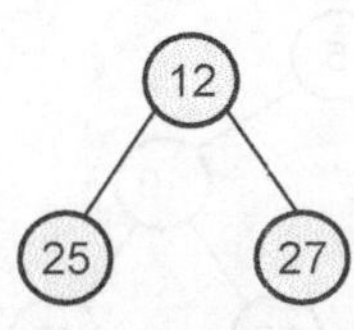

Step 4 : Insert 30

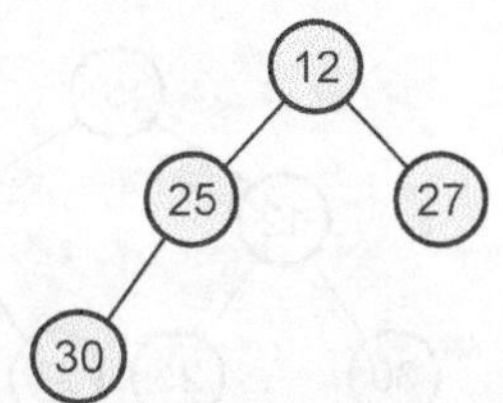

Step 5 : Insert 5

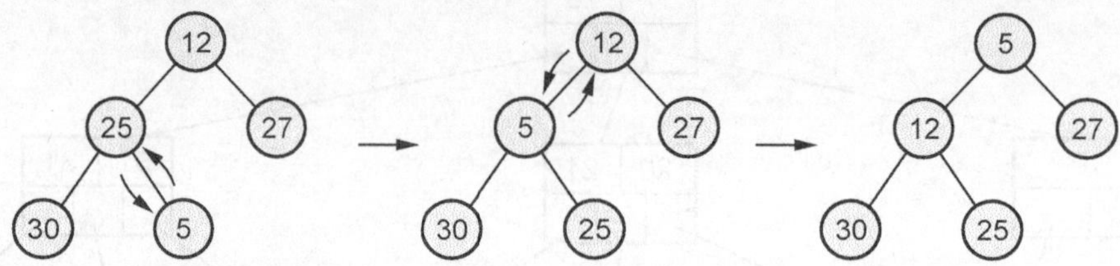

Step 6 : Insert 10

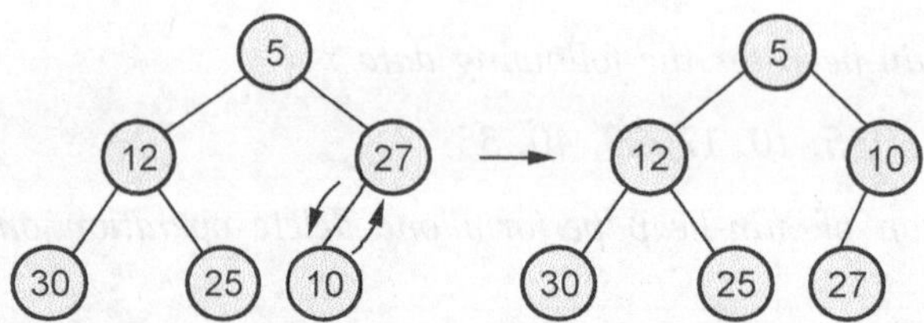

Step 7 : Insert 17

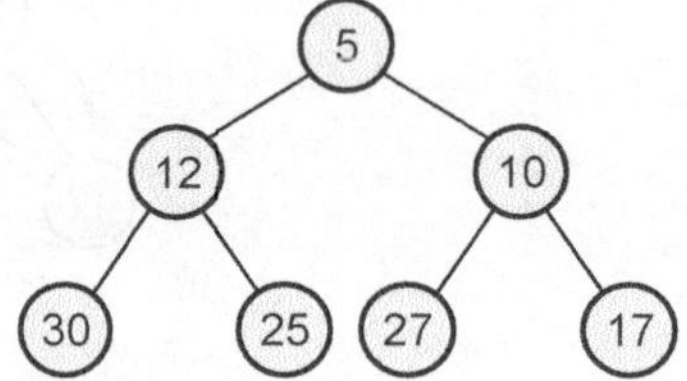

Step 8 : Insert 29

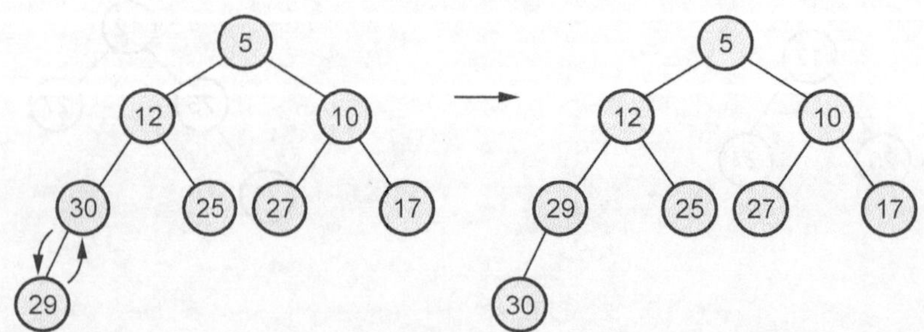

Step 9 : Insert 40 **Step 10 :** Insert 35

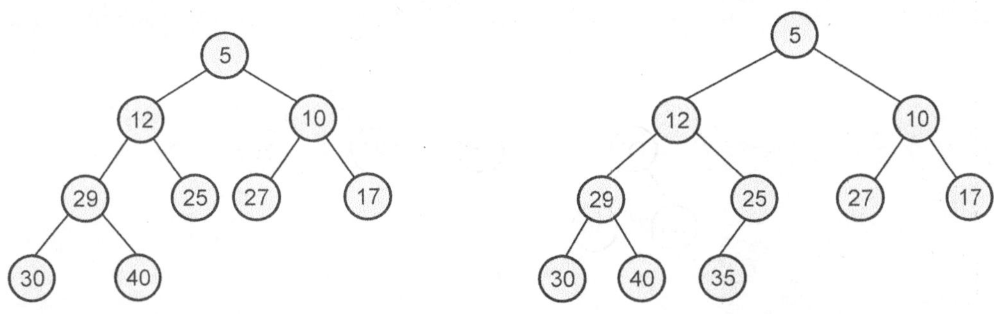

This is required min-heap.

For deletion operation, we need to delete a root node. The process of deleting a root node is illustrated as follows.

1) 2)

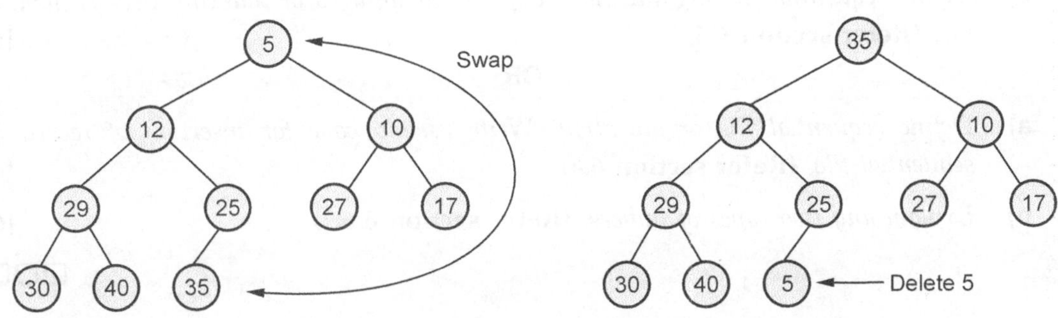

3) Now heapify the tree to maintain Min heap.

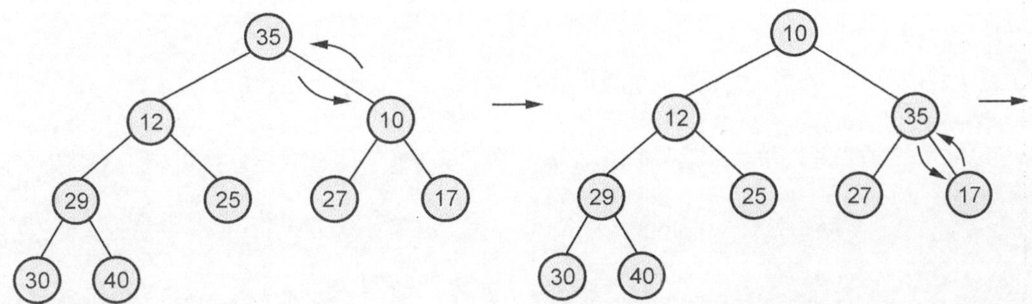

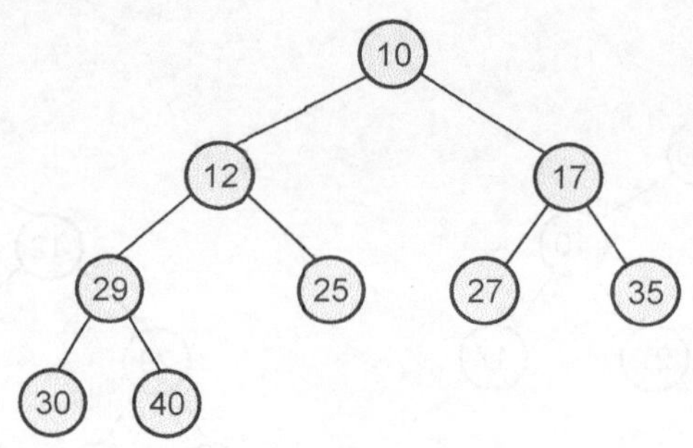

b) *Write short note on :*

i) Red - black tree **(Refer section 5.9)** **[6]**

ii) K - dimentional tree **(Refer section 5.10)**

Q.7 a) *Explain Linked organization of a file.* **(Refer section 6.7)** **[6]**

b) *Define sequential file organization. Explain advantages of indexing over sequential file.* **(Refer section 6.4)** **[6]**

OR

Q.8 a) *Define sequential file organization. Write pseudo code for insertion of record in sequential file.* **(Refer section 6.4)** **[6]**

b) *Explain any two types of indices.* **(Refer section 6.6.1)** **[6]**

❑❑❑